Letters of Anton Chekhov

LETTERS

of

ANTON

CHEKHOV

Selected and edited by

AVRAHM YARMOLINSKY

The Viking Press / *New York*

Letters translated by Bernard Guilbert Guerney appear on pages

7, 12, 15, 24, 64, 82, 84, 85, 88, 91, 92, 93, 95, 96, 104, 107, 110, 111, 112, 113, 114, 118, 119, 120, 122, 124, 125, 127, 130, 131, 133, 134, 152, 154, 157, 159, 163, 165, 170, 171, 173, 178, 179, 180, 181, 183, 184, 185, 186, 187, 188, 190, 191, 194, 198, 201, 203, 204, 205, 206, 208, 209, 214, 216, 217, 218, 219, 222, 224, 230, 233, 234, 238, 246, 249, 250, 252, 258, 259, 261, 262, 263, 264, 266, 269, 271, 272, 273, 275, 276, 277, 278, 279, 280, 283, 284, 285, 289, 290, 291, 292, 293, 295, 297, 298, 366, 367, 370, 371, 375, 376, 377, 378, 383, 384.

Letters translated by Lynn Solotaroff appear on pages

133, 135, 296, 301, 304, 309, 310, 311, 315, 317, 318, 319, 320, 323, 324, 327, 328, 329, 330, 334, 337, 338, 339, 342, 345, 346, 349, 353, 357, 359, 361, 364.

To Babette

who worked with me ungrudgingly on these pages

Foreword

Chekhov once confessed to a fellow alumnus of his medical school that he suffered from what he called "autobiographophobia." Was he wary of that literary genre because he felt that it bred complacency and deception, no matter how veiled? He could not bear showing himself as other than he was. In any case, whenever the request came to commit to paper something about his personal history, he set down as brief and bare an account as possible. He limited himself to some data about his activities as an author and to the more notable events in his life, not omitting his having learned "the mystery of love" at the age of thirteen. Only on one occasion did he picture, feelingly, the boy he had been and the man he had struggled to become. He wrote here with patent indirection, as it were withdrawing himself from the account, and presenting the metamorphosis to another writer as a theme for a story. Elements of an autobiography, with flashbacks and premonitions as well as gaps, are offered in the letters. They, of course, delineate Chekhov with greater intimacy than that found in his fictions, revealing in detail, as they do, what he thought and felt and what he did, his moods and musings, his interests, opinions, convictions, his sympathies and antipathies. We catch a glimpse of his workshop, and of the man in his idle moments. He is uncommonly candid. Here is no reticence, here are no euphemisms. There is no shrinking from phrases that prudish editors were to expurgate, though they seemed to have had no scruples about publishing his matter-of-fact dwelling on how "the Lord smote him in his bowels," as He had punished King Jehoram aforetime.

Chekhov took obvious pleasure in the crude, homespun vernacular. He wrote in unbuttoned ease. This was natural on pages that were never meant for publication. Some passages from several of the letters that Chekhov had penned during his journey to Sakhalin alone formed an exception. They were incorporated in a short series of travel sketches published in the Petersburg daily, *New Times*.

What adds to the engaging quality of Chekhov's letters is their irrepressible humor. Chekhov began by supplying the comic sheets with what in later years he dismissed as "trash." There were also pieces barbed with satire, aimed at the vulgarity of the newly rich, the stupidity of officialdom, the crushing oppressiveness of the police State. He was not defending certain principles, he was simply attacking what disgusted him in the world around him. With maturity, he wrote more substantial pieces, both stories and plays. Less here than in his letters, the bantering tone kept recurring. Yet his literary career ended with a play that (despite the insistence to the contrary of the members of the Moscow Art Theater) he repeatedly declared to be a comedy. He made his wife laugh with a comic story that he improvised on his deathbed.

A prominent characteristic of the man was his relish for what life had to offer. In spite of his ailments, he retained an enormous gusto for food: sturgeon, roast duck, veal cutlets, the "extraordinarily delicious aromatic oatmeal" that he savored in Germany during his last days. His mouth waters when a shop for delicacies opens in Yalta. He writes to a friend that music and wine are superb corkscrews for him. If on the road a cork gets stuck in his soul or in his head, he has only to drink off a glass of wine and he has wings and the cork is gone. He turns aside in dismay as he eyes the ill-dressed women in a German watering place.

For travel he had a passion that amounted to a compulsion. In his last letter, wanting information from his cousin George, the employee of a steamship company, he writes that he prefers a steamer to a train because trains are faster and he would get home too soon—he had not had his fill of wandering. Despite the limited means of his early years and later his increasing ill health, he was always eager to be on the go:

> For to admire and for to see,
> For to be'old the world so wide.

And he was at pains to write of his journeys, as when, in his twenties, he refreshed his memories of his shabby birthplace, with its plethora of stuffy piety and its absence of privies. He dwelt with equal distaste on both. Again, he gave an ample account of his adventures when, at thirty, he made, by carriage and boat, over treacherous roads and waters, the quixotic trek across Siberia to the penal colony of Sakhalin. Notwithstanding the incredible hardships that he met with, he managed to write about them to his kinfolk and others. These are among the many letters that testify to the strength of his family feeling.

On the homeward journey, by way of the Indian Ocean and the Black Sea, he made a point of catching the glimpses that they afforded of several exotic places. Like what he saw on his earlier visits to the Ukraine and the Caucasus and his later ones to some of the glories of Europe, they naturally furnished material for his letters. When the onset of his fatal illness condemned him to exile on what he called "the Devil's Island" of Yalta and, again, "a warm Siberia," his loneliness made him all the more avid for communication. His wife called him a "loner," and, of course, he needed privacy for his art, but to some extent he was a gregarious loner. What he had to say to his siblings and other friends, to men and women of letters, to people of the theater, was never a received opinion—he was the least doctrinaire, the least dogmatic of men—but always his personal, perceptive, individual, sometimes own-wayish response to experience.

His uncertain health—he was still far from being a certified invalid—had been no obstacle to his making the strenuous trip to Sakhalin. He had the vague hope that his scrupulous if amateur study of conditions in the penal colony would alleviate the convicts' lot. While on the dismal island he managed, singlehanded, to take a census of the population. (Half a dozen years later he would volunteer for the tiresome, tiring job of census-taking at home.) The infirm flesh inhabited by this courageous spirit was equally no barrier to his preparations, in his capacity as physician, for contending with an expected cholera epidemic. Characteristically, he admitted to a correspondent that he had no liking for the peasants for whom he exerted himself. His honesty was equal to his humanity. When, in an often misquoted statement, he wrote to a storyteller who asked his advice that "an author must be humane to the tips of his fingernails," he might have been describing himself. He labored to organize help for famine-stricken villagers, being concerned particularly with the children. Visiting the area on one occasion, he was nearly lost in a blizzard. He busied himself with various civic activities: the building of rural schools, the founding of a medical journal, the effort to establish a haven for convalescent patients in Moscow and a hospital for alcoholics on a Finnish island. He dreamed of setting up a colony in which members of the literary fraternity could rest, refresh themselves, and work. He devoted himself to these matters while remaining an apolitical man. They were the expression— he was no joiner—of individual initiative, of the private conscience, of his abiding sense of justice. He wrote to his wife, when there were differences between her and his sister, "One must dread injustice, you must be without reproach on the score of justice, absolutely without reproach. . . ." In regard to this there could be no wavering—nor with respect to what was for him the supreme value: freedom from every form of coercion or bondage.

A puzzling feature of the letters is the record that they give of Chekhov's friendship with Suvorin, whom he admired as a critic, detested as an advocate of the autocracy, valued for such liberal impulses as he showed, and delighted in as a companion. When Suvorin took an active stand against the supporters of Dreyfus, notably Zola, it was the sign for Chekhov to break with his old friend.

In the letter to Suvorin which states that he believes Dreyfus to be innocent, Chekhov declares that "great writers and artists should engage in politics only to the extent needed to defend themselves from politics." Apparently he meant the term to refer to the despotic regime under which he lived or to the despotic regime that he feared would be set up by the advocates of revolution. He was suspicious of politics controlled by violent fanatics—he once remarked that freedom was more seriously threatened by the left than by the right. He noted with pleasure the absence from the streets of Nice of both policemen and Marxists. As a matter of fact, he early observed that there would never be a revolution in Russia. A gradualist, he pinned his hopes to the civilized individual with a conscience. Somehow he managed to combine a bent for practicality with millennial hopes.

The Dreyfusard might sometimes show an animus against what he considered Jewish traits, but as a young man he was involved with a Jewish girl, and, though he gave way to his reservations, he seems to have thought of marrying her. In any event, racism was foreign to his nature. With uncanny premonition he wrote that anti-Semitism grows in a soil that "reeks of the slaughterhouse." His relationship with Suvorin was ultimately renewed, though not on the old intimate footing. The letters testify to Chekhov's feelings about the man, as strong as they were mixed, and to his lasting memory of what Suvorin had done for him as a young writer. Among other things the letters reveal Chekhov's ability to include among his friends such diverse characters as Tolstoy, the evangelical anarchist, whom he revered, and Gorky, the budding revolutionary, to whom he was greatly attracted.

Chekhov's attitude was as ambivalent as the next man's. Thus, loving Tolstoy this side idolatry, he had no patience with Tolstoyan asceticism, along with other elements of the sage's thinking. He despised the vulgarity and greed of the bourgeoisie, which he observed with particular distaste during his stays in Nice and his visit to Monte Carlo, yet he appreciated carriages on springs and other creature comforts. The letters not infrequently show Chekhov contradicting himself on various points. He left no doubt in the minds of his friends that he was an unbeliever. This was in part due, as he makes plain, to the brutal aspect of his father's piety. Yet as a mature man, secular-minded, Chekhov seldom concluded a letter without calling down heavenly blessings on his addressee. Probably they were a matter of habit ingrained in childhood. Another trait that was certainly formed when he was a boy, clerking in his father's grocery store, and in the grim years after its failure, was that of noting the price of every purchase in rubles and copecks, and even when poverty was behind him, he had the impulse to keep expenses down. The role that money played among his elders had so depraved him, he remarked, that he should take a sulphuric acid bath to rid himself of his old skin and then grow a new one. Chekhov could be reckoned a materialist, but he found a place in his holy of holies, along with the human body (the first-named of the things he venerated), for such disembodied values as "inspiration, love, and freedom."

It is clear that he was able to believe in the civilizing effects of education, since he did not doubt that human beings were malleable creatures. He held that progress, however slow, was certain. He believed, too, in the supremacy of science, which he watched making giant strides. He took satisfaction in being a physician partly because this was his strongest bond with science. At the same time he affirmed that he was himself not one of those artists, nor would he want to be, who thought that you can get at the essence of a thing by the intellect alone. If to some extent his medical knowledge nourished his fictions, he dealt with his characters not as patients but as human beings (psychopathology exerted a particular attraction over him). Not astonishingly his letters are peppered with references to medical matters. They supply material for a chart of his own illness, though he tried to conceal it from his family and sometimes from himself.

Sickness imposed prohibitions that made for the large drab patches in his life. Having to guard his health, to pamper himself like the Russian ladies at Yalta and Nice, to lavish attention on his miserable body, filled him with shame and disgust. In addition to the cruel effects of physical distresses was the different restraint that censorship, or the fear of it, put on his freedom to write. This was a constant source of vexation. The letters bring this out as they evoke the atmosphere of social stagnation and political reaction that followed the assassination of Alexander II. Chekhov's adulthood coincided with the last two decades of the nineteenth century and the start of the twentieth. He knew that he was living in what he called "a flabby, sour, dull time." He suffered from the intellectual poverty, the spiritual impotence about him. A master of short fiction, an innovator in that genre as in drama, he regarded himself, like the rest of his generation, as a dwarfish descendant of giant predecessors. (He had his moments of pride, tinged with bitterness, when he contemplated what he could do, given time and strength.) The artists of his generation, he lamented, were offering lemonade rather than strong drink. He insisted that the writer was not "a confectioner, not a cosmetician, not an entertainer," but a man under contract to tell the truth. Further, the writer, no less than the scientist, must be completely objective, must be a witness. Yet again, he declared as emphatically that a writer must have a purpose. If he clung to the idea of freedom, he included in it, though not admitting as much, freedom to contradict himself.

One of the most affecting features of the letters is what they have to say of his brief, close, unique marriage, cemented, it would seem, by separations. It is the major subject of the letters of his last four years, those of his intimacy with Olga Knipper. At the time he was occupied with such concerns as filling the shelves of the Taganrog public library, helping a student to transfer from one university to another, giving advice to literary aspirants. But the dominant theme is the relationship between the dedicated actress and the mortally sick writer, devoted to his wife's art as to his own. It was a fundamental assumption with him that whatever the differences between the sexes, their equality should in nowise be infringed. He repeats his conviction that he and his wife have behaved toward each other in an exemplary fashion, so that, as he wrote her a year and a half before he died, he wished every couple might be granted the same blessing. Few of his stories equal the pathos, veined with jocularity, of those pages.

It will be remembered that in spite of his unwillingness to write about himself, he had offered to a friend as the theme for a story a sketch of the basic change that he had undergone. That theme is implicit in the body of the letters and helps to give them their force and grace. "Write a story, do, about a young man, the son of a serf, a former grocery boy, a choirsinger, a high school pupil and university student, brought up to respect rank, to kiss the hands of priests, to truckle to the ideas of others—a young man who expressed thanks for every piece of bread, who was whipped many times, who went without galoshes to do his tutoring, who used his fists, tortured animals, was fond of dining with rich relatives, was a hypocrite in his dealings with God and men, needlessly, solely out of a realization of his own insignificance—write how this young man squeezes the slave out of himself, drop by drop, and how, on awaking one fine morning, he feels that the blood coursing through his veins is no longer that of a slave but that of a real human being." In a word, he was free. Of course, Chekhov spent his whole life under a despotic regime. In addition to the political situation there was the bondage that his illness laid upon him. Yet he was inwardly free. The fact is unmistakable in his letters. Of all the reasons for which we read them, this is not the least.

That Chekhov's epistolary legacy clamored to be published was recognized early on. A collection of three hundred and twenty-five letters appeared under a Moscow imprint in 1909, five years after the writer's death. Chekhov's sister, Mariya, his literary executrix, edited a six-volume compilation of nearly nineteen hundred items, which came out between 1912 and 1916. Thereafter more books were issued, comprising some nine hundred letters. One of these volumes, brought out in 1924, contains Chekhov's part of his correspondence with his wife, supplemented by excerpts from some of her letters to him. Though published in Berlin, the text is in the original. Two years later Constance Garnett's translation of this book appeared in London. Other letters found their way into miscellanies and periodicals.

In the spring of 1944 the Council of the People's Commissars ordered the publication of the complete corpus of Chekhov's writings. This edition, in twenty volumes, was seven years in the making, the last eight volumes (1948–51) being devoted to the letters. The most comprehensive collection in existence, it consists of nearly forty-two hundred items, including telegrams and even trivial notes. Obviously, Chekhov belonged to the race of letter-writers. Although he professed to love telegrams, perhaps as exemplars of the verbal economy that he prized, he would have smiled ironically at such pious custody of the negligible. The edition is a scholarly one, provided with notes of various kinds, several meticulous indexes, and many illustrations (chiefly reproductions of photographs), and the letters are given in full, except for suppressed passages, which will be touched upon later.

A generous two-volume selection from the letters in the complete collection, with some editorial changes, was issued in the 1950s and reprinted in the 1960s. The number of copies brought out so far, at a fantastically low price, is a million and a half. Thus, at a time when the Soviet authorities were engaged in emphasizing the doctrine that literature, like the other arts, justified its existence only as ancillary to the Party-State, they were paradoxically willing to disseminate writing that was to this doctrine as fire is to ice. Implicit in his stories and plays, Chekhov's antipathy to the unborn totalitarian regime is clearly manifested in the letters. A new edition of his complete writings is under way in Moscow. It will include a more nearly exhaustive text of the letters than was previously available.

The Chekhov archives, many of them housed in the Lenin Library, Moscow, contain some seven thousand letters addressed to him. He is said to have preserved all the communications that he received and to have been scrupulous about penning replies. Presumably a number of these, hitherto unpublished, are extant and some may yet come to light. Indeed, a little more than one hundred letters unknown before or known only in part were published in 1960. To date a limited number of the communications to him have been brought out. Among them are those from his wife, his sister, his brother Aleksandr, and from many noted literary figures, such as Bunin.

The Soviet editors state that as far as possible they restored the cuts in the text due to prerevolutionary censorship. On the other hand, here and there one comes across excisions. Unlike those made under the old regime, most of them are plainly indicated by three dots in brackets. To judge by the context, and by those letters that had previously been published in full, some of the suppressed material was held to be offensive on the grounds of ribaldry or an approach to it. In a letter to Suvorin, Chekhov mentioned his brief visit to Ceylon, "the site of paradise," on his way home from Sakhalin. "When I have children," he wrote, "I'll say to them not without pride, 'You sons of bitches, in my time I had dalliance with a Hindu maiden—and where? In a coconut grove, on a moonlit night.' " This passage is suppressed in the complete Soviet edition and also in the selected letters published years later, when official prudery was slightly relaxed. Fortunately, the passage appears, among others, in the prerevolutionary collection edited by the writer's sister. As has been noted, Chekhov was anything but a prude. This made the censoring of what he wrote to his family and other intimates a troublesome task for the guardians of Soviet morals.

The letter mentioned above also exemplifies an excision of material regarded as ideological heresy. Chekhov makes an observation, by no means rare with him, that shows plainly his readiness to "kow-tow" (in the Soviet vocabulary) to the West. The British, he concedes, exploit their colonials, but also bestow upon them the benefits, material and spiritual, of civilization. The Russians, too, he admits, exploit their non-Russian nationals, but in return give them nothing. These remarks are replaced in the complete collection by three dots in brackets, but are allowed space in the selected letters.

Again, Chekhov writes from Nice, praising as "intelligent and elegant" all that was said and published about Alphonse Daudet on the occasion of his death. Then he reflects that, should Tolstoy die, the journalists would manage to comment on the event, but his fellow novelists would only "scratch themselves." He concludes with an exhortation that could not be printed in an era of inordinate vainglory officially prescribed: "We should send our young literati abroad to study; by God, we should!" These lines do not appear in the complete collection of the letters, nor is their absence indicated in the usual manner. They are, however, printed in the selected letters.

There are also deletions of a baffling kind. In a letter penned when he was a young man, Chekhov spoke of considering marriage to a Jewess. These lines are cut, together with reference to the matter in a subsequent letter. Truly, the workings of the mind of the Soviet bureaucrat are inscrutable.

The eight volumes of letters are prefaced by a statement that they contain all the epistolary material at hand either in manuscript or in print. But aside from the deletions mentioned, at least one letter is excised in its entirety, though it is free of anything objectionable from the Soviet viewpoint. It was printed in the 1909 *Yearbook of the Russian Imperial Theaters*. The addressee is Vsevolod Meyerhold, a greatly gifted actor with the Moscow Art Theater, who as a director was to become the progenitor of the Soviet theater. An admirer of Chekhov, he had urged the Yalta exile to come to Moscow without fear of cold weather, for the ardent love of his devotees would warm him even in the Arctic. Meyerhold is mentioned on more than one page of the com-

plete collection, apparently by oversight, but his name is excluded
from all the indexes. As a rule, a purged dissenter—and Meyerhold
was one—was given the silence treatment. The innocent letter is, however, printed in the selected letters—another sign that time had somewhat weakened Stalinist rigor.

In any case, no serious damage was done to the text by Soviet
censorship, whether prompted by prudery, chauvinism, xenophobia,
unwillingness to offend non-Russian nationals, or some unfathomable
reason. It should be added that the sedulous labors of those concerned
with the task of compiling the collected letters brought to light a
plethora of new material.

The chief obstacle to putting together the more telling letters in a
single, not too formidable volume, intended for the common reader, is
having to decide what one can bear to omit. The present editor solved
his problem by offering only certain letters in full, as they came to the
addressee. Other letters have sizable excisions—for example, of discussions of the appropriateness of one or another stage personality
for a given role, of a catalogue of books that Chekhov procured for the
Taganrog Municipal Library, or of passages about the comings and
goings of relatively obscure acquaintances and the state of their health.
Further, conventional salutations and greetings at the close are not
seldom dispensed with, as are also the pious good wishes, which are so
little in character. What would otherwise have been cut is sometimes
saved by a glint of humor. Chekhov speaks of a headachy letter as "incoherent." He was incoherent at other times, too, and such passages
have sometimes been omitted. All excisions are indicated by three
asterisks.

Chekhov's sensitiveness to the texture of prose is amply evident in
what he had to say to other writers, whether amateurs or professionals.
Yet as a letter-writer he was sometimes strangely careless. Occasionally
the editor found it desirable, in order to clarify matters, to alter a
phrase or amplify the paragraphing. Like other Russian writers, Chekhov all too often resorted to ellipses, and these have not always been
retained. Yet the editor was invariably guided by the wish to reduce
to a minimum any tampering with the text.

A word about certain technical matters. To begin with, the trans-
literation of Russian names and of a few other words seldom departs
from that used by the Library of Congress. In the case of well-known
figures—for example, Tchaikovsky and Chaliapin—the spelling of

whose names in English is dictated by foreign usage, that spelling is adopted. A person is identified the first time he or she is mentioned or, more often, the first time he or she appears as an addressee. The feminine form of the patronymic and family name is retained: Anton Pavlovich Chekhov, but Mariya Pavlovna Chekhova. At the head of a letter the initials of the addressee's name and patronymic are given, together with the family name. Throughout, even when the letters were written in foreign parts, the dates are according to the Old Style calendar, twelve days behind the Western calendar in the nineteenth century and thirteen in the twentieth. It is hoped that the footnotes will supply sufficient information to those in search of it.

A.Y.

Editor's Note

Some of the letters have been
translated by Bernard Guilbert Guerney,
others by Lynn Solotaroff. A list of
the pages on which their work appears
may be found on the copyright page.
Their renderings have been revised by
the editor, who has englished the
rest of the Russian text.

Contents

Letters of Anton Chekhov

$\begin{bmatrix} 1879 \end{bmatrix}$

TO M. P. CHEKHOV[1]

Taganrog,[2] *April 6–8, 1879*

Dear brother Misha,

I received your letter when my terrible boredom was at its peak, I sat yawning beside the gate, and hence you can judge how very welcome your huge missive was. Your handwriting is good and in your whole letter I didn't find a single grammatical mistake. There is only one thing I don't like: why do you exalt yourself as "a worthless, insignificant little brother"? You are aware of your insignificance? All Mishas, brother, need not be alike. Be conscious of your failings—do you know when? In comparison with God, perhaps, with intelligence, beauty, nature, but not with human beings. Among people you must be conscious of your dignity. You know, don't you, that you're not a swindler, you're honest? So respect the honorable fellow in you and know that such a person is not a nonentity. Don't confuse humility with insignificance.

Georgy, our cousin, has grown up. He is a good boy. I often play knucklebones with him. He has received the parcels you sent him. You

[1] Mikhail Pavlovich Chekhov (1865–1936), the youngest of the Chekhov brothers, nicknamed Misha or Mishka. He graduated from the Law School of Moscow University. According to his brother he was then eager to marry, "if only to a broken frying-pan." When he did take a wife, Chekhov has described her as "very nice, simple-hearted, and an excellent cook." Mikhail held positions in the civil service, and wrote short stories, articles, sketches, playlets, for the weeklies. He was his famous brother's first biographer. He also translated works by Upton Sinclair, Jack London, and other novelists.

[2] A small port on the sea of Azov, founded by Peter the Great. Here Anton Pavlovich Chekhov was born on January 17, 1860, the third son in a family which was to include five boys and one girl. The Chekhovs owned a grocery and a house built on borrowed money. In 1876 the father, having become insolvent, to avoid "the debtors' pit," absconded to Moscow, where his two elder sons were studying and where he was soon joined by his wife, their youngest son, and daughter. Anton remained in Taganrog, together with his brother Ivan. The latter stayed with their aunt; Anton was left alone to fend for himself. While completing his secondary education at the local school, a classical Gymnasium, he did tutoring to earn his bread and—the family being in dire straits—to send small sums to Moscow.

do well to read books. Form the reading habit. In time you'll prize it. Mme. Beecher-Stowe brought tears to your eyes? I read the book some months ago for a scientific purpose and after finishing it I experienced the unpleasant sensation that mortals feel when they stuff themselves with raisins or currants. Dubanos, whom I promised you, has run away, and I know all too little about where he keeps himself now. I shall manage to bring you something else. Read the following books: *Don Quixote*, seven or nine parts. A good thing. Cervantes' work is indeed believed to measure up to Shakespeare. I advise all our brothers to read Turgenev's "*Don Quixote* and *Hamlet*," if they haven't done so yet. You, my boy, will not understand it. If you want to read an entertaining travel book, try Goncharov's *Frigate Pallas*. Give Masha [3] a special greeting from me. Don't worry if I come late. Time flows fast, no matter how you brag of boredom. I shall bring a boarder with me who will pay 20 rubles a month and on whom we'll keep an eye.[4] I'm about to put through a deal with his mamenka. Pray!! Twenty rubles is too cheap though, if you consider Moscow prices and Mamasha's character —she'll want to feed the boarder like a Christian. Our teachers charge 350 rubles, and the poor boys get only the gravy of the roast.

A. Chekhov

[3] The nickname of Chekhov's only sister, Mariya Pavlovna Chekhova (1863–1957). She taught history and geography in a Moscow high school for girls. Developing an interest in painting, she studied under well-known Russian masters. Added to her other concerns was the management of the household. Probably because of her devotion to Anton, she never married. Of all the members of the family, she was closest to him and, indeed, became his literary executrix. The directorship of the Chekhov museum in Yalta was her responsibility.

[4] Shortly after graduating from high school, on June 15, 1879, Chekhov was to rejoin his family in Moscow and enter the university there in the department of medicine. Delayed by the red tape involved in securing the stipend granted by the municipality, he reached Moscow early in August, accompanied by two classmates who were to board with the Chekhovs.

[1883]

TO N. A. LEIKIN[1]

Moscow, January 12, 1883

Gracious sir, Nikolay Aleksandrovich!

In response to your amiable letter I am sending you several items. I have received the fee and I also get the weekly (on Tuesday); I thank you for both. I thank you further for the flattering invitation to continue contributing. I contribute to *Splinters* with special zest. The policy of your journal, the way it looks, and the skill with which it is managed will attract to you, as they already have, others beside myself.

Through thick and thin I too stand for brief items, and if I were in charge of a humorous journal, I would kill everything tending to prolixity. In Moscow editorial offices I alone revolt against *longueurs* (which, however, does not on occasion prevent me from offering them to some people. You cannot help asking for trouble). At the same time I confess that limits "from this point to this" cause me considerable grief. Sometimes it is not easy to put up with these restrictions. For instance . . . You reject anything over a hundred lines, which is reasonable. . . . I have a topic. I sit down to write. The thought of "a hundred" and "no more" jogs my elbow from the very first line. I tighten, as far as possible, sift, cut—and sometimes (as the author's flair prompts me) to the detriment of the substance and (above all) the form. Having done the tightening and the sifting, I begin to count. Having counted 100–120–140 lines (more I did not write for *Splinters*), I get frightened and . . . do not send off the piece. As soon as I start the fourth page of a sheet of notepaper doubts begin eating me, and I do not dispatch the item. Most often I am quickly reduced to gnawing off the end and mailing what I would rather not offer. As an example of my plight, I am sending "The Only Remedy." I am dispatching this piece, which

[1] N. A. Leikin (1841–1906), a prolific author of novels, essays, skits, and humorous stories, was also the publisher and editor of the comic weekly *Splinters*, a Petersburg publication, to which Chekhov contributed during 1882–87.

[5]

I have tightened, making it as short as I can, but it seems to me that it's devilishly long for you. Yet it also seems to me that if I had made it twice as long it would have had twice as much salt and substance. I have smaller items—but I am afraid you would not find them acceptable. Some time I may send them, but I can't make up my mind. . . .

The upshot of it all is the request: enlarge my space to 120 lines. . . . I am certain that I shall rarely take advantage of this privilege but the knowledge that I have it will keep my elbow from being jogged.

In fine, accept the assurance of the respect and devotion of your most obedient servant,

Ant. Chekhov

P.S. For the New Year I prepared an envelope for you weighing one and a half ounces. The editor of *The Spectator* came and made off with it. I couldn't stop him: a friend. Our editors inveigh against Muscovites working for Petersburg, too. But Petersburg scarcely deprives them of as much as the censors swallow. In the wretched *Alarm Clock* some 400–800 lines are crossed out in each issue. They don't know what to do.

TO N. A. LEIKIN

Moscow, after April 17, 1883

Much esteemed Nikolay Aleksandrovich!

I am sending you several stories in response to your letter.

You observe, à propos, that my "Willow" and "Thief" are somewhat serious for *Splinters*. Perhaps, but I wouldn't have sent you pieces not good for a laugh had I not been guided by certain considerations. I think that a serious piece—tiny, say about 100 lines—will not irritate the eye much, all the more so since the masthead of *Splinters* does not contain the words "humorous" and "satirical." It does not limit the contents to indisputable humor. A featherweight thing, in the spirit of the weekly, having a plot and expressing protest in the right tone, is read gladly, as far as I have noticed; that is, it's not dry. By the way, among the little pieces in your weekly by "Y," [1] our wittiest contributor, there are trifles that are somewhat serious, but slim, graceful, so that they can be eaten after dinner instead of dessert. They do not cause

---

[1] Pen name of Viktor Viktorovich Bilibin, secretary to the editor and publisher of *Splinters*.

friction, quite the contrary. Again, Liodor Ivanovich [2] does not always crack jokes, and nevertheless scarcely a reader of *Splinters* skips his verse. Short pieces, no matter how serious (I'm not speaking of mathematics), make light reading. . . . God save us from dryness, but a warm word, spoken at Eastertime to a thief who is a deportee, will not kill an issue. (Besides, truth to tell, it is hard to follow close on humor's heels! Sometimes you will run after humor and then blurt out something so inept that willy-nilly you take refuge in seriousness.) For Pentecost I'll send you something green, à la "Willow." I will be serious only on high holidays.

"Agafapod Yedimitzyn" is the pseudonym of my brother Aleksandr. In recent years he has been a contributor to Moscow periodicals, and is now an official. An assiduous worker, he lived fairly well by his pen. The fellow was a humorist, but he deviated into lyricism, phantasmagoria, and, methinks . . . is lost to authorship. You want to drop lyricism, but it's too late, you're stuck. His letters are full of humor, nothing funnier could be invented, but when he takes to scribbling for a journal there is trouble, he begins to stumble. If he were younger, he could be made into an outstanding writer. He does have a genuine sense of humor. Consider this alone—that he joined the staff of the Taganrog customs-house after all the goods there had already been stolen. I have written to him, and he is sure to send you something.

And now I remain always at your service,

A. Chekhov

TO A. P. CHEKHOV[1]

Moscow, May 13, 1883

* * * I've read your reply to my letter. I am surprised, to some extent. Brother dear, some places you haven't understood enough, other places you have understood overmuch. Nobody was asking you to jettison yourself. Since I know what a poor swimmer you are, could I, without having gone batty, give you this lethal advice? The talk had been about

[2] L. I. Palmin, who wrote verse.

[1] Chekhov's eldest brother, Aleksandr (1855–1913), familiarly called Sasha, was an alumnus of Moscow University, where he studied physics and mathematics. He contributed to humorous weeklies and to *New Times*, edited such journals as *The Fireman* and *The Blind*, and did much hack work. The close relationship between the two brothers was marked by severe admonitions, combined with affection, on the part of the younger.

creative works, about subjectivity. Don't go leaning so hard, brother dear, on that disposition of yours being like your uncle's. Karamzin [2] and Zhukovsky [3] whine at every word, yet they write least of all concerning themselves. (By the way, I congratulate you on having an uncle [4] who has a medal. Vanka [5] will now croak from envy.) Next: really, must you be getting *Light and Shades* to be familiar with Nikolka's [6] works? Why, you saw him less than five years ago. How many pictures did he have when you were leaving? Next, sir: when I wrote about Mariya I did not mean her to typify a pupil at the diocesan school or a student taking the courses for young ladies at an institution of higher learning. She is what she was even when you were here. There's no need of any propaganda whatsoever (you may actually land in the cooler, first thing you know); I was speaking about the disregard, past and present, for one's personality. As for Mishka, I said nothing and was thinking you yourself would call him to mind. He and Mariya had suffered to the same extent.

However, let's go on. —In speaking of envious newspapermen I had *newspapermen* in view—but tell me, if you please, what sort of a newspaperman are you? Brother, I have undergone so much, and have come to hate things so, that my wish would be for you to forswear the repute borne by the Utkinas and the Kicheyevs.[7] *Newspaperman* means crook, at the very least, something which you yourself have been convinced of on more than one occasion. I am in their company, I work with them,

[2] Nikolay Mikhailovich Karamzin (1766–1826), statesman and writer, author of a patriotic history of Russia, and some odes.

[3] Vasily Andreyevich Zhukovsky (1783–1852), one of the forerunners of Pushkin; a translator of verse from several languages into Russian.

[4] Mitrofan Yegorovich Chekhov (1836–94); the medal was awarded to him in his capacity as churchwarden.

[5] Nickname of the writer's third brother Ivan (1861–1922), variously called also Vanya, Jean, and "the positive man." He taught in a provincial school, later in Moscow.

[6] Nickname of Nikolay (1858–89), the second of the Chekhov brothers. He studied at the Moscow School of Painting, Sculpture, and Architecture, contributed cartoons to comic weeklies, illustrated his brother's stories. He died of tuberculosis on the Lintvarevs' estate, where the Chekhovs rented a summer cottage. "A good, strong, Russian talent," his famous brother wrote of him in 1883.

[7] L. N. Utkina was the publisher of the humorous weekly *The Alarm Clock*, and she used to pay contributors with the furnishings of the editorial room. The Chekhov museum at Yalta exhibits a wall clock received by Nikolay in payment for illustrations he had contributed.

The second reference is to two Kicheyevs, Nikolay Petrovich, editor of *The Alarm Clock*, and Pyotr Ivanovich, verse writer and drama critic. Chekhov had an eye on the latter when he coined the word *Kicheyevshchina*, to denote "a vile disease—the unwillingness of people in the very same group to understand one another."

I shake hands with them, and people are saying that, as seen at some distance, I have come to look like a crook. I grieve, and hope that sooner or later I shall isolate myself, *à la* yourself. You're no newspaperman but the one who *is* a newspaperman is the fellow who, as he smiles right into your eyes, is selling your soul for thirty false pieces of silver and, because you are a better and bigger man than he, is seeking on the sly to ruin you at the hands of somebody else: there, that's the sort of newspaperman I was writing you about. But you, brother, are a puzzle, a whiff, a gas, a nonentity—a newspaper manikin. I am a newspaperman, because I write a lot, but this is temporary. I won't die one. If I shall write, it will inevitably be from afar, from behind a tiny chink. Don't be envying me, brother dear! Outside of jitters, writing doesn't give me a thing. The 100 rubles I take in monthly go back into the belly, and I haven't the strength to change my drab, indecent coat for something less threadbare. I pay coming and going and am left with *nihil.* More than 50 goes bang for the family. There is nothing with which to go to Voskresensk.[8] As for Nikolka, he too has devilish little money. I find consolation in the fact that I have no creditors breathing down my neck, at least. I received 70 rubles from Leikin for April, and it's the 13th already, yet I haven't even enough to hire a cab.

If I were living by myself I'd be living like a rich man, but now, well—by the rivers of Babylon, there we sat down, yes, we wept. —Pastukhov led me off to supper at Testov's;[9] promised me 6 copecks a line. With him I could earn not 100 but 200 rubles a month. But, as you can see yourself, it would be better to set out on a visit without pants, with your [. . .] bare, than to be working for him. *The Alarm Clock* I can't stand, and should I agree to scribble for it, it won't be otherwise than painful to me. To the devil with these sheets! If they were all as honest as *Splinters* I'd be riding horseback. My stories are not mean-spirited and, they say, are better than others as to form and content, while sundry Andryushki Dmitriyevy[10] are promoting me as one who belongs among the top-notch humorists, among the better—even the best

[8] A town near Moscow, which after the Revolution lost its name, related as it was to the word "resurrection," and is now Iskra. Ivan was a school principal there and, thanks to the largesse of a rich merchant, occupied a house so spacious that it accommodated some members of the family during the warm season, when they were glad to escape from Moscow.

[9] Nikolay Ivanovich Pastukhov, publisher of *Moscow Broadside,* a cheap gazette. Testov's was a well-known Moscow restaurant.

[10] A contemptuous reference to Andrey Mikhailovich Dmitriyev, who published under the pseudonym of Baron Galkin.

—ones; my stories are recited at literary evenings, but—it's better to be bothering with [...] than to be taking money for what is mean-spirited, for making sport of a drunken shopkeeper when—and so on. The devil with them! We'll wait and see, but for the time being we'll keep going around in our drab coat. I'll immerse myself in medicine, which offers salvation, even though I myself don't believe to this very day that I am a medico, and this means that—at least people say so, yet to me it makes no difference whatsoever—this means that the branch of science I had hit on was not meant for me.

However, let's go on. —You write that my mudslinging has thoroughly bespattered Tretyakov,[11] who is dying of consumption. Consumption has nothing to do with this, nor has dying. At the very beginning of the letter I stipulated that I was jeering neither at Ivan nor at Pyotr (who are no concern of mine whatsoever), but at the system. —I was writing to you as a man of letters and as to one of my best friends. —What, then, are consumption and mud doing here? I haven't a thing against Leonid Vladimirovich personally but, on the contrary, I begin to be bored whenever I recall his face; I did have in view a certain shortcoming which does not pertain to him alone, inasmuch as he is not the only member of the gentry. I thought, and think, that congratulatory letters are beyond your power and mine, that they could be successfully replaced by conversations about this, that, and the other. —I thought that, in one way or another, you would respond concerning the above-mentioned shortcoming, would minimize it, justify it, would write to what extent I was just, to what extent unjust (after all, the theme is a good one), but you let go full blast with consumption and mud. —It would have been better, really, if you had written, "Judge not!"—condemnation being the sole offense of my letter, an offense which is redeemed, it seems to me, by its literary strain. Let's go on. . . .

Your *Easter Night* I have tucked away in the archives and will send you the honorarium for it next year. By the way: *Word of the Times, the Clang of Metal* is printed and I received the money. Only recently did I learn that the money I received included an honorarium of my own. At 5 copecks per line. I'll pay up through anybody who'll be going to visit you. The *Spectator* is interred and its requiem sung. No more resurrections for it. Leikin writes that he was moved twenty times to print your "Pipe" but still was not able to decide: no matter how he tried he failed to understand the ending. He asks you to send things in. Write.

11 Leonid Vladimirovich Tretyakov, a university friend of the addressee.

You'll get some rejections, you'll grieve a little, feel sorry for yourself a little, but then you'll get the hang of it and will be getting the wherewithal for Nestlé's Flour for Infants. The money will come in handy, and especially in Taganrog, where an extra twenty-five-ruble note is more impressive than it is in Moscow. By the way, next year you will rent a cottage for me in the quarantine area for the whole summer. I will arrive as a physician and will live with you the whole summer. There will be money and we'll live it up. Concerning our trip south I can say nothing positive. To my great grief half the examinations will come toward the end of vacation, which has spoiled the summer for me to a great extent.

Of what use will our aunt be to you? What a catch! The idea of dragging her almost 800 miles to palp the hens! Why, she'll miss Aleksey [12] so much that she'll eat you up alive and, on the sly, will stuff your offspring with potatoes! Mother is begging hard to go to you. Take her, if you can. Mother is still spry and isn't as heavy as Aunty. Aunty is less talkative but is harder to get along with. She is given to covert malice.

Father is telling everybody that you have a remarkable post. When tipsy he discourses on your uniform, your rights, and so on. Describe your uniform for him, please, and drag in an account of just one official holiday when you stood in the midst of an assembly of the great ones of this world.

"Well, now, how about Sasha—ah?" he will begin, usually after the third glass. "The customs-house in Taganrog is first class! Whoever is in the civil service there—" and so on. . . . * * *

TO N. A. LEIKIN

Moscow, August 21–24, 1883

Much esteemed Nikolay Aleksandrovich!

What I am sending you herewith is botched. The anecdotes are pale, the story lacks polish and is too petty. I have a better subject, and I could have written and earned more, but fate is now against me. I write

[12] Feodosiya Yakovlevna Dolzhenko, a sister of Chekhov's mother, was a zealous proselytizer for Orthodoxy.

Aleksey Alekseyevich Dolzhenko, her son, was described by Chekhov as a player on the violin and the zither, "one of the finest human beings . . . unusually witty, honest and decent." Chekhov left him 1000 rubles in his will.

under the foulest conditions. Before me is my nonliterary work,[1] merci-lessly walloping my conscience, while the infant of a relative [2] who has come to stay with us howls in one adjacent room, and in another Father is reading "The Sealed Angel" aloud to Mother. . . . Someone wound the music box, and I hear "Fair Helen." . . . For a writer it is hard to imagine a worse setup. My bed is occupied by a relative, who now and then comes up to me and starts a medical conversation: "My little daughter must have colic—that's why she cries. . . ." I have the misfor-tune of being a medico, and there is not one individual who doesn't consider it necessary to engage me in talk about medicine. Whoever is tired of discussing medicine broaches the subject of literature.

A peerless setup. I scold myself for not having gone to the dacha, where I would have had a good night's sleep, written a story for you, where, above all, medicine and literature would have been left alone.

In September I will betake myself to Voskresensk, weather permit-ting. Your last story is a delight. . . .

The little one is roaring!! I swear I will never have children. . . . The French have few children, probably because they are learned people and write stories for *Amusant*.[3] It is said that the authorities want to compel them to have more children—a theme for *Amusant* and *Splinters* in the form of a caricature: "The State of Affairs in France." A police officer enters and demands children.

Farewell. I am thinking of how and when I can do some zzzzing.

I have the honor of being

A. Chekhov

TO A. P. CHEKHOV

Moscow, between October 15 and 20, 1883

Our villainous brother, Aleksandr Pavlovich!

First of all, don't be a lummox and forgive me for having taken so long to answer your letters. It isn't so much laziness as the lack of leisure that is to blame for my silence. There isn't a minute of free time. I even abstain from games of solitaire because I have no time. I'm having my final examination before graduation (despite your wish, you animal,

---

[1] Boning for university examinations.
[2] Chekhov's brother Aleksandr.
[3] A French comic weekly.

that I should flunk my promotion to the fifth term), having passed which I shall attain to the calling of Kachilovsky.[1] The cat is harmed by the tears of the mouse; even thus am I affected by my negligence of past years. Woe is me! I am forced to learn almost everything from the very beginning. Aside from the examinations (which, however, still merely await me) there are, at my disposal, the cadavers to be worked on, clinical studies with the inevitable *historiae morbi,* making the rounds of the hospitals. —I work, and feel my incapacity. Memory has become poor as far as cramming is concerned, I have aged, there's laziness, there's literature—there's a whiff of the little brown jug about you, etc. I'm afraid of failing one of my examinations. I want to rest up but—summer is still so far off! The thought that the whole winter still lies ahead sends ants crawling all over my back.

And we have news. I begin a second page. On October 14 my close friend Fyodor Fedoseyevich Popudoglo died. For me it's an irreplaceable loss. He was not a man of talent, although his portrait is in *The Alarm Clock.* He was a literary old-timer and had a wonderful flair where letters were concerned, and such people are precious for beginners. Secretly, like a thief in the night, I would make my way to his quarters on Sadovaya Street and he would open his heart to me. He took a fancy to me. I knew his very bowels. He died of meningitis, although treated by such an accomplished physician as myself. He was treated by twenty doctors and I was the only one of them who diagnosed his illness correctly. May the Heavenly Kingdom be his; may his memory last forever! He died of alcohol and boon companions, whose *nomina sunt odiosa.* Unreason, negligence, a careless attitude toward his own life and those of others—that is what he died of—at the age of thirty-seven.

Second piece of news. N. A. Leikin came to see me. He is a nice fellow but stingy. He spent five days in Moscow and kept begging me to persuade you not to sing the swan song about which you wrote to him. He likes your stories, and if they are not printed it is solely because of "a misunderstanding," and because you don't know *Splinters.* Here are his words: "How cleverly he showed up the customs-house and what a lot of material he has, but no! he writes about some Chinese '*tam-od-dzyu,*' as if scared of something. . . . He should have put it straight on the line with '*tamozhnya*' [Russian for customs-house] and Russian names. The censorship has nothing against it." If you don't indulge in

[1] A physician in Taganrog.

Chinese gibberish, you come out with horrible lyrics. Write, and you will find your own path. The charm of extra earnings will make up for the first failures. And these failures are trifling: your stories are printed in *Splinters*.

Together with Leikin came N. S. Leskov,[2] my favorite author. He used to call at our home, took me along to the Salon,[3] to Sobolev Alley.[4] He gave me an autographed copy of his works. I am riding with him one night. Half-tipsy, he turns to me and asks, "Know who I am?"—"I know." —"No, you don't! I'm a mystic—." —"I know that too." He stares at me with his aged eyes and vaticinates: "You'll die before your brother." —"Could be." —"I anoint thee with oil, even as Samuel anointed David. Write!" He resembles an exquisite Frenchman and, at the same time, an unfrocked priest. He's a man worth attention. When I live in Petersburg I'll be his guest for a while. We parted good friends.

As for fish and wine: you'll have to deal with *Vater*, who is a specialist in matters juridical. I haven't any money, I confess, and besides, there's no time to earn it. I'm not hunting for a position for you out of sheer egoism: I want to spend the summer with you down south. Don't look for a summer cottage, for you may find something that I shan't like. We'll look together. You smack your lips so in describing your red tidbits and your blue ones [5] that it's hard to recognize the lyricist in you. Don't be eating that garbage, brother! Why, that's abomination, uncleanliness. The only good point about the blue ones is that they are crisp, but marinated ones stink with a damp-vinegary stink (certainly horrible). Eat meat, brother. You'll get skinny in that low-down Taganrog if you're going to stuff yourself with the garbage they sell on the marketplace. For you do overeat, and when you're drunk you're even likely to gorge yourself with a lot of unripe stuff. Your wife knows just as much about housekeeping as I do about obtaining eiderdown—for that reason alone be careful about your food and eat with discrimination. Meat and bread. At least don't feed Mosevna,[6] when she grows up, with whatever comes to hand. Let her know nothing of aunt's spice cookies, her father's special sauce, your "Let's have a bite," and her mama's "bestest" morsel. Train her in the aesthetics of the stomach, at

2 Nikolay Semyonovich Leskov (1831–95), a great storyteller with an idiosyncratic style; also a brilliant punster.
3 A place of amusement in Moscow.
4 The Red Light district.
5 The red ones were tomatoes; the blue, eggplants.
6 The nickname of A. P. Chekhov's little daughter, Mariya, who was to die the next year.

least. By the way, speaking of aesthetics. Excuse me, my dear, but don't be a parent in words only. Teach by example. Clean linen mixed with soiled, scraps of food left on the table, foul rags, your spouse with her dress disarranged, and wearing around her neck a ribbon as dirty as Kontorskaya Street—all this will ruin the little girl even in her earliest years. Appearances affect a child before all else, and appearances have been devilishly downgraded in your house. Upon my honor, I could not recognize you when you were living with us two months ago. Could it possibly be you, who used to live in a tidy room? Discipline the housemaids, brother! By the way, speaking of another sort of cleanliness. Don't swear out loud. You will both corrupt the housemaid and soil Mosevna's eardrums with your utterances. Were I in Anna Ivanovna's [7] place I would give you a drubbing every minute. Regards to Anna Ivanovna and my sprig of a niece. A little girl is held in high regard among us.

As yet they aren't printing your things over at *The Alarm Clock*. When they start printing them I'll notify you.

Chekhov

TO N. A. LEIKIN

Moscow, December 10, 1883

Esteemed Nikolay Aleksandrovich!

* * * I am extremely tired, ill-tempered, and sick. My tired state was brought on by my studies and the pursuit of daily bread, of which I had to earn double the usual ration last month, because my brother the artist came back from his hitch as a conscript only yesterday. I was obliged to work the devil knows where—which is why I did not contribute a story to your last number. I have done such a heap of writing and have gotten so tired that I durst not write for *Splinters:* I knew that I would write nonsense. To my tired state add a hemorrhoid (the fiends brought it). I wasted three days last week lying about in a fever. Thought I had caught typhus from patients, but, glory be to God, that cup passed from me.

Nikolay has returned, and things will ease up.

* * * And I am not sending you a story this time either. Having examinations on December 16 and 20. Dread writing. Don't be angry.

---

[7] A. P. Chekhov's common-law wife.

When I'm free I will be the most assiduous of your contributors. And in my head, too, things are disposed somehow differently now: the humorous bent is missing altogether!

I ask your indulgence and send regards.

Your humble servant,
A. Chekhov

[1884]

TO N. A. LEIKIN

Voskresensk, June 27, 1884

Last evening, respected Nikolay Aleksandrovich, I received your letter and read it with pleasure. * * * Now I am answering it.

Have just returned from an autopsy which took place seven miles from Voskresensk. I was traveling there in a devil-may-care troika, accompanied by a decrepit, barely breathing, good-for-nothing court inspector, a little, white-haired man, a kindly soul who for twenty-five years has been dreaming of attaining to the position of judge. I was making the examination together with a county physician, in a field, under a green young oak, near a country road. The dead man was a stranger to the locality, and the peasants on whose land the body had been found begged us with tears in their eyes, for Christ's sake, not to perform the autopsy in their village. "The women and the children will not sleep for fear. . . ." The inspector, scared by rain clouds, made difficulties at first, but then, deciding that the record of the proceedings could be set down roughly in pencil, and seeing that we were ready to do the cutting up in the open, yielded to the peasants' entreaties. An alarmed hamlet, witnesses, a policeman with a badge, the dead man's widow wailing two hundred steps from where the autopsy was to take place, and two peasants in the role of guards close to the corpse. Near the silent guards a dying bonfire. The peasants must guard the body day and night without pay until the authorities arrive. The corpse, dressed in a red shirt and new pants, is covered with a sheet. On the sheet there is a towel with an icon lying on it. We ask the policeman for water. . . . Water is available, a pond is hard by, but no one offers a bucket: we'll befoul it. One peasant resorts to cunning: the Manekhino villagers steal a bucket from the Tukhlov villagers. Nobody's sorry if a neighbor's bucket is ruined. Impossible to understand how and where they manage to steal it. They are terribly glad of their feat, and grin. . . .

The autopsy reveals twenty broken ribs and a swollen lung, and the stomach smells of alcohol. A violent death, caused by strangulation. The drunken man had been crushed by something heavy, probably a peasant's heavy knee. On the body many abrasions caused by "rocking." [1] The Manekhino peasants found the body and rocked it for two hours so zealously that the future lawyer defending the suspected murderer will have the right to ask the expert if the ribs had not been broken as a result of the "rocking." The inspector is so far gone in decrepitude that not only a murderer but an ailing bug can hide from his dimming eye....

You are probably tired of reading, but I feel like writing. I shall add one more characteristic detail and hold my peace. The murdered man was a factory hand. He had been walking from the Tukhlov tavern with a barrel of vodka. Polikarpov, the witness, who was the first to notice the corpse near the road, declared that a barrel was close to the body. However, passing the body an hour later, he no longer saw the barrel. Ergo, the Tukhlov tavern-keeper, who has no right to sell vodka to be drunk off the premises, had stolen the barrel to remove evidence.

But enough about this. You are disgusted with the examination of wet nurses.... But what about the examination of prostitutes? Medicos (of course, learned ones) who touched upon the question of "the insult to the moral feeling" of those subjected to examination, debated the matter and arrived at this conclusion: "they have the goods, we have the money." If food inspectors may certify apples or ham without insulting the seller, then why should not goods offered by wet nurses and prostitutes be certified? Who fears to offer insult should refrain from buying.... If you're afraid to insult a wet nurse by palping her and hire her without such an examination, she will regale you with goods beside which rotten oranges, ham infected with trichinae, and poisoned sausage pale.

* * * This is an awfully long letter! Every other day I go to the zemstvo [2] hospital, where I receive patients. I should be doing this every day, but I am lazy. The zemstvo physician is a friend of mine.

Votre A. Chekhonte [3]

[1] The practice of rocking the body of a drowned person to and fro, in order to remove water from the windpipe and save his life.

[2] Zemstvo: an elected county council administering certain local affairs such as schools, roads, taxes.

[3] A name invented by a high school teacher of Chekhov's and used by him as one of his pseudonyms.

Zvenigorod, July 14, 1884

Esteemed Nikolay Aleksandrovich!

At present I am in the city of Zvenigorod, where, by the will of the fates, I occupy the post of a zemstvo physician who has persuaded me to replace him for two weeks. Half the day is occupied by receiving patients (thirty to forty a day), the remaining time I rest or am dreadfully bored, seated at the window and gazing at the dark sky, which for the third day has been pouring down a bad, ceaseless rain. Before my window there is a hill with pine trees, to the right the house of the county police officer, farther to the right a mangy burg that was once upon a time a metropolis, to the left a recently abandoned rampart, farther to the left a grove, and from behind it peers Savva the consecrated.[1] Facing the river is the back porch, or more correctly, the back entrance, near which a privy stinks and a sucking pig grunts.

This is Saturday. I don't want to miss the post, because I am in a hurry to dispatch an urgent piece of work. As for the story, I'll scribble it at night and send it off tomorrow. Address letters to me at Voskresensk. They will be forwarded to me punctually.

I was in Moscow and heard that L. I. Palmin had married his old woman.[2]

I saw him but he told me nothing about this. Don't tell him that I passed on to you that prosaic piece of news about this poet. . . . Perhaps the news is no longer news to you!

Farewell.

Your A. Chekhov

[1] A well-known hermitage.
[2] Pelageya Yevdokimovna Palmina, Palmin's common-law wife.

$\begin{bmatrix} 1885 \end{bmatrix}$

TO N. A. LEIKIN

Moscow, March 22, 1885

Esteemed Nikolay Aleksandrovich!

I send you Easter greetings and wish you prosperity and every form of success. In order not to pour more gall into your holiday mood, I am sending my stuff long before the fixed date. At present I have no *feuilleton*, because there's literally *no* material. Moscow offers nothing but suicides, bad pavements, and exhibitions at the riding academy. I'll go and see the local superknow-it-all, Gilyarovsky,[1] who has recently become the little czar of Moscow reporters, and ask him for some raw material. If he has any, he will give it to me, and I shall send a survey as usual for Tuesday evening. If, however, he has nothing, and the reading of tomorrow's paper proves just as fruitless, you will have to do without a survey for this issue. Of course, I could write about the town council, the pavements, Yegorov's tea house. But in all this, what is of interest for *Splinters?* I imagine that your contributors have sent you all sorts of holiday stuff, and the absence of a survey will not force you to work at an extra story during the holiday. And I too am sending you three little things. Only one of them may be worthless, while the other two seem to me good. Enclosed herewith are also captions for drawings. I am glad to rush to help, but I can do nothing about the way my mind works—I start thinking up a caption, but what turns out is a story or nothing at all. Were I living in the capital and a party to the tricks you and Bilibin concoct, I would have been more useful, for it is easier to think with others to stimulate you. . . . But *hélas!* I shall never be a Petersburger. . . . I am so firmly settled in the swamps of Moscow that

---

[1] Vladimir Alekseyevich Gilyarovsky (1853–1935) dropped out of high school when he was eighteen and tried various occupations, including those of longshoreman, factory hand, circus performer, fireman, horse trainer in the Kalmuck steppes. In 1881 he settled in Moscow, became a reporter, and contributed to comic journals. His first book, *Slum People*, was burned by order of the censors. His verse, stories, and reminiscences of his experiences as a hobo appeared in book form.

you will not pull me out with any kind of honey cake. . . . Family and habit . . . If it had not been for these two, I would not give you any rest and would exhaust you with pleas for a position. . . .

"The Pharmacy Price List" is a fashionable theme. I think it could be used. I suggest that you also take advantage of the scandalous bankruptcies of our time. . . . In Moscow firms crash one after another. . . . One goes broke, drops into a pit, and drags another after it. . . . The same in Petersburg, in Kharkov . . . A parallel between the ninth and nineteenth centuries is good for Cyril and Methodius.[2] . . . Draw a neat cottage with the sign "School." Around it decently dressed and well-fed peasants . . . That is the ninth century. Alongside it is the nineteenth century: the same cottage, but already dilapidated and overgrown with nettles. . . .

In the ninth century there were schools, hospitals. In the nineteenth there are schools, pothouses. . . . Generally speaking, something is gabbling in my head, but I am too lazy to put it in order. . . . It is the foulest sloth, that of the mind. . . . To send an unfinished project is indelicate, so forgive me. . . .

When they have finished arranging the flat, and my sister stops playing scales, perhaps then I shall bring some pieces to completion, but now even the Lord will forgive me. . . . Palmin has moved. . . . A regular Wandering Jew! Apparently, such is his nature—he can't be satisfied with a place. . . . If his nature has nothing to do with it, of course, it is his wife's fault. . . . A lovely phrase: the woman plays the devil! * * *

Good-bye; I shall prepare something for the Cyril and Methodius anniversary. Is it true that there was a case of cholera in Kronstadt? I am glad that my brother Aleksandr pleased you. The fellow is not a bad worker and has a good deal of horse sense. . . . Humor is his innate vice. . . . If he chooses the right path and gives up lyrics, he will have a huge success.

Your A. Chekhov

[2] The two Greek missionaries who preached Christianity to the Slavs. April 6, 1885, was the thousandth anniversary of the death of Methodius.

TO N. A. LEIKIN

Esteemed Nikolay Aleksandrovich!

Your letter reached me in our new quarters. My flat is beyond the Moscow River, and the neighborhood is altogether provincial, clean, quiet, cheap, and . . . doltish. The butchery of *Splinters* acted on me like a blow with the blunt side of an ax. . . . On the one hand, I was sorry to have wasted my labors, on the other . . . it was somehow stifling, terrifying. . . . Of course, you are right: it is better to draw in one's horns and chew bast than to endanger a journal by lashing an ax with a whip. We'll have to wait, be patient. . . . I think, though, that we shall have to go on shrinking indefinitely. What is permitted today will demand a visit to the committee tomorrow, and the time is near when even mention of the rank of "merchant" will become forbidden. Yes, literature earns an uncertain piece of bread, and you were clever to have been born before me, when it was easier to breathe and to write. . . .

I had not intended to send something this week. You had three pieces of mine and I regarded a rest as legitimate, all the more so since moving wore me out. Now, having received your letter and learned the fate of my three pieces, I am sending you a story that I wrote not for *Splinters* but for any publication that would find it acceptable. The story is longish but it has to do with actors, which is appropriate, in view of the opening of the season, and, meseems, humorous. Tomorrow I shall sit down and write "September, October, and November," provided, of course, I am not prevented by my medical practice, etc.

You advise me to make a trip to Petersburg, to have a talk with Khudekov,[1] and you say that Petersburg is not China. . . . I myself know that it isn't China, and you are aware that I have long been conscious of the need for that trip, but what can I do? As I am the breadwinner of a large family, I never have a spare 10-ruble bill, and for this trip, no matter how cheap and uncomfortable it would be, a minimum of 50 rubles is needed. I don't know how to squeeze this sum out of the family and indeed, I can't. If I allow them one course at dinner instead of two courses, I shall begin to pine with remorse. I had

[1] Sergey Nikolayevich Khudekov was publisher of *The Petersburg Gazette*.

hoped that I would snatch enough for the trip out of the honorarium that I got from *The Petersburg Gazette*. But it has turned out that I earn no more as a contributor to the *Gazette* than I used to, for I give it everything that I used to send to *Entertainment, The Alarm Clock,* etc. Allah alone knows how hard it is for me to keep my balance and how easy it is to stagger and lose my equilibrium. Should I earn 20–30 rubles less next month, it seems to me that my balance will go to the devil and I shall be in a mess. As far as money goes, I am badly scared, and probably because of this monetary, by no means commercial cowardice, I avoid borrowing and taking advances. I am not a stay-at-home. If I had money, I would be roaming towns and villages endlessly. . . .

I must not write more than I do; for medicine is not law practice: if you don't work, you fall behind. Consequently, my literary earnings are a constant quantity. They can diminish, increase they cannot. . . .

I congratulate you on your purchase—I love awfully everything that in Russia is called an estate. This word has not lost its poetic nuance. And so in the summer you will rest in the lap of Nature. . . .

Palmin came to see me yesterday and will come again on Tuesday. On Tuesdays I have soirees, with girls, music, singing, literature. I want to introduce our poet to society, or he will turn sour.

Your A. Chekhov

[1886]

TO A. P. CHEKHOV

Moscow, January 4, 1886

Quarantine-Customs-House Official Sasha!

I congratulate you and all your vale [of tears] on the New Year, on new happiness, on new infants. . . . May God grant you all that is best! You are probably sulking because I do not write you. . . . I, too, am sulking and for the very same reasons. . . . Animal! Lummox! Progenitive clerk! Why don't you write? Can it be that your letters have lost their former charm and power? Can it be that you have ceased to consider me your brother? Can it be that after this you're not a swine? Write—I repeat it a thousand times—write! Just a peep or two, but let's hear from you. . . . Things are going well here, except, perhaps, that Father has bought up more lamps. He has a mania for lamps. By the way, if I find it in my desk, I'll enclose a certain rarity with this; I request its return after you've read it.

I've been in Petersburg and, while staying at Leikin's, survived all the torments which the Scripture bids us "suffer unto the end." . . . He fed me magnificently but, the beast, all but choked me with his lying. . . . I became acquainted with the editorial staff of *The Petersburg Gazette,* where I was received like the Shah of Persia. Chances are you will be working on that sheet, but not before summer. Do not rely on Leikin. He's trying every which way to trip me up on the *P.G.* He'll trip you up, too. Khudekov, ed. of the *P.G.,* will be staying with me in January. I'll have a good talk with him.

But, for the love of Allah—do me a favor, chuck those oppressed collegiate registrars of yours! Is it possible your smeller isn't sensitive enough to warn you that this theme has had its day by now and makes one yawn? And wherever, in that Asia of yours, do you unearth those torments which the miserable bureaucratic wits go through in your stories? Verily, I say unto thee—merely reading them makes one feel creepy! The story "Spick and Span" is magnificently conceived, but . . .

there are the bureaucrats! If, instead of a bureaucrat, you had put in a benign burgher, without stressing his being an official and his tendency to pull rank, your "Spick and Span" would have been as delectable as all those boiled lobsters which Yerakita [1] slurped down. Also, do not permit any shortening or reworking of your stories. . . . For it is a loathsome thing to see the fine Leikinian hand in every line. . . . Withholding permission is difficult, however; it is easier to resort to a means within grasp: do your own shortening, *nec plus ultra*— and do your own revamping to the utmost. The more you shorten the more often you will get into print. But, above all: insofar as possible be vigilant, keep your eyes open, and huff and puff, rewriting five times, shortening, etc., bearing in mind that all of Petersburg is watching the labors of the Bros. Chekhov.

I was overwhelmed by the reception extended to me by the Petersburg people. Suvorin,[2] Grigorovich,[3] Burenin [4] . . . Welcome, acclaim, glorification, all this scared me—because I had been writing sloppily, in an offhand way. There, if I had known that I was being read thus, I would not have written so like a hack. . . . Remember, then: you are being read. Furthermore, don't use the names and family names of people you know in your stories. It is in poor taste: there is the familiarity, and then, too . . . those you know lose respect for the printed word. . . . I have made the acquaintance of Bilibin. A very decent fellow, this, whom you can, in case of need, trust *fully*. In two or three years he'll be playing a prominent role in the newspaper field of Peters-

[1] A Taganrog broker whom the Chekhov brothers remembered for having on one occasion eaten an enormous dish of lobsters.

[2] Aleksey Sergeyevich Suvorin (1814–1912), a novelist, playwright, journalist, editor. He made a fortune as a publisher. He began as a liberal, but the Petersburg daily, *New Times*, which he acquired in 1876, became the mouthpiece of chauvinism and of the interests of the ruling classes. In 1886 Chekhov, then unknown, started contributing to the paper. Many of his stories and his only novel first appeared in its columns. He had a deep respect for Suvorin's discernment in matters of literature, and, with some of his views, his own coincided. But he detested the man's reactionary stance. He took comfort in the thought that he could occupy an independent position with regard to the paper and not be besmirched by its policies. Nevertheless, in 1893 he ceased offering his work to *New Times*, although he maintained friendly relations with Suvorin, who, paradoxically, contributed to a few of Chekhov's causes. Their intimate relations did not survive Suvorin's adherence to the enemies of Dreyfus and Zola, although Chekhov kept in touch with his old friend to the end.

[3] Dmitry Vasilyevich Grigorovich (1822–99) won his reputation as a novelist in the mid-nineteenth century and was thus one of the survivors of the Golden Age of Russian literature. Chekhov dedicated his book of short stories, *In the Twilight* (1887), to him.

[4] Viktor Petrovich Burenin, a *feuilleton* writer for *New Times*.

burg. He will wind up as editor of a *News,* or a *News Times,* or some such thing. Consequently, a useful man. . . .

Once more, for the love of Allah!—when did you manage to fill [. . .] with so much chill? And whom do you want to astonish by your pusillanimity? That which may be dangerous for others is for a university man merely something to laugh at, to laugh at condescendingly, yet you yourself are bucking with all your might to be a coward among cowards! Why this dread of envelopes with the return addresses of editorial offices? And what can people do to you if they find out that you write? You ought to spit on the whole lot of them—let them find out! Why, they won't beat you up, won't hang you, won't fire you. . . . By the way—Leikin, on meeting the director of your department at a Loan Association started snowing him under with reproaches for the persecution you're enduring because of your authorship. The man became confused and began swearing by God. . . . Bilibin writes, yet at the same time serves ever so diligently in the Post and Telegraph Department. Levinsky [5] publishes a humorous journal—and fills sixteen posts. Think of how severe the restrictions are for the military, but even they are not embarrassed about writing openly. There is a need of hiding things, but to go into hiding—no, no! No, Sasha, it's high time to turn over to the archives, together with the oppressed bureaucrats, the persecuted newspaper correspondents. . . . It is more realistic nowadays to depict collegiate registrars who make life impossible for their Excellencies, and correspondents who poison existence for others. . . . And so on. Don't be angry about the moralizing. I'm writing this because I feel sorry, vexed. You are a good scribbler, you could be getting twice as much as you do now, yet you are eating wild honey and locusts owing to some misapprehensions or other lodged in your skull. . . .

I still haven't married and have no children. Living isn't easy. This summer, probably, there will be money. O, if only there would be!

Write, write! I often think of you and rejoice when I realize that you exist. . . . Don't be a lummox, then, and don't forget

Your A. Chekhov

Nikolay dawdles. Ivan, just as before, is nothing but a downright Ivan. Sister is dizzy, as if she had been inhaling charcoal fumes: admirers, symphonic performances, a spacious apartment. . . .

[5] Vladimir Dmitriyevich Levinsky, editor of *The Alarm Clock.*

Moscow, February 1, 1886

Kindest of humorists and assistant barrister, most unselfish of secretaries, Viktor Viktorovich!

Five times I started writing to you and five times was prevented from doing so. At last I nailed myself to a chair and am writing. [...]

I have just returned from visiting the notable poet, Palmin. When I read him the lines from your letters relating to him, he said, "I respect that man. He is highly gifted!"

Whereupon his Inspired Highness lifted the longest of his five fingers and was good enough to add (thoughtfully, of course), "But *Splinters* will corrupt him! Have some brandy."

We talked for a long time and about many things. Palmin is a typical poet, if you admit the existence of such a type. A poetic personality, always rapturous, chock full of themes and ideas. . . . Conversation with him does not tire one. True, talking to him you have to drink a great deal, but then you can be sure that during the three or four hours of palaver you will not hear one dishonest word, not one banal phrase, and sobriety is a small price to pay.

* * * Many thanks for the trouble you took about the clipping and for sending me the original. In order not to be indebted to you (financially) I am sending you for the postage a 35-copeck stamp which you sent me some time ago with the honorarium and which I was never able to get off my hands. Now you be burdened with it!

* * * Your gloating over the prohibition of my "Attack on Husbands" by the censorship redounds to your honor. Shake hands. Nevertheless it would have been much pleasanter to receive 65 rubles instead of 55. To get back at censorship and all gloaters over my misfortune I and my friends have thought up a "Cuckolding Society." The statutes have already been submitted for approval. I have been elected chairman by a vote of 14 to 3.

* * * Now about a fiancée [1] and Hymen . . . With your permission I postpone these two items until next time, when I shall be free from

---

[1] Dunya Yefimovich Efros (also called Dunichka, Israelite, and Nose) was a close friend of Chekhov's sister. Four weeks later Chekhov wrote to Bilibin, "I have definitely parted from my fiancée, i.e., she parted from me. But I haven't bought a revolver yet and I don't keep a diary. Everything in the world is changeable, inconstant, approximate, and relative."

the inspiration communicated to me by the talk with Palmin. I am afraid to say too much, and talk nonsense. When I speak about a woman I like, I usually prolong the talk to *nec plus ultra*, to the Pillars of Hercules, a trait that has been mine since before my school days. Thank your fiancée for remembering me and for her attention and tell her that my marriage is probably—alack and alas! Censorship does not permit it. . . . My she is a Jewess. Should a wealthy Jewess have enough courage to embrace Orthodox Christianity with its consequences —very well; if not, it's not necessary. Besides, we have already quarreled. Tomorrow we'll make up and a week later quarrel again. Vexed that religion is in her way, she breaks pencils on my desk and photographs—and this is characteristic. A terrible shrew. It is certain that a year or two after the wedding I shall divorce her. But . . . finis.

> *Privately practicing physician,*
> *A. Chekhov*

TO A. S. SUVORIN

Moscow, February 21, 1886

Gracious sir, Aleksey Sergeyevich!

I have received your letter. Thanks for the flattering opinion of my work and the speedy publication of my story.[1] You can judge for yourself how refreshingly and even inspiringly the kind attention of an experienced and gifted man like yourself has acted upon me as an author.

I share your opinion of the wretched ending of my story and I thank you for the useful suggestion. I have been writing for six years, but you are the first who has taken the trouble to advise a cut and to motivate it.

A. Chekhonte, my pseudonym, is probably both fanciful and bizarre. But it was thought up in the foggy dawn of my youth, and I am used to it and so don't notice its oddity.

---

[1] "Requiem."

I write relatively little, no more than two or three short stories a week. I shall have some leisure for contributions to *New Times,* but I am glad that you did not make delivery of the work at a fixed date a condition of my being one of your authors. Such a condition means haste and a sense of pressure, which interferes with work. Having to meet a deadline is inconvenient for me, because I am a physician occupied with my practice. . . . I can't guarantee that tomorrow I won't be torn away from my desk for a whole day. . . . There is constant risk of not meeting the deadline. . . .

For the time being the fee you offer is completely satisfactory. If, in addition, you will have your newspaper sent me—I see it very rarely— I shall be very grateful.

This time I am sending a story [2] that is exactly twice as long as the previous one and, I fear, twice as bad. . . .

I have the honor to be

yours respectfully,
A. Chekhov

TO V. V. BILIBIN

Moscow, March 11, 1886

There is hope that in the days to come I shall have my hands full and so I am answering your letter now, esteemed Viktor Viktorovich, when there is a free hour at my disposal!

Primo: your adventures with the dramatic censorship [1] had the same effect on me as Mayne Reid has on high school boys; today I sent them a one-acter.[2]

You shouldn't have angled to have *Splinters* raise my fee. If, because of the 10 rubles added to your pay, Leikin, to keep within his budget, will have to contribute two little scenes, then how many such pieces will he have to turn out, should I also get a raise? Have a heart, take pity on the man! [. . .]

You are probably right when you say that it is too soon for me to marry. . . . I am frivolous in spite of being only one year younger than

2 "The Witch."
1 A skit of Bilibin's was rejected by the Theatrical-Literary Committee.
2 The first version of "On the Harmfulness of Tobacco."

you. Sometimes I still dream of high school: homework left undone, and fear of being called on by the teacher. Ergo, I'm young.

Ears of Corn [3] hit the bull's eye! You are "hard"! Just the opposite. Your only fault is softness, you're cottony (forgive the expression). If you're not afraid of similes, as a feuilletonist you resemble the lover to whom the woman says, "You're going about it gently. . . . It must be more forceful!" [. . .]

Precisely, you are going about it gently. . . .

Merci for the theme.[4] Shall utilize it.

"The Witch" in *New Times* brought me about 75 rubles—more than a month's pay from *Splinters*.

I am reading Darwin. Magnificent! I simply love him. I have not read Stulli's *Marriage*. He taught history and geography at our high school, and he boarded with us. If you see him, remind him that the wife of Tournefort, our French teacher, when she felt her time was near, surrounded herself with candles. [. . .]

Have no themes at all. I don't know what to do. Spotted fever, which in the shortest time carried off *six* members of my class, is raging in Moscow, I'm afraid. I fear nothing, but of this fever I am afraid. It is as if there were something mystic about it. . . .

I know "The Witch" is not to your taste, indeed, many people did not like it, but what's to be done? In the absence of themes, the devil nudges your hand to write such pieces. . . .

However, it's time to sleep.

Your A. Chekhov

TO N. P. CHEKHOV

Moscow, March, 1886

Little Zabelin! [1]

* * * You have often complained to me that people didn't "understand" you! Even Goethe and Newton didn't complain of that. . . . Christ alone

---

[3] A monthly that printed a survey of the comic press, describing a *feuilleton* by Bilibin as "illiterate, hard, pretentiously provocative."

[4] The theme suggested by Bilibin was as follows: a newly appointed bureaucrat is afraid of his subordinate, an old rat who has sharpened his teeth on official papers. While presenting a report to his superior, the bureaucrat is vexed by the thought that the underling is making game of him. Chekhov did not use the suggestion.

[1] A broad hint at Nikolay's morbid weakness for liquor. Zabelin, a Zvenigorod landowner, was an alcoholic.

did, but He was speaking not of His ego, but of His teaching. You are perfectly well understood. And if you don't understand yourself, it is not the fault of others.

I assure you that as a brother and a friend I understand you and sympathize with you heartily. I know all your good qualities as I know my five fingers; I value and deeply respect them. I can even enumerate those qualities if you like, to prove that I understand you. I think you are kind to the point of spinelessness, sincere, magnamimous, unselfish, ready to share your last penny; you are free from envy and hatred; you are simple-hearted, you pity men and beasts; you are trustful, not spiteful, and do not remember evil. You have a gift from Heaven such as others do not possess: you have talent. This talent places you above millions of people, for only one out of two million on earth is an artist. Your talent sets you apart: even if you were a toad or a tarantula, you would be respected, for to talent everything is forgiven.

You have only one fault. Your false position, your unhappiness, your intestinal catarrh are all due to it. It is your utter lack of culture. Please forgive me, but *veritas magis amicitiae.* . . . You see, life sets its own terms. To feel at ease among cultivated people, to be at home and comfortable with them, one must have a certain amount of culture. Talent has brought you into that circle, you belong to it, but—you are drawn away from it, and you waver between cultured people and the tenants vis-à-vis.

Cultured people must, in my opinion, meet the following conditions:

1. They respect human personality, and for this reason they are always lenient, gentle, civil, and ready to give in to others. They do not raise a rumpus over a hammer or a lost eraser; when they live with you they do not make you feel that they are doing you a favor, and on leaving they do not say, "Impossible to live with you!" They overlook noise, cold overdone meat, jokes, the presence of strangers in their rooms.

2. They feel compassion not only for beggars and cats. Their hearts ache over what the naked eye does not see. Thus, for instance, if Pyotr knows that his parents do not sleep nights because they see him seldom (and that when he is drunk), he will spit on vodka and hasten to see them. They sit up nights in order to help the Polevayevs, to keep their brothers at the university, and to buy clothes for their mother.

3. They respect the property of others and therefore pay their debts.

4. They are candid, and dread lying as they dread fire. They do not

lie even about trifles. A lie insults the listener and debases him in the eyes of the speaker. They do not pose; they behave in the street as they do at home; they do not show off before their inferiors. They do not chatter and do not force uninvited confidences on others. Out of respect for the ears of other people they often keep silent.

5. They do not belittle themselves to arouse compassion in others. They do not play on other people's heartstrings so as to elicit sighs and be fussed over. They do not say, "People don't understand me" or "I have frittered away my talent! I [...]," because all that is striving after cheap effect; it is vulgar, stale, false.

6. They are not vain. They do not care for such paste diamonds as familiarity with celebrities, the handclasp of the drunken Plevako,[2] the raptures of the first comer in a picture gallery, popularity in beer halls. . . . They laugh at the declaration "I represent the press!!" which befits only the Rodzeviches and Levenbergs.[3] When they have done a copeck's worth of work they do not strut about with their briefcases as though they had done a hundred rubles' worth, and they do not brag of having entree where others are not admitted. The truly talented always keep in the shade, among the crowd, far from the show. Even Krylov[4] said that an empty barrel is noiser than a full one.

7. If they possess talent they respect it. They sacrifice peace, women, wine, vanity to it. They are proud of their talent. They do not carouse with riffraff: they are aware that their calling is not just to live with such people but to have an educative influence on them. Besides, they are fastidious.

8. They cultivate their aesthetic sense. They cannot fall asleep in their clothes, see the cracks in the wall full of insects, breathe foul air, walk on a spittle-covered floor, eat off a kerosene stove. They seek as far as possible to tame and ennoble the sexual instinct. [...] The kitchen is not their main interest. What they want from a woman is not a bedfellow, not equine sweat, not a cleverness that shows itself in the ability to fake a pregnancy and to lie incessantly. What they need, especially if they are artists, is freshness, elegance, humanity, the capacity for being not a [...] but a mother. They do not swill vodka offhand. They do not sniff at cupboards, for they know that they are

[2] Fyodor Nikiforovich Plevako was a Moscow lawyer.
[3] Two-bit journalists.
[4] Ivan Andreyevich Krylov (1769–1844), the Russian La Fontaine.

not pigs. They drink only when they are free, on occasion. For they need *mens sana in corpore sano.*

And so on. That is what cultivated people are like. In order to educate yourself and not be below the level of your surroundings it is not enough to read *Pickwick Papers* and memorize a monologue from *Faust.* It is not enough to come to Yakimanka [5] only to leave a week later.

What is needed is continuous work, day and night, constant reading, study, will power. Every hour counts.

Trips to Yakimanka and back will not help. You must make a clean break. Come to us; smash the vodka bottle; lie down and read— Turgenev, if you like, whom you have not read, give up your conceit, you are not a child. You will soon be thirty. It is time!

I am waiting. . . . We are all waiting. . . .

Your A. Chekhov

TO D. V. GRIGOROVICH

Moscow, March 28, 1886

Your letter, my kind, ardently beloved bearer of good tidings, struck me like a thunderbolt. I nearly cried, I got all excited, and now I feel that your message has left a deep mark on my soul. As you have been kind to my youth, so may God succor your old age. For my part, I can find neither words nor deeds with which to thank you. You know with what eyes ordinary people regard the elect such as you, and so you can imagine how your letter has affected my self-esteem. It is better than any diploma, and for a fledgling writer it is bounty for the present and the future. I am almost in a daze. It is not within my power to judge whether I merit this high reward. I can only repeat that it has overwhelmed me.

If I have a gift that should be respected, I confess before the purity of your heart that hitherto I have not respected it. I felt that I did have talent, but I was used to thinking it insignificant. Purely external causes are enough to make one unjust to oneself, suspicious, and diffident. And, as I think of it now, there have been plenty of such causes in my case.

[5] The street on which the Chekhovs lived.

All those who are near to me have always treated my writing with condescension and have never stopped advising me in a friendly manner not to give up real work for scribbling. I have hundreds of acquaintances in Moscow, among them a score or so of people who write, and I cannot recall a single one who would read me or regard me as an artist. In Moscow there is a Literary Circle, so-called: gifted writers and mediocrities of all ages and complexions meet once a week in a restaurant and give their tongues free rein. If I were to go there and read them even a fragment of your letter, they would laugh to my face. In the five years that I have been knocking about newspaper offices I have come to accept this general view of my literary insignificance; before long I got used to taking an indulgent view of my labors, and so the fat was in the fire. That's the first cause. The second is that I am a physician and am up to my ears in medical work, so that the saw about chasing two hares [1] has robbed no one of more sleep than me.

I am writing all this for the sole purpose of exonerating myself to at least some degree in your eyes. Up till now my attitude toward my literary work has been extremely frivolous, casual, thoughtless. I cannot think of a *single* story at which I worked for more than a day, and "The Huntsmen," which you liked, I wrote in a bathing-cabin. I wrote my stories the way reporters write notices of fires: mechanically, half-consciously, without caring a pin either about the reader or myself. . . . I wrote and tried my best not to use up on a story the images and scenes which are dear to me and which, God knows why, I treasured and carefully concealed.

What first impelled me to self-criticism was a very friendly and, I believe, sincere letter from Suvorin. I began to plan writing something decent, but I still lacked faith in my ability to produce anything worth while.

And then against all expectations came your letter. Excuse the comparison, but it had the effect on me of a governor's order to leave town within twenty-four hours: I suddenly felt the urgent need to hurry and get out of the hole in which I was stuck. . . .

I agree with you entirely. The instances of cynicism that you point out I myself recognized when I saw "The Witch" in print. Had I written the story in three or four days instead of in twenty-four hours, they would not have been there.

I will stop—but not soon—doing work that has to be delivered on

[1] The allusion is to the Russian proverb: chase two hares, and you catch neither.

schedule. It is impossible to get out of the rut I am in all at once. I don't object to going hungry, as I went hungry in the past, but it is not a question of myself. . . . To writing I give my leisure: two or three hours during the day and a fraction of the night, that is, an amount of time that is good only for short pieces. In the summer when I have more spare time and fewer expenses I shall undertake some serious piece of work.

I cannot attach my real name to my book [2] because it is too late: the vignette is ready and the book is in print.[3] Even before you did so, many Petersburg people advised me not to spoil the book by using the pseudonym, but I disregarded the advice, probably out of *amour-propre*. I thoroughly dislike my book. It is a hodgepodge, a messy bag stuffed with a student's trifles, tampered with by censors and editors of humorous periodicals. I believe that many, having read it, will be disappointed. Had I known that I was read and that you kept your eye on me, I would not have published my book.

All my hope is pinned to the future. I am only twenty-six. Perhaps I shall succeed in achieving something, though time flies fast.

Forgive this long letter and do not hold it against a man who for the first time in his life has made bold to indulge in the pleasure of writing to Grigorovich.

If possible, send me your photograph. I am so overcome by your kindness that I feel like writing you not a sheet, but a whole ream. May God grant you happiness and health, and believe the sincerity of your deeply respectful and grateful

A. Chekhov

TO A. P. CHEKHOV

Moscow, April 6, 1886

Well, enough of this, you customs officer; why such strong language? Where could "the ghost of a have-been" have come from, and why don't you recognize yourself in the mirror?

[2] *Motley Stories.*
[3] As a matter of fact, the title page bears both the actual name and the pseudonym Chekhonte.

1. Davydov [1] will remit the money, and if he hasn't done so yet, that is because he's stone broke.

2. *The Cricket* owes you money. *The Alarm Clock*, too. Tomorrow Mishka will collect your crumbs and send them to you. Generally speaking, when it comes to payment, turn to Mishka. A good lawyer. *The Cricket* pays promptly, and you will get 8 copecks a line. * * *

These days I work for *New Times*, where I am paid 12 copecks a line. I shall manage to drag Gil [2] into the Petersburg press; while uneducated, he is talented. Couldn't I do the same for you, all the more so since you are a thousand times better educated and more gifted than the corks who contribute to *Action* and *The Observer*? [3] Work, my dear! Be on your guard, plug away, don't squander time fussing. Don't turn yourself and your work into Nestlé's flour. . . . At first it would be well for you to work for *The Petersburg Gazette;* from there before long you will move to *New Times*. Both newspapers are pitch dark to you. You don't know what they need. . . . Couldn't you look up these papers in Novorossisk? *New Times* is certainly received in Novorossisk. Look up the Saturday issues. Leikin is no longer the vogue. I have taken his place. Nowadays I am the rage in Petersburg, and I'd like you not to lag behind. . . .

Can it be that you are leaving Novorossisk? Couldn't you wait till fall? If you do, I give you my word of honor that I'll visit you in the summer. [. . .] on the debts. The dead and the talented have no shame. Kolka [4] owes 3000, and it doesn't matter. We'd live it up gloriously! Your departure goes against the grain with me, all the more so since I am sure that Petersburg will give you nothing but new debts. . . . Wait till fall! I shall be in Petersburg then, I'll acquaint Grigorovich and the rest with your person and—who knows? Grigorovich is an actual councillor of State and a bearer of a decoration. . . . He will find a better berth for you than you will yourself. All the Ministers know him. . . . So remember: plug away at short stories. I speak from experience. Write. Write to Mother. Let me know by what route I can best reach you. Greetings. . . .

Your A. Chekhov

---

[1] Vladimir Vasilyevich Davydov, editor of *The Spectator*.
[2] V. A. Gilyarovsky.
[3] Respectively, a radical journal and a monthly with an anti-Semitic bias, both published in Petersburg.
[4] Chekhov's brother Nikolay.

Dearest Aleksandr Pavlovich, Mr. Chekhov!

If you haven't given up the desire to write to me, my address is Doctor Chekhov, Voskresensk, Province of Moscow.

I have just returned from Petersburg, where I spent two weeks. I had a splendid time there. I got very close to Grigorovich and Suvorin. There are too many details to be set down in a letter. I'll give them to you when we see each other. Do you read *New Times?*

"The City of the Future" is a magnificent subject on account of both its novelty and its appeal. I think that if you overcome your laziness you will do rather well, but you are such a sloth! "The City of the Future" will be a work of art only on these conditions: (1) no politico-economico-social verbal effusions; (2) objectivity throughout; (3) truth in the description of characters and things; (4) extreme brevity; (5) audacity and originality—eschew clichés; (6) warmheartedness.

In my opinion, descriptions of nature should be extremely brief and offered by the way, as it were. Give up commonplaces, such as: "the setting sun, bathing in the waves of the darkening sea, flooded with purple gold," and so on, or: "Swallows, flying over the surface of the water, chirped gaily." In descriptions of nature one should seize upon minutiae, grouping them so that when, having read the passage, you close your eyes, a picture is formed. For example, you will evoke a moonlit night by writing that on the mill dam the glass fragments of a broken bottle flashed like a bright little star, and that the black shadow of a dog or a wolf rolled along like a ball, and so on. Nature becomes animated if you do not shrink from making physical phenomena resemble human actions.

In the area of mental states there are also particulars. May God save you from generalities. It is best to avoid descriptions of the mental states of your heroes; the effort should be to make these clear from their actions. Don't have too many characters. The center of gravity should be two: he and she.

I am writing this as a reader with a distinct taste. I write also so that you should not feel alone. Loneliness is very trying for an author. Poor criticism is better than none. . . . Isn't that true?

Send me the beginning of your tale. . . . I'll read it and send it back to you the next day with my opinion. Do not be in a hurry to finish it, because no one in Petersburg will read your manuscript before the end of September: some are abroad, others in the country.

I am glad that you have undertaken serious work. At thirty a man should be set in his ways and a person of character. Still an inexperienced youth, I may be forgiven if I busy myself with rubbish. However, my five stories in *New Times* have caused a commotion in the capital which fairly suffocated me.

The fees from *The Cricket* and *The Alarm Clock* have been forwarded to you by Misha in two installments.

And now be well and do not forget your

A. Chekhov

The weather is bad: windy.

TO M. V. KISELEVA[1]

Moscow, December 13, 1886

First of all, respected Mariya Vladimirovna, permit me to present to you a printed tale [2] about how noted authors utilize acquaintance with [...].[3] The *feuilleton* I am sending you brought me 115 rubles. Well, how then can one help gravitating to [...]? [3]

* * * With your permission, I am stealing for my stories from your two latest letters to Masha two descriptions of weather. Remarkable— you have a completely masculine manner of writing. In every line (except where you touch upon children) you are a man. Of course, this should flatter your self-esteem, for, speaking generally, men are a thousand times superior to and more accomplished than women.

In Petersburg [4] I rested, that is, I spent whole days roaming the city, paying visits, listening to compliments, which my soul detests. Alas and

---

[1] M. V. Kiseleva was a writer in a small way, daughter of the director of the Imperial Theaters and wife of Aleksey Sergeyevich Kiselev, a landowner from whom the Chekhovs rented a summer cottage on the estate near Moscow known as Babkino, 1885–87.

[2] The story "Mire," about an attractive Jewess who seduced two men for mercenary reasons. Chekhov discussed it in another letter to the same correspondent, below.

[3] Derogatory terms, probably, for Jewess and Jews.

[4] Chekhov and his sister arrived in the capital in late November or early December, staying for a week or so.

alack! In Petersburg I am becoming fashionable, like *Nana*. While Korolenko,[5] who is serious, is barely known to the editors, all Petersburg reads my trash. Even Senator Golubev [6] reads it. . . . This flatters me, but my feeling for literature is offended. I am ill at ease with a public that courts literary toy dogs only because it fails to notice elephants, and I am thoroughly convinced that not a single dog will know me when I begin working seriously. * * *

How is Counterfeiter? [7]

Finally, having wished your entire family all earthly good, I am respectfully and devotedly,

A. Chekhov

---

[5] See note to first letter to him, p. 62.
[6] Mme. Kiseleva's son-in-law, Ivan Yakovlevich Golubev.
[7] A dog of Mme. Kiseleva's, so named by Chekhov because of its distrustful look.

[1887]

TO M. V. KISELEVA

Moscow, January 14, 1887

Your "Larka," esteemed Mariya Vladimirovna, is very nice; it has rough spots, but brevity and the masculine style of the story redeem everything. Since I don't wish to set myself up as the sole judge of your literary offspring, I am sending your story, having read it, to Suvorin, an extremely understanding person. I will let you have his opinion in due time. . . . And now permit me to respond to your criticism of my "Mire." Even your praise of my "On the Road" has not allayed my wrath as an author and I hasten to avenge myself for "Mire." Look out and hold tight to your chair so as not to faint. Well, here goes. . . .

Every critical article, even an unjustly abusive one, is usually met with a silent bow—such is literary etiquette. Retorting is ruled out, and those who engage in it are justly reproved as inordinately vain. But since your critique was, as you said, in the nature of "an evening talk on the terrace of a wing of the main house at Babkino, in the presence of Ma-Pa,[1] Counterfeiter, and Levitan,"[2] and as the discussion, passing over the literary aspect of the story, assumed a general character, I shall not sin against etiquette if I allow myself to continue the conversation.

To begin with, let me say that I dislike, as you do, the kind of literature that we are discussing. As a reader and an average man, I tend to shy away from it, but if you ask my honest and sincere opinion about it, I will say that the question of its right to exist is still open and subject to argument, although Olga Andreyevna[3] thinks she has settled it. Neither I nor you nor all the world's critics have any data reliable enough to justify rejecting that literature. I don't know who is right: Homer, Shakespeare, Lope de Vega, the writers of antiquity generally,

---

[1] A nickname of Chekhov's sister.
[2] Isaak Ilyich Levitan (1860–1900), a noted landscape painter. Chekhov was to doctor this close friend when he wounded himself trying to commit suicide.
[3] O. A. Golokhvastova was a playwright.

who were not afraid of exploring the "dunghill," but who were morally firmer than we are, or contemporary writers, prim on paper but as far as their souls and their lives are concerned, coldly cynical. I don't know who shows bad taste: the Greeks, who were not ashamed of celebrating love as it really exists in beautiful nature, or the readers of Gaboriau, Marlitt, Boborykin.[4] Like nonresistance to violence, freedom of the will, and such, this problem can be solved only in the future. We can merely speak of these problems, we are not competent to solve them. Reference to Turgenev and Tolstoy, who avoided the "dunghill," does not clarify the problem. Their squeamishness proves nothing; certainly there was a generation of writers before their time who not only dismissed as dirt "rascals of both sexes," but who also would not describe peasants and officials below the rank of titular councillor.[5] Nor does the reference to the corrupting influence of the trend in question solve the problem. Everything in this world is relative and approximate. There are people who are corrupted even by children's literature, who read with peculiar pleasure the suggestive passages in the Psalms and in Solomon's parables, and there are also those who, the more they know of life's filth, the more they gain in purity. Publicists, jurists, and physicians, initiated into all the secrets of human sinfulness, are not known to be immoral; and the morality of realistic writers most often exceeds that of archimandrites. When all is said, no literature can outdo the cynicism of real life; you won't intoxicate with one glass someone who has already drunk up a whole barrel.

2. It's true that the world teems with "rascals of both sexes." Human nature is imperfect, and it would therefore be strange to see none but the righteous on earth. To think that it is the duty of literature to pluck the pearl from the heap of villains is to deny literature itself. Literature is called artistic when it depicts life as it actually is. Its purpose is truth, honest and indisputable. To limit its functions to special tasks, such as the finding of "pearls," does it mortal injury, just as if you forced Levitan to picture a tree without its dirty bark and yellowed leaves. I agree that a "pearl" is a good thing, but a writer is not a confectioner, not a cosmetician, not an entertainer; he is a man with an obligation, under contract to his duty, his conscience; he must do what he has set out to do; he is bound to fight his squeamishness and

---

[4] Pyotr Dmitriyevich Boborykin (1836–1921), a long-lived, versatile, and prolific writer of sensational fiction, which offered few compensations for his slovenly prose.
[5] The lowest civil rank.

dirty his imagination with what is dirty in life. He is like any ordinary reporter. What would you say if a reporter, out of fastidiousness, described only honest mayors, highminded ladies, and virtuous railroad magnates?

For chemists there is nothing unclean on earth. A writer should be as objective as a chemist; he must give up everyday subjectivity and realize that dunghills play a very respectable role in a landscape, and that evil passions belong to life as much as good ones do.

3. Writers are children of their time, and so, like the rest of its public, they must submit to the external conventions of living together. They certainly must be decorous. That is all we have the right to demand of realists. However, you say nothing against the execution and form of "Mire." Consequently I must have been decorous.

4. I confess I rarely converse with my conscience when I write. This is due to habit and to the pettiness of my efforts. That is why, when I set down this or that opinion on literature, I do not have myself in mind.

5. You write, "Were I the editor, I would have returned the *feuilleton* to you for your own good." Why, then, go no further? Why not mete out punishment to editors who print such stories? Why not issue a stern reprimand to the Central Press Administration for not banning immoral newspapers?

Lamentable would be the fate of literature (both major and minor) if it were left to the mercy of personal views. That's first. Second, no police would consider itself competent in matters of literature. I agree that you can't do without restraint and the stick, for cheats make their way into literature too, but no matter how you rack your brains, you will not devise a better police for literature than criticism and the authors' own conscience. Since the creation of the world, you know, people have puzzled over it, but have invented nothing better. . . .

You would like me to suffer a loss of 115 rubles and have the editor disgrace me. Others, including your father, are enraptured with the story. Still others send Suvorin abusive letters, reviling both the newspaper and me, etc. . . . Who is right, then? Who is the supreme judge?

6. You write further, "Leave the writing of such rubbish to abject, unfortunate scribblers like Okreitz, Pince-Nez, Aloe. . . ." May Allah forgive you, if you wrote those lines sincerely! The condescendingly disdainful tone you take toward little people, only because they are little, does no credit to the human heart. In literature low ranks are as in-

dispensable as in the army—thus speaks the head, and the heart must say it even more emphatically. . . .

Ugh! I have tired you out with my verbosity. . . . Had I known that my objections would be so longwinded, I would not have started writing to you. . . . Please, forgive! * * *

You read my "On the Road" —Well, how do you like my audacity? I write of intellectual matters and am unafraid. In Petersburg I caused a furor. Somewhat earlier I dealt with "nonresistance to evil" and again astounded the public. Compliments had been offered me in the New Year issues of all the papers, and in the December issue of *Russian Wealth*, the magazine that prints Lev Tolstoy, there is an article by Obolensky [6] (two sheets) [7] entitled "Chekhov and Korolenko." The lad is enthusiastic about me and argues that I am more of an artist than Korolenko. He's probably lying, but nevertheless I am beginning to feel that I have performed a unique service to my fellow authors. I alone, a scribbler of newspaper trash who has not appeared in the bulky monthlies, have attracted the attention of lop-eared critics— This has never happened before. . . . *The Observer* railed at me—and did that journal catch it! At the end of last year I felt like a bone thrown to the dogs. * * *

I have written a play on four sheets of letter paper. It will run for 15–20 minutes. The tiniest drama in the world.[8] Generally speaking, it is much better to write little pieces than big ones: they make few claims and the thing is a success—what more is wanted? I wrote my drama in an hour and five minutes. I have started another, but haven't finished it, because I have no time. * * *

Devotedly and respectfully,

A. Chekhov

---

[6] Leonid Yegorovich Obolensky, a respected critic and publicist, an editor of *Russian Wealth*, who was Chekhov's senior by fifteen years.

[7] One sheet was equivalent to sixteen printed pages.

[8] Originally called "Kakhas"; the title was changed to "Swan Song."

Moscow, January 17, 1887

Uncorrupted sir!

* * * Thank you. If it were not for you, the remittances would have come a week later. I apologize for having troubled you and I would be glad if you agree to take 1/100 per cent as commission. * * *

With a sinking heart I am waiting for Leikin. He will again wear me out. I am not getting along with this Quasimodo. I refused a raise and also refused punctual delivery of contributions, and he bombards me with tearful-pompous letters, accusing me of the shrinkage of subscriptions, perfidy, duplicity, and the like. He lies, saying that he receives letters from subscribers asking why Chekhonte does no writing. He is cross with you for not contributing. I shall demand 12 copecks a line.

I'd be glad to give up working for *Splinters*, for I am disgusted with trifles. I want to turn out something bigger, or not write at all. * * *

As I shall again be broke by the end of January, to avoid borrowing, which affects me morbidly, and the family's complaints, I shall again trouble you for a remittance. Help me, and in return I will send a prescription.

What a stupid situation! Two hundred rubles were remitted to me and the same day I received 20 rubles from *The Alarm Clock*, but all I have left now is 30 rubles, and that sum, too, will be gone by January 22. Please tell me, dear heart, when shall I live like a human being, that is, work and not be out of pocket? At present I slave and am hard up, and I ruin my reputation by having to produce trash. * * *

What kind of work do you do for *New Times?* Is it creative?

Do let me hear from you. In view of your straitened circumstances, and in order not to swell the proletariat, stop procreating. Such is the desire of Malthus and Pavel Chekhov.

Be well, and greetings to all.

We (including your sister) beg your blessing, and I remain your loving brother

Antonius and Medicine Chekhov

Besides medicine, my wife, I have also literature—my mistress, but I do not mention her—those living in sin will perish sinfully.

TO F. O. SCHECHTEL[1]

Petersburg, between March 11 and 14, 1887

The world's most gifted architect!

* * * Seated in a most depressing hotel room, I am getting ready to make a clean copy of a story I have finished. I am bored. The boredom is compounded by uncertainty and lack of money. I don't know when I'll leave the city. I am so nervous that my pulse is irregular. This plaintive missive is by no means intended to plunge you into sentimental melancholy or to dispose you to lend me money, but to prevent you from being sore at me for not having looked in regularly on Darya Karlovna.[2]

I do, however, have a request: do not forget to bestir yourself to secure me a free trip to Taganrog and back. Arrange it so that the return ticket is not dated. No matter what happens, even if there is an earthquake, I must get away from here, for my nerves can't stand it any longer.

I want to leave not later than March 31. I will go, though with no more than a single ruble, but I'll go in any case.

The weather is splendid in Petersburg, but the effect is spoiled by lack of money and by my spring overcoat having been borrowed by a common acquaintance of ours. Everywhere I am made much of, but no one has the bright idea of handing me one or two thousand rubles. * * *

> *Yours wholly, including my boots, my*
> *galoshes, my teeth, my vest, and the rest,*
> A. *Chekhov*

---

[1] This friend, Franz (Fyodor) Osipovich Schechtel (1859–1926), was a fellow student of Nikolay's at the Moscow School of Painting, Sculpture, and Architecture. His work for the Moscow Art Theater earned him membership in the Academy of Architecture.
[2] Schechtel's mother.

Taganrog, April 7, 1887

Christ has risen, dear Nikolay Aleksandrovich!

I received your letter yesterday. It was brought me by a letter carrier with a good-natured mug and wearing a russet overcoat. Having delivered the letter, he put his bag near a tray on a bench and sat down in the kitchen to drink tea, without the slightest concern about the other addressees. Stark Asia! All around there's such Asia that I can't believe my eyes. Sixty thousand inhabitants busy themselves exclusively with eating, drinking, procreating, and they have no other interests, none at all. Wherever you go there are Easter cakes, eggs, local wine, infants, but no newspapers, no books. . . . The site of the city is in every respect magnificent, the climate glorious, the fruits of the earth abound, but the people are devilishly apathetic. They are all musical, endowed with fantasy and wit, highstrung, sensitive, but all this is wasted. . . . There are neither patriots, nor captains of industry, nor poets, not even decent confectioners.

On Saturday I am going to Novocherkassk, where I act as best man at the wedding of a wealthy Cossack girl. Having got plastered on Don wine, I shall return to Taganrog on the 14th and make my way to the Donetz region. My Taganrog address [1] is still valid. * * *

Oh, what women there are here!

Yesterday I was driven out to the shore. The sea is wonderful! There is only one trouble: intestinal catarrh, caused by a change of water and food. Ever so often I have to run. And the latrines are in the courtyards here, back of the beyond. . . . If you don't get there in time, you may be subject to many unpleasant accidents.

I have written a story [2] for *The Petersburg Gazette* and I shall take it to the station together with this letter. * * *

Your A. Chekhov

[1] He gives the address, which is that of his uncle Mitrofan.
[2] "A Cossack."

TO F. O. SCHECHTEL

Taganrog, April 11, 1887

Dearest Maestro!

I am in the south!!! However, that does not mean that I am warm. For six days now a cold wind has been blowing in Taganrog, so that you are forced to put on a warm overcoat.

I am bored and feel poorly. I have diarrhea. Money is scarce. The future is uncertain. The townspeople have become disgusting. Poor food. Dirty streets. My sleeping arrangements are peculiar.

When the wind stops I will travel farther. My address is M. Ye. Chekhov's house. Letters received here will be forwarded.

Taganrog is a very good city. If I were as gifted an architect as you, I would raze it.[1]

* * * Good-bye. Avoid wine and women.

Your A. Chekhov

How are Nikolay's mad dogs faring?

TO M. P. CHEKHOVA

Taganrog, April 7–19, 1887 [1]

Benevolent readers and pious listeners!

I continue [2] with trepidation, following chronological order.

April 2. The ride from Moscow to Serpukhov was boring. My fellow travelers happened to be assertive, self-possessed people who talked about nothing but the price of flour. * * * At Tula *Schnapps trinken,* mild fuddle, and *schlafen.* I slept doubled up à la Fyodor Timofeich,[3] the tip of my boots close to my nose. I woke up in Oryol, where I mailed a postcard to Moscow. The weather is good. There is little snow on the ground.

---

[1] In spite of his distaste for his native town, Chekhov was active in trying to elevate its cultural standards. He spent time, energy, and money on this task. To the end of his life he maintained a lively correspondence with Dr. Iordanov, the civic-minded head of the municipal library.

[1] Chekhov's visit to his birthplace and neighboring towns lasted from April 2 to May 15. The present letter chronicles only the period from April 2 to April 14.

[2] On April 1 and 2 Chekhov had mailed home two brief notes dealing with his trip.

[3] The family tomcat.

At twelve, Kursk. An hour's wait, a glass of vodka, men's room with washing facility, cabbage soup. Changed trains. The coach is chock full. * * * As we roll along, I fall asleep. I wake up in Slasyansk, where I mail a postcard. Here new companions: a landowner like Ilovaisky [4] and a conductor. We criticize the railroads. The conductor relates how three hundred coaches belonging to the Asovsk railroad were stolen by the Lozovo-Sevastopol railroad and painted its color.

Khartzyzsk. Midday. Wonderful weather. The fragrance of the steppe, the air resounding with birdsong. I see old friends—kites flying over the steppe. Tumuli, pumps, buildings going up—all familiar and well remembered. At the buffet a portion of extraordinarily delicious, rich vegetable soup. Then a stroll on the platform. Young ladies. At the last window of the second floor of the station house sits a girl (or a married woman, the devil knows which) in a white blouse, languid, beautiful. I look at her, she looks at me. . . . I put on my pince-nez, she puts on hers. Oh, wonderful vision! I contracted inflammation of the heart, and rode on. The weather is devilishly, outrageously splendid. Khokhols.[5] Oxen, kites, white cottages, southern streams, branches of the Donetz railroad with a single telegraph wire, daughters of landowners and lease-holders, ginger-colored dogs, greenery—all this flashes by as in a dream. Hot. The conductor is getting tiresome. Only half my meat patties and my pastries have been consumed and they are beginning to smell bitter. I shove them under someone's seat together with the rest of the vodka.

Five o'clock. The sea is in sight. There it is, the Rostov line, twisting beautifully, the prison, the poorhouse, yokels, freight cars, the Belov hotel, St. Michael's Church with its uncouth architecture. I am in Taganrog. I am met by Yegorushka,[6] a fellow with a powerful frame, dressed to kill: a hat, gloves, costing 1 ruble 50 copecks, a cane, and the rest. I do not recognize him, he recognizes me. He hires a carriage and we are off. The impression of Herculaneum and Pompeii: no people, but, instead of mummies, sleepy country bumpkins and dunderheads. All the houses are rundown, haven't been plastered for a long time, the roofs not painted, the shutters closed. . . . Beyond Police Street drying and hence viscous and lumpy mud, through which you can

[4] Member of a well-known southern landowning family.

[5] The word, which means "forelock," is also a somewhat derogatory folk name for a Ukrainian. In former times the Ukrainian men left a long forelock on their shaved heads.

[6] Yegor, or Georgy, Mitrofanovich Chekhov, a cousin.

drive at a walking pace and cautiously, at that. We reach our destination.

"It's, it's, it's . . . Antonichka!"

"Da-a-arling!"

Next to the house is a bench resembling a box in which toilet soap is packed. The porch is in a state of agony—ideal cleanliness is all that is left of its pretense of ostentation. Uncle is as before, but markedly grayer. As always he is kind, gentle, and sincere. Lyudmila Pavlovna [7] says that she has forgotten to use the expensive tea, and generally finds it necessary to apologize and make excuses where they are not called for. She casts suspicious glances: perhaps I disapprove of her? Nevertheless, she is glad to regale me with goodies and show me much kindness. Yegorushka is a good and, by Taganrog standards, a proper youth. He plays the dandy and likes to study himself in the mirror. Bought himself a lady's gold watch for 25 rubles and keeps company with young misses, born exclusively to fill the vacuity of boys' heads. Outwardly Vladimirchik [8] looks like the thin, stooping Mishchenko who used to be with us, is meek and reticent, obviously a pleasant sort. He is preparing to be a luminary of the Church, is entering a seminary and dreams of the career of a metropolitan. So Uncle will have not only his halva but also a metropolitan. Sasha has not changed. Lelya is scarcely distinguishable from Sasha. What is outstanding is the unusual affection for their parents and each other. Irina [9] has grown stout. As formerly, everywhere on the walls wretched portraits and oleographs that came as prizes with spools of cotton manufactured by Coats and Clark. What is striking is the pretension to luxury and elegance, but of taste there is as much as there is femininity in a swamp-boot. Crowding, heat, not enough tables, and absence of all conveniences.

The nurse, Volodya, and another of the smaller children sleep in one room; the parents and a third child occupy another. Yegor sleeps in the anteroom on a chest. Intentionally, there is no supper; otherwise the house would long ago have exploded and vanished into thin air. * * * Hot air comes from the kitchen and from the stoves, which are kept going in spite of the warm weather. The water closet is far away, next to a fence; thugs hide there now and then, so that at night defecation is more dangerous than poison. The only tables are card tables and

[7] Chekhov's aunt.
[8] Vladimir, or Volodya, Mitrofanovich Chekhov, a younger cousin.
[9] The nurse.

round side tables for decorative purposes. There are no cuspidors, not one decent wash basin, the napkins are dingy. * * * I hate Taganrog taste, I can't bear it. I would run from it to the ends of the earth.

Selivanov's house is vacant, abandoned. The sight of it is dismal, I would not take it for any money. I wonder how we could have lived in it. * * *

After tea I go out with Yegor for a walk on Grand Street. The sun is setting. The street is decent, paved better than those in Moscow. There is a smell of Europe. On the left aristocrats promenade; on the right, democrats. A thousand and one young ladies: tow-haired, brunettes, Greek, Russian, Polish . . . The fashion: olive-green dresses and blouses. Not only the aristocracy (mangy Greeks) but the entire new part of town wears this olive-green color. Bustles are small; only Greek women wear large bustles, the others haven't the courage.

It is dark when I am back in the house. Uncle dons the uniform of a church warden. I help him put on his big medal, which he had never worn before. Laughter. We make our way to St. Michael's. It's dark. No conveyances for hire. Silhouettes of yokels and longshoremen on their way from church to church flash along the streets. Many of them carry small lanterns. The Mitrofan church is very effectively lighted from the bottom to the top of the cross. Loboda's house with its bright windows stands out in the dark.

We reach the church. Gray, skimpy, and dull. Little candles stick up in the windows—that's illumination. Uncle's face is flooded with the most beatific smile. That takes the place of the electric light. The interior is nothing to write home about, like the church at Voskresensk. We sell candles. Yegor, as a dandy and a liberal, does not take part in the selling, but stands aside and looks at everything with an indifferent eye. But Vladimirchik is in his element.

A procession with the Cross and banners. It is led by two fools waving a censer with a mixture producing Bengal fire, which gives off smoke and sparks. The public is pleased. In the vestibule of the temple stand the founders, benefactors, and other pillars thereof. With Uncle at their head and icons in their hands, they wait for the return of the procession. Vladimirchik is perched on the wardrobe and pours incense into a brazier. The smoke is so thick that you can hardly breathe. Now the priest and the bearers of banners enter the vestibule. Solemn silence ensues. All eyes are on Father Vasily.

"Papashka, do I pour some more?" Vladimirchik suddenly shrills from the top of the wardrobe.

Matins begin. I go to the cathedral with Yegor. There are no carriages for hire, and so we have to walk. In the cathedral everything is proper, ceremonious, solemn. The choir is magnificent, the voices are superb, but the discipline is poor. * * *

From the cathedral we walk home. My legs ache and are numb. We break fast: delicious Easter cake, disgusting sausage, dingy napkins, stuffy air, and the smell of children's blankets. Uncle breaks his fast at Father Vasily's. Having eaten and drunk heartily of the local wine, I go to bed and fall asleep to the sound of "It's . . . it's . . . it's. . . ."

In the morning an invasion of priests and choristers. * * * [10] As I made my way through the New Market to Mme. Zembulatova,[11] I realized how filthy, empty, lazy, illiterate, and boring Taganrog is. Not a single literate sign, and even "Rasia [12] Tavern"; the streets are deserted, the mugs of the longshoremen express self-satisfaction, the dandies wear long overcoats and caps, the new part of the city is dressed up in olive green, gallants, misses, peeling plaster, universal indolence, ability to be content with paltry earnings and an uncertain future—all this right before your eyes is so disgusting that Moscow with its grime and spotted fever seems likable.

At Mme. Zembulatova's, wine and twaddle. I go back home to Uncle's. Dinner: soup and fried chicken ("On a holiday one cannot do without fowl, child! Why not allow oneself a choice morsel?"). * * *

Back home, I found fat Father Ioann Yakubovsky, who graciously took interest in my medical practice and, to Uncle's delight, remarked condescendingly and solecistically, "It is pleasant to parents that they have such good children." Father Deacon also interested himself in me and said that the St. Michael's choir (a pack of hungry jackals, led by a bibulous choirmaster) was considered the best in town. I agreed, though I knew that neither ecclesiastic understood the least bit about singing. The beadle, seated at a respectful distance, looked sideways with longing at the jam and wine that the priest and the deacon were relishing.

By 8 P.M. Uncle, his household, including the nurse, as well as the rabbits, the dogs, the rats that live in the storeroom, were all fast asleep.

[10] The omitted passage deals with visits to former neighbors and acquaintances.
[11] Her husband was a physician who had been a schoolmate of Chekhov's and his classmate at the University.
[12] An illiterate spelling of "Rossiya."

Willy-nilly I too had to go to bed. I sleep in the parlor on a couch. It had not grown longer, it is as short as it ever was, and hence when I get into bed I am forced to lift up my legs in an unseemly way or to lower them to the floor. I recall Procrustes and his bed. I cover myself with a pink quilted blanket, stiff and stuffy, which becomes intolerably offensive at night, when the stoves, lit by the nurse, make themselves felt. Yakov Andreyich [13] is allowed only in dreams and reveries. In Taganrog only two individuals permit themselves this luxury—the mayor and Alferaki; [14] the rest of the citizenry must either piss in bed or take a long trip outdoors.

April 6. I wake up at 5 o'clock. The sky is overcast. A cold, obnoxious wind is blowing, reminding me of Moscow. Boring. I wait for the cathedral chimes and go to late mass. It's pleasant, decent in the cathedral, not boring. The singing is good, not vulgar, the public consists exclusively of misses in olive-green dresses and chocolate-colored blouses. There are many pretty ones, numerous enough to make me sorry that I am not Misha, who needs pretty girls so much. . . . Most of the local girls have a good figure, a beautiful profile, and are not averse to a serious flirtation. There are no gallants here, unless you count Greek brokers and impaired members of the Kamburov family, and as a result, officers stationed here and newcomers have the field to themselves.

From the cathedral I go to Yeremeyev's.[15] I find his wife at home—a nice little lady. Yeremeyev is pretty well fixed and as I look at his spacious apartment, I can see that Aleksandr was mistaken when he kept saying that you can't do well in Taganrog. No end of visitors, all of them local bigwigs—small, cheap little people, among whom, however, you can find some fair specimens. I got acquainted with officer Djeparidze, a local celebrity who had fought a duel; met several doctors. At 3 o'clock Yeremeyev comes home, half-seas-over. He is in raptures over my visit to the town and swears eternal friendship; our acquaintance had always been slight, but he assures me that he has only two true friends in the world: me and Korobov. We sit down to dinner and swill the local wine. The dinner is decent; spring chickens and no hard rice. * * *

April 7, 8, 9, 10. Days of greatest boredom. The sky is overcast and

---

13 Chekhov's name for a chamberpot.
14 A rich merchant.
15 A physician at whose sister's wedding Chekhov was to play a part.

it is chilly. I run day and night. The nights are an ordeal: darkness; wind; creaking doors, hard to open; groping in the dark courtyard; suspicious silence; no newsprint. . . . I bought Hunyadi,[16] but the local stuff is an outrageous fake, bitter. Every night I am reduced to pitying and cursing myself for my voluntary acceptance of torture, for having left Moscow to betake myself to the land of *ersatz* Hunyadi, darkness, and a privy way off beside the fence. The constant discomfort of camping out, in addition to ceaseless "But you haven't eaten enough, but you should eat more." Only one consolation: Yeremeyev and his wife and their comfortable apartment. Furthermore, Fate has spared me: I haven't run across Anisim Vasilyevich; nor have I been forced to discuss politics. If I do meet him, I'll blow my brains out. * * *

April 11. * * * Every day I make the acquaintance of girls who visit Yeremeyev to find out what kind of bird this Chekhov who writes is. Most of them are neither homely nor stupid, but I am indifferent because I have intestinal catarrh, which deadens all feelings.

Yegorushka is employed by the Russian Steamship Company. He leaves for work at five in the morning, returns for dinner, at five o'clock he goes back to work, and at nine, tired and hungry, he promenades with girls in the municipal park. A hard-working, decent fellow. Smokes, keeping it a secret from his father. Lyudmila Pavlovna hides her son's sin and is afraid that her husband will smell it out. Yegorushka is free from both the store and the church—he has no time for them; he works every day, including the high holidays. Is permitted to return home late and talk about women. Vladimirchik looks at his brother's life and licks his lips. * * *

Uncle accompanies the tax assessor on his rounds. Aunt trembles when she sees that magistrate. * * * Obviously he is a crafty rascal who knows how to profit from his position. He poses as a general, and Uncle and others believe that he has that rank. * * *

April 14. Alas! the bitter cup did not pass from me: yesterday that human dynamo and chatterbox, the police clerk, Anisim Vasilyevich, called. He entered and proceeded to talk in a Kamburov voice, but as loudly and shrilly as is beyond the powers of a hundred young Kamburovs together.

"But, Lord, for sure I told Yere where I live, so why didn't you drop in? My boy Firs is sailing the seas, and did Nikolay Pavlych finish *Messalina?* Are his pictures on show? And how is it with you?"

---

[16] A laxative.

He related that the chief of the city police had made him give his word of honor that he would not scribble for the newspapers, and that the head of the provincial police promised to deport him to the Urals within twenty-four hours if he dared write a single line, and so on. Then he held forth about the weather, socialists, Italy, immorality, gophers—speaking interminably, with modulations, interjections, and so earsplittingly that I almost fainted and led him out into the court-yard. He stayed until evening; to get rid of him, I went to the park, he followed me; from there I went to Yeremeyev's, he followed me. Yeremeyev was not in and I returned home—the police offal followed me, and so on. He promised to call for me today and accompany me to the cemetery.[17]

My intestinal catarrh continues to drive me out of the house to a certain spot and back again. My cold is gone but in its place a new ailment has appeared—inflammation of a vein in my left shank. Two or three inches of the vein are as hard as slate and painful. My infirmities are countless. The verse in Scripture, "In sorrow shalt thou bring forth children," is fulfilled as far as I'm concerned. But my offspring is not Yegor, not Vladimir, but stories and tales, of which now I can't even think. Writing disgusts me. * * *

I meant to take a trip on Wednesday, but the vein in my leg interfered. Until Saturday I loafed about in the park, at the club, and with young ladies. Though life in Taganrog is dull and tiresome, it makes a definite impression, it's not hard to get used to. During my stay in Taganrog I did justice only to the following items: remarkably savory pretzels to be had at the market, the wine, caviar, excellent cabs, and Uncle's sincere cordiality. Everything else is bad and mediocre. True, the young ladies here are not bad-looking, but one has to get used to them. They move abruptly, they behave frivolously with men, elope with actors, guffaw, fall in love easily, whistle for their dogs, drink wine, etc. There are even cynics among them. * * *

On Saturday I was on my way. At the Morskaya station the air was wonderful and caviar 70 copecks a pound. In Rostov an hour's wait. In Novocherkask I have to wait twenty hours. I stay overnight at the home of an acquaintance. Deuce only knows where I had to spend nights: in beds with bedbugs, on couches, on small couches, on chests. The last night I slept on a divan in a long, narrow drawing room under a mirror; Yakov Andreyich looked like a soup tureen embellished with

---

[17] A local Easter custom similar to the American Memorial Day.

tender half tints. I am in Novocherkask. I've just had breakfast: caviar, butter, marvelous Caucasian wine, and juicy meat patties with scallions.

The young lady at whose wedding I was to be best man has postponed it till Friday. On Thursday I must again be in Novocherkask, but today at 4 o'clock I travel farther. At Zverevo I shall have to wait nine hours.

In the meantime, good-bye.

A. Chekhov

TO M. P. CHEKHOVA

Cherkask, April 25, 1887

I am now on my way from Cherkask to Zverevo, and thence by the Donetz railway to Kravtzov's.

Yesterday and the day before there was the wedding, a real Cossack bridal, with music, women bleating like goats, and a revolting drinking bout. So many motley impressions that it is impossible to set them down on paper, and I must put it off till I return to Moscow. The bride is sixteen. The marriage ceremony took place in the local cathedral. I acted as best man in a borrowed frock coat, enormously wide trousers, and without a single stud. —In Moscow such a best man would get it in the neck, but here I was the greatest swell.

I saw a lot of wealthy marriageable girls. An enormous selection, but I was so drunk the whole time that I took bottles for girls and girls for bottles. Apparently, thanks to my drunken condition, the local maidens decided that I was witty and "a wag." The girls here are a flock of sheep: if one gets up and leaves the ballroom, all the others file after her. One of them, the smartest and the most daring, wishing to show that she knew something about fine manners and diplomacy, kept striking me on the hand with her fan and saying, "Oh, you naughty man!" while at the same time her face wore an expression of fear. I taught her to say to her swains, "How naïve you are!"

Apparently in obedience to a local custom, the newlyweds kissed every minute, kissed so vehemently each time that their lips made an explosive noise, and I had a taste of cloying raisins in my mouth, and got a spasm in my left calf. Their kisses did the inflammation in my left leg no good.

[55]

I can't tell you how much fresh caviar I ate and how much wine I drank. It's a wonder I didn't burst! * * *

As soon as I left Uncle's my intestinal catarrh vanished. Evidently the odor of sanctity has a laxative effect on the intestines. * * *

My money is coming to an end and I have to live like a pimp. Wherever I go I live at other people's expense, and I'm beginning to resemble a Nizhny Novgorod cardsharper, who eats the bread of others but radiates self-assurance.

At Zverevo I'll have to wait for the train from nine in the evening till five in the morning. When I was there last I slept in a second-class car on a spur. At night I went out of the car to relieve myself; it was miraculous: the moon, the boundless steppe; a desert with ancient grave mounds—the silence of the tomb, and the coaches and rails standing out boldly against the dim sky—a dead world, as it were. An unforgettable picture. It is a pity that Mishka could not come with me. He would have gone mad with all these impressions. * * *

Good-bye. I hope everybody is well.

A. Chekhov

TO M. P. CHEKHOVA

Ragozin Ravine, April 30, 1887

* * * I am staying at the Kravtzovs', a little house built of flat stones and with a thatched roof and sheds. Three rooms with clay floors, curved ceilings, and windows opening vertically. Rifles, pistols, sabers, whips hang on the walls. Cartridges, instruments for repairing rifles, tins of powder, and bags of small shot—all this fills the wardrobes and is piled on the window sills. The furniture is lame and chipped. I have to sleep on a consumptive couch, which is not upholstered and is very hard. Latrines, ashtrays, and other amenities are unknown, unless you travel for some half a dozen miles. To relieve yourself (irrespective of the weather), you have to walk down into the ravine and choose a bush; you are warned not to sit down until you have convinced yourself that under the bush there is no troublesome rattlesnake or some other creature.

The population: old man Kravtzov [1] and his wife, also Pyotr,[2] a

---

[1] Gavril Pavlovich Kravtzov was a retired Cossack cavalry officer, owner of the ravine on which his farmstead was located.

[2] G. P. Kravtzov's son, whom Chekhov had tutored.

Cossack cornet, and several other children, as well as Nikita, a shepherd, and Akulina, a cook. Of dogs there is no end, and they are all ferocious, allowing no one to pass, day or night. I need a constant escort, or else the number of Russia's men of letters will diminish by one. The worst creature is Mukhtar, an old hound from whose mug dirty tow is suspended instead of hair. He hates me and every time I leave the house he rushes at me with a savage roar.

Now about food. In the morning tea, eggs, ham, and lard. At noon goose soup—a liquid resembling the slops left after fat marketwomen have bathed, then roast goose or turkey, with marinated sloe, fried chicken, porridge with milk, and sour milk. Neither vodka nor pepper is to be had. At 5 o'clock millet porridge with lard is cooked in the forest. In the evening, tea, ham, and all the leftovers from dinner. Omission: after dinner coffee is served—to judge by its taste and smell, it is prepared from dried cornel.

Sports: hunting bustards, bonfires, trips to Ivanovka,[3] target practice, baiting dogs, making preparations for Bengal lights, political discussions, building stone towers.

The main occupation is rational agronomy, which was introduced by the young cornet, who acquired 5 rubles' and 40 copecks' worth of books on agriculture. The main branch of the economy is ceaseless day-long killing. They kill sparrows, swallows, bumblebees, magpies, ravens, so that they should not eat the bees; they kill bees so that they should not damage the blossoms of the fruit trees, and fell trees so that they should not impoverish the soil. The result is a peculiar cycle based on the latest scientific data.

We go to bed at nine. Sleep is disturbed by the howls of the dogs in the courtyard, and under my couch another hound barks fiercely in response to them. A discharge of firearms wakes me up: through the window my hosts fire rifles at some animal that is damaging the economy. To leave the house at night it is necessary to wake up the cornet, or else the dogs will tear you to pieces. The result is that the cornet's sleep depends on the quantity of tea and milk that I had drunk previously. * * *

Farewell. Greetings.

A. Chekhov

---

[3] The nearest railway station, about fifteen miles away.

TO N. A. LEIKIN

Yesterday, kind Nikolay Aleksandrovich, I went to the post office at Ivanovka (a distance of 15 miles) and picked up two letters from you. * * * Here the post office is considered a luxury, and so the stations are very few and they are idle. No one drives out to get mail. Should you be in the habit of driving for nothing, as they say—that is, just to fetch newspapers—you risk getting the reputation of a loafer, a free-thinker, a socialist. * * *

I am now going to Slavyansk, and thence to Holy Mountains, a monastery, where I shall spend three or four days, fasting and praying. From there I shall return to Taganrog.

Horrible: I have 53 rubles—no more. I am forced to clip my wings and lick my lips when I should be eating. I travel third class and as soon as only 20 rubles are left in my pocket, I shall make for Moscow, so as not to be reduced to beggary.

Oh, if I had 200–300 rubles to spare, I would make the sparks fly! I would travel all over the world! *The Petersburg Gazette* fee will go to the family. I pin high hopes on my pay from *Splinters*, which I asked Viktor Viktorovich to send me to Taganrog.

Recently I have been staying in the Switzerland of the Don region, in the middle of the so-called Donetz Ridge: mountains, ravines, groves, streams, and steppe, steppe, steppe. . . . I was staying at a retired Cossack cavalary officer's, who is living on his holding, without near neighbors. I ate goose soup, slept on a wooden couch, was waked by gunfire (chickens and geese are not slaughtered here, but shot) and by the yelping of dogs being punished; nevertheless, I had the time of my life. No end of impressions. Had Viktor Viktorovich been with me for one day, he would have taken to his heels, or imagined that he was somewhere in Singapore or Brazil.

Generally speaking, I am satisfied with my trip. Only the lack of money is disagreeable. Incredible but true: I left Moscow with 150 rubles.

Good-bye. The horse is at the door. About hemorrhoids later. Today I shall be on the road until dark.

Greetings to the family.

Your A. Chekhov

TO M. P. CHEKHOVA

Taganrog, May 11, 1887

I continue with trepidation. From the Kravtzovs I went to Holy Mountains. I board a train, which takes me to Kramatorovska. * * * It is 7 P.M. when I reach that station. Here oppressive heat, smell of coal gas, a lady [...] and a wait of an hour and a half. From there I change to another train and arrive at Slavyansk, rather late at night. The coachmen refuse to drive to Holy Mountains in the dark and advise me to spend the night in the town, which I do very readily, for I feel jaded and I limp with pain like forty thousand Leikins. The station is three miles from the town, and fare for a shared carriage is 30 copecks. The town is something like Gogol's Mirgorod.[1] There is a barber shop and a watchmaker, so presumably in a thousand years there will be a telephone. Circus posters are pasted on walls and fences, alongside of them there are burdocks and excrement; pigs, cows and sundry domesticated creatures promenade on green, dusty streets. Houses peep out cordially and affectionately, like good-humored grannies; the pavements are soft, the streets wide, and the air is fragrant with lilac and acacia; the singing of nightingales, the croaking of frogs, barking, a harmonica, a woman's squeal—all that is heard from afar.

I put up at Kulikov's hotel, and paid 75 copecks for a room. After sleeping on wooden couches and in troughs it was delightful to see a bed with a mattress, a wash basin and—oh, magnanimity of Fate!—beloved Yakov Andreyich. (Having traveled far and wide, I have come to the conclusion that Yakov Andreyich is much more useful and pleasing than Yakov Sergeyich Orlovsky[2] or even Yashenka M.) Green boughs and westerly breezes push through the wide-open window. Stretching and screwing up my eyes like a tomcat, I order food and for 30 copecks I am served a mighty portion, larger than the biggest chignon, of roast beef, that is equally entitled to be called not only roast beef but also a chop, a beefsteak, and a little meat pillow with which I would certainly have cushioned my side had I not been as hungry as a dog and as Levitan on a shoot.

A glorious morning. Because of the holiday (May 6) the bells in the local cathedral are ringing. Mass is over. I see police officers, army officers, justices of the peace, and representatives of other angelic ranks

[1] The town in a story of that title.
[2] An acquaintance of Chekhov's.

emerge from the church. I buy 2 copecks' worth of sunflower seeds and for 6 rubles hire a carriage with rubber tires to take me to Holy Mountains and (in two days) back. We drove out of town through lanes literally submerged by the green foliage of cherry, apricot, apple trees. Birds sing tirelessly. Apparently mistaking me for Turgenev, Khokhols whom we pass doff their caps. Grigory Palenichka, my coachman, keeps jumping down from his seat to straighten the harness or lash out at the boys running after the carriage. * * *

I arrived in Holy Mountains at noon. The place is extremely beautiful and striking: the monastery stands on the bank of the Donetz River, at the foot of a huge white rock on which, crowded together and overhanging each other, a small garden, oaks, and age-old pines are heaped. It looks as if the trees feel packed to suffocation on the rock and as though an unknown force were pushing them up and up. They are literally suspended in the air, and look as if they would tumble down at any moment. Cuckoos and nightingales are never quiet, day or night.

The monks, very pleasant people, gave me a very unpleasant room with a mattress like a pancake. I spent two nights at the monastery and got no end of impressions. On account of the Feast of St. Nicholas fifteen thousand pilgrims flocked to the place, eight-ninths of them old women. I didn't know that there were so many old women in the world, or I should have shot myself a long time ago. . . . The services are endless: at midnight they ring the bells for matins, at 5 A.M. for early Mass, at 9 for late Mass, at 3 for nones, at 5 for vespers, at 6 for compline. Before each service you hear the weeping sound of a bell in the corridors, and a monk runs along crying in the voice of a creditor who implores his debtor to pay at least five copecks on the ruble, "Lord Jesus Christ, have mercy on us! Pray come to matins!"

It is awkward to remain in your room, so you get up and go. . . . I found a nice spot for myself on the bank of the Donetz and stayed there all the time that the services were going on.

I've bought an icon for Aunt Fedosiya Yakovlevna.

All of the fifteen thousand pilgrims get monastic grub free: *shchi* with dried gudgeon and gruel. Both are delicious and so is the rye bread.

The bell-ringing is remarkable. The singers are poor. I took part in a procession of the Cross in rowboats.

I give up describing Holy Mountains, because there's too much to say, and all I would do would be to crumple up the picture.

On my return trip there was a six-hour wait at the station. Tedium.

In one of the trains I noticed Sofya Khodakovskaya; [3] she seems to paint herself all the colors of the rainbow and bears a strong resemblance to a dead cat.

A night in a third-class coach of a moribund, foul, dawdling freight and passenger train. I was a worn-out son of a bitch.

Now I am back in Taganrog. Again "it's, it's, it's," again the short couch, Coats's oleographs, stinking water in the wash basin. . . . I am driven to the outlying districts of the city and I promenade in the gardens. Many orchestras and a million girls. * * *

I study local life. I was at the post office, in the bathhouses, saw Kasperovka. A discovery: Taganrog has a Butcher Street. * * *

If I send a wire to the country address reading: "Tuesday suburban train Aleksey," it means that I shall arrive on Tuesday aboard that train and please have Aleksey meet me. Of course, not necessarily Tuesday, for neither the day nor the hour when I shall return home and sit down to work is known to me. When I write, I am nauseated. I have no money, and if it were not for my ability to sponge on people I wouldn't know what to do.

There is the scent of acacia. Lyudmila Pavlovna has grown stout and has every appearance of a Jewess.[4] No mind can fathom the depth of her intelligence. When I listen to her, I am utterly at a loss before the inscrutable fate that sometimes creates such rare pearls. An incomprehensible creature! I have not forgotten anatomy, but looking at her cranium I begin to doubt the existence of a substance called brain.

Uncle is charming and all but better than anyone in town.

A. Chekhov

[3] Daughter of a Taganrog customs officer.

[4] In the complete eight-volume edition of Chekhov's letters, this sentence ends with three dots in brackets, designating a suppressed word or words. In the two-volume *Selected Letters*, the omission is restored. It is *zhidovka*, the feminine form of *zhid*, which, with its derivatives—not unlike the English "Yid" and its synonyms—has a derogatory connotation. Oddly enough, along with *yevrey*, the neutral word for Jew, and its forms, Chekhov used the offensive words in letters to his family and friends, his scrupulous humanity and devotion to justice notwithstanding. That devotion is clearly exemplified in an incident of his schooldays, recalled by a classmate. An upperclassman, on being called a "Yid," slapped the offender and was himself expelled. Chekhov rallied the classmates of the expelled boy to sign a declaration to the effect that they would boycott classes unless the Jewish boy were reinstated, which he was.

TO V. G. KOROLENKO[1]

Moscow, October 17, 1887

Many thanks, dear Vladimir Galaktionovich, for the book[2] you sent me and which I am now reading. As you already have my books, I must limit myself willy-nilly to sending you my gratitude.

By the way, in order that my letter may not be too brief, let me say that I am exceedingly glad to have made your acquaintance. I say it sincerely and from the bottom of my heart. In the first place, I deeply prize and love your talent; it is dear to me for many reasons. Secondly, it seems to me that if you and I live ten or twenty years longer, we shall not avoid having much in common. Of all successful Russian writers now, I am the most frivolous and featherbrained; I am far from being irreproachable; speaking figuratively, I loved my pure Muse but did not respect her, was unfaithful to her, and more than once took her to places that did not befit her. You, on the other hand, are serious, firm and steadfast. As you see, there is a great difference between us. Nevertheless, having read you and now having become acquainted with you, I think that we shall not be alien to one another. Whether I am right or wrong, I am pleased to think so.

By the way, I am sending you a clipping from *New Times*.[3] I shall clip the subsequent installments by this Thoreau, of whom you will learn from the present enclosure, and keep them for you. The first chapter is promising: there are thoughts, there is freshness and originality, but difficult to read. The architecture and the construction are impossible. Thoughts beautiful and ugly, light and ponderous are heaped one upon another, are crowded, squeeze the juices out of each other, and it looks as though any moment they will be so crushed that they will squeal.

---

[1] V. G. Korolenko (1853–1921), an eminent writer, largely of short fiction, was most congenial to Chekhov but, unlike him, was in active opposition to the existing order. He was exiled to Siberia and in 1885, after half a dozen years, was permitted to return home. He fascinated the public with stories that offered a delightful blend of humor and fantasy, compassion for the underdog (as exemplified in part by the Siberian natives), and faith in human goodness. In the name of justice and freedom he hailed the revolutionary movement, and after seizure of power by the Bolsheviks he denounced the new regime as a betrayal of the principles he valued.

[2] A collection of Korolenko's stories.

[3] Chapter I of Thoreau's *Walden or Life in the Woods* (1854), the Russian title being *In the Woods*.

When you come to Moscow I shall hand you the Thoreau clippings, meanwhile good-bye and keep well.

My play [4] will probably be staged in the Korsh theater. If it is, I shall let you know the date. Perhaps you will chance to be in Moscow at the time. Then you'll be welcome.

Your A. Chekhov

TO A. P. CHEKHOV

Moscow, November 20, 1887

Well, the play has come off.[1] . . . I describe everything in order. First of all, Korsh [2] had promised me ten rehearsals and gave me only four, of which only two can be called rehearsals, for the others were in the nature of tournaments in which messieurs the artists practiced controversy and mutual abuse. Only Davydov and Glama knew their parts, the others followed the prompter and their inner conviction.

Act I. I am behind the scenes in a cubicle resembling a prisoner's cell. The family is in an orchestra box: they tremble. Contrary to expectation, I am cold-blooded, and not agitated. The actors are tense, nervous, and cross themselves. Curtain rises. Enter the person for whom the benefit is being given. Diffidence, ignorance of the parts, presentation of the bouquet, combine to make me unable, from the first phrase, to recognize my play. Kiselevsky, on whom I placed great hopes, did not pronounce a single phrase correctly. Literally: *not one.* In spite of this, and the prompter's mistakes, Act I was a great success. Many curtain calls.

Act II. A crowd on the stage. Guests. Don't know their lines, confuse everything, talk nonsense. Every word cuts me like a knife in my back. But—oh, Muse!—this act, too, was successful. Curtain calls for everyone and two curtain calls for me. Congratulations on success.

Act III. Not badly played. Huge success. Three curtain calls for me, and during them Davydov shakes my hand and Glama, like Manilov,[3] presses my other hand to her heart. The triumph of talent and virtue.

[4] *Ivanov.*

[1] The première of *Ivanov* took place in Moscow on November 15, 1887. Vladimir Nikolayevich Davydov played the part of Ivanov.

[2] Fyodor Adamovich Korsh was founder, owner, and manager of the theater in Moscow that bore his name.

[3] A character in Gogol's *Dead Souls*, a model of sentimentality.

Act IV. Doesn't go badly. Curtain calls. Next a very long, tiresome intermission. Unaccustomed to getting up and filing into the buffet between two scenes, the public grumbles. Curtain rises. Beautiful. A view of the supper table through the proscenium arch (the wedding). The orchestra plays flourishes. The best men come in; they are drunk and so, you see, they clown and kick up their heels. A pothouse, a booth for a side show, filling me with horror. Then, enter Kiselevsky. This is a gripping, poetic passage, but my Kiselevsky doesn't know his lines. He's drunk as a fiddler, so the short poetic dialogue turns into something tedious and abominable. The audience is baffled. At the end of the play the hero dies because he cannot bear the insult dealt him. The public, grown cool and tired, cannot understand this death (which the actors had introduced, against my better judgment; I have a variant). Curtain calls for the actors and for me. During one of these curtain calls a frank hissing, partly muffled by applause and stamping, is heard.

On the whole, weariness and vexation. It is disgusting, although the play had a substantial success (denied by Kicheyev [4] and company).

The theater people say that they had never seen such turbulence, never heard such general applause and hissing or so much heated discussion of a play. And at Korsh's an author was never called before the curtain after Act II.

The play will be performed a second time on the 23rd, with a variant and other changes: I banish the best men.

Details when we meet.

Your A. Chekhov

TO A. P. CHEKHOV

Moscow, November 24, 1887

Well, my dearest Gusev,[1] at last everything has settled down, has fallen into place, and, as before, I am sitting at my desk and with an unruffled spirit turning out stories. You can't conceive what went on! The devil alone knows the result of such insignificant trash as my little

---

[4] In *Moscow Broadsides* he stigmatized the play as "profoundly immoral" and "chaotic." An equally negative notice appeared in another Moscow newspaper.

[1] Probably a teasing suggestion that Aleksandr is a goose. The Russian word resembles the English in sound and colloquially has the same connotation.

play (I sent one set of proofs to Maslov).[2] I already wrote you that at the first performance the excitement among the public and backstage was such as the prompter, who has been working in the theater for thirty-two years, had never seen in all his born days. They were noisy, they were gabbling, they were clapping, they were hissing; there was almost a free-for-all at the buffet while up among the gallery, the students wanted to pitch somebody out and the police led two of them away. The excitement was general. Sister almost fainted; Dyukovsky,[3] who was overcome by palpitation of the heart, fled, while Kiselev clutched his head for no known reason and vociferated most earnestly, "Well, what am I to do now?"

The actors were under nervous strain. Everything that I wrote to you and Maslov about their acting and their attitude toward their work must not go beyond the letters, of course. It becomes necessary to justify and explain a great deal. . . . It turns out that a daughter of the leading lady in my play had been at death's door—what did play acting matter at that point? Kurepin [4] did the right thing by praising the actors.

The day after the performance there appeared in the *Moscow Broadside* a review by Pyotr Kicheyev, who disparages my play as brazenly cynical and immoral balderdash. The *Moscow News* praised it.

The second performance didn't go badly, though it was not without surprises. The actress whose daughter was sick was replaced by another who went on without rehearsal. Again there were curtain calls after Act III (twice) and after Act IV, but no hisses this time.

And that's it. My *Ivanov* is being given again Wednesday. Now all have calmed down and gotten into their grooves. We have made a note of November 19 and shall celebrate the date every year by a spree, inasmuch as this day shall long be held memorable by the family. * * *

Your Schiller Shakespearovich Goethe

---

[2]Aleksey Nikolayevich Maslov, a fellow writer of no great account who used the pen name Bezhetsky.

[3] Mikhail Mikhailovich Dyukovsky, a school inspector.

[4] Aleksandr Dmitriyevich Kurepin, a Moscow journalist, editor of *The Alarm Clock*, later a contributor to *New Times*.

[1888]

TO A. N. PLESHCHEYEV[1]

Moscow, February 9, 1888

* * * I hasten to start work on small pieces, yet I have an irresistible longing to undertake something big again.[2] Oh, if you knew what a subject for a novel[3] sits in my noddle! What wonderful women! What funerals, what weddings! If I had money, I would make off for the Crimea, seat myself under a cypress, and complete a novel in one or two months. Imagine, three sheets are already written! However, I am lying: if I had money in hand, I would live it up and all the novels could fly away head over heels.

When the first part of the novel is ready, I'll send it to you to read, but not to print in *The Northern Herald*, because my novel does not fit a publication subject to preliminary censorship.

I am greedy, I like to have my works teeming, and for that reason my novel will turn out to be long. Besides, I am attracted to the characters I depict, they are dear to me, and so I am disposed to busy myself with them for a long time. * * *

Tomorrow I shall be a guest at a wedding in the house of a tailor who writes fairly good verse and who patched up my jacket out of respect for my talent (*honoris causa*). You are probably sick of my trifles, and so I cease.

Keep well. May your creditors be damned. They're an importunate breed, worse than mosquitoes.

Cordially yours,
A. Chekhov

Doesn't *The Northern Herald* have the habit of sending proof to authors?

[1] Aleksey Nikolayevich Pleshcheyev (1825–93), poet, fiction writer, critic, and literary editor of *The Northern Herald*. In his youth he served a long term in Siberia as a political exile. In 1890 he inherited a large fortune and went abroad, dying in Paris.
[2] Chekhov had recently completed a long narrative, "The Steppe," which was to appear in *The Northern Herald*.
[3] This never materialized. The only work of Chekhov's in the genre of the novel is *The Duel*, serialized in *New Times* in 1891.

Moscow, April 28, 1888

Guskov! [1]

I am answering your latest letter. First of all, I invite you to keep your head and keep your eye on the root of things. In the second place, I have this further to say:

It is possible to take care of your children,[2] but on the indispensable condition that you vow in the name of whatever you please that neither earthquake, nor flood, nor fire, nor sword, nor plague will prevent you from being punctual, that is, on a definite date you will send me a definite sum of money. . . . The essence of the matter is money. Neither grandfather's piety, nor grandmother's kindness, nor papa's tender feelings, nor the uncles' magnanimity can take the place of money. Remember that, as I remember it every moment. . . . If you are certain that it is within your power to meet this condition, then, read on.

Fifty rubles a month is enough. No less. The children will be under their grandmother's care. Which one? Not Yevgeniya Yakovlevna: [3] To live with Yevgeniya Yakovlevna means to live with me. . . . My quarters are *crowded*, and there is positively no room for children. I pay 750 rubles rent. If we move to a flat with two more rooms for the children, the nurse, and the children's things, the rental will come to 900 rubles. However, even in a spacious flat we would be crowded. As you know, I have a group of adults living under one roof only because, owing to some incomprehensible circumstances, they must not separate. Living with me are Mother; sister; Mishka, the student (who will not leave even after he has graduated); Nikolay, who is idle and has been left by his mistress, and who drinks and is in tatters; also our aunt and Alyosha (these two are only roomers).[4] Add to this that from 3 P.M. till dark and on all holidays Ivan lounges about, and in the evening Father comes in.[5] All these people are nice, jolly, but touchy,

---

[1] The salutation is derived from the word for "gosling"—a less derogatory term than some of his other appellations for his brother.

[2] Aleksandr had written that his wife was dying and the nurse had typhus. He asked Chekhov to inquire if their mother and sister could not take care of the children temporarily.

[3] Chekhov's mother.

[4] The son of the aunt, a widow, who is the sister of Chekhov's mother.

[5] The father apparently lived in his humble place of employment.

pretentious, uncommonly talkative, tramp noisily, are hard up. . . . I am dizzy. . . . If two children's beds and a nurse are added, I would have to stuff my ears with wax and put on black spectacles. . . . If I had a wife and children, I would gladly take on even a dozen more children, but with my family as it is now, depressed by the abnormality of living together, vociferous, disorderly in money matters, and artificially pasted together, I cannot take in another soul, especially one that has to be brought up, given a start in life. Furthermore, early in May my entire family goes south. To take the children with us and back is inconvenient and expensive.

The children can live with their grandmother Fedosiya Yakovlevna.[6] I already spoke to her about it, informed her as to your motives and my own, and she gladly consented. Aleksey [7] is a good fellow and will probably have nothing against this arrangement.

Living with her has these conveniences for the children: (1) quiet; (2) the adults' good will; (3) absence of irritations, such as music, guests, piety, looking askance at the progeny of a sinful union, etc.

For 50 rubles Aunt will give the children living quarters, food, a servant, my medical help (the flat 18–25 rubles, firewood provided by Alyoshka, nurse 5–6 rubles, the rest spent on grub and incidentals). Condition: the children must be brought from Petersburg by you or by a servant; no one in Moscow can fetch them. The rooms must be rented by September 1. Until then the kids will stay with our aunt in my quarters (for that reason 25 rubles a month will be sufficient until September).

I have a headache; that's why my letter is probably incoherent. I am sorry if it is. Generally, my head is no good. I think you will understand me. That is, me and my innards you may not understand, but do grasp my arguments and reasons. Write to me but not to our aunt. Write her later, after we come to an understanding, or there will be much unnecessary talk. Talk has worn me out. Keep well and, if possible, brisk.

Your A. Chekhov

Tear up this letter. Generally, get into the habit of tearing up letters—they are scattered all over your quarters.

In the summer come to see me. It is cheap.

[6] Actually the children's great-aunt.
[7] The great-aunt's son.

Moscow, May 3, 1888

Dear Alba,[2]

* * * I have sent a story[3] to *The Northern Herald*. I am a little ashamed of it. Very boring and so much philosophizing that it's cloying. It's unpleasant, but I could not help dispatching it, for I need money as I do air. Tomorrow I'll finish a story for *New Times*. During the summer I'll write nothing but trifles.

Leman[4] writes me that you (Petersburg authors) "have agreed to print on the jackets of your books announcements of those by others," and he invites me to join you and warns me that "only those persons are included who are united by a sense of solidarity." I agreed to join you, and in my response I posed this question: "How do you know with whom I feel solidarity and with whom I do not feel solidarity?" How you Petersburg folk love hot air! Can it be that you aren't stifled by such expressions as solidarity, unity of young writers, community of interests, and the like? Solidarity and such stuff I understand on the stock exchange, in politics, in religious (sectarian) affairs, etc., etc., but solidarity of young literary people is impossible and unnecessary. We cannot think and feel identically, our aims differ or we don't have any, we know each other little or not at all, and consequently there is nothing to which solidarity can firmly attach itself. Is it needed? No. To help one's colleague, to respect his personality and his work, to refrain from gossiping about him, not to envy him, not to lie to him or to play the hypocrite with him—for all this you have to be not so much a young writer as just a human being. Let us be ordinary human beings, let us take the same attitude *toward all;* then an artificially blown-up solidarity will not be needed. The persistent urge toward the private, professional, coterie-like solidarity that you want will generate involuntary espionage, suspicion, control, and without our wishing it, we shall become something like a Jesuit order. . . .

---

[1] Ivan Leontyevich Leontyev-Shcheglov (1855–1911), an artillery officer who wrote fiction and plays. The second half of his hyphenated name was his pseudonym. Chekhov often addressed him as "Jean."

[2] A reference to Herzog von Alba, a character in Goethe's tragedy *Egmont*.

[3] "An Unpleasantness."

[4] Anatoly Ivanovich Leman, a writer of fiction and of works on musical instruments.

Dear Jean, while I do not feel solidarity with you, I promise you, for the rest of your life, complete freedom as a literary man; i.e. you may write as you please for any publication, have the mental make-up of, say, even a Koreisha,[5] betray your convictions and leanings a thousand times, etc., etc., and my relations with you as a human being will not change one iota, and I shall always carry announcements of your books on the jackets of mine. This I can always promise my other colleagues, and I should also like to have the same done for me. In my opinion, this is what most normal relations are. They alone make possible respect, even friendship, and compassion in life's difficult moments.

I have chatted too long, however. May Heaven protect you.

Your A. Chekhov

TO A. S. SUVORIN

Sumy, May 30, 1888

Esteemed Aleksey Sergeyevich!

* * * I live on the shore of the Psel river, in the wing of an old manor house. I rented the dacha sight unseen, on a guess, and for the time being I have not repented it. The river is wide, deep, abounds in islands, fish, and crawfish. But above all there is so much space that it seems to me that for my hundred rubles I acquired the right to occupy a limitless area. Nature and life are built on the same pattern, which has now grown so antiquated that they are rejected in publishers' offices; just as antiquated is the barking of dogs that is heard from afar, like nightingales that sing day and night; old unkempt gardens; country houses tightly boarded up, sad and very poetic, inhabited by the souls of beautiful women; not to mention serfs, old flunkeys who have one foot in the grave; virgins yearning for the most banal kind of love. Not far from us there is such a hackneyed cliché as a water mill (sixteen wheels) with a miller and his daughter, who always sits at the window and is apparently waiting for something. It seems to me that everything I now see and hear has long been familiar to me from old romances

---

[5] A holy fool, believed by some to have prophetic powers. He was kept in a psychiatric hospital, where visitors came to consult him.

and fairy tales. The only whiff of novelty that I have felt had to do with a mysterious bird, a bittern, which nests somewhere far away among the reeds, day and night emitting a cry that resembles partly the sound of a knock on an empty barrel, partly the bellowing of a cow locked up in a shed. Every Khokhol has seen this bird at some time in his life, but each describes it differently, consequently none of them has had a good look at it. There is novelty of a different kind, too, but it is of rather recent origin.

Every day I paddle over to the mill, and in the evening, with the maniacal fisherman from Kharitonenko's plant, I make my way to the islands to fish. There is some interesting talk. By Whitsunday all the maniacs will spend the night on the islands and fish all night long. Me too. There are admirable types. The family of my landlady [1] turned out to be very likable and hospitable.

* * * You write that neither the talk about pessimism nor the tale of Kisochka [2] bring it at all nearer to a solution. It seems to me that it is not the task of fiction writers to solve such problems as God, pessimism, etc. The writer's business is to depict only who spoke or thought about God or pessimism, and how and under what circumstances. The artist ought not to judge his characters or what they say, but be only an unbiased witness. I heard two Russians engaged in a disjointed talk about pessimism, settling nothing, and I must reproduce this conversation just as I heard it, but it is the jurors, that is, the readers, who will evaluate it. My business is to be talented, that is, to be able to distinguish important testimony from trivia, to illuminate the figures and speak their language. Leontyev-Shcheglov reproaches me for having finished my story [3] with the phrase "There is no making head or tail of anything in this world!" His opinion is that an artist who is a psychologist, and precisely for that reason, is *obligated* to make sense of things. I don't agree with him. It is time for writers, particularly artists, to confess that in this world you cannot make head or tail of anything, as Socrates long ago confessed and Voltaire, too. The crowd thinks that it knows everything and understands everything, and the stupider it is, the broader, apparently, is its horizon. If, however, the artist, in whom the crowd has confidence, will be audacious

---

[1] Aleksandra Vasilyevna Lintvareva, owner of the Luka estate, near the city of Sumy, Province of Kharkov. The Chekhovs rented a dacha from her from 1888 to 1890.

[2] A character in Chekhov's story "Lights," on which Suvorin commented in a letter not preserved.

[3] "Lights."

enough to declare that he understands nothing of what he sees, this alone will be a great contribution to thinking and a long step forward.

* * * Now about the future. Late in June or early in July I shall go to Kiev, thence down the Dnieper to Yekaterinoslav,[4] then to Aleksandrovsk and so as far as the Black Sea. I shall visit Feodosiya. If you are really going to Constantinople, couldn't I join you? We would call on Father Paisius,[5] who will prove to us that Tolstoy's doctrine comes "from the devil." All of June I shall be at work, and therefore I'll probably have enough money for the trip. From the Crimea I shall make my way to Poti,[6] from Poti to Tiflis,[7] from Tiflis to the Don Region, from the Don to Psel. In the Crimea I shall start a lyrical play. * * *

Your sincerely devoted A. Chekhov

TO M. P. CHEKHOVA

Feodosiya, July 14, 1888

Mademoiselle sister!

* * * I slept well, in a first-class stateroom in a bed. At five o'clock in the morning I arrived in Feodosiya—a grayish-brown, wretched town, with a gloomy, boring look. No grass, puny trees, coarse soil, hopelessly arid. Everything incinerated by the sun, and only the sea, which cares nothing for small towns and tourists, smiles. Sea bathing is so wonderful that after a dip I began to laugh for no reason whatever. The Suvorins, who live in the best dacha, were glad to see me; it turned out that my room had long been made ready and that they had long been waiting for me to start excursions. An hour after my arrival I was driven to a certain Murza, a Tartar, to have something to eat. We were a large company: the Suvorins, the general attorney for maritime affairs, his wife, local moneybags, Aivazovsky.[1] . . . About eight Tartar dishes were served, very savory and very rich. The meal lasted till five in the afternoon and everyone was drunk as a lord. Murza and the attorney (a middle-aged man of affairs, a Petersburger) promised to

---

[4] Now Marx.

[5] A Taganrog monk who, in being ordained abbot, became deranged and fell into the habit of saying that everything, including his rank, came from the devil.

[6] A seaport in what is now the Georgian Soviet Republic.

[7] Now Tbilisi.

[1] Ivan Konstantinovich Aivazovsky (1817–1900), a noted painter of seascapes.

take me to Tartar villages and show me the harems of the wealthy denizens. I'll go, of course.

It is too stuffy to write. I think that I shall not put up with this heat long. I'll return soon, although the Suvorins insist on keeping me here until September. * * *

Your A. Chekhov

TO I. L. LEONTYEV-SHCHEGLOV

Feodosiya, July 18, 1888

I am writing to you, dear Captain, from the shores of the Black Sea. I am staying with General Suvorin in Feodosiya.[1] We spend the whole day in conversation. The night, too . . . And little by little I turn into a conversation machine. We have already solved no end of problems, and we have mapped out no end of others that no one has yet broached. We talk, talk, talk, and in all probability we shall die of inflammation of the tongue and vocal cords. To be with Suvorin and keep mum is as easy as to visit Palmin and not guzzle. Suvorin is really incarnate sensitivity. He is a grand man. In art he is what a setter is in hunting snipe, that is, he acts with devilish flair and is always aflame with passion. He is a poor theoretician, is not thoroughly versed in any science, the scope of his knowledge is very limited, in every field he is self-taught—hence his essentially canine innocence and wholeheartedness, as also the independence of his outlook. Lacking in theories, involuntarily he had to develop the riches with which Nature endowed him, involuntarily he developed his instinct till it reached the dimensions of a great intellect. It is pleasant to talk to him. An when you grasp his conversational manner, his sincerity, which most talkers lack, even chatting with him is almost a delight. I fully understand your Suvorin-*Schmerz.* * * *

Your A. Chekhov

[1] After nearly a fortnight in this Crimean town, Chekhov left for the Caucasus, accompanied by Aleksey, Suvorin's elder son. The two wanted to include Bukhara and Persia in their itinerary, but Aleksey, having received a telegram about his brother's death, left for home, and in August Chekhov was back in the family's summer cottage on the Lintvarev estate.

TO M. P. CHEKHOVA

Feodosiya, July 22, 1888

Dear family!

Hereby I inform you that tomorrow I am leaving Feodosiya. My idleness is driving me out of the Crimea. I haven't written a line and haven't earned a copeck. If my vile *dolce far niente* lasts one or two weeks more, I shall be left without a copeck and the Chekhov family will be reduced to wintering in Luka. I had dreamed of writing a play in the Crimea, and two or three stories, but it has turned out that under the southern sky it is easier to fly to heaven alive than to write even one line. . . . I get up at eleven o'clock, go to bed at 3 A.M., and all day long drink and talk, talk, talk endlessly. I have turned into a talking machine. Suvorin, too, is idle and we have solved all the problems there are. A life of feasting, as full as a bowl, of being sucked in . . . *Dolce far niente* on the beach, chartreuse, punch, fireworks, sea bathing, gay suppers, excursions, romances—all that shortens the days and makes them barely noticeable; time flies, flies, and you doze off to the sound of the waves and your head refuses to work. Hot days, stuffy, Asiatic nights . . . No, I must leave!

Yesterday I was driven to Shakh-mamai, Aivazovsky's estate, some fifteen miles from Feodosiya. A luxurious estate, almost fabulous; such estates could probably be seen in Persia. Aivazovsky himself, a hale old man in his seventies, is a blend of a good-natured Armenian and an over-fed bishop; is full of dignity, has soft hands, offers them in the manner of a general. None too clever, his is a complex nature and worthy of attention. He is a combination of a general and a bishop and an artist and an Armenian and a naïve grandfather and an Othello. Married to a young and very beautiful woman, whom he rules with a heavy hand. Acquainted with sultans, sheikhs, and emirs. Had a hand in Glinka's opera *Ruslan and Lyudmila*.[1] Was a friend of Pushkin's, but did not read him. In his entire life he has not read one book. When he is offered some reading material, he says, "Why should I read, if I have my own opinion?" I spent a whole day and had dinner with him. A long, slow dinner, with endless toasts. By the way, at dinner I

---

[1] Mikhail Ivanovich Glinka (1803–57), the composer, owed to Aivazovsky two Tartar melodies used in Act II of this opera.

made the acquaintance of Tarnovskaya,[2] a woman doctor, the wife of a well-known professor. She is a corpulent lump of meat, running to fat. If she were stripped to her skin and painted green, she would be a frog from the swamps. Having talked to her, I mentally crossed her off the list of physicians.

I see many women, the best of them is Suvorin's wife. She is as original as her husband, and she does not think like a woman. She talks a lot of rubbish but if she wants to speak seriously, she shows intelligence and independence. Is head over heels in love with Tolstoy and therefore cannot stand contemporary literature. When you speak to her about it, you feel that Korolenko, Bezhetsky,[3] myself, and others are her personal enemies. Has an uncommon gift for chattering nonsense without stopping, but chatters in a talented and interesting manner, so that you can listen to her all day without boredom as to a canary. Generally speaking, she is an attractive, intelligent, good woman. Evenings she sits on the sandy beach and cries, mornings she laughs boisterously and sings gipsy songs.

* * * I shall remit money one of these days.

* * * I kiss everyone.

A. Chekhov

TO K. S. BARANTZEVICH [1]

Sumy, August 12, 1888

Greetings, dear Kuzma Stanislavovich!

Having returned from journeys to far parts, I find two letters from you on my desk. I shall save the answers to them for the end of this letter, and now only tell you where I was and what I saw. I was in the Crimea, and New Athos,[2] in Sukhum, Batum, Tiflis, Baku. . . . I saw prodigious marvels. The impressions were so new and sharp that all I experienced seems a dream. I saw the sea in all its expanse, also the Caucasian shore, mountains, mountains, mountains, eucalyptuses, tea

---

[2] Praskovya Nikolayevna Tarnovskaya, one of the earliest Russian women physicians, advocated education for her sex.

[3] The pen name of Maslov.

[1] Kazimir Stanislavovich Barantzevich (1851–95), a minor novelist in the humanitarian tradition.

[2] A monastery.

shrubs, waterfalls, pigs with long pointed snouts, trees wrapped in lianas as in veils, small clouds spending the night on the breast of giant rocks,[3] dolphins, fountains of petroleum, subterranean fires, the fire-worshipers' temple, mountains, mountains, mountains. . . . I endured the Military-Georgian road. It is not a road, but poetry, a marvelous, fantastic story composed by a demon and dedicated to Tamara.[4] Imagine yourself perched on a mountain eight thousand feet high. Now please walk, in your mind, to the edge of the abyss and look down, far, far down. You see a narrow floor, along which a little white ribbon is twisting—the white-haired, grumbling Aragva. Before you see it, little clouds, groves, ravines, rocks, meet your gaze. Now lift your eyes a bit and look ahead of you: mountains, mountains, mountains, and on them insects—cows and human beings. . . . Look up, and there is a terrifyingly deep sky. A fresh mountain breeze blows.

Imagine two high walls and between them a long, long corridor; the ceiling is the sky, the floor—the bed of the Terek; an ash-colored snake is twisting at the bottom. One of the walls has a shelf along which a carriage, in which you are seated, is dashing.[5]

The snake is angry, roaring, bristling. The horses tear along like devils. The walls are high, the sky is higher. From the top of the walls curly trees peer down curiously. You are dizzy! This is the Daryal canyon or, in Lermontov's words, the gorge of Daryal.

[Oh, messrs the natives are swine. Not a single poet, not one singer. To live somewhere close to Gavaur or near Daryal and not compose fairy tales—that's swinish.] [6] * * *

Your A. Chekhov

TO A. N. PLESHCHEYEV

Sumy, August 27, 1888

I am answering your latest letter, dear Aleksey Nikolayevich. There will be a story for the October issue of *The Northern Herald* without fail.[1] It will run to one or two sheets. An advance will hardly

[3] A slightly altered quotation from a lyric by Lermontov.
[4] A ghostly queen who figures in a ballad by Lermontov which is based on a Georgian legend of a fatal enchantress.
[5] Here Chekhov drew a diagram of the scene.
[6] The passage in brackets is omitted from the complete edition of the letters, and appears in the *Selected Letters*.
[1] "The Name-Day Party."

be needed: I have no money, I'll live half-starving, but shall try not to take money beforehand, for I shall need advances in the summer, when I am idle and need spare, crazy cash. It is worth starving in the winter for the sake of spring and summer debauchery.

Yesterday I returned from Poltava province. I visited the Smagins [2] again, again covered no end of miles, and got worn out, dusty and frayed, like a son of a bitch. I was traveling for a special purpose—to buy (?!?) a farm. By means of all manner of tricks and transactions with a bank I want to acquire some 50 acres with a garden and a stream. The price of the farm is 3000 rubles. I'll pay interest on a loan, and in the future gradually repay it. I haven't agreed on the price but probably shall, and no sooner will cheerless October arrive than I shall sign myself thus: "Poltava landowner, physician, and littérateur, Antoine Shponka." [3]

This is the news that concerns you. You will not refuse to visit me on the farm, will you? Poltava province is a hundred times warmer and more beautiful than the Crimea; the spot is salubrious, cheerful, hospitable, lively. . . . Stay with me two or three months, we'll drive out to the towns of Sorochintzy, Mirgorod,[4] visit the Smagins, the Luka estate, etc. I buy the property so that you and all my good friends, from whom until now, speaking in all conscience, I have received nothing but kindness, should regard this mangy farm of mine as their own, and will have a place where they can relax. If I actually do buy the property, I shall build cottages on the shore of the Khorol [5] and lay the foundation for a literary colony.

Another piece of news (in confidence): the Lintvarev sisters are planning to marry my brother Ivan, the teacher, to Vata.[6] If this happens, Vata's very nice Mamasha will be my relative, on which I congratulate myself. Vata is a capital fellow. She's a wonderful housewife and rules her wonderful Mamasha with a heavy hand. * * *

Wait, *Russian Thought* will yet perform stunts of another kind! [7]

---

[2] Hospitable landed gentry.
[3] A character in a comic story by Gogol.
[4] These towns owed their fame to Gogol's tales of the Ukraine.
[5] A river.
[6] The nickname of Valentina Nikolayevna Ivanova, a relative of the Lintvarevs.
[7] *Russian Thought* was exempted from preliminary censorship. A. M. Yevreinova, the editor of *The Northern Herald* (see below, p. 94), requested the same privilege, arguing with the head of the Press Bureau that the contributors to her magazine also wrote for *Russian Thought*. The response was that *Russian Thought* was "wholly ours. They write what we want. They consult us about everything." Pleshcheyev,

Under the banner of science, art, and a protest against the suppression of free thought, among us in Russia there will reign toads and crocodiles of a sort that even Spain did not know at the time of the Inquisition. Well, you will see it! Narrowmindedness, great pretensions, inordinate self-love, and complete absence of a literary and social conscience will do their work. All these Goltzevs and Co. will so pollute the atmosphere that every man coming from the fresh air will find literature fiendishly disgusting, and every charlatan and wolf in sheep's clothing will have a place where he can lie, play the hypocrite and die "with honor." * * *

Be well.

Yours cordially,

A. Chekhov

TO A. S. SUVORIN

Sumy, August 29, 1888

Esteemed Aleksey Sergeyevich!

On September 2 my summer ends, and I go to Moscow. My address is the same as last year's: Moscow, Kudrinskaya-Sadovaya Street, Korneyev's house. When you travel home by way of Moscow, then, if there is time, drop in on me or at least let me know—I'll call on you and see you off to the station.

All these days I have been occupied by the thought of your encyclopedic dictionary.[1] If you really publish it, let me know in good time: I shall give you my views, which may be helpful.

The day before yesterday I returned from Poltava province. I was looking at a farm, did not agree on the price, and withdrew. I happened to arrive there just at threshing time. Bumper crops. Whoever sowed wheat got 70 to 80 rubles' worth of grain per desyatin,[2] in spite of low prices, and rye weighed so much that in one day, in my presence,

---

who had heard the story from the editor of *The Northern Herald*, recounted it to Chekhov, adding that *Russian Thought* was plotting against *The Northern Herald* and perhaps even bribing the censors.

Chekhov's attitude toward V. A. Goltzev, editor of *Russian Thought*, underwent a *volte face* after they met. In 1892 Chekhov began contributing to *Russian Thought*, and his acquaintance with Goltzev soon ripened into friendship.

[1] Suvorin's plan did not materialize.

[2] One desyatin is 2.7 acres.

a 6-HP machine threshed 1200 poods,[3] and the sheaves were so heavy that the workers were quite worn out! The work is grueling, but jolly, like a barn dance. In my childhood, when I stayed with my grandfather on Count Platov's estate, I had to sit for days on end from dawn to dusk at the threshing machine, and write down the poods and pounds of the threshed grain. The whistles, the hissing, and the deep sound, like a whirring top, emitted by the machine during the work, the creaking of wheels, the indolent gait of the oxen, the clouds of dust, the black, sweaty faces of dozens of men—all this engraved itself on my memory like the paternoster. And now, I spent hours on end at the threshing, and I felt exhilarated. The threshing machine looks alive when it is working, it has a sly, playful expression; the men and the oxen, on the contrary, seem machines. In the Mirgorod county hardly any farmers own a threshing machine, but they can rent one. It plays the part of a prostitute, that is, it travels all over the neighborhood and offers itself to anyone who wants it. It charges 4 copecks a pood, that is, some 4 rubles a day. Today it is buzzing in one place, tomorrow in another, and everywhere its arrival is an event, like the visit of a bishop.

I liked the farm I was considering. A very cozy, poetic little place. Magnificent soil, a water meadow, the Khorol, a pond, an orchard with an abundance of fruit, a hatchery, and a row of lindens. It is situated between two huge villages, Khomutz and Bakumovka, without a single doctor, so that it would be suitable for an excellent medical dispensary. Everything very cheap [...]. I have not agreed to pay the unfair price asked by the owner of the property, who is a Cossack. It is 300 rubles more than I can and will give him.

In case the owner accepts my offer, I am leaving power of attorney with a friend so he can obtain the deed of purchase, and perhaps before October is here I shall join the crowd of Shponkas and Korobochkas.[4] Should the purchase go through, I shall take advantage of your offer and accept 1500 rubles from you, but please only on condition, an indispensable one, that you will regard this sum as a usual debt, that is, without regard to kinship or friendship. You will not interfere with my liquidating it, without allowing me any rebates or concessions. Otherwise this debt of mine will put me in a position such as you can guess. Until now when I got into debt, I would engage in hypocrisy—

[3] A pood equals 36 pounds.
[4] Small landowners, the first a character in a short story by Gogol, the second an unforgettable figure in *Dead Souls*.

a very disgusting, psychopathic state. Generally speaking, I am exceedingly sensitive about money matters and lie unwillingly. I'll tell you frankly and confidentially: when I was beginning to work for *New Times* I felt as if I were in California (before *New Times* I received no more than 7 or 8 copecks a line), and I promised myself to write as often as possible in order to get more—and there is nothing bad about this. But when we became better acquainted and when you became an intimate friend, my sensitiveness reared, and work for the paper, entailing receipt of honoraria, lost its real value for me, and I started talking and promising more than performing; I began to fear that our relationship might be darkened by someone's thinking that I needed you as a publisher, not as a human being, etc., etc. All this is foolish, offensive, and only proves that I attribute great importance to money, but I cannot help it. Perhaps I shall decide to occupy a position on the paper with a definite assignment and a salary only when we have become cool to each other, and in the meantime I shall be useless to you. As a friend I shall not lose sight of the paper or of the encyclopedic dictionary, and *pour plaisir* shall take charge of some department of the dictionary, shall, from time to time, say once a month, write a piece for the Sunday issue, but not for thousands would I accept a steady place on the paper, even if you threatened to cut my throat. This doesn't mean that my relation to you is more cordial and sincere than that of others. It means that I am terribly corrupted by this: I was born, grew up, was schooled, and began writing in an environment in which money played a shockingly large part. Forgive this unpleasant frankness; what may seem inexplicable must once and for all be explained.

To be on the safe side, I have written to my brother to put aside for you my royalties and 25 per cent of my honoraria. In that way the debt can be amortized in one and a half to two years.[5] * * *

> *Yours cordially,*
>
> *A. Chekhov*

I shall not write sizable pieces for some time. I'll return to trifles. I missed them. * * *

[5] Aleksandr had a clerical position in the office of *New Times*. The property was not purchased.

TO A. N. PLESHCHEYEV

Moscow, October 4, 1888

Dear Aleksey Nikolayevich,

If your letter had arrived two hours earlier, my story [1] would have gone to you, but now it is on the way to Baskov Lane.[2]

I should be glad to read what Merezhkovsky wrote.[3]

Meanwhile, good-bye.

After reading my story, write me. You will not like it, but I am not afraid of you and Anna Mikhailovna.[4]

I am afraid of those who look for a tendency between the lines and who insist on seeing me as necessarily either a liberal or a conservative. I am not a liberal, not a conservative, not a gradualist, not a monk, not an indifferentist. I should like to be a free artist and nothing more, and I regret that God has not given me the power to be one. I hate lying and violence, whatever form they take, and I am equally repelled by secretaries of consistories and by Notovich and Gradovsky.[5] Pharisaism, stupidity, and tyranny reign not in shopkeepers' homes and in lock-ups alone: I see them in science, in literature, in the younger generation. That is why I have no partiality either for gendarmes, or butchers, or scholars, or writers, or young people. I regard trade-marks and labels as prejudicial. My holy of holies is the human body, health, intelligence, talent, inspiration, love, and absolute freedom—freedom from force and falsehood, no matter how the last two manifest themselves. This is the program I would follow if I were a great artist.

However, I've chattered too long. Be well.

Your A. Chekhov

---

[1] "The Name-Day Party."
[2] Address of the editorial office of *The Northern Herald.*
[3] A favorable comment on Chekhov's work contributed to *The Northern Herald.*
[4] Pleshcheyev's wife.
[5] Respectively, a journalist and a publicist who contributed to liberal publications.

TO A. N. PLESHCHEYEV

Moscow, October 9, 1888

Forgive me, dear Aleksey Nikolayevich, for using ordinary paper in writing to you; there isn't a sheet of proper stationery around, and as for waiting until some is bought from a store, I don't feel like it and have no time for it.

Many thanks to you for having read my story [1] and for your last letter. I treasure your opinions. In Moscow I haven't anybody to talk with, and I'm glad I have kind people in St. Petersburg who don't find it a bore to correspond with me. Yes, my amiable critic, you are right! The middle of my story is dreary, drab, and monotonous. I wrote it indolently and sloppily. Having become accustomed to little stories which consist only of beginnings and endings, I am bored and take to chewing the cud when I feel that I'm writing the middle of a story. You are also right in not hiding but coming out flatly with your suspicion: Am I not afraid that I'll be taken for a liberal? This furnishes me with an occasion for looking into my innards. It seems to me I could be more readily accused of gluttony, of drunkenness, of frivolity, of indifference, of whatever you like, with but one exception: never of a desire to seem or not to seem to be something. —I never concealed myself. If I like you, or Suvorin, or Mikhailovsky,[2] I do not make a secret of it anywhere. If I find something appealing about the heroine of my story, Olga Mikhailovna, a liberal and, in the past, attending university courses, I make no secret of her appeal in the story—something which, it would seem, is sufficiently clear. Nor do I make a secret of my respect for the zemstvo, which I love, as well as for trial by jury.

True enough, what is suspicious about my story is its tendency toward balancing pluses and minuses. But then, you know, I'm not balancing conservatism and liberalism, which do not represent the essence of the matter for me; but the falsity of the chief characters and their truthfulness. In the story Pyotr Dmitrich lies and plays the buffoon during a trial, he is ponderous and hopeless, yet I can't withhold the fact that he is an attractive and softhearted person by nature. Olga Mikhailovna, my heroine, lies at every step, yet there's no need of

---

[1] "The Name-Day Party."

[2] Nikolay Konstantinovich Mikhailovsky (1842–1904), publicist, literary critic, theoretician of Russian Populism. He advised Chekhov to break with Suvorin.

keeping secret the fact that this lying pains her. The Ukrainophile won't do as your evidence. I did not have Pavel Lintvarev in mind. Christ be with you! Pavel Mikhailovich is a sensible, modest fellow who thinks for himself without foisting his ideas on anybody else. The Ukrainophilism of the Lintvarev family—it's the love of warmth, of the native dress, of the native language, of one's native land! It is likable and touching. But I had in mind those grave idiots who scold Gogol because he did not write like a true Khokhol—wooden, ungifted, and pallid idlers who, being as empty-headed as they are empty-hearted, nevertheless try to be apparently above mediocrity and to play a part, to which end they slap labels on their foreheads.

As for the man of the '60s, why, I tried to be careful and brief in depicting him, even though he deserves a whole essay. I spared him. What we have here is a faded, stagnant, ungifted nonentity who had usurped the '60s; in the fifth year of high school he had caught five or six ideas belonging to others, had stuck to them, and will stubbornly keep muttering them to the very day of his death. This is not a charlatan but a little simpleton who has faith in what he is muttering, yet has little understanding or none at all of what he is muttering. He is stupid, deaf, heartless. You ought to hear how, in the name of the '60s, which he does not understand, he grouses against the present, which he does not see; he slanders the students, both sexes, women, writers, and everything that is contemporary, and he regards this as the very essence of a man of the '60s. He is as boring as a hole in the ground and is as pernicious as a gopher to those who believe him. The '60s are a sacred period, and to allow stupid gophers to usurp it means vulgarizing it. No, I won't cross out either the Ukrainophile, or this goose that I'm fed up with! I was fed up with it even when I was in high school; I am fed up with it right now. When I am depicting types of that sort, or when I speak of them, it's neither conservatism nor liberalism I think of but their stupidity and pretensions. * * *

Stay healthy and cheerful. The prize [3] has knocked me out of my rut. My thoughts are whirling more foolishly than ever before. All my people bow to you, and I bow to yours. It's cold.

Your A. Chekhov

[3] The Department of Russian Language and Literature of the Academy of Sciences awarded five hundred rubles, half of the Pushkin Prize for excellence in literature, to Chekhov in October 1888, for *In the Twilight,* a collection of his stories published the previous year.

TO D. V. GRIGOROVICH

Moscow, October 9, 1888

* * * Of course, the prize means happiness for me, and if I were to say that I don't find it exciting I'd be lying. I feel as if I had graduated once more somewhere, from some third institution of learning in addition to high school and university. I've kept trotting from corner to corner yesterday and today, like a man in love; I'm not working, and all I do is think.

Of course—and this is beyond any doubt—I do not owe this prize to my own self. There are young writers who are better and more sorely needed than I; Korolenko, for instance, is very far from being a bad writer and is an honorable man and would have received the prize if he had sent in his book. The idea of trying for the prize was put forth by Ya. P. Polonsky,[1] Suvorin supported it and sent my book to the Academy. And you yourself were there and stood up for me staunchly.

You'll agree that if it hadn't been for the three of you I would have had as much chance of seeing that prize as of seeing my ears. I don't want to play the modest violet and to assure you that all three of you were partial, that I'm not worthy of the prize and so forth—that would be old stuff and a bore; all I want to say is that I do not owe my happiness to my own self. I thank you a thousandfold and shall be grateful to you all my life.

I haven't been working for the piddling press, as far back as the first of the year. My short short stories I print in *New Times*, while whatever is more or less substantial I turn over to *The Northern Herald*, where they pay me 150 rubles per sheet. I'm not going to leave *New Times*, since I am attached to Suvorin; besides that, you see, *New Times* does not belong to the piddling press. I have no definite plans for the future. I have a desire to write a novel, a marvelous theme is available, at times a passionate longing to sit down and start in on the novel seizes me—but, apparently, there is not enough strength. I have made a beginning—and am timid about going on. I have resolved that I'll write it without hurrying, during the favorable hours only, correcting and polishing; I will spend several years on it; but as for writing it straight off, in a single year—I haven't enough spirit for that, one

---

[1] Yakov Petrovich Polonsky (1820–98), a novelist, short-story writer, poet.

[*84*]

dreads one's incapacity, and besides there is no need for haste. I have a knack for disliking this year what was written the year before; it seems to me that in the year to come I shall be stronger than I am now, and that is why I am now in no haste to risk things and take a decisive step. For, should the novel turn out to be a poor one, why, my gamble will lose me everything for all time to come.

Those ideas, women, men, pictures of nature that I have accumulated for the novel will remain whole and unharmed. I won't squander them on trifles—and that's something I promise you. My novel takes in several families and a whole district, with its forests, rivers, ferries, railroad. In the center of the district are two main figures, a man and a woman, near whom others, pawns, are grouped. As yet I have no political, religious, and philosophical view of the universe; I change it every month and will be compelled to limit myself solely to descriptions of how my chief characters make love, get married, give birth, meet death, and how they talk.

Until the hour for my novel strikes I'll go on writing that which I like—i.e., very short stories running to 1–1½ sheets and less. Stretching out trifling themes to cover a big canvas is boring, even though it pays off. Yet it is a pity to touch on large themes and expend images which are dear to me upon work to be done on schedule, the work of a day laborer. I'll bide a while till a more convenient time. * * *

I spent the summer gloriously. I stayed in the Kharkov and Poltava provinces, I visited the Crimea, Batum, Baku, I crossed the Caucasian mountains. Countless impressions. If I were living in the Caucasus, I would be writing fairy tales there. An amazing country!

I shall not be in Petersburg earlier than November, and I shall go to see you the day of my arrival. Meanwhile, let me thank you from the bottom of my heart, and wish you health and happiness.

Cordially,

your devoted A. Chekhov

TO A. S. SUVORIN

Moscow, October 10, 1888

Word of the prize had an overwhelming effect. It spread through my room and through Moscow like the awesome thunder of immortal Zeus.

Every day now I walk about like a man in love; Mother and Father spout dreadful nonsense and rejoice beyond words; Sister, nervous and aspiring, guarding our reputation with all the austerity and pettiness of a lady at court, is making the rounds of her close friends and spreading the news abroad. Jean Shcheglov discourses on literary Iagos and the five hundred enemies I'll acquire for the five hundred rubles. I met the Lensky couple [1] by chance, and they made me pledge my word that I would have dinner with them; I happened to meet a certain lady who adores people of talent and she, too, invited me to dine; the inspector of the vocational school made a special trip to congratulate me and wanted to buy my "Kashtanka" [2] for 200 rubles, "to make something" on the deal. * * * I repeat once more: the second- and third-rate writers of newspaper fiction ought to put up a monument to me, or at least present me with a silver cigar case: I have blazed a trail for them into the prestigious thick periodicals and to laurels, and the hearts of decent folk. For the time being this is my one good deed; just the same, everything I wrote and for which I was given the prize will not live in the memory of men for even a decade.

I am having terrific luck. I passed the summer magnificently, happily, having spent practically nothing but pennies and without running up any particularly big debts. The Psel [3] smiled at me, and so did the sea, and the Caucasus, and the farmstead, and the book trade likewise (I received monthly remittances for my *In the Twilight*). In September I worked off half of what I owe and wrote a novelette, [4] sort of, running to 2¼ sheets, which brought me more than 300 rubles. *Twilight* has come out in a second edition. And suddenly, like a bolt from the blue, this prize!

My luck is running so well that I am squinting up at the heavens warily. In a short while I'm going to hide under the table and I'll squat there quietly, without raising my voice. Until I resolve to take a serious step— write a novel, that is—I'll keep myself to myself, quietly and unobtrusively, writing unpretentious little stories, little plays; I won't scale a mountain and I shan't fall off but will be working at an even pace, the way Burenin's pulse works: I will heed the Ukrainian who said, "If I was Czar I'd steal me a hundred rubles and git." As long as I am a

---

[1] Actors associated with the Maly Theater in Moscow.
[2] A story for children.
[3] The river that flowed through the estate where he had summered.
[4] "The Name-Day Party."

little czar in my ant hill I'll steal a hundred rubles and run off. However, it seems I'm already starting to write nonsense.

People are talking about me now. Make hay while the sun shines. An advertisement of both my books ought to be run three times in succession and also on the 19th, when the prize will be announced officially. The 500 rubles I'll put aside toward buying a farmstead. The takings from the book will go toward the same end.

What am I to do with my brother? [5] Nothing but grief there. In a sober state he is intelligent, shy, truthful, and gentle, but drunk he is unbearable. Having downed two or three glasses he gets fearfully excited and starts in lying. He wrote that letter [6] out of a passionate desire to voice or perpetrate a harmless but effective lie of some sort or other. He hasn't reached the stage of hallucinations yet, because he drinks comparatively little. I recognize by his letters when he is sober and when he is drunk: some letters are profoundly decent and sincere, others are mendacious from start to finish. He is beyond a doubt a victim of alcoholism. What is alcoholism? It is as much of a psychosis as morphine addiction, masturbation, nymphomania, etc. Most frequently alcoholism is inherited from the father or mother, from grandfather or grandmother. But there are no drunkards in our line. Grandfather and father would occasionally get high with their guests, but this did not hinder them from buckling down to business right on time or from awakening in time for an early morning church service. Wine made them good-natured and witty; it gladdened the heart and enlivened the mind. My brother the teacher and I never drink *solo*, we don't know what's what in wines, we can drink all we want to, but our heads are clear when we awaken. One day this summer a certain professor from Kharkov and I took it into our heads to get drunk. We drank and drank and then dropped the whole thing, since it hadn't worked for us. In the morning we awakened utterly unaffected. Yet Aleksandr and my artist brother lose their minds after two or three glasses and at times crave a drink. . . . God knows whom they take after. All I know is that Aleksandr doesn't drink without reason, but gets drunk whenever he is unhappy, or is discouraged about something. * * *

Your A. Chekhov

---

[5] Chekhov's brother Aleksandr.
[6] A drunken letter addressed to Suvorin, his employer.

TO A. S. SUVORIN

Moscow, October 27, 1888

* * * In conversations with the writing fraternity I always insist that it's none of the artist's business to solve narrowly specialized problems. It's bad when an artist tackles something that he does not understand. We have specialists around for special problems; it's their business to judge about the peasant commune, about the destinies of capital, about the harmfulness of hard drinking, about boots, about women's diseases. As for the artist, he must judge only about that which he understands; his orbit is just as limited as the orbit of every other specialist—this I repeat, and this I always insist upon. That his sphere is free from questions and is solidly packed with nothing but answers can be claimed only by one who has never written and has had nothing to do with images. The artist observes, selects, surmises, composes—actions which by themselves presuppose a question at their very beginning; if at the very beginning he has not put a question to himself, then there is nothing to surmise about and nothing to select. In brief, I shall conclude with psychiatry: if one is to deny that question and intention exist in creative work, it becomes necessary to admit that the artist creates without premeditation, without design, under the influence of an affect; therefore, if some author were to boast to me that he had written a tale without a previously thought-out intention but by inspiration alone, I would call him a madman.

In demanding from an artist a conscious attitude toward his work you are right, but you are confusing two concepts: *the solution of a problem* and *the correct posing of a question*. Only the second is obligatory for an artist. Not a single problem is solved in *Anna Karenina* and in *Eugene Onegin*, but you find these works quite satisfactory only because all the questions in them are correctly posed. The court is obliged to pose the questions correctly, but it's up to the jurors to answer them, each juror according to his own taste. * * *

You write that the hero of my "Name-Day Party" is a figure to which I ought to have devoted much attention. Good Lord, I'm not an insensible beast, I understand this. I understand that I mutilate my chief characters and mar them, that I let good material go to waste. —I must say in all conscience that I would willingly spend half a year working without a break on "The Name-Day Party." I like to take it easy, and I see nothing at all attractive about rapid-fire publication. I would willingly, with pleasure, with feeling, working intermittently, describe my hero *in his entirety*, describe his soul while his wife was giving birth, his trial, his nasty feeling after acquittal, describe how the midwife and the doctors drink tea at night, describe the rain. —This would afford me nothing but pleasure, since I love to rummage and fuss. But what am I to do? I start in on the story on September 10 with the thought that I am obliged to finish it by October 5—the final deadline; should I miss it, I would be guilty of deception and would be left without money. The beginning I write calmly, without constraint, but in the middle I already begin to lose heart and to be afraid that my story will prove too long: I must remember that *The Northern Herald* hasn't too much money and that I am one of its expensive contributors. That's precisely why a beginning of mine always turns out to be a most promising one, as if I had begun a novel; the middle is all mussed, timorous, while the ending, like that of a short-short, is a display of fireworks. Willy-nilly, in doing a story, you worry first of all about its framework: out of the mass of heroic and semiheroic characters you take just one person—wife or husband; you place against the background and draw only this person, and this person is the one you will also emphasize; as for the rest, you scatter them in the background, like small change, and you'll get something in the nature of the vault of heaven: one great moon and a mass of very little stars. The moon, however, does not pan out, because it can be understood only when the stars around it are also understood, yet these stars have not been finished. And what I produce turns out to be not literature but something stitched together after the method Trishka used on his kaftan.[1] What can one do? I don't know, I really don't know. I will rely on time, which heals all things.

In all conscience, once more—I say that I haven't yet begun my literary activity, even though I have received the prize. Subjects for five novellas and two novels are languishing in my head. The idea for one of the novels was in fact conceived long ago, so that some of its *dramatis personae* have grown old by now without having been written about. There's a veritable army of people in my head, pleading to get out and awaiting commands. Everything that I have written up to now is poppycock by comparison with what I would write and would

[1] Trishka's kaftan is a byword, derived from a fable by Krylov. Trishka is distantly related to our Simple Simon.

write with rapture. It is a matter of utter indifference to me whether I write "The Name-Day Party" or "Lights," or a skit or a letter to a good friend—it's all wearisome, automatic, flabby, and there are times when I feel sorry in a vexed way for the critic who attaches significance to "Lights," for instance; it seems to me that I am taking him in with my productions, even as I take in many people with my serious or inordinately jolly mien. —I do not relish my success; the subjects roosting in my head are annoyingly jealous of those that have already been used in my writing; I feel offended because the poor stuff has already been made use of, whereas the good material is lying about the warehouse like rubbishy books. Of course, a great deal in this wail is exaggerated, much *imaginary*, but there is some truth in it, and a large measure, at that. What do I call good material? Those images that seem the choicest to me, that I love and jealously guard from being wasted and against getting their throats slit for the sake of a "Name-Day Party" deadline. —If I am mistaken in my love, then I am in the wrong; but then, it's possible that I'm not mistaken in my love! Either I am a fool and a conceited fellow, or I really am an organism capable of being a good writer; everything that is being written now is not to my liking and brings on boredom, whereas everything that is roosting in my head interests me, I find it touching and exciting—and from this I deduce that everybody is doing what is unnecessary, whereas I am the only one who knows the secrets of how things ought to be done. Most probably all those who write think thus. However, the devil himself would break his neck with these questions.

In deciding how I am to act and what I am to do *money won't help*. An extra thousand rubles won't solve the problem, while a hundred thousand is something written on the sky with a pitchfork. Besides, whenever I am in the money I become extremely carefree—I don't know why, perhaps it's due to my being unaccustomed to money—and lazy: at such times I find the ocean only knee-deep. —What I need is solitude and time.

Forgive me for monopolizing your attention with myself. It just flowed from the pen. For some reason I'm not working now.

Thank you for printing my pieces. For God's sake, don't stand on ceremony with them: shorten, lengthen, change, discard, and do what you please. I give you carte blanche. I shall be glad if my efforts don't usurp other people's space. * * *

Your A. Chekhov

TO A. S. SUVORIN

Moscow, November 3, 1888

* * * To think scientifically is a good thing in all areas, but the trouble is that scientific thought concerning creativity will in the end inevitably be reduced to a pursuit of "little cells" or "centers" controlling creative ability, and in due time some dull-witted German or other will discover these little cells in the temporal part of the brain, another German will disagree with him, a third German will agree, while a Russian will run through some article concerning these little cells and will fire off a report of his own in *The Northern Herald*, *The Herald of Europe* will get busy picking this report to pieces, and for three years a foolish infection will be suspended in the Russian air, giving the dullards income and popularity, but affording intelligent people only irritation. * * *

Your A. Chekhov

TO A. S. SUVORIN

Moscow, November 7, 1888

* * * It is not the public which is to blame for the atrocious state of our theaters. The public is always and everywhere the same: intelligent and foolish, cordial and pitiless—depending upon its mood. It always was a herd which needed good shepherds and dogs, and it has always gone wherever it was led by the shepherds and the dogs. You are outraged because it laughs uproariously at flat jokes and applauds resounding phrases, but then it is none other than that same foolish public that fills the house when *Othello* is put on and, when it listens to the opera *Eugene Onegin*, weeps as Tatyana writes that letter of hers.

As a general thing the public, for all its foolishness, is nevertheless more intelligent, sincere, and good-humored than Korsh, the actors, and the playwrights, who imagine themselves more intelligent. Mutual misunderstanding. * * *

The Dramatic Society I regard as a commercial institution. It has one aim only: to try to have its members take in as much as possible. This is so excellent an aim that by comparison all other aims aren't worth an empty eggshell. Viktor Krylov [1] is a son of a bitch, but in view

---

[1] Viktor Aleksandrovich Krylov (1836–1906), a playwright.

of the Society's aim I would be the first to vote for him as president. As long as icons rather than live wires preside, there won't be any order in the Society.

Regards to all of you. We're having the foulest sort of weather.

Your A. Chekhov

TO A. N. PLESHCHEYEV

Moscow, November 13, 1888

Oof! I have at last finished copying the story,[1] have packed it up and sent it off to you, dear Aleksey Nikolayevich. Have you received it? Read it? Angry at me, are you? The story is altogether unsuitable for reading in a family circle of anthology lovers; it is without grace and gives off the dank odor of sewers. But, at least, my conscience is at peace: in the first place, I have kept my promise; in the second, I have rendered the late Garshin[2] that tribute which I wanted to render and was able to. It seems to me, as a medico, that I described the psychic pain correctly, according to all the rules of the science of psychiatry. As for the wenches—I was, in time of yore, a big specialist in that department. [...]

Your A. Chekhov

TO A. S. SUVORIN

Moscow, between November 20 and 25, 1888

* * * You say that writers are the chosen people of God. I'm not going to get into any argument about that. Shcheglov calls me a Potemkin[1] in literature, and so it's not up to me to talk of the thorny path, the disillusionments, and so on. I don't know if I have ever suffered more than shoemakers, mathematicians, conductors; I know not who speaketh

---

[1] "An Attack of Nerves," written for and contributed to an anthology published in memory of Garshin.

[2] Vsevolod Mikhailovich Garshin (1855–88), a writer whose short stories were expressive of his supersensitive, compassionate nature, and sharply conveyed his awareness of evil. In a fit of acute depression he committed suicide.

[1] Statesman and warrior, he is widely remembered as chief among the lovers of Catherine the Great.

with my lips, God or someone else who is worse. I will permit myself to testify to just one minor annoyance which experience may have made you too familiar with. Here is what it's all about. You and I love ordinary people, whereas we are loved because we are regarded as extraordinary. I, for instance, am invited everywhere; they wine and dine me everywhere as if I were a general at a wedding; my sister's indignation is aroused since she is invited everywhere because she is the sister of a writer. Nobody wants to love us for our ordinary selves. Hence it follows that if on the morrow we should appear as ordinary mortals in the eyes of our good friends, they will cease to love us and will merely pity us. And that is vile. Vile, too, is the fact that we are loved for the sort of thing which we often dislike in ourselves and have no respect for. It's vile, my having been right when I wrote "The First Class Passenger," the story in which I have an engineer and a professor discussing fame.

I'll go off to the farmstead. The devil with them. You have your Feodosiya.[2]

By the way—about Feodosiya and the Tartars. The Tartars have been robbed of their land, yet no one gives a thought to their well-being. What the Tartars need is schools. Write about this, urging that the funds now being wasted on the kraut University of Dorpat,[3] attended by the useless Germans, ought to be allotted by the Ministry to schools for Tartars, who are useful to Russia. I would write about this myself, only I don't know how. . . .

Stay well and happy.

Your A. Chekhov

TO A. S. SUVORIN

Moscow, December 23, 1888

Dear Aleksey Sergeyevich,

* * * There are moments when my spirits positively sink. For whom and for the sake of what am I writing? For the public? But I don't see it and have less belief in it than I have in a hobgoblin: it is uneducated, badly brought up, while its better elements are careless and insincere

---

[2] Seaport in the Crimea where Suvorin had a house.
[3] Now Tartu, Estonia, noted for its university, which was founded by a Swedish ruler in the seventeenth century.

in their attitude toward us. Whether I am necessary to this public or not is something that I can't grasp. Burenin says I am not necessary and that I am busying myself with trifles, the Academy has awarded me the prize—the devil himself will be at a loss. Write for money? But I never have money, and because I am not accustomed to having it, I am almost indifferent to it. For money I work listlessly. Write for praise? But praise only irritates me. The literary society, the students, Yevreinova,[1] Pleshcheyev, young ladies, and so on, praised my "Attack of Nerves" extravagantly, but it was Grigorovich alone who noted the description of the first snowfall in it. And so on, and so on. But if we had criticism I would know that I deal with vital subjects—whether good or bad does not matter; I would know that to people who have dedicated themselves to the study of life I am just as necessary as a star is to an astronomer. And I would then put my back into the work, and I would know for the sake of what I would be working. But at present I, you, Muravlin,[2] et al. resemble maniacs writing books and plays for their personal pleasure. Personal pleasure is, of course, a good thing; one feels that while one is writing—but afterward? However . . . there, I'm closing the valve. In a word, I feel hurt about Tatyana Repina,[3] and I feel pity not because the heroine poisoned herself but because she lived her allotted years, died a martyr's death, and was depicted for no reason whatsoever and without any benefit to people. Countless tribes, religions, languages, cultures have vanished because there were no historians and scientists. Thus there are vanishing before our eyes countless lives and works of art, thanks to a total absence of criticism. It will be said that criticism has no point for us, because all contemporary works are wretched and don't amount to anything. But that is narrow-minded. Not only life's pluses are studied, but its minuses as well. The mere conviction that the '80s have not produced a single writer will furnish enough material for a work in five volumes. * * *

I sent Khudekov, for 100 rubles, a story [4] that I am asking you not to read: I am ashamed of it. Last evening I sat down to write a fairy

---

[1] Anna Mikhailovna Yevreinova (1844–1919), author of scholarly works, editor and for a time publisher of *The Northern Herald*.

[2] Pseudonym of Dmitry Petrovich Golitzyn (1860–1917), writer; eventually a prominent bureaucrat and an extreme reactionary.

[3] The heroine of Suvorin's play with the same title. Chekhov had a hand in its production.

[4] "The Gardener and the Evil Spirit."

tale [5] for *New Times*, but a woman [6] presented herself and dragged me off all the way to Plyushchikha Street to see the poet Palmin who, in a drunken state, had fallen and bashed his forehead so badly as to expose the bone. I fussed with him, this drunkard, for an hour and a half, maybe two, tired myself out, made everything on me stink of iodoform, got my dander up and came home all tired out. Today it was already late to write. In general, I am finding life tedious and, at times, I begin to hate it—something that never happened to me before. Lengthy, stupid conversations, guests, people asking me for favors, handouts of a ruble, or two rubles, or three, having to pay cabbies for patients who don't give me a cent—in a word, everything is so balled up that one might as well run out of the house. People borrow money from me and don't pay it back, walk off with my books, don't consider my time of any value. The only thing lacking is an unrequited love. * * *

Your Chekhov

TO A. S. SUVORIN

Moscow, December 26, 1888

* * * You write that one must work not for the sake of criticism but of the public, that it is still premature for me to be complaining. It is pleasant, of course, to think that one is working for the sake of the public, but how do I know that I am working precisely for the public's sake? I myself, because of the pettiness of my work and a thing or two besides, derive no gratification from it; as for the public (I did not call it vile), in its attitude toward us it is careless and insincere; one will never hear the truth from it, and therefore there's no telling whether it needs me or not. It is premature for me to complain, but it is never premature to ask myself: Is it real work I am busying myself with or trifles? Criticism keeps mum, the public lies, and my intuition tells me that I am busying myself with rubbish. Am I complaining? I don't remember what the tone of my letter was, but if I did, it wasn't on my own account but on that of our whole fraternity, which I feel infinitely sorry for.

All week long I have been as spiteful as a son of a bitch. Hemor-

[5] Later called "The Bet."
[6] The woman was Palmin's wife.

rhoids with itching and bleeding, visitors, Palmin with his bashed forehead, boredom. In the evening, at the beginning of the holidays I was busy with a patient who died before my eyes. Generally speaking, not very cheerful themes. Spite is pettiness of soul so to speak. I confess and I damn myself. I am particularly vexed with myself because I confide in you the secrets of my melancholy, which is highly uninteresting and shameful at an age as rich with blossom and as glorified by poets as mine.

For New Year's I'll try to send a fairy tale and after the first of January I'll mail you "The Princess." * * *

Cordially yours,

A. Chekhov

TO A. S. SUVORIN

Moscow, December 30, 1888

* * * The director [1] considers Ivanov a superfluous man in the Turgenev vein; Savina [1] asks, "Why is Ivanov such a scoundrel?" You write, "It is necessary to endow Ivanov with something which will make evident why two women persist in clinging to him, and why he is a scoundrel, whereas the doctor is a great man." If that is how the three of you have understood me it means that my *Ivanov* is worthless. I probably lost my wits and have written something altogether different from what I wanted to write. If Ivanov, my handiwork, turns out to be a scoundrel or a superfluous man, and the doctor a great man, if it is beyond understanding why Sarah [2] and Sasha [3] love Ivanov, it is evident that my play hasn't come off and putting it on is out of the question.

Here is how I understand my chief characters. Ivanov belongs to the gentry, is a university man, not remarkable in any way; by nature he is easily excitable, ardent, greatly inclined to infatuations, honest and straightforward, like the majority of the educated gentry. He lived on

---

[1] Fyodor Alekseyevich Yurkovsky, manager of the Aleksandrinsky Theater in Petersburg; Mariya Gavrilovna Savina (1854–1915) was an actress associated with the same theater.

[2] A Jewish woman who has renounced her faith, her family, and her fortune to marry Ivanov.

[3] A young girl, an heiress, who is loved by Ivanov and who, loving him, hopes to redeem him.

his estate in the country and had a post in the zemstvo. What he did and how he conducted himself, what engrossed and what infatuated him can be seen from the following speech, addressed by him to the doctor (Act I, scene 5): "Don't go and marry either Jewish girls, or female psychopaths, or bluestockings. —Don't war with thousands singlehanded, don't fight with windmills, don't go butting your forehead against walls. May God preserve you from all sorts of country estates managed on rational principles, schools out of the ordinary run, fiery speechifying." There you have some of the things in his past. Sarah, who had seen his rationally managed estates and other chimerical projects, tells the doctor about him: "This is a remarkable man, doctor, and I'm sorry you didn't know him two or three years ago. He is moody nowadays, he won't talk, won't do anything, but before—what a delight." (Act I, scene 7.)

His past is resplendent, like that of the majority of Russia's intellectuals. There is not—or there hardly ever is—a single Russian member of the gentry or a single university man who refrains from boasting about his past. The present is always inferior to the past. Why? Because Russian excitability has one specific property: it soon gives way to fatigue. On the spur of the moment, having hardly hopped off his school bench, a man will take on a burden beyond his strength, will take on, all at the same time, not only the schools but also the muzhik, and a rational economy, and reads *The Herald of Europe;* he delivers speeches, writes to a Minister, wars against evil, applauds the good; he loves, but not just simply, not in any old way but, infallibly, it is the bluestockings whom he loves, or female psychopaths, or [...], or even prostitutes, whom he rescues, and so on and so on.

However, hardly has he managed to live to the age of thirty or thirty-five than he already begins to feel fatigue and boredom. He hasn't as much as even a passable mustache to his name yet, but he already speaks ex cathedra: "Don't you go and get married, old man—trust my experience." Or: "What, essentially, is liberalism? Just between the two of us, Katkov [4] was often right." By now he is all set to negate not only the zemstvo but rational economy, and science, and love. —My Ivanov tells the doctor (Act I, scene 5): "You, my dear friend, finished your studies only last year, you are still young and vigorous—but I am thirty-five. I am entitled to give you advice." Such is the tone of these prematurely fatigued people. Further on, with a sigh of authority, he gives the ad-

[4] Mikhail Nikiforovich Katkov (1818–87), an influential reactionary journalist.

vice: "Don't go and marry thusly and thusly"—see one of the quotations given above—"But choose for yourself something sort of run-of-the-mill, grayish, without vivid hues, without excessive sounds. In general, build your whole life according to hackneyed patterns. The grayer and the more monotonous the background is, the better. As for the life I have lived, how wearisome, ah, how wearisome!"

Conscious of boredom and physical fatigue, he does not understand what is happening to him and what has occurred. Horrified, he says to the doctor (Act I, scene 3): "There, you say that she will die soon, yet I feel neither love nor pity but fatigue, some sort of void. To anyone just looking at me this would seem dreadful, but I myself don't understand what is happening to my soul." Caught in such a situation, narrow-minded and careless people usually throw all the blame on their milieu, or else enroll themselves in the category of superfluous persons and Hamlets and quietly settle for that. But Ivanov, a straightforward fellow, openly declares to the doctor and the public that he does not understand himself: "I don't understand, I don't understand.—" That he sincerely does not understand himself is evident from the long monologue in Act III in which, conversing eye to eye with the public and making his confessions to it, he actually weeps!

The change that has taken place in him outrages his decency. He seeks outward causes and fails to find them; he takes to seeking them within himself and finds only an indefinite feeling of guilt. That feeling is Russian. A Russian, whether someone in his household has died, or he has fallen ill, or if he is in debt to somebody, or is making a loan himself, always feels himself guilty. All the time Ivanov is expiating some guilt or other of his and, at every nudge, the feeling of guilt grows within him. In Act I he says, "It's probable that I am dreadfully guilty, but my thoughts are all tangled, my soul is fettered in some sort of indolence, and I haven't the strength to understand myself." In Act II he says to Sasha: "Day and night my conscience aches; I feel profoundly guilty, but I don't understand just what my guilt consists of."

To fatigue, boredom, and the feeling of guilt add one more enemy. It is loneliness. If Ivanov were a government clerk, an actor, a priest, a professor, he would have become habituated to his situation. But he is living on a country estate. He is in a provincial place. The people there are either drunkards, or addicted to cards, or like the doctor. None of them has any concern with his feelings and the change within him. He is lonely. The long winters, the long evenings, the empty garden, the empty rooms, the grousing Count, the ailing wife. —No place to get away to. That is why he is plagued at every moment by the question: Where can he find a spot for himself?

Now the fifth enemy. Ivanov is fatigued, he does not understand himself, but life is indifferent to all that. It presents him with its legitimate demands and willy-nilly, he must find solutions for these problems. The sick wife a problem, a heap of debts a problem, Sasha clings to him—a problem. What solutions he finds for all these problems should be evident from the monologue in Act III and the content of the two last acts. Such people as Ivanov do not solve problems but collapse under their weight. They are at a loss, lift their hands helplessly, fidget, complain, do foolish things, and, in the very end, surrendering to their undisciplined, crumbling nerves, can no longer find any ground underfoot and join the ranks of the "broken" and the "misunderstood."

Disenchantment, apathy, the ready yielding to fatigue, deterioration of the nerves are the inevitable consequence of inordinate excitability, and such excitability is characteristic to an extreme degree among our young men and women. Take literature. Take the present times. —Socialism is one kind of excitement. But where is it? It is in Tikhomirov's [5] letter to the Czar. The Socialists have taken wives and are criticizing the zemstvos. Where is liberalism? Even Mikhailovsky is saying that all the checkers are mixed up nowadays. —And what price all Russian fads? The war has tired us out, Bulgaria has tired us out to the point of irony, Zucchi [6] has tired us out, so have operettas.

A ready yielding to fatigue (Dr. Bertenson, too, will confirm this) does not find expression only in whining or a feeling of boredom. The life of a man who is tired out cannot be represented thus: [7] It is very uneven. Not all worn-out people lose their capacity for getting extremely excited, but this lasts only for a very brief while, moreover, and each spell of excitement is succeeded by still greater apathy. This can be graphically represented thus.[8] The descent, as you can see, does not follow an inclined plane but takes a somewhat different course.

[5] Lev Aleksandrovich Tikhomirov (1850–1923), a spokesman of the terrorists who were responsible for the assassination of Alexander II, ended by becoming a pillar of the autocracy. He addressed to Alexander's successor an abject petition, protesting his repentance and begging permission to return to Russia (he had earlier escaped abroad) and as a loyal subject to atone for his past.

[6] An Italian ballerina.

[7] Here Chekhov drew a gently rippling line.

[8] Here Chekhov drew a rippling line with several high peaks, the line itself gradually descending.

Sasha declares her love. Ivanov cries out in rapture: "A new life!"—but next morning believes in this life just as much as he believes in the existence of a hobgoblin (monologue, Act III). His wife insults him; he flies off the handle, becomes excited and hurls a cruel insult at her. He is reviled as a scoundrel. If this fails to dispatch his crumbled brains, he gets excited and condemns himself.[9]

To avoid exhausting you, I pass on to Doctor Lvov. This is a type of the honest, direct, ardent, narrow and rectilinear man. It is of such that clever people say: "He is stupid, but he has a sense of honesty." Whatever resembles breadth of vision or immediacy of feeling is alien to Lvov. The commonplace personified, this, a walking bias. He looks at every phenomenon and person through a cramping frame; his judgments about everything are preconceived. He worships him who shouts "Make way for honest toil!"; as for him who does not shout this, he is a scoundrel and a kulak. There is no middle-of-the-road. He was brought up on the novels of Mikhailov [10]; in the theater he saw the "new people" portrayed on the stage—i.e., the kulaks and the sons of this age, as drawn by the new dramatists, the go-getters (Proporyev, Okhlyabyev, Navarygin, and so on). He had put this in his pipe, but had packed it in so tightly that while reading *Rudin*, he inevitably asks himself, "Is Rudin [11] a scoundrel or not?" Literature and the stage have so conditioned him that he approaches every person in life and literature with the same question. . . . If he would have had the luck of seeing your play he would have considered a crime on your part your failure to state clearly whether Messrs. Kotelnikov, Sabinin, Adashev are scoundrels or not. For him this question is important. That all men are sinners does not suffice him. You must dish up saints and scoundrels for him!

He was already prejudiced when he arrived in the district. He saw kulaks in all the well-to-do muzhiks at once and, at once, saw a scoundrel in Ivanov, whom he didn't understand. A man has an ailing wife yet he visits a rich woman living near by—there, isn't he a scoundrel? Evidently he is killing off his wife to marry the rich woman. . . .

Lvov is honest, direct, tells the truth no matter what it costs him. He will, if need be, throw a bomb under a carriage, give some inspector one in the snout, won't hesitate to call a man a scoundrel. He won't stop

[9] He commits suicide.
[10] Pseudonym of Aleksandr Konstantinovich Sheller (1838–1900), author of many ideological novels popular in the 1870s and 1880s. He also edited a Petersburg weekly.
[11] The leading character in Turgenev's novel of that title. He is a young man whose idealism finds expression in rhetoric rather than action.

at anything. He never feels any gnawings of conscience: he is an "honest toiler," intent on destroying the "power of darkness"!

Such people are needed and, for the most part, are of a likable sort. To caricature them, even in the interests of the stage, is dishonest—and besides there is no point in doing so. True, caricature is sharper and therefore more understandable, but it is better to leave the drawing unfinished than to smear it. . . .

Now about the women. What do they love men for? Sarah loves Ivanov because he is a good sort, vehement, brilliant, and makes speeches as fiery as those of Lvov (Act I, scene 7). She loves him as long as he is aroused and interesting, but when he begins to turn misty before her eyes and to lose a definite countenance she no longer understands him and, by the end of the third act, speaks her mind directly and brusquely.

Sasha is a young lady formed in the latest mold. She is educated, bright, honest, and so forth. In the country of the blind the one-eyed man is king, and so she singles out the thirty-five-year-old Ivanov. He is the best of all. She had known him when she was small and had seen at close range how active he was at that time, when he was not yet tired out. He is a friend of her father's.

What we have here is a female whom the males vanquish not by the brightness of their plumage, or by their suppleness, or by their courage, but by their complaints, bellyaching, failures. Here is a woman who loves men during the period of their decline. Hardly have Ivanov's spirits hit bottom than the girl is right there, all set. That is all she had been waiting for. Goodness gracious, she now has so noble, so sacred a task! She will resurrect one who has fallen, help him regain his footing, bestow happiness upon him. It is not Ivanov but this task she is in love with. "Life," said Daudet's d'Argenton, "is not a novel!" Which is something Sasha does not know. She does not know that for Ivanov love constitutes only a superfluous complication, an additional stab in the back. Well, what's the upshot? Sasha has her hands full with Ivanov for all of a year, but he still won't come to life and keeps right on declining more and more.

My fingers are aching; I am winding this up. . . . If all the things mentioned above are not in the play then putting it on is out of the question. It means that I have not written what I wanted to write. Withdraw the play. I do not want to preach heresy from the stage. If the public leaves the theater feeling that the Ivanovs are scoundrels but that the Doctors Lvov are great men I will have to hand in my resignation and abandon my pen to the devil. You won't get anywhere with corrections and insertions. No corrections whatsoever can bring a great man down from his pedestal and no insertions whatsoever are likely to make a scoundrel over into a run-of-the-mill sinner. Sasha can be made to come out right at the final curtain, but I can no longer add anything to Ivanov and Lvov. I don't know how to do it. But if I were to add something, my feeling is that I would injure the play even more. Do trust my feeling, for it is that of the author.

* * * Frankly speaking, what tempted me about the production of the play was neither fame nor Savina. . . . I was figuring on earning about a thousand rubles. But it is better to borrow this thousand than risk committing a folly. Don't tempt me with success! Success in my case (provided I don't die) still lies ahead. I am betting that, sooner or later, I shall skin the theater to the tune of six or seven thousand. Want to bet?

* * * Oh, have I worn you out with this letter! Enough. Basta!

Happy New Year! Hurrah!

You lucky people, you will be drinking—or have already drunk—real champagne, but I shall be drinking slops!

My sister is ill. Aches, high temperature, headache, and so on. The same with the cook. Both in bed. It's typhus, I'm afraid.

Forgive me, dear man, for a desperately lengthy, wearisome letter.
* * *

Your A. Chekhov

* * * I have read over this letter. In the characterization of Ivanov the word "Russian" often occurs. Don't get in a temper over this. When I was writing the play I had in view only that which was necessary—that is, nothing but typical Russian traits. Thus inordinate excitability, a sense of guilt, proneness to fatigue are purely Russian characteristics. Germans never get excited, and that is why Germany doesn't know what disillusioned, or superfluous, or fatigued people are. The excitability of Frenchmen constantly maintains the same pitch, without going through abrupt rises and falls, and that is why the Frenchman even in his most decrepit dotage is normally excited. In other words, Frenchmen have no occasion to expend their powers on excessive excitement; they do spend them cleverly—that is why they don't go bankrupt.

Clearly, in the play I didn't use such terms as Russian, excitability, proneness to fatigue, and so forth, being certain that the reader and spectator would pay attention and have no need of such signs as: "This is a watermelon, not a plum." I tried to express myself simply, to avoid sly tricks, and was far from suspecting that readers and spectators would pounce on my chief characters because of a phrase, or stress dialogues concerning a dowry, and the like.

I wasn't able to write a play. A pity, of course. Ivanov and Lvov appear to my imagination as living people. I am telling you in all conscience, sincerely, that these people were born in my head—not of seafoam, not of preconceived notions, not of "cerebration," not by chance. They are the result of the observation and study of life. They stay in my mind, and I feel that I haven't lied by so much as one centimeter, that I haven't exceeded wisdom by a single note. But if they have turned out to be lifeless and blurred on paper, the fault is not theirs but that of my inability to communicate my thoughts. Which means that trying my hand at plays is still premature for me.

[1889]

Moscow, January 2, 1889

Most Wise Secretary!

I congratulate your radiant self and your offspring on the New Year, and wish you new happiness. May you win two hundred thousand and get to be an Actual Privy Councillor and, above all, enjoy good health and have our daily bread in an amount great enough to satisfy a glutton like yourself.

On my last visit to you when we were together and when we parted, it was as if a misunderstanding had occurred between us. I am going to visit you soon again; in order to put an end to this misunderstanding I find it necessary, sincerely and in all conscience, to let you know the following. I was seriously angry at you, and I was still angry when I left, of which I now repent. On my first visit what tore me away from you was your *horrible*, utterly outrageous treatment of N.A.[1] and of the cook. Do forgive me magnanimously, but such treatment of women, no matter what they are like, is unworthy of a decent and loving individual. What heavenly or earthly authority gave you the right to make them your bondwomen?

The constant use of language of the basest sort, a raised voice, reproaches, capricious acts at breakfast and dinner, eternal complaints that your life is like a convict's and your work accursed—come, isn't all that an expression of crass despotism? No matter how insignificant and blameworthy a woman may be, no matter how close she may be to you, you have no right to sit in her presence without your pants on, to be drunk in her presence, to use words that even factory hands refrain from using when they see women around them. You regard decorum and good upbringing as prejudices, but then one must spare something, at least—at least feminine weakness and children; one must spare the poetry of life, at least, if the prose is over and done with. Not one decent

---

[1] Natalya Aleksandrovna, the second wife of the addressee.

husband or lover will permit himself to talk to a woman [...], coarsely, for the sake of a funny story, to speak in ironic terms of relations in bed, [...]. This sort of thing corrupts a woman and alienates her from the God she believes in. A man who respects a woman, a man well bred and capable of love, would not permit himself to appear before a housemaid without his pants, to shout at the top of his voice: "Katka, bring the pisspot here!" Of nights, husbands sleep with wives, observing every propriety of tone and manner, and, come morning, they hasten to put on neckties, to avoid offending women by their unbecoming appearance—negligence in dress, that is. This is pedantic, but it has as a basis something that you will understand, if you happen to recall what a terribly educative role, with respect to breeding, environment and details play in the life of man. Between a woman who sleeps on a freshly laundered sheet and one who snoozes on a soiled sheet and goes off into peals of laughter as her lover [...], there is the same difference as between a drawing room and a pothouse.

Children are sacred and pure. Even among cutthroats and crocodiles they maintain their angelic rank. We may crawl into any pit you like, but we are in duty bound to envelop them in an atmosphere befitting their rank. You can't be foul-mouthed in their presence with impunity, or insult the servant, or tell Natalya Aleksandrovna with rancor, "Get out! To the devil with you! I'm not holding you!"

You can't make children the plaything of your mood, now kissing them tenderly, then stamping your feet at them in a frenzy. It is better not to love than to love with a despotic love. Hatred is considerably more honest than the love of a Nasser-Eddin,[2] now appointing his fervidly beloved Persians as satraps, then impaling them on stakes. One must not take the name of children in vain, yet you have a way of referring to every penny that you give or wish to give to another as "taken from the children." If anyone takes something away, it means that he *has given*, yet to speak of one's good works and handouts isn't altogether pretty. It is akin to reproaches. For the most part, men live for their families, but rare is the man who would dare to claim that as meritorious, and one is hardly likely to encounter, outside of yourself, such another hero who, as he hands over a ruble as a loan, would say, "I am taking this away from my children." One must be lacking in respect for children, lacking in respect for their sacredness, to be able to maintain, while one is well fed, well clothed, in a tipsily gay mood

2 Nasser-Eddin (1848–96), the Shah of Persia.

every day, that *all* of one's earnings go for the children only! Come, come!

I ask you to recall that despotism and lying ruined your mother's life. Despotism and lying mangled our childhood to such a degree that one feels queasy and fearful in recalling it. Remember the horror and revulsion we felt when at dinner Father would raise hell over the soup being too salty or curse out Mother as a fool. Nowadays Father simply can't forgive himself all these things.

Despotism is triply criminal. If the dread Judgment Day is not a fantasy, you will at that Judgment be liable before the Sanhedrin to a greater extent than Chòkhov [3] and I. Ye. Gavrilov.[4] It is no secret from you that the heavens have endowed you with that which is lacking in ninety-nine men out of a hundred: you are by nature infinitely magnanimous and gentle. For that very reason a hundred times more will be asked of you. In addition to that, you're a university man and are considered a journalist.

Your painful situation, the wretched character of the woman with whom you have to live, the idiocy of cooks, having to work like a convict sentenced to hard labor, an accursed life and so on, cannot serve as justification for your despotism. It is better to be the hanged than the hangman.

Natalya Aleksandrovna, the cook, and the children are weak and defenseless. They have no rights whatever over you, whereas you have the right to throw them out of the house at any minute and to mock at their weakness as much as you please. Do not make them feel this right.

I have interceded to the best of my ability and my conscience is clear. Be magnanimous and consider the misunderstanding at an end. If you are a straightforward man and not a sly one, you won't say that this letter shows evil intentions, that it is insulting, for instance, and was inspired by ill feeling. All I seek in our relations is sincerity. For I have no further need of anything else. You and I have nothing to divide.

Write that you, too, aren't angry, and consider the black cat that crossed our path as nonexistent.

Regards from the whole family.

Your A. Chekhov

[3] Mikhail Mikhailovich Chekhov (1851–1909), a cousin of the writer.
[4] Ivan Yegorovich Gavrilov was a Moscow merchant who employed both Mikhail M. and Pavel Yegorovich Chekhov (1824–98), Anton's father, in his warehouse. It was his mispronunciation of the family name that made Chòkhov a family joke among the Chekhov brothers.

* * * It would afford me great pleasure to read a paper before the Literary Society on how the idea of writing *Ivanov* came to me. It would be a public confession. I had cherished the daring dream of summing up everything that has been written until now about glum and whining people and of putting an end to these writings with my *Ivanov*. It seemed to me that a need to depict the despondent man was felt by all the fiction writers and playwrights of Russia and that all of them were writing instinctively, without any definite images in mind and without any viewpoint regarding the task. As far as my conception went, I came close to scoring a bull's-eye but the execution is worthless. I should have waited! I am glad that I didn't listen to Grigorovich two or three years ago and didn't write a novel. I can imagine how much good stuff I would have spoiled had I heeded the advice. "Talent and freshness will overcome everything," says he. Talent and freshness can ruin a great deal—that's nearer the truth. Outside of a plenitude of material and talent, something of no lesser importance is needed. Maturity is needed, for one thing; secondly, a *sense of personal freedom* is indispensable, yet only of late this sense began to burn within me. Hitherto I did not have it; its place was successfully taken by my frivolity, sloppiness, and disrespect for the work.

What writers of noble birth took from nature for nothing commoners purchase at the cost of their youth. Write a story, do, about a young man, the son of a serf, a former grocery boy, a choir singer, a high school pupil and university student, brought up to respect rank, to kiss the hands of priests, to truckle to the ideas of others—a young man who expressed thanks for every piece of bread, who was whipped many times, who went out without galoshes to do his tutoring, who used his fists, tortured animals, was fond of dining with rich relatives, was a hypocrite in his dealings with God and men, needlessly, solely out of a realization of his own insignificance—write how this young man squeezes the slave out of himself, drop by drop, and how, on awaking one fine morning, he feels that the blood coursing through his veins is no longer that of a slave but that of a real human being.* * *

Your Chekhov

TO A. N. PLESHCHEYEV

Greetings, dear Aleksey Nikolayevich!

I am writing you after serving my term of hard labor. Oh, why did you approve my *Ivanov* when it came before the Committee? What witless demons put it into Fyodorov's [1] head to choose my play for his benefit performance? I am worn out, and no honorarium can make up for the unbearable tension I suffered from all last week. Formerly I attributed no significance to my play and regarded it with condescending irony: I was through with it, and to the devil with it. But now when unexpectedly and suddenly I found it in the works, I realized what a bad job it was. The last act is particularly bad. All week long I was messing about with the play, scribbling variants, corrections, insertions. Fashioned a new Sasha (for Savina), changed Act IV beyond recognition, polished up Ivanov himself, and was so fagged out, started hating my play to such a degree, that I was ready to end it with Kean's [2] words: "Give Ivanov the stick, the stick!"

No, I don't envy Jean Shcheglov. I understand now why he guffaws so tragically. To compose a good play for the theater, you must have a special talent (one can be an excellent novelist and at the same time compose the plays of a cobbler); but to compose a bad play and then attempt to make a good one out of it, to try all manner of tricks, to cross out, to write in, to insert monologues, to resurrect the dead, to bury the living—for this you must have a much greater talent. This is as difficult as to buy a soldier's old pants and insist on cutting a dress coat out of them. In this case you will not start guffawing tragically, but neigh like a horse.

I shall come to Petersburg on January 21 or 22. First of all I'll call on you. We ought to spend an evening together and drink some claret. Vodka disgusts me more and more every day, beer I don't drink, red wine I dislike, so what is left is champagne, for which, until I marry a wealthy witch, I shall substitute claret or something like that.

When I am done with my Bolvanov,[3] I'll start writing for *The North-*

---

[1] The stage name of F. A. Yurkovsky, manager of the Aleksandrinsky Theater, Petersburg.

[2] Edmund Kean, the English tragedian, who acted in a play by Dumas père, in which he urged that a character be subjected to the bastinado.

[3] *Bolvan* is the Russian for "blockhead"—the word used here is a play on Chekhov's *Ivanov*.

ern Herald. Fiction is a peaceful, holy occupation. The narrative genre is a lawful wife, the dramatic is a spectacular, blustering, impudent, and tiresome mistress.

I will not publish *Ivanov* in *The Northern Herald*.[4]

I am stone broke. I live on the charity of my "Boor" and of Suvorin, who for 100 rubles bought several of my stories for his *Cheap Library*. May Providence guard both of them.

Suvorin is now in Moscow staging his *Tanya*.[5] Lensky is playing Adashev amazingly. I am sure that the Moscow ladies, having seen Adashev-Lensky, will get themselves lovers-journalists. Lensky is passionate, ardent, spectacular, and uncommonly attractive. That's good. The public must see journalists not in caricatures and not tiresomely clever, as in Davydov's [6] skin, but in a pink light pleasing to the eye. Yermolova is good as Tatyana.

Little by little I am at work on my novel.[7] I don't know if anything will come of it, but while I'm writing it, I fancy that after a good dinner I am lying in a garden on hay that has just been mown. A wonderful rest. Oh, shoot me if I go off my head and occupy myself with what is not my business!

Where is Georginka? [8] Tell him that I should be glad to see him at the theater on January 26.[9] Let him learn how plays should not be composed. And, by the way, he ought to provide himself with material for summer conversations. I shall place a ticket at his disposal.

Rassokhin [10] has received a copy of the Garshin miscellany. I received 3 rubles. The money will be passed on. I am an honest man. Greetings to your family. If Nikolay Alekseyevich [11] is still in the dungeon, give the prisoner my regards! My family bows low to you.

Your A. Chekhov

---

[4] After its success on the stage, the play was published in the issues of that journal for March 1889.
[5] The title of this popular play, in which Chekhov had a hand, was *Tatyana Repina*.
[6] Vladimir Nikolayevich Davydov, the actor who played the role of Ivanov at the première of that play.
[7] This project never materialized.
[8] Georgy Mikhailovich Lintvarev, a son of A. V. Lintvareva. He was a pianist.
[9] The date of a rehearsal, presumably the dress rehearsal, at the Aleksandrinsky Theater.
[10] Sergei Fyodorovich Rassokhin, editor of the lithographed *Theatrical Library*.
[11] The addressee's son, an army officer confined to the guard house because of a scandal perpetrated in the company of drunken comrades.

TO A. M. YEVREINOVA

Moscow, March 10, 1889

Respected Anna Mikhailovna!

I have received my fee. Thanks. It was more than I expected, and I fear that you have not deducted my debt. I do owe something to the office, don't I?

Yesterday I finished and made a fair draft of a story, but it was for a novel ¹ of my own which is occupying me at the present time. Ah, what a novel! If it weren't for the thrice-accursed conditions of censorship I would promise it to you for November. There's nothing in the novel that would stir up revolution, but the censor will mangle it just the same. Half of the characters say, "I don't believe in God"; there's one father whose son is doing a life term at hard labor for armed resistance; there's a district inspector of police who is ashamed of his police uniform; there's a chief of the local nobility who is hated, and so on. Rich material for the red pencil.

I have a lot of money now—sufficient to live on till September; I am not bound by any promises. —The most suitable time has come for the romance (the literary, of course, and not the matrimonial sort). If I don't write it now, then when am I to write it? That's how I reason, although I am almost positive that I'll be fed up with the novel in two or three weeks and will again put it aside.* * *

You just wait: I'll buy up all the bulky, highbrow periodicals and stop their publication, leaving only *The Northern Herald*. That's when we'll get us electrical illumination, a majestic doorman, our own printing plant, carriages with rubber tires for the staff; we'll invite Milan ² to become a contributor (in charge of foreign affairs), hire Ashinov ³ as a doorman—and we'll have forty thousand subscribers. Though, incidentally, I haven't seen my rich bride even once. And she hasn't seen me either. Here's what I'll write her: "Fall in love not with me but with an idea" ⁴—and that's how I'll touch her heart.* * *

Sincerely devoted,

A. Chekhov

¹ The projected *Stories from the Life of My Friends*, which was never completed.
² Milan, King of Serbia; compelled to abdicate his throne on March 6, 1889.
³ Nikolay Ivanovich Ashinov was an adventurer who, together with a monk, attempted to establish a military settlement of volunteers in Abyssinia, calling himself the hetman of the free Cossacks.
⁴ Slightly misquoted from Turgenev's *Virgin Soil*.

Moscow, March 11, 1889

* * * Well, what do you think? I am writing a novel!! I write, I write, and there is no end in sight to my writing. I started it—the novel, that is—in the beginning thoroughly correcting and shortening what had already been written. I have by now outlined clearly nine physiognomies. What an intriguing plot! I have called it: *Stories from the Life of My Friends,* and I am writing it in the form of separate finished stories, closely bound together by having in common the plot, the ideas, and the characters. Each story has a title of its own. Don't think that the novel will be a crazyquilt. No, it will be an authentic novel, an entity, where every character will be organically indispensable. Grigorovich, to whom you conveyed the contents of the first chapter, got frightened because I took a student who will die and so will not move through the whole novel—i.e., will prove superfluous. But for me this student is a nail from a big boot. He's a detail.

I am barely managing the technique. I'm still weak in that department and feel that I'm making no end of crude mistakes. There will be boring stretches, there will be stupidities. Unfaithful wives, suicides, tight-fisted peasants who exploit their fellows, virtuous muzhiks, devoted slaves, argumentative little old ladies, kind little old nurses, county wits, red-nosed army captains, and "new" people—all of these I'll try to avoid, although in places I betray a strong tendency toward stereotypes.* * *

By the way, recently, among its excerpts from newspapers and periodicals, *New Times* cited from some newspaper or other a note eulogizing German chambermaids for working like convicts *all day long* and getting only two or three rubles a month for it. *New Times* subscribes to this eulogy and tacks on something on its own: our trouble, now, is that we keep a lot of superfluous servants. The way I see it, the Germans are scoundrels and poor political economists. In the first place, one can't use the same tone in speaking of servants that one uses in speaking of prisoners; in the second, a servant has legal rights and is made of the same flesh as Bismarck; servants are not slaves but free workers; in the third place, the higher the pay for the work, the happier the State, and each one of us must strive to pay labor more. Nor am I saying anything about the Christian point of view.* * *

Your A. Chekhov

[111]

Moscow, April 8, 1889

Holiday greetings to you, to Anna Ivanovna, Nastya, and Borya,[1] and I wish you wealth, fame, honor, serenity, and gaiety all your life.

The weather in Moscow is vile: mud, cold, rain. The painter [2] persists in maintaining a temperature of 39 degrees [Centigrade]. I visit him twice daily. My mood resembles the weather, I don't work, but read or pace from corner to corner. I'm not sorry, however, that I have time to read. Reading is more cheerful than writing. I think that if I were to live another forty years and read all that time, read and read and study how to write like a talented man, i.e. briefly, at the end of the forty years I would fire so huge a cannon at all of you that the heavens would shake. But now I am only a Lilliputian, like the rest.

Here everyone is tidying up, cleaning, baking, cooking, polishing, beating the rugs, running up and down stairs. Help! I am about to visit the painter. Keep well. Come, and then we shall sail down the Volga or to Poltava.

Your A. Chekhov

TO A. N. PLESHCHEYEV

Moscow, April 9, 1889

* * * I am a pusillanimous fellow, I don't know how to look circumstances straight in the eye, and therefore you will believe me when I tell you that I am literally unable to work. It's three weeks now that I haven't written a line! I have forgotten all my subjects and I'm not thinking of anything that might be of interest to you. I am hideously boring.

The novel has advanced considerably and, in anticipation of high tide, has run aground on a shoal. I am dedicating it to you—I've already written you about that. I base this novel on the life of good people, their faces, deeds, words, thoughts, and hopes; my aim is to kill two birds with one stone: to depict life truthfully and, while I am at it, show to what extent this life deviates from the norm. The norm is not known to me, just as it is not known to any one of us. All of us know what a

---

[1] Suvorin's wife and children.
[2] Chekhov's brother Nikolay, who was ill with typhoid and tuberculosis.

dishonorable act is, but just what honor is we do not know. I'll keep to the framework which is nearer the heart and which has already been tested by people stronger and more intelligent than I. This framework is man's absolute freedom—freedom from coercion, from prejudices, ignorance, the devil; freedom from passions and so forth.* * *

On Monday there will be a general meeting of the Dramatists. They want to elect me to the committee. I don't understand a thing about their committee, and I won't accomplish anything worth while for them. They might at least take into consideration the fact that for nine months I do not reside in Moscow. Apparently the session won't be a peaceful one. I'll be sticking up for five or six hundred rubles to be given to the widow of Yuryev, instead of the three hundred voted by Petersburg. It is shameful for a Society which lays out more than fifteen thousand for its clerical staff to be paying three hundred rubles to the widow of its chairman. In general, my tongue is itching and I want to chatter for a bit.* * *

Your wholly devoted A. Chekhov

TO A. S. SUVORIN

Sumy, beginning of May, 1889

I don't believe my eyes. Not long ago it rained and was cold, and now I sit at an open window and listen to nightingales, hoopoes, orioles, and other creatures vocalizing in the green garden. The Psel is majestically gentle, the tones of the sky and the land stretching below it are warm. The apple and cherry trees are in blossom. Geese waddle along with their goslings. In short, spring with all its appurtenances.* * *

I get up early, go to bed early, eat a lot, write and read. The painter [1] coughs and is cross. He is in a bad way.

For lack of new books I am backtracking, reading what I have read before. Among other things I am reading Goncharov and I keep wondering. I keep wondering at myself: why up to now have I considered Goncharov a first-rate writer? His *Oblomov* is a thing of no import whatsoever. The blown-up figure of Ilya Ilyish himself is really not so big as to have made it worth while to write a whole book about him. A bloated lazybones (there are many of his breed around), by nature uncomplicated, run-of-the-mill, petty; to elevate a character like that

---

[1] Chekhov's brother Nikolay.

to the status of a social type is to pay him tribute over and beyond his due. I ask myself: if Oblomov were not a lazybones, what would he be? And I answer: nothing. And if that's the case, let the fellow snooze to his heart's content. The other characters are small potatoes, have a whiff of Leikin about them, are negligently drawn and half-concocted. They are not typical of their time and do not contribute anything new. Schtoltz does not inspire me with any confidence whatsoever. Here, the author says, is an excellent fellow, but I don't believe it. What we have is a sly knave, who is thoroughly self-satisfied. He is half-concocted and three-quarters stilted. Olga is concocted and dragged in by the hair. But the main trouble is that the novel is permeated with chill, chill, chill. —I am striking Goncharov from my scroll of demigods.

But then, how direct, how powerful Gogol is, and what an artist! His "The Carriage" is, all by itself, worth two hundred thousand rubles. Uninterrupted delight, and that's all there is to it! The greatest Russian writer, this. In *The Inspector General* the best act is the first; in *The Marriage*, Act III is the worst of all. I'm going to read him aloud to our folks.* * *

Be happy, and in your orisons may I be remembered,

Your Akaky Tarantulov [2]

TO A. S. SUVORIN

Sumy, May 4, 1889

* * * You write that I have grown lazy. This does not mean that I have become lazier than I was. I work now just as much as I worked three to five years back. To work, and to have the appearance of a man who works from nine in the morning until dinner and from evening tea until bedtime has become a habit with me, and in this respect I am a bureaucrat. But if my labor does not result in two novellas a month, or an income of ten thousand a year, it isn't laziness that is to blame but my psycho-physical make-up: I don't love money enough to go in for medicine in a big way, and as for literature, I am short on passion and,

[2] Akaky Tarantulov was Chekhov's signature to a dramatic scene that he included in a Letter to the Editor appearing in *New Times* on April 22, 1889. The farce, which the author called "a little foolishness," was an attack on a clique in the Society of Dramatic Writers and Operatic Composers which, Chekhov feared, might destroy that institution; he was a recent but active member of its administrative committee.

consequently, on talent. The flame within me burns evenly and sluggishly, without flare-ups and crackling; that's why I never happen to dash off three or four sheets at one sitting in a single night, or to get so carried away by my work as to hinder myself from going to bed if I want to sleep. Hence I commit neither outstanding stupidities nor do I perform outstanding feats of intelligence.

In this respect I am afraid that I am very much like Goncharov, whom I do not like and who, when it comes to talent, towers over me by ten heads. There is a paucity of passion; and then, add psychopathy of this sort: for no clear reason it is two years now since I fell out of love with seeing my works in print, became indifferent to reviews, to chit-chat about literature, to gossip, to successes, to failures, to the big honorarium—in a word, I have become a perfect fool. My soul is subject to a kind of stagnation. I explain this by the stagnation in my personal life. I am not disenchanted, not tired out, not having the blues, but suddenly everything has simply become somehow less interesting to me. I'll have to pour a little more gunpowder under me.* * *

Bring me some forbidden books from abroad.* * *

God is doing the smart thing: He has taken Tolstoy [1] and Saltykov [2] to the other world and in this way reconciled what seemed to us irreconcilable. Now both are rotting and both are equally indifferent. I hear people are rejoicing over the death of Tolstoy and this joy strikes me as gross beastliness. I have no faith in the future of those Christians who, although they hate gendarmes, at the same time hail the death of another and see death as an angel of deliverance. You cannot picture to yourself how extremely repulsive it is when women rejoice over this death.* * *

Your A. Chekhov

---

[1] Dmitry Andreyevich Tolstoy (1823–89), Minister of Education, later Minister of Interior Affairs, was an extreme reactionary.

[2] Mikhail Yevgrafovich Saltykov (also known as Saltykov-Shchedrin and as N. Shchedrin, his pen name; 1826–89) belonged to the serf-owning gentry. A civil servant with radical convictions, he was the author of numerous sketches satirizing the ruling class and the rich; he also wrote a remarkable novel depicting the moral deterioration of a landed family. His last work was his autobiography.

Sumy, May 8, 1889

Pseudo-playwright who loses sleep because of my laurels!

I begin with Nikolay. He has chronic tuberculosis—an incurable illness. There are temporary improvements, and worsening *in statu* in the course of the illness; the question must be: how long will the process last? But not: when will the patient recover? Nikolay is spryer than he was. He strolls in the courtyard, eats, and grumbles at Mother properly. He is terribly capricious and hard to please.

We brought him here first class and for the time being refuse him nothing. He gets everything he needs and wants. They call him General, and I think that he believes himself to be a General. Holy relics.

You ask how you can help Nikolay. Help him any way that you can. The best help is monetary. If there had been no money, by now he would be lying around in a hospital for unskilled workmen. Ergo, money is the main thing. If you have no money, if you can't help, there is no claim on you. Besides, the sum needed is sizable, you can't get off with five or ten rubles. * * *

Once before I wrote you from Sumy. Among other things I asked you to send me *The Novorossisk Telegraph*. Now, not as a service, but as a friendly act, I would request you to send me the issues of the Kiev newspapers from May 1 to 15. First send me the issues of the 1st to the 7th, then of the 8th to the 15th.[1] By registered mail. I shan't trouble you again.

Now about your play. Your aim was to present a person who doesn't whine,[2] and then you took fright.[3] Your purpose seems clear to me. Only he who is indifferent doesn't whine. Those who are indifferent are either philosophers, or petty, egotistical individuals. The attitude toward the latter would be negative, toward the former positive. Of course, those indifferent blockheads who feel no pain even when seared with red-hot irons are out of the question. If you mean by a person who doesn't whine one who is not indifferent to his surroundings, but who cheerfully and patiently endures the blows of fate

---

[1] Chekhov was apparently interested in the plays being given in Kiev. At the time two of his one-acters were being staged.

[2] The character was to be in contrast to Ivanov, the whiner, in Chekhov's play.

[3] "Sometimes I become despondent," Aleksandr had written his brother, "and want to chuck the play, but after a while I come back to it."

and regards the future with hope, then here, too, your aim is clear. Many alterations must not discourage you, for the more mosaic-like the work, the better. Thereby the characters in a play only gain. Above all, beware of the personal element. The play will be worthless if all the characters resemble you. In this respect your piggy bank is hideous and only causes annoyance. Why Natasha, Kolya, Tosya? As though there were no life but yours?! And who is interested in knowing your and my life, your and my thoughts? Give people human beings, not yourself.

Beware of highflown language. Flunkeys must not use vulgar solecisms. Rednosed retired captains, drunken reporters, starving writers, consumptive working wives, honest, immaculate youths, high-minded virgins, good-natured nurses—all those have already been described and must be avoided like the pit. One more piece of advice: go to the theater, say, three times, look closely at the stage each time. Make comparisons, this is important. Act I must last as much as a whole hour, the others no more than thirty minutes. Act III eclipses everything, but not to the point of killing the last act. Finally, remember the censorship. It is severe and vigilant.

I should advise you to use a pseudonym for the plays. It's more convenient for you, and in the provinces you will not be mistaken for me, and besides, you will avoid being compared with me, which disgusts me no end. You are one thing, I another; but people pay no attention to that, they are impatient. If your play is good, I'll catch it; if poor, you'll catch it.

Don't be hasty in submitting it to the censorship committee or in having it staged. If you fail to have it staged in an imperial theater, we'll take it to Korsh's theater. It should not be staged before November.

If•I manage to compose something for the theater, it would be convenient: you could take my play to the committee together with yours. They know me there and they will act promptly. They usually keep my plays no longer than three to five days; casual plays get stuck there for months.

Heartfelt greetings to the "Captains Cook" [4] and to Natasha Aleksandrovna. I wish you bodily health and the salvation of your soul.

Your A. Chekhov

[4] A reference to the children.

TO A. N. PLESHCHEYEV

My compliments to you, dear Aleksey Nikolayevich!

* * * The money earned by *Ivanov* and my books [1] is almost gone. I cannot get along without an advance. I'll take advances from all my publishers, run through them and then, lifting my eyes to Heaven, I'll start calling for help: "God of Abraham, Isaac, and Jacob, who hath slain Goliath, fed five thousand with five barley loaves, let the earth yawn and swallow my creditors, for thine is the glory, the honor and worship, Father and Son and Holy Ghost, Amen."

It is boring without you, no one to talk to and no one to listen to. The young are inclined mostly to controversies and debates; but I am too lazy for conversational tournaments, peaceful talk is more after my heart. Speaking generally, it is dull to live in the country without the people to whom the heart is accustomed. If I married Sibiryakova,[2] I would buy a huge estate which I would put at the disposal of the ten people I love. But as I shall not marry Sibiryakova and shall never win two hundred thousand, I must reconcile myself to my fate and live on dreams. * * *

I feel sorry about Saltykov. His was a strong, tough head. The scoundrelly spirit that dwells in every petty Russian intellectual of the middling sort who has frittered his soul away in swindling has lost in him its most stubborn and troublesome foe. Every newspaperman knows how to muckrake, even Burenin knows how to deride, but it was only Saltykov who knew how to contemn openly. Two-thirds of his readers disliked him, but he was believed by all. Nobody doubted the sincerity of his contempt.

Write me a letter, my dear. I love your writing; when I see it, I grow cheerful. Besides, I shall not hide it from you, my correspondence with you flatters me. Your letters and Suvorin's I treasure and shall bequeathe to my grandchildren: let the sons of bitches read them and know what went on in times long past. * * *

Your A. Chekhov

---

[1] By this time Chekhov had published three books of stories.

[2] A millionaire's widow whom, according to groundless gossip, Chekhov was going to marry.

TO A. S. SUVORIN

I am answering your letter concerning Bourget [1] on the chance that you haven't yet left for abroad. I'll be brief. You write, among other things, "Let the science that deals with the physical world take its normal course, but at the same time let there also be left something that offers refuge from this exclusive concern with the physical world." The science dealing with the physical world takes its normal course, and those places where one may find refuge from exclusive concern with the physical world also exist, and by the look of things nobody is encroaching on them. And even if there is any assault and battery, it is directed only against the natural sciences and not against the sanctuaries that offer refuge from these sciences.

The question is put more correctly and less offensively in my letter than in yours, and I am closer to the "life of the spirit" than you. You speak of the right of these or those kinds of knowledge to exist, whereas I speak not of a right but of peace. I want people not to see war where there is none. The different kinds of knowledge have always abided in peace with one another. Anatomy and *belles lettres* have an equally illustrious origin, the very same goals, the very same enemy—the devil—and they have absolutely nothing to wage war about. There is no struggle for existence among them. If a man knows the theory of the circulation of the blood he is rich; if, over and beyond that, he masters the history of religion and the lyric "A wondrous moment I recall," [2] he becomes not poorer but richer, ergo, what we are dealing with is only pluses. That is why geniuses have never waged war, and why, in the case of Goethe, the naturalist managed to live serenely side by side with the poet.

For it is not the different kinds of knowledge that wage war—not poetry and anatomy—but delusions, i.e., people. When man does not understand, he senses a discord within himself; he seeks the reasons for this discord not in his own self, as he should, but outside himself, whence comes the war against what he does not understand. Throughout the Middle Ages alchemy gradually, in a natural, peaceful way, developed into chemistry, astrology into astronomy; the monks did not

[1] Paul Bourget (1852–1935), French novelist.
[2] By Pushkin.

understand, saw a war, and themselves engaged in fighting. Our own Pisarev [3] was, in the '60s, just such another militant Spanish monk. * * *

Your A. Chekhov

TO P. I. TCHAIKOVSKY

Moscow, October 12, 1889

Most esteemed Pyotr Ilyich!

I am preparing to go to press this month with a new book of my stories; these stories are as dreary and tedious as autumn, all uniformly monotonous, and their artistic elements form a thick mixture with the medical ones, but just the same all this does not deter me from venturing, in all diffidence, to address a request to you: grant me permission to dedicate this book to you. I wish very much to receive an affirmative answer from you, since this dedication would, first of all, afford me great pleasure and, secondly, it would gratify, even if only to a slight extent, that profound feeling of respect which compels me to think of you every day. The thought of dedicating the book to you settled firmly in my head the very day when, lunching with you at the home of Modest Ilyich,[1] I learned from you that you were a reader of my stories.

If together with your permission you would send me your photograph, it would be more than I deserve, and I would be content forever and ever. Forgive me for troubling you, and allow me to wish you all the best.

Wholly dedicated,
A. Chekhov

TO P. I. TCHAIKOVSKY

Moscow, October 14, 1889

I am very, very touched, dear Pyotr Ilyich, and thank you infinitely. I am sending you both photograph and book,[1] and would send you even the sun, if it belonged to me.

[3] On Pisarev, see below, p. 203.

[1] The composer's brother.

[1] Both photograph and book were inscribed. The inscription in the latter (*Stories, 1889*) was: "The future librettist, A. Chekhov." Both author and composer anticipated collaborating on an opera based on Lermontov's novel *A Hero of Our Time*.

You left your cigarette case at my place. I am sending it on to you. It is three cigarettes short: they were smoked by a violoncellist, a flautist, and a pedagogue.

Thank you once more and permit me to remain

Cordially and faithfully yours,
A. Chekhov

TO A. N. PLESHCHEYEV

Moscow, October 21, 1889

Greetings, dear Aleksey Nikolayevich!

Many thanks for your letter. As regards my health and mood, about which you inquire, it cannot be said that they are bad. I manage fairly well, now and then there are good minutes, and in general, in the language of the stock exchange, the mood is slack.

* * * Svobodin [1] is by no means at fault. If the play [2] is really poor, and if the authorities don't allow it, what is to be done? The only thing he is guilty of is extravagance: coming to see me cost him no less than 100 rubles.

Not a word about this play of mine. Whether it has been eaten up by mice, or whether the directors presented it to the Public Library, or whether it burned up with shame because of the lie perpetrated by Grigorovich,[3] who loves me like his own son—all these things could have happened, but I know *nothing*. I have received no notices or explanations from anyone, I know nothing, and I am making no inquiries for fear that my inquiry will be interpreted as a plea or as the

[1] Pavel Matveyevich Svobodin, an actor with the Aleksandrinsky Theater.

[2] *The Wood-Sprite*. A benefit was a performance, the receipts from which were given to an actor or actress as a supplement to his or her salary; the beneficiary chose the play. Pleshcheyev had written to Chekhov that as Svobodin had chosen *The Wood-Sprite* for his benefit, he should have protested more vigorously against its rejection by the official Commission in charge of the Imperial Theaters. A Commission member had urged Svobodin to give up the play for his benefit, arguing that the Grand Dukes would dislike it and so stop attending the Russian theater.

The Wood-Sprite, with a new fourth act, was staged later in 1889, and ten years later another version of it, under the title *Uncle Vanya*, was staged by the Moscow Art Theater.

[3] Pleshcheyev had written to Chekhov that "the double-faced" Grigorovich, who was a member of the unofficial Theatrical Committee, which was dissatisfied with the play, had nevertheless praised its second act to Suvorin.

[*121*]

irrepresible desire to be crowned by Aleksandrinsky laurels. I am as vain, you know, as a pig.

For the stubborn silence of Messrs. the members of the court-martial that tried my *Wood-Sprite*, I can only account by ardent sympathy with my talent or by the desires to prolong that paradisiacally sensuous delight with which my pleasant ignorance provides me. Who knows? Perhaps my play has been declared a work of genius. Is it not enchanting to guess?

The Petersburg Gazette announces that my play has been recognized by the Theatrical Committee as "a capital dramatized tale." Very nice. That means that I am either a poor playwright, with which I readily agree, or that all the gentlemen who love me as their own sons and entreat me for God's sake to be faithful to myself in my plays, to avoid clichés and offer complex ideas, all of them are hypocrites.

* * * I shall soon be issuing a new book.[4] I collect stories and I have ruined several days rewriting several things completely. * * *

Cordially yours,

A. Chekhov

TO A. S. SUVORIN

Moscow, October 28, 1889

* * * You write that it is impossible to think of anything more despicable than our liberal opposition. Well, what about those who are not part of this opposition? They are hardly any better. The mother of all Russian evils is gross ignorance, and that is inherent in all parties and trends to the same extent. And, because you praise German culture and emphasize universal literacy, you shall dwell in paradise, and I therefore respect you profoundly. * * *

Your A. Chekhov

---

[4] A collection of stories entitled *Gloomy People*. It included the story called "Volodya," a totally different version of "His First Love," originally published in 1887.

Moscow, December 3, 1889

Much esteemed Mariya Vladimirovna!

This morning a certain goose came to me from Prince Urusov [1] and asked me for a short story for *The Russian Huntsman,* which is edited by this Prince. Of course, I refused, as I refuse everyone who draws near my pedestal with entreaties. In Russia there are now two inaccessible heights: the top of Elborus and I.

Having received the refusal, the ambassador, greatly saddened, all but died of grief and at last proceeded to plead with me to recommend writers of stories familiar with the chase. I fell to thinking, and very opportunely recalled a lady writer who is dreaming of a monument and who for years has been ill with envy of my literary fame. In short, I gave him your address, and one of these days you will receive an invitation to deliver by January a huntsman's story, short, of course, full of poetry and all sorts of beauties. More than once you have observed the chase, with hounds, etc., and it will not be difficult for you to create something suitable. For instance, you could write a piece like "Ivan Gavrilov" or "A Wounded Elk." In the second story, if you have not forgotten, huntsmen wound an elk, she has the look of a human being, and no one has the heart to kill her. Not a bad subject, but dangerous in this respect, that it is hard to avoid sentimentality; the piece has to be written in the style of a police report, without words that arouse pity, and should begin like this: "On such and such a date huntsmen wounded a young elk in the Daraganov forest." But should you moisten the language with a tear, you will deprive the subject of its sternness and of everything deserving attention. . . .

I am teaching you how to write. You will say: What impertinence! Maybe so, but you cannot imagine how delightful it is to feel important and to gloat over the envious!

In case Prince Urusov sends you the invitation and you accept it, don't forget to add the following postscript: "As for my terms, I shall not make any exception for your journal and shall accept 80 to 100 rubles a sheet—the usual honorarium for a journal." * * *

Cordially,

your devoted A. Chekhov

[1] Aleksandr Ivanovich Urusov, publisher and editor of the illustrated weekly *The Russian Huntsman.*

TO A. S. SUVORIN

Moscow, December 18–23, 1889

[1] . . . Essays, *feuilletons*, foolish pieces, skits, dull stories, a great many mistakes and absurdities, tons of paper covered with writing, the Academy's prize, a life like Potemkin's, and, with all that, not a single line that in my view is of serious literary significance. There was a mass of work done under pressure, but not a minute of serious labor. When, the other day, I read Bezhetzky's "A Family Tragedy," this story moved me to pity for the author; it's a feeling that I experience when I see my own books. The element of truth in this feeling is the size of a fly. But my hypochondria and my envy of other people's work blow it up to the size of an elephant. I long, passionately, to hide away somewhere for five years or so and busy myself with painstaking, serious work. I must study, learn everything from the very beginning, for, as a man of letters, I am an all-around ignoramus; I must write conscientiously, with feeling, with sense—write not five sheets in one month but one sheet in five months. I must leave home, must start living on 700 to 900 rubles a year, and not three to four thousand as now, I must spit on much, but there is more Khokhol laziness than audacity in me. * * *

In January I'll be thirty. Vile. But I feel as if I were twenty-two.

Your A. Chekhov

---

[1] The beginning of this letter is lost.

[1890]

TO A. N. PLESHCHEYEV

Moscow, February 15, 1890

I am answering your letter, dear Aleksey Nikolayevich, by return mail. Did your name day come round? Yes, but I forgot it!! Forgive me, dear friend, and accept my belated felicitations.

Is it possible that *The Kreutzer Sonata* did not prove to your liking? I won't say that it is a work of genius, a work for all time—I am no judge on these points—but in my opinion, in the mass of that which is now being written among us and in Europe, it is hardly possible to find anything to equal the significance of its intent and the beauty of its execution. To say nothing of its artistic merits, which are in places astonishing, one feels grateful to the story if only for one thing: its extreme power to arouse thought. While reading it one can barely restrain oneself from crying out, "This is true!" or "This is preposterous!" Certainly, the story has very vexing shortcomings. Aside from all the things you have enumerated, there is still another, which one doesn't feel like forgiving the author—to be precise, the audacity with which Tolstoy discourses on what he knows nothing about and what, out of stubbornness, he does not want to understand. Thus, his judgments on syphilis, on foundling asylums, on women's abhorrence of copulation, etc., not only can be controverted but also are a direct exposure of a man who is ignorant, who throughout the course of his long life had never gone to the trouble of reading two or three books written by specialists. Yet, just the same, these shortcomings scatter like feathers in the wind; in view of the merits of the tale, one simply does not notice them, but if one should, one would merely feel vexed because this tale has not escaped the lot of all the works of man, all of which are imperfect and none of which is immaculate.

So my friends and acquaintances in Petersburg are angry at me? What for? For my having bored them insufficiently by my presence, which I myself became bored with ever so long ago! Set their minds at rest, tell them that I ate many dinners, many suppers while in Petersburg, but *have not captivated* a single lady, tell them I felt certain each day that I would leave in the evening on an express train; tell them I was kept back by my friends and the *Maritime Journal*, which I had to go through, page by page, all the way back to 1852.[1] While living in Petersburg I accomplished in one month as much as my young friends could not have accomplished in a whole year. However, let them keep on being angry!

All day long I sit, read, and take notes. In the head and on paper nothing but Sakhalin. Mania. *Mania Sakhalinosa.*

Your A. Chekhov

TO A. S. SUVORIN

Moscow, between February 19 and 21, 1890

* * * All day long I read and write, read and write. . . . The more I read, the stronger my conviction that two months will not be enough to do one-fourth of what I planned, but I cannot stay in Sakhalin more than two months: the rascally steamers don't wait! The work is diversified, but tedious. One has to be a geologist, a meteorologist, an ethnographer, but I am not used to this, and I am bored. I shall be reading about Sakhalin until March, while the money lasts, and then I'll return to stories. * * *

In my Sakhalin work I shall look like so learned a son of a bitch that you will only throw up your hands. I have already stolen a great deal from other people's thoughts and knowledge, which I shall pass on as my own. In our practical age you cannot do otherwise. * * *

I have read that the Queen of Rumania has written a play about the life of the common people (?) and that it will be staged in a Bucharest theater. An author who may not be hissed. Me, I would be delighted to hiss. * * *

Respectfully,

Heinrich Block and Co.[1]

P.S. How are your much esteemed horses? Would be good to have a ride somewhere.

[1] This reading was in preparation for Chekhov's trip to Sakhalin.
[1] A Moscow bank.

TO A. P. CHEKHOV

You infusorium!

I must become acquainted with newspaper material on Sakhalin—in the greatest detail, if possible, since I am not interested solely and one-sidedly in the data which that material can furnish. Data are, of course, in a class by themselves but, Gusev, one also needs historical illumination of the facts that constitute the gist of these data. The articles were written either by people who had never been in Sakhalin and hadn't the least notion of what the whole business is about, or by people who have a pecuniary interest in Sakhalin and have managed to make a pile, while appearing innocent. The audacity of the first group and the dodges of the second are factors of obfuscation and putting the brakes on progress which are bound to be of greater value to the investigator than disinterested information, which for the most part is casual and false; these factors excellently characterize our society's attitude toward this business in general, and the prison business in particular. As for an author and his motivation, you will understand only after you will have read his article in its entirety.

At any rate, spare the Public Library your visits. What you have already done will suffice. The rest will be transcribed by Sister, whom I have hired and who will start her pilgrimages to the Rumyantzev Library the third week in Lent. And for you, ninny, I'll find other work. Bow down at my feet and ask my forgiveness. Everything you will have to do you will find listed in a letter that you will receive during the fourth or fifth week in Lent. —Now, about lice I can tell you only one thing: dirt is the death of me! Oblomov's man Zachar and Aleksandr Chekhov say that there's no getting rid of lice and bed-bugs—this is very scientific; yet I, just imagine, have repeatedly seen families which had no conception of these creatures. There are very many things that are effective against lice. Ask at a druggist's about a decoction of sibanilla.

All of us are in good health. Greetings to Natalya Aleksandrovna, Kuka,[1] and my godson.

Your benefactor,

A. Chekhov

---

[1] The nickname of the elder child.

TO A. S. SUVORIN

Moscow, March 9, 1890
(The Feast of Forty Martyrs and of
Ten Thousand Larks)

Both of us are mistaken about Sakhalin, but you probably more than I. I am going there fully convinced that my trip will not result in any valuable contribution to either literature or science: I lack the knowledge, the time, and the pretensions for that. My plans are not those of a Humboldt or a Kennan,[1] I want to write one hundred to two hundred pages and thereby pay off some of my debt to medicine, toward which, as you know, I have behaved like a pig. Perhaps I shall not be able to write anything; nevertheless the journey does not lose its attraction for me: by reading, looking around and listening, I shall get to know and to learn a great deal. I haven't left yet, but thanks to the books that I have been obliged to read, I have learned much of what everyone should know under penalty of forty lashes, and of which I was formerly ignorant. Besides, I believe that the trip will mean six months of incessant work, physical and mental, and this I need, for I am a Khokhol[2] and have already begun to be lazy. One must keep in training. My trip may be a trifle, the result of obstinacy, a whim, but consider and tell me what I lose by going. Time? Money? Shall I be undergoing privations? My time is worth nothing, money I never have anyway, as for privations, I shall travel by carriage not more than twenty-five to thirty days—and all the rest of the time I shall be sitting on the deck of a steamer or in a room and constantly bombarding you with letters.

Suppose the trip gives me absolutely nothing, still, won't the whole journey yield at least two or three days that I shall remember all my life, with rapture or with bitterness? And so on, and so on. That's how it is, sir. All this is unconvincing, but neither do your arguments convince me. You say, for instance, that Sakhalin is of no use and no interest to anybody. But is that so? Sakhalin can be of no use or interest only to a country that does not exile thousands of people there and

---

[1] At the invitation of the Czar, Alexander von Humboldt explored Siberia in 1829; in the 1880s George E. Kennan made a thorough study of the Siberian penal system for *Century* magazine.

[2] Having been born in Taganrog, which lies on the border of Ukrainian territory, Chekhov sometimes called himself a Khokhol to account for his laziness, allegedly a southern characteristic. As a matter of fact, both his parents were of Great Russian stock.

does not spend millions on it. After Australia in the past and Cayenne,[3] Sakhalin is the only place where you can study colonization by criminals. All Europe is interested in it, and it is of no use to us? No longer ago than twenty-five or thirty years, our own compatriots in exploring Sakhalin performed amazing feats that make man worthy of deification, and yet that's of no use to us, we know nothing about those men, we sit within four walls and complain that God made a botch of man. Sakhalin is a place of unbearable sufferings, such as only human beings, free or bond, can endure. The men directly or indirectly connected with it solved terrible, grave problems and are still solving them. If I were sentimental—I am sorry I am not—I would say that to places like Sakhalin we should make pilgrimages, like the Turks who travel to Mecca, and navy men and criminologists in particular should regard Sakhalin as military men do Sevastopol. From the books I have been reading it is clear that we have let *millions* of people rot in prison, destroying them carelessly, thoughtlessly, barbarously; we drove people in chains through the cold across thousands of miles, infected them with syphilis, depraved them, multiplied criminals, and placed the blame for all this on red-nosed prison wardens. All civilized Europe knows now that it is not the wardens who are to blame, but all of us, yet this is no concern of ours, we are not interested. The vaunted '6os did *nothing* for the sick and the prisoners, thus violating the basic commandment of Christian civilization. In our time something is being done for the sick, but for prisoners nothing; prison problems don't interest our jurists at all. No, I assure you, we need Sakhalin, and it is important to us, and the only thing to be regretted is that I am the one to go there and not someone else who is better equipped for the task and is more capable of arousing public interest. As for me, I go after trifles. * * *

We have been having student riots on a large scale. They began at the Petrovsky Academy, where the authorities forbade the students to bring young women into their rooms, suspecting not only prostitution but also the political corruption of the girls. From the Academy the trouble spread to the university, where, now surrounded by heavily armed Hectors and Achilleses on horseback and with lances, the students make the following demands:

1. Complete autonomy of the universities.

[3] The French deported convicts to Cayenne, and because of the high mortality, the place became known as "the dry guillotine."

2. Complete freedom of instruction.

3. Free admission to the universities without distinction of creed, nationality, sex, or social status.

4. Admission of Jews to the universities without any restrictions and granting them the same rights as other students.

5. Freedom of assemblage and recognition of student organizations.

6. Establishment of university and student tribunals.

7. Abolition of the police function of inspection.

8. Reduction of tuition.

I have copied this with some abbreviations from a proclamation. I think the fire is blazing strongest in a crowd of [...] of the sex which is eager to get admission to the University, while its preparation for this is five times as bad as that of the male, whose preparation is wretched and who, with rare exceptions, does miserably at the university.

* * * And now permit me out of respect for you to throw myself into an abyss and smash my head.

Your A. Chekhov

TO M. I. TCHAIKOVSKY

Moscow, March 16, 1890

Dear Modest Ilyich,

* * * I sit at home without venturing out and read about how much Sakhalin coal cost per ton in 1863 and the cost per ton of coal in Shanghai; I read about amplitudes and NE, NW, SE, and other winds which will be buffeting me as I observe my own seasickness near the shores of Sakhalin. I read about soil and subsoil, about sandy clay and clayey sand. However, I haven't gone out of my mind yet, and yesterday I actually sent off a story to *New Times;* will send *The Wood-Sprite* to *The Northern Herald* shortly—will do so most unwillingly, since I don't like to see my plays in print.

In one and a half or two weeks my book [1]—the one I have dedicated to Pyotr Ilyich—will be coming out. I am ready to stand day and night as guard of honor near the entrance to the house where Pyotr Ilyich lives

[1] *Gloomy People.*

—such is the extent of the respect I feel for him. If we were to talk of ranks, he now holds a place in Russian art second only to Lev Tolstoy, who has long occupied the first place. (The third I present to Repin,[2] while for myself I take the ninety-eighth.) I have long cherished in secret the insolent dream of dedicating something to him. This dedication, I thought, would be a partial, minimal expression of that enormous estimate that I, as a writing fellow, had formed concerning his magnificent talent and which, because of my lack of musical gifts, I am unable to commit to paper. Regrettably, I had to turn my dream into reality by means of a book which I do not consider a superior one. It is made up of gloomy, psychopathological sketches and bears a gloomy title, so that my dedication may prove far from suiting the taste of the admirers of Pyotr Ilyich—and the taste of Pyotr Ilyich himself.

Are you a Chekhovist? I thank you sincerely. No, you are not a Chekhovist, but simply a tolerant person. Stay well. Wishing you all the best,

Your A. Chekhov

TO I. L. LEONTYEV-SHCHEGLOV

Moscow, March 22, 1890

* * * You write that you want to start a knock-down-drag-out scrap with me, "particularly on matters of morality and artistry," you speak vaguely of some transgressions of mine, deserving of friendly reproof, and even threaten me with "influential newspaper criticism." If one crosses out the word "artistry" the whole quoted phrase gains clarity, but it takes on a significance which, to tell the truth, troubles me not a little. What is it, Jean? How am I to understand this? Is it possible that when it comes to concepts of morality I part company with such people as yourself, and even to such an extent that I deserve reproof, as well as the special attention of influential critics? I cannot accept the notion that you have in mind some sort of cunningly contrived higher morality, since there are no lower, or higher, or middling moralities, but there is only one—to be precise, that morality which gave us in times of yore Jesus Christ, and which now hinders me, you, and Barantzevich

---

[2] Ilya Yefimovich Repin (1844–1930), a celebrated Russian painter.

from stealing, offering insults, lying, and so forth. As for me, if I am to credit the tranquillity of my conscience, I have never in my life, either in word or deed or intent, or in my stories or skits, coveted my neighbor's wife, or his manservant, or his ox, or any cattle of his; I haven't stolen, haven't played the hypocrite, haven't flattered those in power or sought anything from them, haven't blackmailed anybody, and haven't been a fancy man. True, all the days of my life were spent in idleness; I have laughed for no reason, have been a glutton, a drunkard, a lecher, but then, all this is a private matter, and all this does not deprive me of the right to think that when it comes to morality I do not stand out from the general run on either the plus or the minus side. No high deeds, no vile misdeeds—I am just like the majority; of sins there are plenty, but with morality we are quits, since I am paying for the said sins at usurious rates with those difficulties that sins bring in their wake. But if you want to start a knock-down-drag-out scrap with me because I am no hero, why, chuck your ferociousness out of the window, and replace your invective with your endearing tragic laughter—that will be better.

As for that word "artistry," I dread it more than merchants' wives dread brimstone. When people tell me about things artistic and inartistic, about what is scenic or not scenic, about tendentiousness, realism, etc., I lose my head, turn into a hesitating yes-man, and respond with banal half-truths which aren't worth a penny. I divide all creative works into two sorts: those that are to my liking and those that are not. I have no other criterion, and, should you ask me why Shakespeare is to my liking and Zlatovratsky [1] is not, why, I wouldn't be able to answer you. Perhaps in time, when I'm smarter, I shall acquire a criterion, but for the present all discussions concerning "artistry" merely make me tired and strike me as a continuation of all those scholastic dialogues wherewith people used to tire themselves out during the Middle Ages.

If criticism, the authority of which you cite, knows what you and I don't, why has it kept mum until now? Why doesn't it disclose to us the truth and immutable laws? If it had known, believe me, it would long ago have shown us the way and we would know what to do. * * * But criticism keeps pompously quiet or gets off cheap with idle, worthless chatter. If it presents itself to you as influential, it is only because it is

[1] Nikolay Nikolayevich Zlatovratsky (1845–1911) was a novelist with a marked populist bias.

immodest, insolent, and loud, because it is an empty barrel that one involuntarily hears.

Let's spit on all this, however, and sing an aria from another opera. Please, don't pin any literary hopes on my Sakhalin trip. I am not going there for the sake of observations and impressions, but simply to be able to live for half a year as I have not lived until now. Don't expect anything from me, Uncle. If I have the time and the ability to do something worth while, thank God, if not, don't carp. I'll be leaving after Easter week.

Dear little staff captain with mustaches, be well and happy.

Your A. Chekhov

TO A. S. SUVORIN

Moscow, April 1, 1890

* * * You upbraid me about objectivity, styling it indifference to good and evil, absence of ideals and ideas, etc. You would have me say, in depicting horse thieves, that stealing horses is an evil. But then, that has been known a long while, even without me. Let jurors judge them, for my business is only to show them as they are. I write: You are dealing with horse thieves—know, then, that these are no beggars but men with full bellies, that these men belong to a cult, and that stealing horses is not simply stealing but a passion. Of course, it would be gratifying to couple art with sermonizing, but, personally, I find this exceedingly difficult and, because of conditions imposed by technique, all but impossible. Why, in order to depict horse thieves in seven hundred lines I must constantly speak and think as they do and feel in keeping with their spirit; otherwise, if I add a pinch of subjectivity, the images will become diffused and the story will not be as compact as it behooves all short short stories to be. When I write, I rely fully on the reader, on the assumption that he himself will add the subjective elements that are lacking in the story. Be of good cheer.

A. Chekhov

TO V. M. LAVROV[1]

Moscow, April 10, 1890

Vukol Mikhailovich!

The following is the sort of phrase I happened to read in the March issue of *Russian Thought*, on page 147, in the bibliographical section: "Only yesterday, even the high priests of unprincipled writing, such as Messrs. Yasinsky[2] and Chekhov, whose names—" and so on. Usually one does not respond to criticism, but in the present instance what we are dealing with may not be criticism but simply calumny. I might well not have responded even to calumny except that within a few days I am leaving Russia for a long period, perhaps never to return, and I find it beyond my strength to refrain from a response.

An unprincipled writer—or, what is the selfsame thing, a blackguard—I have never been.

True enough, all my literary activity has consisted of an unbroken run of blunders, occasionally coarse, but an explanation for that can be found in the dimensions of the gift bestowed upon me, but not at all in whether I am a good or a bad fellow. I have not gone in for blackmailing, I have neither written libels nor played the informer, I have not flattered, have not lied, have not insulted others; in short, I have many stories and leading articles that I would willingly discard because of their worthlessness, but there is not a single line of the sort for which I would have to feel ashamed now. If we admit the proposition that in speaking of lack of principles you are referring to the melancholy circumstances that I, an educated man who frequently appears in print, have done nothing for those I love, that my activity has not left a trace —activity on behalf of the zemstvo, of the new court system, of freedom of the press, of freedom in general, and so on—well, in that respect *Russian Thought* should in all fairness consider me its comrade, rather than accuse me, since *Russian Thought* itself has not, up to the present, accomplished any more than I in the direction indicated—and it is not you and I who are to blame for this.

Even if I am to be judged superficially as a writer, I hardly deserve to be accused publicly of a lack of principles. Up to now I have been

---

[1] V. M. Lavrov (1852–1912), publisher and editor of *Russian Thought*. According to Chekhov, it was the monthly which "expressed the best strivings of the Russian intelligentsia." The quarrel with Lavrov was patched up in 1892.

[2] Yeronim Yeronimovich Yasinsky (1850–1931) used the pen name of Maxim Belinsky; a journalist and a novelist, he wrote in the French naturalist tradition.

leading a cloistered life, living within four walls; you and I meet once in two years; Machtet,[3] for instance, I haven't seen even once in my life; you can judge from that how often I leave the house; I have always emphatically declined to participate in literary evenings, in soirees, in sessions, and the like; I have not showed up in a single editorial office without an invitation, have always tried to have my acquaintances see the physician in me rather than the author; in short, I have been a discreet writer, and this letter of mine is the first indiscretion during the entire decade of my activity. My relations with my fellow writers are excellent: never have I taken upon myself the role of being their judge or the judge of those journals and newspapers for which they work, considering myself incompetent and finding that in the present subordinate position of the press every word against a journal or a writer is manifestly not only merciless and tactless but also downright criminal. Up to now I ventured to turn down only those journals and newspapers the poor quality of which was evident and proven, but whenever I had to choose among periodicals I gave preference to those which, because of material circumstances, or for other reasons, were in greater need of my services, and that is why I worked not for you and for *The Herald of Europe* but *The Northern Herald,* and also why I received only half of what I would have received if I had a different view of my obligations.

Your accusation is calumny. I cannot ask you to retract it, since it has already done its worst and could not be hewed out with an ax; neither can I explain it away by carelessness, lightmindedness, or something of that sort since, as I know, your editorial office is staffed with incontrovertibly decent and educated persons who, I hope, write and read articles not thoughtlessly but with an awareness of responsibility for every word of theirs. All that is left me is to point out your error to you, and to ask you to believe in the sincerity of the painful feeling that caused me to write you this letter. That after your accusation any contacts between us—not only of a business nature but even on the basis of an ordinary hat-tipping acquaintanceship—are impossible goes without saying.

A. Chekhov

[3] Grigory Aleksandrovich Machtet came to New York in 1872, together with several other radical young compatriots. Lured by rumors of freedom in the United States, "a rosy Arcady," they made a vain attempt to organize a Russian settlement which would become a school for communists. Returning home the following year,

TO M. P. CHEKHOVA

Volga, Steamer Aleksandr Nevsky

early morning, April 23, 1890

My Tungus ¹ *friends!*

Did it rain in your area when Ivan returned from the monastery? In Yaroslavl the rain beat down so hard that I had to put on my leather coat. My first impression of the Volga was spoiled by rain, the tear-stained windows of the railway compartment, and the wet nose of Gurlyand,² who came to meet me at the station. In the rain Yaroslavl seemed to look like Zvenigorod, but its churches remind me of the Perervinsky Monastery. There are many signs grossly misspelled, it is dirty, jackdaws with huge heads stalk along the pavement.

My first duty on board the steamer was to give free rein to my talent, i.e., I went to sleep. On awakening, I saw the sun. The Volga is not bad: water meadows, sun-drenched monasteries, white churches, an amazing expanse; wherever you look, it's cozy, inviting you to sit down and cast a line. Lady monitors roam the bank and nibble the tufts of green grass; now and then a shepherd's horn is heard.³ White seagulls hover over the Volga looking like the younger Drishka.⁴

The steamer is none too good. Its best feature is the water closet. It is elevated, having four steps beneath it, so that an inexperienced person like Ivanenko might easily mistake it for a royal throne. The worst on the steamer is the dinner. I give you the menu complete with the original spelling: sorrl soup, sawsajes with cabaj, sterjen frittrs, baked cat pudding; "cat" turned out to be "kashka." ⁵ Since I earned my money in the sweat of my face, I should have preferred the reverse, i.e., that the dinner were better than the water closet; particularly since after the spree at Korneyev's,⁶ my innards have been completely clogged, and I can manage without a water closet until we get to Tomsk.

---

he was later deported to Siberia as a political prisoner. By then he had broken into print, but remained a minor literary figure.

¹ The Tunguses (now called Evenks) are a nationality in eastern Siberia. The reference may have been a family joke.

² A law student in Yaroslavl.

³ This jocular reference to cows may have been suggested by the fact that the school in which Chekhov's sister taught was headed by someone whose relatives ran a dairy farm.

⁴ Reference to an acquaintance of the Chekhovs'.

⁵ Confusion of *koshka* (cat) and *kashka*, a diminutive of *kasha* (porridge).

⁶ Owner of a Moscow house in which the Chekhovs lived.

Kundasova [7] is on board. I haven't any idea where she is going, or why. When I start questioning her about this, she launches into some extremely foggy conjectures about someone who arranged to meet her in a gulley near Kineshma; then she bursts into fits of uncontrollable laughter and begins to stamp her feet or jab her elbow into anything at hand without sparing [. . .] your tendons. We have passed Kineshma and the gulleys, yet she remains on board, which of course makes me very happy. By the way, yesterday, for the first time in my life, I saw her eat. She eats no less than others, but mechanically, as though she were munching oats.

Kostroma is a fine town. I saw Ples, where the languid Levitan lived; saw Kineshma, where I strolled along the boulevard and observed the local swains; stopped at a druggist's there to buy some potassium chlorate for my tongue, which had turned into Moroccan leather from the spree. When the druggist caught sight of Olga Petrovna, he was delighted and disconcerted, and so was she; apparently they have known each other for some time and, judging by their conversation, have strolled through the gulleys near Kineshma many times. So that's where the swains are! The druggist's last name is Kopfer.

It's chilly and rather tiresome but on the whole amusing.

The steamer whistles incessantly, its whistle a sound between a donkey's bray and an aeolian harp. In five or six hours I'll be in Nizhny. The sun is rising. I slept artistically during the night. My money is intact—because I'm always clutching at my belly.

The tugboats are very charming, each of them pulling four or five barges along; it is like an elegant, young intellectual who is trying to flee while his fat tub of a wife, his mother-in-law, sister-in-law, and wife's grandmother are holding him by the coattails.

I greet Mamasha and Papasha with a bow to the ground, all the others with a bow from the waist. I trust that Semashko,[8] Lidiya Stakhiyevna,[9] and Ivanenko are behaving themselves. It would be interesting to know who is carousing with Lidiya now until 5 A.M. Ah, how glad I am that Ivanenko has no money! * * *

Your A. Chekhov

[7] Olga Petrovna Kundasova, a flighty young woman who was an acquaintance of the Chekhovs.

[8] Marian Romualdovich Semashko, an acquaintance of the Chekhovs who was a cellist.

[9] L. S. Mizinova. See below, p. 187.

TO M. P. CHEKHOVA

The Steamer Perm *on the Kama River*
April 24, 1890

My Tungus friends!

I am sailing along the Kama but cannot determine where we are—somewhere near Chistopol, I think. Nor can I wax rhapsodic about the beauty of the shores, since it is fiendishly cold; the birch is not yet in leaf, there are strips of snow here and there, small ice floes are drifting—in short, all aesthetics have gone to the devil. I'm sitting in the deckhouse, where people of every social rank are seated at table, and, listening to their conversations, I ask myself, "Isn't it time you people had tea?" If I had my way I'd do nothing but eat from morning till night; since I haven't the money to eat all day, I sleep and then sleep some more. I don't go up on deck—it is cold. At night it rains, and during the day there is a nasty wind blowing.

Ah, caviar! I eat, eat, and simply cannot get done with it. In this respect it is like a ball of cheese. Luckily it is not salty.

It's a pity I didn't think of sewing myself a little sack for tea and sugar. I have to order these with each glass, which is tiresome and expensive. I wanted to buy some tea and sugar in Kazan this morning but overslept.

Rejoice, O Mother! It seems I'll be spending twenty-four hours in Yekaterinburg and shall see our relatives. Perhaps their hearts will soften and they'll give me three rubles and an eighth of a pound of tea.

From the conversations now under way, I gather that a circuit court is traveling with me. Not gifted people, but the merchants who occasionally put in a word or two seem intelligent. You come across awfully rich people.

Sturgeon is cheaper than mushrooms, but you soon get tired of it. What else is there to write about? Nothing . . . Oh, but we do have a general and a skinny, fair-haired fellow on the ship. The former dashes back and forth from his cabin to the deck and is forever sending his photograph off somewhere; the latter is made up to look like Nadson [1] and tries to create the impression that he is a writer; today at dinner he lied to some woman, telling her that Suvorin had published a book of his; naturally, my face registered the appropriate degree of awe.

---

[1] Semyon Yakovlevich Nadson (1862–87), a popular poet.

Except for what I've spent on food, all my money is intact. The scoundrels don't want to feed me gratis!

I'm neither cheerful nor bored but my soul seems as insipid as gelatine. I'm glad to sit motionless and silent. Today, for instance, I hardly said five words. But then I'm lying: I talked to a priest on deck.

People of non-Russian stock have begun to turn up. There are a great many Tartars—honorable and modest folk.

One great convenience: you lock your cabin when you leave and again when you go to bed, so that I'll get to Perm [2] without having any thing stolen. * * *

Your A. Chekhov

Forgive me for writing only of eating. Were it not for eating, I'd have to write about the cold—I lack subjects.

The court has decreed that tea be served. Invitations have been extended to two candidates for judicial positions, who are traveling as office staff. One looks like the sartorial poet Belousov,[3] the other like Yezhov.[4] Both listen respectfully to Messrs. the chiefs, don't dare to have an opinion of their own, and pretend they are acquiring wisdom by listening to clever talk. I love exemplary young people.

TO M. P. CHEKHOVA

Yekaterinburg,[1] April 29, 1890

My Tungus friends!

The Kama is a most tedious river. To appreciate its beauties one must be a Pecheneg,[2] sit motionless on a barge near a barrel of petroleum or a sack of dried Caspian roach, continually swilling rotgut. The banks are bare, the trees are bare, the ground is brown, with strips of snow, and the devil himself couldn't raise a sharper and more disgusting

[2] Now Molotov.
[3] Ivan Alekseyevich Belousov was a tailor in his youth, later wrote and translated verse, and published his reminiscences. He was prized by Chekhov.
[4] N. M. Yezhov, a contributor to *New Times,* who wrote fiction.
[1] Now Sverdlovsk.
[2] The Pechenegs were nomads who, in the Middle Ages, roamed the steppes be tween the lower reaches of the Volga and the Urals. Chekhov used the name as a synonym for a benighted savage.

wind. When a cold wind blows and ruffles the water, which now after the floods is the color of coffee slops, one is chilled and bored and wretched. The strains of accordions coming from the banks sound dismal, and the figures in ragged sheepskin coats standing stock-still on the barges that we pass seem petrified by some endless sorrow. The towns on the Kama are gray; the only occupation of their inhabitants, it seems, is the manufacture of clouds, boredom, wet fences, and mud in the streets. The wharves are crowded with the intelligentsia, for whom the arrival of a steamer is an event. Everything about these gentry suggests "the second fiddle"; apparently not one of them earns more than 35 rubles and they are probably all dosing themselves for some ailment or other.

I have already written that my fellow travelers include a circuit court: the presiding judge, his associate, and the prosecutor. The president: a sturdy, elderly German in good health, a convert to Orthodoxy, pious, a homeopath, and obviously a gay dog; the associate, an old man like the ones our poor Nikolay used to draw, is stooped, coughs, and likes off-color stories; the prosecutor, aged forty-three, dissatisfied with life, a liberal, a skeptic, and very kindly. During the entire trip the trio was busy eating, settling important matters, eating, reading, and eating. There was a library on board and I saw the prosecutor reading my *In the Twilight*. The talk was about me. Hereabouts the favorite is Mamin-Sibiryak,[3] who describes the Urals. They talk more about him than about Tolstoy.

I was two and a half years sailing to Perm—or so it seemed to me. We landed there at 2 A.M. The train was scheduled to leave at 6 P.M. It was raining. Rain, cold, mud—brrr! * * *

Waking up yesterday morning on board a train and looking out of the window, I felt disgusted with nature: the ground was white, the trees were covered with hoarfrost and a regular blizzard was chasing the train. Now isn't that revolting? Aren't they sons of bitches? . . . I have no rubbers, I pulled on my big boots and walking to the buffet for coffee I perfumed the whole Ural province with their tarry smell. When we got to Yekaterinburg, there was rain, sleet, snow. * * *

In Russia all the towns are alike. Yekaterinburg is exactly like Perm or Tula, or like Sumy and Gadyach. The ringing of the bells is magnificent, velvety. I stopped at the American Hotel (not bad at all) and

[3] Dmitry Markisovich Mamin-Sibiryak (1852–1912). His novels dealt realistically with the life of the Ural miners.

immediately wrote to A. M. Simonov [4] to say that I meant to stay in my hotel room two days and take Hunyadi, which, let me say not without pride, I drink with signal success.

The people here inspire the new arrival with a feeling akin to horror. They have prominent cheekbones, big brows, broad shoulders, tiny eyes, and huge fists. They are born in the local cast-iron foundries and are brought into the world not by a midwife, but by a machinist. A fellow like that comes into your room with a samovar or a decanter and you expect him to murder you. I move aside. This morning just such an individual came in—high-cheekboned, big-browed, sullen, towering to the ceiling, several feet across the shoulders, and wearing a fur coat besides.

Well, I thought, this one is sure to murder me. It turned out that it was Simonov. We talked. He is a member of the zemstvo board; manages his cousin's mill, where they have electric light; edits *The Yekaterinburg Week*, which is censored by the Chief of Police, Baron Taube; is married, has two children, is growing rich, gaining weight, getting old, and lives "substantially." He says he has no time to be bored. Advised me to visit the museum, the plants, the mines; I thanked him for the advice. He invited me to tea, I invited him to have dinner with me. He did not invite me to dinner, and generally did not insist on my coming to see him. From this Mamasha may conclude that the relatives' heart has not softened, and that Simonov and I are not essential to one another. * * * Relatives are a tribe to which I am as indifferent as I am to Frosya Artemenko.[5]

> *Your Homo Sachaliensis,*
>
> *A. Chekhov*

P.S. Ask Lika not to leave *wide margins* in her letters.

TO M. P. CHEKHOVA

Krasnyi Yar—Tomsk, May 14–17, 1890 [1]

My magnificent Mamasha, excellent Masha, sweet Misha, and all my intimates!

[4] A relative.
[5] A casual acquaintance of the Chekhovs.
[1] This letter chronicles Chekhov's Siberian trip from May 4 to May 16.

In Yekaterinburg I received a telegram from Tyumen: "The first steamer from Tomsk leaves May 18." That meant that willy-nilly I had to race along in a carriage. I did so. I left Tyumen on May 3, having spent two or three days in Yekaterinburg, using them to repair my coughing and hemorrhoiding person.

Both post and private coachmen are available for travel in Siberia. I hired the latter: it was all the same to me. Your humble servant was placed in a wicker basket drawn by a pair of horses. You sit in this vehicle, look on God's world like a little siskin, without a thought in your head. The Siberian plain commences at Yekaterinburg and ends the devil knows where. I would say that it looks very much like our southern steppe, were it not for the small birch groves here and there and the cold wind pricking your cheeks. Spring hasn't arrived here as yet. There is no trace of greenery, the forests are bare, only some of the snow has melted, the lakes are under lackluster ice. On May 9, St. Nicholas' Day, there was a frost, and today, the 14th, there was a snowfall of over three inches. Only the ducks speak of spring. Oh, how many ducks! Never before in my life have I seen such a multitude of ducks. They fly over your head, flutter by the side of the carriage, swim in the ice holes of the lake and in puddles. In short, I could have shot a thousand of them in one day with a poor fowling-piece. Wild geese are heard honking, they too are numerous here. Files of cranes and swans often catch the eye. In the birch groves heathcocks and hazel-hens are seen flying. Hares, which are not shot and eaten here, stand up nonchalantly on their hind legs, with their ears pricked up, their eyes inquisitively following all comers. They run across the road so often that this is not considered a bad omen.

Traveling is a cold business. I have my sheepskin on. My body is comfortable, but my feet and legs are freezing. I wrap them in my leather overcoat, but it doesn't help. I am wearing two pairs of trousers. Well, you ride and ride. Mileposts flash by, puddles, birch groves. We pass tramping settlers, a file of convicts under guard. We have met vagabonds with pots on their backs; these gents roam the Siberian highway freely. On occasion they will do in an old woman in order to use her skirt for puttees, or they'll remove from a milepost a metal sign with a number on it, just on the chance that it may come in handy. Again, they will bash in the head of a beggar they meet or gouge out the eyes of their fellow deportee, but they won't touch a traveler. As far as robbery is concerned, travel hereabouts is entirely safe. From Tyumen to Tomsk neither the coachmen on the post vehicles nor the self-employed drivers can recall that anything has been stolen from a traveler. When you enter a station you leave your things in the courtyard; when you ask if they won't be stolen, the reply is a smile. It is even bad form to mention burglaries and murders on the highway. It seems to me that were I to lose my money at a station or in a vehicle, if the coachman found it, he would return it to me without fail, and wouldn't brag about the matter.

Generally speaking, people here are good, kindly, and with pleasing folkways. The rooms are tidy and the furniture simple, with some pretensions to luxury; the sleeping accommodations are soft, with featherbeds and big pillows; the floors are painted or covered with home-made linen rugs. All this is due to the general prosperity, to the fact that a family has an allowance of 43 acres of excellent black earth which produces rich crops of wheat (30 copecks is the price of 36 pounds of wheat flour). However, not everything is explained by material welfare, the people's way of life must not be overlooked. On entering a Siberian bedroom at night you are not assailed by the peculiar Russian stench. True, handing me a teaspoon, an old woman wiped it on her behind, but then they will not serve you tea without a tablecloth, people don't belch in your presence, don't search for insects in their hair; when they hand you water or milk, they don't put their fingers in the glass; the plates and dishes are clean, kvas is as transparent as beer. In sum, such cleanliness as there is here can be only dreamed of by the Khokhols, who are cleaner than Katzaps.[2] The bread they bake here is delicious; the first days I could not get my fill of it. Equally tasty are the pies, tarts, and turnovers; family bread resembles Ukrainian spongy rolls. Pancakes are thin. The rest of Siberian cookery is not for the European stomach. * * *

By evening the puddles and roads begin freezing and at night there is a full-fledged frost, calling for a fur coat. Brrr!

The mud having become hillocks, the carriage jolts, turning your innards inside out. By daybreak you are worn out by the cold, the bouncing, the jingling of the bells on the harness; you yearn for warmth and bed. While the horses are being changed, you curl up in a corner and fall asleep immediately, but a minute later your coachman tugs at your sleeve and says, "Get up, friend, it's time!" On the second

[2] The familiar, somewhat derogatory name of the Great Russians.

night I developed a sharp toothache in my heels. It was intolerable. I asked myself: aren't they frostbitten?

I can't go on writing. The district police officer has arrived. We get acquainted, start talking. Until tomorrow.

It was my jack boots that caused the pain in the heels. The backs are too narrow. * * * In Ishim I had to buy felt boots and traveled in them until they fell apart from dampness and mud.

Tea in the peasant hut in the small hours. On the road tea is a true blessing. Now I know its value and I drink it frantically. It warms you up, banishes sleep, you eat a lot of bread with it. You sip it, and you talk with the peasant women, who are sensible, fond of children, kind-hearted, diligent, and freer than they are in Europe. Their husbands do not scold and beat them because they are as tall and strong and intelligent as their masters. When their husbands are absent, the women do the driving. They like punning. The children are pampered and allowed to sleep long hours. They take tea and eat with the adults, and repay it in kind if the latter tease them.

There is diphtheria. Smallpox is widespread, but, oddly enough, it is not as infectious as it is elsewhere; two or three patients will die—and that's the end of the epidemic. There are no hospitals or doctors. The sick are treated by male nurses. Bloodletting and cupping are practiced on a grandiose, brutal scale. On the road I examined a Jew with cancer of the liver. He was emaciated and scarcely breathing, but this did not prevent the nurse from placing twelve cupping glasses on him. By the way, a word about the Jews. Here they till the soil, work as coachmen, run ferryboats, trade, and are called peasants, because they are peasants *de jure* and *de facto*. They are universally respected and, according to the police officer, are not rarely elected village elders. I saw a tall, lean Jew scowling with distaste and spitting when the policeman was telling risqué stories, an undefiled soul; his wife cooked a delicious fish soup. The wife of the Jew with cancer regaled me with pike roe and excellent white bread. Exploitation by Jews is unheard of. I might as well say something about the Poles. Some of them are exiles, deported from Poland after 1864. They are kind, hospitable, and most urbane people. Some of them are well-to-do, others are poor and work as clerks at the stations. At Ishim, for an excellent dinner and a room where I had a good sleep I paid one ruble to Pan Zaleski, a Polish nobleman who kept a tavern. A conscienceless moneygrubber to the marrow of his bones, the table he set, his manners, were those of a gentleman.* * *

Would you like me to tell you something about the Tartars, too? Here you are. There are not many of them here. Good people. In the Kazan province even priests speak well of them, and in Siberia they are "better than the Russians"—that's what I was told by the police officer in the presence of Russians, who confirmed this opinion by silence. My God, how rich Russia is in good people! Were it not for the cold that robs Siberia of the summer, and were it not for the officials who corrupt the peasants and the exiles, Siberia would be the richest and happiest land.* * *

During the first three days of my journey my collarbones, shoulders, vertebrae, and coccyx began to ache, what with the shaking and jolting. There was no sitting, walking, lying down. To make up for all that, my headaches and chest pains vanished, my appetite grew beyond belief, and the hemorrhoids modestly effaced themselves. The tension, the exertion of lifting heavy luggage, and perhaps also the farewell drinking parties in Moscow made me spit blood in the morning, and this caused me to be despondent and exposed me to dismal thoughts. All this ceased by the end of the trip; it's a long time since I have coughed as little as now, after a fortnight spent outdoors. Indeed, after the first three days on the road my body grew used to the jolts, and the time came when I stopped noticing how morning gave way to midday, followed in its turn by evening and night. The days flashed by rapidly, as in a lingering illness. You think that morning has not gone yet, but the driver advises me to stay overnight, to avoid losing the way in the dark. And indeed, I glance at the watch and find that it's past 7 P.M.

The driving is fast, though less so in spring than in winter. Uphill the horses go at a gallop, and before the coachman is seated on his box and the carriage leaves the courtyard, it takes two or three men to hold the horses. They resemble those used by Moscow firemen. On one occasion we almost ran over several old women, another time we all but dashed into a file of prisoners.

Now here is an adventure that I owe to Siberian driving. Only I beg Mamasha not to "oh" and "ah" and lament, because it all ended happily. In the small hours of May 6 a very nice old man was driving me in my tarantas drawn by a pair of horses. I was drowsy and, having nothing to do, watched snakelike flames sparkling in the fields and the birch groves: it was the burning of last year's grass, which is set on fire here. Suddenly I hear a drumming noise of wheels. A posting station troika is dashing at top speed, heading for us like a bird. My old man hastens to turn right and the troika flies past us, and in the uncertain light I make out someone driving a huge, heavy coach. It is followed by another coach also going at full speed. We hasten to turn right. . . . To my bewilderment and horror, it turns not right, but left. I barely have time to think, "My God, we'll collide!" when a terrible crash is heard, the horses tangle, a dark mass, the yokes fall, my carriage rears up, and I am on the ground with my luggage on top of me. But that is not all. A third troika is bearing down on us. In the natural course of events, this last troika should have crushed me and smashed my bags, but, God be praised, I was not asleep, broke no bones in tumbling and jumped up so fast that I was able to yell "Stop!" at the third troika. It came to a halt, but not before it had landed into the other. . . . Of course, if I had been asleep in my carriage, or if the third coach had followed hard on the second, I would have returned home either an invalid or a headless horseman. Results of the collision: broken shafts, torn harness, yokes and baggage scattered on the ground, dazed, worn-out horses, the thought of a narrow escape. It appears that the first driver had lashed his horses, but the drivers of the other two troikas were asleep and their horses just followed the first coach. Having recovered from the stupefaction, my old man and the other three drivers engaged in ferocious cursing. Oh, how they cursed! I thought it would come to blows. You cannot imagine how alone I felt in the midst of this savage, cursing horde, in the field, before dawn, within sight of fires near and far consuming the grass but failing to warm the cold night air even slightly. Oh, how oppressive it was! You hear the cursing, look at the broken shafts and at your smashed luggage, and it seems to you that you are in another world, and that you will be trampled to bits. . . . After an hour's cursing my old man began to tie the shafts and the harness together with a little rope—my belt came in handy. Somehow we dragged ourselves to the station, halting now and then.

Early in the morning there was a downpour with a high wind. It rained day and night. I put on my leather overcoat, which protected me from rain and wind. A wonderful overcoat. The mud became unconquerable. Coachmen were reluctant to drive at night. But what was worst and what I shall not forget my whole life was fording the river at night. The coachman and you begin to shout. Rain, wind, ice floes crawl downstream, splashing is heard. . . . Suddenly, joy: a bittern calls. These birds inhabit the shores of Siberian waterways. Seemingly, geography means more to them than climate. Well, an hour later, there appears a huge ferry, shaped like a barge, with enormous oars resembling lobster claws. Ferrymen are nasty folk, mostly deportees, sent here for vicious behavior, by order of the peasant communes to which they belong. Unbearably foul-mouthed, they shout and beg money for vodka. The crossing is slow, intolerably so! The ferry crawls. . . . Again a sense of aloneness, and the bittern seems to call on purpose, as if to say, "Don't be afraid, uncle, I am here. The Lintvarevs sent me here from the shores of the Psel."

On May 7 a private coachman whom I asked for horses said that the. Irtysh had flooded the fields, that yesterday Kuzma, having driven out, was barely able to return, and that it was necessary to wait. I ask: how long? The answer is: the Lord knows.* * * Well, suspecting that the Irtysh flood was invented only so as not to drive me at night through the mud, I protested and ordered the horses to be hitched up. The peasant, who had heard about the flood from Kuzma and had not seen it himself, scratched his head and agreed; the old drivers encouraged him, saying that in their youth they had feared nothing. We are off. . . . Mud, rain, fierce wind, cold, and I am wearing felt boots. Do you know what such boots are when wet? They are made of jelly. We drive on and on, and before my eyes there stretches a vast lake dotted with tiny islands, and with small bushes sticking out here and there—the flooded meadows. Far off there is the steep opposite shore of the Irtysh, white with snow. . . . We begin to make our way across the lake. What prevented me from turning back was stubbornness and an incomprehensible daring ardor, the same ardor that made me jump from a yacht to bathe in the Black Sea, and indulge in not a few other follies. Perhaps a psychotic attack. We drive, selecting islets and strips of land. The direction of the road is indicated by the washed-out bridges. To drive along the strips of land it is necessary to lead the horses one by one. The coachman unhitches them and I jump into the water in my felt boots and hold on to the horses. Entertaining! With it all, rain and wind . . . save us, Queen of Heaven! Finally we reach an island with a roofless hut on it. Wet horses wandering over wet manure. A peasant with a long stick comes out of the hut and undertakes to guide us. He measures the depth of the water with the stick and tests the ground. May God give him health, he led us to a long tongue of land that he called a "ridge" and told us to turn right or left—I don't remember which—to reach another ridge. We followed his advice.

We're driving on. . . . The felt boots are as wet as a latrine. They squelch, my socks blow their noses. The coachman is silent, and clicks his tongue despondently. He would gladly drive back, but it's too late, darkness is falling. . . . Finally, oh joy! We reach the Irtysh. The bank is gullied, slippery, disgusting, not a trace of vegetation; muddy water with whitecaps lashes it and angrily jumps back as though averse to touch a bank that apparently can only be inhabited by toads and the souls of murderers. The river neither booms nor roars, but it seems as though on its bed it were knocking on coffins. A damnable impression! The other bank is steep, brown, barren.

A hut occupied by ferrymen. One of them comes out and announces that the weather is too bad for the ferry to leave. The river is wide, he says, and the wind high. And so I had to spend the night in the hut. I remember the night, the snoring of the ferrymen and of my driver, the howling of the wind, the drumbeat of the rain, the growling of the Irtysh.* * *

In the morning they would not ferry me because of the wind. We crossed the river in a rowboat. The rain lashes, the wind blows, the baggage is soaked; the felt boots, which at night were drying on the stove, again turn to jelly. Oh, my dear leather overcoat! If I didn't catch cold, I owe this to it alone. When I come home, rub it with suet or castor oil. Once ashore, I sat on my luggage a whole hour waiting for horses, which were to be brought up from the village. I remember how slippery it was climbing up the bank. In the village I warmed up and had tea. The deportees came to beg alms. Every day each family in the village leavens a pood of wheaten flour to bake bread for the deportees. It is a kind of tax.

The deportees take the bread and barter it for vodka. One of them, a raggedy, shaven old man, whose eyes had been gouged out by his fellow deportees in a tavern, having heard that a traveler was in the house and taking me for a merchant, began reciting and chanting prayers. He chanted prayers for health and for the repose of the dead, and an Easter canticle. What didn't he chant! Then he started lying to the effect that he came from a merchant family in Moscow. I noticed the contempt in which this boozer held the peasants on whom he sponged.

On the 11th I obtained post horses. Out of boredom I read the complaint books at the stations. I made a discovery that struck me: the entries of the postal stations are provided with privies. They are invaluable in damp and rainy weather. Oh, you can't appreciate this!

On the 12th they would not let me have any horses. I was told that travel was impossible, since the Ob was in flood and had inundated the meadowland. I was advised to take a side road to Krasnyi Yar, thence to go by rowboat to Dubrovino, where post horses would be available. I started for Krasnyi Yar with horses hired from a private coachman. I reach it in the morning and am told that there is a rowboat, but that I shall have to wait a while, because grandfather had sent a workman off in it to row the district policeman's clerk to Dubrovino. Well, I'll wait. One hour passes, a second hour, a third. . . . Noon comes, evening. . . . *Allah kerim*, how much tea did I drink, how much bread did I eat, how many thoughts did I think! And how long I slept! Night comes, then dawn, no boat. Finally the workman returns in the boat at 9 o'clock. We're off. Thank heaven! How smoothly we move! There is no wind, the rowers are skilled, the islands we pass beautiful. The flood had caught cattle and people off guard. And I see peasant women going out in boats to the islands to milk the cows. These cows are lean, despondent; because of the cold there is no fodder at all to be had.

We covered eight miles. At the Dubrovino posthouse I had tea and with it I was served—just imagine!—waffles. The woman who runs the place must be a deportee or the wife of one. At the next station the clerk, an old Pole, to whom I gave antipyrin to relieve his headache, complained of his poverty and told me that Count Sapieha, Chamberlain of the Court of Austria and a Pole, who helped Poles, had recently passed through Siberia. "He stopped near this station," the clerk told me, "but I never knew it! Holy Mother of God! He would have helped me. I wrote to him in Vienna, but got no reply—" and so on. Why am I not Sapieha? I would send this poor fellow back to his native land.

On May 14 I was again refused horses. The Tom is in flood. What a nuisance! Not a nuisance, but a calamity! Tomsk thirty-five miles away, and then this, so unexpectedly! In my place a woman would have burst into sobs. Some kind folks found a way out for me: "You go as far as the Tom, Your Honor—it's only four miles from here; there they'll row you across to Yar, and from there Ilya Markovich will drive you to Tomsk." I hire a private coach and go to the Tom, to the spot where the boat ought to be. I drive up: no boat. It has just gone off with the mail and isn't likely to come back soon, since there's a gale blowing. I begin my wait. The ground is covered with snow, the rain is mixed with granulated snow, and then there's the wind. . . . An hour passes, then another, no boat. Fate is mocking me! I go back to the station. Here three troikas and a postman are getting ready to set out in the direction of the Tom. I tell them there is no boat. They remain. Fate rewards me: the clerk, in answer to my hesitant query as to the chances of getting a bite to eat, tells me that the stationmaster's wife has cabbage soup. Oh rapture! Oh, most radiant day! And the woman's daughter actually brings me excellent cabbage soup, with wonderful meat, roast potatoes, and a cucumber. I have not dined so well since the meal I had at Pan Zaleski's inn. Having downed the victuals, I went the limit and made coffee for myself. A spree!

At dusk the mailman, an elderly fellow, who had obviously been through thick and thin and who dared not sit in my presence, started getting ready to drive to the Tom. So did I. We were off. As soon as we reached the river, an incredibly long boat came into view. While the mail was being loaded onto the boat I witnessed a strange phenomenon: thunder, and at the same time snow and a cold wind. We finished loading and cast off. Sweet Misha, forgive me for being glad that I didn't take you with me! How clever I was not to have taken anyone with me! At first our boat moved over the meadow close to shrub willows. As often happens before or during a storm, a gust of wind suddenly swept over the water, raising mighty waves. The boatman seated at the rudder thought that we should weather the storm among the willow shrubs, but others disagreed, saying that if the storm grew more violent, we would spend the night in the shrubs and drown anyway. The matter was put to a vote and it was decided to move on. My ill luck that so mocks me! What was the point of all these jokes? The men were rowing silently, concentrating on their task. . . . I remember the figure of the mailman, who had had such a tough time. I remember a soldier who suddenly turned as purple as cherry juice. . . . The thought flashed through my mind that if the boat should capsize, I would first of all jettison my sheepskin and my leather overcoat—then the felt boots, then, etc. But now the shore looms closer and closer. . . . You relax more and more, the heart contracts with joy, you take a deep breath as though you have suddenly finished a heavy task, and you jump onto the wet, slippery bank. . . . Thank God!

At Ilya Markovich's we are told that the road is too bad for driving after dark and that we must stay the night. Well, I do. After tea I sit down to go on writing this letter, interrupted by the arrival of the police officer. He is a thick mixture of Nozdryov, Khlestakov,[3] and dog. He is a drunkard, a lecher, a liar, a singer, a raconteur, and with all that a goodhearted fellow. He brought with him a large chest stuffed with dossiers, a bed with a mattress, a gun, and a clerk. The clerk is an intellectual who studied in Petersburg, a fine, outspoken liberal, a man with nothing against him, who got to Siberia for some unknown reason, infected to the marrow of his bones with all diseases, owing his alcoholism to his superior, who called him Kolya. The man in power sends for a cordial. "Doctor!" he yells. "Drink another glass and I'll bow down at your feet!" Of course, I drink. The man in power guzzles mightily, lies recklessly, indulges shamelessly in ribaldry. We go to bed. In the morning they again send for liquor. They swill vodka till 10 o'clock, and finally we leave. Ilya Markovich, the convert, whom the peasants here worship, gives me horses to take me as far as Tomsk.

I, the police officer, and the clerk got into one carriage. As long as we were together on the road the police officer was telling whoppers, swilling liquor from a bottle, bragging that he did not take bribes, admiring nature, and shaking his fist at the tramps we passed. After covering ten miles, we halted at the village of Brovkino. . . . We stopped at a Jew's shop and stepped down for a "rest." He ran to get liquor, his wife cooked the soup I have already mentioned. The police officer called for his two village subalterns and the local road contractor, and in his drunken state began giving them a tongue-lashing, not embarrassed in the slightest by my presence. He swore like a Tartar.

I soon parted company with the police officer and his clerk and reached Tomsk the evening of May 15. You can judge what the road was like from the fact that in the last two days I covered only some fifty miles.

Tomsk is sunk in mud. About that city and the life there I'll write you shortly. Meanwhile farewell.* * * I embrace, kiss, and bless you all.

Your A. Chekhov

P.S. Forgive me that this letter is like vinaigrette sauce. Incoherent. What could I do? Sitting in a hotel room, one couldn't do better. Excuse

[3] The bully in Gogol's *Dead Souls*, and the braggart in his *Inspector General*, respectively.

the length. It's not my fault. I lost control of my hand and besides I wanted to talk to you as long as possible. It is 3 o'clock in the morning. My hand is tired. There is a snuff on the candle wick, and the light is poor. * * *

TO A. S. SUVORIN

Tomsk, May 20, 1890

Hello, at last! Greetings from the Siberian Man, dear Aleksey Sergeyevich! I missed you and our correspondence dreadfully.

However, I'll begin at the beginning. At Tyumen they told me that the first steamer to Tomsk would leave on May 18. It became necessary to race along by carriage. The first three days every sinew and joint ached, but then I became used to things and felt no aches whatsoever. But lack of sleep and the constant fuss with the baggage, the jouncing and starvation, made me spit blood, thus spoiling my mood, which was indifferent anyway. During the first few days things were bearable, but then a chill wind sprang up, the floodgates of heaven opened, the rivers flooded the meadows and the roads. Often it was necessary to change from the carriage to a boat. About the war I waged against the flood and the mud you will read in the enclosed pages; I said nothing there about my big boots, which proved tight, and that I waded through the mud and water in felt boots, and that those felt boots of mine turned into jelly. The road was so abominable that in the last two days of my travels I covered only fifty miles.

When I was leaving I promised to keep sending you notes on my journey, beginning at Tomsk, since the road between Tyumen and Tomsk has already been described and exploited a thousand times. But in your telegram you expressed a wish to have my Siberian impressions as soon as possible and were harsh enough, sir, to reproach me with having a poor memory—i.e., of having apparently forgotten you. To write on the way was positively impossible; I kept a brief diary in pencil and can offer you now only what I noted down in this diary. In order not to write at too great length and not to become confused I have divided all my recorded impressions into chapters. Am sending you six chapters. They are written *for you personally*. I wrote them only for you and was not afraid of being too subjective in my notes, and was not afraid that there would be more of Chekhovian emotions and thoughts than of Siberia in them. If you find any lines of interest and worth printing, hand them over to benevolent publicity, after signing them with my name and printing them in separate chapterettes, a tablespoonful every hour. You can give them a general title, *From Siberia,* then *From Transbaikal,* then *From the Amur,* and so on.* * *

Throughout my journey I went hungry as a dog. I stuffed my belly with bread so as not to daydream of turbot, asparagus, and so on. I had daydreams even about buckwheat groats. Daydreams about food for hours on end.

In Tyumen I bought some sausage for the road, but what sausage! When you put a piece in your mouth it's filled with a stench as though you had entered a stable at the very moment when the drivers are removing their footcloths; when you begin to chew, you feel as though you had sunk your teeth into a dog's tail smeared with tar. Pfui! I took one or two mouthfuls and threw away the sausage.

I received a wire and a letter from you in which you write that you want to publish an encyclopedic dictionary. I don't know why, but the news of this dictionary rejoiced me greatly. Go ahead, my dear! If I'm up to the job, I give you November and December: these months I shall be living in Petersburg. I'll work day and night. * * *

Ah, what expenses! *Gewalt.*[1] Thanks to the rising water I had to pay the drivers double and occasionally triple rates everywhere, since the work is infernal, as hard as a convict's. My suitcase, my dearest little trunk, proved unsuitable for travel: it took up a lot of space, poked me in the ribs, rumbled thunderously and, most important of all, threatened to get smashed. "Don't take any trunks along on a long journey!" kindhearted folk had told me, but I recalled this advice only midway of my journey. Oh, well! I am leaving my suitcase in Tomsk as a settler, and to replace it I have bought something made of hide pulled off carrion, that has the advantage of spreading out as flat as you please on the floor of the tarantas. Paid 16 rubles for it. To continue: racing to Amur with relays of horses is torture. You'll smash both yourself and all your baggage. I was advised to buy a vehicle. Bought same today for 130 rubles. If I fail to sell it in Sretensk, where my traveling with horses comes to an end, I'll be left high and dry and will send up a howl. Today I dined with Kartamyshev, editor of *The Siberian Herald.* The local Nozdrev,[2] an expansive nature. —Spent 6 rubles on drink.

[1] The use of the word in the sense of a cry for help indicates that Chekhov had an ear for Yiddish, which he heard in his native town and perhaps elsewhere.

[2] A character in Gogol's *Dead Souls,* a blustering braggart.

Stop! I am informed that the assistant to the Chief of Police wants to see me. What's up?!?

False alarm. The police officer turns out to be a lover of literature and even a writer. He has come to pay respects. He went home to fetch a drama of his and, apparently, wants to treat me to a reading of it. He will be back any moment and will again interfere with my writing to you. * * *

Stop! The police officer is back. He did not read his play, even though he had brought it, but he did treat me to a story. Not bad, but too regional. He showed me a gold nugget. Asked for vodka. I can't remember a single Siberian intellectual who, on coming to see me, hasn't asked for vodka. He had acquired a "lady friend"—a married woman; also let me read a petition for divorce addressed to His Imperial Majesty. Then he proposed to take me on a sight-seeing tour of the Tomsk brothels.

Am writing this on coming back from the brothels. Disgusting. Two A.M. * * *

I shall not describe Tomsk. In Russia all cities are alike. Tomsk is a boring town, not sober, no beautiful women at all, Asiatic lawlessness. The city is remarkable by reason of the fact that Provincial Governors die in it. * * *

Your A. Chekhov

TO M. P. CHEKHOVA

Krasnoyarsk, May 28, 1890

What a murderous road! I barely, barely crept up to Krasnoyarsk, and I repaired my vehicle twice: first the trigger broke—an iron upright contraption connecting the front of the carriage with the axletree, then what they call a ring broke under the front of the carriage. Never in my life have I laid eyes on such a road, such terrible slush, and a roadway so horrible, so neglected. I'm going to write up this disgrace in *New Times* and so will say nothing about it for the present.

The last three stages were magnificent—as you get closer to Krasnoyarsk you seem to be descending into another world. You emerge from the forest onto a plain which looks very much like our Donetz steppe, only here the mountain ridges are more grandiose. The sun is shining its head off, the birches have burgeoned, although only three stages back they had shown no signs of their buds bursting open. Glory be, I have at last rolled into summer, where there is neither wind nor icy rain. Krasnoyarsk is a beautiful civilized town; Tomsk, by comparison with it, is a pig in a skullcap, in bad taste. The streets clean, paved, the houses of stone, big, the churches fine.

I'm alive and absolutely well. The money is all here, the luggage is also all here—I did lose the woolen socks—and found them shortly.

So far—if one avoids mentioning the carriage—everything is going well and there is nothing to complain about. But the expenses are frightening. Nowhere is impracticality in everyday matters as telling as on the road. I pay more than is necessary, do what isn't necessary, don't say that which is necessary, and on every occasion expect that which does not happen.

Misha, don't get ready for Japan yet; it seems that I shall return by way of America.

I'll be in Irkutsk in five or six days; will stay there about the same number of days, after which I'll be off, galloping to Sretensk—and that will be the end of my transportation by carriage. There, more than two weeks have gone by in this incessant galloping of mine, my thoughts moving only in this one direction, this was my life; every day I saw the rising of the sun, from start to finish. I've gotten so used to all this that it seems to me I have been galloping and carrying on my war against the miry road all my life. When there is no rain and the road is free from mudholes, everything becomes somehow odd and even a bit boring. And how filthy I am, and what an ignominious mug I have! And how threadbare my unhappy clothes are! * * *

With reference to Mother's department: I still have one and a half jars of coffee; I feed on honey and locusts. Today I am going to dine— and in Irkutsk, at that. The nearer the east, the dearer everything becomes. Rye bread—rye flour, I mean—is already 70 copecks for 36 pounds, while on the other side of Tomsk the same amount is 25 to 27 copecks, and 30 copecks will get you 36 pounds of wheat flour. The tobacco they sell you in Siberia is mean and loathsome. I shiver, since the tobacco I have brought with me is already coming to an end. * * *

For God's sake, let there be no sicknesses and no incidents! Be of good cheer to the marrow of your bones.

Your Homo Sachaliensis,
A. Chekhov

* * *

Greetings, my most kind Nikolay Aleksandrovich!

I send you the warmest regards from Irkutsk, from the depths of Siberia. I arrived in Irkutsk last night, and am very glad I did, since the journey knocked me out completely, and I was missing my relatives and friends, to whom I have not written for a long time. And now, what is there of interest to write you about? I'll begin by saying that the trip is unusually long. I have covered over two thousand miles by carriage from Tyumen to Irkutsk. From Tyumen to Irkutsk I waged war against cold and rivers in flood; the cold was terrible; on the Feast of Ascension there was a frost and a snowfall, so that I didn't get a chance to take off my sheepskin coat and felt boots until I got to the hotel at Tomsk. As for the rivers in flood, they are a plague of Egypt. The rivers overflowed their banks and inundated the meadowlands for miles around, and the roads with them; it was constantly necessary to exchange my carriage for a boat—and as for boats, they weren't to be had for nothing; for a good boat one had to pay with one's heart's blood, since it was necessary to sit for days and nights on end in the rain and the cold wind, and wait and wait. . . . From Tomsk to Krasnoyarsk there was a desperate war against insuperable mud. My God, it's fearful even to recall it! How many times I had to have my carriage repaired, to trudge beside it, to curse, to crawl out of it and climb back into it again, and so on. There were times when the ride from one station to the next took six to ten hours, and from ten to fifteen hours were needed to repair the vehicle. The heat and dust during the trip from Krasnoyarsk to Irkutsk were dreadful. Add to this hunger, dust in your nose, eyes glued together for want of sleep, eternal fear that something may break in the carriage (which was my own), and boredom. But just the same I am content and thank God for having given me the strength and opportunity to make this journey. I have seen and lived through a great deal, and everything is exceedingly interesting and new to me, not as a man of letters but simply as a human being. The Yenisey river, the *taiga*, the stations, the drivers, untamed Nature, the wild life, the physical agonies caused by the hardships of travel, the delights of resting—altogether everything is so wonderful that I can't even describe it. For one thing, during more than a month I have been out in the fresh air day and night, which is interesting and wholesome; for a whole month I have seen the sunrise from beginning to end.

From here I am going to Baikal, then to Chita, and on to Sretensk, where I exchange my horses for a steamer and sail down the Amur to my journey's end. I am in no hurry, since I have no wish to be in Sakhalin before the first of July. * * *

Your Homo Sachaliensis,

A. Chekhov

TO M. P. CHEKHOVA

Listvenichnaya Station, on the
shore of Lake Baikal, June 13, 1890

I am living through confoundedly foolish days. On June 11—day before yesterday, that is—in the evening, we left Irkutsk in the hope of boarding the Baikal steamer, which was to put off at four in the morning. From Irkutsk to Lake Baikal there are only three posting stations. At the first station we were notified that all the horses were out and therefore going on was impossible. Willy-nilly we had to stop for the night. Yesterday morning we left this station and toward noon arrived at Lake Baikal. Went to the wharf and on inquiring received the answer that the steamer would not start out before Friday, June 15. Which means that, until Friday, we must needs sit on the shore, contemplate the water, and wait. Since there is never a thing which doesn't come to an end eventually I have nothing against waits and I always wait patiently, but the rub is that on the 20th, at Sretensk, there will be a steamer starting down the Amur; if we miss that we'll have to wait for the next steamer, which will be leaving on the 30th. Good sirs, whenever shall I hit Sakhalin?

We drove toward Lake Baikal along the bank of the Angara, which has its source in Lake Baikal and empties into the Yenisey. Look at the map. The river banks are picturesque. Mountains and mountains; on the mountains—forests with never a break. The weather wonderful, calm, sunny, warm; I rode along and, for some reason, felt that I was exceptionally well; so fine was my mood that it is actually beyond description. All this was due, probably, to being no longer stuck in Irkutsk, and because Angara's bank looks like Switzerland. Something new and original. We rode along the bank, rode up to Angara's estuary and turned to the left, and there it was, the shore of Lake Baikal, which, in Siberia, is called the Sea of Baikal. A mirror. The other shore is, of course, out of sight: sixty miles away. Shores high, steep, rocky, forested. Promontories visible to right and left, jutting into the lake, something like Aiu-Dag or Feodosiya's Tokhtebel. Much like the Crimea. The Listvenichnaya posting station is situated right near the water and bears a striking resemblance to Yalta; if the houses were white it would be altogether Yalta. Only there are no buildings on the mountains, since the mountains are too sheer and you can't build on them.

We settled in a small shed, reminiscent of any dacha in Kraskovo. Not far from the windows, five to seven feet away from the foundation, the lake begins. We're paying a ruble a day. Mountains, forests, the mirror of Lake Baikal—all this is poisoned by the thought that we'll have to be stuck here until Friday. What are we to occupy ourselves with here? In addition we still don't know what there is for us to eat. The population subsists on nothing but wild garlic. There is no meat, no fish; nobody gave us any milk but only the promise of some. We had to cough up 16 copecks for a puny loaf of white bread. I bought some buckwheat grits and a very small chunk of smoked pork and ordered them to cook me a gruel—it had no taste, but there was nothing to do about it: eat one must. All evening we searched the village, on the chance of someone selling us a chicken, and failed to find it. —But then, there is vodka! [...] And yet it would seem that procuring meat and fish would be considerably easier than procuring vodka, which both costs more and is harder to transport. No, drinking vodka must be considerably more interesting than catching fish in Baikal or raising cattle.

At midnight a wretched little steamer arrived; we went to take a look at it and, while we were at it, to ask if there wasn't something to eat on board. We were told that we would be able to get dinner on the morrow, but that at this hour of the night the galley fire was out, and so on. We expressed gratitude for the morrow—it held out hope, after all. But, alas—the captain entered and said that, at four in the morning, the wretched little steamer was leaving for Kultuk. Many thanks! In the buffet (where you couldn't turn around, it was so cramped) we drank a bottle of sour wine (35 copecks) and saw some amber beads on a plate: salmon roe. Went home—and to sleep. I have come to loathe sleeping. Every day you make your bed on the floor by spreading your short sheepskin with the wool outside, putting a rolled-up overcoat and a small pillow at the head; you sleep on these hillocks in pants and vest—civilization, where art thou?

It's raining today and the lake is hidden by fog. "Engrossing!" as Semashko would say. It's tedious. Ought to settle down to writing, but one doesn't feel like working in bad weather. I can foresee merciless tedium; if I were alone it would not matter so much, but there are lieutenants and an army physician traveling with me, all of whom love to talk and to argue. It's little they know but they talk about everything. One of the lieutenants is, over and above that, a braggart, something of a Khlestakov. Travel absolutely must be solo. To be with one's thoughts sitting alone in a carriage or in a room is considerably more interesting than being with others. Besides the military men, we have Innokentii Alekseyevich traveling with us, a student in the technical school at Irkutsk, a boy who looks like the Neapolitan lad whose pronunciation was so odd, but who is cleverer and kindlier. We took him along to see that he gets to Chita.

Felicitate me: I sold my traveling carriage in Irkutsk. I won't say how I came out on the deal, for if I do dear Mama will keel over in a faint and won't sleep for five nights running. . . . * * *

The fog has lifted. I see clouds on the mountains. Oh! Devil take you! You'd think it was the Caucasus.

Good-bye.

Your Homo Sachaliensis,
A. Chekhov

TO M. P. CHEKHOVA

En route from the Cossack village of
Pokrovskaya to Blagoveshchensk,
June 23–26, 1890

I have already written you that we are stranded on a shoal. Near Ust-Strelka, where the Shilka merges with the Argun (see map), the steamer, which draws two and a half feet of water, dashed against a rock, sprang several holes and, getting its hold full of water, settled on the river bed. They took to pumping out the water and patching up the holes: a stripped sailor crawls into the hold, stands up to his neck in water, and gropes for the holes with his heels; each hole is covered from within by canvas smeared with grease, a plank is placed over this, and a prop is put against the plank, which prop rises, like a column against the underside of the deck above—and there is your repair. The pumping went on from five in the evening until night but the water did not subside; the work had to be put off until morning. In the morning they found several new holes and again fell to patching and pumping. The sailors pump away while we, the public, stroll about the decks, chat, eat, drink, nap; the captain and his mate do the same things as the public and are not in any hurry. To the right is the coastline of China, to the left is the Pokrovskaya village with its Amur Cossacks; stay in Russia, if you want to; if you want to, leave for China—not prohibited. During the day unbearable sultriness, so that one has to put on a silk shirt.

Dinner is served at twelve, supper at seven in the evening.

As ill luck would have it, the *Herald*, the steamer that was to meet ours, approaches the Cossack village. The *Herald*, thronged with passengers, also can proceed no further and both steamers are stuck there. The *Herald* has a military band aboard. This results in nothing short of a gala. Music was playing on our deck all day yesterday, diverting the captain and the sailors and, consequently, hindering the repairs to the steamer. The female half of the passengers grew hilarious: music, officers, sailors— oh! The finishing-school misses were particularly enraptured. Yesterday, in the evening, we went strolling through the village where the very same music was played, this time ordered by the Cossacks. Today we are going on with our repairs. The captain promises that we shall be off after dinner, but he promises indolently, looking somewhere away to one side—evidently lying. We are taking our time. Upon my asking one of the passengers when we would be leaving at last, he asked in his turn, "Why, is it bad here?"

True enough. Why shouldn't we stay put, as long as we aren't bored?

The captain, his mate, and the ship's agent—the acme of amiability. The Chinese passengers in Third Class are good-natured and amusing. Yesterday one Chinese passenger was squatting on the deck and singing something ever so lugubrious in a falsetto; while he was at it his profile was funnier than any caricature could possibly be. All were watching him and laughing, but he was paying them no attention whatsoever. He had his fill of singing falsetto and launched into tenor—God, what a voice! It was the bleating of a sheep or the mooing of a calf [crossed

[*160*]

out: "but not singing at all"]. The Chinese remind me of gentle tamed animals. Their queues are black, long, like those of Natalya Mikhailovna. A propos of tamed animals: there is a fox cub housed in the washroom. You are washing, but it sits there and watches you. If it has not seen people for a long time it begins to whimper.

What strange things they talk about! They talk only about gold, gold fields, the Volunteer Fleet, about Japan. In Pokrovskaya every muzhik—and even the priest—digs for gold. The settlers, who go in for this also, get rich here just as quickly as they get poor. There are fellows in coarse overcoats who drink nothing but champagne, and walk to the pothouse only on a runner of red velveteen, which is unrolled from the hut smack up to the pothouse door. * * *

The Amur region is extraordinarily interesting. Devilishly original. The life seething here is something that the Europeans haven't as much as an inkling of. It—this life, that is—reminds me of tales about life in America. The river banks are so very wild, original, and luxuriant that you long to remain and live here forever. I am writing the concluding lines on June 25. The steamer is shaking and interferes with my writing. We are sailing again. I have already sailed more than six hundred miles on the Amur and have seen a million most magnificent landscapes; my head is spinning with delight. One cliff I saw was such that if Kundasova got the notion of amusing herself at the foot of that cliff, she would expire in ecstasy, and if I, with Sofya Petrovna Kuvshinnikova,[1] in command, were to arrange a picnic at that spot, we would be in a position to say to each other, "Die, Denis—you will never do anything better!"[2] Astounding nature. And how sultry the weather! What warm nights! There is fog of mornings, but it's a warm fog.

I survey the shores through binoculars, and I see the devil's own plenty of ducks, geese, loons, herons, and all sorts of creatures with long bills. Now there's a place to lease a dacha!

Yesterday, in the small town of Reinovo, the owner of a gold mine called me in to see his ailing wife. As I was leaving he thrust a packet of bills into my hand. I became embarrassed, refusing the money repeatedly, and thrust it back into his hands, assuring him that I myself was very rich; we had a long discussion as we tried to persuade each

[1] A neighbor of the Chekhovs in the country, the wife of a physician and herself a painter. Her affair with the well-known landscape painter I. I. Levitan is reflected in Chekhov's story "The Grasshopper."

[2] Potemkin, on having heard a reading of a comedy by Denis Fonvizin, said to the author, "Die, Denis—you will never write anything better!"

other but, just the same, when it was all over there were 15 rubles remaining in my hand. Yesterday, too, the owner of a gold mine was dining in the same cabin with me; he had the face of Petya Polevayev; [3] he drank champagne at dinner instead of water and treated us to champagne as well.

The villages here are the same as on the Don; there is a difference in the buildings but it doesn't amount to much. The inhabitants don't observe the fasts and eat meat even during Passion Week; the girls smoke cigarettes and the crones smoke pipes—that's the accepted thing. It's strange, at times, to see peasant women with cigarettes. And what liberalism! Ah, what liberalism!

The air on board the steamer becomes red-hot from the talk. People aren't afraid to speak out here. There is no one to make arrests and no place to which to transport anyone—play the liberal to your heart's content. The folk here are for the most part independent, self-reliant and not devoid of logic. If a misunderstanding of some sort arises in Ust-Kara, where convicts are serving their terms (there are many politicals among them who are not sentenced to hard labor), all of Amur gets stirred up. There are no secret denunciations. A fugitive political can go freely by steamer all the way to the ocean without any fear of the captain turning him in. This *laissez-faire* can also be explained in part by the total indifference to everything that is going on in Russia. Everyone says, "What's it to me?"

I forgot to write you that in Transbaikal it is not the Russians but the native Buryats who are the coachmen. Odd folk. Their horses are vipers. More ferocious than fire-brigade horses. There's no harnessing without trouble. The off-horse's legs are hobbled while it is being harnessed; hardly is the hobble removed than the troika is off, flying to the devil so fast that one loses one's breath. If you don't hobble the horse while it's being harnessed, it kicks, gouges the shafts with its hoofs, tears the harness, and creates the impression of a young devil who has been caught by his horns.

We are getting close to Blagoveshchensk. Keep well and cheerful and don't become estranged from me. You have already become estranged, no? Low obeisances and friendly kisses to all.

Antoine

I am in perfect health.

[3] An acquaintance of N. P. Chekhov's during his early years in Moscow.

Blagoveshchensk, June 27, 1890

Greetings, my precious one!

The Amur is a very fine river; what I have derived from it is more than I could have anticipated, and I have been wanting for a long time to share my transports with you, but the scoundrelly steamer kept shaking for all of seven days and hindered me from writing. In addition to that I am utterly unable to describe such things of beauty as the banks of the Amur; I throw in my hand when I am confronted by them and admit that I am a beggar. Well, how is one to describe them? Picture to yourself the Suram Pass in the Caucasus which has been compelled to be a river bank—and there's the Amur for you. Crags, cliffs, forests, thousands of ducks, herons, and all sorts of beaky rapscallions, and a wilderness with never a break. To the left, the Russian river bank; to the right, the Chinese. If I want to, I gaze at Russia; if I want to, I gaze at China. China is just as much of a desert and a wilderness as Russia is: one rarely comes upon villages and upon the tiny huts of the border guards. Everything in my head is mixed up and pulverized—and this is not at all hard to figure out, Your Excellency! I sailed on the Amur for more than 660 miles and saw millions of landscapes, and yet the Amur had been preceded by Lake Baikal, by Transbaikal. —Really, I have seen such riches and have had so many delightful experiences that even dying is no longer frightening. People on the Amur are original, life is interesting, not like ours at all. The only thing people talk about is gold. Gold, gold, and nothing else. I'm in a foolish mood, don't feel like writing, and write briefly, and swinishly; today I sent you four small pages about the Yenisey and the *taiga*; later on I'll send you something about Lake Baikal, Transbaikal, and the Amur. Don't throw away these pages; I'll collect them and, using them as a score, will narrate what I don't know how to convey on paper. I have now transferred to the *Muraviev*, a steamer which, so they say, does not shake; I'll write—perhaps.

I am in love with the Amur; I would willingly live close to it for a couple of years. It is beautiful, and spacious, and free, and warm. Switzerland and France have never known such freedom. The least exile breathes more easily on the Amur than the foremost general in Russia. If you were to live here for a while you would write very many good things and fascinate the public, but I don't know how to do it.

From Irkutsk on one begins encountering Chinese, and here they are thicker than flies. A most good-natured lot, these. [...]

From Blagoveshchensk on you start coming upon the Japanese—or, more correctly, Japanese women. These are diminutive brunettes with oversized, ingenious coiffures, with beautiful torsos and, as it seemed to me, with short thighs. They dress beautifully. Predominant in their language is the sound of *ts* [...].

When I invited one of the Chinese to the buffet to treat him to vodka, before drinking he extended his glass to me, to the man behind the counter, to the waiters, and kept saying *"Kussai!"* [1] Chinese ceremonies. He did not gulp his drink, the way we do, but downed it in small swallows, with a bite of something after each swallow, and later, by way of thanking me, gave me several Chinese coins. An awfully polite folk. They dress as the poor do, yet beautifully; they eat with gusto, ceremoniously.

The Chinese will take the Amur away from us—that's beyond doubt. They won't take it away by themselves but it will be handed over to them by others—the English, for instance, who are lording it in China and building up a stronghold there. The people living along the Amur are a sarcastic lot; they all laugh because Russia is bothering about Bulgaria, which isn't worth a bent penny, but has forgotten about the Amur entirely. This isn't shrewd and it isn't wise. However, about politics later, when we see each other.

You telegraph me to return by way of America. I myself was thinking of that. But people are scaring me off: it will prove expensive. The money can be remitted not only to New York but even to Vladivostok, through the Irkutsk branch of the Bank of Siberia, where I was most amiably received. I haven't run out of money yet, even though I am spending it recklessly. I took a loss of 160 rubles on the sale of my carriage, and my fellow travelers, the lieutenants, borrowed more than a hundred rubles from me. It is hardly likely, however, that a remittance will be needed, after all. Should any need of it arise, I shall turn to you in good time. I am in perfect health. Judge for yourself: by now it is more than two months that I am spending both days and nights under the open sky. And what a lot of gymnastics I go through! * * *

I bathe in the Amur. To take a bath in the Amur, to talk and dine

---

[1] Oddly, the Chinese pronunciation of the Russian word for "eat."

with smugglers of gold—isn't this interesting? I run to board the *Yermak*. Good-bye. Thanks for the news of your family.

Your A. Chekhov

TO A. S. SUVORIN

Aboard the Baikal, *Tartar Strait,*
September 11, 1890

Greetings!

I am sailing through the Tartar Strait, from North Sakhalin to South Sakhalin. I am writing this letter without knowing when it will reach you. I am well, even though I have staring at me from every direction the green eyes of cholera, which has set a trap for me. In Vladivostok, Japan, Shanghai, Chefoo, Suez, and, it seems, even on the moon— cholera everywhere, everywhere quarantines and fear. Sakhalin is expecting cholera and vessels are quarantined. In short, it's a bad business. There are Europeans dying in Vladivostok; one of the deaths, incidentally, was that of a general's lady.

I lived on North Sakhalin for exactly two months. I was received with extraordinary courtesy by the local administration, even though Galkin [1] hadn't written a single word about me. Neither Galkin, nor Baroness Muskrat,[2] nor the other geniuses whom I was foolish enough to turn to for help, rendered me any help whatsoever; it became necessary to act at my own risk.

General Kononovich, the administrator of Sakhalin, is an educated and decent fellow. We hit the right note quickly enough and everything went well. I'll bring back certain papers showing you that the circumstances in which I was placed from the very beginning were most propitious. I saw *everything;* ergo, the question no longer consists of *what* I saw but *how* I saw it.

[1] Mikhail Nikolayevich Galkin-Vrasky, head of the Main Prison Board. On January 26, 1890, Chekhov petitioned him for assistance with his visit to Sakhalin for "scientific and literary purposes." The Sakhalin administration granted him the freedom of the island, but he was strictly forbidden to have any contact with political prisoners. Galkin, on his part, not only failed to give Chekhov the help for which he petitioned, but tried to interfere with the publication of his book on Sakhalin.

[2] In Russian, *Vykhukhol,* Chekhov's jesting reference to Baroness Ikskul von Hildeband.

I don't know what I'll wind up with, but what I have done is not a little. It would suffice for three dissertations. I got up daily at five in the morning, went to bed late, and all my days were passed under the severe pressure of the thought that there was still a great deal that I had not done; but now that I have finished with penal servitude I have the feeling that apparently I saw everything but failed to notice the elephant.

Incidentally, I had the patience to take a census of the entire population of Sakhalin. I made the circuit of all the settlements, stopped in at all the huts and talked with all and sundry; in taking the census I employed a card system, and I have already recorded about ten thousand convicts and settlers. In other words, there is not a solitary convict or settler who hasn't had a talk with me. I was particularly successful with a census of the children and am pinning quite a few hopes on it.

I had dinner with Landsberg,[3] I sat in ex-Baroness Hembruck's [4] kitchen. . . . I called on all the celebrities. I was present at a flogging, and for three or four nights afterward I dreamt of the executioner and the revolting "mare." [5] I had talks with those whose chains were forged to their wheelbarrows. Once, when I was having tea down in a mine, Borodavkin, a quondam merchant from St. Petersburg, deported here for arson, took a teaspoon out of his pocket and proffered it to me. But, in sum, my nerves were shattered and I have vowed not to take any more trips to Sakhalin.

I would write you more, if it weren't for a lady who is sitting in the cabin and laughing loudly and chattering away with no let-up. I haven't the strength to write. She has been behaving this way since last evening. . . . * * *

Tomorrow from afar I shall see Japan, the island Matsmai. It is now midnight. The sea is blacked out, a wind is blowing. I don't understand how the steamer can navigate through the pitch darkness in the wild, little-known waters of the Tartar strait.

When I recall that I am separated from the world by more than sixty-five hundred miles I am overcome by apathy. It seems to me that it will take a hundred years for me to get home. * * *

Your A. Chekhov

It's tedious.

[3] Karl Khristoforovich Landsberg, a convict, formerly an officer of the Guard.
[4] A convict.
[5] A board to which a man to be flogged was tied.

TO YE. YA. CHEKHOVA[1]

Korsakov, South Sakhalin,
October 6, 1890

Greetings, dear Mama!

I am writing you this letter almost on the eve of my return to Russia. From day to day we expect a steamer of the Volunteer Fleet, and hope that it will dock here not later than October 10.[2] I am mailing this letter to Japan, whence it will travel via Shanghai or America to you. I am staying at Korsakov, which has no telegraph or post office and where steamers call only once in a fortnight. Yesterday a steamer came and brought me a pile of letters and telegrams. * * * Strangely enough, it is rainy and cold where you are, but on Sakhalin ever since my arrival the weather has been clear and warm; some mornings may be chilly, with hoarfrost, and one of the mountains is bright with snow, but the earth is green, the trees have not shed their leaves, and everything in nature is like May at the dacha. That is Sakhalin for you!

* * * At midnight I heard the roar of a steamer. Everyone jumped out of bed: hurrah, the steamer is here! We dressed and went to the dock, carrying lanterns; we peered into the distance—no mistake, the lights of a steamer. The majority voted that it was the *Petersburg.* I was glad. We piled into a boat and made for the steamer. . . . We sailed and sailed and finally made out the dark hull of a steamer through the fog; one of us shouts hoarsely, "What's the steamer's name?" "The *Baikal*" is the response. Pah, confound it, what a disappointment! I was sick and tired of Sakhalin. For three months on end I have seen no one but convicts, and people who could talk of nothing but penal servitude, lashes, and convicts. A dismal life. You are eager to be off for Japan and from there to India.

I am well, except for attacks of shimmering in the visual field which I have frequently now, and each of which is followed by a severe head-ache. I had such an attack yesterday and today again, and that is why I have a headache while I am writing this letter, and an oppressive feeling in my whole body. The hemorrhoids too make themselves felt.

The Japanese consul, Kuze-San, is living in Korsakov with his two secretaries, my friends. Their manner of life is European. Today the

---

[1] Yevgeniya Yakovlevna Chekhova, Chekhov's mother.
[2] Chekhov left on October 13.

local administration paid them a formal visit for the purpose of presenting them with the decorations bestowed upon them, and I, too, was of the company, in spite of my headache, and had to drink champagne.

Staying in the south, I traveled three or four times from Korsakov to Nai-buchi, which is lashed by real ocean waves. Look at the map for the eastern shore of the southern section—and you will find miserable, poverty-stricken Nai-buchi. The waves cast ashore a boat with six shipwrecked American whalers; they are now staying here and stroll the streets with dignity; they are waiting for the *Petersburg* and will sail with me.

* * * I shall bring no furs; there are none in Sakhalin.

Keep well, may all of you be protected by

Your Anton

I shall bring presents to everyone.

No more cholera in Vladivostok and Japan.

TO A. S. SUVORIN

Moscow, December 9, 1890

Greetings, my precious one!

Hurrah! There, I am at home at last sitting at my desk, praying to my molting penates, and writing to you. I have a pleasant feeling now, as if I had never left home. I'm well, and happy to the marrow of my bones. Here is a report, of the briefest sort, for you. It wasn't two months I spent on Sakhalin, as you have it in you paper, but three, plus two days. My work was intensive; I made a full and detailed census of the entire population of the island and saw *everything*, except an execution. When we meet, I will show you a whole trunkful of odds and ends about the convicts, raw material that cost me plenty. I know a great deal now, but I came back with a wretched feeling. As long as I was staying in Sakhalin, I only felt a certain bitterness in my innards, as if from rancid butter; but now, in retrospect, the island seems to me a perfect hell. For two months I worked hard, without sparing myself in any way, while during the third month I began to feel the strain of the bitterness I spoke of, the tedium, and the thought that cholera was heading from Vladivostok to Sakhalin and that I was running the risk of having to winter in the penal colony. But, thank Heaven, the cholera let up, and on October 13 the steamer bore me away from Sakhalin.

I stopped at Vladivostok. About our Maritime Region and our east coast generally, with its fleets, its problems, its dreams of the Pacific, I shall say but one thing: it's all appalling poverty! Poverty, ignorance, and paltriness, such as can drive one to despair. One honest man to ninety-nine thieves, who desecrate the name of Russia. . . . We bypassed Japan, since there was cholera there. For that reason I did not buy any Japanese articles for you, and the 500 rubles you gave me for such purchases I spent upon my own needs, which, according to law, gives you the right to have me deported to Siberia. The first foreign port we touched was Hong Kong. The bay is wonderful; the sea traffic is such as I haven't seen the like of even in pictures; there are splendid roads, horse-drawn streetcars, a railway going up the mountain, museums, botanical gardens; no matter where you look you see the Englishmen's tender solicitude for the men in their service; there is even a club for sailors. I rode in jinrickshas, which is to say, in vehicles drawn by men; bought all sorts of rubbish from the Chinese; and waxed indignant as I listened to my Russian fellow travelers upbraiding the English for their exploitation of the natives. Yes, thought I, the Englishman exploits Chinese, sepoys, Hindus, but then he gives them roads, aqueducts, museums, Christianity; you too exploit, but what do you give?

When we left Hong Kong the steamer began to roll. It had no cargo and it swung through an angle of 38 degrees, so that we were afraid it would capsize. I am not subject to seasickness; this discovery was a pleasant surprise. On the way to Singapore we threw two corpses into the ocean. When you see a dead man, wrapped in canvas, go flying head over heels into the water, and when you recall that there are several miles to the bottom, a fear comes over you, and for some reason you imagine that you yourself will die and be cast into the sea. The horned cattle we were carrying sickened. Dr. Shcherbak and your humble servant having passed sentence upon them, they were slaughtered and thrown into the ocean.

Singapore I don't remember well because while I was touring it I felt sad for some reason and all but wept. Ceylon came next—the site of Paradise. Here I covered some seventy miles by rail and had my fill of palm groves and bronze-skinned women. When I have children, I'll say to them, not without pride: "You sons of bitches, in my time I had dalliance with a dark-eyed Hindu maiden—and where? In a coconut grove, on a moonlit night!" From Ceylon we sailed for thirteen days and nights without a single stop and grew dazed with boredom. I can stand heat well. The Red Sea is dismal. As I gazed on Mount Sinai I was deeply moved.

God's world is good. Only one thing isn't good: ourselves. How little there is in us of justice and humility, how poor is our conception of patriotism! The drunken, bedraggled, good-for-nothing of a husband loves his wife and children, but what's the good of that love? We, so the newspapers say, love our great country, but how is that love expressed? Instead of knowledge—inordinate brazenness and conceit, instead of work—laziness and swinishness; there is no justice; the concept of honor does not go beyond "the honor of the uniform," the uniform which is the everyday adornment of the prisoners' dock. What is needed is work; everything else can go to the devil. The main thing is to be just—the rest will be added unto us.

I am passionately eager to have a talk with you. My soul is on the boil. I want no one but you, for only with you can one talk. To hell with Pleshcheyev. To hell with actors.* * *

How glad I am that I managed without Galkin-Vrasky! He didn't write a single line in my behalf, and I appeared in Sakhalin as a complete stranger.* * *

I firmly embrace you and your entire family, but only a bow to The Denizen [1] and Burenin, both of whom should long since have been deported to Sakhalin.* * *

May Heaven protect you.

Your A. Chekhov

TO I. L. LEONTYEV-SHCHEGLOV

Moscow, December 10, 1890

Greetings, dear Jean!

* * * I am not going to describe my voyage to Sakhalin and my stay there, since a description, even the briefest, would turn out to be endlessly long in a letter. All I shall say is that I am up to my chin in satisfaction, that I have had my fill and am so enchanted that I wish

---

[1] Pen name of Aleksandr Aleksandrovich Dyakov, a contributor to *New Times.*

for nothing more and would not feel wronged if I were struck down by paralysis or carried off to the other world by dysentery. I can say *I have lived! That will do me!* I was both in Hell, as represented by Sakhalin, and in Paradise—i.e., on the island of Ceylon. What butterflies, midges, what flies, roaches!

The trip, especially across Siberia, resembles a severe, lingering illness. It is oppressive to ride, ride, and ride, but then how light and airy are the memories of everything experienced!

I spent three months and three days on Sakhalin. About the results of my Sakhalin labors I shall tell you when we see each other.* * *

I was well the whole time, but in the archipelago, where we had a storm, and the icy nor'easter was blowing, I caught cold; now I cough, blow my nose endlessly, and evenings have fever. Time for a bit of doctoring.

My people are radiant with joy.

Ah, my angel, if you only knew what darling beasties I have brought along from India! They are mongooses, each the size of a middle-aged kitten, very cheerful and sprightly beasties. Their good points are daring, curiosity, and attachment to man. They go forth to do battle against a rattlesnake and are always victorious, having no fear of anyone or anything; as for their curiosity, there isn't a single bundle or parcel in a room that they will leave unopened; on encountering anyone the first thing they do is to clamber into his pockets for a look: what's in there? When they are left by themselves in a room they *start crying.* Really, it's worth while coming here from Petersburg to take a look at them.* * *

Your A. Chekhov

TO A. S. SUVORIN

Moscow, December 17, 1890

My dear, I've just wired you that there will be a story.[1] It is a suitable one, but it's long and narrow, like a centipede; it has to be cleaned up and copied. I shall send it to you without fail, for I am a man who is not lazy and who works.

The figure of Pleshcheyev with his inheritance of two million seems to me comical. We'll see how he will take his millions in tow! What

1 "Gusev."

good are they to him? Three rubles each twenty-four hours will suffice for you to smoke cigars, swallow fifty sweet patties, and drink
seltzer.

I have brought back about ten thousand cards—statistics, and a lot
of papers of all sorts. I would like to be married now to some sensible
miss, so that I might have her help in putting all this trash to rights, for
it would go against my conscience to pile that drudgery on my sister,
since she has plenty of work as it is.

I am growing a little pot-belly [. . .]. After the tropics I caught cold:
I cough, run a high temperature of evenings, and my head aches.

Grigorovich was never a yard-keeper in a poor section of Petersburg
—that's why he holds the Kingdom of Heaven so cheap. He's mistaken.

To live forever, it seems to me, would be just as trying as going without sleep one's whole life.

If the sun sets just as beautifully in the Kingdom of Heaven as it does
in the Bay of Bengal, I herewith venture to assure you that the Kingdom
of Heaven is a very good thing. . . .

Tell me, when will they promote Leikin to the rank of Privy State
Councillor? This literary Huge White Sturgeon writes me, "I got rid of
sixteen pounds this summer," he writes about hen turkeys, about literature and cabbage. The tone of his letters is surprisingly equable, calm.

When I come I shall tell you everything from the beginning. How
wrong you were when you advised me not to go to Sakhalin! * * *
There are myriads of midges in my head now, no end of things, and I
have a world of plans. And what a moping, vacuous creature I would
be if I had sat at home. Before my trip *The Kreutzer Sonata* was an
event for me, and now I find it ridiculous and foolish. Perhaps the trip
matured me or else it made me lose my mind. The devil only knows.* * *

Your A. Chekhov

[1891]

TO M. P. CHEKHOVA

Petersburg, January 14, 1891

I am tired out, like a ballerina after five acts and eight tableaux. Banquets, letters which one is too lazy to answer, conversations and all sorts of bosh. Right now I've got to take a cab to Vasilievsky Island, to dine there, yet I am bored and I have to work. I will stay here for three days more and see: if this ballet continues I'll either go home or to Ivan in Sudoroga.[1]

I am enveloped by a dense atmosphere of ill will, extremely vague, and to me inexplicable. They are tendering me dinners and chanting banal dithyrambs to me and at the same time are all set to devour me. Why? The devil knows. If I had shot myself I would have afforded great pleasure to nine-tenths of my friends and admirers. And in what petty ways people express their pettiness! Burenin berates me in a *feuilleton,* even though it is not customary for newspapers to berate their own contributors; Maslov (Bezhetsky) no longer goes to dine with the Suvorins; Shcheglov tells all the gossip current about me, and so on. All this is dreadfully foolish and boring. They're not people, but some sort of mold.* * *

Your A. Chekhov

TO A. F. KONI[1]

Petersburg, January 26, 1891

Gracious sir, Anatoly Fyodorovich!

* * * My brief Sakhalin past appears to me so huge that when I want to talk about it, I do not know with what to begin, and every time it seems to me I don't say what should be said.

---

[1] Russian for "convulsion." A jesting reference to Sudogda, a small town where Ivan was teaching school.
[1] A. F. Koni (1844–1927), a jurist and public figure of the liberal persuasion, counted Turgenev, among other literary men, as a friend, and was himself a writer.

I shall try to describe in detail the condition of the Sakhalin children and adolescents. It is extraordinary. I saw hungry children, thirteen-year-old girls who were prostitutes, fifteen-year-old pregnant girls. Girls start in as prostitutes at the age of twelve, sometimes before menstruation. Church and school exist only on paper, it is the convict environment, the convict set-up that shape the children. Among other things I set down a conversation with a ten-year-old boy. I was taking a census in Upper Armudan, a village; the settlers are one and all beggars and have the reputation of desperate card players. I come into a hut; no one at home but a white-haired, hunched, barefoot little boy sitting on a bench. He is deep in thought about something. We start a conversation:

I: What's your father's name?

HE: Don't know.

I: How is that? You live with your father and don't know his name? Shame.

HE: He isn't my real father.

I: What do you mean: not real?

HE: He just lives with Ma.

I: Is your mother married or a widow?

HE: A widow. She came because of him.

I: Because— What does it mean: because of him?

HE: Killed.

I: You remember your father?

HE: No. I'm unlawful. I was born in Kara.[1]

One of my fellow passengers on the steamer that took me to Sakhalin was a prisoner in leg irons who had killed his wife. With him was his daughter, a child of about six. I noticed that when the father was going down from the upper deck to where a latrine was located he was followed by several soldiers, and his daughter. While the prisoner was in the latrine, a soldier carrying a rifle stood at the door with the little girl. When the prisoner, returning, walked up the stairs, she climbed behind him, holding on to his fetters. At night the little girl slept in a heap with the prisoners and the soldiers.

I remember that when I was in Sakhalin I attended a funeral. The wife of a settler who had gone to Nikolayevsk was being buried. At the freshly dug grave stood four convict porters—ex officio, I and a

---

[1] An infamous gold-mining district.

local official who wandered through the cemetery in the capacity of Hamlet and Horatio, a Circassian who had roomed with the deceased, also a woman convict: out of pity she had brought the dead woman's two children—one an infant, the other a four-year-old boy by the name of Alyosha. He wore a woman's jacket and blue pants with bright patches on the knees. Cold, damp, water in the grave, the convicts laugh. The sea is within sight. Alyosha peers into the grave with curiosity; he wants to wipe his chilled nose but the long sleeves of his jacket interfere. When the grave is filled up, I ask him, "Alyoshka, where is Ma?" He waves his hand like a landowner who has lost his money gambling, laughs, and says, "Shovelled under."

The convicts laugh; the Circassian turns to us and asks what he should do with the children—he is not obliged to feed them.

I did not find any contagious diseases in Sakhalin; there is very little inherited syphilis, but I saw blind children, filthy, covered with sores— all conditions caused by negligence.

Of course, I shall not settle the problem of the children. I do not know what should be done. It seems to me that charity and remnants of sums allotted to prisons and the like will not do. I believe it is wrong to rely on philanthropy, which in Russia is fortuitous, and on remnants which don't materialize. I prefer the State Treasury.* * *

Allow me to thank you for your cordiality and for your promise to visit me, and also to remain

> *Yours sincerely, respectfully, and devotedly,*
> *A. Chekhov*

TO M. P. CHEKHOVA

Petersburg, March 17, midnight, 1891

I have just seen the Italian actress, Duse, in Shakespeare's *Cleopatra.* I don't understand Italian, but she acted so well that it seemed to me that I understood every word. A remarkable actress. Never before have I seen anything like it. [I looked at this Duse and was mortified by the thought that we have to form our characters and taste on wooden actresses like N. and her kind, whom we call great because we haven't any better. Looking at Duse, I understood why one is so bored in a Russian theater.] [1]

Today I sent you a draft for 300 rubles. Did you get it?

After Duse it was pleasant to read the enclosed address.[2] My God, what a decline of taste and of the sense of justice! And this is the work of students, devil take their souls! Solovtzov [3] and Salvini both equally find "a fervent response in the heart of youth." A penny for all those hearts.

Tomorrow at half past one we leave for Warsaw.[4] Keep alive and well, all of you. Greetings to everyone, even to the mongoose, who does does not deserve a greeting.

I shall write.

Yours heartily,

A. Chekhov

TO M. P. CHEKHOVA

Vienna, March 20, 1891

Czechs, my friends!

I am writing from Vienna, where I arrived yesterday at four in the afternoon. The trip was pleasant. From Warsaw to Vienna I traveled like a railway Nana, in a luxurious coach of the "International Society of Sleeping Cars": beds, mirrors, huge windows, carpets, etc.

Oh, Tunguses, my friends, if you knew how wonderful Vienna is! It cannot be compared to any of the cities I have seen in my whole life— wide streets, exquisitely paved, a multitude of boulevards and plazas, all the houses six and seven stories high, and stores—they are not stores but sheer vertigo, reveries! Billions of ties alone in the windows! What amazing articles made of bronze, porcelain, leather! Enormous

---

[1] This bracketed passage appears only in the prerevolutionary collection of Chekhov's letters edited by his sister. It is omitted from the Soviet *Complete Chekhov*. No part of the letter appears in the Soviet *Selected Letters*.

[2] The address by the students of the Kharkov Technological Institute was presented to N. N. Solovtzov on the occasion of his benefit. It concludes, "May God grant us more talents like yours, and Russian drama will long find a fervent response in the hearts of youth."

[3] Nikolay Nikolayevich Solovtzov, the manager of a Kiev theater, formerly an actor in Moscow.

[4] Chekhov traveled abroad in the company of Suvorin and Suvorin's son Aleksey.

churches, yet they do not oppress you by their bulk, but caress the eyes because they seem to be woven of lace. The Cathedral of St. Stephen and the *Votivkirche* are especially admirable. They are not edifices but tea biscuits. The Parliament, the City Hall, the University, are magnificent. Everything is magnificent, and only today and yesterday I understood fully that architecture is really an art. And here art is offered not piecemeal, as with us, but it stretches in belts for miles. Many monuments. In every side street, without fail, a bookshop. In their windows you notice Russian books too, but alas, they are not by Albov [1] or Barantzevich or Chekhov, but by all kinds of anonymous authors writing and printing abroad. I saw Renan and *The Secrets of the Winter Palace*, etc. Oddly enough, here everyone may read and say whatever he pleases.

Know, ye natives, what manner of cabs are here, deuce take them. No buggies, but only brand-new, pretty carriages drawn by one or, more frequently, two horses. The horses are wonderful. On the box sit dandies in short coats and top hats, reading newspapers. Civility and courtesy.

Dinners are good. There is no vodka, they drink beer and tolerable wine. One thing is objectionable: they charge for bread. Before handing you the check they ask, *"Wieviel Brödchen?"* i.e. how many rolls did you gobble? And they charge for each roll.

The women are beautiful and elegant. And in general everything is deucedly elegant.

I haven't completely forgotten the German language. I understand and make myself understood.* * *

I miss home and all of you, and furthermore I feel guilty at having left you again. But it doesn't matter! I shall return and stay home a whole year without a break. A bow to all, all! * * *

Every good wish. Do not forget me, sinner that I am. I embrace, bless, and bow to each of you, and remain

Your loving A. Chekhov

---

[1] Mikhail Nilovich Albov (1851–1911), a writer of fiction, co-editor of *The Northern Herald*.

I am now in Venice, where I arrived from Vienna day before yesterday. One thing I can tell you—in all my life I have never seen any cities more remarkable than Venice. It is utter enchantment, brilliance, joy of life. In lieu of streets and alleys, canals; in lieu of cabbies, gondolas; the architecture is amazing, and there isn't the least spot that would fail to arouse historic or artistic interest. You float along in a gondola and see the palazzos of the doges, the house where Desdemona lived, the houses of famous artists, houses of worship. And in these houses of worship the sculpture and painting are such as we have never dreamed of even in our dreams. In a word: enchantment.

All day, from morning to evening, I loll in a gondola and float through the streets or ramble over the famous Piazza of St. Mark. This piazza is as even and clean as a parquet floor. Here one finds the Cathedral of St. Mark (something which is beyond description), the Palazzo of the Doges, and certain edifices which are to my sensations what scored notes are to singers. I sense the amazing beauty and find it delectable.

And in the evening! Oh Lord, my God! In the evening, being unaccustomed to it all, you could die. You are riding in a gondola—warmth, stillness, stars. There are no horses in Venice, and so it's as quiet here as in an open field. Gondolas darting all around. . . . Here's a gondola riding along, with little lanterns hung all over it. Seated in it are a double bass, violins, a guitar, a mandolin, and a cornet, two or three ladies, several men—and you hear singing and instruments. They sing operatic arias. What voices! I leave them a little behind, and there is another boatful of singers, and then another and, right up to midnight there hovers in the air a medley of tenors, violins, and all sorts of sounds that take hold of your soul.

Merezhkovsky, whom I met here, has lost his mind with ecstasy. For a Russian, poor and humiliated, it is not hard to lose his mind here, in a world of beauty, richness, and freedom. You long to remain here forever and, when you stand in a church and listen to the organ, you long to embrace Catholicism.

The mausoleums of Canova and Titian are magnificent. Here great artists are buried in churches, as kings are; here art is not despised, as with us: the churches shelter statues and paintings, no matter how nude they are.* * *

However, stay well. I wish you all the best. Should you ever happen to be in Venice, it will be the best thing in your life. You ought to see the glass industry here! Your bottles, by comparison with those produced here, are so hideous that the mere thought of them makes me feel queasy.

I'll be writing you again but, for the present, good-bye.

Your A. Chekhov

TO M. P. CHEKHOVA

Venice, March 25, 1891

Ravishing, blue-eyed Venice sends greetings to all of you. Ah, Signori e Signorine, what a wondrous city this Venice is! Picture to yourselves a city made up of houses and churches such as you have never seen: an inebriating architecture in which everything is as graceful, light, as the birdlike gondola. Such houses and churches can be built only by men possessing enormous artistic and musical taste and endowed with a leonine temperament. Now imagine that on the streets and in the lanes instead of pavement there is water; picture a city in all of which there is not a single horse, imagine that instead of cabbies you are seeing gondoliers on their astonishing boats, light, dainty, beaky birds which barely touch the water and twitch at the least wave. And everything, from sky to earth, is inundated by sun.

There are streets as wide as Nevsky Prospekt, and there are some where, by spreading your arms, the whole street can be blocked. The center of the city is the Piazza of St. Mark with its famous Cathedral named after the same saint. The Cathedral is magnificent, especially from the outside. Alongside it is the Palazzo of the Doges, where Othello had his explanation with the Doge and the Senators.

Generally speaking, there isn't the least spot which fails to stir up recollections or to move you. The small house where Desdemona lived, for instance, creates an impression that is difficult to get rid of.

The best time in Venice is the evening. First of all, there are the stars; secondly, the long canals, in which the stars and lights are reflected; thirdly, gondolas, gondolas, and gondolas—when it is dark they seem alive. Fourthly, you want to weep, because you can hear music and superb singing coming from every side. Here's a gondola floating by, with little multicolored lanterns hanging all over it; there is light enough to make out a double bass, a guitar, a mandolin, a violin. —Here's just such another gondola—with men and women singing— and how they sing! Grand opera, absolutely.

Fifthly, the weather is warm. . . .

In short, he who doesn't go to Venice is a fool. Living here is cheap. Room and board come to 18 francs a week per person (i.e., 6 rubles and, by the month, 25 rubles); a gondolier charges 1 franc (i.e., 30 copecks) per hour. Admission to museums, the Academy, and so on, is free. Ten times cheaper than the Crimea, and yet the Crimea stacks up against Venice as a cuttlefish against a whale.

I am afraid Papasha is angry at me because I did not say good-bye to him. I ask his forgiveness.

What glass they have here, what mirrors! Why am I not a millionaire? * * *

Next year we will all take a country house in Venice for the summer.

There is a booming in the air because of the pealing of churchbells. My Tungus friends, let us embrace Catholicism! If you but knew how splendid the organs in the churches are, what sculpture there is here, what little Italian lasses there are, on their knees with prayer books!

However, stay well, all of you, and don't forget me, great sinner that I am.* * *

Addio.

Your A. Chekhov

TO M. V. KISELEVA

Rome, April 1, 1891

The Pope of Rome has entrusted me with congratulations for you on your saint's day and with wishes that you may have just as many rubles as he has rooms—and of rooms he has eleven thousand! Rambling through the Vatican I withered away with fatigue, and when I returned to my room it seemed to me that my legs were made of cotton wool.

I dine at a *table d'hôte*. Just imagine: sitting opposite me are two darling Dutch girls; one of them looks like Pushkin's Tatyana, and the other like Tatyana's sister Olga. I keep looking at them throughout dinner and in my imagination I see a tidy little white house with a turret, excellent butter, superb Holland cheese, Holland herrings, a benignly visaged pastor, a sedate teacher—and I want to marry a darling Dutch girl, and I want to be depicted on a serving tray together with her near the tidy little house.

I have seen everything and clambered everywhere I was bidden to clamber. If they gave me anything to sniff, I sniffed. But so far all I feel is fatigue and a hunger for cabbage soup with buckwheat grits. Venice had cast its spell over me, had made me lose my mind, but when I left it Baedeker and inclement weather beset me.* * *

Neckties are astonishingly cheap here. Dreadfully cheap, so that even I, likely as not, may take to eating them. Two for a franc.

Tomorrow I am off to Naples. Wish that I may chance upon a beautiful Russian lady—a widow or a divorcée, if possible.

The guidebooks say that a romance is a *sine qua non* in traveling through Italy. Oh, well, devil take it, I agree to everything—if there has to be a romance, let there be a romance!

Do not forget the great sinner, yours with sincere devotion and respect,

A. Chekhov

My greetings to messieurs the starlings.

TO M. P. CHEKHOV

Nice, April 15, 1891

Yesterday a postcard from Papasha arrived, forwarded from Rome; the said postcard informed me that a house for the summer has already been taken.[1] Well, glory be to God for that. Am very glad for the sake of all of you and for my own. Move in, with God's help, little by little. Subscribe for *Russian Bulletins* and *News of the Day*, and notify *New Times* and *Splinters* about the change of address; as for *The Historical Herald* and *The Northern Herald*, I'll subscribe for them myself.

We are living in Nice, at the seashore. The sun is shining, it is warm, greenery everywhere, the air is fragrant, but there's wind. An hour's ride from Nice is famous Monaco, and there you will find a spot called Monte Carlo, where they play roulette. Imagine the assembly halls of

---

[1] Near the town of Aleksin, Tula province.

the nobility, beautiful, high-ceilinged, but more spacious. There are huge tables in these halls; on the tables is the equipment for roulette, a game I'll describe for you when I get back. Day before yesterday I rode over there—and lost. Gaming exerts a horrible fascination. After losing I, along with Suvorin *fils*, fell to thinking, and I thought up a system according to which one is absolutely bound to win. Yesterday we rode over there, each of us taking along 500 francs; on the first stake I won a couple of gold pieces, then more and more; my vest pockets were weighed down with gold; I handled French coins dated as early as 1808, and coins from Belgium, Italy, Greece, Austria. —Never before did I see so much gold and silver. I began to play at five, and by ten I didn't have a franc in my pocket and I had only one thing left: satisfaction at the thought that I had already bought a return ticket to Nice. There you are, my dear sirs! You will say, of course, "What a vile thing to do! We're struggling with poverty, yet he's playing roulette over there." You are perfectly right, and I give you permission to cut my throat. But, personally, I am very well satisfied with myself. At least I am now in a position to tell my grandsons that I played roulette and that I am familiar with the feeling aroused by this game.

Near the Casino with its roulette there is another sort of roulette— the restaurants. They fleece you frightfully and feed you magnificently. There isn't a serving that isn't a complete composition before which one must genuflect in reverence, yet by no means venture to eat it. Every morsel is over-rich with artichokes, truffles, all kinds of nightingale tongues. —And, O Lord my God, how utterly contemptible and abominable this life is, with its artichokes, palms, fragrance of oranges! I love luxury and riches, but the impression made on me by the roulette luxury of this place is that of a luxurious water closet. There is a somewhat hovering in the air which, you feel, insults your decency, which vulgarizes nature, the sound of the sea, the moon.

Yesterday I attended a Sunday service in the local Russian church. Peculiarities: in lieu of willow wands, palm fronds; in lieu of choirboys, ladies, because of which the singing takes on an operatic shade; one puts a foreign coin in the plate; the churchwarden and guards speak French; and so on. Bortnyansky's Cherubic Canticle Number 7 and a simple paternoster were sung magnificently.

Venice, of all the places I have been to so far, has left me with the most radiant recollection. Rome, in general, resembles Kharkov, while Naples is filthy. As for the sea, it does not ravish me, since I became fed up with it as far back as November and December. What the devil, it turns out that I have been traveling without a break for a whole year. I had hardly come back from Sakhalin than I went off to Petersburg, then I went to Petersburg again and on to Italy.

If I don't get back in time for Easter, just remember me in your prayers when you break your fast, and accept my absentee felicitation and assurance that on Easter eve, away from you, I shall be feeling dreadfully low.

Are you saving the newspapers?

Regards to everybody: Aleksey and his aunt, Semasha, handsome Levitan, golden-curled Likisha, our old cook, and everybody in general. There, stay well, all of you; may Heaven guard you. I have the honor to report myself and to remain wearily yours,

Antonio

Regards to Olga Petrovna.[2]

TO M. P. CHEKHOVA

Paris, April 21, 1891

Today is Easter. And so, Christ is risen. This is the first Easter I am spending away from home. I arrived in Paris Friday morning and set out for the Exposition at once. Yes, the Eiffel Tower is very, very high. The rest of the Exposition's structures I saw only from the outside, since the cavalry was being kept inside, in full readiness against anticipated disorders.[1] Demonstrations were expected on Friday. The common people were surging through the streets, yelling, whistling, wrought up, and the police kept dispersing them. All it takes to disperse a mob here is about ten policemen. The police makes a concerted onslaught and the crowd runs as if it had gone mad. In one of these onslaughts I, too, was honored: a policeman grabbed hold of my shoulder blade and started shoving me ahead of him.

Massive movement. Streets swarming and seething. Not a street but is Terek, the turbulent river. Noise, hubbub. The sidewalks are taken up with little tables, at the little tables are Frenchmen who, out in the street, feel right at home. A superb lot. However, there's no describing Paris; I'll put off its description until my homecoming.

2 Kundasova.
1 In connection with May Day.

I attended matins at the embassy church.

The retired diplomat Tatishchev [2] has latched on to us. Going every-where with us as a sort of aide-de-camp is the Parisian correspondent I. Yakovlev-Pavlovsky,[3] who at one time lived with us together with the Fronsteins in the Moiseyevsky house. Pleshcheyev is here together with his daughters and his son. Plenty of company, in short. A whole Russian colony.

Tomorrow, or the day after, we are leaving for Russia. I'll be in Moscow Friday or Saturday. I'll be taking the Smolensk route home, and so, should you want to meet me, come to the Smolensk station.

If they won't let me leave here on Tuesday, or even on Wednesday, I'll nevertheless be back in Moscow no later than Monday, and I there-fore ask Ivan not to leave but to wait.

I'm afraid you have no money.

Misha, for the salvation of your soul, get my pince-nez fixed. Put in lenses of the same strength as yours. Without glasses I am simply a martyr. I was at the Salon exhibition, and did not see half the paintings, because of nearsightedness. And, incidentally, Russian painters take their art much more seriously than the French do. By comparison with the landscape painters here, whose work I saw yesterday, Levitan is king.

This is the last letter. Good-bye. I started out with an empty trunk but shall return with a full one. Each one of you will be rewarded ac-cording to your deserts.

Wishing you good health,

Your A. Chekhov

TO A. S. SUVORIN

Aleksin, May 10, 1891

Your letter received. *Merci.* The numeral 1 is used as a signature by Dedlov-Kign, man of letters and an interesting traveler, whom I know by hearsay but have not read. Yes, you're right—my soul needs balm. I would now read with pleasure, and even joy, something serious not only about myself but in general. I am longing for serious reading, and

[2] Sergey Spiridonovich Tatishchev (1846–1906), was a contributor to *New Times.*
[3] I. Yakovlev was the pen name of Ivan Yakovlevich Pavlovsky, who was associated with *New Times.* As a high-school student he had boarded with the Chekhovs in Taganrog.

all Russian criticism of late does not nurture but merely irritates me. I would read with rapture something new about Pushkin or Tolstoy—it would be balm for my idle mind—.

I, too, am pining for Venice and Florence and would be ready to climb Vesuvius once more; Bologna, on the other hand, has tarnished and been effaced from my memory; and as far as Nice and Paris are concerned, when I recall them "I read and loathe the record of the years. . . ." [1] * * *

On Monday, Tuesday, and Wednesday I write the Sakhalin book; on the other days, except Sunday, I am writing a novel and, on Sundays, short short stories. I am working with a will but, alas, I have a numerous family and I, the writing member, am like unto a lobster stuck in a creel with other lobsters: sort of cramped. The weather all these days remains magnificent; the spot where the summer villa is located is dry and wholesome, plentifully wooded. Lots of fish and lobster in the Oka. I can see railway trains and steamers. On the whole, if it weren't for the crowding I would be very very deeply contented. When will you be in Moscow? Write me, please. The French Exposition won't be to your liking—prepare yourself for that. But the Oka will be to your liking when, at five in the morning, at Serpuhov, we board a mangy tub of a steamer and sail off to Kaluga.

I have no intention of getting married. I would now wish to be a little bald-headed ancient, seated at a huge desk in a fine study.

Stay well and be at peace. A low bow to all your people. Write me, please.

Your A. Chekhov

TO A. S. SUVORIN

Bogimovo,[1] May 20, 1891

I have moved to other summer quarters. What open space! The second floor of a large mansion is at my disposal. The rooms are huge, two of them are the size of your drawing room, even larger; one has columns; there is a gallery for musicians. When we were placing our furniture we were worn out by the unaccustomed pacing of such enormous

---

[1] A line from Pushkin's "Remembrance."

[1] After only a week or two at Aleksin the Chekhovs left for their new summer quarters, a few miles away.

rooms. A beautiful park, a pond, a stream with a mill, a boat—the details of all this are simply enchanting.* * *

Crucians take the bait readily from a fishing rod. Yesterday I forgot all my sorrows; now sitting beside the pond and catching crucians, now choosing a corner near the abandoned mill and catching perch. The details of everyday life are also engaging.

The last two manifestoes—concerning the Siberian railway and the transported convicts—were very much to my liking. The Siberian railway is called a national project and the tone of the manifesto guarantees its expeditious completion; as for the convicts who will have served such and such terms as compulsory settlers and deported peasants, they are permitted to return to Russia, but without the right to live in the province of either capital. The newspapers let this pass without paying any attention, and yet it is something unprecedented in Russia—this is a serious step toward the abolition of life-term penalties which for so long have weighed on the social conscience as unjust and in the highest degree cruel.* * *

Be well.

Your Chekhov

TO A. S. SUVORIN

Bogimovo, May 27, 1891, 4 A.M.

* * * You write that I am a man of stuccoed brick, and I don't contribute anything to the paper. But enter into my situation. My literary activity is in such a state of muddle and disorder that the devil himself would break a leg there. I did make a start on a novella—but the trip abroad intervened; there is no time to go on with it now—I've got Sakhalin on my neck. I would get down to writing bagatelles and have already tried to do so, but the thought that I must get rid of Sakhalin by fall paralyzes any capability. Wait, dear man, I will shortly throw the penal servitude off my back and will be wholly yours, from head to heels. I give you my word of honor that the Sakhalin book will be in the printer's hands this fall, since I am already writing and writing it, cross my heart, and if you don't believe me, I can send you material proofs. Thanks to my getting up with the chickens, no one hinders me

from working and my task is proceeding under a full head of steam even though it is sticky, pernickety work, like a sheepskin that's not worth dressing: for the sake of a single mangy line of some sort or other, one is forced to rummage among papers for a full hour and reread all kinds of wearisome stuff. To write about climate or to compile from fragmentary notes an historico-critical piece on a penal colony—my God, what a bore this is! * * *

TO L. S. MIZINOVA[1]

Bogimovo, June 12, 1891

Bewitching, astounding Lika!

Having become infatuated with that Circassian, Levitan, you have absolutely forgotten about having given brother Ivan a promise to come to us on June 1, and are not answering my sister's letters at all. I, too, wrote to you in Moscow, inviting you, but my letter also remained the voice of one crying in the wilderness. But even if high society receives you in the drawing room of Malkiel the tadpole,[2] you are badly brought up just the same and I do not regret having chastised you with a horsewhip on one occasion. Do understand that the daily expectation of your arrival not only makes us languish but puts us to expense. Ordinarily, at dinner, all we have is yesterday's soup, but when we are expecting guests we also prepare a roast of boiled beef, which we buy from the female cooks round about.

We have a magnificent garden, shaded alleys, discreet nooks, a river, a mill, a boat, moonlit nights, nightingales, tom-turkeys. —In the river and the pond there are very clever frogs. We often go out for strolls, during which I close my eyes and bend my right arm into a pretzel, making believe that you are walking arm in arm with me.* * *

Here is my signature [drawing of a heart pierced by an arrow].* * *

[1] Lidiya Stakhiyevna Mizinova (1870–1937), familiarly addressed as Lika, a close friend of Chekhov's, if not more, and the object of his persistent teasing. On completing her secondary education she taught at the same high school for girls as did Chekhov's sister. Later she attended a dramatic school, studied painting, and was sent abroad to prepare for an operatic career, which she failed to achieve. For a while she was associated with the Moscow Art Theater but left the stage to marry an actor. Her affair with I. N. Potapenko is partially reflected in *The Sea Gull.*
[2] A member of a Moscow family with which the Chekhovs were acquainted.

TO A. S. SUVORIN

Bogimovo, July 24, 1891

* * * Thank you for the 5-copeck raise. Alas, it won't improve my affairs. In order to accumulate capital, as you write, and to emerge out of the whirlpool of petty fears and worries about pennies, only one way has been left me—the immoral. To marry a rich woman or to claim *Anna Karenina* as a work of mine. And since this is impossible I have given up my affairs as a bad job and have left it to them to follow whatever course may best suit them.* * *

TO A. S. SUVORIN

Bogimovo, August 18, 1891

At last I have finished my long, tiresome story [1] and am sending it to you at Feodosiya by registered mail. Read it, please. It is too long for a newspaper, and does not lend itself to the possibility of being divided into installments. However, you know best. If you postpone printing it until autumn then I shall read proof in Moscow. The story will not suffer by it, but *New Times* will gain financially, for my proofreading always reduces the number of lines.

The story runs to more than 4 printed sheets. This is dreadful. I knocked myself out, and I was dragging the end along just as if it were a wagon train on a miry night in autumn, at a walk, with stops: that's why I was late. Half the honorarium, if you don't reject the story, will go to pay my indebtedness to your newspaper, while the other half will go to fill my belly. If you put off printing the story until autumn, telegraph your esteemed office to send me 300 rubles as soon as possible against the story, for as things are the wind is whistling through my pockets and I haven't the wherewithal for going away. The money is to be sent only on the condition, of course, that the work is acceptable, etc.

Alas, I shan't come to see you. I am saying this in a sepulchral voice. I haven't the wherewithal for going away, but I don't want to contract any new debts.* * *

Your A. Chekhov

---

[1] *The Duel*, Chekhov's only novel.

Bogimovo, August 18, 1891

Today, together with the story, I sent you a letter, and here's another for you, in answer to the one from you just received. In speaking of Nikolay and the doctor who was treating him you stress that "all this is done without love, without any sacrifice of little personal conveniences." You are right in saying this about people in general, but what would you have the physicians do? What if, in reality, the "gut burst," as your children's nurse put it—what is one to do then, even if one should feel the urge to give up one's life for the sick man? Usually, when those in the household, the relatives and servants, are taking "all measures" and are straining every nerve, the doctor sits there and looks like a fool, discouraged, dismally ashamed of himself and his science and trying to preserve outward composure. . . . Physicians go through loathsome days and hours—may God withhold this from every man. True enough, ignoramuses and cads are no rarity among physicians, even as among writers, engineers, and people in general, but it is only physicians who go through the loathsome hours and days which I am speaking of, and for that, in all conscience, much must be forgiven them.

As for the opinion that "man is not sufficiently clubbed over the head —he deserves being lashed," I would be ready to agree with you, perhaps, if you would demonstrate that man has up to the present been taking delight in a state of utter bliss and that he has not been beaten and clubbed into stupor by fate. * * *

A country wife was carting rye and tumbled head first off the cart. Smashed herself dreadfully: concussion of the brain, strain of the neck tendons, vomiting, great pain, and so on. They brought her to me. Moans, ohs and ahs, she implores God for death, yet her eyes are fixed on the peasant who brought her and she mumbles, "Have done with the lentils, Kyrilla, thresh them later on, but get to threshing oats now." I tell her that talk about oats could be put off, for, really, there is now something of a more serious nature to talk over, but she tells me, "He's sure got very good oats!" A bustling, greedy country wife. Such find it easy to die.

I shall leave for Moscow on September 5. I have to look for new quarters.

All the best!   *Your A. Chekhov*

Bogimovo, August 30, 1891

The story is to your liking—well, glory be to God. Of late I have become devilishly overanxious. It constantly seems to me that the trousers I have on are atrocious, and that I'm not writing the way I should, and that I'm not giving the right powders to patients. Must be a psychosis, this.* * *

Sakhalin is coming along. There are times when I want to sit over it for three or five years and work on it frantically, yet at times, during the hours of overanxiety, I would be ready to spit on it. And yet, by God, it would be a good thing to give up three years to it! Much of what I would write would be nonsense, for I am not a specialist, but, really, I shall write something sensible. And the virtue of *Sakhalin* is that if it survives me by a hundred years it would be a literary source and an aid to all those who are engaged and interested in penology.

You are right, Your Excellency: I have done a lot this summer. If there were one more such summer I would, like as not, write a novel and buy me an estate. It's no joke: I not only filled the larder but actually paid off a thousand rubles on what I owe. When I come to Moscow I'll take 150 or 200 rubles for my *Boor* from the Society—and that is how God provides for us of the gaily whistling brotherhood.* * *

Please pass the word to your son that I envy him. And I envy you as well. And not because the women have left you but because you are bathing in the sea and staying in a warm house. It's cold in my barn of a room. I would now like to have rugs, an open fireplace, bronzes, and learned discourses. Alas, I shall never be a Tolstoyan! In women what I like above all is beauty, and in the history of humanity, culture, which finds its expression in rugs, carriages on springs, and keenness of thought. Ah, if one but could turn as quickly as possible into a little old man and sit at a huge desk! * * *

TO A. S. SUVORIN

Moscow, September 8, 1891

* * * Death gleans men one after another. It knows its business. Write a play: an old chemist has invented an elixir of immortality—take it in dosages of fifteen drops and you will live forever; however, the

chemist smashed the vial with the elixir, out of dread that such wretches as he and his wife would go on living forever. Tolstoy denies immortality to mankind, but, my God, how much of the personal is involved here! Day before yesterday I read his Epilogue.[1] Kill me, if you will, but it is more stupid and stifling than *Letters to a Governor's Lady*,[2] which I despise. Devil take the philosophy of the great ones of this earth! All great sages are as despotic as generals, and as rude and indelicate as generals, because they feel certain of their impunity. Diogenes spat at beards, knowing that he would not suffer for it: Tolstoy reviles doctors as blackguards and reveals his ignorance of great issues because he is that same Diogenes whom you are not going to haul off to the police station and whom you are not going to revile in the newspaper. And so, to the devil with the philosophy of the great ones of this earth! All of that philosophy with its holy simpleton epilogues and letters to a Governor's lady is not worth one little filly from "Strider." [3]

A bow to my schoolmate Aleksey Petrovich,[4] and wish him good health, a playful mood, and seductive dreams. May he dream of a naked Spanish girl with a guitar.* * *

Your A. Chekhov

TO YE. M. SHAVROVA[1]

Moscow, September 16, 1891

We old bachelors smell like dogs? So be it, but as for physicians who specialize in women's diseases having the souls of libertines and cynics, do allow me to dispute the point. Gynecologists have to deal with fierce prose, such as you have never even dreamed of and to which, perhaps, if you knew it, you would attribute, with that ferocity which is natural to your imagination, an odor worse than a dog's. He who constantly sails the seas loves dry land; he who is always immersed in prose longs passionately for poetry. All gynecologists are idealists. Your doctor reads poems: your intuition was a true prompter; I would add that he

[1] The epilogue to *The Kreutzer Sonata.*
[2] Letters to the wife of the Kaluga Provincial Governor in *Selected Passages from Correspondence with Friends*, by Gogol.
[3] "Strider, the Story of a Horse," by Tolstoy.
[4] A. P. Kolomnin, Suvorin's son-in-law, a lawyer.
[1] Yelena Mikhailovna Shavrova (1874–1937), a young writer of short stories whom Chekhov advised and encouraged, and whose work he helped to place.

is a great liberal, a bit of a mystic, and dreams of a wife *à la* Nekrasov's Russian woman. The well-known Snegirev [2] never mentions "the Russian woman" otherwise than catching his breath. Another gynecologist I know is enamored of a mysterious veiled lady whom he had beheld from afar. A third attends all first nights—and afterward, near the coat room, loudly scolds playwrights, asserting that they are obligated to depict none but ideal women, and so on.

Also, you have overlooked the fact that a foolish fellow or a mediocrity cannot be a good gynecologist. The mind, even a seminarist's mind, shines more brightly than a bald spot, yet you noticed and stressed a bald spot but jettisoned the mind. You also noticed and stressed that a corpulent man—brrr!—exudes some sort of grease, but have completely overlooked his being a scientist—i.e., that for several years he has been thinking and doing something which has placed him above millions of men, above all the Verochkas and Greek women in Taganrog, above all sorts of banquets and wines.[3] Noah had three sons: Shem, Ham and (I think) Aphet. The only thing Ham noticed was that his father was a sot but completely overlooked that Noah was a genius, that he had built the ark and saved the world. Those who write are not under any obligation to ape Ham. Put that in your pipe and smoke it. I dare not request you to love one who is a gynecologist and a scientist, but I do dare to remind you of justice, which is more precious to the objective writer than the air he breathes.* * *

TO A. S. SUVORIN

Moscow, October 19, 1891

How magnificent that "Little Letter" [1] of yours turned out to be! Written ardently and beautifully, and the thoughts are sound. To hold forth now about laziness, drunkenness, and so on is as bizarre and tactless as to try to improve the mind of a man who is vomiting or who is suffering from typhus. Like power in any shape, a full stomach always holds a dose of insolence, and this dose expresses itself first of all in the well-fed lecturing the starving. If during a grave sorrow an offer of consolation

[2] Vladimir Fyodorovich Snegirev, an eminent gynecologist.
[3] References to a story by the addressee.
[1] The "Little Letters" were a special department of *New Times* conducted by Suvorin. In this one he inveighs against General N. M. Baranov, Governor of the Nizhny Novgorod province, for accusing the starving peasants of laziness.

is disgusting, then what would be the effect of moralizing to the starving, and how stupid and offensive moralizing must seem. According to the well-fed, a man who is 15 rubles in arrears is already a good-for-nothing, a fellow who may not drink; and have they figured out the arrears of States, of prime ministers, marshals of the nobility, and bishops, all taken together? And how deep in debt are the Guards, those select troops? Only tailors know.

Now, sir, here is my itinerary. First I shall get off my neck the piece for *The Collection*.[2] It is a sizable story, running to 1 or 2 sheets, the kind that is boring and hard to write, without a beginning or an end; I'll get it off—and deuce take it. Then I'll make my way to General Baranov's province. I'll have to sail up the Volga and travel by carriage. Then I shall pay you a visit. I'd rather not go to Zaraysk.[3] In winter I don't know how to judge estates. What is snowed under and surrounded by naked trees I simply don't understand and am prejudiced against.

You have directed the office to send me 400 rubles? *Vivat dominus Suvorin!* So on account of *The Duel* I have received 900 rubles from your firm.[4] Altogether you owe me about 1400 rubles for *The Duel*. Therefore 500 will go to the payment of my debt to you. Thank you for that. By spring I have to discharge my entire debt, or else I shall pine away, for with spring I want to start taking advances again in all the editorial offices. I'll take the money and be off to Java.

* * * Oh, friends, how boring it is! If I am a physician, I need patients and a hospital; if I am a man of letters, I have to live among people, not on Malaya Dmitrovka Street, with a mongoose. I need at least a bit of social and political life, at least a tiny bit, and this life within four walls, without Nature, without human beings, without a fatherland, without health and appetite—this is not life, but some sort of [...] and nothing else.

For the sake of all the perch and pike that you will catch on your Zaraysk estate, I beg you to publish the English humorist Bernard.[5] Have it set in print.

A low obeisance to your family. Keep well for a thousand years.

Your A. Chekhov

[2] A publication to be sold for the benefit of the Famine Fund. What Chekhov actually contributed was not a story but a chapter from his book on Sakhalin.
[3] Suvorin was planning to buy an estate in that neighborhood.
[4] Suvorin had bought the novel for serialization in *New Times*.
[5] Lazare Bernard, the editor of *Punch*.

TO A. S. SUVORIN

Moscow, October 25, 1891

* * * Run *The Duel* not in two installments a week but just one. Running two installments infringes on a long-established custom of the newspaper and makes it look as if I were taking one day a week from others, and yet it's all the same to me and to my story if it is run in one installment or two installments a week.

The members of the literary brotherhood in Petersburg don't talk of anything but the impurity of my motives. Just now I received the pleasant news that I am marrying the rich Sibiryakova. On the whole I receive lots of good news.

I wake up every night and read *War and Peace*. One reads it with such interest and such naïve wonder as if one had never read it before. Remarkably well done. But I dislike the passages in which Napoleon appears. As soon as Napoleon comes on, straining and all sorts of tricks instantly begin, in order to prove that he was more stupid than he actually was. All that is done and said by Pierre, Prince Andrey, or that utterly insignificant Rostov—all that is well done, intelligent, natural and touching; but all that Napoleon thinks and does is not natural, not intelligent, inflated and of no significance whatsoever. When I'll be living somewhere in the provinces (something which I now am dreaming of day and night) I'll practice medicine and read novels.

I shall not come to Petersburg.

Had I been around Prince Andrey I would have cured him. It is odd to read that the wound of a prince, a rich man attended by doctors day and night, benefiting from the care of Natasha and Sonya, was emitting a putrid smell. What a mangy thing medicine must have been at that time! Tolstoy, as he was writing his stout novel, must have involuntarily become saturated with hatred for medicine.* * *

Your A. Chekhov

TO YE. P. YEGOROV[1]

Moscow, December 11, 1891

Esteemed Yevgraf Petrovich!

Here is the story of my unsuccessful journey to see you. I was getting ready to go to you not with a correspondent's ends in view but at the

[1] Yevgraf Petrovich Yegorov, a zemstvo chief in the province of Nizhny Novgorod.

behest of—or, rather, by agreement with—a small circle of persons who wish to do something for the famine victims. The rub is that the public has no confidence in the administration and is therefore refraining from making contributions. There are a thousand fantastic fairy tales and cock-and-bull stories current about embezzlements, barefaced steals, and the like. People are shying away from the diocesan authority and are indignant about the Red Cross. A zemstvo chief, master of the never-to-be-forgotten Babkino estate, came right out with it and told me categorically, "There is stealing going on in Moscow at the Red Cross!" With such an atmosphere as that prevailing, the administration, no matter how long it waits, is hardly likely to receive any considerable aid from those who could give. And yet at the same time the public wants to be philanthropic and feels the prick of conscience.

In September the intellectuals and plutocrats of Moscow were forming into small groups; they pondered, they talked, they bustled about, they called in knowledgeable people to advise them; all talked about how to circumvent the administration and organize relief on their own. They decided to send agents of their own into the provinces affected by famine, men who would familiarize themselves on the spot with how matters stood, organize soup kitchens and so forth. Some of the people heading the groups, men who can throw their weight around, made trips to see Durnovo,[2] to request his permission, but Durnovo refused to grant it, declaring that the organization of relief could appertain only to the diocesan authority and the Red Cross. In a word, private initiative was blocked at the very start. Everybody lost heart, became dispirited; some grew rancorous, and some washed their hands of the whole thing. One must have the audacity and authority of Tolstoy [3] to go against all sort of prohibitions and prevalent attitudes and do what duty dictates.

Now, sir, concerning myself. My attitude toward private initiative was one of full sympathy, since every man is free to do good as he wishes; but all arguments about the administration, the Red Cross, and so on seemed to me inopportune and impractical. I supposed that with a certain amount of equanimity and good nature it was possible to circumvent everything terrible and ticklish, and for this there was no

[2] Ivan Nikolayevich Durnovo (1830–1903), Minister of the Interior.
[3] Tolstoy set up soup kitchens for the famine sufferers without having recourse to the authorities.

need to make a trip to the Minister. I went to Sakhalin without a single letter of recommendation. Nevertheless, I did all that I wanted to do there; why then, couldn't I make a trip to the famine-stricken provinces? I also recalled such administrators as yourself, as Kiselev, and all the zemstvo chiefs and tax inspectors of my acquaintance—men of the utmost decency and deserving the greatest confidence. And I decided to combine, if possible and though in a small area, two powers: the administration and private initiative. I wanted to see you as soon as possible and to seek your advice. The public has faith in me, it would have faith in you as well, and I could count on success. Remember, I sent you a letter.

At that point Suvorin arrived in Moscow; I complained to him at length that I did not know your address. He telegraphed to Baranov,[4] and Baranov was kind enough to send your address. Suvorin was down with influenza; usually when he comes to Moscow we are inseparable for days on end and discuss literature, of which he has superb knowledge. Well, this time we discussed it too, and the upshot was that I caught his influenza, took to my bed, and started coughing my head off. Korolenko was in Moscow and he found me suffering. A pulmonary complication made me languish a whole month; I did not set foot out of the house and did just nothing at all. Now my affairs are on the mend, but I am still coughing and losing weight. And there you have the whole story. If it hadn't been for the influenza, why, the two of us just might have fleeced the public of two or three thousand, or more, depending on circumstances.

The irritation that the press rouses in you is wholly understandable. The reasoning of journalists is just as irritating to you, who are familiar with the true state of things, as the reasoning of a layman on diphtheria is irritating to me, a medico. But what would you have us do? Just what? Russia isn't England and it isn't France. Our newspapers are not rich and have very few people at their disposal. To send a professor of the Petrovskaya Academy or Engelhardt [5] to the Volga is costly; you can't send an able and gifted staff member, either—he is needed at home. *The London Times* would, at its own expense, have taken a census in the famine-stricken provinces, planted a George Kennan in each district, paying him 40 rubles a day—and the results would be

<hr>

[4] Nikolay Mikhailovich Baranov, Governor of the Nizhny Novgorod province.
[5] N. A. Engelhardt was a journalist connected with *New Times*.

sensible; but what can *Russian News* or *New Times* do, when they consider an income of a hundred thousand as the riches of Croesus?

As for the correspondents themselves, they are townsmen, who know the village only through the writings of Gleb Uspensky.[6] Their position is false in the extreme. Flutter into a district, take a whiff, write your piece, and get going again. A correspondent has neither material resources, nor freedom, nor authority. For 200 rubles a month he gallops on and on and implores God for but one thing: not to arouse anybody's rancor over his involuntary and unavoidable pack of lies. He feels at fault. However, it isn't he who is at fault but Russian darkness. The Western correspondent has at his disposal superb maps, encyclopedic dictionaries, statistical studies; in the West a correspondent can do his work sitting at home. But how are things with us? Among us a correspondent can derive information only from talk and rumors. Why, throughout this whole Russia of ours we have up to now investigated only three districts: the Cherepov, the Tambov, and some other. That's in all of Russia, mind you! The newspapers are lying, the correspondents are rapscallions, but what are we to do? *Yet it is out of the question not to write.* If our press were silent, the situation, you will agree, would be still more dreadful.

Your letter and your project for buying up their cattle from the peasants have dislodged me from my inertia. With all my soul and all my energies I am ready to obey you and to do whatever you wish. I have been thinking the matter over for a long time, and here is my opinion: we cannot count on the money-bags. It's too late. Every rich man has already shelled out the thousands that he was fated to shell out. We can now rely only on the average man who contributes his half-rubles and rubles. Those who, in September, were prating about private initiative have found refuge in all kinds of Commissions and Committees and are already at work. Which means there is only the average man left. Let's announce a subscription. You write a letter to the editor and I'll have it printed in the *Russian News* and in *New Times*. In order to combine the two previously mentioned powers, both of us can sign the letter. If this should be inconvenient for you in view of your official standing, a third person could write a letter to the effect that such-and-such have been organized in Sector 5 of the Nizhny Novgorod district and, glory be to God, things are coming along success-

[6] Gleb Ivanovich Uspensky (1843–1902), a writer who preferred rural themes.

fully and it is requested that contributions be sent to P. Yegorov, zemstvo chief, to be reached at such and such an address, or to A. P. Chekhov, or to the editorial office of this or that newspaper. The only thing needed is to write at some length. Write, in detail, and I'll add a thing or two—and the trick is done. It is necessary to write about contributions but not about any loan. Nobody will fall for a loan: it's scary. It is hard to give, but to take back what one has given is still harder.

I have only one rich acquaintance living in Moscow—she's V. A. Morozova, a well-known philanthropist. I called on her yesterday with your letter. I talked, dined. At present her chief interest is the Committee on Literacy, which organizes free lunches for schoolboys, and she is giving everything to that. Since literacy and horses are incommensurate, V. A. promised me the cooperation of the Committee in the event of your wishing to organize free lunches for schoolboys and sending her detailed information. I felt *awkward* about asking her for money right then and there, since people take her money, with no end to it, and harry her as if she were a fox. I merely asked her that in case any Commissions and Committees of one sort or another came calling on her, not to forget us either, and she gave me her promise she wouldn't forget. Your letter and your ideas have also been communicated to Sobolevsky, the editor of *The Russian Bulletins*—just in case. I am spreading the news everywhere that the enterprise has already been organized.

Should the rubles and half-rubles materialize, I'll be sending them on to you without any delay. And you may consider me at your disposal, and please believe that it would mean true happiness for me to accomplish something, at least, since up to now I have done exactly nothing for the famine-stricken and for those who are helping them. * * *

Your A. Chekhov

TO A. I. SMAGIN [1]

Moscow, December 11, 1891

* * * Well, here's what it's all about, my dear sir! I am stuck in Moscow, yet at the same time something I have undertaken in the Nizhny

[1] Aleksandr Ivanovich Smagin, a landowner who was a zemstvo chief.

Novgorod province is already seething, seething! I and a friend of mine, a zemstvo chief, the finest of fellows, in the most backward district of that province, where there are no landed proprietors, or doctors, or even intellectual girls, of whom there are plenty even in Hell nowadays—well, he and I have cooked up a little deal on which we think we will make a hundred thousand or thereabouts. Outside of all sorts of undertakings to help the victims of the famine, we are in the main trying to save next year's crop. Because the muzhiks are selling their horses for next to nothing, for mere pennies, there is a serious danger that the fields will not be plowed for spring sowing and that thus the story of the famine will be repeated all over again. Well, then, we're buying up the horses and feeding them and, come spring, we'll return them to their owners. Our enterprise is already on a firm footing, and in January I'll make a trip there to contemplate its fruits.

Here's my reason for writing you this. If, while a noisy feast is on, it should befall you or someone else to collect even only a half-ruble for the benefit of the famine victims, or if some Korobochka [2] bequeathes all of a ruble for the same cause, and even if you yourself win one hundred rubles playing Old Maid—then, in your orisons be all of us sinners remembered and do set aside a mite for us from your bountifulness! This need not be done right now but whenever you will—yet no later than spring. In spring the horses will no longer be ours. Each contributor will receive a most detailed accounting of every copeck expended—in verse, if he wishes it, written to my order by Gilyarovsky. In January we shall appear in the papers. Direct the largesse either to me or straight to the combat zone: Epiphany Station, Province of Nizhny Novgorod, for Yevgraf Petrovich Yegorov, zemstvo chief. * * *

Yours with my whole soul,

A. Chekhov

---

[2] A miserly, serf-owning crone, about whom Gogol furnishes a side-splitting passage in *Dead Souls*.

[1892]

TO A. P. CHEKHOV-

Moscow, February 23, 1892

My fireman brother!

I've come to believe in forebodings and prophecies: when in childhood you irrigated your bedding of nights and later in adolescence when, in addition to irrigation, you occupied yourself with hurrying to conflagrations, and loved to talk about a fire brigade running up a stone staircase—already then it should have been foreseen that you would be the firemen's editor.[1] And so, congratulations. Put out fires, Sasha, with your gifted pen at Sheremetyev's expense, and we shall jubilate.

Now give ear. I have betrayed Khoklandia,[2] its songs and lobsters. The estate [3] has been purchased in the Serpukhov district, a dozen miles from the railroad station of Lopasnya. Be impressed: 575 acres, 432 of them wooded, two ponds, a mangy stream, a new house, an orchard, a piano, three horses, cows, a springless carriage, a sulky, carts, a sledge, hotbeds, two dogs, birdhouses for starlings, and other items too numerous for your fireman's mind to comprehend—all that was purchased for 13,000, a part of the sum borrowed. I shall pay 490 rubles a year interest on the debt, that is, half of what I paid hitherto as rent for the flat and the summer cottage. . . . Average effort can make the property, what with lumber and other things, yield an income of a thousand rubles, and with greater zeal over two thousand. Leasing the hayfield brings 250 rubles.

Thirty-eight acres have already been sown to rye. In March I shall sow clover, oats, lentils, peas, and whatever belongs to a kitchen garden. If I croak, I shall leave it to my relatives to pay the interest.

Come to see us, Sasha! You can stay in the hen coop, and for your

---

[1] In January 1892 Chekhov's brother Aleksandr became editor of *The Fireman*, a journal launched by Count A. D. Sheremetyev.
[2] A jocular reference to the Ukraine, where Chekhov had been looking for land.
[3] Located near the village of Melikhovo, and so referred to by that name.

entertainment I shall arrange a fire alarm. There are minnows in the ponds, mushrooms in the woods, the air is pleasant, better relations in the house. On March 1 we move, bidding farewell to Moscow. And so I shall no longer pay rent for a flat and a dacha. Our own butter, alva,[4] too. I shall try to pay off the debt in four years.

Send *The Fireman* to the following address: Lopasnya Station on the Moscow-Kursk Railroad, A. P. Chekhov.

Yesterday Garin-Vinding[5] told me that he wanted to send you an article entitled "Fires in Theaters."

Greetings to your people, and keep well. If you make a killing, remit some money.

Landed gentleman A. Chekhov

In the program of the journal you omitted the section: litigation relating to arson and insurance.

TO A. S. SUVORIN

Moscow, March 3, 1892

* * * I make discoveries every day. What a horror it is to have dealings with liars! The painter from whom I bought the estate lies, lies, lies, without any need, stupidly—as a result there are disappointments, day in and day out. At every moment one expects new deceptions—hence the irritation. People have grown used to saying and writing that it is only the shopkeepers who use false weights and measures, but you ought to take a good look at the gentry! It's loathsome to look at them. They aren't people but ordinary kulaks, even worse than kulaks, for a village kulak grabs yet works, whereas my painter grabs, gorges, and quarrels with the servants. Just imagine: ever since last summer his horses haven't seen one grain of oats or a wisp of hay but are filling their bellies with nothing but straw, even though each horse does the work of ten. His cow gives no milk because she's hungry. His wife and his mistress live under the same roof. The children are filthy and in rags. The place stinks of cats. Bedbugs and enormous cockroaches. The

---

[4] A Greek word apparently current in Taganrog, meaning several things relating to a farm.

[5] Dmitry Viktorovich Garin-Vinding was an actor and writer whose pen name was D. Garin.

painter puts on an act of being devoted to me with his whole soul, and at the same time is teaching the muzhiks to cheat me. Since it is hard to make out by sight which is my land and which is my forest, the muzhiks were instructed to show me a large forest belonging to a church as mine. But the muzhiks disobeyed. In general, it's all nonsense and vulgarity. The disgusting thing is that all this hungry and grubby rabble thinks that I too shiver over every copeck just as it does, and that I, too, am apt to swindle. The muzhiks are cowed, thoroughly frightened and irritated. —I am sending you a note about country estates. I shall make inquiries on the spot. * * *

All the best.

Your A. Chekhov

TO I. L. LEONTYEV-SHCHEGLOV

Melikhovo, March 9, 1892

* * * Yes, men like Rachinsky [1] are very few here below. I, my dear fellow, understand your delight. After the stifling air you inhale among the Burenins and Averkiyevs [2]—the world is full of them—Rachinsky, a humane, pure-hearted visionary, is a spring breeze. I am ready to lay down my life for him, but, dear friend . . . permit me this "but" and don't be cross—I would not send my children to his school. Why? In my childhood I received religious instruction and religious education, with church singing, the reading of the Acts of the Apostles, and of designated psalms, as part of the divine service, with regular attendance at matins, with the duty of helping at the altar and ringing the church bells. And what was the result? When I recall my childhood now, it appears to me dismal enough; I have no religion now. You know, when my two brothers and I formed a trio in the middle of the church and chanted the canticles, "May my prayer be a censer" [3] and "The Archangel's Voice," [4] the members of the congregation were touched and they envied our parents, but at the same time we felt ourselves to be little convicts. Yes, dear friend! I understand Rachinsky, but the children whom he teaches I do not know. Their souls are dark-

[1] Sergey Aleksandrovich Rachinsky was a professor at the University of Moscow who advocated religious education for children.
[2] Lesser literary figures. Chekhov could not abide Averkiyev.
[3] Sung at the Lenten service.
[4] Sung at the festival of the Annunciation.

ness to me. If there is joy in their souls, then they are happier than my brothers and I, whose childhood was misery. * * *

Your A. Chekhov

TO A. S. SUVORIN

Melikhovo, March 11, 1892

* * * I am doing no end of reading. Have read Leskov's *Legendary Characters* in the January issue of *The Russian Review*. Divine and piquant. A fusion of virtue, piety, and lechery. But very interesting. Read it, if you haven't read it yet. I reread Pisarev's [1] criticism of Pushkin. Horribly naïve. The man dethroned Onegin and Tatyana, while Pushkin gets off without as much as a scratch. Pisarev is the grandpa and papa of all the critics nowadays, including Burenin. The same pettiness and dethroning, the same chill and egocentric wit, and the same coarseness and lack of consideration for people. One can become brutalized not by the ideas of Pisarev, which are nonexistent, but by his coarse tone. His attitude toward Tatyana, particularly toward her dear letter, which I love tenderly, strikes me as simply disgusting. His criticism stinks of the insistent, cavilling prosecutor. However, the deuce with him! * * *

Your A. Chekhov

TO A. S. SUVORIN

Melikhovo, March 17, 1892

* * * It is uncomfortable to live in the country, the season of impassable roads has started, but in nature something amazing, poignant, is happening that with its poetry and novelty makes up for all the discomforts of life. Every day there are surprises, one better than the other. The starlings have flown back, water is gurgling everywhere, on the thawed

---

[1] Dmitry Ivanovich Pisarev (1840–68), a brilliant youth who endeared himself to the radical wing of the intelligentsia by his crudely materialistic and utilitarian ideology. His brash essays were written in prison, where he was confined for a vitriolic attack on the regime, the manuscript having been seized by the police before it was run off on a clandestine press.

patches grass already shows green. A day lasts an eternity. You live as in Australia, at the end of the world, your mood is calm, contemplative, animal, in the sense that you don't regret yesterday or wait for tomorrow. From here, from far off, people seem very good, and this is natural, because in retiring to the country we hide not from people but from our vanity, which, in the city, where you are surrounded by people, is unreasonable and inordinate. As I watch spring, I am terribly eager for a paradise in the Beyond. In a word, there are moments when I am so happy that I superstitiously pull myself up and remember my creditors, who one day will banish me from my lawfully acquired Australia. And justly!

Your A. Chekhov

TO A. P. CHEKHOV

Melikhovo, March 21, 1892

Fireman Sasha!

We have received your journal and rapturously read the biographies of famous heads of the Fire Department and the lists of the decorations bestowed upon them. We wish you, Sashechka, would receive the Order of the Lion and the Sun.

We are living on our own estate. Like unto a certain Cincinnatus I spend all my time in toil and eat my bread in the sweat of my face. Mamasha was preparing for communion today and drove to church behind our own horse; Papasha tumbled out of the sleigh—that's how impetuous the pace of the steed was!

Papasha is philosophizing just as before and asking such questions as: Why is snow lying here? Why are trees over there, but none over here? He spends all his time reading the papers and then tells Mother that a society is being formed in Petersburg to fight the classification [1] of milk. Like all the men of Taganrog he is unfit for any work other than that of lighting church lamps. With the peasants he is stern of speech. * * *

Well, sir, as far as my financial affairs are concerned, they're in quite a bad way, since the expenses of the estate exceed its income tenfold.

---

[1] Presumably he meant adulteration.

I recall Turnefort: [2] "She has to give birth but there is no candle." And so I say: We have to sow but there are no seeds. Geese and horses have to eat, but the walls of the house don't help. Yes, Sashechka, not only Moscow loves money. * * *

Well, Sasha, when my estate is sold at auction I'll buy a house with a garden in Nezhin and live there until my hoary old age. "All is not lost yet!" I shall say when a foreigner settles on my estate.

You will be acting basely and abominably if you won't come to us this summer to live the life of Cincinnatus if only for a day. Just recently a lovely little estate right alongside of mine was sold for three thousand. House, outbuildings, garden, pond, 135 acres. There, that should have been yours! What a lot of raspberries, strawberries! * * *

Your Cincinnatus

TO L. S. MIZINOVA

Melikhovo, March 27, 1892

Lika, there is a cruel frost out of doors and in my heart, and so I am not writing you the long letter you wanted to receive.

Well, how have you solved the problem of a summer residence? You are a liar and I don't believe you: you don't want to live near us at all. Your summer residence is in the Myasnitskaya quarter, under the fire tower: that's where you are, heart and soul.[1] But we—we mean nothing at all to you. We are but the starlings of yesteryear, whose song has long since been forgot.

A. I. Smagin stayed with us two days. The rural policeman was here today. The mercury in the thermometer went down to −10. I let fly at this mercury with all the swear words beginning with the letter S,[2] and for answer get its cold glittering stare. —But when will it be spring? Lika, when will it be spring?

Accept the above question literally and do not seek for a hidden meaning in it. Alas, I am already an old young man, my love is no sun and

[2] An instructor in the Taganrog high school. It is uncertain how he spelled his name.
[1] The address of Kuvshinnikova, which was frequented by Levitan, about whom Chekhov liked to tease Mizinova.
[2] Perhaps including an allusion to SOB, which begins with the same letter in Russian.

does not make a spring either for me or for the bird I love! Lika, it is not you whom I so ardently love. I love in you my sufferings of the past and my now perished youth.

TO L. S. MIZINOVA

Melikhovo, March 29, 1892

Dear Melita,[1]

* * * All of us are awaiting your arrival with impatience. The rooms have taken on a decorous look, the place has become spacious, and we spent all day yesterday cleaning up the little shed which will house our dear guests. * * *

Write me, if only a couple of lines, Melita. Do not consign us to premature oblivion. Go through the motions, at least, of still remembering us. Deceive us, Lika. Deception is better than indifference.

You will be comfortable with us. Even though our country place is lacking in some comforts we shall try to see that you won't need them. * * *

There's no money, Melita. The atmosphere is a trifle on the suffocating side. There are no wickets in the windows. Father has filled the place with incense. I stunk it up with turpentine. There are aromas issuing from the kitchen. Headache. No privacy. But, above all, no Melita, and no hope that I shall see her today or tomorrow. * * *

Yours from head to heels, with all my soul and all my heart, until my tombstone, to the point of self-oblivion, of stupefaction, of frenzy.

Antoine Tiekoff (the pronunciation of Prince Urusov)

TO A. S. SUVORIN

Melikhovo, March 31, 1892

It was cold, everyone felt dejected, the birds flew southward, and I did not write you so as not to infect you with my bad mood. Now the birds have returned, and I am writing. Everything is as it has been: neither tedious nor jolly. I lead an existence that is mainly vegetative, which

[1] A character in Grillparzer's *Sappho*, then playing in Moscow.

is constantly poisoned by the thought that it is necessary to write, always write. I am writing a tale.[1] Before publishing it, I should like to send it to you, for your opinion is worth its weight in gold, but I must make haste, because there is no money. This story abounds in argument and there's nothing in it about love. It has a plot and a dénouement. The bias is liberal. It runs to a couple of sheets. But I should have consulted you, to avoid heaping up a lot of boring rubbish. You have admirable taste, and I believe in your first impression as I believe that there is a sun in the heavens. If they do not print my story right away, and allow me a month or two for corrections, permit me to send you proof. * * * Locked up in an egotistical shell of self-esteem—and participating in the intellectual movement only indirectly, one risks making a damn fool of oneself against one's will. Won't you permit me to send you proof?

* * * Living is cheaper in the country than in the city, but I'm having bad luck. Oats cost 80 copecks instead of 15, there is no hay, pasture is only *in spe,* but I have six nags, in addition to fowl. They are eating me alive. * * * As a farm hand and landowner I am worthless. All I know how to do is dig runnels and shovel snow into the pond. When I drive in a nail, it is crooked.

* * * This letter will probably reach you on Easter Eve. Christ has risen! May God give you everything good. Hearty greetings to Anna Ivanovna and the children.

When I write a play I shall need Börne.[2] Where can I get his books? He is one of those intellectuals whom Jews and narrow people so love.

After the Divorce,[3] Daudet's new novel, portrays three women admirably, but is hypocritical, at least in its finale. If an Old Believer or an Arab inveighed against divorce, that would be understandable, but Daudet in the role of a preceptor of morals who demands that spouses grown repulsive to each other should not separate is horribly ludicrous. The French are sick of naked wenches, and so want to play at morality for gastronomical reasons.

Your A. Chekhov

---

[1] "Ward Number 6."
[2] Ludwig Börne (1786–1851), a brilliant publicist of Jewish birth. He was a leader of the Young Germany radical movement.
[3] The title of the two Russian translations of the novel *Rose et Ninette.*

Melikhovo, April 6, 1892

* * * There, for all of a month we've been living on our own farmstead, which we at last found and bought. My sister has, I believe, already written you about this in detail. Five hundred and seventy-five acres, poor forest land, garden, park, river one mile from the house, a pond in the garden, a spacious house, etc. No repairs required, glory be to God. Life here is tranquil and salubrious, but not cheap, since wretched old nags called horses eat up a thousand poods of oats a day, a pood costing 90 copecks hereabouts.

At Easter both matins and an afternoon mass were sung in our church. A lot of guests came from Moscow and joined in the singing.

We're already in the midst of real spring. Warm, clear, noisy. We stroll through garden and field, taking delight in space, to which we had grown so unaccustomed while living in Moscow. All around our property are woods, woods, woods, so that there's a prospect of richly rewarding mushroom hunts. We have sowed 38 acres of rye; my people also want a spring sowing, but that's not my department and it won't be in the future; I'll busy myself with the orchard and, if there should be any spare money, with bees. Such a wealth of raspberries and strawberries as we've got! And currants, too. Plenty of plum and apple trees; I didn't see any cherry trees, though; however, they say there are cherry trees, too. The best thing we have is an alley of lindens, which reminds one of the alley in Bogimovo. * * *

I get up at four or five and go to bed—I am ashamed to say it!—at ten. We dine at twelve. I want to go to America or somewhere still more remote because I have become dreadfully fed up with myself. * * *

Good-bye! May God protect you.

Your heartily devoted
A. Chekhov

TO A. S. SUVORIN

Melikhovo, April 8, 1892

[. . .] Since Good Friday I have had guests, guests, guests . . . and I haven't written a single line. * * *

[1] Natalya Mikhailovna Lintvareva, the youngest daughter of Aleksandra Vasilyevna Lintvareva.

Levitan, the artist, is staying with me. Last evening we were out shooting. He shot at a snipe, and the bird, hit in the wing, fell into a puddle. I picked it up: a long beak, big black eyes, and beautiful plumage. It looked astonished. What were we to do with it? Levitan frowned, shut his eyes, and begged me with a tremor in his voice, "My dear fellow, hit his head against the gunstock. . . ." I said, "I can't." He went on nervously shrugging his shoulders, twitching his head, and begging me; and the snipe went on looking at us in astonishment. I had to obey Levitan and kill it. One more beautiful enamored creature gone, while two fools went home and sat down to supper. * * *

Be well and prosperous. See you in Moscow!

Your A. Chekhov

TO L. A. AVILOVA[1]

Melikhovo, April 29, 1892

Esteemed Lidiya Alekseyevna!

I have never written verse. Only once, though, I wrote a fable for a little girl's album, but this was a long, long time ago. The fable is still alive, many people know it by heart, but the little girl is already twenty years old, and as for me, obedient to the general law, I am already an old literary dog who looks down on versifying and yawns. Probably things appear under my shingle, written by a person of the same name or by an impostor. There are many Chekhovs.

Yes, it's fine in the country now. Not only fine but actually amazing. Real spring, trees burgeoning, weather hot. Nightingales sing and frogs clamor in a range of voices. I haven't a penny, but then, the way I reason, it isn't the man with a lot of money who is rich, but the one who can afford to be living now in the luxurious setting furnished by early spring. I was in Moscow yesterday but almost smothered there from boredom and all sorts of unpleasantnesses. Imagine, if you will: an acquaintance of mine, a lady of forty-two, recognized herself in the twenty-year-old heroine of my "Grasshopper" (*The North*, Nos. 1 and 2), and all Moscow is accusing me of libel. The main evidence consists

---

[1] Lidiya Alekseyevna Avilova (1865–1943), a writer of short stories and author of reminiscences: *Chekhov in My Life*. In these memoirs she asserts that she had a love affair with Chekhov, but the letters that would substantiate this have been lost or tampered with. The romance may have been a figment of her imagination.

of superficial similarities: the lady paints, her husband is a doctor, and she lives with a painter.

I am finishing a tale,[2] a very boring one since woman and the element of love are entirely absent from it. I can't bear such tales, and as for writing this one, I did it inadvertently somehow, and frivolously. I can send you an offprint, if I know your address after June.

I'd like to write a comedy, but the Sakhalin work interferes.

I wish you all the best, chiefly—health.

Oh, yes! I once happened to write you that one must be indifferent when writing dolorous stories. And you did not understand me. When working on such stories you may weep and moan, you may suffer right along with your characters but, I suppose, you must do it in such a way that the reader will not notice it. The more objective the telling, the more powerful the effect produced. That's what I meant to say.

Sincerely, devotedly,

A. Chekhov

TO P. V. BYKOV[1]

Melikhovo, May 4, 1892

Much esteemed Pyotr Vasilyevich!

Yeronim Yeronimovich[2] wrote me that you are close to the editorial board of *World-wide Illustrations*. When the occasion presents itself, be so kind as to inform the board that the advertisement in which they describe me as "highly gifted" and print the title of my story[3] in letters suitable for a poster has produced a most disagreeable impression on me. It resembles the advertisement of a dentist or a masseuse and in any case this does not appeal to the intellect. I know the value of publicity and am not opposed to it, but for a man of letters modesty and an attitude toward readers and fellow writers that suits literature is the best and most effective publicity. Generally speaking, I have had no luck with *World-wide Illustrations*. I asked for an advance and was

2 "Ward Number 6."
1 P. V. Bykov was *de facto* editor of the newspaper *World-wide Illustrations* and eventually of several collections of Chekhov's stories.
2 Yasinsky, a journalist and fiction writer.
3 "In Exile."

treated to an advertisement. There has been no advance—let that pass—
but my reputation should have been spared this. Forgive me if this
letter—my first one to you—is peevish and dull. . . .

I earnestly beg you to pardon me and to believe that I turned to you
with a complaint solely because I respect you sincerely.

A. Chekhov

TO A. S. SUVORIN

Melikhovo, May 28, 1892

Life is short, and Chekhov, for whose reply you are waiting, would like
it to flash by brightly and with a crackle; he would travel to Princes
Islands and to Constaninople and to India again and to Sakhalin. But,
first, he has a noble family which needs protection. Second, there is a
large measure of cowardice in him. I call peering into the future by no
other name than cowardice. I am afraid to get entangled and each
journey considerably complicates my financial affairs. No, do not tempt
me needlessly! Don't write me about the sea.

I wish you would return from abroad in August or September; then
I would travel with you to Feodosiya; otherwise I would not get a
glimpse of the sea this summer. I itch terribly for a steamer and freedom generally. Smooth, unctuous life disgusts me.

It is hot here. Warm rains. Ravishing evenings. Within a mile there
is good bathing and good sites for picnics, but there's no leisure to bathe
or go picnicking. Either I write, gnashing my teeth, or settle problems
not worth a penny with carpenters and farm hands. Misha has been
hauled over the coals by his chief for spending weeks with me instead
of staying at home, and now I have to keep house alone, which I don't
hold with, because it's fiddle-faddle, and resembles a gentleman's
amusement rather a serious business.

I bought three mousetraps and I catch twenty-five creatures daily
and take them to the forest. It is wonderful in the woods. Landowners
are foolish to be surrounded by parks and orchards, instead of living in
the woods. In a forest you sense the presence of deity, not to speak of
the fact that it is more advantageous—there is no stealthy felling of
trees and the care of the woods is easier. If I were you, I would buy
500 to 600 acres of good forest land, provide it with roads and paths,

and build a castle in it. A road cleared through a forest is more majestic than tree-lined avenues.

What shall I do with Monte Cristo? [1] I abridged him so that he resembles a man who has recovered from typhus. The stout fellow turned into a puny one. The first part, in which the count is well off, is very interesting and well done, but the second, aside from a few passages, is unbearable, because there Monte Cristo does foolish things and utters nothing but bombastic nonsense. However, in general the novel is effective. Shall it be postponed till fall?

* * * To judge by the papers, life is burdensome everywhere. They write that cholera is on the way to Transcaucasia and that it has already visited Paris. Before you sail for Constantinople, find out if the vessels arriving from the Black Sea ports have not been placed in quarantine. Quarantine is a surprise that God forbid anyone should encounter. Nowadays it is known tenderly as "the three-day observation."

In central Russia the horses have influenza. They die. If you believe that everything that happens in nature is designed and purposeful, then obviously nature is straining every nerve to get rid of debilitated organisms and those she doesn't need. Famines, cholera, influenza. . . . Only the healthy and strong will remain. But to reject the doctrine that there is a purpose in things is impossible. Our starlings, young and old, suddenly flew away somewhere. This was baffling, because the time for the migration of birds was still far off. But unexpectedly we learned the other day that clouds of southern dragonflies, mistaken for locusts, had flown across Moscow. The question arises: how did our starlings learn that on such-and-such a day, miles from Melikhovo, multitudes of insects would be flying? Who informed them? Verily this is a great mystery. But it is a wise mystery. The same wisdom, it occurs to one, is hidden in famines and the illnesses that succeed them. We and our horses represent the dragonflies, and famine and cholera—the starlings.

I bought a wonderful croquet set in your store. A good set and decently priced.

So write me when you plan to leave. May God grant that you win or inherit three hundred thousand, to enable you to buy an estate near Lopasnya. Keep well.

Your A. Chekhov

[1] Chekhov made an abridgment of Dumas' *The Count of Monte Cristo* which Suvorin was to publish. The plan was not carried out. A close friend of Chekhov's drew a caricature showing him at work on the novel and Dumas watching the process and crying.

TO A. S. SUVORIN

Hot and no rains. Nature languishes and so do people. The rye is as tall as a man, it must be harvested in twenty days, but oats are still an inch high. No happy prospect for crops. But then there aren't any mosquitoes. When I learned that Jean Shcheglov had chosen Vladimir for his permanent domicile, I was horrified: mosquitoes will eat him alive, and it is the seat of boredom, historical, endless! The most boring of all the provincial cities, not even a theater. It would have been better to settle in Tula or Voronezh.

I am writing a little love story.[1] I write with pleasure, finding delight in the very process of writing, and with me the process is laborious, slow. When I have a headache or when I hear people talking nonsense, I write gritting my teeth. My head aches often and even more frequently I have to listen to balderdash.

I have an interesting subject for a comedy, but I haven't yet invented the ending. Whoever will contrive new endings for plays will open a new era. The endings, deuce take them, don't come easily. The chief character either gets married or shoots himself, no way out. The title of my future comedy is *The Cigarette-case*.[2] I shall not start composing until I invent an ending as intricate as the beginning. And once I have got the ending, I shall finish the piece in two weeks.

* * * I would go to Feodosiya with pleasure. Of course, solo. Send word in any case that I am coming and that I should not be regarded as an impostor. I shall finish the story and then I shall make off to the Crimea to compose the comedy. I like huge houses. As for sea bathing, it will do me no harm, for I don't feel very well. During which month will you be returning? Why, in God's name, shouldn't we live in Feodosiya together the whole of September or October? For me this would be enchanting, I would be in seventh heaven. If you aren't tired of me, think it over and let me know. By fall my financial affairs will be in good shape, and I shall not whine, "I must write." If we exchange letters beforehand, I shall meet you in Feodosiya.

Our chambermaid, who impressed us by her zeal, turned out to be a professional thief. She stole money, handkerchiefs, books, photographs.

[1] "Neighbors."
[2] There is no trace of it.

. . . Every guest missed 5 or 10 rubles. I can imagine how much money she must have stolen. I'm not in the habit of locking my desk or counting my money! I think that she must have stolen about two hundred. During all of March and April I thought that too much money seemed to be disappearing. * * *

Your A. Chekhov

TO A. S. SUVORIN

Melikhovo, June 16, 1892

* * * My soul cries out for breadth and heights but, willy-nilly, one must lead a life that is petty and narrow, given over to filthy rubles and copecks. There is nothing more vulgar than lower-middle-class life with its pennies, grub, preposterous talk, and conventional virtue that nobody needs. My soul has wasted away because of the awareness that I am working for the sake of money and that money is the center of my activity. This nagging feeling, together with the justice of it, makes my writing a contemptible occupation in my eyes, I have no respect for what I write, I am listless and bore my own self, and I am glad I have medicine which, no matter what, I am following not for the sake of money, after all. Really, one should take a bath in sulphuric acid, peel off one's skin, and grow new wool. * * *

Your A. Chekhov

TO L. S. MIZINOVA

Melikhovo, June 28, 1892, 4 A.M.

Noble, decent Lika!

As soon as you wrote me that my letters do not obligate me in any way I breathed a sigh of relief, and here I am now, writing you a long letter without any fear that some aunt of yours will, upon seeing these lines, make me marry such a monster as yourself. I, for my part, also hasten to reassure you that, in my eyes, your letters have only the significance of fragrant flowers but not of documents; inform Baron Stackelberg, your cousin, and the dragoon officers that I shall not stand in their way.

We Chekhovs, in contradistinction to the Ballasses,[1] believe in letting young girls live. That is a principle with us. And so, you are free. * * *

Quiet, peace, and concord reign here—if you don't take into account the din created by the children of my older brother. But it's hard to write just the same. You can't concentrate. In order to think and compose it becomes necessary to go off to the truck garden and weed the poor dear grass, which isn't interfering with anybody. I have a sensational bit of news. *Russian Thought* has, in the person of Lavrov, sent me a letter brimming with delicate sentiments and assurances. I am deeply touched, and, if it weren't for my vile habit of not answering letters, I would have answered that I consider our misunderstanding of two years ago at an end. At any rate, my child, I am sending to *Russian Thought* that liberal tale [2] which I began when you were here. Now there's an odd incident for you!

Does Levitan of the dark eyes full of African passion still haunt your dreams? Are you still getting letters from your septuagenarian rival [3] and, like a hypocrite, answering her? There's a great big crocodile ensconced within you, Lika, and, essentially, I am doing the right thing in heeding common sense instead of my heart, into which you have sunk your teeth. Away, away from me! Or no, Lika—let come what may! Allow my head to turn dizzy from your perfume and help me to tighten the loop of the lasso you have already thrown around my neck. I imagine how gloatingly you triumph and with what demoniac laughter you read these lines. Oh, I think I am writing nonsense. Tear up this letter. Forgive its illegibility and don't show it to anyone. Oh, oh!

Basov [4] wrote me that you have started smoking again. That's vile, Lika. I despise your character.

It rains daily but nevertheless the earth is dry.

Well, good-bye, maize of my soul. With abject deference I kiss your powder box and I envy your old boots that see you every day. Write me about your successes.

May all go well with you and don't forget him whom you have vanquished.

King of the Medes

---

[1] Admirers of the addressee, like those previously mentioned.
[2] "My Patient's Story."
[3] S. P. Kuvshinnikova.
[4] A relative of the addressee.

TO N. A. LEIKIN

Melikhovo, July 13, 1892

Forgive me, kindest Nikolay Aleksandrovich, for having taken so long to answer your letter. Because of cholera, which has not reached us yet, I have been called in by the zemstvo as a health officer, a district has been assigned to me, and now I am riding around, visiting villages and factories and gathering material for a medical convention. There is no time even to think of literary work. In 1848 cholera was raging in my district; we estimate that this time, too, it will be no less severe—although, naturally, God disposes. The districts are extensive, so that the physicians will be spending all their time merely in exhausting drives from place to place. There are no barracks: the tragedies will be played out in huts or in the open air. There are no assistants. The promises of disinfectants and drugs are unlimited. The roads are abominable and my horses are even worse. As for my health, already by noon, I begin to feel fatigue and a desire to hit the hay. That's without the cholera; but what things will be like with the cholera, we'll see.

Aside from this epidemic I expect an epidemic of another disease which will inevitably attack my farmstead. It's impecuniousness. With the cessation of literary work my income ceased as well. Without counting the three-ruble fee received today from a patient with gonorrhea, my income is exactly nil. * * *

Your A. Chekhov

TO L. S. MIZINOVA

Melikhovo, July 16, 1892

You, Lika, are a captious one. In ever character of my letter you see irony or malice. A splendid disposition you've got, I must say. In vain do you think that you'll wind up as an old maid. I bet that in time you will evolve into an evil-tempered, cantankerous, shrill-voiced hag who'll go in for usury and yanking the ears of all the urchins in the neighborhood. The miserable titular councillor in his skimpy, rust-colored bathrobe who will have the honor of calling you his spouse will be constantly stealing your liqueur and thus drowning the bitterness of domestic life. I often see in my imagination two respectable persons—you and

Sappho—sitting at a small table and swilling liqueur as you recall your past, while in an adjoining room, hugging the stove with a timid and hangdog look about them and playing checkers, are your titular councillor and a little Hebrew [1] with a big bald patch, whose surname I would rather not give. * * *

So, be well. This time I'm not saying anything tender because you will see in it only irony. And, of course, I shall not sign my name. I shall not sign it out of stubbornness.

TO N. M. LINTVAREVA

Melikhovo, July 22, 1892

Esteemed Natalya Mikhailovna!

* * * There have been rumors that your sister Yelena Mikhailovna passed by our place on her way to Khotun. Day before yesterday I heard that she had been assigned to the Belopesotzky complex of villages. Could we have thought, three years ago, that we would have to fight together against cholera in the Serpukhov district? The Khotun medical section borders on mine of Melikhovo, the latter designated formally on July 17. Which means that fate itself wants us to be "estimable colleagues." Yelena Mikhailovna will be confronted with having to organize her section; her patience will be very sorely tried, since our zemstvo is noted for its dilatoriness and has saddled the doctors with all the heavy work of organization. I am as furious as a chained watchdog; I have twenty-three villages, yet up to the present I haven't gotten as much as one cot and, probably, never will get that assistant who was promised me at the Medical Council. I drive from factory to factory begging, as if for alms, for premises to shelter my future patients. From morning to evening I am driving about, and I am already exhausted, even though cholera hasn't appeared yet. Last evening I was soaked by a downpour, slept away from home, went home on foot through the mud, and kept swearing all the time. My laziness has been profoundly mortified. I think that Yelena Mikhailovna won't find matters any easier, either. But that is so only at first. In a week or two everything will get into its rut and we shall settle down. The cholera, we must suppose, will not be particularly severe. And even severe cholera is not

[1] The reference is, of course, to Levitan.

terrible, inasmuch as the zemstvo has provided the physicians with the most extensive powers. That is, I didn't receive a copeck, but I can rent as many huts and hire as many people as I wish, and in serious situations can order a medical squad from Moscow. The zemstvo workers here are intelligent; colleagues are efficient, knowledgeable people; while the peasants have become so used to medicine that it will hardly be necessary to convince them that we physicians are not to blame for the cholera. In all probability, they won't beat us up. * * *

Yours with my whole soul,

A. Chekhov

TO A. S. SUVORIN

Melikhovo, August 1, 1892

My letters chase after you, but there's no catching up with you. I wrote you often—and to the St. Moritz address, among others. But, to judge from your letters, you weren't receiving anything from me. In the first place, there is cholera in Moscow and in the environs of Moscow, and it will reach our locality any day now. Secondly, I have been appointed a cholera doctor, and my section includes twenty-five villages, four factories, and one monastery. I am organizing things, building barracks, etc., and I am lonely, inasmuch as everything having to do with cholera is alien to my soul, and work which demands constant travel, discussions, and petty cares tires me out. No time to write. Literature has long since been cast aside, and I am miserable and destitute, since I found it suited me and my independence to forgo the remuneration received by physicians in charge of sections. I am bored, but cholera, if one takes a bird's-eye view of it, offers much that is of interest. It's a pity you're not in Russia. Material for "Little Letters" is going to waste. There is more of good than of bad, and in this cholera differs sharply from famine, which we observed last winter.

Now everybody is pitching in. Ferociously. In Nizhny at the fair, they are working miracles which are liable to compel even Tolstoy to adopt an attitude of respect for medicine and, in general, for intervention in life by people of culture. It looks as though cholera has been lassoed. There has been a decrease not only in the incidence of infections but in the rate of mortality. In enormous Moscow there are not more than fifty cases of cholera a week, yet in the Don region it seizes a thousand a day—an impressive difference. We, district leeches, are prepared, we have a definite program of action, and there are grounds for thinking that in our areas we too will lower the rate of mortality for cholera. We have no assistants, we shall have to act simultaneously both as physicians and medical orderlies; the peasants are coarse, unclean, mistrustful; but the reflection that our labors will not go for naught makes all this almost unnoticeable. Of all the Serpukhov doctors I cut the sorriest figure: my horses and carriage are mangy, I don't know the roads, of evenings I can't see a thing. I get tired out very quickly but, mainly, no matter how I try, I can't forget that it is necessary to write, and I very much want to spit on cholera and sit down to my writing. And I want to have a chat with you. Utter loneliness.

Our efforts on the farm have been crowned with complete success. Ample crops, and after we have sold the produce, Melikhovo will yield over a thousand rubles. The truck garden is brilliant, whole mountains of cucumbers, marvelous cabbage. If it weren't for the damn cholera, I could say that I never spent a better summer than this one. * * *

Your A. Chekhov

TO A. S. SUVORIN

Melikhovo, August 16, 1892

I'm not going to write you any more, even if you were to cut my throat. I wrote to Abbazia; to St. Moritz I wrote ten times, at least. Up to now you haven't sent me a single correct address and that's why not a single letter of mine has reached you, and my lengthy descriptions of and lectures on cholera have all gone for naught. That hurts. But what hurts most of all is that after a whole series of my letters dealing with the plight that cholera has caused us, you up and write me from your gay, turquoise-blue Biarritz that you envy me my leisure! May Allah forgive you!

Well, sir, I am alive and in good health. The summer was splendid—dry, warm, abounding in the fruits of the earth—but, beginning with July, all of its charm came to be utterly spoiled by news of cholera. While in your letter you were inviting me now to Vienna, now to Abbazia, I was already the physician appointed by the Serpukhov zemstvo for a section; I tried to grab the cholera by its tail and went full steam ahead with the organization of the new section.

I have twenty-five villages, four factories and one monastery in my section. In the morning I see patients, and when the morning is gone I travel. I ride about, deliver lectures to the Pechenegs, treat the sick, get angry, and, since the zemstvo hasn't given me as much as a copeck for the organization of admission centers, I go cadging among the rich— now this one, now that one. I have turned out to be a superb mendicant; thanks to my beggarly eloquence my section now has two superb barracks, fully equipped, and five barracks, not superb but abominable. I have relieved the zemstvo even from expenses for disinfection. Lime, vitriol, and all sorts of smelly slops I obtained begging from the factory owners for all of my twenty-five villages. In short, A. P. Kolomnin ought to be proud of having studied in the same high school that I attended.

My soul is tired. Tedium. Not to belong to one's own self, to think only of diarrhea, to be startled of nights by the barking of watchdogs and knocking at the gate (have they come to fetch me?), to be driving repulsive nags over unknown roads, and to be reading only about cholera and to be waiting only for cholera and at the same time to be utterly indifferent to this disease and to the people whom you serve— all this, my dear sir, is the kind of mess which won't prove at all wholesome.

There is already cholera in Moscow and the district of Moscow. One must expect it at any hour. To judge by its progress in Moscow one must regard it as declining and assume that the Comma [1] is losing its virulence. We must also consider that to a great extent it is susceptible to the measures taken against it in Moscow and among us. The intelligentsia works briskly, sparing neither life nor money; I see it every day and am touched, and when I also recall how The Denizen [2] and Burenin poured out their bilious acids upon this same intelligentsia I find it a little hard to breathe. In Nizhny physicians and people of culture in general worked wonders. I was wild with rapture on reading about the cholera. In the good old days, when thousands sickened and died, men could not so much as dream of the overwhelming victories that are now being achieved before our eyes. It is a pity you are not a physician and cannot share my gratification—that is, truly feel deeply

[1] The cholera micro-organism, so called because of its shape.
[2] This contributor to *New Times* was one of Chekhov's *bêtes noires*.

and realize and evaluate all that is being done. However, one cannot speak of all this briefly. * * *

Of course, there's no time even to think of literature. I'm not writing a thing. I refused any pay, so as to preserve for myself at least a minimal freedom of action, and therefore I abide without a penny. I am waiting until the rye is threshed and sold, and until such time I shall subsist on *The Bear* [3] and mushrooms, of which we have no end. Incidentally, never have I lived as cheaply as now—even our bread is baked from our own milled grain. I think that in two years all my domestic expenses won't exceed a thousand rubles a year. * * *

You see at what length I write although I am not certain that my letter will reach you. Imagine my cholera-begotten boredom, my cholera-begotten solitude, and forced literary inactivity, and write me oftener and at greater length. Your disgust with the French I share. The Germans are far superior, though for some reason they're called obtuse. I love Franco-Russian sympathies as much as I do Tatishchev. There's something mischievous in these sympathies. But on the other hand, I am immensely delighted by Virchow's [4] visit to us.

We have a bumper crop of delicious potatoes and marvelous cabbage this year. How do you get along without shchi? [5] I don't envy you either your sea, or your freedom, or the good mood that you enjoy abroad. There is nothing better than the Russian summer. And incidentally, I am not very eager to go abroad. After Singapore, Ceylon, and perhaps our Amur, Italy and even the craters of Vesuvius don't seem enchanting. Having been in India and China, I saw no great difference between Russia and foreign parts.

Living in Biarritz now is my neighbor, the owner of the famous Otrada,[6] Count Orlov-Davydov, who has run away from cholera; all he had doled out to his doctor for the fight against cholera was five hundred rubles. His sister, a countess living in my section, when I drove over to her place to talk about a barrack for her workers, behaved toward me as if I were a hired man who had come to look for a job. I was hurt and lied to her that I was a rich man. I told the same lie to the archimandrite who refused to grant permission for the use of any

[3] In a letter to another friend Chekhov had written about this playlet, "My *Bear* [usually translated *The Boor*] should have been called Milch-cow. It has brought in more than any of my tales. Oh, the public!"

[4] Rudolph Virchow was an eminent German scientist, and leader of the liberal opposition to Bismarck.

[5] A meat and vegetable soup, the chief ingredient of which is cabbage.

[6] Russian for "Delight," the count's estate.

quarters for victims of cholera who, presumably, might happen to be stricken in his monastery. In answer to my question as to what he would do with those who would fall sick in his hostelry he answered me, "They are people of substance and will pay you themselves." Do you understand that? But I flared up and told him that I wasn't interested in any payment, since I was rich, but in safeguarding the monastery. . . . Most stupid and most offensive situations occur. . . . Prior to Count Orlov-Davydov's departure I called on his wife. Enormous diamonds in her ears, a bustle, and no knowledge of how to conduct herself. A millionairess. In the presence of such personages one experiences the foolish mood of a divinity student, when one feels urged to do or say something rude for no reason whatsoever.

I know a priest, an excellent fellow, a widower who has illegitimate children, who calls on me often and stays a long time.

Do write, or there will be trouble.

Your A. Chekhov

TO A. S. SUVORIN

Melikhovo, October 10, 1892

* * * I gave my word to be physician of a section until October 15, on which date my section will officially cease to be. I shall dismiss my assistant, close up the barrack, and, if there should be any cholera, I shall cut a somewhat comic figure. Add that the physician heading one of the adjoining sections has come down with pleurisy and consequently, if cholera should occur in his section, I would have to take it over too, as duty to a colleague.

Up to now I haven't had a single case of cholera, but I have had epidemics of typhus, diphtheria, scarlatina, and so on. At the beginning of summer there was a lot of work, but then, as fall approached, there was less and less.

Because of the cholera, my literary activities for the past summer were almost nil. I wrote little, and of literature I thought even less. I have, however, written two short tales,[1] one decent, the other wretched, which I shall publish, perhaps in *Russian Thought*. I received a friendly letter from Lavrov and have made up with him in all sincerity.

During the summer life was difficult, but now it seems to me that I

[1] "Ward Number 6" and "The Story of an Unknown Man."

have never had as good a summer as this one. In spite of the cholera turmoil and impecuniousness, which kept me in its paws until fall, I liked life and wanted to live. How many trees I planted! Thanks to our *Kulturträgerei*, Melikhovo became unrecognizable to us, and now seems cozy and beautiful, although, perhaps, essentially it's worthless. Such is the power of habit and the consciousness of proprietorship. And it's amazing, how pleasant it is not to pay rent. New acquaintances have been made and new relationships formed. Our former fears of the peasants now seem to us absurdity. I served in the zemstvo, presided at the Medical Council, visited factories—and I liked all this. I am already regarded as one of their own, and when they pass through Melikhovo they spend the night. Add to this that we have bought a carriage with good springs and a top, built a new road so that we don't have to drive through the village, are digging a pond. . . . What more? In a word, until now everything has been new and interesting, what it will be like later, I don't know. It's snowing already, cold, but Moscow doesn't lure me. So far no signs of boredom. * * *

The intelligentsia hereabouts is very nice, and interesting, above all, they are honest. Only the police are not congenial.

We have seven horses. We have a calf with a broad muzzle. There are two puppies, Muir and Merrilees.[1] * * *

Your A. Chekhov

TO A. S. SUVORIN

Melikhovo, October 18, 1892

* * * I am far from cheating myself, my dear man, about the true condition of affairs; not only am I bored and dissatisfied, but as a doctor I am cynical enough to be convinced that from this life we can expect only evil—errors, losses, illnesses, weakness, and all kinds of dirty tricks. Nevertheless, if you only knew how pleasant it is not to pay rent, and with what delight I left Moscow yesterday. It is a new thing for me to realize that I am not obligated to live on such and such a street in such and such a house. Today I was strolling in the snowy fields; there was not a soul near me, and it seemed to me that I was strolling on the moon. . . . For touchy people, neurasthenics, the desert

[1] A British firm, well known in Russia.

is the most comfortable habitat. Here nothing frets your pride, and so you don't rage over what is not worth an eggshell. Here there is room in which to move about and you read more. The only bad thing is the absence of music and singing, and also that wild horses won't drag you here. Other things are either replaceable or can be easily obtained in Moscow for money, and Moscow is but a stone's throw from me.

Winter. My section is already closed, but patients keep coming nevertheless. Yesterday I took two tales to *Russian Thought*. I shall work all winter long without getting up, in order to leave for Chicago in the spring. From there across America and the Pacific to Japan and India. After what I saw and felt in the Orient, I am not drawn to Europe, but if I had time and money I would go to Italy and Paris again.

* * * There were eleven cholera cases in our neighborhood. These are the blossoms, the berries will come in the spring. High mortality is a serious matter. We are poor, you know, and uncultivated, because we have much land but a scanty population.

Write me something about Tolstoy.

On October 20 there will be a zemstvo meeting. I understand that they propose to thank me for organizing my section. From August to October 15 I registered five hundred patients on cards; I probably received no less than a thousand. My section turned out to be an outstanding one, in that it had a doctor, a medical assistant, two excellent barracks, patients were visited and reports sent to the sanitary bureau, but no more than 110 rubles and 76 copecks were spent. I place the lion's share of the expenses on the shoulders of the neighboring manufacturers, who did the work of the zemstvo.

Please write to me. It is good that you weren't present at Svobodin's funeral. Generally speaking, never attend funerals.

Your A. Chekhov

TO I. L. LEONTYEV-SHCHEGLOV

Melikhovo, October 24, 1892

Had it not been for the pilot of *The Week*, who sent me your address and wrote about you, I wouldn't know what planet you are on and what is happening to you. It is a long, long while since I have written to you, dear Jean, and a long, long while since I have seen your tragic handwriting. —Well, sir, as you know, I have already moved out of Moscow and am living on an honorably acquired estate. I've gone deeply into debt (nine thousand!!), the weather is venomous, the roads cannot be traveled, either on wheels or runners, but one is not drawn to Moscow nor does one wish to leave the house to go anywhere. It is warm indoors and it is spacious outdoors; outside the gate is a bench on which one can sit awhile and, contemplating the umber field, meditate on this and that. . . . Stillness. No dogs howling, no cats miaowing, and the only thing one can hear is a little wench running all over the garden and trying to put the sheep and calves where they belong. I pay interest and assessments, but all this comes to only one half of the rental of an apartment in Moscow.

As a cholera doctor I see the sick, who are, every now and then, too much for me, but, after all, they are three times easier to bear with than discussions of literature with visitors in Moscow. It is warm here, and spacious, and the neighbors are interesting, and living is cheaper than in Moscow, but, dear captain—there's old age! Old age, or being too lazy to live, I don't know which, but one does not particularly want to live. One does not want to die but living, too, has become a bore, somehow. In short, the soul is having a taste of what the cold sleep is like. * * *

Your A. Chekhov

TO A. S. SUVORIN

Melikhovo, November 25, 1892

It is not difficult to understand you, and you should not have scolded yourself for failing to express yourself clearly. You are an inveterate drunkard, and I treated you to sweet lemonade, so, granting lemonade its due, you correctly observe that there is no alcohol in it. What our works lack is precisely spirits that intoxicate and captivate, and you made that crystal clear. And why is this so? Leaving aside "Ward Number 6" and me, let's talk about things in general, which is more interesting. Let's talk about causes, if it doesn't bore you, and let's deal with the entire epoch. Tell me in all conscience, has any one of my contemporaries, people thirty to forty years old, given the world even a drop of alcohol? Aren't Korolenko, Nadson, and all present-day playwrights lemonade? Have Repin's or Shishkin's canvases bowled you over? The stuff is nice, talented, you admire it, and at the same time you cannot forget that you'd like to have a smoke.

Science and technology are passing through a great period now, but for our writing fraternity it is a flabby, sour, dull time; we ourselves are sour and dull, and can only beget gutta-percha boys,[1] and the only one who does not see it is Stasov,[2] whom Nature has endowed with the rare ability to get drunk even on slops. The cause of this is not our stupidity, or our lack of talent, or our insolence, as Burenin thinks, but a disease which for an artist is worse than syphilis and impotence. We lack "something"—that is true, and it means that if you lift the skirt of our Muse, you will find the spot level. Remember that the writers whom we call eternal or simply good and who intoxicate us have one very important characteristic in common: they move in a certain direction and they summon you there too, and you feel, not with your mind alone, but with your whole being, that they have a goal, like the ghost of Hamlet's father, who did not come and trouble the imagination for nothing. Some, depending on their caliber, have immediate objects: abolition of serfdom, liberation of their country, politics, beauty, or, like Denis Davydov,[3] simply vodka; others have remote objectives: God, immortality, the happiness of mankind, and so forth. The best of them are realistic, and paint life as it is, but because every line is permeated, as with sap, by the consciousness of a purpose, you are aware not only of life as it is, but of life as it ought to be, and that captivates you. And we? We! We paint life as it is, and beyond that neither whoa! nor giddap! Whip us and we cannot go a step farther. We have neither immediate nor distant aims and our souls are a yawning void. We have no politics, we don't believe in revolution, we have no God, we are not afraid of ghosts, and I personally am not afraid even of death and blindness. One who desires nothing, hopes for nothing, and fears nothing cannot be an artist. Whether it is a disease or not—that is a question of name and doesn't matter, but it must be admitted that our situation is unenviable. I do not know how it will be with us in ten or twenty years, when circumstances will have changed, but in the meantime it would be rash to expect something of real worth from us, regardless of

[1] An allusion to "The Gutta-percha Boy," a story by D. V. Grigorovich.

[2] Vladimir Vasilyevich Stasov (1824–1906), an art critic.

[3] Denis Vasilyevich Dadydov (1784–1839), a versifier whose early work was valued for its spirited praise of martial valor and of the pleasures of drink. He fought as a partisan in the War of 1812.

whether we are gifted or not. We write automatically, obeying a long-established routine, according to which some people are in the government service, others in trade, still others write. . . . You and Grigorovich consider me intelligent. Yes, I am, at least to the extent that I don't hide my illness from myself, don't lie to myself, don't cover my vacuity with other people's rags, such as the ideas of the '60s and the like. I won't throw myself down a stair-well like Garshin, nor shall I delude myself with hopes for a better future. I am not to blame for my illness, and it is not for me to doctor myself, for the disease, it must be supposed, has ends that are hidden from us and that have not been visited upon us without reason. * * *

Your A. Chekhov

TO A. S. SUVORIN

Melikhovo, December 3, 1892

That the writers and artists of the latest generation lack an aim in their work is a curious phenomenon that is entirely legitimate and logical, and if Sazonova,[1] for no reason at all, got scared by a bogey, that doesn't mean that my letter[2] was wily and disingenuous. You yourself discovered it to be insincere only after she had written you, or you would not have sent her my letter in the first place. In my letters to you I am often unjust and naïve, but I never write what is not in my heart.

If you are looking for insincerity, you will find tons of it in her letter. "The greatest miracle is man himself and we shall never tire of studying him." Or: "The aim of life is life itself." Or: "I believe in life, in its bright moments, for the sake of which one *can*, indeed one *must*, live; I believe in man, in that part of his soul which is good. . . ." Can all this be sincere, and does it mean anything? This isn't an outlook, it's caramels. She underscores "can" and "must" because she is afraid to speak of what is and what has to be reckoned with. Let her first say what is, and only then I will listen to what one can and must do. She believes in "life," and that means that if she is intelligent, she believes in nothing, and if she is a country wife, she believes in a peasant God and crosses herself in the dark.

[1] Sofya Ivanovna Sazonova was a contributor to *New Times*.
[2] The previous letter to Suvorin (November 25), which began the present discussion of purposiveness in art.

Under the influence of her letter you write me about "life for life's sake." Thank you very much. You've got to admit that her letter with its paean to life is a thousand times more funereal than mine. I write that we are without aims, and you realize that I consider aims necessary and would gladly go looking for them, but Sazonova writes that one must not allure man with all manner of good things that he will never get: "prize that which is," and in her opinion all our trouble comes from the fact that we keep pursuing lofty and distant aims. If this isn't a country wife's logic, it's the philosophy of despair. He who sincerely believes that man needs lofty and distant aims as little as a cow does, that "all our trouble" comes from pursuing these aims—has nothing left him but to eat, drink, sleep, or if he is fed up with that, he can take a running start and dash his head against the corner of a chest.

I'm not scolding the lady, I'm only saying that she is far from being a very jolly person. She is apparently nice enough, but all the same you shouldn't have shown her my letter. She is a stranger to me and I feel awkward about it now.

Hereabouts people are already riding tandem and cooking cabbage soup with smelts. We have already had two snowstorms that ruined the roads, but now the weather is calm and it smells of Christmas. * * *

Your A. Chekhov

TO A. S. SUVORIN

Melikhovo, December 8, 1892

Oh, if only you knew how exhausted I am! I am so tired that I am utterly tense: guests, guests, guests. . . . My farm is located on the Kashira highway, and every passing intellectual considers it necessary and a matter of duty to drop in on me in order to warm up, and sometimes stays the night. A whole legion of physicians alone have come down on me! Of course, it is a pleasure to be hospitable, but there are limits. . . . You know, I left Moscow to get away from visitors. And now the Astronomer [1] has arrived and is going to spend the night. . . . What a chatterer!

[1] The nickname of Olga Petrovna Kundasova. Chekhov nicknamed her the Astronomer because she was once on the staff of the Moscow Observatory.

And I have to write, write, and I must not spare the horses, because for me not writing means getting into debt and having the blues. I write a piece in which there are a hundred characters, summer, autumn [2]—and all this falls apart, gets entangled, is forgotten. . . . A plague on it! Take a trip to Petersburg? But in Petersburg I work sluggishly and accomplish little. Go to Moscow and take a room in a hotel there? But in such a room I'd perish of boredom. I shall probably end by coming to Petersburg without having written half a sheet and having scattered on the way whatever had been in my head. I envy you having an apartment in Tsarskoe Selo,[3] though I don't believe that you will remain alone there. Even there people will find you. . . .

The Astronomer was in the Caucasus and now is on her way to Petersburg to study mathematics. She also wants to occupy herself with literature—to turn out compilations that had never before appeared in Russian periodicals, but she says it is impossible to start work right away because a minimum of four years is needed for preparatory labors. This prima donna apparently believes that she will live 386 years.

Your A. Chekhov

2 Probably "Three Years."
3 The suburb of Petersburg now called Pushkin.

[229]

$\begin{bmatrix} 1893 \end{bmatrix}$

TO J. I. OSTROVSKY[1]

Melikhovo, February 11, 1893

Most esteemed Josif Isayevich!

* * * You know, in general outline, my so-to-speak *curriculum vitae.* Medicine is my lawful wife, literature my illegitimate spouse. Of course, they interfere with each other, but not so much as to exclude each other.[2] * * * I am not rich and I live chiefly on what I earn. The older I get, the less and the more lazily I work. I feel old age upon me already. My health is not so good.* * *

Your A. Chekhov

TO A. S. SUVORIN

Melikhovo, February 24, 1893

I haven't yet seen *Russian Thought*, but I am looking forward to it. I do not like Protopopov.[1] He is an argumentative man who racks his brains, is sometimes just but dry and heartless. I am not acquainted with him personally and have never seen him; he has often written about me, but I have never read him. I am not a journalist; I have a physical aversion to abuse directed against no matter whom, I say—physical, because after reading Protopopov, The Denizen, Burenin, and other judges of humanity, the taste of rust remains in my mouth and my day is ruined.

---

[1] A doctor who had been a schoolmate of Chekhov's.

[2] In a letter of 1897 addressed to his Czech translator, Chekhov wrote: "I look upon medicine as my lawful wife and literature as my mistress, who is dearer to me than a wife."

[1] Mikhail Alekseyevich Protopopov was a journalist and literary critic. He had published an article in the monthly mentioned, attacking Suvorin and *New Times.* The chief purpose of this letter was to persuade the addressee not to engage in a public controversy with Protopopov.

It is simply painful. . . . Stasov called The Denizen a bedbug; but why, why did The Denizen revile Antokolsky? [2] This is no criticism, you know, not a matter of world view, but hatred, bestial, insatiable spite. To what end does Skabichevsky [3] damn people? Why this tone, as if not artists and writers are being judged but common criminals? I cannot, I cannot understand.

* * * My tale will be completed in the March issue.[4] "Continuation follows" instead of "End" is my error. While reading final proof, I wrote the former phrase instead of the latter word. You won't like the finale, I crammed things together. I should have made it longer. But to write at length would also have been risky, for there are few characters, and when in a fairly long story the same two figures keep reappearing, it becomes boring, and these figures grow dim. However, why talk about us old duffers? When will you send me your novel? I am hungry for it, so I can write a long critique of it.

Good Lord! How magnificent *Fathers and Children* is! Words fail, one is reduced to shouting for help. Bazarov's illness is done with such power that I felt weak and had the sensation of having caught his infection. And Bazarov's end? And the old parents? And Kukshina? This is done with diabolical skill. Simply a work of genius. *On the Eve* I don't like, all except Yelena's father and the finale. This abounds in the tragic. "The Dog" is very good. The language is marvelous. Please reread it, if you have forgotten it. "Asya" is a dear. "The Quiet Spot" is too crowded and unsatisfactory; *Smoke* I dislike altogether. *A Nobleman's Nest* is not superb, as *Fathers and Children* is, but the finale also resembles a miracle. All of Turgenev's women and girls are unbearably contrived and, forgive the term, false, except Bazarov's mother, and mothers generally, especially society ladies, who, however, resemble each other (Liza's mother, Yelena's mother) and Lavretzky's mother, a former serf, and also peasant women. Liza, Yelena, are not Russian girls, but some sort of Pythias, vaticinating, abounding in pretensions not befitting their rank. Irina in *Smoke* and Odintzova in *Fathers and Children*, generally lionesses, volcanic, seductive, insatiable, questing for something, all of them are rubbish. In comparison with Tolstoy's Anna Karenina all these ladies of Turgenev's with their tempting shoulders are worthless. The negative types, where Turgenev caricatures slightly

2 Mark Matveyevich Antokolsky, an eminent sculptor.

3 Aleksandr Mikhailovich Skabichevsky, a historian of literature.

4 The reference is to "The Story of an Unknown Man," which was being serialized in *Russian Thought*.

(Kukshina) or jests (descriptions of balls), are drawn remarkably and so flawlessly that it is impossible to pick holes in them. The descriptions of nature are good, but . . . I feel that we no longer respond to such descriptions and that something else is needed.[5]

My sister is improving. My father, too. We expect cholera, but are not afraid of it; we are ready, though not to die, but to spend zemstvo funds. If cholera comes, it will take up much of my time.

Stay alive, be well, at peace. A bow to your wife.

Wholly your A. Chekhov

We have received a lot of Ukrainian lard and sausage. What bliss!

TO A. P. CHEKHOV

Melikhovo, April 4, 1893

* * * I was planning to write to Suvorin, and haven't written him a single line, and therefore my letter,[1] which made the dauphin and his brother so indignant, is sheer invention. But once such things are said, then so be it: the old structure is cracking and must collapse. I am sorry for the old man, he has written me a penitential letter; I shall probably not have to break with him definitively, but as regards the editorial office and the dauphins, no kind of relationship with them smiles to me at all. In recent years I have grown indifferent and I feel my *anima* so free from the cares of the vain world that it is all the same to me what is said and thought in the office. Furthermore, as regards my convictions, I am divided by 5516 miles from The Denizen and Co. As publicists, they simply disgust me, as I have already declared to you more than once.

What I cannot get indifferent to is that *volens-nolens* you have to bear with the scrapes that you get into nearly every month.* * *

[5] In a letter to Olga Knipper of February 13, 1902, Chekhov was to write, "I am reading Turgenev. Of his work, one-eighth or one-tenth will remain; in twenty-five to thirty-five years all the rest will be relegated to the archives."

[1] Aleksandr had written to Chekhov on March 31 that he did not know the contents of Chekhov's letter "to old Suvorin," but did know its consequences. Suvorin's younger and elder sons "reproached you for black ingratitude," Aleksandr wrote to his brother. "You, they say—owe the old man everything, from the first to the last thread—from money to fame. Without him you would be a zero. But you, in gratitude, stick your nose into family affairs and set him against his children. They talk about this aloud in the office, in my presence."

A neighbor's wife is giving birth. Whenever a dog barks I expect that someone has come to fetch me. I have already made three visits.* * *

Your A. Chekhov

TO A. S. SUVORIN

Melikhovo, April 26, 1893

Greetings, congratulations on your return.* * * Well, I am going to write, first of all, about my own self. To begin with, I am sick. The sickness is vile, foul. Not syphilis, but worse—hemorrhoids, [. . .] pain, itching, tension, there is no sitting down, no walking about, and such irritation throughout the body that you are tempted to put your neck in a noose. It appears to me that no one wants to understand me, that everybody is stupid and unjust; I turn rancorous, I say foolish things; I think that all the members of my household will heave a sigh of relief when I go away. There, that's the kind of comeuppance it is, sir! My sickness can be accounted for neither by a sedentary life (since I was lazy and still am), nor by my dissolute conduct, nor by heredity. * * * In fine, an operation is mandatory.

Otherwise everything is fine. The chill spring has, it would seem, come to an end. I stroll through the fields without galoshes and bask in the sun. Am reading Pisemsky.[1] Great, great talent! His best work is *An Artel of Carpenters*. His novels tire one out with their details. Everything of his that is of a topical character, all these needlings directed at the critics and liberals of that day, all the critical comments aspiring to accuracy and contemporaneity, and all the so-called profound thoughts tossed off here and there—how petty and naïve all these things are by present-day standards!

There, that is just it: the novelist who is an artist must bypass everything the significance of which is of a temporary nature. Pisemsky's people are alive; his temperament is powerful. Skabichevsky in his *History* accuses him of obscurantism and betrayal, but, my God, among all the contemporary writers I do not know one who is as passionately and devotedly liberal as Pisemsky. All his priests, government clerks,

---

[1] Aleksey Feofilaktovich Pisemsky (1820–81), a novelist and playwright whose work was noted for its realistic and socially conscious character. His satire was directed against the gentry and officialdom, but also was scornful of starry-eyed radicals.

and generals, with never an exception, are scoundrels. Nobody has spat so copiously as he upon the old judicial system and military service. Incidentally, I have also read Bourget's *Cosmopolis*.[2] Bourget offers not only Rome but the Pope, and Correggio, and Michelangelo, and Titian, and the Doges, and a belle of fifty, and Russians, and Poles, but how watered down and affected and mawkish and false all this is by comparison even with that same crude and rather simple-hearted Pisemsky of ours.* * *

I probably won't go to America, because there isn't any money. I haven't earned anything: I was ailing and nursing a grudge against the weather. What a good thing it was, my getting away from the city! Tell all the Fofanovs, Chermnys,[3] *et tutti quanti* who live by literature that the country is immeasurably cheaper than the city. I experience this every day. My family no longer puts me to any expense, since quarters, bread, vegetables, milk, butter, horses are all our own and not boughten. As for work, there is so much of it that there isn't time enough. Of the whole Chekhov family I am the only one who lies down for a rest or sits at a desk while all the others are working from morning till evening. Drive the poets and fiction writers into the country! Why should they lead lives of poverty and semi-starvation? City life cannot offer a poor man any rich material as far as poetry and art are concerned. Writers live imprisoned within four walls and see people only in editorial offices and beer-halls.

Many sick people come. Many consumptives, for some reason. However, keep well, my dear.

The drought has begun.

Your A. Chekhov

TO A. S. SUVORIN

Melikhovo, July 28, 1893

I would immediately tool over to see you in Petersburg—that's the sort of mood I am in now; but there is cholera 14 miles from here, and I am the physician for this section and in duty bound to stay put in one spot, without any excursions. It would be possible to run off for two or three days, except that my female assistant gobbles morphine and is

[2] A novel that appeared in a Russian translation in 1893.
[3] Minor literary figures.

already three-quarters poisoned, and there isn't anybody with whom I could leave the section and the sick. There is only one thing left: to imagine that you have come to me at Melikhovo, which is so repellent to you, and brought along cigars from Ten-Kate, at 6 rubles and 50 copecks a hundred—"the kind Atava smokes."

My life this spring was revolting. I've already written you about that. Hemorrhoids and a repulsive psychopathic mood. I felt rancorous and depressed, and the family would not forgive me this mood—hence daily bickerings and my deathly craving for solitude. And spring proved abominable, cold. And there was no money. But a zephyr sprang up, summer set in—and all the troubles were gone, as if they had been waved away. Summer was amazing—a very rare summer. A plenitude of clear warm days and a profusion of moisture—such a happy conjunction must probably occur no oftener than once in a hundred years. A harvest to wonder at. Millet rarely ripens in the province of Moscow, but it is now waist high. If the harvests were always like that one could subsist on the produce of the estate alone, or even the hay alone, of which, with a certain effort, up to ten thousand bales of 36 pounds each could be mowed on my place. Last fall I dug a pond and planted trees around it. Now veritable clouds of minnows are already swimming about in it. And it's quite tolerable for a dip.

In the spring I didn't smoke at all and didn't drink at all, but now I smoke a cigar or two, and I find that it's very good for one's health not to smoke. You would do well to quit smoking. However, all these things are trifles and small talk. I didn't write a play about life in Siberia [1] and forget about it, but on the other hand I did turn in my *Sakhalin* for publication. I call it to your attention. Forget what you once read in my quarters, for it was false. I was occupied with the work a long time, and long felt that I was not on the right track, until at last I caught on to what was false. It consisted precisely in my wish to teach someone, as it were, with my Sakhalin, yet at the same time keeping something back and restraining myself. But no sooner had I begun to show what a freak I had felt myself to be on Sakhalin and what swine one found there, than things eased up for me and my work went swimmingly, even though it turned out to be a little humorous. The opening chapters will appear in the October issue of *Russian Thought.*

I have also written a bit of a tale that will run to 2 sheets—"The Black Monk." Well, if you would come, I would let you read it. Yes,

[1] There were one or two newspaper reports that he did write such a play.

sir! And coming here would not be so difficult. My carriages and horses are now fairly decent, the road is not so bad; the place is crowded and there is no privacy, but from these ills one can escape into the woods. I have no desire whatsoever to write a play.* * *

I have news: two dachshunds—Bromine and Quinine, dogs with an ugly appearance. Crooked paws, long bodies, but extraordinary intelligence.

Medicine is exhausting and trivial to the point of vulgarity. Occasionally I have to pay visits four or five times a day. You return from Krukovo and a messenger from Vaskino is already waiting in the courtyard, and peasant women with infants overpower me. In September I give up medical practice for good.

You want a mild spree. But I want one *dreadfully*. I am drawn infernally to the sea. To spend a week in Yalta or Feodosiya would be a true delight to me. Good as it is to be at home, it would be a thousand times better, it seems, to be aboard a steamer. I want freedom and money. To be lolling on deck, guzzling wine and chatting about literature—and in the evening ladies.

Won't you take a trip south in September? The Russian south, of course, since I won't have money enough to go abroad. We might take the trip together, if you have nothing against it.* * *

All the best!!

Write!!!

Your A. Chekhov

TO A. S. SUVORIN

Melikhovo, August 7, 1893

* * * My head has been aching for two days now. Have just come back from a factory to which I drove through the mud in a racing sulky and where I examined the sick. In the forenoon I was taken in a cart to see an infant who had diarrhea and was vomiting. In short, there isn't any time to think of literature. You are glad because I can drink wine at your expense, but when will that come about—that is, when shall I be drinking wine at your expense? What hurts is your going abroad. When I read about that in your letter it was just as if shutters had been closed within me. In case of trouble or boredom where am I to go?

Whom am I to turn to? There are devilish moods when one wants to talk and to write, yet I don't correspond with anybody but you, and there is nobody whom I talk with for any length of time. This doesn't mean that you are better than all those whom I know, but it does mean that I have grown used to you and that you are the only one with whom I feel free. Let me know your address, at least. I'm going to write you and send you off-prints—if I don't croak from cholera or diphtheria. But, probably, the latter contingency will not arise during late autumn and by then I shall be wining and dining with the St. Petersburg Decadents.* * *

Your A. Chekhov

TO L. S. MIZINOVA

Melikhovo, August 13, 1893

Dear Lika, I am not writing to you because there is nothing to write about; life is so empty that one feels only the flies biting—and nothing more. Do come here, darling little blonde—we'll talk, we'll quarrel, make up; without you I am bored, and I would give five rubles for the opportunity of talking with you for the space of even five minutes. There is no cholera, but there is dysentery, there is whooping cough, there is foul weather with rain, with humidity, with coughing. Hasten to us, pretty little Lika, and sing something. The evenings have grown long, and there is no human being nearby who might wish to dispel my boredom.

I shall be off to Petersburg when I am entitled to do so—i.e., after the cholera. Probably in October I shall already have installed myself there. I am thinking of putting up a building in that district and dream of resettling there. However, all this is vulgar. The only thing that is not vulgar is poetry, of which I feel the lack.

Money! Money! If I had the money I would be off to South Africa, about which I am now reading very interesting letters.[1] One must have a purpose in life, and when you travel you do have a purpose in life.* * *

Ivanenko,[2] the gawk, continues to be a gawk and to step upon roses, mushrooms, dogs' tails, and so on. Is he going to teach at Ivan's school? What do you know about this? I am limitlessly sorry for him, and I

[1] Probably *Letters from Africa* by Henry Sienkiewicz, translated from the Polish.
[2] A. I. Ivanenko was an unemployed flautist who lived with the Chekhovs.

would give him a piece of land and build him a house, if it were proper and if it were not taken amiss. He is, you know, already an old man!

I, too, am an old man. It seems to me that life wants to make game of me a bit, and that's why I hasten to set myself down as an old man. When, having frittered away my youth, I shall want to live in a human way and shall not be able to, I shall have an excuse: I am an old man. All this is silly, though. Forgive me, Lika, but, truly, there is nothing to write about. What I need is not to write, but to sit near you and talk.

I'm going to supper.

Our apples are ripe. I sleep seventeen out of the twenty-four hours. Lika, if you have fallen in love with somebody and already forgotten me, at least don't laugh at me. * * *

Keep well, my dear Lika, and do not forget me. Even if you become enamored of a Tisha, nevertheless drop me a line.

Your A. Chekhov

TO A. S. SUVORIN

Melikhovo, August 24, 1893

About short stories I am not joking, because short short stories I shall place with a newspaper, that is *New Times*. I have every intention of writing such pieces. My dream: to build me a house in the woods, which I already own, set out roses, give orders that no one be received, and write these stories. I have chosen a marvelous spot for the house.

My plan a silly joke? But it would be even sillier if, in debt as I am, I should ask you to send me another thousand rubles to Serpukhov. You write that my books will bring me twenty to thirty thousand rubles. Excellent. It is also said that I shall enter Paradise. But when will that be? Meanwhile one wants to live in the present, one wants the sun, of which you write.* * *

We have built a new kitchen, as well as quarters for the help, which has dealt a heavy blow to my pocket. We exterminated the cockroaches —and this, you see, is likewise an historical event. Rains rage, the spring crops are rotting in the fields.

I will start building my house in April. A two-story house. I shall be living there in solitude, without any female servants. Women are uncleanly and talk far too much about their industriousness. Before the house spreads a broad field with a distant view—a village, more than a mile away. The park takes up 55 acres or thereabouts. All these things depend, of course, on one contingency: that I do not use up for the winter's living expenses all the money I take in for *Sakhalin*. Yet I have already eaten up 1100 rubles. Tell Witte [1] to entrust me with cooking up some project or other, and pay me for it. Despite all these grandiose plans and dreams of solitude, of a two-story house and so on, I clearly realize that, sooner or later, I shall wind up bankrupt—or, more correctly, with the liquidation of all plans and daydreams.

My quarters are crammed. You can imagine: Ivan and wife; Ivanenko, who has been living here more than a year, while waiting to have a place found for him in Moscow. At dinner they needle one another. Stupid and boring.* * *

Your A. Chekhov

TO L. S. MIZINOVA

Melikhovo, September 1, 1893

Darling Lika, you have fished the word egoism out of a dictionary of foreign words and regale me with it in each letter of yours. Give that word as a name to your lapdog, do.

I eat, sleep, and write for my own pleasure? I eat and sleep because all people eat and sleep; even you are no stranger to these weaknesses, despite your ethereality. As for writing for one's own pleasure—why, my bewitching one, you managed to twitter as you did merely because you have no firsthand familiarity with the whole burden and oppressive force of this worm gnawing at life, no matter how small that worm may seem to you.

I succeed in everything? Yes, Lika, in everything—except, perhaps, that right now I don't have a cent, and I don't see you. However, I am not going to argue with you. Have it your way. The only thing I can't share with you, my friend, is my amazement: that you, without rhyme or reason, should have hit on the notion of telling me off.

On my way to Petersburg I shall drop in on you, without fail, but I am counting on the kindness of fate: perhaps you'll visit Melikhovo once more before my trip to Petersburg.

[1] Count Julius Witte, Minister of Finance.

During one of the winter months I shall settle in Moscow and live there for ten or fifteen days.

It is cold, Lika, it is abominable.

Your A. Chekhov

I shall be in Moscow probably about September 10.

TO A. S. SUVORIN

Melikhovo, November 11, 1893

I am alive and well. The cough is worse, but still I think I am far from consumption. Smoking I've reduced to one cigar every twenty-four hours. During the summer I sat in one spot, treated sick people, visited patients, expected cholera. I received a thousand patients, wasted much time, but there was no cholera. I wrote nothing, and simply took advantage of the time free from medicine to read, and put my bulky Sakhalin book in order. * * *

Pascal is drawn well,[1] but there is something in his innards that isn't good. When I get diarrhea at night, I place a cat on my stomach that warms me like a compress. Clotilde or Abishag is the cat that warms King David. Her earthly lot is to warm an old man, and nothing else. An enviable lot! I am sorry for Abishag, who did not compose psalms but in the sight of God was probably purer and more resplendent than the ravisher of Uriah's wife. She, a human being, a person, is young, and naturally desires youth, and one must be, excuse me, a Frenchman to make her—in the name of the devil knows what—a warming pan for a white-haired Cupid with stringy cock's legs. It offends me that Pascal, not some younger and stronger man, used Clotilde; old King David, exhausted in the embrace of a young girl—this is an unripe muskmelon that has already been touched by the autumnal frost of early morning but still imagines it can ripen—to every fruit its time, as they say. And besides, what nonsense: is sexual potency a sign of real life, of health? [...] All thinkers were already impotent at forty, and every primitive at ninety keeps ninety wives. Serf-owners preserved their procreative powers and impregnated Agashkas and Grushkas until the moment when, at a most advanced age, they were struck down by apoplexy. . . . I am not moralizing, and probably my own old age

---

[1] The hero of Zola's novel *Docteur Pascal.*

will not be free from attempts to "draw my bow," as Apuleius puts it in *The Golden Ass*. Judging humanly, there is little that is objectionable in the fact that Pascal slept with a young girl. That's his private business. But what is bad is that Zola praised Clotilde for sleeping with Pascal, and it's bad that Zola called this perversion love. * * *

Recently I've become frivolous and at the same time I am drawn to human beings as never before, and literature has become my Abishag and I've become so devoted to it that I've begun to despise medicine. But in literature I love not those novels and stories that you expect from me, or that you have ceased to expect, but the fact that during many hours I can read lying on the couch. For writing I haven't enough passion. * * *

I wish you all the best. * * *

Your A. Chekhov

TO V. A. GOLTZEV[1]

Melikhovo, December 28, 1893

Potapenko and Lika have just arrived here; Potapenko is already singing. But how sad it is that you could not come! The weather is excellent, and we have wine, but above all, you could rest from Moscow impressions, of which you seem to be dreadfully sick. Furthermore, it would not have done us any harm to talk of this and that, for example, about the proof [2] that was waiting for you, but since you failed to come, it went to bed; however, I'll mail it to you not later than New Year's.

Ah, my story [3] in *The Russian Bulletins* was given a haircut, so thoroughly that with the hair the head, too, was cut off. Purely childish chastity, and amazing cowardice. If they had deleted several lines, it wouldn't much matter, but they sliced off the middle, gnawed off the end, and my story lost so much that it turned my stomach.

Well, let us assume that it is cynical, but then it shouldn't have been printed at all, or it would have been just to say a word to the author, or deal with the matter by letter, all the more so since the piece did not get into the Christmas number and its publication was postponed indefinitely.[4] But all this is uninteresting. Excuse the boredom.

---

[1] Viktor Aleksandrovich Goltzev (1850–1906), critic, publicist, and editor of the distinguished liberal monthly *Russian Thought*.
[2] Of "A Woman's Kingdom."
[3] "Big Volodya and Little Volodya."
[4] It was printed in the issue of December 28.

* * * Write me when you can come. Besides New Year's, you know, there is also Epiphany.

We could talk about a play, which we might compose together, if you wish. I do. Think it over.

I have no money, none, and there won't be any soon, deuce take it. I had counted on January pay from *The Russian Bulletins,* but after the incident with the story I have lost all appetite for that pay. Don't say anything about it to Sablin.[5]

It would be most convenient and peaceful if I evaded contributing further to the paper, citing lack of time as the main cause.

Bring your little girl. A dachshund of ours has whelped—if she likes we shall present her with a puppy. And give her a sleigh ride.

At midnight on the 31st remember me in your orisons, just as I shall remember you.

Keep well, my dear.

Lika, too, has started singing.

Your Antoine

[5] Mikhail Alekseyevich Sablin (1842–98), a contributor to *The Russian Bulletins.*

$\left[\,1894\,\right]$

TO A. S. SUVORIN

Melikhovo, January 2, 1894

You laugh at my thoroughness, aridity, pedantry, and at the descendants who will value my work,[1] but I repay evil with good: I read your latest Letter about the schism [2] with delight, and offer you high praise. A magnificent Letter, and its success is wholly intelligible. First, it is fervent, second, liberal, third, very intelligent. Your liberal position is always remarkably winning. But when you attempt to develop conservative views, or even use conservative expressions (like "at the foot of the Throne") you remind one of an enormously ponderous bell with a crack in it which produces a false note.

My *Sakhalin* is an academic work and I shall win the Archbishop Makarius prize [3] with it. Medicine cannot now accuse me of infidelity: I have rendered just tribute to learning and to that which the old writers used to call pedantry. And I rejoice because the rough garb of the convict will also be hanging in my wardrobe. Let it hang there! To run *Sakhalin* in some journal won't do, of course—it isn't journalistic work; as a book, however, I think it will prove of some use. At any rate, you laugh in vain. He laughs best who laughs last. Don't forget that I shall shortly be seeing your new skit. * * *

Your A. Chekhov

TO A. S. SUVORIN

Melikhovo, January 25, 1894

* * * I think I am mentally fit. True, I am not especially eager to live, yet this is not, properly speaking, a disease, but something probably

---

[1] *The Island of Sakhalin.*

[2] The mid-seventeenth-century break between the innovating Russian Orthodox Church and the Old Believers. These were being persecuted by both Church and State, and Suvorin attacked the persecutors.

[3] A jesting invention of Chekhov's.

temporary and, indeed, a normal occurrence in everyday life. In any event, if an author depicts a person mentally ill, it does not mean that he himself is a mental case. I wrote "The Black Monk" in a state of cold reflection and without any gloomy thoughts. I simply took it into my head to picture megalomania.[1] As for the monk scudding along over the fields, I saw him in a dream, and after I woke up in the morning I told Misha about it. So tell Anna Ivanovna[2] that poor Anton Pavlovich has not yet, thank God, gone off his rocker, but at supper he overeats and as a result dreams of monks. * * *

May angels and archangels, cherubim and seraphim guard you.

Your A. Chekhov

TO A. S. SUVORIN

Yalta, March 27, 1894

Greetings!

There, by now it is almost a month that I've been in Yalta, in dreariest Yalta, at the Hotel Russia, in Room No. 39, while in No. 38 is Abarinova, your favorite actress. Spring weather, warm and radiant, the sea is all that a sea ought to be, but the people are in the highest degree tedious, dull, lackluster. I acted foolishly in giving up all of March to the Crimea. I should have taken a trip to Kiev and there devoted myself to the contemplation of sanctuaries and the Khokhol spring.

I am still coughing, but, just the same, on April 5 I shall move on northward toward my penates. I cannot stay on here any longer. Besides, there's no money. I took along only 350 rubles. If you deduct the traveling expenses coming and going, there will be 250 rubles left—and with such funds you won't be overindulging your appetite. If I had a thousand, or fifteen hundred, I would go to Paris, and that would be fine for many reasons.

In general, I am well; I am ill in certain particulars. For instance—coughing, an irregular pulse, hemorrhoids. Once the irregularity of the pulse happened to last for six days without a break, and the sensation

---

[1] "If I had not become a writer," Chekhov told a friend, "I would probably have become a psychiatrist."

[2] Suvorin's wife.

during all that time was disgusting. After having given up smoking for good I no longer have gloomy and anxious moods. Perhaps it is due to my having given up smoking that Tolstoyan morality has ceased to move me; in the depth of my soul my attitude toward it is inimical—and that, of course, is unjust. There is muzhik blood flowing through my veins, and you won't bowl me over with muzhik virtues. Since my childhood I had come to have faith in progress, and could not help but have that faith, inasmuch as the difference between the time when they used to flog me and the time when they ceased to flog me was a terrible one. I loved intelligent people, sensitiveness, courtesy, wit; and as for some people picking their corns, or their foot clouts emitting a stifling odor—I regarded such things with the same indifference with which I regarded young ladies walking about in curlpapers of mornings. Tolstoy's philosophy, however, had moved me greatly, had possessed me for six or seven years, and this possession was due not so much to the basic theses, which had been known to me earlier, but to the Tolstoyan manner of expression, his reasonableness, and, probably, a *sui generis* hypnotism.

Now, however, something within me protests; shrewdness and justice tell me that there is greater love for man in electricity and steam than in continence and abstention from meat. War is an evil and law is an evil, but it does not follow that I must needs go about in bast sandals and sleep atop the oven with the hired hand and his wife, and so on, and so on. The gist of the matter does not consist in that, however, nor in the *pro et con*, but in the fact that, somehow or other, Tolstoy is water over the dam as far as I am concerned; he is no longer in my soul, and he has departed from within me, saying: I leave your house untenanted. I am free from having anyone billeted upon me.

I am fed up with discourses of every sort, and as for such nitwits as Max Nordau, I cannot read them without revulsion. Feverish patients do not want to eat, but they do want to have something and express their vague longing by calling for "something sort of sour." So I, too, want something sort of sour. And this is not accidental, since I notice precisely the same mood all around me. Everybody, it seems, was in love, has now fallen out of love, and is in search of new infatuations. It is very possible, and looks very much as though it would come to pass, that the Russian people will once more live through an infatuation with the natural sciences, and that the materialistic movement will once more be the vogue. The natural sciences are working wonders now, and they may advance upon the public like Mamai [1] and subdue it with their massiveness, their grandiosity. However, all this lies in the hand of God. Once you launch into philosophizing, though, your head will start going round and round.

A certain German in Stuttgart sent me 50 marks for a translation of a story of mine. How do you like that? I am for the Convention,[2] yet some swine has published in the papers an allegation that, during an interview, I had come out against the Convention. Also, certain phrases which I simply could not be capable of uttering are ascribed to me. * * *

Your A. Chekhov

TO L. S. MIZINOVA

Yalta, March 27, 1894

Darling Lika, thank you for the letter. Even though you are trying to work up a scare in that letter about your dying soon, and even though you are teasing about having been spurned by me, I thank you just the same. I know very well that you won't die and that nobody has been spurning you.

I am in Yalta and I am bored—even very bored. The local aristocracy, so to say, is putting on *Faust*, and I attend the rehearsals, and take delight in contemplating a veritable flowerbed of raven, auburn, flaxen, and blond little heads, listen to the singing, and eat; at the home of the headmistress of the girls' high school I eat *chebureks* [1] and mutton with buckwheat grits; invited by well-born families, I eat shchi with spinach; at the confectioner's, I eat, in my room at the hotel, I eat.

I go to bed at ten, I rise at ten, and after dinner I rest, but just the same I am bored not because "my ladies" are not around, but because the spring up north is better than the local variety, and because I cannot for even a moment get rid of the thought that I am obligated, that I am in duty bound, to write. To write, write, and write. I am of the opinion that true happiness is impossible without idleness. My ideal: to

---

[1] The supreme Tartar ruler of the fourteenth century, who laid waste a large section of what was to become Russia, the devastation leaving an indelible impression on the memory of the Russian people.

[2] The International Copyright Convention.

[1] Small pies made of thinly rolled unleavened dough and filled with mutton—an Oriental dish.

be idle and to love a plump girl. For me the highest delight is to ramble or lounge and do nothing at all; my favorite occupation is collecting whatever is worthless (scraps of paper, wisps of straw, and so on) and doing whatever is useless. At the same time I am a littérateur and am obliged to write even here, in Yalta. When you get to be a great singer, Lika dear, and they pay you a good salary, do bestow alms upon me: marry me off to yourself and board me at your expense, so as to enable me to do nothing. But, if you really should up and die, then let this be the task of Varya Eberle [2] whom, as you know, I love. I have become so frazzled by incessant thoughts of the obligatory, inevitable work that, for a week now, I have been tortured without let-up by an intermittent pulse. An abominable sensation.

I have sold my fox-lined overcoat for 20 rubles! It cost 60 rubles, but since it had already shed 40 rubles' worth of its fur, the price it fetched was not too low. The gooseberries haven't ripened here yet, but it is warm, bright, the trees are burgeoning, the sea has a summery look about it, the young ladies thirst for emotions but, just the same, the north is better than the Russian south—at least in the spring. With us of the north Nature is more melancholy, more lyrical, more Levitanesque, whereas here it is neither this nor that, just like good, sonorous but frigid verses. Owing to an intermittent pulse I have been abstaining from wine for a week, and because of that the setting here strikes me as even more impoverished. How are you doing in Paris? How are the Frenchmen? Are they to your liking? Oh, well—go right ahead.

Mirov gave a concert here and cleared 150 rubles. He bellowed like a white sturgeon, yet was enormously successful. I am dreadfully sorry I never studied singing; I, too, would have been able to bellow, since my throat abounds in the elements of râle and my octave, so they tell me, is a true one. I would be earning a living and enjoying my success with the ladies.

This June it won't be I who will come to Paris but you who will come to Melikhovo; you will be driven there by longing for your native land. You won't manage without revisiting Russia, if only for a day. You talk it over with Potapenko. This summer he, too, will be taking a trip to Russia. Traveling with him will turn out to be cheaper. Let him buy the ticket, and you simply forget to reimburse him (it won't

[2] Varvara Apollonovna Eberle, a singer who was a friend of Mizinova and of the Chekhov family.

be the first time for you). However, if you won't come here, I shall go to Paris. I am convinced, however, that come you will. It is difficult to conceive that you would forgo seeing Grandpa Sablin.

Be well, Lika, tranquil, happy, and content. I wish you success. You are a clever girl.

Should you care to pamper me with a letter, address it to Melikhovo, for which I will be leaving shortly. I shall answer your letters promptly. I kiss both your hands.

Your A. Chekhov

My lowest bow to V. A. Eberle.

TO A. S. SUVORIN

Melikhovo, July 11, 1894

You wrote that you would come to see me one of these days; I was waiting but instead of you only a newspaper kept coming, with the "Little Letters," from which I concluded that you are stuck fast in Petersburg and have changed your mind about taking trips anywhere. I am not drawn to Yasnaya Polyana. My brain has become flabby and does not pant for strong impressions. I would prefer a cabana by the sea and small talk about trifles.

Here's my plan. Between July 20 and 22 I'm going to Taganrog to treat an uncle who has fallen seriously ill and insists on my help. He is the most excellent of men and to turn him down would be awkward, even though I know my help is of no use. I shall stay in Taganrog for one day, two or three days, take a dip in the sea, visit the local cemetery, and then head back for Moscow; there, having done with *Sakhalin* and sent up thanks to heaven, I declare myself a free man, ready to go wherever I please. If there is any money I'll go abroad, or to the Caucasus, or to Bokhara. However, it is in the area of my finances that the difficulties will most probably occur, so that changes in my plan are inevitable. You might tell Witte, the Minister of Finance, that instead of distributing subsidies right and left, or promising a hundred thousand to some fund, he ought to arrange things so as to enable littérateurs and artists to ride on the government-owned railways free. With the exception of Leikin (mention him not at night!) all Russian men of letters are living in what is practically a state of semistarvation, inasmuch as every man of letters, even one who turns out a hundred sheets a year, if so the fates decree, is saddled with the devil's own plenty of obligations. And there is nothing more wearisome and unpoetic, so to say, than the prosaic struggle for existence, which deprives life of joy and brings on apathy. However, all this has nothing to do with the matter at hand. If you are going with me to Taganrog—a most appealing town—then let's go. In August I'll be at your service: we'll move on to Switzerland.

* * * If you have any new tidbit, do write. Write me about Taganrog too. I am inviting you to this town on the basis of your declaration that it is all one to you where you go, as long as it isn't abroad. As for me, I have of late begun to have dreams of taking a trip across the steppe and living there under the open sky, even if it be for no longer than a day and a night. About ten years ago I went in for spiritualism, and the spirit of Turgenev which I had raised answered a question of mine with: "Your life is nearing its sunset." And, truly, I am now experiencing as intense a desire for all manner of things, as though carnival had already arrived. It looks as if I could lap up everything: both life abroad and a good novel. And some kind of force, just like a premonition, is urging me to make haste. However, it may be no premonition at all but simply regret because life is flowing along so monotonously and sluggishly. A protest of the soul, so to say. * * *

I bow low and pray heaven that your sins may be pardoned and all blessings granted you.

Archimandrite Antonius

TO A. S. SUVORIN

Melikhovo, August 15, 1894

* * * It may happen occasionally that you pass the third-class buffet and see some cold fish, fried a long time ago, and reflect apathetically: who needs this unappetizing fish? At the same time there is, indubitably, a need for this fish, and it is eaten, and there are people who find it tasty. The same thing may be said about the works of Barantzevich. This is a bourgeois writer who writes for the better kind of third-class passengers. For this public Tolstoy and Turgenev are much too luxurious, too aristocratic, a trifle alien and indigestible. A public that finds corned beef with horseradish delectable but rejects artichokes and asparagus. Share their point of view: imagine a dingy, depressing

courtyard, intellectuals, ladies ,who look like cooks, the stench of the kerosene stove, the poverty of interests and tastes—and you will understand Barantzevich and his readers.

He is not colorful; this is partly because the life he depicts is not colorful. He is fraudulent (so-called "good books"), because bourgeois writers cannot help but be fraudulent. What we have here is writers of perfected gutter literature. Such writers sin along with their public, while the bourgeois writers play the hypocrite along with it and flatter its narrow little virtue. * * *

Good-bye, Your Excellency. Be well. My lowest bow to Anna Ivanovna, and all good wishes.

Your A. Chekhov

Where did you get the idea that I drink too much vodka? I cannot take more than three glasses at a time.

TO M. P. CHEKHOVA

Odessa, ca. September 14, 1894

* * * Vocational courses have been started in Taganrog, in which adolescent little girls of fifteen to twenty learn the art of sewing according to the latest fashions *(modes et robes)*. Sasha, our late uncle's daughter, who is now seventeen or eighteen, a dear, good little girl, was taking these courses and, by the mayor's account, was considered the star pupil. And really, she does sew beautifully. She has a great deal of taste. One day, in a talk with me, the mayor happened to complain that he simply could not find a teacher for these courses, that he would have to write to Petersburg for a teacher, and so on. I responded by asking, "If I should take my cousin, whom you praise so highly, to Moscow, and apprentice her there to the best modiste, would you then engage her as one of your teachers?" He answered that he would be delighted to do so. The stipulated salary of a teacher is 50 rubles a month—and incidentally this money would certainly come in handy for uncle's family, which will now be in need. Well, then, think about it: isn't it possible to do something for the little girl? She could be supported in Moscow for a winter and I would give her 15 or 20 rubles a month for a place to live; she could stay with you, which would not inconvenience

you much since—I repeat—she is a fine little girl. For the main thing is that she must be helped. Think about it until I arrive—and after that we'll talk it over. * * *

Your A. Chekhov

TO A. S. SUVORIN

Melikhovo, November 27, 1894

* * * I served as a juror in Serpukhov. Landed gentry, factory owners, and Serpukhov merchants—there's your jury panel. Through an odd chance I landed on the jury for every trial, without a single exception, so that the upshot was that it even aroused laughter. I was the foreman of the jury at all the trials. Here is my conclusion: (1) jurors are not characters dragged in from the street but people mature enough to be representatives of so-called social conscience; (2) among us kind people have an enormous authority, irrespective of their being nobles or peasants, educated or uneducated. A pleasant impression, on the whole.

I have been appointed as trustee of a school in a village bearing the name Talezh. The teacher receives 23 rubles a month, has a wife and four children, and is already gray, despite his being only thirty. So cowed is he by need that, no matter what you may start talking to him about he will bring the subject around to the problem of a salary. In his opinion poets and prose writers must write only about additional salaries; when the new Czar changes the ministers the salary of teachers will probably be increased, and so on. * * *

Your A. Chekhov

TO T. L. SHCHEPKINA-KUPERNIK[1]

Melikhovo, November 28, 1894

I shall be ecstatic when you come to me, but I am afraid that your delicious cartilages and little bones will be dislocated. The road is terrible. The tarantas, in agonizing pain, keeps leaping up and loses wheels at every step. The last time that I was driving from the station, because

---

[1] Tatyana Lvovna Shchepkina-Kupernik (1874–1953), author and translator, a close friend of Chekhov's.

[*251*]

of the jolting ride my heart was torn from its moorings, so that I am now incapable of love.

They say that your tale will be printed in *The Week*. I rejoice for you and congratulate you heartily. *The Week* is a solid and engaging journal.

Good-bye, dear friend.

Your A. Chekhov

TO YE. M. SHAVROVA

Melikhovo, December 4, 1894

* * * I am perfectly well. My novella, "Three Years," will appear in the January issue of *Russian Thought*. The project was one thing but what resulted was something else, rather flabby and not silken as I wanted it to be but cambric. You are an expressionist, you will not like it.

I am fed up with one and the same thing all the time; I want to write about devils, about terrifying, volcanic women, about wizards—but, alas! the demand is for well-intentioned tales and stories from the life of the Ivan Gavriloviches and their spouses.

Wishing you all the best,

Your A. Chekhov

TO A. S. SUVORIN

Melikhovo, December 5, 1894

* * * The public expects something out of the ordinary,[1] and the newspapers do not satisfy its expectations; its wishes, however, are extremely vague. Even the rumors are not definite; there is nothing but a persistent amorphousness of some kind. The Russian has always been more interested in foreign politics than in his own, and, as he listens closely to the talk around him, he can perceive how great the extent of the Russian intellectual's naïveté and superstition is and how meager his knowledge. As an infant the intellectual was injured by his nurse; his education was a process of cowing him so that he is afraid of having an

---

[1] On the occasion of the ascension to the throne of Nicholas II.

opinion of his own, and he has so little faith in himself that if he were to offer an ovation to Yermolova [2] today, he would feel badly about that ovation tomorrow. Come what may, however, everybody is in an expectant mood and hoping for something or other and, on meeting, everybody smiles. * * *

[2] Mariya Nikolayevna Yermolova, an actress.

[1895]

Moscow, January 10, 1895

Many thanks for having joined our company—and so generously, at that. Here is how we assist the person concerned: [1] give her 40 rubles a month and deceive her by saying that we have borrowed the money for her from a wealthy merchant and will not ask for payment of the loan before the expiration of three years. She does not accept any assistance from *us,* because it would embarrass her, so that, willy-nilly, it becomes necessary to lie. * * *

I am ailing, on and off—must have caught a cold. A hell of a cough has created for me the reputation of a valetudinarian, upon meeting whom people inevitably ask, "What is it—you seem to have lost weight?" Nevertheless, I am, on the whole, perfectly well and am coughing only because I have gotten into the habit of coughing. * * *

Thank you for your letter. Dash off some more lines for me about something. If you come here we might have a talk about the grain crisis.[2] The way I see it, this crisis will prove of great service to Russia. The horses are well fed, the pigs are well fed, the wenches are merry and walking about in rubber galoshes, cattle is bringing high prices— the muzhiks won't sell even calves. The kulaks alone are in a bad way— which is just what was needed.

Keep well.

Your A. Chekhov

---

[1] O. P. Kundasova.
[2] Brought about by a limitation on the export of grain.

TO V. V. BILIBIN

Moscow, January 18, 1895

* * * I am not writing a play, and besides, I do not want to write. I have grown old and the fervor is no longer there. What one wants is to write a novel a hundred miles long. When your play is ready, write me—do you need any pull with Korsh?

I live in the country; at rare intervals I drop in on Moscow, where I eat oysters. Getting old. No money. No decorations. No ranks. Debts there are.

I keep reading your works and I recall the past, and whenever some youthful humorist crosses my path I read him *Borodino* [1] and tell him, "Not you dare claim that you are mighty knights!" You and I were at one time very liberal, but I, for some reason, was considered a conservative. Not so long ago I looked through some back numbers of *Splinters*, already half-forgotten, and I was struck by the derring-do which at that time was so marked in you and me, and which is not to be found nowadays in a single one of the latest geniuses. * * *

Keep well.

Entirely yours,

A. Chekhov

TO A. S. SUVORIN

Melikhovo, January 21, 1895

* * * Fie, fie! So women take away one's youth? Not mine. In my time I have been a shop assistant, not an owner, and destiny pampered me very little. I have had few romantic affairs, and I bear much the same resemblance to Catherine that a walnut bears to an ironclad. As for silk chemises, all that they mean to me is that their softness makes them agreeable to handle. I do feel predisposed to comfort, but debauchery does not entice me, and I would be unable to appreciate Mariya Andreyevna,[1] for instance.

For my health's sake it is necessary for me to go to some distant place for eight or ten months. I shall go to Australia or to the estuaries of the

---

[1] A poem by Lermontov, from which the following quotation comes.
[1] The wife of I. N. Potapenko.

Yenisei. Otherwise I'll croak. Very well; I'll come to Petersburg—but shall I have a room in which I could hide? That is a question of considerable importance, for I shall be obliged to write all of February to earn the wherewithal for my voyage. Ah, how necessary it is to get away! My whole chest is wheezing, and the hemorrhoids are enough to make the devils queasy—there will have to be an operation. No, the deuce with it, with literature—I should have practiced medicine. But then, I have no business arguing about this. I am obliged to literature for the happiest days of my life and for what I am chiefly drawn to. * * *

Wholly yours,

A. Chekhov

TO YE. M. SHAVROVA

Melikhovo, February 28, 1895

You are right, the subject is risqué. I cannot tell you anything definite, I can only advise you to lock up the story in a chest and keep it there a whole year and then reread it. Then it would be easier for you to see it clearly; as for me, I am afraid to give you an opinion because I may be mistaken.

The story is somewhat thin: its thesis sticks out of it, the details spread like spilled oil, the characters are barely sketched. There are superfluous characters—for instance, the heroine's brother, the heroine's mother. There are superfluous episodes—for instance, the events and conversations before the wedding; in fact, everything that has to do with the wedding. But if these are deficiencies, they are not important ones. What is important, as I see it, is that you fail to control the formal aspect of the story. In order to settle such problems as degeneration, psychosis, etc., one must have scientific knowledge of them. The importance of the meaning of the disease (let us call it by the letter S, out of modesty) you exaggerate. In the first place, S is curable; in the second, if the doctors find that the patient has a certain serious illness, for instance, tabes or cirrhosis of the liver, and that it was caused by S, then they can make a relatively favorable prognosis, since S is subject to cure. In degeneration, in general nervousness, in debility, and the like, the cause is not S alone, but a combination of various factors, such as vodka, tobacco, the intellectuals' habit of eating too much and doing too little physical work, bad upbringing, the conditions of city life, etc., etc. And besides S, there are other diseases no less serious. For instance, tuberculosis. It seems to me, too, that it isn't the business of the artist to lash out at people because they are ill. Is it my fault if I have migraine? Is it Sidor's fault that he has S, that he is more susceptible to it than Taras? Is it Akulka's fault that her bones are tubercular? No one is guilty, and if there are guilty ones, it concerns the Board of Health, not the artist.

The physicians in your story behave vilely. You make them forget the secrecy to which they are sworn; moreover, they send a gravely sick paralytic into the city. Is it possible that the unhappy victim of the mysterious S was driven in a jolting tarantas? Also, the lady in your story treats S as a bugaboo. That's wrong. S is not a vice, not the product of evil will, but a disease, and the patients who suffer from it need warm, cordial treatment as much as any others. It's wrong for a wife to abandon her sick husband because his illness is infectious or foul. Whatever her attitude toward S, the author must be humane to the tips of his fingernails.

* * * I should like you to picture something full of the joy of life, luminously green, like a picnic. Leave it to lechers to represent cripples and black monks. I shall soon begin to write humorous stories, for my entire psychopathological repertory is exhausted.

I am building a bathhouse.

I wish you everything good, earthly and heavenly. Send me more "official papers." I love to read your stories. Only allow me to set you one condition: no matter how severe my criticism may be, it does not mean that a story is not fit to be published. My captiousness is one thing, publication and payment are another.

Your A. Chekhov

TO A. V. ZHIRKEVICH[1]

Melikhovo, March 10, 1895

Much esteemed Aleksandr Vladimirovich!

* * * Verse is not my province; I have never written any, my memory refuses to retain it, and, precisely as is the case with music, I am merely

---

[1] A. V. Zhirkevich (1857–1927) was a military jurist and a writer.

sensitive to verse but unable to say definitely why it makes me experience delight or boredom. Formerly I made attempts to correspond with poets and to express my opinion, but nothing came of all this as far as I was concerned and it did not take long for me to turn into a bore like a man who had the right feelings but who expounded his thoughts uninterestingly and vaguely. Nowadays I usually confine myself to writing: "I like this" or "I don't like this." Your poem [2] was to my liking.

As for the short story you are writing—it is another matter entirely; I am ready to write a critique of it running to even twenty sheets, and if you send it to me in due course and should wish to learn my opinion, why, it would give me great pleasure both to read it and to write you more or less definitely about it and I shall feel free to do so. * * *

Your sincerely dedicated A. Chekhov

TO A. S. SUVORIN

Melikhovo, March 16, 1895

* * * Your "Little Letter" dealing with athletic games for students may prove of benefit if you treat this theme persistently and frequently. Such games are absolutely necessary. That sort of thing is good for the health, and it's a pleasure to look at, and it's liberal—liberal in the sense that nothing so promotes the fusion of the classes as street and social games do. Such games would offer opportunities for friendship to our young men and women, who lead lonely lives; they would fall in love with one another more often. However, these games should not be instituted until the Russian student is no longer starving. No croquet, no stealing, will make the studiosus vigorous on an empty stomach. * * *

May the heavens, seen from the earth and seen from Sirius, protect you. In your orisons may I be remembered, write me two or three lines. Has the Astronomer called on you?

Your A. Chekhov

2 A long piece called *Pictures of Childhood*, published as a book in 1894.

TO A. S. SUVORIN

Melikhovo, March 23, 1895

* * * Very well—I'll get married, if that's what you want. But my conditions are: everything must be as it had been before this—that is, she will have to live in Moscow, while I'll live in the country and will make trips to see her. As for that bliss which persists day in and day out, from morning to morning—I won't be able to take it. When I am told every day about one and the same thing in the same never-varying tone, I become ferocious. I become ferocious in the company of Sergeyenko,[1] for instance, because he looks very much like a woman ("intelligent and responsive") and because in his presence the notion pops into my head that my wife may possibly look like him. I promise to be a splendid husband, but give me the sort of wife who, even as the moon, will not appear in my heaven each and every night: I won't write any better just because I get married.

And so you are going to Italy. * * * Greet her for me. I love her passionately, although you told Grigorovich that I lay down in the Piazza di San Marco and said, "It would be pleasant now to be lying down on the grass in our Moscow Province!" Lombardy made such a strong impression on me that it seems to me I remember every tree, and I see Venice with my eyes closed.

I've been living at Melikhovo for four years now. My calves have grown into cows, the woods are taller by more than a foot. My heirs will profit from the timber, and will call me an ass, for heirs are never satisfied. * * *

Wholly your A. Chekhov

TO A. S. SUVORIN

Melikhovo, April 13, 1895

* * * I am getting through with *The Polanietski Family* by Sienkiewicz —it's a Polish paschal cake of curds with saffron. If you take Paul Bourget and add some Potapenko, squirt Warsaw eau de cologne over the mixture, and dilute it to half-strength, your end product will be Sienkiewicz. The chronicle of the Polanietskis is beyond doubt inspired by the *Cosmopolis* of Bourget, by Rome, and by marriage (Sienkiewicz

---

[1] A former schoolmate of Chekhov's who became a writer.

married not so long ago); here also are the catacombs, and the old eccentric professor sighing for idealism, and Leo XIII, who is in the company of the saints, with a visage not of this earth, and an admonishment to revert to the prayer book, and the slander of the Decadent, who is dying because of morphine addiction, after having confessed and received Holy Communion—i.e., after having repented, in the name of the Church, of his errors. There is the devil's own plenty of discussion on domestic felicity and on love, and the wife of the hero is so utterly faithful to her husband, and comprehends God and life—with her *heart*—so subtly that, in the upshot, one feels overcome by mawkishness and embarrassment, as if after a slobbery kiss. Sienkiewicz has, apparently, never read Tolstoy, nor is he Nietzsche, while his comments on hypnotism are those of a philistine, but to make up for all this, every page of his is simply mottled with Rubenses, Borgheses, Correggios, Botticellis—and this for the sake of showing off his culture before the bourgeois reader and to show the fig—but only on the sly—at materialism. The intent of the novel: to lull the bourgeoisie in its golden dreams. Be true to your wife, pray with her according to the prayer book, accumulate money, love sport—and it's in the bag for you, in this world and the next. The bourgeoisie is ever so fond of so-called "positive" types and of novels with happy endings, since both soothe it with the reflection that one can both accumulate money and maintain one's innocence, be a beast and at the same time be happy.

We have a pitiful kind of spring. The snow is still lying in the fields and there is no riding either on runners or on wheels, and cattle are longing for grass and freedom. Yesterday a drunken old peasant, having taken off his clothes, was bathing in the pond. His decrepit mother was beating him with a stick, and everyone stood round them and guffawed. Having bathed, the peasant walked home barefoot in the snow, his mother after him. On one occasion this aged woman came to me to be treated for bruises—her son had given her a beating. To keep on postponing the enlightenment of the dark masses is so vile! * * *

Your A. Chekhov

TO A. S. SUVORIN

Melikhovo, October 21, 1895

Thanks for the letter, for the warm words and the invitation. I will come, but probably not before the end of November, since I have a devilish lot of work. First of all, this spring I shall be building a new school in the village, in my capacity of trustee. It is necessary, well in advance, to ready the plan, the estimates, to take trips now here, now there, and so on. Secondly, if you can imagine such a thing, I am writing a play [1] which, probably, I also shall finish no earlier than toward the end of November. I am writing it not without enjoyment, even though I am frightfully unfaithful to stage conventions. A comedy; three female roles, six male; four acts; a landscape (view of a lake); lots of literary talk, little action; a ton of love.

* * * Me, I am horrified . . . and here's the reason why. *The Surgical Chronicle.* [2] is published in Moscow—a splendid periodical which enjoys success even abroad. It is edited by Sklifasovsky and Dyakonov, well-known surgeons and scientists. The number of subscribers increases with every year, but still, toward the end of the year there is a deficit. Up to January of the coming year (1896) this deficit is covered, as it has always been, by Sklifasovsky but, having been transferred to Petersburg, he has lost his practice, has run out of extra funds, and now neither he nor anybody else on earth can tell who will cover the liability in 1896, in the event of there being one, and yet, to judge by analogy with past years, one must expect a deficit of 1000–1500 rubles. On learning that the periodical was perishing I grew hot under the collar; such an absurdity as the perishing of a periodical which one can't do without and which in no more than three or four years will be yielding a profit—the absurdity of its perishing for lack of a ridiculous sum struck me like a blow on the noddle and I rashly promised to find a publisher, feeling quite certain that find one I would. And I zealously sought one; I begged, humiliated myself, journeyed hither and yon, dined with the devil knows whom, but found nobody. Soldatenkov [3] was the only one left, but he is abroad and won't be back before December, whereas this problem must be settled by November.

How I regret that your printing plant is not in Moscow! If it were, I

1 *The Sea Gull.*
2 A medical journal of which Chekhov was a founder.
3 Kuzma Terentyevich Soldatenkov was a Moscow publisher and owner of a picture gallery.

wouldn't have played so ridiculous a role as that of the unsuccessful broker. When we see each other I shall paint for you a true picture of the tribulations I lived through. If it weren't for the building of the schoolhouse, which will cost me about 1500, I would undertake the publication of the periodical myself, at my own expense—that is how painful and hard it is for me to reconcile myself to a manifest absurdity. On October 22 I shall be off to Moscow and shall propose to the editors, as a last resort, that they should ask for a subsidy of one and a half or two thousand a year. If they agree, I shall tool over to Petersburg and start hustling. How does one go about it? You will teach me? In order to save the periodical I am ready to go to anybody at all and to cool my heels in the anteroom of anybody at all and, should I succeed, I would sigh with relief and a feeling of satisfaction, inasmuch as saving a good surgical journal is just as useful as performing twenty thousand successful operations. In any event, advise me as to what I am to do. * * *

Your A. Chekhov

TO A. S. SUVORIN

Moscow, October 26, 1895

* * * No, do not tempt me needlessly. I cannot come before November. I shall not leave until I finish the play. And having arrived, I shall stop not with you but at the France on Bolshaya Morskaya, for I have work up to my ears; if I stayed with you I should walk about and look for someone to chat with, and in a week, no more, I should start chasing myself out of Petersburg, frightened by my idleness. I intend to stay in Petersburg no less than a month. If you emphatically insist on my stopping with you I shall come to Petersburg without letting you know and shall stay in the France for three weeks, then I shall move to your quarters looking as though I had just come from the station and shall spend a week with you.

Tolstoy's daughters are very appealing. They deify their father and believe in him fanatically. And this means that Tolstoy is really a great moral force since, if he were insincere and not irreproachable, the first ones to regard him skeptically would be his daughters, because daughters are like sparrows: you won't take them in with chaff. —The bride and the mistress you can cozen to your heart's content, and to the beloved women's eyes even a jackass appears to be a philosopher, but daughters are a different breed altogether.

You write, "This note entitles you to draw 100 rubles for her at the bookstore." However, the note was not enclosed, nor do I see the Astronomer herself; they say that she has left for Batum to be with her sister. As regards *The Surgical Chronicle*, that journal itself, all the surgical instruments, bandages, bottles of carbolic acid bow to you down to the ground. Of course, great joy. We have made the following decision: if there is a chance of a subsidy, I shall go and start soliciting and if the subsidy is granted, the 1500 rubles will be returned to you. In November I shall see Sklifasovsky and if possible I shall go to see Witte to save these most naïve people. They are babes. It would be hard to find more impractical people. Be that as it may, the 1500 will be returned to you sooner or later. In gratitude for my endeavors my hemorrhoidal knot will be removed free of charge—an operation which is unavoidable and which is beginning to disturb me. You will be glorified when you come to Moscow and will be shown the new hospital near the Novo-Devichy Monastery. Hospitals should be visited, just as cemeteries and circuses are.* * *

Your A. Chekhov

TO A. S. SUVORIN

Melikhovo, November 10, 1895

* * * My play is moving ahead; for the time being everything is going swimmingly, but what may befall later on, toward the end, I know not. Shall finish in November. Pchelnikov,[1] through Nemirovich, has promised to give me an advance in January (if the play is found suitable), so they must be considering a postponement of the play's production until the following season. It must be because of the play that my pulse is more frequently intermittent; I fall asleep at a late hour and, in general, feel wretched, although since my return from Moscow I have been leading a life of moderation in all respects. I ought to go in for sea-bathing and get me a wife. I am afraid of a wife and family routine, which would hinder me and which, I imagine, does not jibe, somehow,

[1] Pavel Mikhailovich Pchelnikov, business manager of the Moscow Imperial Theaters.

with my disorderliness,* but still this is better than bobbing about in the sea of life and weathering the storm in the frail bark of depravity. Besides, by now I actually have no love for mistresses. [. . .]

* * * I did not use your 1500 rubles for *The Surgical Chronicle* but just the same they were mighty helpful to me. When it became known that you wanted to support the periodical, and when I showed your letter, in which you wrote of the 1500 and of the possibility of a subsidy, the business went like a house afire. Sytin [2] undertook the publication on satisfactory terms; he assumes all the expenses and pays the editors 2 rubles for each subscriber, retaining 6 rubles for himself.* * *

Your A. Chekhov

* You have spoiled my handwriting. After your letters it is difficult to write legibly.

TO A. S. SUVORIN

Melikhovo, November 21, 1895

Well, sir, I have finished my play. I began it *forte* and wound it up *pianissimo*—contrary to all the precepts of dramatic art. The end product was a novella. I am more dissatisfied than satisfied and, while reading my new-born play, I became convinced once more that I am no dramatist. The acts are very brief, there are four of them. Although so far this is only the skeleton of a play, a project which will yet undergo a million changes before the coming season, I have nevertheless ordered two copies to be printed on a Remington (a machine that prints two copies simultaneously)—and I'll send you one. Only don't give it to anybody to read.* * *

[2] Ivan Dmitriyevich Sytin, publisher and book dealer. He changed his mind almost at once about issuing the periodical. Further, the surgeon Pyotr Ivanovich Dyakonov, a co-editor of the journal, insisted that a contribution from such an obscurantist as Suvorin could not be accepted. By the next year the journal had folded.

[1896]

Melikhovo, March 11–13, 1896

Good Lidiya Stakhiyevna!

I shall arrive on Saturday by a fast train at 8 o'clock. Here is the schedule of my stay:

1. When the train stops at the station, having convinced myself that no one is meeting me, I shall hire a cab for 20 copecks and go to the Moscow Grand Hotel.

2. Having surrendered my baggage and taken a room, I shall hire a cab for 10 copecks and go to Theodore's, where I shall get a haircut for 15 copecks.

3. Having been made younger and handsomer by the haircut, I return to my room.

4. At 10 in the evening I shall go to a restaurant in order to eat a half portion of a ham omelette. If Lidiya Stakhiyevna is with me, I shall spare her a small piece of my portion, and if she makes a persistent demand, I shall order for her, at my expense, a bottle of beer.

5. After supper I shall go down to my room and go to bed, glad that I am at last alone.

6. Having awakened in the morning, dressed, washed, I shall be driven to the flea market to buy books.

7. I shall leave Moscow Tuesday morning, having refrained from all excesses and not having allowed anyone to take liberties, in spite of persistent demands.

Good-bye, good Lidiya Stakhiyevna.

Respectfully,
Your A. Chekhov

TO A. A. TIKHONOV[1]

Much esteemed Aleksey Alekseyevich!

In vain do you envy me. Here is no spring whatsoever. Snow; snow drifts; fur-lined overcoats; and, of mornings, the thermometer indicates $-11°$ C. The starlings haven't come winging back yet, while the rooks stalk along the roads despondently, like mutes carrying torches. According to the observations of the muzhiks, the rooks are unusually gaunt this year; evidently, while in flight, they had nothing to eat. Which means that it's cold down south also.

Thanks to *Plowed Land* for the hospitality extended to me, but, alas, I am already beginning to experience pangs of conscience. For a long time now I have been making promises, promises, and that looks a trifle like "procrastinating politics"—or deception, to put it plainly. But, really, I didn't want—and don't want—to deceive you; on the contrary, I very much want to see myself appear in *Plowed Land*—and the whole trouble is that, in the first place, I am a dawdler by nature (I am a *Khokhol*) and writing comes hard to me—a tablespoonful every hour; and, secondly, I am constantly lying in wait for a subject that will prove more appealing, more brightly colored, so as not to bore the reader of *Plowed Land*. Oh, well, there will be a long spring and a long summer; there will yet be time for a great deal, should we remain alive and well, and as soon as my work tots up to more than two or three sheets I shall let you know, without fail.* * *

I press your hand.

Your A. Chekhov

TO A. S. SUVORIN

Melikhovo, June 27, 1896

Railroad pass received; I am celebrating the occasion and sending you a thousand thanks. All that remains to be done now is to think of some place to go. I sent the beginning of a short novel to *Plowed Land*, and

---

[1] The pen name of Aleksey Alekseyevich Tikhonov was A. Lugovoy; he edited the magazine *Plowed Land*.

yesterday received word that Herr Marx [1] is willing to pay me 350 rubles per sheet for it. Which means that by the beginning of August I shall have two thousand rubles, or more, perhaps, so that one might just as well contemplate a distant voyage—say, to the islands of Tahiti. But where to go in the meantime? To you? But then, you are having rainy weather now? You are not disposed to receive guests? I would come for three days with pleasure, but not longer. It is necessary to finish the short novel for *Plowed Land*, and it is necessary to finish the belfry which the peasants have saddled me with. If I do come I will bring along special hand-lines for pike; we shall fish with live bait.

I went to an oculist in Moscow. One of my eyes is farsighted, the other nearsighted. Last year I all but lost my right eye; there was neuralgia, complicated by a rash on the cornea; there is still paresis of accommodation and the pain is still there. I got my orders: a course of treatment involving electricity, arsenic, and sea-bathing. I brought back a heap of spectacles and a magnifying glass to exercise the left eye, which does not know how to read. An out-and-out cripple! * * *

I have conceived an idea—to send one hundred village schoolboys to the exposition in Nizhny Novgorod. The railway people have promised to make the necessary inquiries for me. The teachers will make the trip together with the schoolboys. A low bow and all good wishes.

Your A. Chekhov

TO I. N. POTAPENKO [1]

Melikhovo, August 11, 1896

Dear Ignatzius,

The play [2] is on its way to you. The censor has blue-penciled the passages that he disliked because her brother and her son are indifferent to the actress's love affair with the author. On page 4 I cut the sentence "lives openly with this author," and on page 5 "can love only the young." If the changes, which I have made on slips, are accepted, then

---

[1] Adolph Fyodorovich Marx (1836–1904), a flourishing publisher of books and popular magazines.
[1] Ignaty Nikolayevich Potapenko (1856–1928), novelist and playwright, author of reminiscences of Chekhov.
[2] *The Sea Gull.*

paste the slips securely where they belong, and mayest thou be blessed for ever and ever and mayest thou behold the sons of thy sons! Should these changes be rejected, however, then spit on the play: I no longer want to fuss over it and advise you to do likewise.

On page 5 in the following speech by Sorin [3]—"By the way, please tell me what kind of a person is her author"—substitute "the" for "her." In the same passage, instead of the words, "There's no understanding him. He never says anything," it can read, "You know, I don't like him," or anything else, even something from the Talmud.* That the son disapproves of the love affair is clear from the tone he takes. On the disgraced page 37 he says to his mother, "Why, why has this man come between you and me?" On this same page 37 these words of Arkadima —"Of course, our intimacy cannot please you, but . . ."—may be crossed out. That's all. See the underlined passages in the blue copy.

When will you come to Melikhovo?

Well, then, cross out what may be crossed out, in case Litvinov [4] says beforehand that this is sufficient.

Thanks for the Mignon chocolate. I am consuming it.

On the 16th–17th I am going south, shall be in Feodosiya, shall court your wife. In any event, write me. After the 23rd my address will be: Feodosiya, Suvorin's house.

There is still the Committee, you know!! [5]

If you find quarters for me, I shall spend the winter in Petersburg. One room and a toilet are enough.

Should we take a trip somewhere together? There is plenty of time. We could visit Batum or Borzhom. We could liquor up.

I embrace you.

> *Your debtor,*
> *Antonius*

On page 4 you will have to paste one slip on each copy. On pages 5 and 37 only cross things out. Do, however, as you see fit. Forgive me for wearying you so insolently.

For my part I underlined with a green pencil what may be crossed out and what is most pernicious from the censor's point of view.

* or the words "At her age! Oh, oh, how shameful!"

[3] The brother of Arkadine, the heroine.
[4] The censor.
[5] After having been approved by one censor, a play had to be passed by a committee.

TO M. P. CHEKHOV

Petersburg, October 18, 1896

The play [1] fell through, turned out to be a complete fiasco. There was painful tension in the theater, compounded of bewilderment and disgrace. The actors played infamously, stupidly.

The moral: one should not write plays.

Nevertheless, I am alive, well, and eupeptic.

Your papasha,
A. Chekhov

TO A. S. SUVORIN

Melikhovo, October 22, 1896

In your last letter (dated October 18) you called me an old biddy three times, and you say that I funked. Why such defamation? After the performance I had supper at Romanov's with all due propriety, then went to sleep, slept soundly and next day departed for home without as much as a single plaintive peep out of me. Had I funked, I would have been running around to the editorial offices and to see the actors, nervously imploring them to make allowances, nervously inserting useless corrections in the play, and staying in Petersburg for two or three weeks, going to see my *Sea Gull*, all in a dither, bathed in cold sweat, complaining. —Why, when you called on me that night after the performance you yourself said that the best thing for me would be to leave, and next day, in the morning, I received a letter from you, in which you bade me good-bye. Wherein, then, is the cowardice? I acted just as reasonably and coolly as a man who has proposed, has been rejected, and for whom nothing remains save to depart. Yes, my self-esteem was wounded, but then all this did not come as a cloudburst; I had expected failure and was prepared for it, something which I had forewarned you about in all sincerity.

On getting home I took castor oil, washed in cold water, and now, if you like, am ready to write a new play. I no longer fear fatigue and irritation, nor am I afraid that Davydov [1] and Jean will come to dis-

---

[1] The première of *The Sea Gull*. On the same day he wrote to Suvorin, "I will *never* either write or stage plays."

[1] V. N. Davydov, the actor who played the leading role in Chekhov's *Ivanov*.

cuss the play. I agree with your corrections—and thank you a thousand times. But, please, don't feel sorry about not having been at a rehearsal. For, in reality, there was only one rehearsal, at which no one could understand anything; through the execrable acting one could not perceive the play at all.

I received a telegram from Potapenko: the play was a colossal hit. Received a letter from Veselitskaya (Mikulich), a woman I am not acquainted with, who expresses her sympathy in a tone that conveys the idea of a death in the family—which is altogether out of place. However, all these things are trifles.

My sister is enraptured with you and with Anna Ivanovna, and I am glad beyond words about this, since I love your family as much as my own. She rushed home from Petersburg, probably thinking I would hang myself. * * *

Your A. Chekhov

TO N. A. LEIKIN

Melikhovo, November 20, 1896

Dear Nikolay Aleksandrovich!

* * * You complain of the censorship. It is growing even stricter and more callous, yet it is whispered about that all is well, that new trends are developing, as though censorship has now relaxed, that it is easier to breathe. Tell me, if you please, how do such rumors originate and on what can they be based.[1] Censorship has played havoc with "My Life," that tale of mine in *Plowed Land*. Speaking generally, we must admit that it isn't jolly to be a man of letters nowadays.

Your A. Chekhov

---

[1] It is strange that Chekhov appears not to have perceived the probable connection between the optimistic rumors and the coronation of the Czar, which had taken place some months before the date of this letter.

TO V. I. NEMIROVICH-DANCHENKO[1]

Melikhovo, November 26, 1896

Dear friend,

I am answering the main point of your letter: why, in general, we so rarely carry on serious conversations. When people are taciturn it means either that they have nothing to talk about or that they are constrained. What is there to talk about? We have no politics, we have no social, no intimate circle, even no street life; our urban existence is poor, monotonous, viscous, uninteresting—and talking about it is just as tiresome as carrying on a correspondence with Lugovoy.[2] You will say that we are men of letters and that this fact by itself makes our life rich. Really, now? We have gotten bogged down in our profession, we are up to our ears, it has bit by bit isolated us from the outside world— and as a result we have little free time, little money, few books, we read little and reluctantly, hear little, rarely travel. Talk about literature? But then, we have already talked about it—every year the very same things, the very same things, and everything that we ordinarily say about literature reduces itself to judgments as to who wrote better and who wrote worse; as for conversations on more general, broader terms, they flag, because when you have the tundra and Eskimos all around you, general ideas, being inapplicable to the present, deliquesce and slip away, like thoughts of eternal bliss.

Shall we talk about our personal lives? Yes; that can be interesting now and then, and, if you like, we could converse about them, but there we are constrained, we are secretive, insincere, the instinct of self-preservation restrains us, and we are apprehensive. We are afraid that during our conversation some uncultivated Eskimo who bears no love for us, and for whom we bear no love either, will overhear us; personally, I am afraid that my boon companion Sergeyenko, whose mind you like, will, with index finger raised to heaven, be trumpeting in every house and railroad car the solution of the poser: Why did I get together with N at a time when it is Z who is in love with me?

[1] Vladimir Ivanovich Nemirovich-Danchenko (sometimes referred to as Nemirovich only, 1858–1943), a novelist, playwright, and stage director, was one of the two founders and managers of the Moscow Art Theater. With Stanislavsky he staged *The Sea Gull, Uncle Vanya, Three Sisters,* and *The Cherry Orchard.* He became acquainted with Chekhov in the early 1880s, when both were contributors to *The Alarm Clock.*

[2] A. Lugovoy, pseudonym of Aleksey Alekseyevich Tikhonov (1893–1914), writer, editor of *Plowed Land.*

I fear our morality, I fear our ladies. In short, do not accuse either yourself or me of our taciturnity, of lack of seriousness and of anything at all interesting in our conversations, but accuse the *epoch*, as the critics put it, accuse the climate, space, whatever you please, and leave circumstances to their own fatal, implacable course, placing your hopes in a better future. I am, of course, glad for Goltzev, and I envy him, for at his age I shall be incapable. I like Goltzev very much, I love him.* * *

Your A. Chekhov

TO A. S. SUVORIN

Melikhovo, December 2, 1896

If there is going to be a war this spring I am going. During the last one and a half or two years there were so many adventures of all sorts in my personal life (just the other day there was a fire in our house) that there is nothing left for me to do except to go to the front, like Vronsky —only, of course, not to fight but to heal. The only bright interval during these one and a half or two years was my stay with you in Feodosiya, but as for all the rest, one could simply have dropped it—that's how vile everything was.* * *

Your A. Chekhov

TO A. S. SUVORIN

Melikhovo, December 14, 1896

I have received your two letters about *Uncle Vanya*—one in Moscow, the other at home. Not so long ago I also received a letter from Koni, who had seen *The Sea Gull*. You and Koni have brought me not a few fine moments with your letters, but just the same my soul feels exactly as if it were zinc-lined, I feel nothing but revulsion from my plays, and I have to force myself to read proof. You will say once more that this is not wise, that it is foolish, that it is conceit or vanity, and so on and so on. I know, but what can I do? I would be glad to get rid of this foolish feeling, but I can't, I can't. The fact that my play was a fiasco does not account for this, since most of my plays have been fiascos, and every time the failure was water off a duck's back as far as I was concerned.

On October 17 it was not the play that had no success but my personality. There was one circumstance which struck me during the first act—to wit, those with whom, prior to October 17, I had been as open-hearted as a friend and a crony, those with whom I had dined free of all care, those in whose defense I had broken lances (Yasinsky for instance)—all these had an odd expression, horribly odd. . . . In a word, what had happened had led Leikin to express in a letter his condolence upon my having so few friends, and *The Week* to raise the question: "What Did Chekhov Ever Do to Them?" and *The Theater-Goer* to run in one of its issues (No. 95) an extensive correspondence alleging that the writing fraternity had cooked up a scandal for my benefit at the theater.[1] I am calm now, in my usual mood, yet just the same I cannot forget what happened, even as I would be unable to forget it if, for example, I were to be slapped.* * *

You divide plays into those to be performed, and those to be read. To which category—those to be read or those to be acted—would you assign such plays as *The Bankrupt?* [2] Particularly where Dalmatov and Mikhailov through a whole act carry on a dialogue about nothing but bookkeeping—and make an enormous hit. In my opinion, if the readable play is performed by good actors it, too, becomes playable.* * *

I wish you earthly and heavenly goods, good sleep and good appetite.

Your A. Chekhov

TO F. O. SCHECHTEL

Melikhovo, December 18, 1896

Dear Franz Osipovich,

You evidently have a marriageable girl whom you wish to get off your hands as quickly as possible; but do excuse me: I cannot marry at the present time because, first of all, I have bacilli squatting in me, which are very disreputable tenants; secondly, I haven't a cent, and, thirdly, it still seems to me that I am very young. Allow me to kick up my heels for just two or three years more, and then we shall see—perhaps I

---

[1] The piece in question ended by saying that the scandalous reception of the play was "a settling of private accounts."

[2] By Bjørnstjerne Bjørnson, the Norwegian dramatist and poet.

really will get married. The only thing is, why do you want my wife to "stir me up"? Why, life itself stirs me up as it is, stirs me up briskly.

When shall we see each other? You are coming back on January 7; about the 10th they are taking the census here, in which I have a hand and which, apparently, will drag on until February. I shall have to spend the whole of February going from school to school (as a zealous zemstvo worker). When you return dash off a line or two to me; I shall snatch a day and rush to Moscow. I must see you and want to do so very, very much.* * *

A happy journey to you! However, I do not envy you, because it is now cold abroad, especially in hotels.* * *

I press your hand, and thank you for your letter a thousand times.

Your Chekhov

[1897]

TO YE. M. SHAVROVA

Melikhovo, January 1, 1897

Where did you ever get the idea that I have forgotten you, my esteemed colleague? Oh no, my thought follows you just as persistently as that Moscow officer who is in love with you. The fact is that I am immersed in work, immersed up to my chin: I write and cross out, write and cross out, and on top of that there are sundry "civic matters," a census undertaken *in spe*, trips, patients, and hordes upon hordes of guests. —Makes your head spin! With a setting like that letter writing becomes a test of ingenuity.

I felicitate you on the New Year, on new happiness, on new hopes, and wish you an income of two hundred thousand a week. But, above all, I wish you that which you forgot to wish me in your letter: the desire to live.* * *

Your cher maître,

A. Chekhov

TO A. S. SUVORIN

Melikhovo, January 4, 1897

I congratulate you on the New Year and wish you happiness, health, serenity, and no end of money.

* * * I haven't forgotten that I promised to dedicate *The Sea Gull* to Anna Ivanovna, but have deliberately refrained from doing so. One of my most unpleasant memories is connected with that play, it disgusts me, and its dedication tallies with nothing and seems to be simply tactless.

* * * Your Letter about Gringmut [1] is excellent and it was a big hit

---

[1] The reference is to one of the "Little Letters" in which Suvorin attacked the editorials in *Moscow Bulletins*, an archconservative newspaper. Vladimir Andreyevich Gringmut was its editor.

in our neck of the woods. Generally, the end of the past year was a happy page in the history of the "Little Letters." I love it measurelessly when you are liberal, that is, when you write what you please. The Letter on the subject of the student disturbances [2] is also very good.

When will you come to Moscow? I shall spend all of January taking the census; among the census-takers I shall be in the nature of a company commander. Two or two–three days I shall snatch from time to time and go to Moscow.

Your A. Chekhov

TO A. S. SUVORIN

Melikhovo, January 11, 1897

We are taking the census. The census-takers were issued revolting inkwells, revolting crude badges not unlike some beer brewery labels, and briefcases too small for the census blanks to get into, thus creating the impression of a sword that doesn't fit the scabbard. A shame. From morning on I make the rounds of the huts; since I am not used to their low lintels I keep bumping my head against them and, as if out of spite, my head is aching like hell as it is: I have both migraine and influenza. In one of the huts a girl of nine, adopted from a foundling asylum, broke into bitter tears because all the other girls in the hut were called Mikhailovna, while she was called Lvovna.[1] "Call yourself a Mikhailovna!" I told her. They were all overjoyed and fell to thanking me. This is what is called acquiring friends by telling white lies.

Permission for *Surgery* has been granted. We are going ahead with its publication. Do me a favor, if you will be so kind: order the enclosed advertisement to be printed on your front page and add the charge to my account. The periodical will be a very good one and this advertisement can result only in palpable, substantial good. Cutting off legs, you see, can be good, too.

Your A. Chekhov

---

[2] In this Letter Suvorin responded to the government communiqué regarding the disturbances by declaring that the youth must be treated humanely.

[1] This patronymic derives from the name of the foundling's godfather.

Melikhovo, January 17, 1897

This is my birthday.* * *

Concerning the bubonic plague, whether it will come to us, nothing definite can be said yet. If come it will, it is not likely to frighten us over-much, since both the populace and the physicians have long since become inured to the sudden incidence of mortality, thanks to diphtheria, typhuses, etc. Why, even without the plague we have barely four hundred out of a thousand children surviving to the age of five, while both in the villages and in the factories and back streets of the cities you will not find one woman in sound health. The frightening thing about the plague is that it will appear two or three months after the taking of the census; the common folk will explain the census after a fashion that is all their own and take to lambasting the physicians: "They're poisoning off all the extra people, see, so's there will be more land for the masters." Quarantines are not a serious measure. A certain hope is being offered by Khavkin's [1] inoculations, but, unfortunately, Khavkin is not popular in Russia: "Christians ought to be on their guard against him, seeing as how he's a Yid." * * *

Your A. Chekhov

TO N. M. YEZHOV

Melikhovo, January 23, 1897

Dear Nikolay Mikhailovich,

The enclosed is a letter sent to me by my friend Dr. N. V. Korobov. It deals with a charitable society attached to the first municipal hospital. The moral:

1. It is mainly the destitute who undergo treatment in the municipal hospitals of Moscow and, after being discharged, fall ill again and perish, since they have no clothing sufficiently free from holes to enable them to live in the frost and the dampness. Children weakened by disease and released from the hospitals peg out for the same reason.

---

[1] Vladimir Markovich Khavkin (1860–1930), after graduating from Odessa University, worked at the Pasteur Institute, which sent him to India to study cholera and the bubonic plague. He introduced an anti-plague serum with which eight million Hindus were inoculated. In some backward districts the population threatened the doctor.

Hence the need for charitable institutions in connection with hospitals—societies, day nurseries, and so on, and so on.

2. Charitable societies do exist, but each one is hanging on by a hair, inasmuch as each one is sustained by alms obtained by importuning two or three people. While these persons remain alive so does the society, let them die or turn capricious, the society is no more. Hence it is necessary for honorable Muscovites to provide for these societies by the constant and obligatory participation of one and all. Moscow moneybags spend hundreds and thousands to make of their lesser fellow creatures as many prostitutes, slaves, syphilitics, alcoholics as possible— let them, then, contribute their ten-copeck pieces at least for the treatment and relief of the sufferings, at times unbearable, of these lesser fellow creatures whom they have fleeced and corrupted.

I regret that my friend's letter is brief. Could you not find it possible to see him? He could give you much material about everyday life and some statistics. He is very intelligent. * * *

Your A. Chekhov

TO A. S. SUVORIN

Moscow, February 8, 1897

The census is over. I got quite fed up with the whole business, since I had to enumerate and write at the same time, until I got writer's cramp, and also lecture to fifteen census-takers. The census-takers did excellent work; they were so pedantic as to be laughable. But then the zemstvo chiefs, who had been entrusted with taking the census in the rural districts, behaved revoltingly. They did nothing, understood little, and during moments of utmost difficulty took sick leave. The best one among them turned out to be a toper and a braggart *à la* I. A. Khlestakov [1]—but nevertheless a character, at least as a comic; as for the rest, they were deucedly colorless, and what vexation it was to have anything to do with them.

I am in Moscow, at the Moscow Grand Hotel. Shall stay a short while, ten days or so, and then head for home. All through Lent, and then all through April, I shall again have to bother with carpenters, with caulkers, and so on. Again I am building a school. A deputation

---

[1] A character in Gogol's *The Inspector General*.

from the muzhiks called on me with the request, and I did not have the heart to turn them down. The zemstvo is appropriating a thousand, the muzhiks have collected three hundred rubles—and that's all, but the school will cost no less than three thousand. Which means that I shall again have to be thinking about money all summer long and snatching a bit here and a bit there. Life in the country is, on the whole, full of cares.* * *

Chertkov, the well-known Tolstoyan, had his home raided and searched; they took away everything that the Tolstoyans had collected concerning the Dukhobors [2] and sectarianism, and thus suddenly, as if by sorcery, all the evidence against Pobedonostzev [3] and his angels vanished. Goremykin [4] called on Chertkov's mother and told her: "Your son is offered a choice: either the Baltic provinces, where Prince Khilkov is already living in exile—or foreign parts." Chertkov chose London. He is leaving on February 13. L. N. Tolstoy went to Petersburg to see him off, and yesterday a warm overcoat was taken to L. N. There are many people going to see Chertkov off—even Sytin. And I regret that I cannot do the same. I do not feel at all sentimental about Chertkov, but what they have perpetrated against him makes me profoundly, most profoundly indignant.* * *

Your A. Chekhov

TO A. S. SUVORIN

Melikhovo, March 1, 1897

I passed some twenty days in Moscow and spent all my advances, but now I am at home, leading a life of sobriety and chastity. If you get to Moscow in the third week of Lent I shall come as well. At the present time my mind is occupied with construction (not for myself but for the zemstvo), but I can leave—the only thing is, telegraph to Melikhovo a couple of days beforehand. At a gathering of theater people you will probably get to see the project of an enormous people's theater we are

---

[2] The word means "spirit-wrestlers"; these religious sectarians, persecuted by the authorities, were forced to emigrate in 1898, settling in Canada. The search was made in Chertkov's Petersburg home; he had had a hand in spreading Tolstoy's appeal for help for the Dukhobors.

[3] Konstantin Petrovich Pobedonostzev, an outstanding obscurantist, Curator of the Most Holy Synod.

[4] Minister of the Interior.

planning.[1] *We,* meaning the representatives of the Moscow intelligentsia (the intelligentsia stepping forth to meet capital, and capital not at all a stranger to reciprocity). The theater, the auditoria, a library, a reading room, tea rooms, and so on, and so on, all disposed under one roof, in a clean, handsome edifice. The plan is ready, the statutes are being composed, and the hitch now is just a trifle—we need half a million. There will be a joint stock company, but it won't be a philanthropic enterprise. We anticipate that the government will permit shares of a hundred rubles each.

* * * There is no news—or there is, but it is uninteresting or sad. Much is being said about the bubonic plague and war, about the Synod and the Ministry of Education merging. Levitan, the artist (specializing in landscapes), will evidently die soon. He has distention of the aorta.

As for me, I am not having much luck. I wrote a long story about the way the muzhiks live,[2] but they say it will not pass the censor and that it will have to be cut by a half. Which means further losses.* * *

TO G. M. CHEKHOV[1]

Melikhovo, March 18, 1897

Dear Georgie,

* * * We have snow here; the rooks have winged their way back, but there are no starlings yet; the weather is dank, the highway is getting ruined—in short, it's abominable. But then, to be sure, it must be really spring in Taganrog by now! I envy you, and shall keep on envying you until the middle of April, when it will be fine with us too.

During the sixth week in Lent I shall be off to Petersburg, to which I am being called to have my portrait painted for the Tretyakov Gallery. Shall return about Passion Week and stay home until the end of May. I am going to build this year: building a school in the Novoselki village (halfway between the railway station and Melikhovo).

Now for a favor. Recently the Taganrog high school celebrated its hundredth anniversary, and the director published an historical memoir to mark the event—I read about it in *Universal Illustration*. Be my benefactor: get hold of this history in one way or another and send it to me by registered mail. It would be best if you were to see the director and ask him personally for a copy of his great production for me and, while you are at it, you might find out from him if Veniamin Yevtushevsky [2] has been exempted from tuition fees. I shall tell you *confidentially:* it was I who put up the first semiannual fee for Veniamin on the condition that the philanthropic society (connected with the high school) would pay the second semiannual fee. This condition was transmitted by me to the school council through M. N. Psalti, and if it is accepted I will observe it throughout all the following years, too: pass this on to the director.* * *

Your A. Chekhov

TO L. A. AVILOVA

Moscow, Monday, March 24, 1897

Here is my criminal *curriculum vitae:*

On the eve of Saturday I began to spit blood. In the morning I left for Moscow. At six I went to the Hermitage with Suvorin to dine and as soon as I sat down at the table I had a massive lung hemorrhage. Suvorin took me to The Slavic Bazaar; [1] doctors; I spent over twenty-four hours there; and now I am home, i.e. at the Bolshoi Hotel.

Your A. Chekhov

TO R. F. VASHCHUK[1]

Moscow, March 27, 1897

Dear Madam!

I read your story "In Hospital" in the hospital where I am now. I am responding to you lying down. Your story is very good, starting from

---

[2] A relative of Chekhov's.

[1] The hotel where Suvorin was staying.

[1] Rimma Fyodorovna Vashchuk, while still in high school, sent two of her stories to Chekhov, asking him to tell her if she had "a spark of talent." Later she prepared to teach history and literature.

the place that I marked with a red pencil. The beginning is banal, unnecessary. You must continue, of course, provided that, first, writing gives you pleasure, and, second, that you are still young and that you will learn to punctuate correctly and literarily.

As for the "Fairy Tale," it seems to me that it is not a fairy tale, but a collection of words like "gnomes, fairy, dew, knights"—all that is paste, at least on our Russian soil, on which neither gnomes or knights ever roamed and where you would hardly find a person who could imagine a fairy dining on dew and sunbeams. Chuck it; you have to be a sincere artist, write only about that which is or that which, in your opinion, ought to be; one should paint pictures.

I return to your first story: you should not say too much about yourself; you write about yourself, lapse into exaggeration, and risk getting nothing for your trouble; people will either not believe you or look coldly at your effusions.

I wish you all the best.

A. Chekhov

TO R. F. VASHCHUK

Moscow, March 28, 1897

Instead of being angry,[1] you had better read my letter more carefully. I think I wrote clearly that your story is *very good*, except the beginning, which gives the impression of a superfluous annex. It is not my business to permit or not permit you to write; I spoke of youth, because at thirty to forty years it is already late to begin; I spoke of it being necessary to learn to punctuate correctly and literarily, because in a work of art punctuation marks play the role of notes, and you cannot learn them from a textbook; what is needed is flair and experience. To write with pleasure does not mean to play and amuse yourself. To take pleasure in an occupation means to love it.

Forgive me, it's hard for me to write, I am still lying down.

Read this letter once more and stop being angry. I was wholly sincere, and now I am writing you again because I sincerely wish you success.

A. Chekhov

[1] The young woman's angry reply, to which this letter is a response, was followed by an apologetic letter.

TO A. S. SUVORIN

Moscow, April 1, 1897

The doctors have determined that there is a tubercular process in the apex of my lungs, and they prescribe that I change my way of life. Their finding I understand, but their prescription is beyond understanding, since it is almost impossible. They order me to live in the country, without fail, but then living constantly in the country presupposes constantly fussing with muzhiks, with animals, with all the elements, and to avoid toil and turmoil in the country is just about as hard as to avoid getting scorched in hell. But just the same I am going to try to change my life insofar as it is possible and have already announced through Masha that I am discontinuing my medical practice in the country. This will be both a relief and a great deprivation for me. I am giving up all my official duties in the district and buying a dressing gown; I shall take to warming myself in the sun and eating a lot. I am under orders to eat six times a day and there is indignation because it is considered that I eat very little. I am forbidden to talk much, to swim, and so on, and so on.

Aside from the lungs all my organs have been found healthy. [...] Up to now it had seemed to me that I was drinking only the exact quantity that would do me no harm; but now, after a check-up, it turns out that I was drinking less than I had the right to drink. What a pity!

The author of "Ward Number 6" was transferred from Ward Number 16 to Ward Number 14,[1] which is spacious, has two windows, and three tables, and where the light is Potapenkian. There is not much loss of blood. After that evening of Tolstoy's visit (we talked for a long while), at four in the morning the bleeding resumed at a brisk pace.

Melikhovo is a salubrious spot, precisely on the watershed, up high, so that fevers and diphtheria never occur there. It was decided in a general consultation that I shan't venture anywhere and shall keep on residing in Melikhovo. All that is needed is to arrange the quarters more comfortably. Whenever I get fed up with Melikhovo I'll ride over to a neighboring estate that I have leased to accommodate my brothers, should they come here.

People come to see me all the time, bringing flowers, sweets, good things to eat. In a word, utter bliss.* * *

[1] Chekhov was in the hospital connected with the Medical School of the University of Moscow.

By now I no longer lie down when I write but write sitting up; but, having finished writing, I immediately lie down on my bier.

Your A. Chekhov

Write, please, I implore you.

TO A. P. CHEKHOV

Moscow, April 2, 1897

This is what it is all about. Almost every spring, beginning with 1884, I have been finding blood in my sputum. This year, when you reproached me for having accepted the blessing by the Most Holy Synod, your unbelief pained me and, as a consequence of this, I had a hemorrhage, in the presence of Mr. Suvorin. I found myself in the hospital. Here it was determined that mine was a tubercular process—i.e., it was admitted that I had the right, if I so desired, to call myself an invalid.

Temperature normal, no night sweats, no weakness, but my dreams are haunted by archimandrites, the future appears quite uncertain, and, even though the process has not yet advanced particularly far, it is nevertheless necessary, without putting things off, to write a will, so as to keep you from seizing my possessions. On Wednesday of Passion Week they will sign me out; I shall go to Melikhovo, and there we shall see what happens next. I'm under orders to eat a lot. Which means that it isn't Papasha and Mamasha who will have to put away the grub but me. They know nothing about my sickness at home, and so don't you let anything slip out in your letters, through that inherent malice of yours.

In its April issue *Russian Thought* will be running a tale of mine [1] containing a description (in part) of the fire that broke out in Melikhovo on the occasion of your coming there in 1895.

My profoundest bow and my greetings to your wife and children—with all my heart, of course.

Keep well.

Your benefactor
A. Chekhov

[1] "Peasants."

TO A. S. SUVORIN

If the way one feels can be relied on I am in perfect health, and it seems to me that because of lolling in bed and not doing a thing I have become all puffy. On Thursday at noon, they are releasing me from the hospital; I am leaving for home and shall live there as I lived in the past. About May 5 or 10 I shall arrive in Petersburg, as I have already written to the painter.[1] You write that sloth is my ideal. No, my ideal is not sloth. I despise sloth, just as I despise emotional feebleness and languor. I was speaking not about sloth but about idleness, and I was telling you at the same time that idleness is not an ideal but merely one of the conditions essential to personal happiness.

If the experiments with Koch's new preparation produce favorable results, I shall take a trip to Berlin, of course. Eating is doing me absolutely no good. It is two weeks now that they have been cramming me with food but it is of little use; there is no increase in weight.

I must get married. An ill-natured wife may, perhaps, be able to reduce the number of my visitors by half. Yesterday they kept calling on me all day long, with never a break—it was nothing short of a visitation. They kept calling in pairs—and each one begged me not to talk and, at the same time, put questions to me.

And so, after Thursday, Lopasnya will again be my mailing address. Whatever became of my *Collected Plays?* Seems to have bogged down somewhere. Thanks for the letter. May God grant you health.

Your A. Chekhov

---

[1] Iosif Emmanuilovich Braz, who was painting Chekhov's portrait, which Pavel Mikhailovich Tretyakov had commissioned for the Moscow picture gallery that bears his name. Neither the portraitist nor the sitter was satisfied with the work. The following year Braz tried again while Chekhov was in Nice and produced the portrait that hangs in the Tretyakov Gallery.

TO M. O. MENSHIKOV[1]

Melikhovo, April 16, 1897

Dear Mikhail Osipovich,

My lungs have been acting up a bit of late. On March 20 I was en route to Petersburg, when I began to spit blood, had to stop off in Moscow, and was hospitalized there for two weeks. The doctors diagnosed tuberculosis of the apices, and forbade me almost everything interesting.

Convey my hearty greetings and gratitude to Anna Ivanovna and Yasha.[2] I greatly prize attention and friendly concern.

Today my head aches. A day ruined, but the weather is glorious, it's noisy in the garden. Guests, piano music, laughter—that's indoors; out of doors, starlings.

The censorship has snatched a sizable piece out of "Peasants." [3]

Huge thanks. I press your hand and wish you happiness. My sister sends you a greeting.

Your A. Chekhov

There's no ill wind that brings nobody good. At the hospital I had a visit from Tolstoy, with whom I had a most interesting conversation, most interesting for me, because I listened more than I spoke. We talked about immortality. He takes immortality in the Kantian sense; he holds that all of us (people and animals) will live in a principle (reason, love), the essence and purpose of which is a mystery to us. To me this principle or force presents itself as a formless jellylike mass, my "I"—my individuality, my consciousness, will be fused with this mass—such immortality I don't need, I don't understand it, and Lev Nikolayevich was astonished that I didn't understand it.* * *

---

[1] Mikhail Osipovich Menshikov (1859–1918), a publicist who edited a liberal weekly in the 1890s, but in 1901 joined the camp of the extreme reactionaries and became a contributor to *New Times*.

[2] The addressee's wife and small son.

[3] The Censorship Committee ordered that twenty-seven lines of "Peasants," already printed, be cut and, should the author refuse, that he be arrested.

Melikhovo, April 17, 1897

My dear friend, Aleksandr Ivanovich,

I am home now. Before the holidays I spent two weeks in the Ostrou-
mov section of the Moscow University Hospital, spat blood; the doctors
diagnosed tuberculosis in the apex of my lungs. I feel perfectly well,
have no pain, nothing in my innards troubles me, but the doctors forbade me *vinum*, movement, talk, ordered me to eat a great deal, and
prohibited me from practicing medicine—and I am bored, as it were.

I have heard nothing about the people's theater. At the convention [2]
it was spoken of vaguely and without special interest, and the circle
that had undertaken to draw up the statutes and start things going has
apparently grown cool to the project. This must have been due to the
arrival of spring. Of the members of the group I saw only Goltzev, but
did not succeed in speaking to him about the theater.

There is no news. Literature is at a standstill. In the editorial offices
people drink tea and cheap wine, drink without relish, obviously to
while away the time. Tolstoy is writing a book on art. He visited me in
the hospital and announced that he had abandoned his *Resurrection*,[3]
because he did not like it, and was writing exclusively on art, about
which he had read sixty books.[4] His thesis is not new; in various ways it
has been repeated by wise old men in all ages. Old men have always
been inclined to envisage the end of the world and say that morality
had fallen to its lowest level, that art had degenerated, was played out,
that people had become feeble, and so, and so on. In his book Lev
Nikolayevich wants to convince us that art has now entered its final
phase and is in a blind alley.

I do nothing, feed hemp seeds to sparrows and prune roses, one a day.
As a result the roses bloom luxuriantly. I don't have a hand in farming.

Keep well, dear Aleksandr Ivanovich, thanks for the letter and your
friendly interest. Write me out of deference to my infirmity; and don't

---

[1] A. I. Ertel (1855–1908), a writer of fiction, became involved in radical activities
and was deported to the provinces.

[2] The meeting of actors and other theatrical people in Moscow in early March.

[3] In his diary entry for January 5, 1897, Tolstoy wrote: "Having reached Nekhlyudov's decision to get married, I chucked [the novel] in disgust. Everything in it is
wrong, invented, weak. . . . I am not likely to finish it." He returned to *Resurrection*
in 1898. It was first published as a magazine serial in 1899.

[4] His book on art originally appeared in a periodical in 1897 and 1898.

blame too much my failings as a correspondent. In the future I'll try to answer your letters immediately on reading them.

I press your hand firmly.

Your A. Chekhov

TO N. M. LINTVAREVA

Melikhovo, May 1, 1897

Much esteemed Natalya Mikhailovna!

I am answering your telegram. On March 20 I left for Petersburg, on the way I started spitting blood, in Moscow the priests of Aesculapius arrested me and placed me in a hospital. I stayed there fifteen days. Now I am home, feel well, and in spite of tuberculosis of the pulmonary apexes (râle and blunting) I cough only in the mornings. By winter I shall probably travel to Egypt or to Sochi, but at present there is no particular need for me to go away, because my general condition is not bad, the temperature is normal, and I gain weight. By order of my colleagues I lead a boring, sober, virtuous life and if this lasts another month or two, I shall turn into a goose.

* * * At present an oculist with his assortment of eyeglasses is my guest. For two months he has been selecting spectacles for me. I have so-called astigmatism, because of which I frequently suffer from migraine; furthermore my right eye is nearsighted, my left farsighted. You see what a cripple I am. But this I carefully conceal and try to look like a young man of twenty-eight, in which I frequently succeed, because I buy expensive neckties and use Vera Violetta scent.* * *

Cordial greetings and best wishes to your family.

Your A. Chekhov

TO A. S. SUVORIN

Melikhovo, May 2, 1897

* * * I agree to the arrangement concerning "The Peasants," but the story runs to less than 10 sheets, there will be trouble with the censorship.[1] Shouldn't we add other stories of peasant life? I have something

---

[1] The plan was to publish this novella separately, but Chekhov questioned it because, being a thin book, and therefore cheaper, and so more accessible to the common people, it would be more narrowly regarded by the censors.

of the sort, for instance, "Murder," dealing with schismatics, or the like.[2]

I cannot come to Petersburg before the end of May, as I have not yet settled down and because there is some urgent business demanding my presence. I telegraphed you that I am marrying a rich widow. Alas, this is only a sweet dream! Now not a single fool will have me, as I badly compromised myself by having been hospitalized.

Where have you decided to go? Where will you spend the summer? Won't you stay in Feodosiya? I don't at all know what to do with myself and what would benefit my health: a constitution or sturgeon with horseradish.[3] I want to be at home until August, provided that the weather is decent, dry, then I shall go south and then abroad for the winter or to Sochi (in the Caucasus) where they say the winters are warm and there are no fevers.

I feel fairly well, don't lose weight, and look hopefully to the future. Wonderful weather, almost no money.* * *

Your A. Chekhov

TO A. S. SUVORIN

Melikhovo, May 20, 1897

One school I built last year; the accounts for this building are already settled and handed over to the zemstvo archives. This year I am building another school, which will be completed toward the end of June. And this school is already fully provided for—at any rate, if the funds do run short it will be by considerably less than a thousand and a half. There are more school buildings proposed for the near future, and if you have no objections, and I am alive and well, I shall allocate to each new school under construction a hundred rubles from your contribution and thus you will render assistance not just once but a hundred times. Do you agree? * * *

There is, undoubtedly, something of the publicist in Engelhardt, your new staff member, but what a beclouded head, and no longer young.

---

[2] As a matter of fact, "Peasants" was published in one volume with the novella "My Life."

[3] This refers to a thrust at the liberals made by Saltykov-Shchedrin, to the effect that they could be readily diverted from a dream of a constitution to a dream of sturgeon with horseradish.

He belongs to the same category as Rozanov,[1] so to speak, as far as the timbre of his talents is concerned. What these people have is not a definite outlook, but only enormous, immensely diffused self-love, as well as morbid detestation kept concealed deep within some hidden place of the soul, as if under a crushing gravestone grown over with moss. * * *

Your A. Chekhov

TO A. S. SUVORIN

Melikhovo, June 21, 1897

Greetings!

I, the undersigned, am staying at home in Melikhovo all the time, and by degrees am turning into the landed proprietress Korobochka. I do go to Moscow occasionally, but no visit is ever prolonged. The other day I was at the estate of Morozov,[1] the millionaire; the house was like the Vatican, the flunkeys were in waistcoats of white piqué and had gold chains across their bellies, the furniture was in bad taste, the wines came from Levé, the host's face was utterly expressionless—and I took to my heels.

* * * The harvest will be poor, the prices of grain and hay keep rising. There are no diseases. They are swilling vodka desperately, and there is a desperate lot of filth both moral and physical. I am coming ever nearer to the conclusion that a decent man—who is not a drunkard—can live in the village only with a heavy heart, and blessed is that Russian intellectual who lives not in the village but in a summer cottage.

Your A. Chekhov

---

[1] Vasily Vasilyevich Rozanov (1856–1919), a critic and publicist on the staff of *New Times*. His extreme, original, and reactionary views made bitter enemies for him.

[1] Sergey Timofeyevich Morozov, an industrialist, brother of the notable Maecenas Savva T. Morozov.

TO V. M. SOBOLEVSKY [1]

Dear Vasily Mikhailovich,

I am turning to you with a great request, a very great request which, of course, you did not expect. You did not expect it because, considering what the times are, you are beset by worries and cares and all sorts of embarrassing situations. Here is the matter at issue. We had a priest in our parish, Father Nikolay Nekrasov, a deserving person and one held in respect. He was well liked, indeed, the people loved him, and he was considered one of the best religious instructors in the county. He was promoted for his zeal; they transferred him to a town—to Serpukhov. But this promotion proved to be far from a benefit to him. Nekrasov fell ill in town, he is miserable there, and now sobs aloud, begging to go back to the village. As long as they have not yet assigned a new priest to us they can transfer him back here—and it seems to me that at this point Mikhail Abramovich Morozov, Churchwarden of the Uspensky Cathedral, could exert his influence on our behalf. He could advise us as to what has to be done, to whom we might turn and so on and, if need be, can put in a good word. But for Nekrasov to submit a petition on his own would be awkward—that is not the accepted procedure and, likely as not, he would be reproached with being too fastidious and would be left without a parish. Be so kind as to write to M. A., find out if he can receive Father Nekrasov in order to talk to him, and if he can, when and where. I don't know his address. As a favor, use your influence; I feel so sorry for this poor man! I could give him a medical certificate, and collect hundreds of signatures in his behalf.

If M. A. is not in Moscow, or if he should refuse to exert his influence, couldn't some other kind-hearted man be found among your acquaintances who is in close touch with the clerical authorities? * * *

TO A. S. SUVORIN

* * * I am reading Maeterlinck. I have read his *Les aveugles, L'intruse;* am now reading *Aglavaine et Selysette.* All these are strange, queer

---

[1] V. M. Sobolevsky (1846–1913), jurist, journalist, editor of *The Russian Bulletins.*

pieces, but the impression they create is enormous and, if I had a theater, I would put on *Les aveugles* without fail. Incidentally, a magnificent backdrop is available here—a seascape, with a lighthouse in the distance. Half of the public is idiotic, but one can save the play from being a fiasco by giving the gist of it on the poster—very briefly, of course: "The play is the work of one Maeterlinck, a Belgian writer, a decadent, and the gist of it is that the old man who had been guiding a file of blind men has died without a sound, and the blind men, knowing nothing of this, are sitting and waiting for his return."

* * * I have no end of guests. Aleksandr has left his boys on my doorstep, without either linen or outer clothing; they are living with me and nobody knows when they will leave; apparently they will stay until the end of summer and, perhaps, may stay on forever, which is most amiable on the part of their parents. A cousin has arrived from down south. * * *

Your A. Chekhov

TO A. S. SUVORIN

Melikhovo, August 1, 1897

Olderogge, the psychiatrist, was received most amiably, and the answer he was given was: "Go ahead. For my part I promise you the most extensive support. Submit a comprehensive project to me as soon as possible." [1]

And now Olderogge is in seventh heaven, formulating his project and offering warm prayers for you.

I am home. Waiting until the weather turns foul, so that I may go away, but where to I have not decided yet. Now the winds have started to blow from the north; fall is coming on, and already, even in the warmth of the sun, one feels something autumnal. It is both pleasant and a trifle melancholy, as it were. * * *

Your A. Chekhov

[1] The project was for a hospital—for which a government subsidy was being sought by Olderogge—where alcoholics could be treated. Chekhov had engaged the interest of Suvorin, who had arranged a meeting between the psychiatrist and Witte, the Minister of Finance.

TO A. S. SUVORIN

Nice, October 1, 1897

* * * In Nice I am staying at a Russian *pension*. The room is quite spacious, with windows facing south, with a wall-to-wall carpet, with a couch like Cleopatra's, with a dressing room; hearty breakfasts and dinners, prepared by a Russian cook (borshch and meat patties), just as hearty as those at the Hôtel Vendôme and just as tasty. I pay 11 francs per day. It is warm here; even of evenings there is nothing that resembles autumn. The sea is caressing, appealing. La Promenade des Anglais is overgrown with greenery and shines in the sun; of mornings I sit in the sun and read the newspaper. I stroll about a great deal. Have made the acquaintance of Maksim Kovalevsky, a former Moscow professor dismissed under Paragraph 3.[1] A tall, stout, lively man, and a most good-natured one. He eats a great deal, jests a great deal, and works a very great deal—and one feels at ease and jolly in his company. His laugh is booming, infectious. He lives in Beaulieu, in a pretty little villa of his own. There, too, you will find the artist Jacoby, who calls Grigorovich a scoundrel and a swindler, Aivazovsky[2] a son of a bitch, Stasov[3] an idiot, and so on. Day before yesterday Kovalevsky, Jacoby, and I dined together, and throughout dinner we laughed fit to burst to the great astonishment of the servants. I often eat oysters.

Your A. Chekhov

It's boring without Russian papers and without letters.

TO L. A. AVILOVA

Nice, October 6, 1897

* * * You deplore the fact that my heroes are gloomy. Alas, it is not my fault! With me this happens involuntarily, and when I write, it does not seem to me that I write gloomily; in any event, when I work I am

---

[1] Maksim Maksimovich Kovalevsky (1851–1916), sociologist and historian. In 1887 he had been dismissed from Moscow University, under a paragraph of a statute enacted in 1850 dealing with the dismissal of politically suspect officials. He emigrated to Paris, where in 1901 he founded a Russian school of sociology.

[2] I. K. Aivazovsky was a painter known for his seascapes who taught at the Academy of Fine Arts.

[3] Vladimir Vasilyevich Stasov (1824–1906), an art critic.

always in a good mood. It has been noticed that gloomy people, those of a melancholy disposition, always write cheerfully, but the writings of those full of the joy of life are depressing. But I am full of the joy of life, at least, the first twenty years of my life were pleasurable.

Mornings my health is good enough, and evenings it is magnificent. I do nothing, don't write, and have no desire to write. Have become terribly indolent.

Be well and happy. I press your hand.

Your A. Chekhov

I shall probably live abroad all winter.

TO A. S. SUVORIN

Nice, November 1, 1897

Your letter stunned me unpleasantly. I had been expecting you with such impatience, I wanted to see you, to chat with you, and, truly, you are so necessary to me! I had prepared a huge hamper overflowing with things to talk over, I had prepared marvelous weather for you, really warm weather—and suddenly, this letter. Dreadfully vexing!

Nemirovich, who is on the floor below me at the Pension Russe, was also expecting you. You have your hands full with the theater, and I have something of my own to worry about. The *Surgery* journal is again nearing its last gasp, and again it is up to me to save it, no matter what, since among the physicians I am the only man who has acquaintances and connections in the world of literature and print. The journal, in its scientific aspect, is superb, an altogether European publication. Do advise me: what must I go through to secure a subsidy of three or four thousand a year. If this necessitates calling myself the publisher, why, I would call myself that and then spend a week before Witte's house, barefoot, bareheaded, and with a candle in my hand. Just advise me, but I will submit the petition all by myself, or the editor may submit it.

I was spitting blood again for three or four days; now there's nothing, I'm hopping around and feel splendid. Have written two stories [1] and already sent them off. * * *

Your A. Chekhov

I'll be living in Nice every winter.

[1] "At Home" and "A Pecheneg."

Pension Russe, Nice, November 3, 1897

Ah, Lidiya Alekseyevna, with what pleasure I read your *Forgotten Letters*. This is a fine, well-thought-out, exquisite thing. A small, bob-tailed thing, this, yet there is a world of art and talent in it, and I cannot understand why you don't go on in precisely this vein. Letters are an unsuccessful, boring form and, besides, easy to handle, but I am speaking of the tone of sincere, well-nigh passionate feeling, of the elegant phrase. Goltzev was right when he said that you have an appealing talent, and if, to this day, you don't believe that, your disbelief is something for which you yourself are to blame. You work very little, lazily. I myself am a lazy Khokhol, but then, by comparison with you, I have written mountains of stuff!

In all your stories (with the exception of *Forgotten Letters*) inexperience, uncertainty, and laziness simply stick out between the lines. To this day you haven't become a practiced hand at it, as they say, and are working like a beginner, like a young lady painting china. You have a feeling for landscape, your landscapes are good, but you don't know how to economize and the landscape is constantly staring you in the eye when it is uncalled for, and indeed, one of your stories disappears altogether under a mass of scenic fragments which are piled up along the entire extent of the story from its start to its middle—or almost that. Then, too, you don't work at the phrase; a phrase must be worked at—that is where the art comes in. One must throw out whatever is superfluous, clean the phrase of "to the extent of," "with the aid of"; one must take thought for the musical quality of the phrase, and not tolerate *"stala"* and *"perestala"* ["became" and "ceased"] in the same phrase and almost side by side. Why, my dear girl, such clichés as "The Irreproachable Woman," "At the Breaking-Point"—why, these are nothing but an affront. I will, at the worst, tolerate, side by side, *"kazalsya"* and *"kasalsya"* ["seemed" and "touched"], but as for *"bezuprechnaya"* ["irreproachable"]—it is rough, clumsy, and fit only for colloquial speech, and roughness is something you are bound to feel, since you are musical and sensitive, as attested to by *Forgotten Letters*. I shall save the newspapers containing your stories and will send them to you at the first opportunity, while you, paying no attention to my aspersions, collect some more material and send it to me.

As long as the weather was good everything was going well; but now, when it is raining and the weather is inclement, I have that tickling in my throat again, again blood has appeared—a mean trick.

I write, but only trifles. I have already sent four stories to *The Russian Bulletins*. Keep well. I press your hand.

Your Chekhov

TO M. S. MALKIEL[1]

Yalta, November 5, 1897

Much esteemed Mariya Samoilovna!

I hereby inform you that I have embraced the Islamic faith and have already been registered as a member of the Tartar community of Autka, a village near Yalta. Our laws do not permit us to enter into correspondence with such feeble creatures as women, and if, in obedience to the predilections of my heart, I write to you, I commit a grave sin.

My thanks for your letter, cordial greetings to you and your sister, who tells people's fortunes, and my hope that both of you will land in the harem of some exalted noble who is as handsome as Levitan.

Write again. Be well and prosperous.

Osman Chekhov

TO A. I. SUVORINA

Nice, November 10, 1897

Dear Anna Ivanovna,

Thank you very much for the letter. I am answering immediately on having read it. You ask about my health. I feel hale and hearty, to all appearances, it seems to me, I am completely well, but I have one trouble—I spit blood. There is not much of it, but an attack lasts a long time. The hemorrhage which is still with me started some three weeks ago. As a result, I put up with various privations. I don't leave the house after 3 o'clock in the afternoon, and when I do leave it, only go out on the street. I don't drink anything, don't eat hot foods, don't walk fast, in short, I am not living, but vegetating. And that irritates me, I am in

[1] A Moscow acquaintance of Chekhov's.

a bad temper and it always seems to me that at dinner the Russians make stupid and vulgar remarks, and I force myself not to speak to them impertinently.

But for God's sake don't tell anyone about the blood spitting, this is strictly confidential. I write home that all is well with me, and it is not sensible to say anything different, because I do feel fine—and if they find out at home that I have hemorrhages they will wail.

Now about the little intrigue of mine that you mention. At Biarritz [1] I engaged Margot, a nineteen-year-old girl, to teach me French; when we bade each other good-bye, she said that she would come to Nice without fail. And she is probably here in Nice, but I have not been able to find her. . . . I do not speak French.

The weather here is paradisal. Hot, quiet, the air caresses you. Musical contests are under way. Orchestras pass through the streets, tumult, dances, laughter. I look at all this and think how stupid I was not to live abroad for months, years. Now, it seems to me, if I go on living, I will no longer winter in Moscow in spite of all blandishments. The moment October arrives I leave Russia. I am not moved by Nature here, it is alien to me, but I passionately love warmth, I love culture. And here culture juts out of every shop window, every wicker basket, every dog smells of civilization. * * *

Don't be haughty and grand, write me often. I need letters. I kiss your hand 100 x 100 times and wish you happiness, and thank you again.

Yours heart and soul,
A. Chekhov

TO V. M. SOBOLEVSKY

Nice, November 20, 1897

* * * I do not read proof in order to improve the appearance of the story; usually I finish off the story in the proof and better its musical aspect, as it were. But if it is really inconvenient for you to send proof, have it your way! What can one do! But there is just one thing— please, after having received a story from me, take a post card and

[1] On September 8 Chekhov came to Biarritz from Paris, where, tourist fashion, he had visited the Moulin Rouge and watched the *danse du ventre.* He left Biarritz a fortnight later.

write me just two words: "Story received." I sent you the second story eight days after the first, yet you received it before the first story. Please, don't leave me in uncertainty. * * *

Your A. Chekhov

TO V. M. SOBOLEVSKY

Nice, December 4, 1897

Dear Vasily Mikhailovich,

I am answering your letter point by point. I moved one floor lower because I am constantly going down, but climbing up is not easy for me. Somehow or other I had a spell of spitting blood (there was not much blood but the thing persisted for three weeks) and we, the Aesculapians, decided in a general consultation that for one in my condition having constantly to climb stairs was harmful rather than beneficial—and I changed my quarters. My room is sunny from 7:30 A.M. until sunset, I pay the same (ten francs) as I did on the floor above, while the furnishings here are more luxurious than on the upper floor. As for moving to another hotel, perhaps it would already have been too late, since we'll be going off to Algiers in January, and January is now upon us. And besides, I've grown used to the Pension Russe. It's quiet, they feed you well, the servants are good-natured and honest, and the mosquitoes have already migrated to Egypt.

I am writing considerably less here than I had in mind. To write in a hotel room, at a desk that is not your own, to write after breakfast or dinner (it seems to me that I am eating the livelong day with never a break) and in fine weather, when one yearns to get out of the room—all this is hard, very hard. Here one should read and not write. But, be that as it may, I write just the same. * * *

I keep reading newspapers all day long, studying the Dreyfus affair. The way I see it, Dreyfus is innocent. * * *

Your A. Chekhov

TO A. S. SUVORIN

Nice, December 14, 1897

Nothing new. I don't remember if I wrote you that Dr. Lyubimov, whom you know, has double pleurisy and myocarditis, a serious condition. As for my health, my illness is progressing crescendo and is obviously already incurable: I mean my laziness. Amazing do-nothingness. In every other respect I am as strong as an ox. A great deal of work has accumulated, subjects got mixed up in the brain, and to write in good weather, on a full stomach, at a desk not your own, is penal servitude, and in every way I try to avoid it. * * *

Isn't it time for me to betake myself home? I keep waiting for Kovalevsky, together we'll go to Africa. I shall try to travel as far as possible, so that my jaunt should resemble work at least a little, otherwise I really begin to feel ashamed. I look at the Russian ladies who stay in the Pension Russe—frights, bores, idlers, the self-indulgent sort, and I am afraid of resembling them, and I keep thinking that the cure we, that is, I and these ladies, are undergoing here is most repulsive egotism.

What was said and written on the occasion of Daudet's death [1] was intelligent and graceful. Even Rochefort's [2] comment was good. Yes, we are geniuses, panhumans, fountainheads, but let Lev Tolstoy die and there is no one to write an article. Journalists will turn out something, but the representatives of literature, headed by Grigorovich and Boborykin, will only scratch themselves. We ought to send our young writers abroad, really we ought to.[3]

Your A. Chekhov

TO F. D. BATYUSHKOV [1]

Nice, December 15, 1897

* * * Postscript. In one of your letters you expressed the wish that I send you an international story, on a subject taken from life abroad.

[1] It occurred December 16 N.S. This letter was written December 26 N.S.
[2] French journalist and publicist.
[3] This sentence was suppressed in the eight-volume edition of Chekhov's letters and restored in the *Selected Letters*.
[1] Fyodor Dmitriyevich Batyushkov (1857–1920), a critic and historian of Western literature, who edited the Russian section of *Cosmopolis* and later of another magazine, *God's World*.

Such a story I can write only in Russia, from memory. I am able to write only from memory, I never wrote directly from observed life. What I need is to have the subject filtered through memory, and that there should remain on it, as on a filter, only what is important or typical.

A. Chekhov

TO L. S. MIZINOVA

Nice, December 27, 1897

Dear Lika,

I can only hail your idea of opening a workshop, and not alone because, coming to dine with you and not finding you in, I shall pay court to the pretty little dressmakers, but chiefly because the idea is, in general, a good one. I shall not moralize, but merely say that work, no matter how modest it may seem offhand—whether in a workshop or in a little store—will give you independence, peace of mind and confidence in the future. I, too, would be pleased to open something, so as to struggle for my existence from day to day, like everybody else. In the end the privileged position of an idler tires and bores hellishly.

And I am still in Nice. Late in January or early in February I shall leave for Algeria, Tunis; meanwhile I promenade, breathe the pure air, and wave off mosquitoes, which bite painfully here. The rains have started. Many Russians, but they, excuse me, are boring. * * *

I congratulate your cousin, the one who married another woman without divorcing his wife. Is it you he has married? In any event, to leave an old wife is as pleasant as to crawl out of a deep well.

Write me, dear Lika, don't stand on ceremony and don't be meticulous about exchanging visits, I implore you. Every day I ask myself, why do I get no letters from you. Write longer ones. Keep well and don't mope. Don't be tart like cranberry. Be rakhat-lukum.[1]

Your A. Chekhov

---

[1] Oriental candy made of sugar, flour, and starch, with almonds and other nuts.

⌈1898⌉

TO A. S. SUVORIN

Nice, January 4, 1898

Here, then, is my program. At the end of this January or, rather, the beginning of February, I shall go to Algiers, Tunis, etc., then return to Nice to wait for you (you wrote that you are coming to Nice). After spending some time here, we shall travel together to Paris if you like and from there return to Russia on the train "Lightning" to celebrate Easter.

Your last letter arrived here unsealed.

I visit Monte Carlo very rarely, once every three or four weeks. At first, when Sobolevsky and Nemirovich were here, I gambled for moderate stakes on simple odds (red and black) and would come away with fifty francs one time and a hundred another, but I had to give up the game later since it exhausted me physically.

The Dreyfus case has begun to move, it's on the boil, so to speak, but still has not taken a definite turn.[1] Zola is a noble soul [2] and I (being a member of the Syndicate and having already received a hundred francs from the Jews [3]) am delighted by his fervor. France is a wonderful country and its writers are wonderful.

* * * Judging by the extract published in *New Times*, Lev Nikolayevich's essay on art [4] has nothing interesting to offer. Just the same old story. To say that art has become feeble, reached a dead end, is not what it should be, etc., etc., amounts to saying that the desire to eat and drink has become obsolete, had its day, and is not what is needed. Hunger, to be sure, is a stale joke, we have reached a dead end with our

---

[1] In 1899 a new court-martial tried Dreyfus, but again found him guilty.

[2] The reference is to Zola's open letter to President Faure entitled *"J'accuse!"* that denounced the Army leadership for having forged the evidence against Dreyfus.

[3] It was rumored that among the Dreyfusards were those bribed by a Jewish "Syndicate." In *New Times* Suvorin wrote that this agency "will bribe those who can be bribed and spare no money to corrupt the incorruptible."

[4] Tolstoy's *What Is Art?* was serialized in 1897–98.

desire to eat, regardless of what nonsense philosophers and angry old men may hand us.

Be well.

Your A. Chekhov

TO F. D. BATYUSHKOV

Nice, January 23, 1898

Much esteemed Fyodor Dmitriyevich!

* * * Offprints of the article of yours [1] that you mentioned in your letter, please send me at Nice. I shall probably stay here until April, be bored, and so your paper will be of double service to me.

All the talk here is about Zola and Dreyfus. The overwhelming majority of the intelligentsia is on the side of Zola and believe in the innocence of Dreyfus. Zola has added another eight feet to his stature, his letters of protest have been a fresh wind, and every Frenchman felt that, thank God, there is still justice in the world, and if an innocent man is condemned, there is someone who will step forward for him. The French newspapers are extraordinarily interesting, the Russian are garbage. *New Times* is simply abominable. * * *

Looking forward to your article, I remain respectfully and sincerely

Your A. Chekhov

TO A. A. KHOTYAINTZEVA [1]

Nice, February 2, 1898

The room next to mine is occupied by a lady, forty-six years old, who doesn't come out for breakfast because until 3 o'clock she is busy painting herself. She must be an artist.

I visit the expensive doll [2] every evening and she serves me tea, with a brioche. Murzaki [2] has been gambling, and lost. The baronesses [2] are prospering.

[1] "At a Distance of Half a Century: Balzac, Chekhov, and Korolenko on Peasants" was published in a miscellany, *In Memory of Belinsky*.

[1] Aleksandra Aleksandrovna Khotyaintzeva, a painter, with whom the Chekhov family was acquainted.

[2] References to acquaintances in the Pension Russe, where Chekhov was staying.

[302]

You ask me if I think Zola is right, and I ask you: is it possible that you hold such a low opinion of me as to doubt even for a minute that I am on Zola's side? For one of his fingernails I would not give all who are trying him now at the *Assizes*—all these generals and highly placed witnesses. I read the stenographic reports and do not find anything to indicate that Zola is wrong, and I don't see what *preuves* are needed here.

I have received *Le Rire. Merci!!*

The Carnival is on here. It's jolly. I'm having dinner today at Beaulieu with Kovalevsky.

How's your health? What's new?

A donkey is braying, but at the wrong time.

The weather is delightful.

Be happy.

                                                            Your A. Chekhov

TO A. S. SUVORIN

Nice, February 6, 1898

You write that you are vexed by Zola, but here the general feeling is as if a new, better Zola has been born. In this trial of his [1] he has been cleansed of superficial grease spots as by turpentine, and shines forth before the French in his true splendor. It is a purity, a moral loftiness that no one suspected. Trace the entire affair from the very start. The degradation of Dreyfus,[2] whether just or not, made a painful, dismal impression on everyone (including you, too, as I remember). It was noticed that when he was being sentenced Dreyfus conducted himself as an honorable, well-disciplined officer, while the onlookers, journalists, for instance, shouted at him, "Keep still, you Judas!"—that is, behaved badly, indecently. Everyone came away from the scene disgruntled, with a troubled conscience. Dreyfus's lawyer, Démange, was especially dissatisfied—an honest man who even during the preliminaries had felt that something shady was going on behind the scenes; then the experts, to convince themselves that they were not mistaken, spoke only of

---

[1] The trial of Zola for his exposé (*"J'accuse!"*) of the court-martial that acquitted Major Esterhazy in the Dreyfus case lasted from February 7 to February 23 (N.S.), the defendant being sentenced to a year's prison and a fine. The date of Chekhov's letter is O.S.

[2] It took place on January 5, 1895 (N.S.).

Dreyfus, of his being guilty, meanwhile roaming through Paris, just roaming. . . . One of the experts turned out to be demented, the author of a monstrously absurd scheme, two others were eccentrics. Willy-nilly attention turned to the intelligence department of the Ministry of War, a military consistory occupied with hunting spies and reading other people's letters. Sandher, the chief of the department, suffered, it became known, from progressive paralysis, Paty de Elam[3] turned out to be a counterpart of Tausch the Berliner,[4] Picquart[5] disappeared suddenly, mysteriously, scandalously. Furthermore, a whole series of gross violations of court procedure came to light. Little by little the belief came to prevail that Dreyfus had in reality been condemned on the evidence of a secret document that had been shown neither to him nor to his attorney—and people who had due process at heart saw this as a basic abrogation of law: had the letter been written by Kaiser Wilhelm or by the sun itself, it should have been shown to Démange. All kinds of guesses as to the contents of the letter became current, cock-and-bull stories were repeated. Dreyfus was an army officer, and so the military pricked up their ears; Dreyfus was a Jew, and so the Jews pricked up their ears. . . . Militarism, the Yids, became topics of conversation. Such utterly contemptible figures as Drumont[6] raised their heads, gradually trouble was stirred up on the ground of anti-Semitism, a ground that reeks of the slaughterhouse. When something does not go well with us, we seek for causes outside of ourselves and find them soon enough: "It's the French playing scurvy tricks, the Yids, the Kaiser." Capital, masons, the Syndicate, the Jesuits, buga-boos, are ghosts, how will they relieve our unease? They are, of course, a bad sign. If the French start talking about the Yids, the Syndicate, it is a sign that they feel all is not well with them, that a worm is gnawing at them, that they need these ghosts to appease their disturbed consciences. Then this Esterhazy, a *bretteur* out of Turgenev,[7]

[3] The colonel who conducted the preliminary investigation of the Dreyfus case.

[4] A major who was head of the German secret police.

[5] After Sandher's death, his successor, Colonel Georges Picquart, discovered that Esterhazy, not Dreyfus, had disclosed military secrets to Germany. When he informed the authorities of his findings, he was arrested as a forger and exiled.

[6] Edouard Drumont edited a newspaper that was the chief organ of French anti-Semitism.

[7] The reference is to Turgenev's *The Bretteur*.

a suspicious, impudent character, long despised by his comrades, the striking resemblance of his handwriting to that of the *bordereau*,[8] the Uhlan's letters, the threats that for some reason he did not carry out, finally, the completely secret trial, during which the court handed down the bizarre decision that the document was in Esterhazy's handwriting but not penned by him. . . . Steam was building up, tension was on the increase, the air grew suffocating. The scuffle in the Chamber of Deputies and Zola's letter to boot and his trial were all caused by the nervous strain. What is surprising about it? The best people, the leaders of the nation had to be the first to sound the alarm—that is just what happened. The first to raise his voice was Scherer-Koestner,[9] whom his French intimates call (according to Kovalevsky) "the dagger's blade"—so irreproachable and stainless he is. The second was Zola. And now he is being tried. * * *

I know the case from the stenographic report, which is totally different from what is in the newspapers, and I see Zola plainly. Above all, he is sincere: he builds his judgments solely on what he sees, and not on ghosts, as others do. True, sincere people can make mistakes, but such mistakes cause less harm than reasoned insincerity, prejudices, or political considerations. Even if Dreyfus is guilty, Zola nevertheless is right, because the business of writers is not to accuse, not to persecute, but to side even with the guilty, once they are condemned and suffer punishment. People will say: but politics? but the interests of the State? Well, great writers and artists should engage in politics only to the extent needed to defend themselves against politics. Even without them there are plenty of accusers, prosecutors, and gendarmes, and in any event the role of Paul suits them better than that of Saul. And no matter what the verdict will be, Zola will nevertheless rejoice, his old age will be a good old age and he will die with a conscience at peace or at least at ease. * * *

Your A. Chekhov

---

[8] The list of the military secrets delivered to the German military attaché in Paris.
[9] Vice-President of the Senate.

Nice, February 22, 1898

My dear goddaughter [1] *Olga Germanovna,*

I congratulate you on the addition to the family and hope your daughter will be beautiful, intelligent, engaging, and end by marrying a good fellow, possibly meek and patient, who won't be driven out the window by his mother-in-law. I learned the happy news some time ago, shared in it fully, but did not congratulate you until now because I simply wasn't up to it. I myself had a bellyful—from the most excruciating pain. A dentist broke one of my teeth, then extracted it in three stages, and probably infected me, since infectious periostitis developed in my upper jaw, my physiognomy became distorted, and I was climbing the walls with pain. Typhoid fever set in. An operation was performed the day before yesterday. Now I feel better. (What follows from this point pertains to your husband.)

I can't bring the English almanac but I can mail it; all you have to do is write down the title. You ask me what I think of Zola and his trial. First of all, I judge by the obvious: in support of Zola are all the European intelligentsia and opposed to him, all that is contemptible and suspect. It comes down to this: Imagine that a university administration mistakenly expelled the wrong student. You begin to protest, but they shout back, "You are abusing science!" although all a university administration and science have in common is that officials and professors both wear blue frock coats. You take an oath, try to convince, expose the error. They shout back, "Prove it!" You say, "Kindly let us go to the office and look over the records there." "Out of the question! This is confidential material!" So whatever you do is of no avail. The psychology of the French Government is clear. Just as a respectable woman, having once deceived her husband, makes a number of crude mistakes, falls prey to outrageous blackmail, and finally kills herself—and all for the sake of concealing her initial error—so the French Government, having shut its eyes to a great deal, is pushing ruthlessly ahead now, shifting one way and another merely to avoid acknowledging its mistake.

New Times is conducting a senseless campaign, whereas the majority of Russian newspapers are, if not for Zola, at least opposed to his

[1] Given in marriage to Mikhail by Anton Chekhov, she thus became his god-daughter.

prosecution. The appeal will have no effect even if the outcome is favorable. The issue will be settled of itself, by chance, somehow, owing to the explosion of steam that is accumulating in the minds of the French. It will all work out.

There is nothing new. Discounting the periostitis, everything is fine. My physiognomy is still twisted sideways. Be well. If Mamasha is still with you, give her my regards. I sent a great deal of fragrant soap home. Had you been at Melikhovo, you too might have gotten a piece.

Your Papasha A. Chekhov

TO A. P. CHEKHOV

Nice, February 23, 1898

Brother!!

* * * My health is such that it could only gratify you, my heirs. The dentist broke one of my teeth and then three times tried to pull out the remainder, resulting in an infectious periostitis of the upper gum. The pain was excruciating, and because of the fever, I had to endure the experience that I so artistically depicted in "Typhus," the experience that the intelligentsia suffered looking at your *Platon Andreich.* Nightmare and a sense of distention. Day before yesterday they lanced the boil, and now I am again at my desk and writing. You'll not get your inheritance.

I received the news from Yaroslavl that a daughter was born to Misha. The fresh-baked parent is in seventh heaven.

With regard to Zola's case *New Times* conducted itself just disgustingly. On this subject the old man and I exchanged letters (though in a moderate tone), and thereafter we held our peace. However, I do not wish to write him or to receive letters from him in which he justifies the tactlessness of his paper by saying that he loves the military—I don't want those letters because all this has long been making me sick. I too love the military, but if I had a paper of my own, I would not permit the Cactuses [1] to print Zola's novel *without paying him* [2] while

[1] Pen name of Pyotr Kuzmich Martyanov, who wrote versified "dedications" to Russian authors for *Splinters.* The Chekhovs used the term in derogation of contributors to *New Times.*

[2] The novel in question was *Paris,* which ran for two years in the *Supplement* to *New Times.*

in the newspaper pouring slops on him. And why? Because never had even one of the Cactuses been known for a noble impulse and moral integrity. And anyhow, to attack Zola when he is on trial doesn't befit those concerned with literature. * * *

L'homme des lettres,

A. Tchekhoff

TO A. S. SUVORIN

Nice, March 13, 1898

The weather is magnificent here, sheer enchantment. Warm, even hot; the sky blue, bright, the sea sparkling, the fruit trees in blossom. I stroll without an overcoat, in a straw hat. I have grown as lazy as an Arab, and I do nothing, absolutely nothing, and looking at myself and at other Russians, I am more than ever firmly convinced that a Russian can't work and be his own self unless the weather is wretched. * * *

You have grown attached to the theater, but apparently I retire from it further and further—and I am sorry, for in the past the theater gave me much that was good (and it gives me a fairly good income; this winter my plays were successful as never before in the provinces, even *Uncle Vanya*). Formerly I had no greater delight than to sit in a theater, but now I sit there feeling as though at any moment someone in the gallery will shout: "Fire!" And I don't like actors. This change is due to my being a playwright. * * *

The other day I mailed all the French classics, 319 volumes, to the Taganrog library. Cost me a pretty penny. I am afraid the censorship will be dilatory and may confiscate half of the books.* * *

I am healthy, but no healthier than before, at any rate I have not gained any weight and apparently never shall.

I shall return home after April 10,[1] by way of Paris. * * *

Your A. Chekhov

---

[1] Chekhov had come to Nice in September of the previous year.

TO P. F. IORDANOV[1]

Paris, April 21, 1898

* * * I have purchased a complete account of Zola's case and shall send it to you. Yesterday I saw Bernard Lazare, author of the brochure that served to initiate the hostilities,[2] got from him all the interesting material on Dreyfus's side, and shall send this along too. The Dreyfus case, as it is gradually coming to light, is a huge fraud. The real traitor is Major Esterhazy, and the documents were fabricated in Brussels. The Government knew about this, as did Casimir-Périer[3] who, from the outset, did not believe Dreyfus was guilty, does not believe it now, and withdrew because he did not believe it.

Keep well. I wish you all the best.

Your A. Chekhov

TO L. A. AVILOVA

Melikhovo, July 23–27, 1898

There are so many guests here that I just can't get around to answering your last letter. I would like to write a rather long letter, but my hand grows numb at the thought that someone may come in at any moment and interrupt me. And in fact, as I write the word "interrupt," a little girl comes to tell me that a patient has arrived. I have to go.

The financial issue has already been settled satisfactorily. I clipped my minor stories from *Splinters* and sold the rights to them to Sytin for ten years.[1] Then, as it turns out, I can get a thousand rubles from *Russian Thought*, where, incidentally, I have been given a raise. They were paying me 250, but now it's 300.

Writing has become odious, and I don't know what to do. I'd gladly practice medicine, would accept some post or other, but I no longer have sufficient physical resiliency. These days when I write, or think I must, I feel such disgust, as though (forgive the comparison) I were eating cabbage soup from which a cockroach had been removed.

---

[1] Pavel Fyodorovich Iordanov, a physician, sanitary inspector, and member of the City Council of Taganrog, later mayor of the city. The raising of its cultural level, particularly the improvement of the public library, was one of his concerns.

[2] The reference is to the efforts of the liberals and the radicals that led years later to the rehabilitation of Dreyfus.

[3] The President of France, 1894–95.

[1] In the end the transaction fell through.

Writing itself is not what repels me but this literary entourage, from which one has no escape, and which he carries with him everywhere as the earth its atmosphere.

The weather here is wonderful, one has no desire to leave. I have to write for the August issue of *Russian Thought;* I've already started, but must finish. Be well and content. There's no space left for the rat's tail, so let's just leave the signature docked.

Your A. Chekhov

TO A. P. CHEKHOV

Melikhovo, July 30, 1898

Most Venerable Brother of Mine!

I haven't written until now because guests hindered me, but mainly because there was nothing to write about. Nothing is new except perhaps that we are having the most marvelous weather. Everyone is thriving: Father is disapproving, Mother is in Taganrog, I'm at home working, Ivan is traveling somewhere. Masha attends to the domestic arrangements, Misha is in the Treasury Department, delighting in a happy family life and gradually turning into Gogol's Mizhuev.[1]

* * * We are building a zemstvo school in Melikhovo. We are collecting contributions. We are selling apples. As for literature, the market is bearish. Lacking a desire to write, one does so as though he were eating lenten fare the sixth week of the fast.

I'm dragging out the existence of a bachelor; come fall I'll start to roam again. Such is the vale of life. The conduct of *New Times* in the Dreyfus-Zola case is simply abominable and vile. It is disgusting to read.

If the hospital on the Finnish island is opened, send me an invitation.[2]

Be sensible, pure in thought, and gentle, like your parent, who is gathering apples from under the trees so that people won't steal them.

Your bachelor brother,

Antonius

Regards to the family.

[1] A minor character in *Dead Souls,* he is a decent fellow and a henpecked bore, the opposite of the braggart, bully, and wild liar Nozdryov.

[2] The addressee had a hand in the plan for setting up a hospital for alcoholics—he was one himself—headed by Dr. Viktor Vasilyevich Olderogge, on one of the Aland Islands of Finland. Apparently the hospital never materialized.

TO A. S. SUVORIN

Melikhovo, August 24, 1898

* * * I am building another new school, the third. My schools are considered exemplary—I say this so that you won't think I have squandered your 200 rubles on nonsense. I won't be at Tolstoy's on the 28th; [1] firstly, because it will be damp and cold traveling to his place and, secondly—why should I go? Tolstoy's life is a continuous jubilee and there is no reason to single out a particular day. Thirdly, Menshikov was here and, having come straight from Yasnaya Polyana, told me that Lev Nikolayevich winces and groans at the very thought of people coming to congratulate him on August 28; and fourthly, I won't go to Yasnaya Polyana because Sergeyenko will be there. Sergeyenko and I were students together in high school; he was a comical, jovial, witty fellow, but once he began to fancy himself a great writer and a friend of Tolstoy's (whom, by the way, he exhausts terribly), he became the most tedious person in the world. I dread him—this is a hearse stood on end.

Menshikov said that Tolstoy and his family are very eager for me to visit Yasnaya Polyana and will be offended if I don't come. ("Only not on the 28th, please," Menshikov added.) But, I repeat, it has turned damp and very cold and I have begun to cough again. I am told I have improved considerably, yet at the same time am being driven away from home again. I shall have to go south. I am in a great hurry, doing a little work, and am eager to finish something before my departure, so I haven't a thought to spare on Yasnaya Polyana, even though I ought to go there for a day or two. And I'd like to go.

My itinerary: first to the Crimea and Sochi; later, when it turns cold in Russia, I'll go abroad. Paris is the only place I want to visit, the southern regions don't appeal to me at all. I fear this trip as I would exile.

Your A. Chekhov

Wire me about something. I love to receive telegrams.

---

[1] Tolstoy's birthday.

TO L. S. MIZINOVA

Yalta, September 21, 1898

Dear Lika,

Talk of the devil . . . Chaliapin and Rozhansky [1] are giving a concert here; yesterday we had supper together and talked about you. If only you knew how much joy your letter gave me! You are hard-hearted, you are fat, you cannot understand this joy of mine. Yes, I am in Yalta and shall live here until it snows. I didn't want to leave Moscow, I very much didn't want to, but it was necessary to go away because I am still living in sin with the bacillus—and the story that I have put on weight and even gotten stout is an empty fabrication. And that I am getting married is also a fabrication, spread abroad by you. You know that I shall never marry without your permission. You are certain of this, nevertheless, you spread all kinds of rumors—probably following the logic of an old hunter who doesn't fire a rifle and doesn't let others do so, and merely grumbles and groans, lying on the stove. No, dear Lika, no! Without your permission I shall not get married, and before I do so I shall yet make it tough for you, if you will excuse the crude phrase. Well, do come to Yalta.

I shall wait impatiently for your letter and the pictures, in which, as you write, you resemble an old witch. Send them to me, dear Lika, make it possible for me to see you at least in a photograph. Alas, I do not belong to the number of what you call "my friends": all my requests addressed to you have always remained unsatisfied. I cannot send you my photograph for the reason that I haven't any and that I shan't have any soon. I don't have photographs taken.

In spite of severe prohibition, in January I shall probably take off for Moscow for two or three days, otherwise I will hang myself out of boredom. So we shall see each other? Then bring me two or three neckerchiefs, I'll pay you for them.

From Moscow I shall go to France or Italy.

Nemirovich and Stanislavsky have a very interesting theater company. Beautiful little actresses. Had I stayed a bit longer, I would have fallen for them. The older I grow, the more frequently and more fully the pulse of life beats in me. Make a note of that. But don't be afraid.

---

[1] A. V. Rozhansky was an opera singer in Moscow; his stage name was Sekar.

I'm not going to aggravate "my friends" by daring to do what they dared to do unsuccessfully.

I repeat, your letter made me very, very happy, and I am afraid that you won't believe it and won't answer soon. I swear, Lika, that without you I am bored.

Stay happy, well, and have real successes. Yesterday at supper you were being praised as a singer, and I was glad. May God protect you.

Your A. Chekhov

TO M. P. CHEKHOVA

Yalta, September 27, 1898

Dear Masha,

I received a notice from the post office that a package had arrived. The cap will not be needed soon, since the weather continues summery. It is cool only in the evening, but a summer or fall overcoat is sufficient.

Yesterday I went with Sinani to look at a property that is for sale. It is less than twenty miles from Yalta, on the road to Sevastopol, near the Kekeneis station, between Alupka and Foros. The trip seemed to me very interesting and jolly; if you have ever traveled from Baidar, then you know it. On passing Kekeneis you turn left and drive down to the sea; here the road isn't bad technically but the descent is very steep, I was so frightened that the whole of the following night I was haunted by that precipitous descent. Aside from this road, there is a footpath, too, leading from the highway to the property—it is even pleasant to walk down this way; they say that there is also a side road to Alupka and that soon, in a year or two, a railway will pass close to the property, between it and the sea. Terrible as it is to descend, it is equally delightful, peaceful and quiet when you reach the property. Imagine: (1) a little house of two stories with a red roof; two rooms upstairs, two down; (2) a wing of two rooms—this is no house but a hut such as the Caucasian natives build, very clean; (3) a kitchen with a Russian stove and a range; here it smells of Little Russia; (4) a stable; (5) a new tobacco shed with several partitions. The trees all old. Poplars, cypresses, pomegranates, figs, olives, nut trees; there is one walnut tree that is twice the size of our largest apple tree. The grounds come to some eight acres. There is a vineyard, a tobacco plantation, huge rocks, the size of the wing at Melikhovo. From one of them that is near the house an arched stream gushes. The water is cold. It's cozy in the house and from a balcony a marvelous view of the sea. Alongside, a Tartar hamlet with naïve lanes. Nothing gets stolen. You are treated to grapes and apples. Lots of onions, like the Spanish variety. For a swim in the sea, a fifteen- to twenty-minutes' walk, or take a donkey. You can buy a donkey for 10 rubles. No fodder necessary because all year round a donkey grazes on burrs. There's room for two or three donkeys. For two rubles you can get to Yalta by post chaise or mail coach. The post and telegraph office is two miles away. For a ruble a month a boy will call for your mail every day. Easy to find a cook. Everything touching, cozy, orig- inal, in good taste; a wonderful heavy fragrance of cypresses, but . . . frightening road!! To drive is not so terrifying, indeed, jolly. If I were sure that you wouldn't be scared, I would buy this property at once; by the way, you can have it for only two thousand rubles.[1] It is wildly cheap. The descent is awful but beautiful, and as a painter you will perhaps be tempted by it. Think it over and write me. Below is a plan of the property. The house is new, there is plenty of water. The air is pure as the skies. Not a copeck need be spent on repairs. There is a sideboard in the house, also a wardrobe, a table, and Viennese chairs. All new. So think it over.

Greetings to everybody.

Your Chekhov

TO A. S. SUVORIN

Yalta, October 8, 1898

You write that the public should not be humored; so be it; nor, further- more, should my books be priced higher than Potapenko's and Koro- lenko's. Many of my books are bought here in Yalta, and in the book- stores I have been told that the public often speaks ill of me. I fear that the ladies out walking will go for me with their parasols.

The weather here is warm, altogether summery; today it's windy, but yesterday and the day before it was so balmy that I could not re- strain myself and sent a telegram to *New Times*. We don't wear over- coats and still are warm. The Crimean seashore is beautiful, agreeable,

[1] Several weeks later he did buy the property at the price mentioned.

and I like it better than the Riviera; the only trouble is that there is no culture. With respect to certain conveniences, however, Yalta has progressed even further than Nice, here we have a wonderful sewage system, but the outskirts are sheer Asia.

In *New Times* I read and was puzzled by a notice about the theater of Nemirovich and Stanislavsky and their staging of *Fyodor Ioannovich*.[1] You liked the company so much and they received you so cordially that only some major misunderstanding, about which I know nothing, could have caused the publication of such a notice. What happened? [2]

Incidentally, before leaving Moscow I was at a rehearsal of *Fyodor Ioannovich*. I was pleasantly moved by its intellectual tone and by the breath of true art that was wafted from the stage, although there were no outstanding performers. Irina, in my opinion, is magnificent. Voice, presence, warmth—it was so splendid that you had a lump in your throat. Fyodor seemed to me rather inferior, Godunov and Shuisky [3] good and the old man marvelous, but best of all was Irina. If I had remained in Moscow I would have fallen in love with this Irina.[4]

Keep well. All the best. A low obeisance. I'm going to the bath house.

Your A. Chekhov

TO M. P. CHEKHOVA

Yalta, October 14, 1898

Dear Masha,

Sinani received your telegram yesterday, October 13, at 2 P.M. The telegram is unclear: "How did Anton Pavlovich Chekhov take the news of his father's death?" Sinani was bewildered and thought he had to conceal the news from me. All Yalta knew about Father's death, yet I

---

[1] A play by Aleksey Konstantinovich Tolstoy (1817–75), dealing with a sixteenth-century sovereign, the last representative of the Rurik dynasty, an unworldly but weak-willed and perhaps weak-minded man who provided the playwright with a grateful subject.

[2] The question was never answered.

[3] Leading boyars; Boris Godunov succeeded Fyodor as Czar.

[4] The part was played by O. L. Knipper. Chekhov did not stay in Moscow, but he did fall in love with her and eventually married her.

had no information and not until evening did Sinani show me the telegram. After that I went to the post office and there read a letter just received from Ivan, who informed me about the operation. I am writing this on the evening of the 14th and still have no news, not a word.

Be that as it may, the sad news, completely unexpected, has grieved and shaken me deeply. I am sorry for Father, sorry for us all; the knowledge of your having to endure such distress in Moscow while I live peacefully in Yalta—this I cannot escape from for a moment and it weighs heavily on me. How is Mother? Where is she? If she is not going to Melikhovo (it will be oppressive for her there alone), where do you intend to settle her? In general, there are a great many questions we have to decide. Judging from your telegram to Sinani, you have doubts about my health. If you and Mother are worried, shouldn't I come to Moscow for a short while? Or would Mamasha want to come and stay with me in Yalta to rest up here? She would, incidentally, get adjusted here and if she liked the place, we would settle here permanently. The weather is always warm, you don't need a coat, and life here in winter seems very comfortable. We would spend the winter in Yalta and the summer in Melikhovo or in Kuchukoy, near Yalta.

If Mamasha will agree to come, send me a wire; I will drive to Sevastopol to meet her and from the station take her directly to Yalta in a carriage.

Traveling by the express train is comfortable. People here would receive Mamasha amicably and arrange things pleasantly for her. And were you to get a leave and come here for just a week, it would be a great pleasure for me. Among other things, we would decide what we are to do now. It seems to me that after Father's death, things in Melikhovo will no longer be the same, as though the course of the Melikhovo life ended too with his diary.[1]

Once again, I am completely well. Please write, don't keep me in suspense. I received your parcel.

I will write again tomorrow. Be well. Regards to Mamasha, Vanya, and Sonya.[2]

Your Antoine

---

[1] From his first day in Melikhovo to his last the own-wayish old man kept a diary.
[2] Chekhov's brother Ivan and his wife.

TO A. S. SUVORIN

Yalta, October 17, 1898

* * * I shall probably stay on in Yalta for the winter. I don't feel like going abroad. And, for that matter, I can't possibly go any distance since I have to map out a plan for my further existence. My sister is coming to Yalta in a few days, and together we will decide how we are to live. Most likely Mother will no longer want to live in the country, it would be frightening for her there alone. Perhaps we shall sell Melikhovo and settle in the Crimea, where we shall live together until I am free of bacilli. One way or the other, though the doctors believe I shall still have to spend more than one winter in the Crimea. This is what is termed being unsettled.

You have repeatedly said that I could get five or even ten thousand from the book store [1] on favorable terms, that is, with the debt paid in installments over several years. If you still feel that way, wire me five thousand and inform the store that the debt is to be deducted in small amounts from the monies owing me, at the rate of no more than a thousand a year; otherwise I'll be hard up.* * *

Moon. Sea enchanting. Going out to post this letter.

Your A. Chekhov

TO L. S. MIZINOVA

Yalta, October 24, 1898

Dear Lika,

I have two pieces of news. The first is that my father died. His intestines became strangulated; they caught it too late, drove him to the station over a terrible road, then performed an operation in Moscow, opened his stomach. To go by the letters, he died an agonizing death. Masha has suffered a great deal. And I myself feel wretched.

Second, I am buying (on credit) a piece of land near Yalta [1] in order to have some immovable property where I can spend the winters and at my leisure grow the gooseberries that you detest. The bit of land that I am purchasing is located in picturesque surroundings: views of the sea, the mountains. Own vineyard, own well. It's a twenty-minute

---

[1] Suvorin was owner of a book store, in addition to his activities as a publisher.
[1] Actually, in a suburb of Yalta known as Autka.

[317]

walk from Yalta. I have already drawn up a plan for the house and have not forgotten the guests, to whom I have allotted a little room in the basement; in the absence of guests, hen turkeys will live there.

Be that as it may, I shall hardly get to Paris before April. I want terribly to see you, but I don't want to leave. And I have no money. What's more, it's jolly here, how jolly I can't begin to tell you. The weather is amazing, real summer. No, clearly it's for you to come to Russia, not for me to go to Paris. If, in fact, you do come soon, bring me some ties and handkerchiefs (with the initial "A"). I'll pay you for them. Word of honor, I'll pay! Even if you bring a hundred rubles' worth, I'll pay for it all, I won't stand any interference.

Your photographs are very good. You are even beautiful, which I by no means expected. I'd send you my photograph but I don't have it with me. You can see my portrait in the Tretyakov Gallery. By the way, Braz's portrait is terribly uninteresting.

I am expecting Masha. She is coming to Yalta in a few days so that we can get together and have a talk. After Father's death, after this disaster which lasted for several days and was a strain on everyone, my mother and sister will hardly want to live in Melikhovo. I have already begun to wonder whether we shouldn't all move to the Crimea. It is warm and a comfortable place to live.

Write, Lika. Don't be lazy. My address is simply: Yalta. If you do take it into your head to come to Russia, write me a week in advance.

Where did you ever get the idea I have a bald spot? The nerve?! I know: you are revenging yourself on me because in one of my letters I once pointed out to you in a friendly way, intending no offense whatever, that you are lopsided, thanks to which you, unfortunately, still have not found a husband.

Be well and happy. Don't forget your old admirer.

A. Chekhov

TO M. P. CHEKHOV

Yalta, October 26, 1898

* * * I am buying a piece of land in Yalta and shall build there so that I have a place where I can spend winters. The prospect of endlessly tramping about, putting up with hotel rooms, doormen, haphazard dinners, and the rest simply appalls my imagination. And Mother could spend winters with me. Here winter doesn't exist; it is the end of October and roses and other flowers compete in blossoming, the trees are green, and it is warm. There is an abundance of water. Apart from the house, nothing will be needed, no outbuildings; everything under one roof. There are coal, firewood, quarters for the yard-keeper and everything right in the basement. The hens lay eggs the year round and no special quarters are needed for them, partitions will do. There are a bakery and market nearby, so that it will be warm and very comfortable for Mother. By the way, all autumn long people pick mushrooms and this will be a diversion for Mother. I myself am not going to direct any of the building; it will all be done by an architect. The house will be ready by April. From the standpoint of a city dweller, the piece of land is sizable; it will accommodate an orchard, and a flower bed, and a kitchen garden. As of next year there will be a railroad in Yalta.

The Kuchukoy house is not suitable for sustained all-year-round living. It is a dacha, a very charming one, and worth buying simply because it is charming and is to be had cheaply.

As for marriage, on which you insist—what can I say? There's no use marrying except for love; to marry a girl simply because she is likable is comparable to buying yourself something at the market simply because it's all right. The most important nut in married life is love, sexual attraction, one flesh; all the rest is unreliable and dull, no matter how wisely we calculate. Consequently, it is not a question of a likable girl but a beloved one; as you see, it's just a small matter that's holding me back.

* * * My *Uncle Vanya* is being performed throughout the provinces and is a success everywhere. So you see, one never knows where he'll make it and where he won't. I never counted on this play at all. Be well, write.

Your A. Chekhov

* * *

TO A. P. CHEKHOV

Yalta, November 28, 1898

* * * I am alive and well, at least I am not in pain. I have periods of spitting blood, but they scarcely bother me, and I have grown accustomed to them. My heart is quite strong, which I attribute to my com-

plete abstinence from tobacco and liquor—the latter I leave to dissolute and frivolous people. The weather in Yalta is splendid; warm; in nature —the utmost fecundity. Steamers now come, now go.

Why no word about the islands off Finland, about the hospital for alcoholics?

In its treatment of the Dreyfus case, *New Times* tumbled into a muddy pool and keeps on tumbling. What a disgrace! Brrr!

The lowest obeisance to your honorable family. Be well.

Your Antonio

TO MAXIM GORKY

Yalta, December 3, 1898

Much esteemed Aleksey Maksimovich!

Your last letter gave me great pleasure. I thank you heartily for it. *Uncle Vanya* was written long ago, very long ago; I have never seen it staged. In recent years it has been performed frequently in provincial theaters, possibly because I published a collection of my plays. In general, my attitude toward them is chilly, I lost touch with the theater some time ago and no longer wish to write for it.

You ask me what I think of your stories. What do I think? An unmistakable talent, and a genuine, major talent at that. It came across with extraordinary power, for example, in the story "On the Steppe," and I even felt envious that I had not written it myself. You are an artist, an intelligent man. You have a keen sensibility. You are plastic —that is, when you depict a thing, you see it and feel it with your hands. This is real art. Now you know my opinion, and I am very pleased that I can convey it to you. Very pleased, I repeat, and were we to meet and talk for an hour or two, you would realize how highly I esteem you and what hopes I have for your gift.

Shall I turn now to what is lacking? But that is not so easy. To speak about what is lacking in a talent is comparable to speaking about what is lacking in a large tree growing in a garden; what is mainly in question here is not the tree itself but the taste of the beholder. Isn't that so?

I'll begin by saying that in my opinion you lack restraint. You are like a spectator in a theater who expresses his enthusiasm so unreservedly that he prevents himself and others from listening. This lack of restraint is particularly apparent in the descriptions of nature with which you interrupt the dialogues; reading these descriptions, one wishes they were more compact, briefer—just two or three lines. Frequent mention of "bliss," "whispering," "velvety softness," and the like imparts a certain rhetorical and monotonous quality to these descriptions, and they chill, almost tire one. A lack of restraint is felt also in your depictions of women ("Malva," "On the Rafts") and in the love scenes. This is not breadth—a bold stroke of the brush—but simply a lack of restraint. Then, the frequent use of words that are altogether awkward in the type of stories you write—"accompaniment," "disk," "harmony"—such words are distracting. You often speak of "waves." One detects tension, wariness, as it were, in your depiction of intellectuals; this is not because you have seldom observed intellectuals closely; you do know them, but it seems as though you do not know from what side to approach them.

How old are you? I don't know you, don't know where you are from, and who you are, but it seems to me that while you are still young you ought to leave Nizhny [1] and for two or three years live, rub elbows, so to speak, with literature and literary people—not so that you will learn how to crow like our cock and, generally speaking, become keener, but rather that you should plunge headlong into literature once and for all and come to love it. Besides, one grows old prematurely in the provinces. Korolenko, Potapenko, Mamin, Ertel—these are splendid people; at first you may find them somewhat tedious but after a year or two you will get used to them and appreciate their worth, and their company will more than redeem the unpleasantness and discomfort of life in the capital.* * *

Your A. Chekhov

TO YE. M. SHAVROVA

Yalta, December 26, 1898

Much esteemed colleague!

I have received both books: the spattered blood of the startled heart and the female Nihilist.[1] The first afforded me true pleasure. The second I

[1] Since the Revolution the ancient trade center has been renamed after Maxim Gorky.

[1] One of the books was a collection of Decadent writings entitled *The Blood of a Heart Torn to Pieces.* The other was a novel by Sofya Kovalevskaya, a book for-

read a long time ago. You wrapped *The Female Nihilist* in a sheet, placed it in a package, sealed it, pasted a thousand stamps on it—why such precautions? It should simply have gone by registered mail.

The weather in Yalta is still very fine.

People write me from Moscow and there is a big to-do about the success *The Sea Gull* has had. But since I am unlucky in the theater, fatally unlucky, one of the cast [2] fell ill after the first performance, and my *Sea Gull* will not be staged for a while.

I have so little luck in the theater, so little luck, that were I to marry an actress, she would most likely give birth to an orangutan or a porcupine.

Send me another book and write me again.

Your A. Chekhov

The main thing I forgot: happy New Year!

TO YE. Z. KONOVITZER [1]

Yalta, December 26, 1898

Dear Yefim Zinovyevich,

I wish you and Yevdokyia Isaakovna a happy New Year.* * *

It has been pleasant here, but today it is windy, and cold; I have to keep indoors, eyeing the window dully and envying the people who are not in Yalta this weather.

So my play is a failure? [2] I am unlucky in the theater, terribly unlucky, fatally, and if I were to marry an actress, an orangutan would certainly be born to us—such is my luck!

Keep well, I press your hand.

Your A. Chekhov

bidden in Russia; Shavrova had picked it up in Vienna. The novelist is better known as a mathematician. She was the first woman to teach mathematics at the University of Stockholm.

2 O. L. Knipper, who played the leading part.

1 Editor of *The Courier*, a newspaper.

2 The addressee had written to Chekhov that while the staging of *The Sea Gull* was splendid, the acting was unsatisfactory.

[1899]

Yalta, January 3, 1899

* * * Apparently you did not quite understand me. I was writing to you not about crudity but simply the inappropriateness of foreign, not intrinsically Russian, or seldom used words. With other writers, words such as "fatalistically," for instance, would pass unnoticed, but your works are musical, harmonious, and every rough touch jars terribly. Naturally, it is a matter of taste, and my criticism may simply betoken undue irritability or the conservatism of a man who long ago adopted fixed habits. I can tolerate expressions like "collegiate assessor" and "lieutenant commander" but "flirt" and "champion" (when they occur in descriptions) disgust me.

Are you self-educated? In your stories you are a complete artist and, what is more, a truly educated man. Nothing is less characteristic of you than crudity; you are intelligent and your perceptions are subtle and refined. Your best things are "On the Steppe" and "On the Rafts" —did I tell you that? They are first-rate, masterpieces; they indicate an artist who has been through a very fine school. I don't think I am mistaken. The only weak point is the lack of restraint, the lack of grace. When a man expends the fewest possible movements on a given act, that is grace. In your movements one is aware of a superfluity.

The descriptions of nature are the work of a master; you are a real landscape painter. Except that the frequent attempts to personify nature (anthropomorphism)—when the sea breathes, the sky gazes, the steppe luxuriates, nature whispers, speaks, is melancholy, etc.—such similes make descriptions rather monotone, somewhat sirupy, sometimes dim; in descriptions of nature color and expressiveness are attained only by simplicity, by such simple phrases as: "The sun set," "It grew dark," "It began to rain," etc. And you are one of the few writers to whom this simplicity is to a marked degree natural.

I did not like the first issue of the refurbished *Life*.¹ It somehow lacks seriousness. Chirikov's ² story is naïve and insincere, Veresayev's ³ is a crude imitation of something—of your Orlov ⁴—crude and also naïve. One cannot go far with stories like these. The general tone of your "Kirilka" is well sustained but the effect marred by the character of the recent zemstvo officials.⁵ Never portray recent zemstvo officials. Nothing is easier than the portrayal of disagreeable authorities; the reader likes this, but he is the most unpleasant, the most vapid kind of reader. I have the same aversion to the creatures of the recent zemstvo legislation as I do to the word "flirt," and for that reason I may be wrong. But I live in the country, am acquainted with all the zemstvo officials of my own and the neighboring districts, have known them for some time, and find their personalities and activity completely atypical, of no interest at all. And in this respect I think I am right.* * *

Your A. Chekhov

TO V. A. TIKHONOV¹

Yalta, January 5, 1899

Greetings, dear Vladimir Alekseyevich!

* * * My health is fairly good, but they won't let me go to Moscow and Petersburg; I'm told the bacilli don't tolerate the atmosphere of the capitals. Meanwhile, I want terribly to go to the capital, terribly! I've grown dull here, turned into a philistine, and, it seems, am nearing a point where I may take up with a pockmarked peasant woman who would beat me on workdays and pity me on holidays. Our kind should not live in the provinces. I could put up with Pavlovsk—it is an aristocratic town (I suspect that is the very reason you chose to live

¹ In 1898 this became an organ of nonmilitant Marxism, with Gorky editing the literary department. In 1901, after the appearance there of his poem in prose, "The Stormy Petrel," a veiled invitation to revolution, the magazine was suppressed.

² Yevgeny Nikolayevich Chirikov (1864–1932) was a fiction writer and playwright who emigrated after the revolution.

³ Vikenty Vikentyevich Veresayev was a novelist and physician who wrote under the name of Smidovich. His *Diary of a Doctor* was very popular.

⁴ A character in a story by Gorky called "The Orlov Couple."

⁵ A law passed in 1889 provided for the appointment of such officials from among the gentry only. They combined police and judicial functions and had dictatorial powers over the peasantry.

¹ V. A. Tikhonov (1857–1914), author of fiction and plays, was the editor of the monthly *North*, and wrote reminiscences of Chekhov.

there), a town full of statesmen. In this respect, Yalta is scarcely any different from Yeletz or Kremenchug; even the bacilli are asleep here. * * *

Your A. Chekhov

.TO M. P. CHEKHOVA

Yalta, January 9, 1899

* * * Vanya said that you, that is you, dear Masha, and Mamasha, are disposed to sell Melikhovo. Then do so. Sell it for any sum you like, but no less than fifteen thousand. My conditions: I get fifteen thousand, you, Masha, take the rest; since Melikhovo owes its improvements chiefly to you, you are entitled to this reward. The furniture should be included in the sale; keep what is in the wing, also pictures, linen, rugs, bedding, the saddle, the gun, and all the objects belonging to you and Mamasha, exclusive of such huge pieces as Mamasha's wardrobe. I say all this in case you really want to sell and a buyer is found. If, however, I sell my works to Marx, I shall not be selling Melikhovo, but shall take other steps.

We have a wonderful spring day. It's warm, the sea is calm. I received a telegram from Chaliapin, who saw *The Sea Gull.*

Isn't it possible for us to remove to the Crimea in such a way that afterward we could regularly spend a month or two in Moscow? Away from Moscow, you will be bored, and besides, there's no need for you to limit yourself. You can give up the high school now and confine yourself to painting. If you undertake to manage the business side of my writing, I shall pay you 40 rubles a month—it will be advantageous for me, now that we suffer huge losses. This, à propos. Live as you want to and that is the best you can do.

By the way, about the books. Suvorin is publishing my collected works. I read the first proof and I curse. I have a presentiment that this complete collection of my work will not be issued before 1948. Negotiations with Marx, it seems to me, have already started.

The next time you sew nightshirts for me, please make them a little longer, at least coming below the knee. In a short shirt I resemble a crane. * * *

Be well. I press your hand.

Antonius, Bishop of Melikhovo, Autka, and Kuchukoy

[325]

TO A. S. SUVORIN

Yalta, January 17, 1899

* * * I have read the story by Lev Lvovich [1] entitled "The *Obshchina* [2] Is a Fool." The construction is poor, it would have been better to write simply an essay, without beating about the bush, but the thesis is developed correctly and passionately. I myself am opposed to the *obshchina*. It is sensible when you have to deal with foreign enemies who make frequent raids, or contend with savage beasts, but at present it is a crowd artificially bound together like a band of prisoners. It is said that Russia is an agricultural country. This is true, but has nothing to do with the *obshchina*, at least in our time. The *obshchina* lives by agriculture, but when agriculture begins to be affected by technological culture, it falls to pieces, for the *obshchina* and technological culture are incompatible concepts. By the way, the *obshchina* is responsible for our nation-wide hard drinking and profound ignorance. * * *

Kondakov, the academician, is staying here. The city has chosen both of us to serve on the commission for the arrangement of a Pushkin festival. [3] We want to stage *Boris Godunov*. Kondakov will play the part of Pimen. I am planning a *tableau vivant:* on the stage an abandoned country seat, a landscape, pine trees . . . enter a figure made up as Pushkin, who reads the poem, "In my own land once more." Another *tableau vivant* is "Pushkin's Duel," based on Naumov's painting. * * *

Your A. Chekhov

---

[1] A son of Lev Tolstoy; the story appeared in *New Times*.

[2] The Russian village commune, the members of which collectively held and to some extent tilled the land; this was periodically redistributed by the assembly of householders according to the number of workers or family units in the household. The members of the *obshchina* were jointly responsible for the payment of the poll tax and the discharge of their other obligations. The institution played a vital part in the ideology of the *narodniki* (Populists). Like them, Karl Marx favored the preservation of the *obshchina*, but his Russian disciples pinned their hopes not to the supposed collectivist traditions of the peasants but to the proletariat in the making. Obviously the mystique of Populism, with its idealization of the manual worker, particularly the peasant—an ideology natural to the penitent serf-owner and his heirs— had no appeal for Chekhov.

[3] On the occasion of the hundredth anniversary of Pushkin's birth (May 26, 1799 [O.S.]). Chekhov was not in Yalta when the festival took place. It was a dismal failure.

TO V. F. KOMMISSARZHEVSKAYA[1]

Yalta, January 19, 1899

I am distressed, Vera Fyodorovna; you have set me an impossible task.[2] First, I have never written a review in my life, this is strictly foreign territory for me; second, I do not write for *New Times*. I regret that I cannot fulfill your wish and fear you won't believe how much I regret this. Your wish is sacred to me and being unable to fulfill it leaves me utterly disconcerted. I haven't worked for *New Times* in quite a while, incidentally, not since 1891. Many thanks for the book, it was a pleasure to read. About myself—what can I write you? I am living in Yalta, bored, fed up with everything, including the fine weather, and want to go north. If I have the money, come spring, I will go abroad—to Paris.

Eight performances of my *Sea Gull* have already been given in Moscow and each time to a full house. I am told the performance is extraordinary and that the cast has an excellent grasp of the roles. M. I. Pisarev[3] said that, when he had completed his performance, a "bottle" had burst in the adjoining room and the audience laughed; a Moscow actor said that a vial of ether burst[4] and there was no laughter, it came off well. Be that as it may, I no longer want to write plays. The theater in Petersburg cured me of that.

Why are you forever ailing? How is it you don't seriously try to be treated? Illnesses, after all, particularly female disorders, ruin one's disposition, ruin life, and make it difficult to work. Being a doctor, you know, I understand what this is all about.

You write that you are having success. I'm aware of this, delighted, and at the same time vexed—vexed that I'm given no opportunity to see you. You are a superb actress, but it's a pity you don't have the appropriate entourage, theater, colleagues. You would do well to go to,

[1] V. F. Kommissarzhevskaya was a famous actress associated with the Aleksandrinsky Theater in Petersburg.
[2] She had asked him to review a translation of Nietzsche's *Also Sprach Zarathustra*, which had been adversely judged in a prestigious Russian monthly.
[3] Modest Ivanovich Pisarev, an actor attached to the Aleksandrinsky Theater in Petersburg.
[4] At the end of the play the sound of a shot off-stage is heard. A doctor, to postpone knowledge of the shot from the other characters, especially the mother of the young man who had previously attempted suicide, remarks that something in his "portable medicine chest" must have burst. In Petersburg the noise was explained simply as that of a "bursting bottle," which made the audience laugh, and was an indication of the sloppiness of the performance.

[327]

say, Moscow, the Maly Theater. There at least is something more nearly resembling art, and among the actors are quite a few fine people. You would be an enormous success in Moscow, it staggers my imagination to think of it.

Where will you be this summer? Where are you performing? If it is anywhere near Moscow, I'll come have a look at you. As of April I shall be living at home, near Moscow.

Once again I thank you heartily, wish you health, happiness, and all the good things in this world.

Your A. Chekhov

TO M. P. CHEKHOVA

Yalta, January 20, 1899

Dear Masha,

No doubt Ivan has already told you about my negotiations with Marx. I bargained with him for a long time, long and hard, and finally wired him today that I agree. I receive 75,000 rubles (seventy-five thousand) for future works and those already published; the rate for future works is 250 rubles per sheet; after five years, this increases to 450; after another five, to 650; a supplement of 200 per sheet added every five years thereafter. My future works will become Marx's property once I have published them in journals and newspapers and received an honorarium. The income from the plays will accrue to me and subsequently to my heirs.

* * * What are we to do with Melikhovo? I would offer the second strip of land to the peasants and keep the manor house for myself. But then, let us do what you wish. * * *

TO I. L. LEONTYEV-SHCHEGLOV

Yalta, January 20, 1899

Dear Jean,

A big, huge thanks to you for your letter, for having again shown me your tragic handwriting (which, by the way, has grown more legible). Your friendly congratulations brought home to me a whole sequence of memories. * * *

A bow and a greeting to your wife. I press your hand firmly and wish you all the best, above everything, health and money.

Your A. Chekhov

[*328*]

In the part of your letter dealing with the murder of Roshchin-Insarov,[1] you remark, "What a mess modern life is!" Your attitude toward our times has always struck me as unfair, always seemed to pass through your art like a morbid shudder, damaging its fruits, imparting to them a quality that is not yours. I am far from enthusiastic about the contemporary scene, yet I think one ought to be objective, as fair as possible. If things are not good now, if the present is not to one's liking, the past was simply abominable.

TO L. S. MIZINOVA

Yalta, January 22, 1899

Dear Lika,

Your angry letter, like a volcano, unleashed fire and lava on me; nonetheless, I held on to it and read it with great pleasure. First, I love to receive letters from you; second, I noticed long ago that if you are angry with me it means things are very well with you.

Dear, angry Lika, you rattled on about many things in your letter but said not a word how it goes with you, about your health, your singing, what is new, etc. As for me, I'm living in Yalta as before (not in Bushev's dacha), bored to death, and waiting for spring when I can leave. I have some big news about my life, a real event. Am I getting married? Guess—am I? If so, to whom? No, I'm not getting married, but I'm selling my works to Marx. I'm selling the proprietary rights. The negotiations are in progress and it may happen that in about two or three weeks I'll be living on my income! Now, of course, I won't sell Melikhovo to anyone but you. Let things stay as they have been. * * *

I shall be going to Paris in March; if I don't manage to in March, then in September. By April I shall be back at Melikhovo. Are you coming? You must. If you like, we can go to the Crimea then for about two weeks. My dacha will be ready by June, and Masha, by the way, may come then too.

* * * I am going to Paris strictly to buy a lot of suits, shirts, underwear, ties, handkerchiefs, and the like, and to see you, if by then, knowing I shall come, you don't deliberately leave Paris as you have time

[1] Nikolay Petrovich Roshchin-Insarov was a Kiev actor killed by a scene designer in a fit of jealousy.

and again. If it is somehow inconvenient for you to see me in Paris, couldn't you arrange a meeting somewhere in the vicinity—for instance, at Versailles?

I shall come to Paris alone. And formerly I always came alone. The rumors spread by one of my lady friends are nothing more than charming gossip. Do you want to know who this friend is? You know her very well. She is lopsided and has an irregular profile.

It's raining. Boring. No desire to write. Life is moving one leg after the other.

So, keep well, dear Lika. Send me letters by registered mail. The cost of registration I shall refund to you at Melikhovo by way of provisions, appetizers, and any pleasures that you may wish.

I press your hand.

Your A. Chekhov

TO M. P. CHEKHOVA

Yalta, January 27, 1899

You write: "Don't sell to Marx," whereas the following telegram arrives from Petersburg: "Contract signed and notarized." The sale I made may seem unprofitable and certainly will appear so in the future, but it has the advantage of untying my hands, and for the rest of my life I won't have to deal with publishers and printers. Moreover, Marx publishes in a grand manner. This will be a substantial, not a wretched little edition. I shall be paid 75,000 in three installments; but then, you know this arrangement as well as the others.

What this means is that you will not have to be in charge of my literary output any more, and be a Sofya Andreyevna in miniature.[1] Still, you must arrange your life so that you are free to leave when you want and live where you choose. I approve of your intention and desire not to leave Moscow for any length of time. One should spend at least two months a year in Moscow, a month at least.

And now here are errands. Please see or write Olga Mikhailovna Darskaya and tell her the following. In Yalta the second and third days of the Easter holidays will be devoted to a Pushkin fête; among other things, a performance of *Boris Godunov* will be given. Would it be possible for Olga Mikhailovna to come to Yalta and act the part of

[1] Lev Tolstoy's wife.

[*330*]

Marina, her husband taking that of the Pretender? Her health, incidentally, requires her being in the Crimea during the spring. There are actors for the roles of Pimen and Godunov, but none for Marina and the Pretender; moreover, everyone is eager to have these roles performed by really well-trained artists. If Olga Mikhailovna will not agree to come and take part in the performance, have her wire: "To Chekhov. Yalta. No." I am impatient for her reply. Pimen will be played by the academician Kondakov. I shall most likely be in Melikhovo for Easter, but say nothing about this, don't mention it to Olga Mikhailovna. The proceeds from the performance will go to build a Pushkin School.

* * * Marx originally wanted the income from the plays to accrue to me only "during my lifetime," but I safeguarded the rights of my heirs. He is a tight-fisted German, but even I, according to my attorney, managed to "confound" Marx with my unreasonable demands. I am told that L. N. Tolstoy persuaded Marx to purchase my works. * * *

Your Antonio

TO A. P. CHEKHOV

Yalta, February 5, 1899

Thoughtful Sasha!

* * * After all, speaking generally, *New Times* makes a disgusting impression. The dispatches from Paris [1] cannot be read without loathing, they are not dispatches but sheer forgery and swindle. And Ivanov's [2] self-glorifying articles! And the contributions of that infamous informer, Petersburger.[3] And Amfiteatrov's hawklike raids.[4] This is not a newspaper, but a menagerie, it is a pack of hungry jackals biting each other's tails, it is devil knows what. Olé, shepherds of Israel! [5]

Your brother and benefactor,
A. Chekhov

[1] The dispatches were intended to defame the president of the Supreme Court of Cassation, who was seeking to obtain a second trial for Dreyfus.
[2] Mikhail Mikhailovich Ivanov was a composer and the musical critic of *New Times* who praised his own opera in his columns.
[3] The pen name of Vasily Sergeyevich Lyalin, who conducted a "Little Chronicle" in the paper, and some of whose remarks were those of a volunteer stool pigeon.
[4] Aleksandr Valentinovich Amfiteatrov (1862–1937) was one of the newspaper's feuilletonists.
[5] An adaptation of the opening of Psalm 80.

TO A. S. SUVORIN

In the first place allow me to make a small correction. I telegraphed you as soon as I learned that Marx wanted to buy.[1] And I wired Sergeyenko to see you. Not a minute of secrecy or postponement, and I assure you that what you said to Sergeyenko and repeated in your latest letter to me: the phrase, "Apparently Chekhov did not want to sell to me," is based, speaking the language of class monitors in schools for young ladies, solely on paradoxes. * * *

The contract that was sent me [2] contained all sorts of things, but not a word about the income from my plays. I raised the alarm, and now I am waiting for an answer. . . . "Yes, a farce is something, the rest is rubbish." [3] —I firmly hold to this old truth and I regard income from plays as most reliable.

Out of boredom I read *The Book of My Being* by Bishop Porphyrius.[4] Here is what he said on war: "Standing armies in time of peace are grasshoppers, devouring the bread of the people and leaving stench in the commonwealth, and in time of war they are artificial battle machines which, when they develop, mean farewell to freedom, security and national glory! They are lawless defenders of unjust and prejudicial laws, of favoritism and tyranny."

This was written in the eighteen forties.

Before we mark our devil's dozen years of relationship,[5] send me a calendar. It's annoying not to know people's birthdays. As for how we celebrate that connection—we must think about it and then discuss it.

I see a good deal of Kondakov, the academician, and talk about a section of belles lettres in the Academy. He is enthusiastic, but I consider such a section entirely worthless. Because Sluchevsky, Grigorovich, Golenishchev-Kutuzov, and Potekhin [6] will become academicians, the work of Russian authors and literary activity in Russia generally will

---

[1] Suvorin, with whom he had no contract, had been procrastinating with respect to the publication of Chekhov's collected works, and it was for this reason, among others, that Chekhov was eager to make arrangements with Marx.

[2] From Marx.

[3] A line from Griboyedov's *Woe from Wit*, Act IV, scene 6.

[4] Porphyrius Uspensky (1804–85). He was the author of a voluminous diary, posthumously published. The passage quoted is from an entry dated March 11, 1848.

[5] Chekhov's relations with Suvorin went back to 1886.

[6] In addition to Grigorovich, mentioned earlier, the group consisted of two minor poets and an equally undistinguished writer of prose (Potekhin).

not be more interesting. Besides, an unpleasant and always suspect element will be added—salary.[7] However, we shall see.

Your second letter about Marx and the sale has just been brought to me. I think that the sale is advantageous if I live less than five to ten years, and disadvantageous if I live longer.

Write me if it's true that you will come to Yalta.

Be well and prosperous.

Your A. Chekhov

TO L. A. AVILOVA

Yalta, February 18, 1899

* * * You write that I have an extraordinary ability to live. Perhaps, but, as the saying goes, God deprives a bad-tempered cow of her horns. What's the use of my knowing how to live if I am constantly away from home, as though in exile? I am the man who strolled on Gorokhovaya [1] Street but found no peas. I was free, but didn't use my freedom, I was a man of letters, but involuntarily spent my life with those who cared nothing for letters; I sold my works for 75,000, and already I have received part of the money, but of what use is that to me if for the last two weeks I have been sitting at home without budging and haven't put my nose out of doors. Incidentally, about my business transaction, I sold Marx my past, my present, and my future; I did this, my friend, so as to put my affairs in order. I still have 50,000 (I shall receive them only at the end of two years), which will give me an annual income of 2000. Before my agreement with Marx my books brought in about 3500 annually, and last year I received 8000, probably because of "Peasants." So here you have my commercial secrets. Make what use of them you please, only don't envy me much my extraordinary ability to live.

Nevertheless, be that as it may, if I go to Monte Carlo, I am sure to lose 2000—a luxury of which I dared not even dream heretofore. And perhaps I shall win, not lose? The writer Ivan Shcheglov calls me Potemkin, and he too praises me for my ability to live. If I am Potemkin, why am I in Yalta, why is it so terribly boring here? It is

---

[7] When the section materialized, Chekhov was to learn that outstanding writers elected to it were honorary Academicians receiving no salary.

[1] *Gorokh* is the Russian word for "peas."

snowing, there's a blizzard, there's a draft from the window, heat from the stove, I don't want to write at all, and I don't write anything.

You are kind. I have said this a thousand times and now I say it again.

Be well, wealthy, cheerful, and may heaven protect you. I press your hand.

Your A. Chekhov

TO I. I. ORLOV[1]

Yalta, February 22, 1899

Greetings, dear Ivan Ivanovich!

Your friend Krutovsky [2] came to see me; we talked about the French, about Panama,[3] but I had no time to introduce him to the circle of my Yalta acquaintances, as you wished me to, because, after making some remarks about politics, he went off to the hurdy-gurdies; [4] this was yesterday, today he is in Gurzuf.

I sold Marx everything, both past and future works, and have become a Marxist for life. I am to receive 5000 for every 20 sheets of prose already published, 7000 after five years, an increase every fifth year thereafter, so that when I'm ninety-five I shall collect a terrible amount of money. I shall be paid 75,000 for my previous works. By haggling I managed to secure the proceeds from the plays for myself and my heirs. Yet, alas, I am far from being a Vanderbilt. I've already said good-bye to 25,000, and I shall not receive the remaining 50,000 now but over the next two years, so that I'm not in a position to be truly swanky.

No news of any particular note. I am writing very little. Next season a play of mine [5] that has never appeared in the capitals before will be performed at the Maly Theater—as you see, a bit of an income. Owing to the damp weather that lasted through most of January and February, work on my house in Autka has scarcely begun. I'll have to

[1] Ivan Ivanovich Orlov (1851–1917) was a zemstvo physician with whom Chekhov became acquainted as a young doctor.

[2] Vsevolod Mikhailovich Krutovsky, a horticulturalist, brother of a well-known Siberian physician and author.

[3] Apparently the Panama Canal, in the construction of which the United States was showing a lively interest, was a topic of conversation in Russia at this time.

[4] The wife and sister-in-law of another doctor.

[5] *Uncle Vanya.*

leave before the construction is completed. My Kuchukoy "mayonnaise" (as N. I. Pastukhov, publisher of the *Moscow Leaflet*, calls a majorat), is charming but practically inaccessible. I dream of building a little house there, rather inexpensive but somewhat European, so that I can spend winters there as well. The present two-story cottage is suitable only for summer living.

My telegram about Devil's Island [6] was not intended for publication; it was strictly private. It provoked an indignant outcry in Yalta. The academician Kondakov, one of the old-timers here, said to me about this telegram: "I'm hurt and disappointed."

"What's the matter?" I asked him in bewilderment.

"I'm hurt and disappointed because it was not I who printed this telegram."

Indeed, Yalta in winter is a border region, which not everybody can endure. Boredom, gossip, intrigues, and the most disgraceful slander. Altschuller [7] found it a bitter pill to swallow at first, his esteemed colleagues gossiped outrageously about him.

Your letter contains a passage from Scripture. My reply to your complaint about the tutor [8] and other setbacks is also a passage from Scripture: "Put not your trust in princes nor in the son of man." And I am reminded of another expression concerning the sons of man, the very ones who make life difficult for you: the sons of the times. It is not the tutor, but the entire intelligentsia that is to blame, the entire lot, my dear sir. As long as it is made up of students, young men and women, they are fine, honorable people, our hope, Russia's future; but no sooner do these students strike out on their own, become adults, than our hope and Russia's future go up in smoke, and all that remains in the filter are dacha-owning doctors, greedy officials, and thievish engineers. Remember that Katkov,[9] Pobedonostsev, Vyshnegradsky [10] are

---

[6] To a telegram from the actors who played in the first performance of *The Sea Gull*, Chekhov responded with a wire which read in part, "I sit in Yalta like Dreyfus on Devil's Island."

[7] Isaac Naumovich Altschuller (1870–1943), a Yalta physician who treated Chekhov.

[8] In Russian, a pun on "governor," an example of Aesopian language. Orlov had written to Chekhov that he and other physicians had planned to form a society to meet the medical and economic needs of their district. They directed their statutes, via the Governor, presumably to the Minister of the Interior, who forbade the project. "Oh, how much we could do," Orlov lamented, counting on Chekhov's sympathy, "if we had even a little freedom. . . ."

[9] Mikhail Nikiforovich Katkov (1818–87), a renegade liberal who became the influential editor of a reactionary newspaper.

[10] Ivan Alekseyevich Vyshnegradsky, Minister of Finance.

products of the universities, our professors, not boors at all but professors, luminaries. I do not believe in our intelligentsia, hypocritical, insincere, hysterical, uncultivated, lethargic; I don't believe in them even when they suffer and complain, for their oppressors emerge from their own viscera. I believe in individuals, I see a hope for salvation from distinct personalities scattered here and there throughout Russia—be they intellectuals or peasants, they are a power, though few in number. No man is a prophet in his own country; and the distinct personalities I refer to play an inconspicuous role in society; they do not dominate but their work has its impact. In any event, science is steadily advancing, self-awareness is growing, moral issues are beginning to assume an unquiet character, etc., etc. And all this is happening despite the public prosecutor, engineers, and tutors, despite the intelligentsia en masse, and despite everything. * * *

Your A. Chekhov

TO A. S. SUVORIN

Yalta, March 4, 1899

* * * Here as everywhere much is being said of the student disturbances,[1] and a howl has gone up over the absence of anything about it in the papers. Letters come from Petersburg, the mood there favors the students. Your comment on the riots did not satisfy the public [2]—and no wonder, since it is impossible to discuss the riots in print when you are forbidden to touch on the facts of the matter. The State did not permit you to write, it does not permit you to tell the truth, this is despotism, and on the occasion of this highhandedness you, with a light heart, speak of the rights and prerogatives of the State—somehow this does not make any sense. You speak about the rights of the State, but your point of view is a blinkered one. Rights and justice are the same

[1] Early in February the head of the Petersburg University rudely warned the students that if they disturbed the public peace and order on February 8, the anniversary of the founding of the University, they would be prosecuted in accordance with the penal laws. In response, the students broke up the official ceremonies of the day. As they were leaving the building, they were beaten up by the police, with the result that student riots spread to all the institutions of higher learning.

[2] Writing in *New Times*, Suvorin denounced the students and commended the Czar's mercy and great-heartedness in appointing a commission to investigate the causes of the disturbances. The students reacted by adopting a collective resolution not to subscribe to *New Times*, not even to read it.

for the State as for any juristic person. If the State unjustly transfers a piece of my land to someone else, I bring an action and the court restores my rights to me. Should it not be the same when the State gives me a whipping; if it commits an act of violence, may I not protest against the infringement of my rights? The concept of the State must be based on definite lawful relationships, otherwise it is a bugaboo, a hollow sound that is a terror to the imagination. * * *

Your A. Chekhov

TO L. A. AVILOVA

Yalta, March 9, 1899

* * * I am not going to attend the writers' conference. I shall be in the Crimea or abroad this autumn if, of course, I am alive and free. I shall spend the entire summer at my place in the Serpukhov district. By the way, in what district of Tula province did you purchase an estate? The first two years of ownership are hard, at times very unpleasant, but little by little it all leads to nirvana, sweet habit. I bought an estate on credit, found it very difficult during the first years (famine, cholera), but later things worked out somehow, and I find it pleasant now to recall that somewhere near the Oka River I have a corner of my own. I live peacefully with the peasants, nothing is ever stolen, and when I walk through the village, the old women smile or cross themselves. I address everyone formally except the children and never raise my voice; still, it was medicine, mainly, that cemented these good relations. Things will go well on your estate; just don't listen to anyone's advice, don't let anyone browbeat you, and don't get disillusioned or form any opinion about the peasants during the early stages. The initial attitude of the peasants to all newcomers is surly and insincere, particularly in Tula province. There is actually a saying: "He is a good sort, though he comes from Tula."

So you see, there is something edifying for you. Satisfied? * * *

You ask if I pity Suvorin. Of course I do. He has paid heavily for his mistakes. But those who surround him I don't pity. * * *

Your A. Chekhov

TO I. I. ORLOV

Yalta, March 18, 1899

* * * In Yalta it is already spring: everything is turning green, blossoming, new faces are appearing on the boardwalk. Mirolyubov [1] and Gorky arrive today, the influx is starting, but in two or two and a half weeks I'll probably roll north, closer to you. My house is being constructed but my muse has collapsed utterly: I write nothing and have no inclination to work; I need to breathe a different air; there is such lassitude here in the south! I'm in a foul mood largely because of the letters I receive from friends and acquaintances. Every so often in letters I have to console, lecture, or bare my teeth like a dog. I receive many letters about the student demonstrations—from students and adults; I've even gotten three from Suvorin. And some of the expelled students have come to see me. In my view, the adults—that is, the fathers and the powers that be—have made a terrible blunder. They behaved like Turkish pashas with young Turks and softas,[2] but on this occasion public opinion has eloquently demonstrated that Russia, thank God, is no longer a state like Turkey. I'll show you some of the letters when I see you, but meanwhile, let's talk about you. How are you? Do you intend to come to Yalta? When? If I come to Podsolnechnoye this summer shall I find you there? * * *

Your A. Chekhov

TO L. A. AVILOVA

Yalta, April 6, 1899

* * * If my mother and sister haven't given up on the idea of buying a house, I shall definitely be at Angeres' [1] on Plyushchikha. If I buy a house I'll have absolutely nothing left—neither works nor money. I'll have to take the job of tax assessor.

I'm reading the manuscripts you sent: O Lord, what trash! [2] I read

---

[1] Until 1897 a singer attached to the Bolshoi Theater; later editor of a monthly, *The Magazine for All.*

[2] Muslim students of theology and sacred law.

[1] A Moscow real estate broker.

[2] Chekhov's early stories, which he employed Avilova to copy from old periodicals, for possible inclusion in his collected works.

these and remember the tedium with which I wrote them in the old days when you and I were younger. * * *

Your A. Chekhov

TO A. S. SUVORIN

Moscow, April 24, 1899

* * * Your last letter with the offprint (court of honor) [1] was sent to me yesterday from Lopasnya, I absolutely cannot understand whom and what purpose this court of honor serves and why you felt obliged to agree to appear before a court which, as you have repeatedly stated in print, you do not recognize. A writers' court of honor is nonsense, an absurdity, since they do not constitute a corporate group such as lawyers, army officers. In an Asiatic country where there is neither freedom of the press nor of conscience, where the government and nine-tenths of society regard the journalist as an enemy, where people live so herded together in such wretched conditions and have little hope of better times, diversions such as mudslinging, courts of honor, and the like, put writers in the ludicrous and pitiable position of small animals who, trapped, bite off each other's tails. Even granting the standpoint of the Union [2] that has permitted the court—what does that Union want? What?—to try you for having in print, quite openly, voiced your opinion (whatever it may have been)? This is a risky business, an encroachment on freedom of speech, a step toward making the journalist's position intolerable; for once you have been tried, no journalist can be certain that sooner or later he won't be brought before this bizarre court. The issue is neither the student disorders nor your letters.[3] Your letters could be the occasion for sharp debate, hostile demonstrations against you, abusive letters, but by no means for a trial. The charges against you deliberately, as it were, conceal the main cause of the scandal; they deliberately heap all the blame on the disorders and on your letters to avoid talking about what is primary. I'm at a

[1] After the student riots early in 1899, *New Times* aroused nation-wide indignation by condemning the students and supporting the Government's acts of reprisal. Aleksandr Chekhov, who was working for Suvorin, wrote to his brother, "At last the public understands the true meaning of *New Times* and the stance of its editor." Suvorin was summoned to a so-called court of honor; he chose not to appear at this mock trial, but to respond to the charges in the columns of *New Times*. Copies of these letters of his were sent to his friends, among them, Chekhov.
[2] The Russian Writers' Union of Mutual Defense.
[3] Suvorin's letters in *New Times*.

[*339*]

total loss to explain this, my conjectures leave me at my wit's end. Why is it that once there was the inclination and insistence on engaging in a fight to the finish with you, everything wasn't brought out in the open? In recent years society (not just the intelligentsia, but Russian society in general) has become hostile to *New Times*. The conviction has developed that *New Times* receives a subsidy from the Government and the French General Staff. And *New Times* has done everything possible to encourage this unwarranted reputation; it is hard to understand why it has done so, in the name of what God. For example, no one has been able to understand the exaggerated attitude toward Finland in recent years; to understand the denunciation of newspapers which were banned and allegedly appeared under different names (this, perhaps, could be justified by the goals of "national policy" but it is contrary to what literature stands for); no one has been able to understand why *New Times* attributed to Deschenel and General Bilderling statements they never made, etc., etc.[4] Opinion has it that you are a cruel, implacable man, who seems to be in the good books of the Government. And once again *New Times* did everything to make the public hold on to this prejudice as long as possible. The public placed *New Times* together with the other governmental organs it dislikes; it grumbled, was indignant; the prejudice grew, legends have formed; and the snowball has grown into an avalanche that has begun to roll and will keep on rolling, steadily increasing in size. Yet here in the indictment nothing is said about this avalanche, though precisely because of it they wish to try you. And such insincerity makes me uncomfortable. * * *

Your A. Chekhov

TO M. O. MENSHIKOV

Melikhovo, June 4, 1899

Dear Mikhail Osipovich,

The best to you! You are traveling abroad? I am very glad for you and I envy you. True, in the end you will be worn out, you will be

---

[4] *New Times* had published a conversation that allegedly took place between Paul Deschenel, President of the Chamber of Deputies, and the General, after the funeral of Félix Faure, President of the Republic. The coverage was subsequently denounced by General Bilderling as a fabrication. His statement was published in *New Times*.

bored, but then, later, when you have returned to your beloved northern Palmyra where it is so wet, cold, and dark—when you return home you will have something to remember. I am also glad on Yasha's [1] account. You are traveling, you are in the empyrean, and I am seated in lovable Melikhovo and furiously reading proof, which Marx sends me by the ton. In editing all that I have written until now, I have chucked two hundred stories and everything not belles lettres, and nevertheless what is left comes to two hundred printed sheets, and therefore it will fill twelve to thirteen volumes. Whatever was in the collections known to you is drowned in the mass of material of which the world is ignorant. When I assembled this whole mass I simply threw up my hands in amazement.

My sister wants to sell Melikhovo and has already sent a notice to the papers, but she is not likely to sell it before the fall or even winter. In July I shall go to the Crimea, but in August I shall come back and live in Russia until the late fall.

I did not take part in the Pushkin commemoration. In the first place, I have no frock coat, and, secondly, I am very shy of speeches. As soon as someone begins a speech at a banquet I become unhappy and have the impulse to crawl under the table. These speeches, especially those one hears in Moscow, abound in conscious lying, and besides, they are delivered gracelessly. In Moscow on May 26, and just afterward, it rained, it was cold, the meetings were unsuccessful, but there was much speechifying. And the speaking was not by men of letters but by traders in literature (cattle-dealers). Of all the people I met in Moscow at the time, the only one I found congenial was Goltzev. * * *

I press your hand firmly.

Your A. Chekhov

TO O. L. KNIPPER[1]

Melikhovo, June 16, 1899

What does this mean? Where are you? You so stubbornly send us no news about yourself that we are absolutely lost in guesses and have

---

[1] Menshikov's son, who was accompanying him.

[1] Olga Leonardovna Knipper (1868–1959) is said to have come of a German-Alsatian family that had settled in Russia. She was born in a northeastern provincial town, where her father, an engineer, managed a factory. After the Knippers moved to Moscow the father died, leaving large debts, so that the cultivated and once pros-

already started thinking that you have forgotten us and were married in the Caucasus. If you really are married, to whom is it? Have you decided to leave the stage?

The author is forgotten—oh, how terrible, how cruel, how perfidious! Everyone sends you greetings. There is nothing new, there aren't even any flies. We have nothing. Even calves don't bite.

I had wanted to see you off at the station that time, but fortunately rain prevented me. I had been in Petersburg, had my picture taken by two photographers. Was almost frozen there. I won't be going to Yalta before early July.

With your permission, I press your hand firmly and wish you all the best.

Your A. Chekhov

TO A. S. SUVORIN

Moscow, June 26, 1899

* * * First of all, about the school plans. I have had three schools erected and they are considered model buildings. They are constructed of the best materials, the rooms have ceilings over eleven feet high and Dutch stoves; the teacher's apartment has a fireplace and is by no means small (three to four rooms). Two of the schools were built at a cost of 3000 each, whereas the third, a smaller one, at slightly over 2000. I will send you a picture of the façades of all three schools (I'll ask someone to take photographs); I'll also send along the plans with all the dimensions which, incidentally, were not determined arbitrarily but are based on instructions worked out by the provincial zemstvo. Only don't build this year, wait until summer.

---

perous family had to concern itself with earning a living. The mother taught music, eventually becoming a professor at the Moscow Conservatory. One of the sons became an engineer, the other a director at the Bolshoi Theater. Olga was admitted to the dramatic school of the Philharmonic Society, where she studied under Nemirovich-Danchenko, graduating, like her classmate Meyerhold, with distinction. Chekhov first met her on September 9, 1898, at a rehearsal of *The Sea Gull*. She had the part of Arkadina, the leading role in that play, the part of Yelena Andreyevna in *Uncle Vanya*, of Masha in *Three Sisters*, and of Mme. Ranevskaya in *The Cherry Orchard*. In the memorial performance of *Ivanov* she played Sarra (Sarah). She was to survive her husband by fifty-five years, and was long active on the stage.

This was Chekhov's first letter to his future wife. In May she had visited the family at Melikhovo, spending three days there. Then she went to the Caucasus, where her brother was summering.

You were not mistaken; we are selling our Melikhovo. After Father's death we no longer wish to live there; somehow the whole place has lost its freshness and luster. Moreover, my situation is uncertain: I do not know where I am to live, who I am, where I fit in; and since I'm obliged to spend winters in the Crimea or abroad, the need for an estate is automatically eliminated; to have an estate and not live there is a luxury I cannot afford. And from a literary standpoint, after "Peasants," Melikhovo has been drained of possibilities and lost value for me.

Buyers are coming to look at the place. If they purchase it, fine; if not, I will lock it up for the winter.

I am in Moscow for the present. I go to the "Aquarium," look at the acrobats there, talk to prostitutes. I was in Petersburg but for a very short while. It was cold and nasty and I didn't even stay overnight; I came on Friday and left the same day. I saw Aleksey Petrovich.[1]

My health is tolerable, almost good. Were I permitted to stay in Moscow for the winter, I would most likely go into comerce (with one "m");[2] for example, I'd open a mail-order book business exclusively for provincial buyers, hiring just one helper, who, by the way, would also be required to polish my boots. But, alas, I can't stay in Moscow, I'm being driven back to the swamp.* * *

Your A. Chekhov

TO O. L. KNIPPER

Moscow, July 1, 1899

Yes, you are right: Chekhov, the writer, has not forgotten Knipper, the actress. Moreover, your proposal that we travel together from Batum to Yalta seems to him enchanting. I am ready to go, but here are my conditions: (1) on receipt of this letter, without one minute's delay, you will wire me the approximate date on which you intend to leave Mtzkhet.[1] The wire should read: "Moscow, Malaya Dmitrovka, Sheshkov's,[2] Chekhov, 20th." This means that you will leave Mtzkhet on July 20; (2) I will go straight to Batum and meet you there, bypassing

---

[1] A. P. Kolomnin, Suvorin's son-in-law, a lawyer.

[2] Chekhov is joking about becoming a petty merchant; the spelling of these folk usually left much to be desired, especially in the case of loaned words such as the Russian for "commerce."

[1] A city in the Caucasus where the actress was visiting her brother.

[2] Chekhov's Moscow address.

Tiflis; (3) that you will not turn my head. Vishnevsky considers me a very serious man, and I have no intention of seeming to him as weak as everybody else.

On receiving your telegram, I shall write again and everything will be splendid; meanwhile I send you a thousand cordial wishes and press your hand. Thanks for the letter.

Your A. Chekhov

TO A. I. SINANI[1]

Moscow, August 5, 1899

Much esteemed Abram Isaakóvich,

Moscow is empty and deserted. I did not find Zernov, the president of the University, he is vacationing in the country. I had to write him a letter. Today at 2 o'clock I was in the proctor's office and was told, first, that the president was no longer Zernov, but Tikhomirov,[2] and second, that the proctor's office would do all that was necessary, provided the university did not make difficulties. I went to see Tikhomirov, was kept waiting for an hour and a half in the stifling reception room, then was received most ungraciously. I was told that there were no vacancies and that Weber would have been admitted only if his parents lived in Moscow,[3] and that he should hasten to write or wire to the proctor's office to inform it where his documents should be sent.

There you are! Forgive me for having so miserably failed to carry out your commission; I have been severely punished for it: the interview with the president spoiled my mood and my appetite for some three days.* * *

My cordial greetings to Isaak Abramovich, your mama and sister, and every good wish to you all.

Your A. Chekhov

[1] The addressee, a student, was the son of Isaak Abramovich Sinani, a Yalta tobacconist and bookseller, whose shop was a kind of club for the writers, painters, and actors who came to the city. The elder Sinani helped Chekhov with practical advice in the building of his house, and the two were on friendly terms. The young Sinani secured Chekov's promise to intercede for another Jewish student who wished to transfer to the University of Moscow. In the following letter to Suvorin, Chekhov further described his efforts on the student's behalf.

[2] Aleksandr Andreyevich Tikhomirov, a zoologist of the anti-Darwinist persuasion, was president of the University in 1899–1904 and 1911–17.

[3] An almost impossible condition to meet, since only privileged Jews, of whom there were few, were permitted to reside in Moscow.

TO A. S. SUVORIN

Moscow, August 19, 1899

* * * I wrote you at Veliye Nikolskoye but received no reply. I personally have no news, nor is there any in the papers. The bubonic plague
is not very dreadful. First, it will not strike a particularly large area
but will be confined to isolated points; second, as a mortal danger it is
no more terrible than diphtheria or typhoid fever; third, we now have
inoculations that have proved effective and for which, incidentally, we
are indebted to a Russian doctor by the name of Khavkin, a Jew. In
Russia he is completely unknown, though in England he has long been
hailed as a great philanthropist. The life story of this Jew, so detested
by the Hindus, who almost killed him, is indeed remarkable. So, as a
disease, the plague is not particularly dreadful. What is dreadful is that
it has terrified the masses, gotten a powerful grip on their imagination.
It will work havoc in Spain and may perhaps interfere with the exhibition.[1]

Little is said about the students. Recently I went to the president of
the university to intercede for a student who wished to be transferred
to the university from another district. The petition was refused, and I
myself was received most ungraciously. The president's reception room
and office, with its doorkeeper, reminded me of the department of criminal investigation. I left with a headache.* * *

Your A. Chekhov

TO M. O. MENSHIKOV

Moscow, August 22, 1899

Dear Mikhail Osipovich,

You wrote your latest letter on your way home. Consequently, you are
already in Tzarskoe Selo, your native tundras. Be that as it may, I am
addressing this letter to you at Tzarskoe.

Apparently I am already not a human being, but a floating kidney.
Judge for yourself: on July 20 I left for the Caucasus, thence to the
Crimea, early in August I returned to Moscow, on Wednesday I am
again off to the Crimea, where I shall probably remain during the en-

[1] The Paris World's Fair of 1900.

[*345*]

tire fall and even the winter. In Moscow the weather is repulsive, dismal, it is cold and damp, I don't feel well, I must hurry up and leave, and yet I am loath to be off. How long I shall roam thus, when I shall settle down and give up this nomadic existence—Allah alone knows.

And so address your letters to Yalta; furthermore, I consider it unnecessary to add that it will be a pity if this modest provincial address were to be obliterated in your memory or if it bored you.* * *

We have sold Melikhovo,[1] but on strange terms. The new owner takes possession of the property immediately but payment will be made much later in several installments. * * *

Your A. Chekhov

TO MAXIM GORKY

Yalta, September 3, 1899

Dear Aleksey Maksimovich,

Once again, greetings!

In reply to your letter. First, I am generally opposed to dedications of anything to living people. I once did make such dedications and now feel that it may not have been the right thing to do. This is my attitude in general. In particular, your dedication to me of "Foma Gordeyev" gives me nothing but pleasure and honors me. Only what did I do to deserve this? That, however, is for you to decide; for me all that remains is to bow and thank you.

Strip the dedication of as many excess words as possible, that is, simply write: ". . . is dedicated to so-and-so"—and let it go at that. Only Volynsky [1] likes to write lengthy dedications. And, if you like, here is another piece of practical advice: print more than, at any rate not less than five to six thousand copies. The book will sell quickly. A second printing can be run off simultaneously with the first. Another piece of advice: when reading proof, whenever you can, strike out terms qualifying nouns and verbs. Your writing has so many of these qualifiers that they strain the reader's attention and exhaust him. It is intelligible

---

[1] Late in August 1903, Mariya Chekhova wrote to her brother Aleksandr that the place was "in a lamentable condition. Konshin [the timber merchant who had bought it] has abandoned it, half of the trees have been destroyed," adding that a certain Baron Stuart was buying the farm.

[1] Pen name of Akim Lvovich Flekser, writer of literary and art criticism.

when I write, "The man sat down on the grass"; it is intelligible because it is clear and does not impede the reader's attention. Conversely,
it will be unintelligible and tax the reader's brain if I write: "The tall,
narrow-chested man of average build, who had a short, red beard, sat
down on the green grass, already trampled by passers-by; sat down
noiselessly, timidly and fearfully glancing around him." One's brain
cannot grasp this at once, yet fiction must be grasped at once—on the
spot. Now, one further point: by nature you are a lyricist, the timbre
of your soul is soft. Were you a composer you would refrain from
writing marches. To be insolent, sound off, taunt, denounce furiously—
this is alien to your talent. Hence you will understand if I advise you
to deal mercilessly in the proof with the sons of bitches, lechers, and
runts that turn up here and there in the pages of *Life.* * * *

Your A. Chekhov

TO O. L. KNIPPER

Yalta, September 3, 1899

Sweet actress,

Here are answers to all your questions. I reached my destination [1]
safely. My fellow travelers ceded me a lower berth, then it happened
that only two passengers remained in the compartment: I and a young
Armenian. Several times during the day I had tea, each time three
glasses, with lemon, placidly, unhurriedly. I ate up everything in the
basket. But I find that fussing with a basket and running to the station
to fetch boiling water for tea is a frivolous occupation that undermines
the prestige of the Art Theater. It was cold until we reached Kursk,
then it began to get warm, and in Sevastopol it was quite hot. In Yalta
I put up at my own house and now I live here, under the protection of
the faithful Mustafa. I do not have dinner every day, because it is a

[1] In mid-July Chekhov and Olga Knipper sailed together from the Black Sea port
of Novorossisk to Yalta, where his house was under construction. He put up at a
hotel; she stayed with neighbors of his, the Sredins. In about a fortnight they left
together for Moscow. En route they stopped at Bakhchisaray, whose fountain Pushkin had made famous. One reason for Chekhov's going to Moscow was to be present
at the rehearsals of *Uncle Vanya*, but, falling ill, he hurried back to Yalta late in
August.

long walk to town and again prestige would not permit me to busy myself with a kerosene stove. Evenings I eat cheese. I see much of Sinani. I have already visited the Sredins twice. They studied your photograph and were touched by it, ate the candy. Leonid Valentinovich [2] is fairly well. I do not drink Narzan.[3] What else? I scarcely ever go out into the garden, but keep indoors and think about you. As the train passed Bakhchisaray I thought of you and recalled how we journeyed together. Dear, wonderful actress, remarkable woman, if you knew what joy your letter gave me! I make so low an obeisance to you that my forehead touches the bottom of my well, which has been dug to the depth of 55 feet. I have grown used to you and miss you so much that I can't be reconciled to the thought that I shall not see you until spring; I'm sore, and, in short, if Nadenka [4] found out what is going on in my soul, there would be a scene.

The weather in Yalta is marvelous, but for no reason at all it has been raining for the past two days, now it is muddy and you must wear galoshes. Centipedes crawl along the wet walls and toads and young crocodiles leap in the garden. The green reptile [5] in a flower pot that you gave me and that I brought here safely is now settled in the garden and sunning himself.

A squadron is in port and I watch it through a field glass.

An operetta is on at the theater. Trained fleas keep serving holy art.[6] I have no money. There are frequent visitors. In general, I am bored, it's an idle, senseless boredom.

Now I press your hand firmly and kiss it. Be well, happy, work, bounce about, fall in love, and if possible, do not forget the retired writer, your zealous admirer,

A. Chekhov

[2] Leonid Valentinovich Sredin was a physician afflicted with tuberculosis and settled in Yalta for his health.

[3] A Caucasian mineral water, popular in Russia.

[4] A character invented by Chekhov and figuring in his correspondence with Knipper either as his bride or his jealous wife.

[5] A cactus, known as Queen of the Night.

[6] Trained fleas provided one of the amusements in Yalta for Chekhov and Knipper.

TO V. E. MEYERHOLD[1]

Yalta, October, 1899

Dear Vsevolod Emilyevich,

I do not have the text at hand and so I can discuss the role of Johannes only in general terms.[2] If you will send me the part, I shall go over it, refresh my memory, and be more detailed; but for the present, I shall limit myself to what may have the most immediate practical interest for you.

To begin with, Johannes is an intellectual to the tips of his fingers, a young scholar who has grown up in a university town. There is not a trace of the bourgeois in him. His conduct is that of a cultivated man who is accustomed to the society of decent people (like Anna); in his gestures and appearance he is gentle and youthful, like a man who has grown up in a family that pampered him and who is still under Mama's wing. Johannes is a German scholar and for that reason is self-possessed in the company of men. In the company of women, on the other hand, he becomes as tender as one of them. Highly characteristic of him in this respect is the scene with his wife, in which he cannot refrain from caresses even though he already loves Anna or is falling in love with her.

Now for the question of his nervousness. This ought not to be emphasized lest the neurotic aspect of his nature obscure and overpower what is more important, namely, the loneliness, the kind of loneliness experienced only by noble and, at the same time, healthy organisms ("healthy" in the highest sense). Portray a lonely man, but exhibit no more nervous irritability than the text itself indicates. Do not treat this nervousness as a special phenomenon; remember that in our day almost every cultivated person, even the healthiest, feels most irritable in his own home, among his own family, for the discord between the past and the present is sensed first of all in the family. It is chronic irritability

---

[1] V. E. Meyerhold (1874–1940) was an actor with the Moscow Art Theater, who left the company in 1902 because he disapproved of its emphasis on extreme realism. Having joined the Communist Party early on, he endorsed the Soviet regime, under which he did pioneering, boldly innovative work in stage direction. A dissident artist, he was a victim of the purges of the middle 1930s. The theater that bore his name was closed and he was blacklisted. In 1939 at a conference of stage directors he attacked socialist realism, which led to his arrest and to his death the following year, probably in prison.

[2] Johannes Vockerat in Gerhart Hauptmann's play, *Lonely Lives.* Meyerhold, who was to have the part, had asked Chekhov to help him with it.

free from violent emotion, from convulsive twitching, the kind of irritability that guests do not notice, but the full weight of which is felt first of all by those closest to you—mother, wife—an irritability that is, so to speak, domestic, intimate. Do not dwell on it too much, but portray it as merely *one* typical feature; do not overdo it, otherwise your rendering will be that of an irritable, not a lonely young man. Konstantin Sergeyevich,[3] I know, will insist on this excessive nervousness, will exaggerate it, but do not yield ground, do not sacrifice the beauty and expressiveness of your voice and speech to such a trifling detail as an accent. Do not sacrifice these, for the irritability is, in fact, nothing but a detail, a trifle.

Many thanks for remembering me. Please write me again; it will be a generous act on your part, for I am bored. The weather here is splendid, warm, but this, after all, is only sauce, and what good is sauce without meat?

Be well. Warm regards and best wishes to you.

Your A. Chekhov

TO O. L. KNIPPER

Yalta, October 4, 1899

Dear actress,

You greatly exaggerated everything in your gloomy letter;[1] this is obvious, since the papers' attitude toward the première was altogether friendly. Be that as it may, one or two unsuccessful performances should be insufficient to make you pull a long face and spend a sleepless night. Art, especially the stage, is an area where it is impossible to walk without stumbling. There are in store for you many unsuccessful days and whole unsuccessful seasons: there will be great misunderstandings and deep disappointments—you must be prepared for all this, expect it and nevertheless, stubbornly, fanatically follow your own way.

Of course, you are right. Alekseyev[2] shouldn't have played Ivan the Terrible. It doesn't suit him. When he is a director he is an artist, but

[3] Stanislavsky.
[1] She had written him that the opening of *The Death of Ivan the Terrible,* by A. K. Tolstoy, was a complete failure.
[2] The family name of Stanislavsky.

as an actor he is a rich young merchant who took a notion to toy with art.

I was ill for three or four days, now I sit at home. Of visitors I have an intolerable plethora. Idle provincial tongues wag and I am bored, I am cross, and envy the rat that lives under the floor of your theater.

You wrote your last letter at 4 A.M. If you will imagine that *Uncle Vanya* was not as successful as you wanted it to be, please go to bed and sleep tight. Success has spoiled you, so that you can no longer tolerate mere weekdays.* * *

How are you? Write me oftener. You see I write to you almost every day. An author writes to an actress so frequently—his pride will begin to suffer. Actresses must be treated severely, not be written to. I keep forgetting that I am an Inspector of Actresses.[3]

Keep well, little angel.

Your A. Chekhov

TO G. I. ROSSOLIMO[1]

Yalta, October 11, 1899

Dear Grigory Ivanovich,

Today I sent Dr. Baltzevich 8 rubles, 50 copecks for the photograph and 5 rubles as my annual dues. The photograph, rather indifferent (taken when my enteritis was acute), I am sending you by registered mail.[2] Autobiography? I suffer from an illness: autobiographophobia. To read details about myself and, even more, to write them for publication is a veritable ordeal for me. Enclosed is a separate slip on which are jotted down some dates, very bare, that's all I can do. Add, if you wish, that in the application which I handed to the rector of the university I misspelled the word "medicine."

* * * I regret very much not having attended the dinner and having failed to see the comrades.* * *

---

[3] Chekhov's theatrical friends has given him in jest the title of Inspector of Actresses of the Art Theater.

[1] A neuropathologist who had been a classmate of Chekhov's in the Moscow University medical school.

[2] On May 8, 1899, the fifteenth anniversary of the graduation of Chekhov's class was marked by a dinner, which he was unable to attend. The class arranged for the publication of an album containing photographs and autobiographies of the members. What Chekhov wrote follows his signature.

Won't you come to the Crimea in the summer or in the fall? It is a pleasant place for a rest. By the way, the southern seashore has become a favorite haunt of the zemstvo doctors of Moscow province. Living here is comfortable and cheap for them, and they leave enchanted every time.

If something interesting happens, please write to me. I am bored here, and without letters you might hang yourself, take to drink on the wretched Crimean wine, get involved with an ugly foolish woman.

Keep well. I press your hand and send cordial good wishes to you and your family.

Your A. Chekhov

I, A. P. Chekhov, was born January 17, 1860, in Taganrog. I first attended the Greek school attached to the Church of King Constantine, then the Taganrog high school. In 1879 I was admitted to the medical department of Moscow University. Generally speaking, at the time I had a vague notion of the university departments and I don't recall for what reason I chose the medical department, but in the end I did not repent my choice. In my first year I was already contributing to newspapers and weeklies, and early in the 1880s my literary occupation assumed a steady, professional character. In 1888 I received the Pushkin Prize. In 1890 I went to Sakhalin in order to write a book about our penal colony.

Without counting court reports, book notes, *feuilletons*, notices, everything written from day to day for newspapers and that would be hard to find and collect now, during the twenty years of my literary activity I have written and published more than three hundred sheets of fiction, short and not so short. I also wrote plays.

I don't doubt that the study of the medical sciences seriously affected my literary work; they significantly enlarged the field of my observations, enriched me with knowledge, the true value of which for me as a writer can be understood only by one who is himself a physician; they also had a directive influence and probably because I was close to medicine I avoided many mistakes. Acquaintance with the natural sciences, with the scientific method, kept me always on guard and I tried, wherever possible, to bring my writings into harmony with scientific data, and where this was impossible, I preferred not to write at all. Let me observe that creativity in the arts does not always permit total agreement with scientific data; thus it is impossible to represent on the stage death from poisoning as it actually takes place. But agreement with scientific data must be felt in the conventions accepted, that is, it is necessary for the reader or spectator to grasp clearly that these are only conventions, and that he is dealing with an author who knows the true facts. I do not belong to the fiction writers who have a negative attitude toward science, nor am I one of those artists who think that they can arrive at everything by the intellect alone. I would not want to be one of them.

As regards the practice of medicine, while still a student I worked in the Voskresensk zemstvo hospital (near New Jerusalem) under the well-known zemstvo physician P. A. Arkhangelsky; later I was briefly on the medical staff of the Zvenigorod hospital. During the cholera years (1892–93) I was in charge of the Melikhovo section of the Serpukhov district.

TO A. I. URUSOV[1]

Yalta, October 16, 1899

Dear Aleksandr Ivanovich,

I wanted to visit you in April, to get together with you and thank you for the pleasure [2] you gave me during the winter, but I was prevented by our mutual acquaintances, who told me that you were in severe pain and that you were not up to receiving guests. And after that, you left.

Dear Aleksandr Ivanovich, I implore you, do not be offended: I cannot publish *The Wood Sprite*.[3] I detest this play and am trying to forget it. Whether the play itself is to blame, or the circumstances under which it was written and staged, I do not know, but it would be a real blow to me were some power to drag it into the light of day and force it to live. Here you have a clear instance of perverted parental emotion! [4]

In your letter your wish is stated as a kind, amicable request, and I feel no end of shame now for not sending you the kind of answer I should, and do not know what to do. Give you a promise? If you wish,

[1] A. I. Urusov (1842–1900), lawyer, literary critic, chairman of the Society of Lovers of the Dramatic Art.
[2] Urusov wrote enthusiastic notices of *The Sea Gull* and *Uncle Vanya.*
[3] The addressee had asked permission to have this play printed in a new magazine edited by Diaghilev.
[4] Nevertheless, Chekhov did revise the play, which was staged as *Uncle Vanya.*

I promise to write a new play and send it to Diaghilev. I will write it and send it to you in manuscript.

If you go abroad again, please write me a few lines about your health. I need this both for my sake and that of your acquaintances, who frequently ask me about your health.

I am already living on my own place on the piece of land you saw last year. I had a two-and-one-quarter-story house built, a white house, which the cabmen and Tartars call "The White Dacha." The balcony offers the most marvelous view. There is no trace of the dust that had me so alarmed. My health is fairly good. The bacilli have retreated into the background; what I'm forced to contend with now are hemorrhoids and intestinal catarrh, which wear me out and give me a Lenten look.* * *

Your A. Chekhov

TO O. L. KNIPPER

Yalta, October 30, 1899

Dear actress, good little one,

You ask if I'll get excited. But it was only from your letter, which I got on the 27th, that I learned that *Uncle Vanya* was to open on the 26th. The telegrams started coming on the evening of the 27th, when I was already in bed. They were read to me over the telephone. I woke up every time and ran to the telephone in the dark, barefoot, getting very chilly. Before I had barely dozed off, the bell rang again and again. It was the first occasion when my own fame prevented me from sleeping. The next evening when I went to bed I put my slippers and dressing gown nearby, but there were no more telegrams.

The telegrams were about nothing but the number of curtain calls and the brilliant success of the performance, but I could discern in nearly all of them something strained and elusive which led me to surmise that all of you were not in very good spirits. The newspapers I received today confirmed my conjecture. Yes, dear actress, you Art Theater performers are no longer satisfied with ordinary, average success; you want tumult, cannonade, dynamite. You have been thoroughly spoiled, deafened by constant talk about success, about full houses and not full ones; you are already infected by that poison and in two or three years you will be good for nothing! So much for the lot of you!

How do you fare? How are you feeling? I am in the same place, and I haven't changed. I work and plant trees. But I can't go on writing: visitors have come. They have been here for over an hour. Tea was requested. They went to heat the samovar. How tedious!

Don't forget me, and don't let your friendship for me gutter out, so that we may go away somewhere together in the summer. Farewell for the present. We shall probably not see each other before April. If all of you come to Yalta next spring,[1] you could give performances and also rest here. That would be astonishingly in keeping with art. * * *

Your A. Chekhov

P.S. Actress, write me in the name of all that's holy. I find everything so tedious. It's as if I were in prison. I rage, rage.

TO A. L. VISHNEVSKY[1]

Yalta, November 3, 1899

Dear Aleksandr Leonidovich, childhood friend,

Many thanks for your letter and the poster.[2] Yes, you are right, it's original, but it's not quite appropriate; it would rather suit a benefit performance in the house of some emancipated baroness. Anyhow, everything is splendid, and I thank heaven that after having sailed the sea of life, I have finally landed on so wonderful an island as the Art Theater. When I have children, I will force them to pray to God eternally for all of you.

You were amazed to discover that our cook, Masha, is pregnant, and in your letter you ask me who is responsible. You were the man who visited us most often, you and a young soldier, and who is at fault, I

---

[1] The company did tour the Crimea in April 1900. In Yalta *Uncle Vanya* and *The Sea Gull* were played.

[1] A. L. Vishnevsky (1861–1943), a native of Taganrog, was a member of the Moscow Art Theater Company and acted in *The Sea Gull, Uncle Vanya,* and *Three Sisters,* among other plays.

[2] Advertising *Uncle Vanya,* and with a portrait of Chekhov.

[355]

don't know. And besides, it's not my business to judge my fellow men. If it is not you, then, of course, you won't have to support the baby.

I have a favor to ask of you. Come south in the spring to perform. Plead with Vladimir Ivanovich [3] and Konstantin Sergeyevich.[3] You will be acting and, by the way, taking a rest. In Yalta you will have full houses for five nights, in Sevastopol the same, and in Odessa you will be received like kings, for people love your company already, without having seen it, merely by hearsay.

Write me, please, without letters I am bored.* * *

Your A. Chekhov

TO M. P. CHEKHOVA

Yalta, November 11, 1899

Dear Masha,

I have a ministerial crisis. Mustapha has left and his place has been taken by Arseny, a Russian in a jacket, literate; he used to work in the Nikitsky Garden.[1] He is well thought of, young.

Now I am answering your latest letter. Masha's [2] child must be supported not by Asheshov [3] but by Vishnevsky. To the cook herself he must pay at least 3 rubles a month. It would be better if he were to take Melanya [4] into his house together with the baby. He wrote me that the baby's father was he, and not the soldier, Aleksandr.

It seems to me that no formal declaration of nonpayment of the promissory note [5] should have been made. This is not my style.

Snow on the mountain. It's cold. Only a fool lives in the Crimea now. You write about the theater, a circle, and sundry temptations, as if to tease me; as if you don't know how boring, how depressing it is to go to bed at 9 o'clock, to lie down cross, with the consciousness that there is nowhere to go, no one to speak to, nothing to work at, for anyhow you

[3] Nemirovich-Danchenko and Stanislavsky, respectively.
[1] A botanical garden in the Crimea.
[2] The cook.
[3] Nikolay Petrovich Asheshov, a publicist and literary critic.
[4] The cook's mother.
[5] Given by the timber merchant, Konshin, in partial payment for Melikhovo. He had written to Chekhov to apologize for his failure to make payment on November 1, as agreed.

neither see nor hear your own work. The piano and I are two objects in the house that carry on a soundless, baffled existence, ignorant of why we have been placed here, since no one can play on us.* * *

Your Antoine

TO O. L. KNIPPER

Yalta, November 19, 1899

Dear actress,

You told Vishnevsky, he writes me, that now you would give no more than three copecks to see me. Thank you, you are very prodigal. But a little time will pass, another month or two—and you will not give even two copecks! How people change!

And meanwhile I would give seventy-five rubles to see you.

But fancy, I cannot go on writing: they are ringing the alarm bell. A fire has broken out here in Autka. There is a high wind.

Keep well! I am off to the fire.

Your A. Chekhov

TO V. A. POSSE[1]

Yalta, November 19, 1899

Much esteemed Vladimir Aleksandrovich!

Your letter is still lying on my table awaiting a reply; it served as a harsh reproach to me until, having sent off a reply to the telegram, I finally picked up my pen to write you. The fact is that I am writing a story [2] for *Life* and it will be ready soon—probably by mid-December. Altogether it runs to about three sheets but there's a host of characters, a crush, a jam, and it will take considerable work to diminish the effect of this crowding. One way or another, around December 10 the final draft will be ready and can be set up in type. But here's the trouble: I am overwhelmed by fear that the censors will tear at it. I shall not endure the censors' markings, or so it seems. And since some passages

[1] V. A. Posse (1864–1940), was a radical journalist and the *de facto* editor of the magazine *Life*.
[2] "In the Ravine."

may not pass the censorship, I could not bring myself to make a commitment and give you a definite reply. Now, of course, I am giving you a definite reply but on the condition that you return the story to me if, in places, you think it unprintable—that is, if you also foresee a danger of its being marked here and there by the censors.

Now I have a request. Please don't give me such prominence in your advertisements. Really, it just isn't done. Simply list my name on a line with the others in alphabetical order.

Where is Maxim Gorky?

So, be well. I wish you a lot of subscriptions and more readers—say, a hundred thousand. I press your hand.

Devotedly,

A. Chekhov

TO V. I. NEMIROVICH-DANCHENKO

Yalta, November 24, 1899

Dear Vladimir Ivanovich,

Please don't take offense at my failure to write to you. My correspondence is generally in the doldrums, first, because I am busy with my stories; second, I read proof for Marx; third, I have much ado with sick arrivals who for some reason turn to me. As for the proof for Marx, it is penal servitude. I have barely finished the second volume, and had I known earlier that this would be so far from easy, I would have made Marx give me not seventy-five thousand, but a hundred and seventy-five. The patients who arrive here, mostly penniless, turn to me for help, and I have to speak and correspond a great deal.

Of course, I am bored to extinction here. During the day I work, but in the evening I begin to ask myself, what am I to do, where can I go— and at the time when Act II is on at the theater I am in bed. I get up while it is still dark, as you can imagine. It is dark, the wind howls, the rain beats against the pane.

You are mistaken in thinking that people write to me from the four corners of the earth. My friends and acquaintances don't write me at all.* * *

I am not writing a play. I have a subject: three sisters. But I am not going to start work on the play until I finish the tales that are on my conscience.

My Yalta dacha has turned out to be very comfortable, cozy, warm, attractive. The garden will be extraordinary. I am planting it myself with my own hands. Of rosebushes alone I have a hundred, the noblest, the choicest varieties, also fifty pyramidal acacias, many camellias, lilies, tuberoses, etc., etc.

In your letter one finds a slightly audible trembling note as in an old bell—it is where you write of the Theater, about how the details of theatrical life have worn you out. Oh, don't get tired, don't grow cool! The Art Theater forms the best pages of that book which some day will be written about the contemporary Russian theater. That Theater is your glory, it is the only theater that I love, although I have never set foot there. Had I lived in Moscow, I would have tried to become a part of the administration, if only in the capacity of a watchman, in order to be of even some little help and, if possible, prevent you from cooling toward this institution, so dear to my heart.

There's a heavy downpour. It is dark in the room. Be well, cheerful, happy.

I press your hand. Bow to Yekaterina Nikolayevna [1] for me, and to everyone in the Theater, bowing lowest to Olga Leonardovna.

Your A. Chekhov

TO A. B. TARAKHOVSKY [1]

Yalta, November 26, 1899

* * * Why are you carrying a revolver? You are fulfilling your duty honestly, have justice on your side, so why do you need a revolver? They'll attack you? Well, then, let them. Whatever threats were made, you shouldn't be afraid, whereas constantly carrying a revolver will only ruin your nerves. [2]

[1] The addressee's wife.
[1] Abram Borisovich Tarakhovsky was a contributor to *The Taganrog Herald* and *The Azov Region.*
[2] Threats had been made against Tarakhovsky after he published some articles about life in Taganrog.

Yes, the people's reading room and the people's theater should each have its own location and the municipal library its own. Educational institutions should not be concentrated in one area but scattered throughout the town—that is the first point. Second, one should beware of cramped, crowded conditions, of noise, which is necessary in a theater but so disturbing in a library. Third, when several institutions of the same type are housed under the same roof, one of them is bound to swallow up the others. Fourth, the cooks of the librarian, the theater superintendent, and the rest will quarrel with each other, which will lead to quarrels among those in charge of the institution. Fifth, and most important, being a depository for books, the municipal library should have spacious quarters of its own that are attractive to the public; moreover, there should be some assurance that, as need requires, the library can expand its quarters, but if it is hemmed in by a reading room on one side and a theater on the other, any possibility of expansion is out of the question. After all, given the development of cultural life today, who can be certain that twenty-five or forty years from now the library may not require a five-story building! Theaters, though, are halfway commercial institutions; given sufficient time, they will sprout like mushrooms, and there will be a theater on every block, precisely the kind of theater each requires. As is true, for instance, in Naples.

It is snowing. Life here is passable but dull—ah, how dull! I am working little by little and waiting for spring, when I shall be able to leave. I am overwhelmed by the consumptives who have come here. They turn to me and I am at a loss to know what to do. I have thought up an appeal; we are trying to collect money, but if we fail, I'll have to clear out of Yalta. Read this appeal, and if you think it advisable, publish at least a few lines of it in *The Azov Region*. Emphasize that we wish to build a sanatorium. If only you knew the life led by these poor consumptives whom Russia dumps here to be rid of them, if only you knew—it is an absolute horror! Most appalling is the loneliness and the shabby blankets, which provide no warmth but only provoke one's disgust.* * *

Your A. Chekhov

Greetings to your family.

TO M. P. CHEKHOV

Dear Michel,

It is true that my letters to you have been brief and infrequent; there are many reasons for this. First, over the years I have somehow become cool to correspondence and love only to receive letters, not to write them; second, being obliged to pen about five letters a day, I am getting tired and irritable; third, I have relied far too much on your indulgence. All the other reasons are similar, and I can assure you that your marriage has nothing whatever to do with it. The reference to the marriage was nothing more than a slip of the tongue and should never, incidentally, become the basis for explanations, for this is a dangerous practice. One way or another, I am sorry that I distressed you for so long with my silence. I will try to reform.

Now for current affairs. We are living in Yalta. We have built a house, a small but comfortable house. We pick up what we need in the stores on account, the yard-keeper goes to market every morning. The phone keeps ringing all day, we are plagued with callers. We go nowhere, just sit at home, and I am impatient for the time when I can go to Moscow or possibly skip abroad some way. Our financial situation is none too good, and we are obliged to economize. I am no longer receiving an income from my books; according to the agreement, Marx will not pay me the full balance soon, and what I have received has long since been spent. But with all this economizing, my affairs have not improved, and it is as though there were an enormous factory smokestack over my head into which all my opulence whirls away. I spend little on myself, the house costs next to nothing, but what I spend as a representative littérateur, my literary habits (I hardly know what to call them) snap up three-fourths of whatever gets into my hands. I am working now. If the working mood continues until March, I shall earn about two or three thousand, otherwise I shall be forced to eat up the money from Marx. The house is not mortgaged.

As for Melikhovo, it has been sold in the same manner as my work—that is, with payments made in installments. It seems to me that in the end we shall receive nothing or very, very little. If you go to Moscow, you can learn the details from Masha.* * *

I am besieged by sick people who are sent here from all over with bacilli, with lung cavities, with green faces, but without a cent to their names. One is forced to contend with this nightmare, to resort to all sorts of tricks. Look at the enclosed leaflet and, if possible, print all of it or excerpts from it in *The Northern Region*. Lend us some support.

Now about Polevoy.[1] I don't correspond with Petersburg any more. I do not turn to Marx. With Suvorin I have long since stopped corresponding (the Dreyfus affair); I cannot carry out your commission [2] before spring, when I shall be in Petersburg. But what do you want Polevoy for? He is, you know, a little Yid and his work was outdated a long time ago. There's nothing in it but wretched biography.* * *

Your A. Chekhov

TO P. F. IORDANOV

Yalta, December 11, 1899

Forgive me, most esteemed Pavel Fyodorovich, for not having written you for so long and not having answered your letters.

* * * I have not thanked you for my having been elected to serve as a trustee of the Library, and my conscience torments me. What is done in such cases? Do I have to write to the mayor? Please enlighten me.

I remember, you wanted to make me a member of the Asylum committee. Please, make of me and with me all that can be made of and with me for Taganrog, I put myself completely at your disposal. The membership dues, 100 rubles, I am remitting to you by mail. If the money must be accompanied by a statement, send it to me and I'll sign it. Tarakhovsky wrote me that a Sunday school [1] was opened in Taganrog (I think that's what he said), and that I should join the society sponsoring it. To that, too, I consent.

By the end of this month I shall let you have the titles of the books that I sent you last summer, in agreement with the list of those you wanted. Please check to see if all those books have been received. There was a gigantic discount, so that the Library owes me very little.

The priests got me hitched: made me a member of the diocesan

---

1 Pyotr Nikolayevich Polevoy, author of a history of Russian literature.
2 To obtain Polevoy's history of literature for Mikhail.
1 Elementary teaching by volunteers to illiterates on Sundays.

school committee. This is in the Tavrida province. From the Serpukhov county, where I am a trustee, I get hysterical letters.[2]

* * * While talking to you once in one of Taganrog's wooded spots I told you that close to Moscow there is a school to which zemstvos and cities send teachers during the summer, to study the elements of horticulture. Later, in Moscow, I was told by knowledgeable people that every summer you might send one or two students to that school. In this way, little by little, you will get a staff of people trained in horticulture and capable of supervising the city's public gardens. When I am old I shall apply to you for the position of municipal gardener.

Your A. Chekhov

I sent you the regulations of the horticultural school. Have you received them?

[2] From two women teaching at the village school there.

[1900]

Yalta, January 8, 1900

* * * Here I see much of Kondakov, the academician. We speak of the Academy's Pushkin Division, devoted to belles lettres.[1] Since Kondakov is going to take part in the elections of future Academicians I was trying to hypnotize him and plant in him the idea that Barantzevich and Mikhailovsky should be elected. The first, a man worn out, tormented, indubitably a man of letters who in old age (which has already caught up with him) is in need and employed by a horse-drawn tramway company, just as he was in need and employed in the same way in his youth. A salary and repose would be just the thing for him. As for the second man—that is, Mikhailovsky—he would lay a sound foundation for the new Division and by his election would satisfy three-fourths of the entire writing fraternity. But the hypnosis did not work; my effort did not succeed. The supplement to the decree is just like Tolstoy's epilogue to *The Kreutzer Sonata*. The Academicians have done everything to safeguard themselves against the men of letters, whose society shocks them just as much as the society of Russian Academicians shocked the Germans. Writers of belles lettres can be only Honorary Academicians, but that means nothing, like being an honorary citizen of the town of Viazma or of Cherepovetz: no salary, no right to vote. A neat trick! The ordinary Academicians will be elected from among the professors, but Honorary Academicians will be chosen from among those writers who do not live in Petersburg—those, that is, who cannot attend the sessions and wrangle with the professors.[2]

I can hear a muezzin crying from a minaret. Turks are very reli-

---

[1] On the occasion of the centenary of Pushkin's birth (May 26/June 6, 1899), an imperial decree created a Division of Belles Lettres in the Department of Russian Language and Literature of the Academy of Sciences. The Division was to be composed of honorary professors from among outstanding writers and regular professors, all duly elected.

[2] Chekhov was mistaken. There was no such discrimination.

gious: they have a fast now, going without food all day. They have no religious ladies—that element which shoals religion, just as sand shoals the Volga.* * *

Your A. Chekhov

TO M. P. CHEKHOVA

Yalta, January 15, 1900

* * * Today I received a letter from *The Courier*—an invitation to Goltzev's twentieth anniversary as a writer; contributions are being collected for a library in his name to be opened in Staraya Ruza (there is such a village). This foolish Muscovite sentimentality will embarrass Goltzev himself first of all. No one ever celebrates twentieth anniversaries, and if some official or actor were to celebrate his twentieth anniversary, *The Courier* would be the first to make fun of him. Oh, how good it is that no one knows when I started writing.

We do not receive *The Day's News*. See to it that the paper is sent. If they will not do it free of charge, pay [. . .]. Mother misses a newspaper.

I have purchased in Gurzuf [1] a bit of beach that affords bathing, with the Pushkin rock [2] near the dock and the park. We now own a whole cove, in which one can keep a boat or a cutter. The house is rather mangy, but the roof is tiled, four rooms, big entry. There's a mulberry tree—a large one. Yesterday I was in Gurzuf and dined with that very beautiful lady (so beautiful that it is frightening) with whom Mme. Bonnier acquainted us. Kuchukoy is being sold. For the new cottage we'll need bentwood chairs. Babakay [3] has sent tables and high stools. Not bad. Don't buy lamps, I'll bring them myself when I go to Moscow.

Everything is all right. Keep well. It is raining heavily. Our highway is so muddy that there is no riding, no walking. A gate is being put up.* * *

Your Antoine

[1] A suburb of Yalta.
[2] Legend has it that the poet climbed the rock during his visit to Gurzuf.
[3] Chekhov's contractor.

TO V. M. SOBOLEVSKY

Yalta, January 19, 1900

* * * I am alive, almost well. I ail now and then but not for long, and this winter they did not put me to bed even once, I did my ailing on the go. I worked more than I did last year and I felt more bored. It is bad to be without Russia, bad in every sense. You live here just as if you were seated at the Strelna,[1] and all these evergreens, it seems, are made of tin, and there's no joy to be got out of them. And you don't see anything of interest, since local life lacks taste.* * *

Your A. Chekhov d'Académie [2]

TO F. D. BATYUSHKOV

Yalta, January 24, 1900

Much esteemed Fyodor Dmitriyevich!

Roche [1] asks me for the passages [2] that were cut by the censorship. But there were no such passages. There is one chapter that did not appear either in the periodical or in the book; it is what the peasants say about religion and about the authorities.[3] But there is no need to send it to Paris, just as there was no need to translate "Peasants" into the French language.

I thank you cordially for the photograph. Repin's illustration [4] is an honor that I did not expect and of which I did not dream. It will be very pleasant to receive the original; tell Ilya Yefimovich that I shall await the drawing with impatience and that now he cannot change his mind, since I have bequeathed the drawing to the city of Taganrog, where, incidentally, I was born.

In your letter you mention Gorky. By the way, what do you think of him? I do not like all of his work, but there are parts of it that I like very, very much, and I have no doubt that Gorky is of the stuff of

[1] A suburban restaurant in Moscow.
[2] He was elected an honorary member at the session of January 8, 1900.
[1] Denis Roche (1868–1951), Chekhov's French translator.
[2] In "Peasants."
[3] This chapter has not come to light.
[4] The famous painter's drawing for the dust jacket of the French edition of "Peasants," of which Chekhov was to receive the original from the artist.

which artists are made. He is the real thing. A good man, intelligent, clear-headed, thoughtful, but he carries much unnecessary ballast, for example, provincialism.

You write, "You don't know whence to expect the movement of the waters." [5] But what you do expect? There is movement, but, like the rotation of the earth around the sun, it is invisible to us.

Many thanks for your letter and for having remembered me. I am bored here, sick and tired of the place, I feel as if I have been jettisoned. Furthermore, the weather is nasty, and I am not well. And I keep coughing.

All the best to you.

Devotedly your A. Chekhov

TO V. A. GOLTZEV

Yalta, January 27, 1900

Dear Viktor Aleksandrovich,

I sent you a telegram,[1] but just the same let me congratulate you by letter as well. I am congratulating you, giving you a warm hug, clasping your hand firmly and asking you to believe that I love you and respect you as I rarely respect anybody. For the last ten years you have been one of the people nearest to me.

I am still expecting that young scholar whom you wrote about, but he still does not come. Where is he? Of course we will find a place for him. The weather is most abominable; in February it will worsen but, they say, the air of Yalta possesses curative qualities even when the weather is bad. Beginning with January 17—my name day and the day of my elevation to the rank of an immortal—I was ailing and even indulging in occasional thoughts of how I might put one over on those who had elected me to be one of the "immortals," but nothing happened, I took on new life, and am now hale and hearty—although not without a Spanish fly under the left clavicle. The doctor found that all

---

[5] Batyushkov preceded this remark with the observation that while in his lectures he dealt with the distant European past, contemporary problems were not alien to him.

[1] On the occasion of the twentieth anniversary of *Russian Thought*, of which Goltzev was editor. The glowing telegram declared that the periodical piloted by the addressee expressed the best aspirations of the Russian intelligentsia.

was well with the right lung—better than it was last year. However, outside of all else, the titular ailment is hemorrhoids.[2]

The idea of opening a reading room in Old Ruza does not appeal to me at all. Why, there is nothing in Old Ruza but a ferry and a tea house—that's one; second, you can't open a good reading room anyway; and third, the muzhiks don't get brighter in the least by reading books in reading rooms. What's needed here are scholarships. When the jubilee for the twenty-fifth year of your literary activity rolls around I shall propose that a complete high school and university education is to be granted in your honor to some "cook's son" [3] of the kind that is so objectionable to people who are your antagonists on principle.* * *

Your A. Chekhov

TO M. O. MENSHIKOV

Yalta, January 28, 1900

Dear Mikhail Osipovich,

What illness Tolstoy suffers from I cannot figure out. Cherinov [1] gave me no answer, and it is impossible to draw any conclusion from what I read in the papers and from what you write me now. Stomach and intestinal ulcers would have told on him in other ways. There are no such symptoms or there may have been some bleeding scratches, caused by gallstones passing through and lacerating the sides. Neither does he have cancer, which would first of all affect appetite, general condition, and above all would be betrayed by his face. Most likely, Tolstoy is in good health (aside from the stones) and will live another twenty years or so. His illness frightened me and kept me in a state of tension. I dread Tolstoy's death. If he died, a large vacuum would be formed in my life. In the first place, I have never loved any human being as much as I do him. I am an unbeliever, but of all faiths I regard his as the nearest to me and the one that suits me best. Second, when Tolstoy is part of literature, it is easy and agreeable to be a writer; even the

---

[2] Popularly associated with the sedentary occupation of bureaucrats.

[3] This phrase is traceable to a circular of 1887 issued by I. D. Delyanov, Minister of Education. It prohibited admission to high schools of "children of merchants, footmen, cooks, laundresses, small shopkeepers and the like, who, except for particularly gifted young people, should not be removed from the milieu in which they belong."

[1] A physician who taught in a medical school.

knowledge that you have not accomplished and never will accomplish anything is not so terrible, for Tolstoy makes up for all of us. His activity justifies all the hopes and expectations that are pinned to letters. Third, Tolstoy, with his enormous authority, stands firm, and as long as he remains among the living, bad taste in literature, all vulgarity, insolent or tearful, all harsh, embittered vanities, will remain remote and in deep shadow. Only his moral authority is capable of keeping so-called literary moods and trends at a certain height. Without him, it would all be a flock without a shepherd, or a jumble in which it would be hard to find one's way.

To dispose of Tolstoy, I shall also speak of *Resurrection*, which I read not in snatches, bit by bit, but all in one gulp. It is a remarkable work of art. The most uninteresting part is all that is said about the relationship between Nekhlyudov and Katyusha; the most interesting passages are the ones about the princes, the generals, the aunties, peasants, prisoners, wardens. The scene with the general, the commandant of the Fortress of Saints Peter and Paul, a spiritualist, I read with a palpitating heart—it is so wonderful! And Mme. Korchagina in an armchair, and the peasant, the husband of Fedosya! This peasant calls his old woman a "grappler." Indeed, Tolstoy is a grappler. The tale has no end, what there is cannot be called an end. To write and write and then dump it all on a Gospel text—that is too theological. To settle everything with such a text is as arbitrary a solution as to divide prisoners into five classes. Why five and not ten? Why a text from the Gospel, and not one from the Koran? First you must make people believe in the Gospel and its unique truth, and then rely on a text from it.* * *

I will certainly send you my photograph. I am glad to have the title of Academician, because it is pleasant to know that Sigma [2] now envies me. But I shall be even more gratified when I lose that title as the result of some misunderstanding. And a misunderstanding is bound to occur, because the learned Academicians are very much afraid that we shall be shocking them. They elected Tolstoy reluctantly. They believe him to be a nihilist. At least that is what he was dubbed by a lady who is the wife of an official with the rank of actual privy councillor—on this I congratulated Tolstoy with all my heart.* * *

Your A. Chekhov

Write me!

[2] Pen name of Sergey Nikólayevich Syromyatnikov, a contributor to *New Times.*

TO M. P. CHEKHOV

Yalta, January 29, 1900

Dear Michel,

This is in answer to your letter.

1. Not once in my life have I been in Torzhok and never have I sent from Torzhok any telegrams to anybody. I left Petersburg the day after the performance of *The Sea Gull;* a footman of Suvorin's and Potapenko saw me off.

2. Suvorin knew in detail about my selling my works to Marx and what the conditions were. When he was asked whether he wished to be the purchaser, he answered that he did not have the money, that his children were not allowing him to buy my works, and, most important of all, no one could pay more than Marx did.

3. An advance payment of twenty thousand meant that the works would be bought for twenty thousand, so that I would never climb out of debt.

4. When the deal was closed with Marx, A.S. wrote that he was very glad about the consummation, since his conscience had always tormented him, because he had published me wretchedly.

5. There was no discussion in Nice of the direction taken by *New Times.*

6. The "relations" of which I wrote you (of course, there should have been no free talk about this with the Suvorins) began to undergo a particular change when A.S. himself wrote me that we no longer had anything further to write to each other about.

7. They had begun to print my complete works at the plant but did not go on, since they were losing my manuscripts all the time, did not answer my letters and by such slovenly behavior were placing me in a desperate position; I had tuberculosis, I had to bear in mind that I must not saddle the heirs with my works in a chaotic, worthless state.

8. By rights, of course, I should not have written all this to you, inasmuch as it is boring and too personal, but since you have been bewitched and the matter was presented to you in a different light, there is no help for it; read all these eight points—and put what you read in your pipe and smoke it. There can be no mention, even, of any reconciliation, since Suvorin and I did not quarrel and we are corresponding once more as if nothing had happened. Anna Ivanovna is a darling

woman but she is ever so crafty. I believe that she is well disposed toward me, but when I talk to her I do not forget for a single moment that she is crafty and that A.S. is a very kind man—and that he publishes *New Times*. I am writing this exclusively for you. You alone. * * *

Your A. Chekhov

TO I. L. LEONTYEV-SHCHEGLOV

Yalta, February 2, 1900

Dear Jean,

This is in answer to your last letter. Stanislavsky is known in private life as Konstantin Sergeyevich Alekseyev, Moscow, near Red Gates; Home Owner. The plays are read not only by Stanislavsky but also by V. I. Nemirovich-Danchenko (Carriage Row, Art Theater). Up to now, I believe, they have not put on any one-act plays. If the play proves to their liking they will put it on. "Liking," in their language, means suitable, interesting as regards direction and in other theatrical respects. It would be better if you wrote for this unusual theater a four-act play, a Shcheglovian, truly artistic piece in the nature of *The Gordian Knot*,[1] without reporters and without writers who are noble and old.

Dear Jean, exposés, bile, rancorousness, so-called "independence"—i.e., criticism directed against liberals and new men—these are not at all your *métier*. The Lord has bestowed a kind gentle heart upon you; use it, then—write with a tender pen, with a soul at ease, without giving thought to the offenses that you have suffered. You call yourself an admirer of mine. And I am an admirer of yours, and a most persistent one, because I know you and know of what stuff your talent is made, and no one will dislodge me from my firm conviction that you possess the true divine spark. You, in consequence of circumstances which happened to combine in one way rather than another, are irritated, have bogged down knee-deep in trifles, are tired out by trifles, are oversensitive, have no faith in yourself—hence your constant thoughts of ailments, of need, thoughts of a pension, of Weinberg.[2]

It is still early for you to be thinking of a pension; as for Weinberg,

---

[1] A novel by the addressee.
[2] Pyotr Isayevich Weinberg, a literary historian, a poet and translator who was chairman of the Literary-Theatrical Committee.

if he has cooled toward you, he had a certain right or basis for doing so. You printed a protest, you exposed the Literary-Theatrical Committee, and at the time this made a painful impression on everyone, probably because that sort of thing is not being done. Be objective, look upon everything with the eye of a kind man—your own eye, that is— sit down to persist in writing a novel or a play about Russian life; not a critique of Russian life, but a joyous "Song of the Goldfinch" [3] to Russian life, and to our life in general, which is given to us only once and to spend which on exposing [...], venomous wives and the Committee is to behave thoughtlessly. Dear Jean, regard yourself, regard your gift justly; let your galleon sail the wide-spreading sea—don't keep it docked at Fontanka. Forgive all those who have wronged you, become resigned and, I repeat, buckle down to writing.

Excuse me if I lapse into the sing-song tone of a pious old female. But my regard for you is sincere, it is that of a comrade, and to put you off with a snippet of a businesslike letter would have been ill-timed on my part, to say the least. * * *

TO MAXIM GORKY

Yalta, February 3, 1900

Dear Aleksey Maksimovich,

Thank you for the letter, for the lines about Tolstoy and *Uncle Vanya*, which I have not seen on the stage, thanks in general for not forgetting me. Here in blessed Yalta without letters one could croak. Idleness, a stupid winter with temperature constantly above zero [C], the total absence of interesting women, pigs' snouts on the boardwalk—all this can befoul a man and wear him out in no time at all. I am dog-tired and it seems to me that the winter has lasted ten years.

You have pleurisy? If so, why do you stay in Nizhny? What for? What, by the way, do you find in this Nizhny, may I ask? What glue keeps you sticking to this city? If, as you say, you like Moscow, why don't you live in Moscow? In Moscow there are theaters and many other attractions, and, above all, it is but a step from there to the border, but living in Nizhny you will be stuck there and will never get any further than Vasilsursk.[1] What you need is to see more, to know

[3] Leontyev's pen name was derived from the Russian word for goldfinch.
[1] Perhaps an imaginary town signifying for Chekhov a wretched provincial hole.

more, to have a wider range of knowledge. Your imagination is tenacious, it takes firm hold, but it is like a big stove that isn't fed enough firewood. This is felt in your work generally and particularly in your stories; in a story you present two or three characters, but they stand apart, outside the mass. It is clear that they live in your imagination, but they alone, the mass has escaped your grasp. I exclude your Crimean pieces (for example, "My Companion"), where one gets a feeling not only of the central characters, but also of the human mass from which they emerged, as well as of the atmosphere and the background—in a word, of everything.

You see how I've berated you, all to the end of getting you out of Nizhny. You are young, vigorous, hardy, if I were you I would be off to India and the devil knows where. I would also get one or two more university degrees. I would, and I would—you laugh, but it hurts me that I am already forty years old, and short of breath and afflicted with all sorts of rubbish that prevents me from living freely. Be that as it may, be a good fellow and a good comrade, don't be cross because I sermonize in my letters like an archpriest.

Do write me. I am waiting for *Foma Gordeyev*,[2] which I haven't yet read as carefully as it deserves.

No news. Keep well, I press your hand.

Your A. Chekhov

TO O. L. KNIPPER

Yalta, February 10, 1900

Dear actress,

The winter is very long. I was not well, no one has written to me for practically a whole month—and I had decided that nothing remained for me to do but to go abroad, where it's not so boring. But now it has turned warm, life has improved—and I have determined not to go abroad until the end of the summer, for the Exposition.[1]

But you, why are you blue? Why are you blue? You live, work, hope, drink, laugh when your uncle reads to you [2]—what more do you want?

---

[2] A novel by Gorky.
[1] The Paris Exposition of 1900.
[2] Her uncle Sasha (A. I. Zaltsa) read aloud some humorous things by Chekhov, and by adopting the Chekhovian style in conversation he and Olga's brother put the family in stitches.

With me it's another story. I have been uprooted from my native soil. My life is incomplete. I don't drink, although I like drinking. I like it when it's noisy but I don't hear any noise. In a word, I now endure the condition of a transplanted tree which hesitates between taking root and starting to wither away. If I should sometimes allow myself to complain of boredom in a letter, I have good reason for it. But you? And Meyerhold, too, complains that he leads a boring life. Good Lord! By the way, about Meyerhold. He ought to spend a whole summer in the Crimea, that's what his health demands. A whole summer, by all means.

Well, now I'm in good health. I do nothing because I am getting ready to set to work. I dig in the garden.

You once wrote that for you, little people, the future is veiled in mystery. The other day I received a letter from your chief, Nemirovich. He writes that at the beginning of May the troupe will be in Sevastopol, then in Yalta. Five performances in Yalta, then evening rehearsals. Only the valuable members of the company will remain for rehearsals, the others will rest where they please. I hope that you are valuable. For the director you are valuable, but for the author you are—invaluable. There's a pun for you as an hors d'oeuvre. I won't write more until you send me your portrait. I kiss your little hand.

Your Antonio Academicus

* * * Thank you for your good wishes on the occasion of my marriage.[3] I informed my fiancée of your intention of coming to Yalta in order to make trouble for her. She replied that she would not let me out of her embraces when that "wicked woman" came to Yalta. I observed that to remain in someone's embraces for so long in hot weather was unhygienic. She took offense, and became thoughtful, as if trying to guess in what circle I had learned this *façon de parler,* and after a short while she announced that the theater is evil and that my decision to write no more plays was in every way laudatory, and asked me to kiss her. To this I answered that now, since I have the rank of an Academician, it did not behoove me to kiss frequently. She burst into tears, and I left.

[3] A few days earlier his correspondent had written to him of having been informed that he was marrying a priest's daughter, and so, she said, "you have given in." Chekhov embroidered on the joke.

TO A. S. SUVORIN

Yalta, February 12, 1900

* * * Yes, of course, jurors are human and can make mistakes, but what of it? There are times when, through error, they will give alms to a well-fed man instead of a famished one, but, no matter how much you write on this theme, you won't get anywhere with all your writing but will merely harm those who hunger. Whether the jurors make mistakes or not, from our point of view, we must admit that in each individual case they judge with discernment, that when they act as jurors their conscience is under a severe strain; and if the captain of a steamer navigates carefully, keeping an eye steadily on chart and compass, and if despite all this the steamer is wrecked, would it not be more correct to attribute the wreck not to the captain but to something else—for instance, the fact that the chart has long been out of date, or that the sea bed has changed?

For jurors have to take three conditions into account: (1) Besides the law that is in force, besides the statutes and juridical definitions, there also exists the moral law, which always precedes the law on the books and determines our actions at the precise time when we want to act according to our conscience. Thus, by law, a daughter is supposed to inherit only one-seventh of the estate. But you, following the dictates of a purely moral order, put the law aside and, despite it, make her bequest equal in amount to that of each of her brothers, inasmuch as you know that, by acting otherwise, you would have acted against your conscience. Thus even jurors occasionally find themselves in a situation in which they feel and recognize that their conscience is not satisfied by the law that is in force, that the case in hand has shadings and fine points which cannot be stowed neatly in the Penal Code and that, evidently, there is need of something else for the correct solution of the problem, and for want of this "something" they bring in a verdict, willy-nilly, in which there's a deficiency. (2) Jurors understand that acquittal is not pardon and that acquittal does not free the defendant from the dread Judgment Day in the next world, from the judgment of conscience, from the judgment of public opinion; they solve the problem solely to the extent to which it is a judicial one, and as for that, let A—t [1] decide whether it is a good thing to murder

[1] Signature on an article about a trial written by V. K. Petersen for *New Times*.

children or not. (3) When a defendant appears in court he has already been racked by investigation and imprisonment, and during the trial he relives the racking experience, so that, even though acquitted, he does not leave the court unpunished.

Be that as it may, it turns out that this letter is already almost finished, but essentially I have written nothing. * * *

Your A. Chekhov

Resurrection is a remarkable novel. I liked it very much, but it must be read right off, all of it, at a single sitting. The end is uninteresting and false—false in regard to technique.

TO A. S. SUVORIN

Yalta, March 10, 1900

No winter has lasted for me as long as this one; and time only crawls instead of moving, and now I understand how foolish I was in leaving Moscow. I have lost the habit of the north and have not become used to the south, and in my condition I can think of nothing but foreign parts. Here in Yalta after spring, has come winter: snow, rain, cold, mud—fit to spit on.

During the week following Easter the Moscow Art Theater will be playing in Yalta, it will bring its own scenery and furniture. All four performances announced were sold out in one day, in spite of raised prices. Among other things, Hauptmann's *Lonely Lives* will be performed—in my opinion, a magnificent play. I read it with great pleasure, although I dislike plays. The Art Theater, they say, has staged it marvelously.

No news. One great event, however. Sergeyenko's *Socrates* is being printed in the supplement to *Plowed Land*. It was a great effort for me to read it. It is not Socrates but a captious fellow, somewhat stupid but crafty, whose wisdom and whatever is interesting about him is due to the fact that he takes everyone at his word. Not a whiff of talent, but it's very possible that the play will be successful, for there are such words in it as "amphora," and Karpov [1] will say that it is a play in which the setting is noteworthy.

[1] Yevtikhy Pavlovich Karpov, a playwright and stage director.

News about the Academy. The President is very much distressed both by Korsh's book and by his polemics.[2] The election of ordinary members took place on February 5. Professor Kondakov was elected to the Pushkin Division. Which means that, with Lamansky [3] and Korsh, there will already be three in that Division. Also, Kondakov writes me, "The Division has decided, for the time being, not to hold an election to fill the three remaining seats," and he is of the opinion that he, personally, won't be around when that "for the time being" comes to an end. And there was no official announcement of Kondakov's having been elected—evidently the thing is being kept hush-hush, so as not to get *messieurs les littérateurs* all stirred up.

How many consumptives there are here! What poverty, and how perturbed one feels in their presence! Those gravely ill are not accepted here either as guests at hotels or as tenants of flats; you can picture to yourself, then, what incidents one has to observe here. People are dying from exhaustion, from the milieu, from total neglect—and this is Tauris the Blest! One loses all relish for both sun and sea. * * *

Your A. Chekhov

TO P. P. YAKUBOVICH[1]

Yalta, June 14, 1900

Most esteemed Pyotr Philipovich!

I have had a profound respect for N. K. Mikhailovsky ever since I first came to know him, and I am obliged to him for a very great deal; nevertheless it did take me a long while to reply to your letter. First of all, prior to the period from October 1 to 15—the deadline, as you write, for the submission of manuscripts—I am hardly likely to write anything new, since I have work on hand, and, in general, I find it quite hard to write during the summer. Secondly, this is the sixth invitation I have received during 1900 to contribute to a miscellany—

[2] Fyodor Yevgenyevich Korsh was a professor of philology and a member of the Academy. Suvorin had a controversy with him regarding the authenticity of an alleged epilogue to Pushkin's "Mermaid."

[3] Vladimir Ivanovich Lamansky, professor of philology.

[1] Melshin was the pseudonym of P. P. Yakubovich (1860–1911), a poet, fiction writer, and literary critic. In 1887 he was sentenced to capital punishment for revolutionary activities, but the sentence was commuted to hard labor in Siberia, where he became a settler, eventually being allowed to return to Russia.

i.e., there are plans afoot for the publication of six such collections. —It seems to me that Nikolay Konstantinovich is too big and too notable a figure for the celebration of his forty-year jubilee to be limited to the publication of a miscellany, a book that will consist entirely of articles which, while probably excellent, are nevertheless of an occasional character and will not sell since, as a general rule with but very few exceptions, such collections sell poorly—very poorly.

If I were in Petersburg I would attempt to infect you with that distrust of miscellanies and almanacs that is now so deep-seated within me after participating in so many miscellanies—twenty, or pretty close to that, counting one for each year of my literary activity. I don't know, perhaps I have aged or am tired out, but I still consider a miscellany as insufficient, even if it should be excellently put together and quickly sold out. If the matter depended on me I would announce a contest for a book dealing with the life-work of Nikolay Konstantinovich, a very good and very necessary book, which I would publish sensibly, without haste; I would include a list of works by him and about him, as well as a splendid portrait of him.

—But, come what may, I shall keep an eye on the deadline set by you and, should I start work on something, I shall inform you without delay. For the present allow me to wish you all the best and to remain sincerely and most respectfully yours,

A. Chekhov

TO A. L. VISHNEVSKY

Yalta, August 5, 1900

* * * I am writing the play, have already written a great deal of it, but as long as I am not in Moscow I can form no judgment about the play. Perhaps what I am turning out is not a play but wearisome Crimean fiddle-faddle. It is called *Three Sisters* (as you already know); for you I am readying the role of a high school inspector, husband of one of the sisters. You will be wearing your uniform and will have a decoration on a ribbon around your neck.

Should the play not go into production this season I shall rework it next season.

I envy you for frequenting so often a place I haven't been to for six years by now—the baths, that is. I am covered all over with fish scales now, I am shaggy from head to toe, I walk about without a stitch and howl like a wild creature; the young ladies are afraid of me. * * *

When I am in Moscow, invite me. Sister writes that you have very good quarters, and if you are really satisfied and feel comfortable, then I am glad and I envy you. Keep well, fellow townsman, cheerful, spry, work well, enjoying it, and do not forget

Your A. Chekhov

TO O. L. KNIPPER

Yalta, August 9, 1900

My dear Olga, my joy, greetings!

Today I received your letter, the first since your departure,[1] I read it, then read it again, and now I am writing you, my actress. Having seen you off, I was driven to Kiest's hotel, where I stayed overnight; the following day, out of boredom and having nothing better to do, I drove out to Balaklava. There I hid from ladies who recognized me and were intent on giving me an ovation, spent the night, and in the morning boarded the *Tavela* [2] for Yalta.

The sea was devilishly rough. Now I sit in Yalta, bored, cross, languishing. Alekseyev was here yesterday. We talked about the play,[3] I gave him my word that I would finish it not later than September. You see how clever I am.

I keep thinking that the door will open and you will walk in. But you won't, you are now at rehearsals or in Merzlyakov Lane,[4] far from Yalta and me.

Farewell, may the heavenly powers, the guardian angels, protect you. Farewell, my good girl.

Your Antonio

---

[1] Knipper left Yalta on August 5, Chekhov having accompanied her as far as Sevastopol. This is the first letter in which he used the intimate "thou" in addressing her.

[2] A steamer named after a large estate in the Crimea.

[3] *Three Sisters.*

[4] The location of Knipper's house.

TO O. L. KNIPPER

My darling, my angel,

I don't write you, but don't be cross, be lenient to human weaknesses. All this time I've been poring over my play, meditating rather than writing, yet it seemed to me that I was busy with real work and I had no mind for letters. I am writing the play but I am not hurrying with it, and it is very possible that I shall leave for Moscow without having finished it. There are a great many characters, it is crowded, I'm afraid it will turn out obscure or pale, and so I think it may be better to put it off till next season. By the way, only *Ivanov* I allowed to be produced at Korsh's immediately after writing it. All the other plays I kept by me for a long time, waiting for Nemirovich-Danchenko, and thus I had a chance to make all kinds of corrections. * * *

Of course, I shall send you a telegram; without fail do come to meet me, without fail! I shall take the morning express. On arriving I shall at once sit down to my play. And where shall I put up? At my sister's there is neither desk nor bed for me; I shall have to put up at a hotel. I shall not stay in Moscow long. * * *

Write me more frequently, your letters always give me joy and lift my spirits, which almost every day are as parched and stale as the Crimean soil. Don't be angry at me, my darling. * * *

Your Antoine

TO O. L. KNIPPER

My dear, my nice Olya, remarkable little actress, your latest letter in which you describe your excursion to Sparrow Hills [1] touched me, it's enchanting like yourself. And here I have been keeping indoors for the sixth or seventh day, because I am ill. Fever, cough, a cold. Today, it seems, I am a little better, on the mend, but still—weakness and emptiness, and disgust because I wrote nothing, didn't do a stroke of work.

---

[1] A pleasure-ground for Muscovites; her description of it evokes the autumn scene, the light, the mood these aroused; she wishes that she could have shared those precious moments with him, who alone "would have understood it all."

The play looks at me gloomily, lies on the table, and I think about it gloomily.

You advise me against leaving for Moscow.[2] Early in October Mother will be going to Moscow. I shall have to see her off, so that obviously I can't come to you. This means that over the winter you will forget what manner of man I am, and I shall be enraptured with someone else, should I meet another woman like you—and everything will go on in the old way as it did before.

Tomorrow I shall write you more, in the meantime, keep well, my dear. Altschuller came to see me. Be well, and happy.

Your Ant—

* * * Forgive me, sweet, for this dull letter. Tomorrow I'll write you more cheerfully.

TO O. L. KNIPPER

Yalta, September 22, 1900

Olya, my darling, greetings! How are you getting on? It is a long time since I have written you, a long time. I have some pangs of conscience because of it, though I am not as much to blame as may appear. I have no desire to write, what have I to write about? My life in the Crimea? What I want is not to write to you, but to talk with you, even to be silent, but only with you. Tomorrow Mother goes to Moscow—perhaps I shall soon go too, although I don't understand what I should go there for. What for? To see you and to leave you again? How interesting. To come, to catch a glimpse of the theatrical turmoil and leave again.

I shall go to Paris, then probably to Nice, and thence to Africa, unless the black death is there. It will be necessary somehow to live through or, rather, to drag through this winter. * * *

Are you angry with me, my darling? What's to be done? It is too dark for me to write, my candles don't give enough light. I kiss you fervently, my dear, good-bye, be well and cheerful! Think of me more often. You seldom write.[1] I explain it on the grounds of your being fed

[2] She cited the cold weather.
[1] There were six letters from Knipper dated September 1 to September 19.

up with me and of others having begun to court you. Well, bravo, granny!

I kiss your little hand.

Your Ant.

TO O. L. KNIPPER

Yalta, September 27, 1900

My sweet Olya, my nice little actress, why this tone, this plaintive, somewhat sour mood? [1] Am I really so much to blame? Now do forgive me, my dear, my good girl, don't be cross, I am not so guilty as your oversensitiveness prompts you to suppose. If I have not yet come to Moscow, it is because I haven't been well, there were no other reasons, I assure you, my darling, on my word of honor. Word of honor! You don't believe me?

Until October 10 I shall stay in Yalta and work, then I'll go to Moscow or abroad, depending on the state of my health. In any event I shall write you.

I haven't had any letters at all either from my brother Ivan or my sister Masha. Obviously they are sore, I don't know why. * * *

As for you, be sure to write me in detail how *The Snow Maiden* [2] went, generally what the start of the performances was like, what the mood of the company is, how the public is reacting, etc., etc. Of course, you are not in my situation; you have no end of material for letters, more than you can use, as for me, I have nothing to report, with one exception, today I caught two mice.

No rain here. A drought in Yalta is a drought! Poor trees, particularly those on the hither side of the mountains, they did not have a single drop of rain all summer long and now are yellow; so it occurs that people too have not a single drop of happiness all their lives. Apparently that is how it must be.

You write, "You have a loving, tender heart, I know, why do you harden it?" And when did I harden it? Exactly how did I show my

---

[1] On September 24, 1900, Olga had written: "Why don't you come, Anton? I cannot understand it. I do not write because I am constantly expecting you, because I want terribly to see you. What is preventing you? What is troubling you? I don't know what to make of it. I am terribly uneasy. Every day I want to cry."

[2] A play by Aleksandr Nikolayevich Ostrovsky (1823–86), one of the chief props of the Russian dramatic repertory.

callousness? My heart has always loved you and been tender toward you, I have never hidden this from you, never, never, and you accuse me of callousness for no particular reason, for nothing.

Your letter gives me the impression that you want and expect some sort of an explanation, some sort of a long conversation with grave faces and grave consequences, and I don't know what to tell you except the one thing that I have told you ten thousand times and shall probably go on telling you for a long time, namely, that I love you—and nothing more. If we are not together now, neither I nor you are to blame, but the demon who lodged bacilli in me and the love of art in you.

Good-bye, good-bye, dear granny, and may the holy angels protect you. Don't be cross with me, darling, don't mope, be sensible.

What's new in the theater? Please write.

Your Antoine

TO V. F. KOMMISSARZHEVSKAYA

Moscow, November 13, 1900

Dear Vera Fyodorovna,

I wanted to answer your letter by word of mouth, since I was counting heavily on being in Petersburg, but certain circumstances kept me from going there and so here I am, writing to you. *Three Sisters* are already finished, but their future—their immediate future, at least—is veiled from me by the murk of uncertainty. The play has turned out to be boring, long-drawn-out, awkward—awkward, I say, since it has four female leads, for instance, and its mood, I am told, is gloomier than gloom.

It would prove very, very little to the liking of your artists if I were to send it to the Aleksandrinsky Theater, but, come what may, send the play to you I will. Read it and decide whether it is worth while to take it along on your tour this summer. It is now being read in the Art Theater (there is only one copy, no more); later I'll take it and make a fair copy, and only then shall we print several copies, one of which I shall hasten to send to you.

But how fine it would be if I succeeded in breaking out of here and going to Petersburg if only for a day! Here I feel as if I were a convict at hard labor; during the day, from morning to evening, I turn the wheel—i.e., I dash about, making calls, while at night I sleep like the dead. I came here perfectly well, but now I am coughing again and am rancorous and, they say, I look yellow. * * *

Cordially yours,

A. Chekhov

TO O. L. KNIPPER

Nice, December 17, 1900 [1]

Sunday. Don't remember date.

There, it's the third night now that I am in Nice, yet there isn't as much as one line from you. What meaneth this dream? How would you have me take it? My darling Olya, don't be lazy, my angel, write your old man more often. Here, in Nice, everything is splendid, the weather is astonishing. After Yalta nature and the weather here seem simply paradisal. Bought myself a summer overcoat and am playing the fop. Yesterday sent Act III of play [2] to Moscow, and tomorrow will send IV. In III I changed only a little here and there, but in IV I went in for drastic changes. I fattened up your part a lot. (You are supposed to say "Thank you. . . .") And you, in return, write me how the rehearsals are going, what's what and how things are—write everything. Because you're not writing me I, too, don't want to write. *Basta!* This is my last letter.

Jacoby, the painter, called on me today. Day before yesterday saw Maksim Kovalevsky, a Moscow celebrity, received an invitation from him, and shall shortly be going to dine with him at his summer villa in Beaulieu. Shall shortly be going to Monte Carlo to play roulette.

Write me, darling, don't be lazy. You have a heap of letters from me, I haven't a single one from you. How have I angered you? * * *

They overfeed you here. After dinner one has to nap and not do a thing, and that isn't good. I shall have to change my way of life, eat a little less.

The guests at our Pension are Russian and, to boot, dreadfully boring—dreadfully. And, for the most part, ladies.

---

[1] This date was established by the editor of Vol. VI in the Soviet edition of Chekhov's complete letters.

[2] *Three Sisters.*

I kiss you hard and embrace my darling little woman. Do not forget me. Remember me at least once a week. I embrace you again, and again.

Your Antoine

When you see Leopold Antonovich,[3] tell him that I am not going to Africa now, but am going to work. Tell him that I have left Egypt and Algiers for next year.

TO O. L. KNIPPER

Nice, December 26, 1900

Little actress, why are you worried? I received your telegram and for a long time did not know how to reply. I am as strong as a bull—should that be my reply? But I am ashamed to put it that way. And how are you? Are you still staying indoors, or do you already go to the theater? My good darling, it is of course impossible not to ail, but it's better not to ail. When you are far away, the devil knows what thoughts get into my head and I am even frightened. Don't be ill, dear, when I'm not there, be a clever girl.

Today I visited Monte Carlo, won 295 francs. Nemirovich wired me from Menton; tomorrow we shall meet. I bought a new hat. What else? Did you get the new variant of your part?

* * * Your last letter is very touching, it is written so poetically. My clever one, the two of us should live at least five more years and then let old age lay hold of us; at least, there would still be really something to remember. You are in a good mood, as it should be, only don't grow shallow, my girl.

I kiss you ardently, although apparently you are already tired of this. Or aren't you? In that case I embrace you firmly and hold you in my arms for twenty minutes and kiss you most warmly. Write how the rehearsals are going, which act you have reached, etc. In general, how is the work going; would it not be better to postpone the play till next season? * * *

Write, or I'll smash you to pieces.

Your Antoine

[3] L. A. Sulerzhitsky, a writer and artist. In 1902 he was arrested and exiled to a southern province as a member of the Social Democratic Party.

TO L. V. SREDIN[1]

Nice, December 26, 1900

Dear Leonid Valentinovich! * * *

This is the second week that I have been in and near Nice—and what can I tell you? To live in Yalta all winter long is a good, a very good thing, but this place after Yalta seems simply paradise. Yalta is Siberia! My first two days here, I strolled in a summer overcoat or sat in my room before a door opened on a balcony, and for want of habit I even found this funny. The people in the streets are jolly, noisy, laughing; not a policeman in sight; no Marxists with bloated countenances. But two days ago suddenly and unexpectedly it turned very cold and everything withered. Frosts don't occur here, and where it came from is a complete mystery.

Do you happen to know where my mother and sister are now? If they are in Yalta, write to tell me whether they are well and how they feel. I wrote to them but received no reply. * * * No matter how delightful it may be on the Riviera, nevertheless, without letters it is tedious. Perhaps my house has collapsed? . . .

I press your hand firmly and embrace you. Keep well and happy.

Your A. Chekhov

TO O. L. KNIPPER

Nice, December 28, 1900

* * * Nemirovich is here with his spouse. Beside other women she seems so banal, like the wife of a Serpukhov merchant. Buys the devil knows what, all as cheap as can be. I am sorry she is with him. He himself is as usual, a good fellow, not boring.

It was cold, but now it is warm, we wear summer overcoats. I won 500 francs at roulette. Is it all right for me to gamble?

And I was in such a hurry with the last act, I thought you needed it. It appears that you will not start rehearsing before Nemirovich's return from abroad. And if I'd had this act at hand two or three more days, it would probably have turned out juicier.

[1] L. V. Sredin (1860–1909) was a physician afflicted with tuberculosis and settled in Yalta, a neighbor of Chekhov's there. He was a friend of both Chekhov and Gorky.

* * * Have you recovered? There you are! Though when you are ill you are a good girl and write good letters, all the same you dare not be ill any more.

I dine with many ladies, Muscovites among them, I don't say half a word to them. I sit sulking, holding my peace, and stubbornly go on eating or think about you. Now and then the Moscow ladies turn the talk to the theater, obviously wishing to draw me into the discussion, but I keep still and chew. I am very glad when you are praised. And, you can imagine, you are highly praised. They say you are a good actress.

Well, little child, be healthy and happy. I am yours! Take me and eat me up with vinegar and olive oil. I kiss you ardently.

Your Antoine

⎡1901⎤

Nice, January 2, 1901

Are you depressed now, or merry? Don't be depressed, sweetheart, live and work and write more often to your hermit Antony. I have had no letters from you for a long time.[1] I do not count the letter of December 12 that I received today, in which you describe how you cried when I went away. What a marvelous letter it is, by the way! You couldn't have written it, you must have asked someone else to write it for you. A wonderful letter.

Nemirovich does not come to see me. The day before yesterday I sent him a telegram asking him to come to see me *"seul."* So that's the reason. And meanwhile I must see him to talk about the letter I have had from Stanislavsky. Today I am staying in, as I did yesterday, the whole day. I am not going out. The reason: I have been invited to dinner by a highly stationed personage and I have said that I was ill. No frock coat, no inclination. A Muscovite, Maklakov,[2] came to see me today. What else? Well, nothing else.

Do describe at least one rehearsal of *Three Sisters.* Ought anything be put in or taken out? Are you acting well, my darling? Oh, mind now! Don't make a mournful face in a single act. Angry, yes, but not mournful. People who carry grief in their hearts a long time and are used to it only whistle and often sink into thought. So you may often be thoughtful on the stage during conversations. Do you understand? Of course you understand, because you are clever. Did I congratulate you on the New Year in my letter? Can it be that I didn't? I kiss both your hands, all your ten fingers and your forehead and I wish you happiness and peace and more love, and that it may last a long time, say fifteen years. What do you think, can there be such love? With me there could, but not with you. I embrace you in any case.

Your Toto

[1] She had written him on December 23 and 24 and had wired him on December 26 and 27.
[2] Vasily Alekseyevich Maklakov, a prominent lawyer.

TO O. L. KNIPPER

Dear drunk,

I have just received your letter with the description of the evening at Luzhsky's.[1] You ask about the fate of your letter, or rather, three letters in one envelope. Don't be worried, darling, I received them. Thanks.

In *The Herald of Europe* I have just read Boborykin's tale, *Fellow Students*. A wretched tale, long-drawn-out, but engaging—the Art Theater is depicted in it and M. P. Lilina is praised to the skies. Read it. The discussion is about *The Sea Gull* and *Uncle Vanya*.

I am already cruelly bored here.

Keep well, grow younger and more attractive, so the old man will not be vexed.

You write nothing about how the play is going, whether it can be counted on, and so on and so on. It is very possible that on January 15 I shall leave for Algiers. Nevertheless, send all letters to the old address in Nice, and they will be forwarded to me at Algiers. I want to have a look at the Sahara.

So, keep well. I embrace you warmly, dear heart.

Your Toto, hereditary honorary Academician

TO O. L. KNIPPER

Nice, January 11, 1901

Cruel, ferocious woman, for a century I haven't had any letters from you. What does this mean? Letters are now delivered to me punctually and if I do not get them, only you, my faithless one, are at fault.[1]

One of these days, if the sea is not as rough as it is now, I'll leave for Africa. My address is the same: Nice, rue de Gounod, and it will be known here where I am. I shall not stay long in Africa, some two weeks. The weather is constantly summery, warm, wonderful, flowers, ladies, bicycles, but, hélas! all this is an oleograph, not a painting, at least for me.

[1] Vasily Vasilyevich Luzhsky was an actor with the Art Theater who had roles in most of Chekhov's plays.
[1] Between December 11, 1900, and January 9, 1901, Knipper had mailed him eighteen letters.

Write, dog! Auburn-haired dog! Not to write to me—this is so mean of you! If at least you wrote me what is happening to *Three Sisters.* You haven't yet written me anything about the play, absolutely nothing, except that you attended a rehearsal, or that there was no rehearsal on a certain day. I will surely give you a beating, what the deuce.

Did Masha come to Moscow?

The days are growing longer, soon it will be spring, my nice, good actress, we shall soon see each other. Write, darling, I implore you.

Your Toto

TO M. A. CHLENOV[1]

Nice, January 19, 1901

Dear Mikhail Aleksandrovich,

I am sending you a brief answer to your letter. A certain Mme. Vasilyeva gives the money or, more correctly, is planning to give it. She is a young woman of twenty to twenty-two. I shall read her a part of your letter, namely, that part which deals with skin diseases, for the present I shall pass over syphilis. It seems to me that it is necessary to build a hospital just for skin diseases solely for the sake of science: the city itself will sooner or later establish a hospital for syphilitics, or else another philanthropist will be found. What do you think? The sum offered is 120,000, but it can also be 130,000, depending on what the houses in Odessa that are being sold will bring. Today I shall call on Mme. Vasilyeva and have a talk with her, and so, I believe, in about a month the question will be settled finally, that is, you will have a new hospital.

Judging from the tone of your letter, you think that it is I who am preparing to give money out of my own pocket, alas! I would not be in a position to offer even a twentieth part; I have nothing now.

Again, keep all this a secret, and in the future never tell anyone a word about my having anything to do with the destinies of Moscow medicine. * * *

Keep well. I press your hand. I shall soon write again.

Devotedly,

A. Chekhov

You aren't married yet?

[1] M. A. Chlenov was a dermatologist.

TO M. F. ANDREYEVA[1]

Dear Mariya Fyodorovna,

I did not send you any flowers, but, please, let it be as if I did, or else my discomfiture and vexation will be measureless. Your letter gave me inexpressible pleasure. Immense and extraordinary thanks, and now regard me as your insolvent debtor.

You write that during my last visit I pained you because I seemed afraid to speak frankly with you about *Three Sisters*, etc. God forbid! I was not afraid to speak frankly with you, I was afraid of hindering you and on purpose I tried to hold my peace, and as far as possible restrain myself, precisely in order not to interfere with your work. If I had remained in Moscow, perhaps after the tenth rehearsal I would have made some remarks, and those only about details. They write me from Moscow that you are excellent in *Three Sisters*, that you play simply marvelously, and I am glad, very glad—God grant you health. Consider me your debtor, that's all.

Today I leave for Algiers, where I shall spend some two weeks, and then be off to Russia.[2] I am very sorry that you will be acting in Petersburg, because I don't like that city and have a low opinion of Petersburg taste. Greetings to Andrey Alekseyevich and the children. Keep well, may Heaven's angels guard you.

Devotedly,

A. Chekhov

TO O. L. KNIPPER

Nice, January 26, 1901

Well, my good darling, today I shall probably leave for Algiers. * * * From there I'll make for Yalta, where I shall spend about a month, and then go somewhere with my dog. I hear from my companions that I shall probably stay about two weeks in Algiers, including the time I

---

[1] M. F. Andreyeva was an actress long associated with the Moscow Art Theater, the wife of Andrey Alekseyevich Zhelyabuzhsky. She played the part of Irina in *Three Sisters*, and acted in other Chekhov plays as well.

[2] The trip to Algiers did not take place because the sea was too rough. Instead, Chekhov left for Italy with M. M. Kovalevsky and another friend.

shall spend on my trip to the Sahara. From the Sahara I shall return tropically hot, hellishly passionate.

How are *Three Sisters* doing? Send me as long a telegram as possible, sparing nothing. These last days it has been cold, cold here, as in Yalta, and I am glad to leave. If the sea gets rough, my mamusya, then, in obedience to my companions, I'll make off not for Algiers, but for Italy, Naples, and I shall write you about this no later than tonight. I shall be traveling to Marseilles all night, brr!

As you see, my spirits have perked up, I love to travel. Recently my dream has been a voyage in summer to Spitzbergen or to Solovki.[1]

And you are worn out by guests and rehearsals, my wonderful, remarkable actress? Never mind, bear up. No matter what happens, we shall spend the summer together. Isn't that so? Look out, otherwise I'll give you a beating.

I am off to do some shopping. It's cloudy, the wind seems to be rising. Now I'll go and buy me new, forgive me, pants, and throw out the old ones here in France.

I kiss you warmly and hug you desperately. Do not be cross, do not be depressed, do not pull a serious face, and write as often as possible to the man who loves you in spite of your defects. No, no, darling, I was joking, you have no defects, you are perfect.

I embrace you again.

Your Antonius, priest-monk

TO N. P. KONDAKOV[1]

Yalta, February 20, 1901

Much esteemed Nikodim Pavlovich!

* * * I fled from Nice to Italy, visited Florence and Rome, but I had to flee from everywhere because of the bitter cold, snow and—no stoves. Now I am in Yalta and am warming up.

You ask if I read what they write about me everywhere. No, abroad I rarely looked at Russian papers, but Burenin's abuse I did read. I have never been a petitioner nor did I once solicit one word about me

---

[1] An island in the White Sea.

[1] N. P. Kondakov, an archaeologist and historian of art, was in 1898 elected to the Academy of Science, Department of Russian Language and Literature. Chekhov met him in Yalta, where he spent his summers.

in the papers, and Burenin is well aware of this, and only God knows why he had to accuse me of self-advertising and pour slops on me.

Kovalevsky traveled into Italy with me; we spoke about you more than once, and he sends you his greetings. As yet nothing is known about his professorship,[2] he only laughs gaily; in June he is leaving for America to lecture, and it appears that he has already received ten thousand francs.

In your letter you expressed the wish to write me about the plans of the Art Theater. Thank you, I shall be looking forward to it impatiently. It seems to me that actors with a feeling for their art who are used to the small Moscow theater will be intimidated by and will not make themselves heard in the Panayevsky Theater,[3] that monster. * * *

Your sincerely devoted,

A. Chekhov

TO M. P. CHEKHOV

Yalta, February 22, 1901

Dear Michel,

I am back from abroad and now I can answer your letter. That you will live in Petersburg is, of course, very good and salutary, but as for employment by Suvorin, I cannot tell you anything definite, although I devoted a good deal of thought to it. Of course, if I were you, I would have preferred employment at the printing press, and rejected the newspaper. *New Times* has a very bad reputation at present, only self-complacent, well-fed people work for it (except Aleksandr, who sees nothing). Suvorin is deceitful, terribly deceitful, particularly in his so-called frankest moments, that is, he may speak sincerely, but it is impossible to guarantee that half an hour later he won't act in a fashion contrary to his words. Be that as it may, it is not a comfortable situation, God help you, and my advice can scarcely be of any use to you. As Suvorin's employee, bear in mind every day that it is not at all difficult

[2] Rumor had it that the eminent expatriate would be allowed to return home to lecture.

[3] In Petersburg.

to break with him, and therefore have a Government position in reserve, or be an attorney. * * *

Write me details, if there are any. Mother is well.

Your A. Chekhov

TO O. L. KNIPPER

Yalta, February 26, 1901

Darling, today is already February 26, but no letters from you, no! Why? Do you have nothing to write about, or has Petersburg with its newspapers exasperated you to such an extent that you have given me up too? This will not do, my sweet, this is all rubbish. I read only *New Times* and *The Petersburg Gazette,* and I am not indignant, I knew a long time ago how it would be. From *New Times* I didn't expect, nor do I expect anything but scurvy tricks, and in *The Petersburg Gazette* the theater critic who holds forth is Kugel, who will never forgive you for playing Yelena Andreyevna,[1] the part that belongs to Kholmskaya, that most vapid actress, his mistress. I received a telegram from Posse about how downhearted you all are. Spit, my love, spit on all these notices, and cheer up.

Won't you come to Yalta with Masha in Holy Week, and then we shall return to Moscow together? What do you say? Think it over, my joy.

I felt not quite well, coughed, etc.; now I am better, today I went for a stroll by the sea.

On February 28 *New Times* has a celebration.[2] I fear that the celebration will be marred by a scandal.[3] I am sorry not for *New Times* but for those who will make the row.

How long will you keep from writing me? A month? A year?

I kiss you ardently, ardently, my own. May the Lord bless you.

Your Antonius, priest-monk

[1] In *Uncle Vanya.*
[2] The twenty-fifth anniversary of Suvorin's ownership of the newspaper.
[3] Because of the paper's reactionary stand.

TO O. L. KNIPPER

Yalta, March 1, 1901

My dear, don't read newspapers, don't read at all, or you will quite pine away. Let this be a lesson to you for the future: heed what the elder priest-monk tells you. I said to you—you know—I tried to persuade you that in Petersburg things would not go well with you—you should have listened to me. In any event, your company will never go there again—and thank God.

Personally, I am giving up the theater altogether, I will never work for it again. One can write for the stage in Germany, in Sweden, even in Spain, but not in Russia, where dramatists are not respected, are kicked by hoofs and forgiven neither success nor failure. You are abused now for the first time in your life, that is why you take it so hard, yet you will get over it in time, you will get used to it. But I can imagine how marvelous, how glorious Sanin's feelings are! He probably carries the notices in his pockets and lifts his eyebrows high, high. . . .

We are having remarkable weather here, warm, sunny, apricots and almonds blossoming. I expect you in Holy Week, my poor, berated actress, I expect you, expect you, bear that in mind.

Between February 20 and 28 I sent you five letters and three telegrams, but not a word in response. * * *

Write and tell me when you plan to leave Petersburg. Write, actress. I am well—word of honor.

I hug you.

Your priest-monk

TO N. P. KONDAKOV

Yalta, March 2, 1901

Much esteemed Nikodim Pavlovich!

I thank you heartily for the book.[1] I read it with great interest and much pleasure. It happens that fifty years ago my mother, a native of the Shuya district, would visit her kinfolk, who were icon painters, in Palekh and Sergeyevo (two miles from Palekh). At the time icon painters were very prosperous; in Sergeyevo her relatives lived in a huge two-story house with a mezzanine. When I told Mother about the subject of your book she perked up and started telling about Palekh

[1] *The Present Condition of Russian Folk Painting* (1901).

and Sergeyevo, about this house which was old even then. According to her recollection, icon painters were in easy circumstances, she heard of large orders received from Moscow and Petersburg for the great churches.

Yes, the powers of the people are great and varied, but they cannot resurrect the dead. You call iconography a craft and as such it is a cotter industry; little by little it took on the character of the Jacquot and Bonaker factory, and if you close it, other factories will spring up which will produce pictures on boards, as prescribed, but Kholuy [2] and Palekh will not come to life. Icon painting was alive and strong as long as it was an art, not a craft, when there were gifted masters at the fore. But when "painting" [3] appeared in Russia, when it was taught, and painters were elevated to the rank of the nobility, then came Vasnetzovs and Ivanovs,[4] and in Kholuy and Palekh only craftsmen remained and iconography became a craft.

Incidentally, in the peasants' huts there are practically no icons; the old images had gone up in smoke, the new ones are altogether casual, painted on paper or foil.

I have neither seen nor read *Hannele*, so that I don't know what kind of a play it is. But I like Hauptmann and consider him a great dramatist. * * *

Of late I have been indisposed. I have had a cough of the kind that has not assailed me for a long time.

Your book is written with warmth, indeed, with passion, and one takes keen interest in reading it. Undoubtedly, iconography (Palekh and Kholuy) is dying or moribund; if only someone turned up who would write a history of Russian icon painting! It is a subject, you know, to which one could devote one's whole life.

My heart tells me, however, that I am boring you. The public has laughed at Tolstoy's excommunication.[5] In vain did the bishops insert a Church-Slavic text into their statement. It was all too insincere, or

---

[2] This, like Palekh and Sergeyevo, mentioned above, was a village the inhabitants of which specialized in icon painting.

[3] The term refers to the art as distinct from iconography, which was subject to a set of rules that left no freedom to the worker's imagination.

[4] Viktor Mikhailovich Vasnetzov (1848–1926) and Aleksandr Andreyevich Ivanov (1806–58) were artists who devoted themselves to religious painting not bound by the prescriptions of iconography.

[5] The excommunication by the Most Holy Synod took place in 1901.

smelling of insincerity. Keep well, God guard you, and if possible don't
forget your respectful and devoted

A. Chekhov

TO O. L. KNIPPER

Yalta, March 7, 1901

I have received an anonymous letter to the effect that you have taken
a fancy to someone in Petersburg and are head over heels in love.
Indeed, I myself have long since suspected it, you miserly little Jewess.
And me you have stopped loving, because I, a wastrel, asked you to
bankrupt yourself with one or two telegrams. Well, so be it, but I still
love you out of old habit, and you see on what cheap paper I am writing
you.

You miser, why didn't you write me that you were remaining in
Petersburg for a fourth week and not going to Moscow? And I kept
putting off writing you, in the belief that you were going home.

I am alive and, I think, well, although I go on coughing furiously.
I work in the garden, where the trees are already blossoming; the
weather is marvelous, as marvelous as your letters, which now come
from abroad. The latest ones are from Naples. Oh, how splendid you
you are, darling, and how clever! I read every letter over three times—
this is the minimum. And so I work in the garden; in the study there
is little work done, I don't feel like doing anything, I read proof and
am glad that it takes up time. I rarely go to town, I have no desire to
do so, but the townsfolk visit me for hours on end, so that I grow dejected every time and begin to tell myself that I will leave the place
again or get married so that my wife will chase them out, that is, my
guests. I'll get a divorce from Yekaterinoslav [1] province and get married again. Allow me to make you an offer.

I have brought you some very fine perfume from abroad. Come and
fetch it in Holy Week. Be sure to come, my wonderful darling: if you
don't come, you will hurt me deeply, you will poison my existence. I
have already begun waiting for you, I count the days and hours. It
doesn't matter that you're in love with someone else and have already
been unfaithful to me, I'll forgive you, only do come, please. Do you
hear, my pet? You know I love you, understand that. Already it is hard

---

[1] Taganrog was in that province.

for me to live without you. If plans are being made at your theater for rehearsals at Easter, tell Nemirovich that it is vile and swinish of him.

I have just been downstairs and had tea with ring-shaped rolls. Kondakov, the academician, writes me that he attended a performance of *Three Sisters* and his enthusiasm is indescribable. You haven't written a word about the dinners tendered in your honor. So you might write me now, at least, in the name of friendship. I am a friend of yours, a close friend, you dog, you.

Today I had a long telegram from Solovtzov [2] about a performance of *Three Sisters* in Kiev, an enormous, desperate success and the like. The next play I write will without fail be a comedy, very amusing, at least in conception.

Now, granny, keep well, cheer up, don't be blue, don't mope. I, too, have been honored with a wire from Madame Yavorskaya about *Uncle Vanya*. She used to come to your theater with the airs of a Sarah Bernhardt, no less, sincerely intent on making the whole company happy by her attention. And you nearly got into a fight with her!

I kiss you eighty times and embrace you closely. Remember I'll wait for you. Remember!

Your priest-monk Antonius

TO O. L. KNIPPER

Yalta, March 16, 1901

Greetings, my little dear!

I am certainly coming to Moscow, but I don't know whether I'll go to Sweden this year. I am fed up with gadding about, and besides it seems as if I were getting to be quite an old man as far as health is concerned, so that, by the way, you will acquire in my person not a husband but a grandfather. I dig in my garden now for whole days together, the weather is warm, exquisite, everything's in flower, the birds are singing, there are no visitors, it is simply not life but peaches and cream. I have quite given up literature, and when I marry you, I'll order you to give up the stage and we'll live together like planters. You don't want to? Very well, then, go on acting another five years and then we shall see.

[2] An actor associated with Korsh's theater and himself owner of a theater in Kiev.

Today, out of the blue, I received *The Russian Veteran*, a special army newspaper, and in it I found a notice of *Three Sisters*. It is Number 56, March 11. It's all right, it's laudatory, and finds no fault with the military side.

Write to me, my good darling, your letters give me joy. You are unfaithful to me because, as you write, you are a human being and a woman; oh, very well, be unfaithful, only be the good, splendid person that you are. I am an old geezer, it is impossible to keep from being unfaithful to me, I understand that very well, and if I happen to be unfaithful to you, you will excuse it, because you realize that though the beard turns gray, the devil's at play. Isn't that so?

Do you see Lidiya Avilova? Have you made friends with Olga Chyumina? [1] I suspect you've already begun writing stories and novels in secret. If I catch you, then good-bye. I'll divorce you.

I read about Pchelnikov's appointment [2] in the papers, and I was astonished, astonished that Pchelnikov was not above accepting such a queer position. But they'll hardly take *Dr. Stockman* off your repertory, it's a conservative play, you know.

Though I have given up literature, still I write something now and then, out of habit. Just now I am writing a story called "The Bishop," on a subject that has been in my head for fifteen years.

I embrace you, traitress, a hundred times, I kiss you hard. Write, write, my joy, or else when we are married, I'll beat you.

Your Elder Ant—

TO O. L. KNIPPER

Yalta, April 22, 1901

My dear, wonderful Knipschitz, I did not keep you from leaving,[1] because Yalta disgusts me and because I thought that I should soon see you at large, anyway. In any case, you are cross for no reason, my darling. I have no secret thoughts, I tell you everything I think.

[1] Olga Nikolayevna Chyumina was a writer of verse and a translator.
[2] P. M. Pchelnikov was appointed inspector of the repertory theaters not financed by the Government, and supervisor of their effect on the public.
[1] She had been in Yalta a fortnight: March 30–April 14.

Early in May I'll come to Moscow and, if possible, we shall be married and sail down the Volga, or first sail down the Volga and then be married—whatever you find more convenient. . . . Then all winter or the greater part of it I shall live in Moscow in the same apartment with you. If only I keep well and don't give in to myself. My cough saps all my energy, I think limply about the future and write without any zest. You do the thinking about the future, you be the mistress of the house, I'll do whatever you tell me. Otherwise we shall not live, but just swallow a tablespoonful of life every hour.

So you are left without a role now? That pleases me very much. * * * What shall I find in your theater? What is being rehearsed? *Michael Kramer? The Wild Duck?* There are moments when I am overwhelmed by the strongest desire to write a long skit or a comedy in four acts for the Art Theater. And I shall do so if nothing prevents me, but I shall turn it over to the theater not before the end of 1903.

I shall telegraph you, don't tell anybody, and come to the station alone to meet me. Do you hear? Well, see you soon, my darling, my sweet little girl.

Do not be downhearted, do not think up God knows what; I have nothing whatever that I would hide from you for even a single minute. Be kind, don't be cross.

I kiss you fervently, dog.

Your Antoine

TO O. L. KNIPPER

Yalta, Thursday, April 26, 1901

Dog Olka! I shall come early in May. As soon as you get my telegram, go immediately to the Dresden Hotel and inquire if Room 45 is free, in other words, reserve a cheap room.

I often see Nemirovich, he is very nice, does not put on airs; I haven't yet seen his spouse. I am coming to Moscow chiefly to gallivant and gorge myself. We'll go to Petrovsko-Razumovskoe,[1] to Zvenigorod [2]

---

[1] A picturesque monastery.
[2] A town near Moscow.

—we'll go everywhere, provided the weather is good. If you consent to go down the Volga with me, we'll eat sturgeon.

Kuprin [3] is apparently in love—under an enchantment. He fell in love with a huge, husky woman whom you know and whom you advised me to marry.

If you give me your word that not a soul in Moscow will know about our wedding until it has taken place, I am ready to marry you on the very day of my arrival. For some reason I am terribly afraid of the wedding ceremony and congratulations and the champagne that you must hold in your hand while you smile vaguely. I wish we could go straight from church to Zvenigorod. Or perhaps we could get married in Zvenigorod. Think, think, darling! You are clever, they say.

The weather in Yalta is rather wretched. A fierce wind. The roses are blooming, but not fully; they will, though. The irises are magnificent.

Everything is all right with me, except for one trifle: my health.

Gorky has not been deported, but arrested; [4] he is held in Nizhny. Posse, too, has been arrested.

I embrace you, Olka.

Your Antoine

TO M. P. CHEKHOVA

Moscow, May 20, 1901

Dear Masha,

* * * Well, I went to see Dr. Shchurovsky. He found a dullness both on the left and on the right. On the right a large area under the shoulder blade is affected, and he ordered me to take the kumiss cure immediately in the Province of Ufa. And if the kumiss doesn't agree with me, I must go to Switzerland. The cure takes two months and is most boring and uncomfortable. I just don't know what to do, how to manage. It's boring to stay at the sanatorium, and to take someone along

---

[3] Aleksandr Ivanovich Kuprin (1870–1938), a novelist and short-story writer. After the October Revolution he emigrated, but returned to the Soviet Union.

[4] Gorky was charged with having been active in the Social Democratic organization in Nizhny Novgorod.

would be selfish and therefore unpleasant. I would get married [1] but I don't have the documents with me, they are all in Yalta, in my desk. * * *

Your A. Chekhov

TO M. P. CHEKHOVA

Aksyonovo, June 2, 1901

Greetings, darling Masha!

I am constantly getting ready to write you and simply can't get ready, no matter what; there is a lot to be attended to, things of all sorts and, of course, of a petty nature. About my having married you already know. This action of mine will not, I think, change in the least my way of life and that setting which has been mine up to the present. Mother is probably saying God knows what by now, but tell her that there will be no changes whatsoever—everything will remain as of old. I will keep on living as I have lived up to the present and Mother will follow the same course, and my relations with you will remain unalterably cordial and pleasant, as they have been up to now.

My health is fair—even good for the time being; the coughing has decreased—it is almost nonexistent. Toward the end of July I shall be in Yalta, where I shall stay until October, and then go to Moscow and stay there till December, then go again to Yalta. Consequently I shall have to live apart from my spouse—that, however, is something I have already become accustomed to. * * *

Your Antoine

---

[1] In response to this letter, on May 24 Masha wrote as follows: "For me personally the wedding ceremony is a horror. You too could do without these superfluous excitements. Those who love you will not abandon you, and there is no question of sacrifice on one side or of the slightest egoism on the other. How could the idea have entered your head? What egoism?! You'll always have time to get hitched. Pass this on to your Knipschitz. What must be thought of first and foremost is that you should be well." She concluded her letter thus: "In any event act according to your own judgment. But perhaps in this matter I am prejudiced."

Chekhov's wedding to Olga Knipper took place on May 25, 1901, in the Church of the Holy Cross in Moscow. The four prescribed witnesses were her brother, Vladimir; her uncle, Captain Aleksandr Ivanovich Zaltza; F. I. Seifert, a law student; and D. V. Alekseyev, a student of chemistry. After the ceremony the couple visited Knipper's mother. Chekhov sent a telegram to his own mother, reading: "Dear Mama, bless us, I am getting married. Everything remains as before. I am leaving for the kumiss cure. Health better." Husband and wife then left for the sanatorium.

Dear Masha,

The letter [2] in which you advise me not to get married was forwarded to me here [3] from Moscow and reached me yesterday. I don't know whether or not I made a mistake, but my reason for getting married was chiefly because, first, I am now over forty, second, Olga comes of an excellent family, and third, if it becomes necessary for us to part, I shall do so without debating the matter, as if I had not married her: she is, you know, an independent person, a self-supporting woman. Furthermore, there is the important consideration that this marriage has by no means changed either my way of life or that of those who lived or still live with me. Everything, decidedly everything, will remain as it was formerly, and I shall continue to live in Yalta alone.

Your wish to come here, to the Ufa province, made me very happy.[4] If you have really made up your mind to come, it would be wonderful. Get here early in June; we shall stay here awhile, I'll drink kumiss, and then we shall sail down the Volga as far as Novorossisk, thence to Yalta. The best route for you to take is by way of Moscow, Nizhny, and Samara. The distance is greater but in the end you will gain two or three days. When I told Knipschitz that you were coming, she was very glad. Today she left for Ufa to shop. It is rather boring here, but kumiss is tasty, the weather is hot, the fare is not bad. One of these days we'll go fishing.

I am sending you a check for 500 rubles. If this seems too much money and you will not want to keep all that cash in the house, deposit part of it in the State Bank in my name. Sinani will show you how to do it. Take along about a hundred rubles plus money for railway tickets; I have cash and shall give you enough for the return trip.

The address is: Aksyonovo, The Andreyev Sanatorium, Province of Ufa.

---

[1] The addressee left instructions that this letter should not be published. She herself included part of it, however, in a book that she edited shortly before her death in 1957. The entire letter was not published until 1960.

[2] See Masha's letter of May 24, quoted in note 1 to Chekhov's letter of May 20, p. 401.

[3] A sanatorium where he had arrived with his wife a few days earlier.

[4] Sensibly, she did not come. Eventually sister and wife resumed their friendship.

Kumiss does not upset my stomach. Apparently it will continue to agree with me.

A low bow and greetings to Mamasha. Thank Varvara Konstantinovna [5] for her telegram. Keep well and serene. Write more often.

Your Anton

TO A. F. KONI

Aksyonovo, June 12, 1901

Your photograph, mueh esteemed Anatoly Fyodorovich, which I have just received, is excellent, one of the most felicitous. Hearty thanks for it and for congratulating me on my marriage and in general for remembering and writing me. This place, where I drink kumiss, is horribly boring, the newspapers are of yesteryear, the public is stodgy, Bashkirs [1] everywhere, and if it were not for nature and fishing and letters, I would probably take to my heels.

Of late in Yalta I coughed a great deal and, I think, had fever. In Moscow Dr. Shchurovsky, a good physician, found my condition markedly worse: formerly the dulling was only in the apexes of my lungs, by now it is in front below the collarbone and in the back it has spread to the upper half of the shoulder blade. This somewhat troubled me, I hastened to get married, and went off to drink kumiss. Now I am well, have gained eight pounds, only I don't know to what I owe this improvement: the kumiss or the marriage. I have almost stopped coughing.

Olga sends you greetings and thanks you cordially.

Next year please go to see her in *The Sea Gull* (which will be staged in Petersburg), she is very good in it, it seems to me.

I wish you health and all the best.

Sincerely,
your devoted A. Chekhov

---

[5] Varvara Konstantinovna Kharkeyevich was headmistress of the Yalta high school for girls.

[1] A people of Turkish stock, the basic population of what is now the Autonomous Bashkir Soviet Socialist Republic.

TO M. P. CHEKHOVA

Yalta, August 3, 1901

Dear Masha,

I will you for possession during your lifetime my house in Yalta, the money and royalties from my dramatic works, and to my wife, Olga Leonardovna, the cottage at Gurzuf and five thousand rubles. If you wish, you may sell the immovables. Hand our brother Aleksandr three thousand, Ivan five thousand, and Mikhail three thousand, Aleksey Dolzhenko [1] one thousand, and Yelena Chekhova,[2] if she gets married— one thousand rubles. After your death and Mother's death everything that remains, except the royalties from the plays, is placed at the disposal of the Taganrog municipality for public education; as for the royalties from the plays, they go to our brother Ivan and, after Ivan's death, to the Taganrog municipality also for public education. I promised one hundred rubles to the peasants of the village of Melikhovo in payment for the paved road; I also promised Gavril Alekseyevich Kharchenko [3] (Kharkov, Moskalevka, his own house) to pay for the high school education of his elder daughter until she is granted free tuition. Help the poor. Take care of Mother. Live peacefully.

Anton Chekhov

TO O. L. KNIPPER

Yalta, August 28, 1901

Doggie, my dear puppy, I have just received your letter, read it twice— and I kiss you a thousand times. I like the plan of the apartment, I'll show it to Masha (she left to see Dunya Konovinitzer off on a steamer), everything is splendid, but why did you place "Anton's study" near a certain closet? Want to get a thrashing?

I am answering your questions. I sleep wonderfully, though it's terribly dull to sleep alone (got used to it), eat heartily, talk with guests all day long. I drink kefir [1] every day with zest, my interior has been

---

[1] Aleksey Alekseyevich Dolzhenko, a cousin of Chekhov's.
[2] Daughter of Chekhov's uncle Mitrofan.
[3] Employed in boyhood in the Chekhov grocery.
[1] Fermented milk.

in order so far, I do not rub my neck with eau de cologne—forgot. Yesterday I washed my head.

I looked in on Orlenev [2] yesterday, got acquainted with Leventon,[3] she shares quarters with him.

Masha will take you some almonds from our tree.

You see what kind of husband I am: I write you every day most punctually. I miss you so much! Every morning I prick up my ears, hoping to hear the Hungarian [4] pass by with a bucket. It seems to me that I have become a regular philistine and cannot live without a spouse. * * *

Behave yourself, or I will beat you until it hurts. Write, darling, don't be lazy.

Your Ant.

TO O. L. KNIPPER

Yalta, September 3, 1901

Dear Olka, greetings!

Yesterday I didn't write you, because, first, there were many guests, and, second, I had no time: I sat and worked on my story.[1]

Thank you, my joy, Mother was very glad to have your letter: she read it and then gave it to me to read aloud to her and she took a long time praising you. What you write about your jealousy is perhaps not without grounds, but you are so intelligent and you have such a good heart that what you write about your supposed jealousy doesn't tally with your character.[2] You write that Masha will never get used to you, and so on, and so on. What nonsense! You exaggerate everything, you imagine foolish things, and I am afraid that, for all I know, you will be quarreling with Masha. Here is what I tell you: have patience and keep silent only one year, only one year, and then everything will be straightened out for you. No matter what is said to you, no matter how things seem to you, you play dumb, play dumb. For newly married

---

[2] Pavel Nikolayevich Orlenev, an actor.
[3] The actress Alla Aleksandrovna Leventon.
[4] One of Chekhov's jocular nicknames for his wife.
[1] "The Bishop."
[2] In her letter of August 30 Olga had expressed the wish to keep Chekhov entirely to herself.

couples all the comforts of life depend on this nonresistance in the early days. Do as I say, darling, be sensible!

I shall come when you write, but in any case no later than September 15. You may do what you like, but I don't intend to be patient any longer. I shall stay in Moscow till December, until you chase me out.

Little German, send me Nemirovich's play. I will bring it back intact. I'll read it very attentively.

I'll bring very few clothes with me and buy the rest in Moscow. I'll buy warm underwear and a new overcoat. Also a plaid and galoshes. (I'll come in my old overcoat.) In a word, I shall try to travel without luggage.

I am installing a huge wardrobe for me and my spouse. She is very cross, and I must make life as comfortable for her as possible.

I kiss and embrace my old woman. May God guard you. In a little while we shall see each other. Write, write, darling, write! Other than you I shall never love anyone, not any woman at all.

Be well and merry.

Your husband Anton

TO V. S. MIROLYUBOV[1]

Moscow, October 19, 1901

Dear Viktor Sergeyevich, greetings!

I have received your letter; many thanks. At present I am in Moscow, but no later than next week, probably on Wednesday, I am leaving for Yalta, where I shall stay all winter long, without venturing elsewhere. And, all winter long, I shall be at work. Forgive me, dear man, for having failed to send you the story [2] so far. That is due to my having interrupted work on it, since I have always found it difficult to finish work that has been interrupted.

Now, rest assured, I shall come home, make a fresh start on the story, and send it off to you! * * *

My wife, to whom I have become accustomed and attached, remains in Moscow by herself, and I am leaving alone. She cries but I shan't

[1] The editor of a monthly, *The Magazine for All;* formerly a singer attached to the Bolshoi Theater.
[2] "The Bishop."

let her abandon the stage. In short, it's a muddle. Keep well, dear man. Write me more often.

Your A. Chekhov

Gorky is in Nizhny, in good health. He sent a play [3] to the Art Theater. There's nothing new in it, but it's a good play.

TO O. L. KNIPPER

Yalta, November 7, 1901

You behave like a glutton, because in every letter you write about eating, asking if I eat much and so forth. Ducky, I eat heartily! Please don't fret. I drink no milk, there is none in Yalta, but then I dine and sup like a crocodile, enough to nourish a dozen.

You want to give up the theater? It seemed so to me when I read your letter. Do you? Think it over carefully, darling, and then make your decision. I shall live in Moscow all winter—bear that in mind.

I was traveling from Sevastopol by carriage, it was cold, cheerless, but the worst was that the drivers, while unharnessing the horses, dropped my box with the clock in it. I had to have it repaired, pay 3 rubles, and now, when it strikes, it seems to me that it is indisposed. It keeps time correctly. So does my pocket watch.

I have just caught two mice. Consequently, no one can say that I do nothing. Did you go to see *The Irinsk Commune* [1]? What did you think of it? Write me. I haven't yet received a single long letter from you, not a single letter with discussions about something. And I love you so when you engage in discussions.

I am afraid that you are sick of me or that little by little you are losing the habit of me—I cannot say so definitely, but I am apprehensive.

The weather is calm, it is cloudy and cool; obviously, winter is coming. Did you dine with Luzhsky? [2] For my part, I haven't managed to drop in on him. In *Michael Kramer* [3] he is good, positively good, especially in Act II. In Act III he is hampered, bewildered, nevertheless one

---

[3] *The Vulgarians*. The Russian word (*meshchane*) could also be translated as philistine, lower middle class, smug townfolk; the American equivalent is Babbitts.

[1] A play by A. I. Sumbatov-Youzhin (he used the second half of his name as a pseudonym), an actor, playwright, and director in one of the Moscow theaters.

[2] An actor with the Moscow Art Theater.

[3] A play by Gerhart Hauptmann. Chekhov had attended a rehearsal of the play.

feels him to be quite an actor. In general, all of you have done *Kramer* wonderfully. Alekseyev [4] is very good; and if our theater critics were keen and broadminded people, the play would have been a brilliant success.

Do not forget that you have a husband. Remember!

All is well in our garden, there is great abundance, and yet it is a sorry sight! I despise nature hereabouts, it leaves me cold.

What if you suddenly took off and came to Yalta for two or three days! You would need no more than one week for this. . . . I would meet you in Sevastopol. In Sevastopol I would be living with you. . . . Eh? Well, God keep you in any case!

I love you—you have known this for a long time. I kiss you 1,013,212 times. Think of me.

Your husband Antonio

TO O. L. KNIPPER

Yalta, November 9, 1901

Greetings, my darling!

* * * I instigate all the best writers to write plays for the Art Theater. Gorky has already done so, Balmont,[1] Leonid Andreyev, Teleshev,[2] and others are doing it, too. It would be appropriate if I were given a salary, say one ruble a head.

My letters to you do not altogether satisfy me. After what we experienced, letters are little, we should continue living together. It is sinful of us not to live together. But what's the use of talking about it! God be with you, I bless you, my little Dutchie, and I rejoice that you are cheerful. I kiss you fervently, fervently.

Your Antonio

TO O. L. KNIPPER

Yalta, December 6, 1901

* * * We will go abroad, but not to Italy, not to Nice, let us take off for Norway, the north, from there to Denmark. . . . Do you want to? Shall we go, my dear little nincompoop? And tell your directors that I shan't

---

[4] Stanislavsky, who played the leading part.
[1] Konstantin Dmitriyevich Balmont (1867–1942), poet and translator. He expatriated himself after the Revolution.
[2] Nikolay Dmitriyevich Teleshev, a writer of fiction.

[*409*]

allow you to leave for Moscow before October 1, let them fire you if they like. In August or late in August we'll be having wonderful ripe apples. And pears? Such pears you have never eaten. Were I to give up literature now, my darling, and become a gardener, that would be very good—it would add ten years to my life.

What shall I do about my stomach?

Well, as usual, I kiss you, my joy. Keep well, may God guard you, may there be angels in back of you.

Your Ant.

Today a Greek came and asked for a loan of 600 rubles at interest. A fine reputation I have! [1]

TO O. L. KNIPPER

Yalta, December 13, 1901

My actress, greetings!

I am well again. I don't see any blood, only the weakness hangs on—I haven't eaten properly for a long time now. I believe that in two or three days I shall be hale and hearty. I am taking pills, drops, powders. . . .

You write that on the evening of December 8 you were tipsy. Oh, darling, how I envy you, if you only knew! I envy your liveliness, your freshness, health, high spirits. I envy you because no considerations of hemorrhages and the like prevent you from drinking. I used to be able to get plastered, as they say.* * *

I often think of you, very often, as befits a husband. While I was with you, you spoiled me, and now without you I feel like a person deprived of his rights. Emptiness around me, wretched dinners, no one even calls me on the phone, [and as for sleeping, I say nothing].[1]

I warmly embrace my actress, [my ardent dog].[1] May God keep you. Do not forget me and do not abandon me. I kiss you a hundred thousand times.

Your Anton

[1] In a letter to his wife two days before, Chekhov had written, "Yesterday a wealthy Tartar came and asked for a loan at interest. When I told him that I did not lend money at interest and regarded it as a sin, he was astonished and did not believe me."

[1] The phrases in brackets are material suppressed by the Soviet editor of Chekhov's letters. They appear in an edition of Chekhov's letters to Knipper (Berlin, 1922).

Yalta, December 17, 1901

Dear Viktor Sergeyevich,

I am not well or not altogether well, which is nearer the truth, and I cannot get on with my writing. I spat blood, now there's weakness and spitefulness. I sit with a poultice on my side and take creosote and all sorts of rubbish. Be that as it may, I am not going to cheat you out of "The Bishop." I will send it to you sooner or later.

In *New Times* I read the article [1] by that policeman, Rozanov, from which I learned about your new activities. If you only knew, my dear fellow, how disturbed I was! It seems to me that you must leave Petersburg at once—for Nervi or for Yalta, but leave. What do you, a good, upright human being, have in common with Rozanov, with the foxy, bombastic Sergius,[2] finally with the egregiously sated Merezhkovsky? I would like to write more, much more, but it is best to refrain, all the more so since nowadays letters are read chiefly by those to whom they are not addressed. I shall say only that in the questions which engage you what is important is not the forgotten words, not idealism, but the consciousness of your own integrity, that is, your soul's entire freedom from all kinds of forgotten and unforgotten words, idealisms, etc., and other such unintelligibilities. It is necessary to believe in God and if one has no faith, one ought not replace it with ballyhoo, but seek, seek, seek alone, face to face with one's conscience. . . .

In any case, be well. If you are coming, drop me a line. Tolstoy is here, Gorky is here, you will not be bored, I hope.

No other news. I firmly press your hand.

Your A. Chekhov

TO O. L. KNIPPER

Yalta, December 29, 1901

You are foolish, darling. Never once since I have been married did I reproach you about the theater; on the contrary, I have rejoiced that you are at work, that you have a purpose in life, that you are not aimlessly dangling like your husband. I don't write you about my illness

[1] It announced the foundation of a religio-philosophical society, approved by the Church.
[2] A bishop who was rector of the Petersburg Theological Seminary.

because I am already well. My temperature is normal, I eat five eggs a day, drink milk, and then there is dinner which, since Masha is here, is delicious. Do your work, darling, don't bustle about, above all, do not yield to depression.[1] * * *

Well, my little slattern, good-bye, keep well! Don't dare to mope, don't lament. Laugh! I embrace you and regret that this is all.

There was no letter from you yesterday. What a lazybones you have become! Ah, dog that you are, you dog!

Well, darling, my good, lovely wife, I kiss you warmly and hug you again warmly. I think of you very often, you too think of me.

Your Ant.

TO O. L. KNIPPER

Yalta, December 30, 1901

My darling, hand the enclosed letter to Rayevskaya.[1] If you see Altschuller, buy a pound of candy at Abrikosov's and have him bring it here. Buy some marmalade, too.

It is tedious here without you. Tomorrow I shall go to bed at 9 o'clock in the evening on purpose not to meet the New Year. You are not here, so there is nothing here, and I want nothing.

The weather has taken a turn for the worse. Windy, cold, smell of snow. Obviously winter has started.

I shall write to Nemirovich.

Darling, write me, I implore you! Did I wish you a happy New Year? No? In that case I kiss you warmly and whisper all sorts of silly things in your ear.

Don't forget your husband. You know when he is cross, he is free with his fists!

Well, I hug my spouse.

Husband Ant.

[1] In a letter of December 23 Knipper had written, "It is such torture for me to think that I can't be beside you, to tend you, change compresses, feed you, comfort you. I imagine how you suffered. I give you my word that this is the last such year, my own. I'll do everything to make your life pleasant, warm, no longer lonely, and you'll see, you will be happy with me and you will write, work. In your heart you probably reproach me for not loving you enough. Isn't it true? You reproach me for not chucking the theater, not being a wife to you."

[1] Yevgeniya Mikhailovna Rayevskaya, an actress with the Moscow Art Theater.

[1902]

Yalta, January 20, 1902

How foolish you are, my darling, what a silly! Why are you sulking? What about? You write that everything about your career is exaggerated and that you are a complete nonentity: that I'm tired of your letters, that you are horrified to feel your life narrowing, and so on, and so on. What a silly you are! I didn't write you about my future play not because I have no faith in you, as you write, but because as yet I have no faith in the play. It is just beginning to glimmer in my brain like the earliest ray of dawn, and I myself don't yet know what it is like, what will come of it, and it keeps changing from day to day. If we were face to face, I would talk to you about it, but I mustn't write about it, because I wouldn't be able to put anything down on paper, but would only scribble nonsense and then grow cold to the subject. In your letter you threaten never to ask me about anything, never to meddle in anything; but why do you treat me so, my darling? No, you are a kind soul, wrath will give place to mercy when once more you see how much I love you, how close you are to me, how I can't live without you, my little silly. Give up moping, give it up! Burst out laughing! I am permitted to mope, for I live in a desert, have nothing to do, see no one and am ill every week, but you? Somehow your life is full.* * *

By the way, Gorky is preparing to start work on a new play about the life of people in a flophouse, though I advise him to wait a year or two, not to be in a hurry. A writer must write a good deal, but he ought not hurry. Isn't that so, my spouse?

On January 17, my name day, I was in a disgusting mood, because I felt ill and because the telephone kept clamoring, bringing me telegrams of congratulation. Even you and Masha didn't spare me.

Incidentally, when is your *Geburtstag?*

You write: don't be sad—we shall soon see each other. What does this mean? Do we meet in Holy Week? Or sooner? Don't upset me, my joy. In December you wrote me that you would come in January, you disturbed me, you stirred me up; then you began writing that you were coming in Holy Week—and I commanded my soul to be still, I hemmed myself in, and now again you are suddenly raising a storm on the Black Sea. What for? * * *

And so, my wife, nice, good, golden one, may God protect you, be well and cheerful, think of your husband at least in the evening, at bedtime. Above all, don't be dejected. You know your husband is not a drunkard, not a spendthrift, not a ruffian; in my behavior I am totally a German husband; I even wear warm drawers. . . .

I embrace my wife one hundred and one times and kiss her end- lessly.

Your Ant.

You write, "No matter where I turn—walls everywhere." And where did you turn?

TO O. L. KNIPPER

Yalta, January 21, 1902

My dear Olyukha, no letter from you today. Angry at me? Or are you in a low mood generally? Yesterday I suddenly received a tele- gram from you. My darling, if I fall ill, I will surely wire you, don't worry. If I have nothing to say about my health, it means that I am hale and hearty, strong as an ox.

How vile our cheap journalism is! Every day these people write something about me, about Gorky—and all lies. Disgusting.

It's a pity that you have forbidden me to write about the weather, when there is much that is interesting in that department. There is nothing to do about it, I'll hold my tongue.

You are rehearsing Act II of Gorky's *The Vulgarians* and it is already January, so obviously the play will not be staged this season. Or will you have time for it? Gorky is starting a new play as I have already reported to you, but Chekhov hasn't yet done so.* * *

My good, dear, wonderful darling, be nice, don't be glum, don't mope, and forgive me if on occasion my letters offer you nothing. I am not to blame, or only partly, so have mercy and do not punish me if sometimes my letter does not please you. If you only knew how much

I love you, how I dream about you, then you wouldn't write me anything in a sour vein.

I embrace my wife and kiss her, which I have a perfect right to do, since I am married to her. I even stroke your broad back. So, keep well and cheerful.

> *Your husband in woolen underdrawers,*
> *A., the German*

TO O. L. KNIPPER

Yalta, January 29, 1902

Again on a spree, gay dog! Well, this is good, this is capital, I love you for it, only don't wear yourself out.

How inept to have awarded me the Griboyedov Prize![1] It will get me nothing but Burenin's abuse; besides, I am too old for such encouragement.

You will come for two days? For only two? It is like giving Tanner [2] only a teaspoonful of milk after a forty days' fast. It will merely unnerve me, give us another separation to suffer—and, my darling, isn't it better for you to delay your coming until the end of Lent? Think. To come for two days—this is cruel, realize it! Two days—that's Nemirovich's present, no, thank you! If I endured it till February, I will endure it till the end of Lent. Two days will be just enough to tire you out with the trip and to unnerve me with expectation and then at once distress me with parting. No, no, no!

Your latest letters are very good, my darling, I read them more than once.

I love you, dog, I can't help it.

Write me, I'll write as usual.

> *Your Ant.*

I embrace my gay dog.

If you don't give up your intention of coming at the end of Shrovetide, be informed that I consent to your staying five days—no less! Five days and six nights.

[1] The Griboyedov Prize was awarded to Chekhov for *Three Sisters* by the Society of Playwrights and Opera Composers. Aleksandr Sergeyevich Griboyedov (1794–1829) was the author of a remarkable comedy in verse, *Woe from Wit*, which during his lifetime circulated widely in manuscript.

[2] An American doctor who studied the effect of prolonged starving by subjecting himself to it.

TO M. P. LILINA[1]

Yalta, February 3, 1902

Dear Mariya Petrovna,

You are very kind, thank you very much for your letter. I regret that I cannot tell you anything of interest, for there is nothing new or interesting as far as we in Yalta are concerned, we live as in some forlorn provincial hole, grow old, drink decoctions of medicinal herbs, wear felt boots. . . . There is, however, one item by way of news, a very pleasant one: Lev Tolstoy's recovery. The Count had been very seriously ill, he had contracted pneumonia, from which old men like him do not usually recover. For two or three days we were expecting the end, but suddenly our old man came to and things began to look up. At this writing hope has been considerably strengthened, and when you read these lines, Lev Nikolayevich will probably be in good health.

As for Gorky, he feels fairly well, is spry, but bored, and is preparing to start a new play—he already has the subject. As far as I can judge, in about five years he will be writing excellent plays, but right now he seems to be fumbling.

What you tell me confidentially in your letter about Konstantin Sergeyevich and my spouse made me extraordinarily happy. Thank you, now I shall take measures, this very day I shall start proceedings for a divorce.[2] I am sending an application to the consistory and am enclosing your letter with it. I believe that by spring I shall be a free man, but before May I'll let that wife of mine have it. She is afraid of me, I don't stand on ceremony with her, you know—I do what I damn please!

A bow and a cordial greeting to Konstantin Sergeyevich. I congratulate both of you on the new theater,[3] which, I am sure, will be a success.

A bow to you, I kiss your hand and bow again.

Your sincerely devoted
A. Chekhov

---

[1] An actress, the wife of K. S. Stanislavsky.
[2] The addressee had written in jest that her husband was paying court to Knipper.
[3] The Art Theater had removed to a new building.

TO V. S. MIROLYUBOV

Yalta, March 8, 1902

Dear Viktor Sergeyevich,

* * * I beg you once more: if the censor crosses out even only one word, do not print the piece.[1] I shall send you another story. As it is, while writing, I already cut and abridged much, with an eye to the censorship.

Remember this request of mine, I beg you.

The Art Theater is now in Petersburg. How things are going there I do not know. I don't hear a word from them. Things must be sluggish? Dismal? However, there is no making head or tail of anything, including the public, in this world.

Many thanks for the telegram about my election to the Academy. * * * Write me two or three lines.

Your A. Chekhov

TO V. G. KOROLENKO

Yalta, March 19, 1902

Dear Vladimir Galaktionovich,

During the entire winter I did nothing at all because of illness. Now I am better, I am almost well, but what will come later I don't know, and so I cannot say anything definite about the story for the collection.[1] I shall let you know in July or August—my situation will then be clearer. As regards *Russian Wealth*, I shall send you a story or a novella at the first opportunity. I am in sympathy with what this monthly stands for, I love it and would gladly contribute to it.

Today I received a letter from a member of the Academy [2] giving me this information: "Yesterday (March 11) there was a special session of the Division of Belles Lettres, again in the Marble Palace, on the subject of the Maxim Gorky incident.[3] The meeting heard an imperial

---

[1] "The Bishop," which was to be published in *The Magazine for All*, edited by the addressee. The periodical offered outstanding fiction and scholarly essays, yet was popular.

[1] A miscellany in memory of Gogol, to be issued in commemoration of the fiftieth anniversary of his death.

[2] N. P. Kondakov.

[3] The cancellation of Gorky's election to the Academy.

reprimand to the effect that the Emperor was 'deeply aggrieved' by the election and that henceforth the names of candidates would be submitted for consideration to his Majesty and to the Ministry of the Interior by the Ministry of Education."

By the way, Gorky, who is now living in Olenza, came to see me today. Tolstoy is improving.

All the best to you, I press your hand firmly.

Many thanks for having remembered me and for the letter.

Your A. Chekhov

TO N. P. KONDAKOV

Yalta, April 2, 1902

Much esteemed and dear Nikodim Pavlovich!

I should like very much to see you and talk with you, so as to learn the details of the last Academic elections. Much is still unclear to me; at least, I do not know what to do, to remain an honorary Academician or to resign.

Be well and prosperous.

Your A. Chekhov

TO V. G. KOROLENKO

Yalta, April 19, 1902

Dear Vladimir Galaktionovich,

My wife came from Petersburg with a high temperature ($39°[C]$), very weak, in severe pain; she was unable to walk, she was carried from the steamer. . . . Now she seems to be a little better. . . .[1]

I am not going to hand Tolstoy your statement.[2] When I broached the subject of Gorky and the Academy to him, he remarked, "I do not consider myself an Academician," and again stuck his nose in his book.

[1] Late in March Olga was taken ill in Petersburg and underwent an operation. Chekhov did not hear of it until the beginning of April. In response to a telegram from him, she came to Yalta on April 14. Some six weeks later they went to Moscow together.

[2] The reference is to Korolenko's resignation as an honorary Academician, in protest against the cancellation of Gorky's election to the Academy. Korolenko requested Chekhov to pass the document on to Gorky and to Tolstoy, another Academician.

Somehow it seems to me that there will be no Academy meeting on May 25, for early in May the Academicians will have already left town. It seems to me also that, far from being re-elected, he will be blackballed.[3] I am very eager to see you and talk things over. Won't you come to Yalta? I would come to Poltava, but cannot manage it, what with my wife's illness, which will probably last some three weeks.* * *

I press your hand and wish you all the best. Keep well.

Your A. Chekhov

P.S. Greetings from my wife.

TO M. P. CHEKHOVA

Moscow, June 2, 1902

Dear Masha,

We are again in trouble. Yesterday at 10 P.M. on the eve of Trinity Sunday Olga felt sharp pains in her abdomen (worse than she had had in Yalta), then came groans, screams, sobs; all the doctors had left for their summer cottages; all acquaintances too were out of town. . . . Fortunately, Vishnevsky appeared at midnight, and began running around for a doctor. Olga was in pain all night; this morning a doctor came; it was decided to place her in Strauch's hospital. Overnight she became markedly hollow-cheeked and thin.* * *

I don't know what I shall be doing now, where I shall go and when I'll leave Moscow. Everything is topsy-turvy.

For some reason Anna Ivanovna [1] feels that she is to blame, that's how she looks. All night long she was trying to find a doctor.

I shall write. Meanwhile be well. Greetings to Mamasha.

Your Antoine

Olga has the same illness, which will probably last a year or two.

3 Korolenko wrote Chekhov that some Academicians were planning to have the charge against Gorky under article 1035 annulled, and then re-elect him.
1 Olga's mother.

[*419*]

TO K. S. STANISLAVSKY[1]

Dear Konstantin Sergeyevich,

All this time, since the eve of Trinity Sunday, Olga has been vomiting, now more frequently, now less, but yesterday the vomiting, accompanied by sharp pain, grew more violent. At Strauch's request I called in Taube, a specialist for internal diseases, and today the two of them made the diagnosis. Olga has peritonitis.[2] This is serious, but not dangerous. It was decided to place her in Strauch's hospital, and Vishnevsky got busy arranging transportation. But suddenly Olga partly recovered, the vomiting stopped, her state of mind improved, and she expressed the desire to sleep; and so her transfer to the hospital was postponed or even canceled (depending upon what the situation will be tomorrow). The day before yesterday Olga was forbidden to have any food, except milk, and I think that the abstention has helped her very much.[3]

If Olga is better, with your permission I shall go to your dacha,[4] and within a fortnight I shall take Olga there, if the doctors agree, of course. Your place is very pleasant, I was there before. If I start the play, I shall not take Olga along with me to the dacha, I'll live like a hermit.
* * *

Your A. Chekhov

TO V. I. NEMIROVICH-DANCHENKO

Moscow, June 16, 1902

Dear Vladimir Ivanovich,

For three days Olya has been taking nothing but cream (without bread), she drank four glasses a day—and only now has she stopped

[1] Professional name of Konstantin Sergeyevich Alekseyev (1863–1938). Born into a wealthy merchant family, he was an actor, a teacher of acting, a stage manager, a theoretician of the theater. His meeting with Nemirovich-Danchenko in 1897 led to the founding of the Moscow Art Theater, which opened on October 14, 1898, as a cooperative institution.

[2] Late in September Chekhov wrote to another friend that the peritonitis had followed on a miscarriage.

[3] In a letter to Nemirovich-Danchenko written the same day Chekhov remarked that it was he who had forbidden the patient solid food, and that of all the doctors who treated Olga, he was the only one who was right.

[4] In the village of Lyubimovka, near the Tarasovka station of the Yaroslavl railway.

feeling a heaviness in the abdomen. Today she was already sitting in an armchair; she is allowed chicken soup. Above all, I have been permitted to go on a trip, and tomorrow I leave with Morozov [1] for Perm. By July 5 I shall be back in Moscow.* * *

Your A. Chekhov

TO O. L. KNIPPER

June 18, on the way from Nizhny Novgorod to Kazan, 1902

My dear, good wife Olya,

On the train I had a whole night's wonderful sleep, now (at noon) I am sailing down the Volga. There is a wind and it's cool, but it is very, very good. I sit on deck all the time and look at the shore. It is sunny. Morozov is accompanied by two good-natured Germans, one old, the other young, neither speaks a word of Russian, so that willy-nilly I speak German. If you move from one side of the deck to the other in time, you do not feel the wind at all. My state of mind is good, the journey is comfortable and pleasant, I cough very much less. I am not worried about you, for I know, I am certain that my dog is well, in fact it could not be otherwise.* * *

I'll write every day. Sleep well, remember your husband.

I hug and kiss my extraordinary wife.

Wire what Strauch said.

Your A.

TO O. L. KNIPPER

Perm, June 22, 1902

My sweet darling, little stick, I am already in Perm.[1] I arrived here yesterday, put up at the Club Hotel, this noon I shall board a steamer and sail up the Kama to Usolye, thence to Morozov's estate, then back

[1] Savva Timofeyevich Morozov, a wealthy industrialist who helped to finance the Art Theater and was one of its directors. The itinerary of the trip was as follows: by train to Nizhny Novgorod, then down the Volga to Kazan, up the Kama to Perm in the Urals, whence by train to Usolye, near which Morozov had an estate, and finally back to Moscow. Before that Chekhov visited Morozov's chemical factory, and is reported to have persuaded him to reduce the workers' hours from twelve to eight daily.

[1] Now Molotov.

to Perm and then to Moscow. I don't know when you'll get this letter, probably not soon; but on July 2 I shall be in Moscow. I am tormented by jealousy, I don't believe my wife and that's why I hurry, hurry. I will give you a beating.

The Kama is a wonderful river. We ought somehow to rent a little steamer for the whole family and journey unhurriedly to Perm and back again, and that would be a summer vacation in earnest, of a sort we have never even dreamed of. We must give the matter thought.

Take care of your health, little stick, be sensible. If Alekseyev's summer cottage is ready, we shall move into it on July 3 or 4. We shall waste no time. Thanks for the good telegrams.

I am on my way to the steamer, it's time. I shall be sailing all day, and at midnight board a train. I kiss you and, if you behave, hug you, too. A bow to Vishnevsky and Zina,[2] to your mother, if she is still with you, give my cordial greetings.

Every day I eat sterlet chowder.

By the time I return you must have put on flesh, be corpulent, chubby, like a female theater owner.

I kiss you once more.

Your A.

TO K. S. STANISLAVSKY

Lyubimovka, July 18, 1902

Dear Konstantin Sergeyevich,

Dr. Strauch came here today and found everything in good shape. He forbade Olga only one thing: riding over a bad pavement, unnecessary movement generally, but to my great delight he permitted her, without any reservations, to take part in rehearsals; she can start work in the theater even on August 10. She has been forbidden to travel to Yalta. I shall go there alone in August, return in mid-September and then shall stay in Moscow till December.

I like Lyubimovka very much. April and May cost me not a little, but now, as if to make up for all I went through in the past, I have been granted so much serenity, health, warmth, pleasure, that I can only throw up my hands. The weather is good, the river is good, and indoors

2 A servant of the Knippers.

we eat and sleep like bishops. I send you thousands of thanks straight from the bottom of my heart. It is a long time since I spent such a summer. I fish daily, five times a day, and the catch is not bad (yesterday we had perch chowder), and to sit on the bank is so pleasant that I have no words for it: In short, everything is very good. Only one thing is bad: I'm idling, I don't do anything. I haven't yet started the play; [1] I am only thinking about it. I shall probably not begin work before the end of August.

Olga sends you her compliments, and a low bow. My greetings to your wife and children. Be well and of good cheer, store up strength and energy. I press your hand.

Your A. Chekhov

TO A. N. VESELOVSKY [1]

Yalta, August 25, 1902

Gracious sir, Aleksandr Nikolayevich!

In December of last year I received an announcement of the election of A. M. Peshkov [2] as an honorary Academician. He was then in the Crimea and I hastened to see him, was the first to bring him the news of his election, and the first to congratulate him. Some time later the newspapers stated that, in view of the fact that he had been summoned to be investigated under article 1035, his election was declared invalid. Furthermore, it was definitely indicated that the annulment had originated with the Academy of Sciences, [3] and since I am an honorary Academician, this announcement originated with me, too. I had congratulated Mr. Peshkov cordially and now I was one of those who declared his election invalid. I found this contradiction hard to accept. I could not reconcile my conscience to it. An examination of article 1035 threw no light on the matter. After long reflection I was able to arrive

[1] *The Cherry Orchard.*
[1] Aleksandr Nikolayevich Veselovsky (1843–1918), professor of the history of West European literature, was a member of the Academy of Sciences, and Chairman of its Department of Russian Language and Literature.
[2] Maxim Gorky was the pen name of Aleksey Maksimovich Peshkov.
[3] The issue of *The Government Herald* for March 12, 1902, carried a notice that the election of A. M. Peshkov as an honorary Academician was declared annulled. Two days later the same announcement appeared in several newspapers under the heading, "From the Imperial Academy of Sciences." After the collapse of the autocracy in February 1917, Gorky's rank of honorary Academician was restored to him.

at only one decision, extremely painful and grievous to me, namely, most respectfully to request you to solicit the annulment of my rank of honorary Academician.[4]

With a feeling of profound respect, I have the honor of being your most obedient servant.

Anton Chekhov

TO O. L. KNIPPER

Yalta, August 27, 1902

My darling, my perch, after a long wait I have at last received a letter from you. I am leading a placid life. I don't go into town, I talk with visitors and now and then I write a little. I am not going to write a play this year, my heart isn't in it. And if I do accomplish anything by way of a play, it will be a farce in one act.

Masha didn't give me your letter, I found it in Mother's room on the table, picked it up mechanically and read it—and then understood why Masha was in such low spirits. The letter is terribly bristly and, above all, unjust. Of course, I understood your state of mind when you wrote it and I do understand. And your latest letter is an odd one, and I don't know what is the matter with you and what you are thinking of, my darling. You write, "It was strange to expect you in the south since they knew that I was laid up. It showed clearly unwillingness that you should be near me when I was ill." Who showed this unwillingness? When was I expected in the south? In my letter I swore to you on my honor that I was never urged to come south alone, without you. This isn't right, darling, this isn't right, one must dread injustice, you must be without reproach on the score of justice, absolutely without reproach, all the more so as you are kind, very kind, and understanding. Forgive me, little darling, for these reprimands, there won't be any more, this scares me.* * *

Did I write you about *The Sea Gull*? I wrote to Gnedich [1] in Petersburg begging him not to stage *The Sea Gull*. Today I received his reply: its performance cannot be avoided, for new scenery has been prepared, etc., etc. So there will be abuse again.[2]

---

[4] The day before Chekhov left Yalta for Moscow he was visited by Korolenko and the two decided to resign as honorary Academicians. Korolenko did so on July 25.

[1] A playwright and one of the directors of the Aleksandrinsky Theater in Petersburg.

[2] The allusion is to the fiasco of the first performance of *The Sea Gull* in the same theater on October 17, 1896.

Don't tell Masha that I read your letter to her. However, do as you please.

Chill is wafted from your letters. Nevertheless I go on pestering you with endearments and think about you endlessly. I kiss you a billion times, hug you. Write me more often, darling, at least once every five days. I am your husband nevertheless, you know. Do not leave me so soon, without our having lived together properly, without your having borne me a little boy or a little girl. And when you have had a baby you can do as you like. I kiss you again.

Your A.

TO O. L. KNIPPER

Yalta, August 29, 1902

My dear wife, little actress, my dog, greetings! You ask me to answer the questions in your latest letter. Very well! Yes, already visitors overpower me. Yesterday, for example, they were coming from morning till evening—some just to call, some on business. You write that these visits please me, that I play the coquette when I say that they enrage me. I don't know whether I flirt or not, only the fact is that I am prevented from working and that conversation—particularly with strangers, sometimes exhausts me. You write, "I am very glad that you are so pleased to be in Yalta and that you are so comfortable there." Who wrote you that I am so comfortable there? Why do you ask what Altschuller told me? This doctor often drops in to see me. He wanted to auscultate me, he insisted on it, but I refused. My mood? Excellent. How do I feel? Yesterday I felt wretched and took Hunyadi but today I am fairly well. As usual, I cough more than in the north. I stood the trip [1] very well; but it was very hot and dusty. Your hair is turning gray and you are growing old? That is because of your bad character and because you don't appreciate your husband and don't love him enough. I sleep as usual, that is, very well, couldn't be any better.* * *

My good darling, find out if Colonel Stakhovich [2] could give you a

---

[1] Chekhov arrived in Yalta on August 16, having traveled from Lyubimovka, the Stanislavsky country place, where the couple had spent part of the summer.
[2] Aleksey Aleksandrovich Stakhovich, adjutant of the Moscow Governor General, later an actor in the Art Theater.

letter (his own or someone else's) to Senger,[3] Minister of Education, urging the admittance of a Jew to the Yalta high school. For the last four years this Jew has passed his examinations with the highest marks, yet they don't admit him, though he's the son of a Yalta house-owner. They admit little Yids from other towns, though. Do find out, darling, and write me without delay.

Write about your health, even if only two words, dear old woman. Do you fish? That's a clever girl.* * *

I take my dog by the tail, swing her several times, then stroke and pet her. Keep well, child, and may the Creator guard you. If you see Gorky at a rehearsal, congratulate him and tell him—but him alone— that I am no longer an Academician, that I have sent a statement to the Academy. But tell him alone, no one else. I hug my darling.

Your husband and protector

TO O. L. KNIPPER

Yalta, September 1, 1902

My dear, my own, again I have received a strange letter from you. Again you pile all manner of things on my noddle. Who told you that I don't want to return to Moscow, that I had left for good and would not return this fall? I wrote you, clearly, in Russian, that I would certainly return in September and live with you till December. Didn't I write? You accuse me of failing to be frank, but meanwhile you forget everything I say or write you. And I am simply at a loss as to what to do with my spouse, how to write to her. You write that you tremble when you read my letters, that it's time for us to separate, that there is something about the whole situation that you fail to understand. . . . It seems to me, my darling, that neither of us is to blame for this whole mess, but someone else with whom you have been talking. Distrust of my words, of my movements has been lodged in you, everything seems suspicious to you—and here I can do nothing, I can't and I can't. I shall not undertake to dissuade you, to change your mind, for it is useless. You write that I am capable of living beside you and all the time saying nothing, that I need you only as a pleasant woman and that you yourself as a human being live alone, a stranger to me. . . . My nice, good darling, you know you are my wife, get it into your

[3] Grigory Eduardovich Senger (1853–1919).

head at last! You are a human being, the nearest and dearest to me, I have loved you limitlessly and I still do, but you set yourself down as a "pleasant" woman, alone, and strange to me. . . . Well, God be with you, have it your own way.

I am better, but I cough furiously. No rain, it's hot. Masha leaves on the 4th and will be in Moscow on the 6th. You write that I shall show Masha your letter; thanks for trusting me. By the way, Masha is absolutely not guilty of anything, sooner or later you will be convinced of this.* * *

My darling, be a wife, be a friend, write good letters, do not mope, do not torment me. Be a kind, nice wife, the sort you are really. I love you more than ever, and as a husband I am not guilty of anything before you, get it into your head at last, my joy, my curlicue.

Good-bye, be well and cheerful. Write me every day without fail. I kiss you, my dolly, and embrace you.

Your A.

TO O. L. KNIPPER

Yalta, September 10, 1902

My chubby little dear, don't put yourself out about the little Jew, he's already attending high school. We have had no rain, no rain, and it doesn't look as though we shall ever have it. There is no water. Invisible dust, which, of course, does its work, is suspended in the air. Nevertheless I am much better; I cough less, and already have an appetite.

I am not taking shares in the company [1] headed by Morozov because I failed to receive the sum owed me and I do nct expect to receive it soon or perhaps ever. I do not wish to be a shareholder only nominally. You are an actress and you get paid less than you deserve, and so you can be a shareholder on credit, but not I.

Are you walking now or do you still have to travel by cab? Do you go to the theaters? Generally, what occupies you? What are you reading? If someone goes to Yalta, send me my spittoon and my eyeglasses.

This year I shall certainly go abroad. I cannot winter here for many reasons.

Has Strauch allowed you to have children? Now or later? Ah, my

[1] It was formed to secure the future of the Art Theater, each shareholder contributing at least 3000 rubles. Chekhov did acquire a share and indeed the next spring as a shareholder received 1000 rubles from the Theater's profits.

darling, darling, time is passing! When our child is a year and a half old I shall probably be bald, gray, toothless, and you will look like your Aunt Charlotte.[2]

Oh, if only it rained! Without rain, it's beastly.

I kiss my old woman and I hug her. Write to me, exert yourself, condescend. When will they finish building the theater? Write, darling.

Your husband, A.

TO O. L. KNIPPER

Yalta, September 18, 1902

My good spouse, there has been a real event—at night it rained. When I strolled in the garden this morning, it was already dry and dusty again, nevertheless it did rain, and during the night I heard the noise. The cold is over, it has turned hot again. My health is completely restored, at least I eat a great deal and cough less; I do not drink cream because the local cream upsets my stomach and is very filling. In short, stop worrying, everything is going if not very well, at least no worse than usual.

Today I am sad: Zola died. It is so unexpected and, as it were, so untimely. —I didn't care for him as a writer, but in the last few years, when the Dreyfus case was on everyone's lips, I came to prize him very highly as a man.

And so, we shall soon see each other, my little bug. I shall come and stay with you until you turn me out. I shall have time to bore you, be sure. Tell Naidenov, if his play [1] is mentioned, that he is greatly talented, in any case. I do not write him because I shall soon speak to him—tell him so. * * *

Don't be gloomy, it doesn't suit you. Be cheerful, my darling. I kiss both your hands, forehead, cheeks, shoulders. I stroke all of you, embrace and kiss you again.

Your A.

[2] The sister of Knipper's grandmother.
[1] *The Tenants.*

TO O. L. KNIPPER

Yalta, September 20, 1902

Ilya, my sweet little muzzle, greetings! Your latest letters showed you sunk in melancholy, and perhaps already turned into a nun, while I am so eager to see you! I shall come soon, soon, and, I repeat, stay until you chase me out, even till January. Mother leaves Yalta on October 3—at least that's what she said yesterday. First she will go to Petersburg and then, returning from there, will stay in Moscow with Ivan. That's my advice to her.

Why are you so troubled about my share in the corporation financing the Art Theater under the direction of Morozov? It doesn't matter. When I reach Moscow I'll talk to him about it, but in the meantime, leave him alone, darling.

And so I shall go to Moscow without a spittoon, and in a railway car, oh, what a nuisance it is. Don't send it, the package may come too late. Order Masha [1] to fry a veal croquette, the kind that costs 30 copecks. And get Stritzky's "Export" beer. By the way, nowadays I eat a great deal, but I find that I still have little strength and energy and I have been coughing again, and once more started drinking Ems water. But my mood is not bad, I don't notice how the day passes. Well, these are all trifles.

You are right that if we were to continue to live together I should grow tired of you, for I would get used to you as to a table, a chair. "You and I, both of us, are somehow unfinished creatures." I don't know, darling, whether I am finished or not, but I am certain that the longer we two live together, the broader and deeper my love for you will become. Make a note of this, little actress. If it weren't for my illness, it would be hard to find a man more of a stay-at-home than I.

Day before yesterday there were a few drops of rain and yesterday during the day there were more, and that was all. The sun is as scorching as before, everything is dry. You should have a talk with Taube about your intestines. Has he returned from abroad? Did you inquire? You know, melancholy is caused by intestinal trouble, remember that. In old age, because of this ailment you will beat your husband and your children. Beat them, and at the same time sob.

Altschuller will come tomorrow, will auscultate me—for the first time this fall. I kept putting him off but now it's rather awkward to

[1] The cook.

[*429*]

do so. He kept scaring me and threatening to write to you. (Here in Yalta everyone thinks for some reason that you are a harsh one, and that you keep me under your thumb.)

What else, then? Well, I kiss my little bug. Write me about your health in greater detail. I repeat: see Taube, and again, write. And so I kiss and stroke your back, and then embrace you. Good-bye.

Your A.

Stritzky's beer is called "Export." If you order 20 bottles from him get 10 "Martovsky" beer and 10 "Export." Before coming I shall wire

TO O. L. KNIPPER

Yalta, September 22, 190

My dear philosopheress, my little *Frauchen*, greetings! Today I received from you a magnificent letter—a description of your trip to Lyubi movka, and having read it, I rejoiced that I had such a good, wonderful wife. Yesterday Altschuller visited me and for the first time this fall examined me. Listened, tapped. He found that my health had greatly improved, that, to judge by the change which has taken place since spring, I was getting free from my illness; indeed, he permitted me to go to Moscow—how wonderful! He says I should not go now but wait till the first frosts. So you see! He has it that what helped me was creosote and the fact that I spent the winter in Yalta, but I say that what did it was the rest at Lyubimovka. I don't know who is right. Altschuller insists that I must leave Moscow as soon as I get there. I said: I shall leave in December when my wife lets me. Now the question is: where do I go? It happens that there is bubonic plague in Odessa, and it is very possible that in February or March when I shall be returning from abroad, I shall be quarantined for several days and then in Sevastopol and Yalta I shall be looked upon as a leper Yet I can't return home in winter except by way of Odessa. What am I to do now? Think it over!

We have no rain. Wind.

I read an article by August Scholz about the Art Theater. What rubbish! Sheer laudatory German balderdash, in which more than half of the information offered the public by the way is nothing but lies; for instance, the failure of my plays on the stage of the Moscow

Imperial theaters. Only one item is good: you are called the most gifted Russian actress.

My jackets and trousers are worn out, I have begun to look like a poor relation. . . . You will be ashamed to walk with me in Moscow, so, very well, in the street I shall make believe that you are not acquainted with me—and stick to it until we buy new trousers.

Well, my little light, little muzzle, be hale and hearty. Don't mope, and bridle your nerves. Remember that I hug you and pull you about with all my strength. We shall soon see each other, darling.

Your A.

And so the fact is I am in good health. Make a note of it.

TO O. L. KNIPPER

Yalta, December 4, 1902

Greetings, my angry dog, my ferocious doggie! I kiss you as I write these first lines [. . .]. There's nothing new, everything is as it has been, all is well. The weather is still cold. Today a new church was consecrated here, Mother was there and returned cheerful, buoyant, very pleased to have seen the Czar [1] and the entire ceremony; she had an admission ticket. The bells of the new church ring basso profundo, it is a pleasure.

The new towels get damp quickly, it is inconvenient to dry yourself with them. I have only two towels, but it seems to me that I took three along. I eat heartily, work a little, sleep eleven hours out of every twenty-four. The copy of the contract with Marx that I signed is probably in the hands of the headmistress of the girls' high school, I haven't found it among my papers. Before leaving I handed all the important documents to that lady for safekeeping. Besides, this fuss over the agreement doesn't please me. It will get me nowhere. Having signed a contract you must stick to it honestly, no matter what its provisions.[2]

My good little human being, remember me, write. And remind

[1] Nicholas II.
[2] Some of Chekhov's friends, Gorky among them, regarding the agreement with Marx as disadvantageous to the author, urged him to cancel the contract. Indeed, signatures to a letter to Marx requesting him to release Chekhov from his obligation were being collected, but Chekhov refused to agree to this step.

Nemirovich that he promised to write me every Wednesday. The sow with the sucklings [3] that you gave me delights all visitors.

* * * My darling, my little housewife, I left behind in Moscow the black soap with which I washed my hair (keeps down dust and dandruff), give it to Masha, that she may bring it. Don't forget, my own.

When you go to bed and start thinking about me, remember that I think about you and kiss and hug you. The Lord be with you. Be cheerful and happy, don't forget your husband.

A.

TO O. L. KNIPPER

Yalta, December 12, 1902

Greetings, my actress!

* * * There's shooting in Yalta. The cold has driven thrushes here and they are being hunted. People have no thought of hospitality.

I'm writing a story,[1] but it turns out to be so terrifying that I outdo even Leonid Andreyev. I should like to write a farce but somehow I can't get down to it, and besides, it's too cold to write; it's so cold in the rooms that I am reduced to pacing them in order to warm up. In Moscow it is incomparably warmer. The rooms here are abominably cold, and when you look out of the window you see snow, frozen hummocks and overcast skies. No sun, not any. The solace is that from today on the days will be getting longer, so we are on the way to spring.

My nails have grown, and there is no one to cut them. One tooth in my mouth broke. A button fell off my vest.

During the holidays I am sure to write you every day or perhaps even twice a day—so that you should be in better spirits. * * *

Your A.

---

[3] A bronze figurine that Olga had received from one of her uncles.
[1] An unfinished piece; the characters included two brothers, one of whom was insane, the other condemned to hard labor.

TO O. L. KNIPPER

Yalta, December 14, 1902

My darling, sloven, dog, you will certainly have children, the doctors say so. The only thing needed is to recover your strength. Set your mind at rest: everything is normal and as it should be with you, [all you lack is a husband who lives with you all year round. Now I am going to arrange to live with you for a year without parting,] [1] and you will give birth to a little son who will break the crockery, pull your dachshund by the tail, and you will gaze at him and be content.

Yesterday I washed my head and apparently caught cold, for today I have a headache, can't work. Yesterday I went to town for the first time; it is awfully dull there, in the streets only hideous faces, not one pretty woman, not one attractively dressed.

When I sit down to work on *The Cherry Orchard* I'll write you, dog. In the meantime I am busy with a story,[2] rather uninteresting—at least for me. It is boring.

The earth is covered with green grass, where there is no snow, it is pleasant to look at.

I have received a letter from Efros.[3] He asks me to set down in writing my opinion of Nekrasov. He needs it for a newspaper. It is disgusting, but I shall do it. By the way, I am very fond of Nekrasov, and for some reason there is no other poet whose blunders I so readily forgive. So that's what I'll write to Efros.

One ear came off the sow that you gave me.

Well, my little light, may the Lord be with you, be sensible, don't be blue, don't be bored, and think oftener of your legal husband. As a matter of fact, no one in the world, you know, loves you as I do, and except for me, you have no one. You must remember this and make a note of it.

I hug and kiss you a thousand times.

Your A.

[1] The bracketed passage appears in the edition of the letters prepared by Chekhov's sister. It is suppressed in the Soviet edition.

[2] Perhaps "A Letter," which remains unfinished.

[3] Nikolay Yefimovich Efros, journalist and drama critic, was apparently on the staff of *The News of the Day*. On the occasion of the twenty-fifth anniversary of Nekrasov's death this newspaper asked a number of literary figures if they agreed with Tolstoy that the work of that once popular poet was obsolete. In his brief statement Chekhov repeated what he said in his letter, concluding, "Nekrasov's having had his day or being obsolete is out of the question."

TO O. L. KNIPPER

Yalta, December 15, 1902

My beloved woman, today I received your letter on two short pages. Here are the answers to your questions. I take cod liver oil and creosote regularly, for it is practically my only occupation. I have no dressing gown. I presented my old one to somebody and I forget who it was, but I don't need it because I don't wake up at night. All this time my jacket was cleaned only once. Now that you may not get angry, I shall take appropriate measures. Recently I washed my head. Today I changed my shirt. I will now change my socks. This very minute. The new towels, it seems to me, are poor. They get wet as soon as you take hold of them; they're probably a cheap kind. I need somewhat shorter towels, coarser, thicker and rougher.

Tonight it is snowing, nature treats us scurvily.

Darling, if you are my wife, then, when I come to Moscow see to it that a fur coat is made for me, of some warm but light and beautiful fur, say, fox. The Moscow fur coat almost killed me, it weighs more than a hundred pounds! Without a light fur coat I feel like a tramp. Do your best for me, wife! I don't understand why I didn't have a fur coat made for me during my last visit.

During the holidays I shall write you every day, be assured. When I write you, I myself feel well. You are my extraordinary, wonderful, proper, intelligent, rare wife, without a single defect. In my eyes at least. You do have, however, one defect: you are short-tempered, and when you are in a bad humor it's dangerous to come near you. But this is a trifle. It will pass with time. There is one defect that we have in common—we have married late.

Last year and before that when I woke up in the morning I was usually in a bad mood, my arms and legs ached, but this year there's nothing of the sort, as though I had grown younger. * * *

Your A.

TO O. L. KNIPPER

Yalta, December 20, 1902

My sweet friend, today I received a telegram from Alekseyev as follows: "Gorky's play [1] and the Theater have had a great success. Olga

[1] *The Lower Depths.*

Leonardovna gave the most noteworthy performance in the eyes of the cultivated public." Rejoice, my darling. Your husband is thoroughly satisfied and will drink your health this very day, if only Masha brings some porter.

I am now having some unpleasantness with my teeth. It's uncertain when this stupid music will be done with. Yesterday I received a letter from you that was almost open (again!), and today I had a sad time because Arseny didn't bring a letter of yours from the post office. Furthermore, today's weather is melancholy, warm, quiet, but not a whiff of spring. I sat on the balcony in the sun and kept thinking about you, about Fomka,[2] about crocodiles, about the lining of my jacket, which is torn. I thought that you need a little son who would occupy you, would fill your life. A little son or a little daughter you shall have, my own, believe me, all that's necessary is only to wait, to be quite normal again after your illness. I'm not lying to you, I'm not hiding from you a syllable of what the doctors say, word of honor.

Misha sent me some herring. What else can I tell you? We have many mice. Every day I catch them in a mousetrap. And the mice have probably grown used to it, because they accept it good-naturedly, are no longer afraid of it. There's nothing more to write about, there is nothing or, at least, nothing to be seen, life passes dully and quite emptily. I cough. I sleep well, and all night long I dream, as befits a lazybones.

Write me, little child, write in the greatest detail, so that I may feel that I belong not to Yalta, but to the north, that this cheerless, insipid life has not yet swallowed me. I dream of going to Moscow no later than the first of March, that is, in two months, but I don't know if that's how it will be. God keep you, my good wife, my red-haired dog. Imagine that I take you in my arms and carry you around the room for a couple of hours, and kiss and embrace you. * * * Thank Alekseyev for the telegram.

Tomorrow I shall write. Sleep peacefully, my joy, eat as you should, and think of your husband.

Your A.

---

2 A dog.

TO A. S. SUVORIN

Yalta, December 22, 1902

I am indisposed, in general the sick do not feel well here; the weather in Yalta is all too nasty, it's simply a misfortune! It either rains or a gale is blowing, and ever since I have been here [1] there was only one sunny day. News came today that Gorky's play, *The Lower Depths*, was magnificently performed and had a huge success. I rarely go to the Art Theater, but it seems to me that you exaggerate Stanislavsky's role as director. There is nothing extraordinary about this theater, performances are conducted as everywhere, except that the actors are intellectuals, very decent people. True, they aren't possessed of shining talent, but they are painstaking, they love their occupation and learn their parts. If much of what is staged is a failure, this is because the play is inferior or else because the actors haven't enough fire. Really, Stanislavsky is not to blame. You write that he will chase all the gifted people from the stage, but actually during all the five years that this theater has existed, not a single person with a trace of talent has left.

I learned from Misha's letter that he wants to issue *The European Library;* I wrote to him, as plainly as I could, that such an enterprise is foolish, that *The European Library* is a stolen title, that no one needs translated novels, that none of them is worth a penny, much less five rubles, etc., etc. The fate of this letter is still unknown to me.

You write, "My dear fellow, why do you now find yourself, on your own initiative, in theatrical and neo-literary groups?" I find myself in Yalta, this miserable provincial town, and that is my whole misfortune. Unfortunately, the neo-literati consider me alien, old, their relations with me are tepid, indeed, almost formal; as for the theatrical coterie, my relations with it are limited to letters from my wife, an actress, and nothing more. * * *

Thank you for the letter, it is very interesting.

Your A. Chekhov

I do not see *Liberation*,[2] for some reason I do not see it.

---

[1] Chekhov arrived in Yalta on November 25.
[2] A liberal Russian journal (1902–5), printed first in Stuttgart, later in Paris, and smuggled into Russia.

TO O. L. KNIPPER

Yalta, December 25, 1902

Your letter to Mother came just in time, i.e. yesterday. I am not very well, but better than yesterday; I fancy I am on the mend.

If you knew, my darling, how clever you are! This is clear from your letter, among other things. It seems to me that if I lay even half a night, my nose tucked into your shoulder, I would feel better and would stop being blue. I can't be without you, no matter what.

Yesterday *The Day's News* ran pictures of you in Gorky's play.[1] Vishnevsky looked terrible, Moskvin, Stanislavsky, and you looked wonderful. I was positively touched! Capital fellows. * * *

Dear dog, why am I not with you? Why don't you have a flat in Moscow, where I would occupy a room in which I could work, hidden from my friends? For the summer rent a dacha, in which I could write; then I would get up early, and I would be alone with you, if not every day, at least three days a week.

Dutchie, write me about the wedding.[2] Everything will surely be formal and solemn.

What did Baranov[3] do at the Hermitage? What happened? What was the scandal? Write me all about it.

I embrace my heron, kiss her.

Your A.

TO S. P. DIAGHILEV[1]

Yalta, December 30, 1902

Much esteemed Sergey Pavlovich!

I received *The World of Art* with the article[2] on *The Sea Gull,* and I read the article: many thanks. When I finished reading the article I

---

[1] *The Lower Depths.*
[2] That of Olga's brother, Vladimir.
[3] The Governor of Nizhny Novgorod.
[1] Sergey Pavlovich Diaghilev (1872–1929) was at the turn of the century a leading spokesman for the modernist trend in Russian art. After leaving the country in 1906, he arranged exhibitions of Russian painting abroad and organized the dazzling Ballet Russe, which enchanted the West.
[2] By Dmitry Vladimirovich Filosofov, publisher and critic, who expatriated himself after the October Revolution. He compared the première of *The Sea Gull* with a later presentation.

[*437*]

again had the desire to write a play, which I shall probably do after January.

You write that we spoke about the serious religious movement in Russia. We spoke of the movement not in Russia, but among the intelligentsia. About Russia I shall say nothing; as for the intelligentsia, at present it only toys with religion and chiefly because it has nothing to do. As for the educated segment of our society, it appears to have departed from religion and to be going further and further away from it, no matter what is said and what kind of philosophico-religious associations may be formed. Whether this is good or bad I do not undertake to decide, I shall only say that the religious movement of which you write is a thing by itself, and apart from contemporary culture as a whole, and the latter must not be held to have a causal connection with the former.[3] Modern culture is the beginning of an effort, in the name of the great future, an effort that will continue for tens of thousands of years, to the end that, if only in the distant future, mankind may know the true, real God, i.e. not conjecturing, not seeking for Him in Dostoevsky,[4] but will know Him clearly, know as it knows that two times two is four. Culture today is the beginning of such an effort, but the religious movement about which we talked is a survival, already almost the end of what is dying or dead. This, however, is a long story, that cannot be summarized in a letter. When you see Mr. Filosofov, please tell him of my profound gratitude. I congratulate you on the New Year, and wish you everything good.

Devotedly,
A. Chekhov

[3] In his letter to Chekhov, Diaghilev had observed that the problem of the possibility of a religious movement in Russia was tantamount to the question as to whether contemporary culture was "to be or not to be."

[4] Chekhov was not an admirer of Dostoevsky. He found his work, as he wrote to Suvorin on March 5, 1889, "good, but much too long and immodest. Too pretentious." He is reported to have conceded in conversation that Dostoevsky was greatly gifted but said that he occasionally lacked "flair." "Oh, how he ruined the *Karamazovs* with the speeches by the prosecutor and the lawyer for the defense."

⌈1903⌉

TO O. L. KNIPPER

Yalta, January 1, 1903

A happy New Year to you, my darling actress, my wife! I wish you everything you need and deserve, and chiefly I wish you a little half-German who would rummage in your wardrobe and smudge my desk with ink, much to your delight.

I praise you for having had such a good time at the wedding. Of course, it is a pity that I wasn't there. I would have looked at you and perhaps even done a bit of whirling myself.

Today I received many letters, among them one from Suvorin and another from Nemirovich. The latter sent me a list of plays your theater plans to stage. Not one stands out conspicuously, but they are all good. *The Fruits of Enlightenment* [1] and *A Month in the Country* [2] must be staged, so that you have them in your repertory. Obviously, they are good plays that belong to literature.

Masha saw the New Year in at Mme. Tatarinova's. [3] I met it at home. Tatarinova sent me a wonderful flowering cactus—*Epiphyllum truncatum*. It has been raining since morning.

Write to me, my own, solace me with your letters. My health is magnificent. My tooth has been filled, that means one more saved. In short, everything is more or less in order. . . .

They are calling me to tea. Keep well and cheerful, darling actress. God be with you. I kiss, embrace, and bless you.

Your A.

---

[1] A play by Tolstoy.
[2] A play by Turgenev.
[3] A Yalta acquaintance.

My dear Olya,

On the morning of the 11th, after Masha had left town, I didn't feel quite right; I had a pain in my chest, I felt sick to my stomach, a temperature of 38° [C] and yesterday it was the same thing. I slept well, though I was disturbed by pain. Altschuller looked in. I had to put on a compress again (it is an immense one). This morning my temperature was only 37° [C]. I feel weak, and shall put on a plaster directly, but still I had a right to wire you today that all is well. Now everything is all right. I am getting better, tomorrow I shall be quite well again. I hide nothing from you, do understand that, and don't upset yourself telegraphing. If anything serious, or even resembling anything serious, should happen, you would be the first I should tell.

You are out of sorts? Chuck it, darling. It will all come out in the wash.

Today the earth is covered with snow, it is foggy, cheerless. It saddens me to think that so much time has passed without my doing any work, and that apparently I am no longer a worker. To sit in an armchair with a compress on and mope is not very jolly. Will you stop loving me, darling? In your letter of yesterday you wrote that you had lost your looks. As though it mattered! If you were to grow a nose like a crane's, even then I should love you.

I embrace my own, my good dachshund. I kiss and embrace you again. Write!

Your A.

* * * What have you decided? What will you tell me about Switzerland? It seems to me that we could take a very good trip. On the way we could stop off at Vienna, Berlin, etc., go to the theaters. Eh? What do you think?

Savina is putting on my old skit, "The Jubilee," at her benefit. Again they will say that this is a new play and they will gloat.

Today it's sunny, a bright day, but I sit indoors because Altschuller has forbidden me to go out. My temperature, by the way, is completely normal.

You keep writing, my own, that your conscience is tormeting you because you are living in Moscow and not with me in Yalta. Well, what can we do about it, my dear one? Judge the matter properly: if you were to stay with me in Yalta all through the winter your life would be marred and I would feel the pangs of remorse, which would hardly improve matters for us. I knew, of course, that I was marrying an actress—that is, when I married I realized clearly that you would be spending your winters in Moscow. I do not consider myself passed over or wronged one millionth of a degree—on the contrary, it seems to me that everything is going well, or the way it ought to go and so, darling, don't disconcert me by your remorse. In March we shall start living happily once more and, once more, won't be feeling the loneliness we are feeling now. Calm down, my own, don't be agitated, live, and hope. Hope, and nothing more.

The supplement to *Plowed Land* has arrived: my short stories, with a portrait and, under the portrait, a wretchedly executed facsimile of my signature.

I am working now; probably I won't be writing you every day. Do forgive me.

Let's go abroad. Let's!

Your spouse,

A.

TO O. L. KNIPPER

Yalta, February 5, 1903

Actressetta, it is two days and two nights since I had a letter from you. So does it mean that you have deserted me? You don't love me any more? If this is the case, then write me and I shall send you your nightgowns, which are in my wardrobe, and you send me my high galoshes. But if you still love me, let everything stay as it is.

Yesterday Shapovalov [1] arrived and brought me peppermints and the Order of the Seagull from Stanislavsky. The peppermints I am eating

[1] Lev Nikolayevich Shapovalov, the architect who designed the Chekhov house in Yalta.

and the badge I have hung on my watch chain. I bow down at your dear feet for your kindness.

For the last few days the temperature in my study has been no more than 11 to 12 degrees [C]. Arseny doesn't know how to heat stoves, and the weather is cold—now rain, now snow, and the wind remains high. I write six or seven lines a day—I could do no more, if you killed me. I have intestinal trouble literally every day, but nevertheless I feel well, I don't cough much, my temperature is normal, there is not a trace of pleurisy. * * *

Darling, why don't you write me? Why? Are you angry? What about? Without your letters I am anxious and have a tedious time. Even if you are angry, write all the same. If you cannot write a kind letter, write an abusive one. * * *

Well, I kiss you on the neck and on both hands and I tenderly embrace my joy. Keep well, laugh, live in hopes.

Your passionate husband,

A.

TO O. L. KNIPPER

Yalta, February 11, 1903

My incomparable wife. I agree! If the doctors permit it, we shall rent a house in the vicinity of Moscow, but it must be furnished and have stoves. All the same, here in Yalta I am rarely in the open air. Well, we shall soon talk about it in detail, my darling.

I haven't received Batyushkov's article [1] that you wrote you had sent me. Have you read S. A. Tolstoya's [2] article on Andreyev? I have, and it threw me into a fever, so glaring was the absurdity of this piece. It is indeed incredible. If you had written anything like it, I would have put you on bread and water and given you a beating every day for a whole week. Now Mr. Burenin, whom the countess has praised to the skies, will proudly lift up his mug and grow more impudent than ever.

No letter from you today. You have become so indolent and have begun to forget your husband. * * *

[1] About Chekhov.
[2] In an open letter Tolstoy's wife supported an attack on Andreyev's story "In the Fog," which had been denounced by Burenin as "filthy" and "pornographic."

My body is starting to ache a little; apparently it is time to take castor oil. You write that you envy me my character. I must tell you that by nature I am hot-tempered, peppery, and so on, and so on, but I am used to restrain myself, for it does not become a decent person to let himself go. Formerly I used to carry on like the devil. My grandfather, you know, was by conviction an arrant advocate of serfdom.[3]

The almond buds have already turned white, the garden will soon be in blossom. Today it is warm. I went out into the garden for a walk.

It is dreary without you, my own. I feel like a lonely dunderhead. I sit for hours motionless and all that is needed is for me to smoke a long pipe. I shall start work on the play [4] on February 21. You will have the part of a foolish girl. And who will play the old mother? Who? Mariya Fyodorovna will have to be asked.[5]

Anatoly Sredin [6] has just arrived, bringing the cup, chocolate, anchovies, a necktie. Thank you, my own, thank you. I kiss you a thousand times! I hug you a million times.

It seems to me that Tolstoya's letter is a forgery. Someone imitated her handwriting, for a joke. So, my joy, be serene and well.

Your A.

TO O. L. KNIPPER

Yalta, February 22, 1903

My little gray puppy, greetings! Yes, there you get flowers from Yermolova,[1] while I sit unwashed like a Samoyed. I even begin to growl. [You ask me if at least I wash my neck. My neck I do wash, but the rest of me is as dirty as a galosh.] [2] I want to go to a bathhouse, but Altschuller doesn't let me.

I received a very nice letter from Nemirovich. He writes about my illness, about the play.[3] The illness is well known, and I realize how

[3] The joke is that Chekhov's grandfather was a serf, who succeeded in buying his freedom and that of his wife and children in 1841.
[4] *The Cherry Orchard.*
[5] M. F. Andreyeva, an actress of the Moscow Art Theater who acted in three of Chekhov's plays.
[6] The son of Leonid Valentinovich.
[1] She had presented bouquets to the three actresses who played the sisters after the performance of *Three Sisters* with which the season ended.
[2] The passage in brackets is omitted from the Soviet edition.
[3] *The Cherry Orchard.*

it should and how it should not be treated, about the play I can say nothing. I shall have something to say soon. Your part is that of an arrant fool.[4] Do you want to play a fool?

I shall not escape swallowing castor oil, my darling. It seems that I have had no appetite for more than a week. It is very easy for me not to eat. I could be a monk vowed to fasting.

* * * Now I have to face a tough job: getting my honorarium for *The Sea Gull* from a government office. A baffling task. Apparently it is necessary to submit a document with a 60- or 80-copeck stamp to some department, but which one is not known.

I have received two packages of postcards—photographs of *The Vulgarians* and of *The Lower Depths*. Thank Stanislavsky, darling. Write me, is Vishnevsky getting married or isn't he?

It is turning chilly, a little wind has sprung up. But before dinner it was quite pleasant.

Well, my marvelous booby, my incomparable spouse, extraordinary actress, I embrace you an infinite number of times and kiss you as many times. Do not forget me, there is only a short while, you know, left us to live, we shall soon grow old, bear that in mind. Write, my good little child.

Your A.

TO O. L. KNIPPER

Yalta, February 23, 1903

Dear dog, if Korovin has a room for me, too, that is, a room where I could hide, without hindering anyone, and where I could work, then take the flat. If it is on an upper floor, that doesn't matter, or not very much; I shall climb quietly, slowly.

I tell you nothing about the stories that I am writing [1] because there is nothing new or interesting in them. You set them down, read them over, and see that all this has already been dealt with, that it is old, old. What is needed is something novel, slightly sour.

I want a small room, but warm and chiefly one in which you would

---

[4] At first Chekhov planned to have his wife play the part of Varya; in the end her role was that of the owner of the cherry orchard.

[1] After the publication of "The Betrothed" in December 1902, Chekhov wrote either stories that he did not complete or mere sketches for stories.

not hear the Malkiels [2] when you have no wish to hear them, and where you wouldn't hear how Vishnevsky eats borshch.

The weather has turned cool. I feel not quite well, darling, all night I coughed. How is Misha's little girl?

Well, granny, I bless you. You will have to take care of getting the passports; when I attend to it I get nothing but vexation for my trouble.

To young ladies going abroad to study here's what should be said: (1) first complete your studies in Russia and then go abroad to improve upon them, if you are preparing yourself for work in the sciences; our institutions of higher learning for women, medical schools, for instance, are excellent; (2) do you know foreign languages? (3) Jews go abroad to study from necessity, for they are hampered, but why do you go?

Generally speaking, these young ladies must be given a talking to. Very many of them go abroad only because they don't know how to study.

Write me, granny, don't stand on ceremony. You can write me whatever you please, you know, because you are the wife, the spouse.

I scratch your little back. I envy you, you sly one, you went to a bathhouse!!

Your A.

TO I. N. POTAPENKO

Yalta, February 26, 1903

Greetings, my dear Ignatius; at last we are conversing again! Yes, you are not mistaken, I am in Yalta, I'll probably stay here till April 10–15, then go to Moscow, from there abroad. * * *

Now about the magazine.[1] In the first place, you didn't write what my obligations as an editor would be; about money you say that it's not needed; I cannot live in Petersburg and consequently I cannot participate in the work or influence it, all the more so since I'll spend the whole of next winter abroad. Second, in editing I am opposed to rule by a

---

[2] A Moscow family with which the Chekhovs were acquainted. One of the girls wrote stories for children.

[1] In a letter dated February 21 Potapenko had invited Chekhov to join him in editing a magazine that he was launching, with Mamin-Sibiryak and Nemirovich-Danchenko also on the editorial board.

cabinet, at the head of a magazine there must be one person, one master, with a will not to be gainsaid. Third, Mamin-Sibiryak and Vasily Nemirovich-Danchenko are gifted writers and splendid fellows, but they are not fit to be editors. Fourth, I shall always be ready to contribute to your magazine, that is certain.

The end of the year is still far off, and we can communicate by letter, come to an agreement, and you will perhaps persuade me that I am mistaken.

I cannot brag about my health. All winter long I have been ailing; I coughed, had pleurisy, but now I am apparently well, I even set to work and wrote a story.[2] How are you doing? Have you lost weight? Gained it? I always remember you with a warm, good feeling. My people are all well, there have been no particular changes. However, I got married. But at my age this is somehow not even noticeable, like a bald spot.

I press your hand firmly and embrace you.

Your A. Chekhov

TO A. I. SUMBATOV-YOUZHIN[1]

Yalta, February 26, 1903

Dear Aleksandr Ivanovich,

Many thanks for your letter. I agree with you: it is difficult to evaluate Gorky—one must needs make sense of the mass of what is being written and said concerning him. I have not seen his *The Lower Depths* played and am but poorly informed about it, but then such stories of his as, for instance, *My Fellow Traveler* or *Chelkash* suffice for me to consider him far from being a minor writer in any respect. *Foma Gordeyev* and *Three of Them* are unreadable—they are poor stuff—and *The Vulgarians*, in my opinion, is a high school effort. However, Gorky's achievement consists not in his having been found likable but in his being the first one in Russia—and, generally speaking, the first one in the world—

---

[2] "The Betrothed."

[1] Aleksandr Ivanovich Sumbatov-Youzhin (1857–1927). The second half of his name was his pseudonym. A playwright and an actor, he was also director in one of the Moscow theaters.

to speak up with contempt for and revulsion against vulgarity, and to speak up at the precise time when the public was ready for this protest.

Both from the Christian and the economic point of view—as well as from any point of view you like—vulgarity is a great evil; like a dam across a river it has always served no other purpose than to cause stagnation, and so the tramps, even if uncouth, even if besotted, were nonetheless a trustworthy counterpoise—at least they proved to be so and the dam, even though it did not burst, did spring a turbulent and dangerous leak just the same. I don't know if I am expressing myself intelligibly. There will come a day, as I see it, when the writings of Gorky will be forgotten, yet Gorky himself will not be forgotten even a thousand years hence. That is what I think, or that is how things appear to me, but it is also possible that I am mistaken.

Are you in Moscow at present? You haven't left for Nice and Monte Carlo, by any chance? I recall rather often the years of your youth and mine, when you and I sat side by side playing roulette. And I recall Potapenko too. By the way, I received a letter from Potapenko today— the strange fellow wants to publish a magazine.

I press your hand. Be well and prosperous.

Your A. Chekhov

TO O. L. KNIPPER

Yalta, February 27, 1903

Greetings, actressella! The sky is overcast, the weather gloomy, but nevertheless, I wander about the garden and prune the rosebushes; now I am sitting down, a little tired. It is warm, pleasant. About the play I'll write you in detail around March 10, that is, whether it will be written by the end of March or not. I haven't forgotten about Switzerland, I remember it for I am eager to be alone with you as soon as possible. My health is so-so.

I haven't yet read anything in the papers about *The Pillars of Society*, I know nothing. To judge by your telegram you are not wholly satisfied. If so, I can only give you one piece of advice: spit on it all, darling. It is now Lent, it is already time to rest, to live, and yet the

[*447*]

lot of you go on ruining your nerves, straining yourselves, deuce knows what for. Your only pleasure is that Vishnevsky will deposit another thousand rubles in the bank. And what the devil is that thousand to you?

I recall that when the Art Theater was starting, you were going to disregard the size of the takings. Nemirovich used to say that if the company (not the audience) liked the play, it would be staged thirty or forty times, even if the takings amounted to no more than twenty rubles. Just imagine now writing a play, worried the whole time by the thought that if the takings would be 1580 and not 1600 rubles, the play would not run or would run only with regrets. * * *

There is nothing more to write about, little booby. I want only one thing: to take you by the ear, pull you to me and kiss your forehead and your little chin twenty times. Write me longer letters, yours are shorter than a bedbug's step. A bow to your brother and to your nephew, if they have not yet left.

I embrace you, my own, my darling, my good girl.

Your A.

TO O. L. KNIPPER

Yalta, March 4, 1903

Darling, there is great excitement in Yalta: a branch of the real Petersburg Kuba emporium has opened. Tomorrow I'll go in to have a look at what they have there and I'll write you; perhaps it will no longer be necessary to bring delicatessen from Moscow.

You give me a dressing-down for not having my play ready, and you threaten to take me in hand. Do take me in hand, that is a pleasant threat, it smiles at me, it is the one thing that I desire—to get into your hands. As for the play, you have apparently forgotten that since the time of Noah I have been telling each and every one that I will start work on it late in February or early in March. My laziness has nothing to do with the matter. I am not my own enemy, you know, and if I had the strength I would write not one but twenty-five plays. In fact, I am very glad that the play is not ready, for now you don't have to rehearse, you can rest. To work so immoderately is piggish, to say the least.

It is cool here, but not bad. As regards the coming winter, I am making no decisions as yet, but I don't look forward to it hopefully. For the present I can only say that I shall be in Moscow until December (especially if you get me a fur coat) and then, most probably, I'll have to rush off abroad, to the Riviera, perhaps, or Nervi, staying till February 15, and then back to Yalta. We shall live separately, but nothing can be done about it. There is no way out, no matter how you cudgel your brains. Well, should you be pregnant, I would take you with me to Yalta in February. Would you like that, darling? What do you think? No matter when, I wouldn't care, I would consent to winter even in Arkhangel, if only you were to become a mother.

Will your company go to Petersburg? Yes or no?

And so tomorrow I'll go to Kuba's and get a whiff of European civilization. Are you moving to new quarters? On which floor? If it's very high, I'll take half an hour walking up; no matter. I have nothing to do in Moscow, anyway.

A bath is a bath, but all the same I will first of all go to a bathhouse. I am sorry that you are not in the Gonetzkaya apartment, it is so close to a bathhouse.

Well, granny, I embrace you and give you a flick on the nose, my darling.

Your A.

TO O. L. KNIPPER

Yalta, March 5–6, 1903

My darling actressella, as I am no longer a man of letters but a gourmet, today I went to Kuba's shop, which is now open. They have marvelous caviar, enormous olives, sausage made on the premises and which must be fried at home (very delicious!), cured filet of sturgeon, ham, biscuits, mushrooms. . . . In short, there is no longer any need to bring anything from Moscow, except groats and millet. It seems to me that we should even buy smoked ham at Kuba's for the holidays. I write you about all this because Altschuller was here today and insisted that under no circumstances should I go to Moscow before the middle of April. My darling, my wife, my actress, my own, won't you find it possible to come to Yalta during the Easter week, or if the company goes to Petersburg, on the feast of St. Thomas the following week? We

[449]

would have a glorious time together; I would give you delicious things to drink and to eat, and *The Cherry Orchard* to read, and then we'd make for Moscow together. Altschuller swears that my pleurisy has not yet been absorbed and that I must by no means go to Moscow. Do come here, my own! The company will give you a leave of absence— I'll pull it out of them if your request doesn't work. Write me that you will come, and above all, think it over. Choose what is best and most convenient for you. But I miss you so badly, I so long to see you that I have no patience. I call you, I call you. Don't be cross, darling, first think about it, consider it carefully. And if you decide to come, go at once and reserve a ticket (at Neglinnoye), or there will be none to be had for the holiday. And write me what you decide.

In *The Cherry Orchard* you will be Varvara Yegorovna or Varya, the adopted daughter, twenty-two years old. Only, please, don't be angry. Do not write, telegraph one word: "Coming" or "Impossible."

Well, you write that you don't know how we shall meet, while I feel as if we had parted yesterday, and I shall meet you as if you had never ceased to be mine for a single day.

Today there is no letter from you.

March 6. From the letter of yours that came today it appears that the Petersburg question has not been settled negatively, that you may still go there. If so, come to Yalta after your stay in the capital. Consider everything carefully, and if you don't find it necessary or possible to come, then so be it—I will submit and shall come myself without more ado. It is for you to decide, because you are a busy person with work to do, while I drift about in the world, a good-for-nothing.

There is a high wind today, it's unpleasant. If my play doesn't come out as I conceived it, you may punch my head. Stanislavsky's part is comic, and so is yours.

Now, puppy, keep well. I love you, you may feel as you wish. Your photograph is on display in the Volkov store.

I hug and kiss you.

Your devoted husband A.

Don't buy any more peppermint lozenges. There's marmalade at Kuba's.

TO O. L. KNIPPER

Yalta, March 18, 1903

My remarkable lovely, at last you have sent your address, and every-thing is in order again. Thanks, darling. This morning I received your tearful letter, in which you scold yourself before leaving for the Chernigov Monastery.[1] I read it through, no address! Then and there I was ready to apply for a divorce, when at noon your telegram came.

So I shall come to Moscow the week after Easter, before your return from Petersburg, and meet you, not at the station, but at home, after I have been to the baths and done a little work on the play. By the way, I am having trouble with it. One of the leading characters is not suffi-ciently thought through and is a stumbling block, but I think that by Easter this character will have become clear and I shall be free from difficulties. * * *

Tomorrow I shall write again. Do not talk foolishly, you are not in the least to blame for not living with me in the winter. On the contrary, we are a very decent couple, who do not interfere with each other's work. You do love the theater, don't you? If you didn't, it would be a different matter. Well, Christ be with you. Soon, soon we shall see each other, and I shall embrace and kiss you forty-five times. Be well, little one.

Your A.

TO O. L. KNIPPER

Yalta, March 23, 1903

My dear granny, you are cross with me because of the address, you keep assuring me that you did send it and indeed, several times. Wait, I'll bring you your letters, and you shall see for yourself; in the meantime, let's pass over it in silence, let's not talk about the address, I've quieted down. Furthermore, you write that I am again asking about Turgenev's plays and that you have written me about them and that I forget what's in your letters. I don't forget the least scrap, darling. I reread them sev-eral times and the trouble is that between my letters and your answers no less than ten days pass every time. I have read almost all of Turge-

---

[1] The Stanislavskys were spending the holiday there.

nev's plays. As I wrote you earlier, I don't like *A Month in the Country*, but *The Hanger-On*, which you will stage, is good enough, not badly put together, and if Artyom [1] doesn't make a long-drawn-out thing of it, and doesn't make it seem monotonous, the play will go fairly well. You will have to shorten *The Provincial Lady* somewhat. True? Good roles.

All winter long I had no hemorrhoids, but today I'm a regular titular councillor. The weather is marvelous. Everything is blossoming, warm, quiet, but no rain, I fear for the plants. You write that for three days and three nights you will hold me in your arms, but what about dinner and tea?

I received a letter from Nemirovich. Thank him heartily. I don't write him because I wrote to him recently.

Now keep well, little mongrel. I've already written you about Gorky; he has visited me and I have looked in on him. His health is fairly good. I can't send you the story "The Betrothed" because I haven't a copy. You will soon read it in *A Magazine for All*. I've written such stories before, in fact many times, so that you will find nothing new in it.[2]

May I turn you upside down, then shake you, them embrace you and bite your ear? May I, darling? Write, or I shall call you a harridan.

Your A.

TO SHOLOM ALEICHEM[1]

Naro-Fominskoe,[2] Province of Moscow,
June 19, 1903

Much esteemed Solomon Naumovich!

Generally speaking, I do not write nowadays, or write very little, so I can only give a conditional promise. I shall write a story with

---

[1] The stage name of Aleksandr Radionovich Artemyev, an actor associated with the Art Theater, who performed in four of Chekhov's plays, including *The Cherry Orchard*.

[2] There is reason seriously to doubt this statement: the story strikes an unwonted note of rebellion.

[1] Pen name of the major Yiddish writer Solomon Naumovich Rabinovich (1859–1916).

[2] A celebrated physician, after an examination the previous month, had advised Chekhov to live near Moscow, hence the address, a suburb of the city.

pleasure, if illness does not interfere. As for my published stories, they are wholly at your disposal, and their translation into Yiddish and their publication in a collection for the benefit of the Jews victimized in Kishinev would give me nothing but heartfelt pleasure.

With sincere respect and devotion,

A. Chekhov

I received your letter yesterday, June 18.

TO S. P. DIAGHILEV

Yalta, July 12, 1903

Much esteemed Sergey Pavlovich!

I am somewhat tardy in answering your letter, for I received it not in Naro-Fominskoe but in Yalta, where I arrived the other day and where I shall probably stay till fall. Having read your letter, I considered the matter a long time and tempting as your invitation is, nevertheless I must in the end respond in a way which neither you nor I would have desired.

I cannot be the editor of *The World of Art*, since living in Petersburg is out of the question for me, and surely the magazine isn't going to move to Moscow for my sake; as for editing by mail and by telegraph, it is impossible. Nor would it be of any advantage whatsoever for the magazine to have me as nothing more than its nominal editor. That's first of all. Secondly, even as a picture must be painted by one painter only and a speech must be delivered by one orator only, so a magazine, too, must be edited by only one man. Of course, I am no critic and, as likely as not, may prove no great shakes as the editor of the critical section; but, on the other hand, how could I ever get on with D. S. Merezhkovsky, who is a stanch believer, a believer who is a preacher, whereas I long since lost belief and can merely keep glancing in perplexity at every intellectual who is a believer. I respect Dmitry Sergeyevich and appreciate him both as a man and a literary figure, but then, if the two of us should manage to pull the cart, it would be in different directions.

Be that as it may, whether my attitude in this matter is erroneous or not, I have always thought and am now convinced that there must be one editor, and only one, and that *The World of Art* must be edited by you in particular, and you alone. Such is my opinion and, it seems to me, I am not going to change it.

Don't be angry with me, dear Sergey Pavlovich; it seems to me that if you edit the journal some five more years, you will agree with me. In a periodical, as in a picture or a poem, there must be only one face, you must be aware of only one will. That's how it was until now with *The World of Art* and it was good. So it would be well to continue in the same way.

I wish you all the best and press your hand firmly. In Yalta it is cool or at least not hot—I triumph.

A low bow.

Your A. Chekhov

TO M. P. LILINA

Yalta, September 15, 1903

Dear Mariya Petrovna,

Don't believe anybody, not a single living soul has read my play; for you I have written the part not of a "bigot," but of a very lovely girl, a role with which, I hope, you will be satisfied. I had almost finished the play, but a little over a week ago I was taken ill, started coughing, felt weak, in a word, last year's predicament began all over again. Today it is warm and my health seems to have improved, but nevertheless I cannot work because I have a headache. Olga will not take the play with her,[1] I'll send her all four acts as soon as I can do a whole day's work. It has turned out not a drama, but a comedy, in places even a farce, and I am afraid that I'll catch it from Vladimir Ivanovich.[2] Konstantin Sergeyevich has a big role. Generally speaking, there are not many roles.

I cannot come for the opening; I'll stay in Yalta till November. Olga has put on weight and grown strong over the summer, will go to Moscow, probably on Sunday. I'll remain alone, and, of course, I shall not fail to take advantage of it. As a writer, it is essential for me to observe as many women as possible, to study them and consequently, I regret to say, I cannot be a faithful husband. Inasmuch as I observe women

---

[1] After a stay in Yalta of two months, she was to leave for Moscow within a few days.

[2] Nemirovich-Danchenko.

[*454*]

chiefly for plays, it is my opinion that the Art Theater should raise my wife's salary or grant her a pension.

Your letter didn't give your address, I am sending this to Kammer-herr Lane. You probably attend rehearsals, so you will receive the play soon. I am infinitely grateful to you for your having remembered and written me. A low bow to Igor [3] and Kira [3] and I thank them for re-membering me; but it's a mistake on Kira's part to make much of a St. Bernard, it is a good dog, but awkward and completely useless. My friend Gipsy is quite another matter. The other day I got myself a mongrel, inordinately stupid.

When you see Vishnevsky, tell him that he should try to reduce—this is necessary for my play.[4] Further, be well, happy, successful, of good cheer. Wish that I get well in a hurry and set to work. A low bow to Konstantin Sergeyevich and all your colleagues of both sexes.

Your A. Chekhov

I kiss your little hand.

TO O. L. KNIPPER

Yalta, September 23, 1903

Greetings, my sweet, my better little half! There were two post cards from you today—I am very glad and pleased. I was counting on a tele-gram from Moscow, but God be with you, anyway: I enter into your situation, and I understand. What have they hit upon at the theater that's new? They're not fagged out? Not disappointed?

The fourth act of my play, as compared with the other acts, will be skimpy as to content yet effective. The way your part ends does not seem bad to me. In any event, don't be downhearted; everything is going well.* * *

I wash myself thoroughly. I order a pitcher of ordinary tap water and a small pitcher of icy water; then I mix the two until I get just what is needed. I dress slowly, either because I have become unaccus-tomed to dressing or because I am hindered by shortness of breath.

---

[3] The Stanislavsky children.
[4] Chekhov had privately cast Vishnevsky in the role of Gayev.

Nastya [1] lays out a fresh suit for me every day. I keep my teeth clean, am diligent about spraying. What else? I write my wife almost every day. One of these days P. I. Kurkin [2] will come to see you. He will tell you what his business is while for your part you can ponder and then give him advice. It's quite an important matter.

Small Ball is growing but doesn't bark yet. When you were leaving you forgot to take your cat along. What are your orders—to send it on to you?

Regards to Vishnevsky and tell him to start soaking up suavity and refinement for a role in my play.

Well, chickabiddy, my blessings on you. Don't sulk, don't frown, don't scold your husband. We'll be seeing each other soon. As soon as the morning frosts begin in Moscow I shall come.

Your A.

TO O. L. KNIPPER

Yalta, September 27, 1903

My darling, my pony, I have already telegraphed you that the play is finished—that all the four acts are written. I am already making a copy. My people have turned out to be alive, true enough, but what the play itself is like I don't know. There, I shall send you the play; you will read it and find out.* * *

If only it had occurred to you, my pony, to send me a telegram after the opening performance of *Julius Caesar*! I am writing *The Cherry Orchard* on that same paper which Nemirovich gave me and with the gold pens which I also received from him. Whether this will make for any changes is something I do not know.* * *

The sea is choppy but the weather is fine. Panov [1] has already left. He and Mikhailovsky [2] will be at the opening performance of *The Cherry Orchard*—so they said.

A bow to Schnapp and thank him in my name for not having fright-

---

[1] A domestic, who eventually became an actress in a Ukrainian company.

[2] Pyotr Ivanovich Kurkin, a zemstvo doctor, who had known Chekhov since their student days. His "business" had to do with helping needy young women enrolled in advanced courses.

[1] Nikolay Zakharovich Panov, a painter who made a pencil sketch of Chekhov the year of this letter.

[2] Nikolay Georgiyevich Garin-Mikhailovsky (1852–1906), an engineer whose avocation was writing.

ened you—not making you think his neck had been injured. Small Ball is pleased with life. Little Ace does, at times, sink into pessimism.

Is Sredin [3] doing your portrait? Yes, that is a pleasure, but a pleasure which one can bear up under only once in a lifetime. Why, you have already had your portrait done by him, by this Sredin!

Well, pony, I stroke you, I groom you, I give you the very best of oats and I kiss your forehead and your little neck. May the Lord be with you! Write me, and don't be too angry if I don't write you every day. I am now copying the play; consequently I deserve consideration.

Bows to everybody.

Your A.

TO O. L. KNIPPER

Yalta, October 9, 1903

My pony, don't write me cross, despondent letters,[1] don't forbid me to come to Moscow. No matter what happens, I will come to Moscow, and if you don't give me houseroom, I shall put up at a hotel somewhere. My health is much better, darling, I have put on weight, thanks to the diet, I cough less, and by November 1, I hope, I shall be in fine shape. My mood is excellent. I am copying the play, shall soon finish, my dear, I swear. I'll wire on mailing it to you. I assure you every extra day is only to the good, for my play becomes better and better, and the characters are clear now. Only I am afraid there are passages that the censor will strike out, which will be dreadful.

My own, my dove, darling, pony, don't be uneasy, everything is not as bad as you think, everything is going very well. I swear that the play is ready. I assure you a thousand times. If I didn't send it to you earlier, it is only because I have been copying it too slowly and making changes, as I always do when I copy.

It is raining today, and cool. Two live quails have been brought us.

Darling, I will certainly come to Moscow even if you kill me, and I would have come even if I weren't married; consequently, if I am run over by a cab in Moscow, you won't be guilty.

[3] Aleksandr Valentinovich Sredin, a painter, perhaps a brother of Leonid Valentinovich.
[1] In a letter dated October 6 Knipper had written unhappily, blaming herself for living apart from him.

Act well, carefully; study, darling, observe; you are still a young actress; don't mope, please! For God's sake.* * *

I embrace my joy. The Lord be with you, be at peace and cheerful.

Your A.

TO V. I. NEMIROVICH-DANCHENKO

Yalta, November 2, 1903

* * * For three years I have been getting ready to write *The Cherry Orchard*—and for three years I have been telling you people to invite some actress to play the role of Lyubov Andreyevna.[1] There, now, go ahead and lay out your cards for a game of patience which simply won't come out right, for all your trying.

At present I find myself in a most absurd situation: I am sitting around all by myself and have no idea what I am sitting around for. There's no point in your saying that it's you who are doing the work while nevertheless the Theater is styled the Theater of Stanislavsky. It's only you they talk about, it's you they write about, but as for Stanislavsky—all they do is revile him for his Brutus. If you walk out, well, I too will walk out. Gorky is younger than either of us; he has a life of his own. . . . As for the theater at Nizhny Novgorod, it is no more than an ephemeral thing. Gorky will get a taste of it, take a sniff at it, and drop it. While we are on the subject: theaters for the people, along with literature for the people, are all fiddle-faddle, all candy for the people. The need is not to bring Gogol down to the level of the people but to bring the people up to the level of Gogol.

Right now I would like, ever so much, to go to the Hermitage, eat sturgeon there, and drink a bottle of wine. Time was when I would drink off a bottle of champagne and not get drunk, then I would drink cognac—and that wouldn't get me drunk either.* * *

Your A. Chekhov

---

[1] Mme. Ranevskaya, the owner of the cherry orchard. After some vacillation this important role was given to Knipper.

TO O. L. KNIPPER

Yalta, November 7, 1903

My sweet, my pony—greetings! Nothing new, everything going well—
absolutely everything. Don't feel like writing; what I feel like is going
to Moscow and I am constantly expecting an exit permit from you. * * *
I overslept today—woke up at nine! I don't feel poorly—so it seems.
Except for upset bowels, that is. I ought to change my regimen, lead a
more immoral life; I ought to eat everything—even mushrooms, even
cabbage—and drink everything. Eh? What do you think?

You tell Vishnevsky to walk more and to avoid excitement. Well, my
dumpling, I hug you. Sign me out of here as soon as you can. Can it be
that you aren't curious to see your husband in a new fur coat?

A.

Don't write me about roast duck—don't torture me. When I arrive I
shall finish off a whole duck.

TO O. L. KNIPPER

Yalta, November 21, 1903

Dear pony, of late I have been giving way to my bad character, forgive
me. I am a husband, and they say that all husbands have bad characters.
I was just called to the telephone. It was Lazarevsky,[1] speaking from
Sevastopol; he said he was coming over this evening and might spend the
night, and again I shall be furious. Hurry up, hurry up and summon me
to you in Moscow. Here the weather is clear and it's warm, but I am already blasé, I can't appreciate these delights as they deserve, I need the
Moscow slush and nasty weather; I can no longer do without the theater and literature. And you know that I am married, you will admit
that; after all, I want to see my wife.* * *

No letter from you today. Yesterday I wired you about the fur coat.
Asked you to wait for a letter. I am afraid that you are angry. But
never mind, we shall make up. There is still plenty of time.

The weather is quite summery. There is nothing new. I am not work-

---

[1] Boris Aleksandrovich Lazarevsky (1871–1936), a jurist known as a writer of
fiction.

ing. I keep waiting for you to allow me to pack and start for Moscow. "To Moscow, to Moscow!" This is the cry not of *Three Sisters* but of *One Husband*.

I hug my little hen turkey.

Your A.

TO K. S. STANISLAVSKY[1]

Yalta, November 23, 1903

Dear Konstantin Sergeyevich,

Hay-making takes place June 20–25, by that time the corncrake's rasping cry is no longer heard, the frogs are also silent by then. The oriole alone moans plaintively. There is no cemetery, there was one, but a very long time ago. Two or three gravestones lying helter-skelter are all that remains. A bridge—that's very good. If a train can be shown without noise, without a single sound—go to it. I am not against the same scenery in Acts III and IV, except that it would be convenient to have exits and entrances in Act IV.

I am impatiently waiting for the day and the hour when my wife will at last permit me to come to Moscow. I am beginning to suspect her of being sly with me, for all I know.

The weather is windless, warm, amazing, but when you think of Moscow, of the Sandunov baths, all this delight becomes boring, to no purpose.

I sit in my study and keep glancing at the telephone. Telegrams are read to me over it, and so I wait for the moment when I shall finally be summoned to Moscow.

I press your hand and make a low obeisance to you for the letter. Keep well and prosperous.

Your A. Chekhov

TO O. L. KNIPPER

Yalta, November 29, 1903

By now I don't know what to do, what to think, pony. They persist in failing to summon me to Moscow, and apparently don't want to know

[1] This letter deals with the scenery of *The Cherry Orchard*.

[460]

ne. You ought to write me frankly why this is so, what the reason is, and I would not waste time, but would go abroad. If you knew how drearily the rain hammers on the roof, how much I want to have a look at my wife. Do I have a wife? Where is she?

I shall not write you any more, do what you may.[1] There is nothing to write about and nothing to write for.

If I do get a telegram today I'll bring you sweet wine. If not, a fig for you.

Schnapp, I repeat, is not the right sort.[2] What is needed is a sorry mutt such as you've seen or something of the kind. You can do without a dog.

Well, I hug you.

Your A.

TO A. N. VESELOVSKY

Moscow, December 11, 1903

Much esteemed Aleksey Nikolayevich!

I do not know how to thank you for the letter. I first learned from the newspapers about my election as temporary chairman of the Society of Lovers of Russian Literature,[1] but I did not write to you because I waited for confirmation. This election is an unexpected and undeserved honor, of which I could not have dreamed. My refusal of it is out of the question, all of me belongs to the Society, and I would be infinitely happy if I could show this not only in words but also in deeds. Unfortunately, at present, because of illness, I cannot attend public sessions, and I would appreciate, if possible, a year's or two years' grace. Or perhaps meanwhile I could be useful to the Society as editor or proof-reader, or in some other capacity without residing in Moscow; I do not live in Moscow now, but am only testing the city to find out if I could live here, and at the first hemorrhage or violent attack of coughing I would have to flee to Yalta or abroad.[2]

[1] In this sentence Chekhov does not use the intimate "thou."
[2] The reference is to the dog, mentioned in his previous letter, that he wished to have introduced into the first act of *The Cherry Orchard*.
[1] Veselovsky was chairman of the Society of Lovers of Russian Literature.
[2] A week before Chekhov wrote this letter he had come to Moscow and he stayed there until February 15, when he left for Yalta. In spite of his illness he visited and received friends, saw Gorky's *The Lower Depths*, attended the Art Theater's New Year's banquet. Above all, he was present at the rehearsals of *The Cherry Orchard*. He criticized the acting, made changes in the text, supplied substitutes for passages cut by the censor.

Kindly write to me when I could find you in. I haven't seen you for a long time and would like to have a talk with you and thank you personally.

I wish you all the best.

Sincerely,

your respectful and devoted A. Chekhov

[1904]

TO F. D. BATYUSHKOV

Moscow, January 19, 1904

Dear Fyodor Dmitriyevich,

I assure you that my anniversary (i.e. the twenty-fifth) is still to come and not so soon. I went to Moscow, to enter the University, in the second half of 1879, the first trifle of 10 to 15 lines was printed in March or April 1880, in *The Dragonfly;* [1] if one is to be very lenient and count this trifle as the beginning, then my anniversary is to be marked no earlier than 1905.

Be that as it may, on January 17, when *The Cherry Orchard* opened, my twenty-fifth anniversary was celebrated on such a large scale, so warmly and indeed, so unexpectedly, that I have not yet been able to regain my composure. [2]

It would be well if you came by Shrovetide. I think that only by then will our actors have come to themselves and play *The Cherry Orchard* not with such bewilderment and so lackadaisically as they do now.* * *

Your A. Chekhov

TO O. L. KNIPPER

Sevastopol, February 17, 1904

Greetings, my peerless pony! I am writing this aboard the steamer, which will leave in about three hours. I have had a good trip, all has

[1] It appeared in the issue of *The Dragonfly* for March 9.

[2] It was arranged that the play should open on Chekhov's birthday. He was too fearful of a failure to be present for the first two acts, but called for by friends, he appeared during the intermission before Act IV. There was a tremendous ovation and there were a dozen speeches, a thirteenth being delivered by Chaliapin at the supper following the performance.

gone well. Nastya is on the steamer with Schnapp. He feels quite at home, and is very nice. In the train, too, he conducted himself exactly as he did at home, barked at the conductors, amused everybody; he was delighted to see me, now he is sitting on deck, with his legs stretched out behind him. Apparently, he has already forgotten Moscow, vexing as this may be. Well, darling pony, I shall wait for letters from you. Without your letters, I must tell you, I can't exist. Either you write me every day or else divorce me, there is no middle course.

I hear Schnapp up above, barking at someone. Evidently the passengers are paying attention to him. I'll go and see.

And so all is well, thank God—couldn't be better. Let's hope the sea won't be rough.

I kiss my manageress and embrace her a million times. Write at greater length, don't spare ink, my darling, my nice, good, gifted actress. The Lord be with you. I love you very much.

Your A.

TO O. L. KNIPPER

Yalta, February 20, 1904

My darling, my pony, without you it's tedious, cold, uninteresting, and you have spoiled me to such an extent that going to bed and getting up, I fear that I shan't know how to undress and dress. My bed is hard, cold, the rooms are cold, outdoors it's freezing, wearisome, not a whiff of spring. All day long I have been busy with last year's letters and old newspapers. I seem to have no other occupation now.

Schnapp is either deaf or stupid. It's as though he had never been away from here, he capers about with the other dogs and obediently spends the night in Mother's room. He is very cheerful but understands little.

Nastya does the cooking, but not very well. We need a cook. Today I had fried sturgeon, very rich and tasty, and soup resembling slops. And ice-cold pancakes.

In the train I ate everything (this is in reply to your question), everything except the ham sandwich. I had a good trip. The desk is here already, and I am writing at it. The drawers are hard to open. Generally speaking, it is satisfactory. The other things have not yet arrived. "Kashtanka"[1] has come, an elegant edition, badly illustrated, published by Marx.

I haven't yet been to town, haven't yet been outdoors. I have no wife, she is in Moscow, I live like a monk. I am sorry I didn't take the cup with me. The cup here seemed small to me; perhaps I am mistaken. Arseny has grown lazy or forgetful; Nastya brushed my clothes; I keep my teeth clean. I shall go to the baths in May when I come to Moscow, till then I shall sow Indian corn on my body and thus still earn something.

Today I had a letter from you—the first of this season. Thanks, my angel, I kiss you, embrace you, pat you.

I wish they'd hurry up and beat the Japanese, somehow the newspapers are peculiar and so are the people; there is a good deal of lying, the value of the ruble is down, people are interested in nothing but the war.

What are the misunderstandings between us, darling? When did you irritate me? Bless your heart! During this visit of mine we had an extraordinary, remarkable time, I felt as if I had returned from a campaign. I thank you, my joy, for being so good.

Write to me, or I will thrash you as usual. I kiss, I hug my joy. Be cheerful and keep well.

Your A.

TO O. L. KNIPPER

Yalta, March 3, 1904

My dear, remarkable little half, I am alive, strong as a bull, in good spirits, and there is only one thing I can't get used to—namely, my monkish state.

I have a favor to ask of you, darling. I have already told you, I am a physician and a friend of the Women's Medical School. When *The Cherry Orchard* was announced, the students requested me, as a doctor, to arrange for a performance of the play for the benefit of their auxiliary; they are terribly poor, many of them are expelled for failure to pay tuition, etc., etc. I said that I would take up the matter with the directors, did so, and obtained their promise. . . . Before I left Moscow

[1] A children's story by Chekhov.

Nemirovich told me that it would hardly be practical to arrange the benefit in Petersburg at present: it is wartime, and the takings may be almost nil; would it not be better, he asked, to arrange a literary matinée for the students' benefit, like the one arranged for the Literary Fund. I agreed with him and it ended with his promising to arrange a literary matinée, only he asked to be reminded of this in Petersburg. So, my own, do remind him now, and in general insist that the matinée should take place. Some of the students may call on you in Petersburg, receive them, talk to them, be as gracious as you can, and tell them how and where Nemirovich can be reached.* * *

We shall defeat the Japanese. Uncle Sasha [1] will come home a colonel, Uncle Karl [1] will have a new decoration.

In the fall I will start building a bathhouse. All this, however, is dreams, dreams! * * *

Darling, my pony, keep well, be cheerful and happy. I am afraid that visitors are coming. People here are so boring, unliterary; there is nothing to talk to them about, and when I listen to them, my vision is clouded.

Well, the Lord be with you.

Your A.

TO O. L. KNIPPER

Yalta, April 10, 1904

My sweet little linnet, you are angry at me, you grumble, but really, I am not at fault. It seems to me that I did not talk with Masha about Tsaritsyno at all, I know nothing about it.* * * Generally speaking, I believed that it would be chiefly you who would solve the dacha problem,[1] not I. In such matters, you know, I am a poor stick.

Why on posters and in newspaper advertisements is my play stubbornly called a drama? Nemirovich and Alekseyev positively do not see in my play what I wrote, and I am ready to vouch that neither of them read *The Cherry Orchard* through carefully even once. Forgive me, but I assure you. I have in mind not alone the dreadful stage set of the second act, not alone Khalyutina, replaced by Adurskaya, who does the same thing and decidedly nothing of what is in my text.

[1] Uncles of Chekhov's wife.
[1] The reference is to the possible purchase of a dacha in Tsaritsyno, now Stalingrad.

The weather is warm, but it is chilly in the shade, the evenings are cold. I take walks lazily, because for some reason I gasp for breath. *The Cherry Orchard* is being staged here by touring trash.[2]

I cannot wait to see you, my joy. Somehow I managed to live without you, a day passes, thank God—without thoughts, without desires, only with playing patience and pacing from one corner of the room to another. I haven't been to a bathhouse for a long time, perhaps six years. I read all the newspapers, even *The Government Herald*, and as a result I am turning brown.

How long will you be staying in Petersburg—write me, do me a favor. Do not forget me, think sometimes about the man to whom you were married once upon a time. I kiss my darling.

Your poor stick

TO O. L. KNIPPER

Yalta, April 15, 1904

My sweet, good darling, yesterday there was no letter from you, today again no letter; in this Yalta I am as alone as a comet, and I am not particularly well. The day before yesterday in the local theater (without wings or dressing rooms) *The Cherry Orchard* was staged, the *mise-en-scène* being that of the Art Theater, the actors a vile lot headed by Daryalova (so named, aping the actress, Daryal), and there are notices, and tomorrow there will be notices and the day after tomorrow too. I am called to the telephone, acquaintances sigh, and I, a patient, so to speak, who is being treated here must dream of how to make off. You might perhaps give this humorous subject to Amfiteatrov.[1] However amusing all this may seem, I must confess that provincial actors behave just like scoundrels.

Express trains have already started running, so that I shall arrive in Moscow in the morning, my joy. I shall come as soon as possible, that is, May 1. I can't stay here: upset stomach, actors, the public, telephone calls, and the devil knows what.

What are your takings these days? Really full houses? I can imagine

[2] The Sevastopol municipal theater company.
[1] Aleksandr Valentinovich Amfiteatrov, a writer of *feuilletons* and fiction.

[*467*]

how tired out you all are. Meanwhile I sit still and keep dreaming about fishing and considering how I am to dispose of my whole catch, although in the entire summer I shall land only one gudgeon, and he will be caught due to his suicidal disposition.

Write me, darling, write, or I shall cry for help. I am sending you a clipping from our *Crimean Courier*, read it.

Well, the Lord be with you, my joy, live, and sleep sweetly, dream, and remember your husband. I love you, you know, I love your letters, your acting, your manner of walking. The only thing I don't like is when you dawdle over the washstand.

Your A.

TO O. L. KNIPPER

Yalta, April 18, 1904

* * * My sweet darling, my little child, my own, in Petersburg, on Great Sadovaya Street in the Yusupov Garden there is an I. G. Kebke exhibition—boats, tents, and the like. You might go and have a look at it. The exhibition is held in the house of the Society for the Rescue of the Drowning. Perhaps you will pick out a light, pretty boat, inexpensive. Or you might find out where their store is located and step into it. The lighter the boat, the better. Ask the price, note the name and number of the boat, so that it could be ordered afterwards, and inquire if it can be sent as ordinary goods. The fact is that railroads use a whole flatcar for a boat, so that the cost of transportation jumps to a hundred rubles.

* * * I am dreaming so eagerly about the summer! I so long to be alone, to do some writing, some thinking!

I embrace you, darling.

Your A.

TO O. L. KNIPPER

Yalta, April 20, 1904

* * * Well, I shall send you one or two more letters, and then I shall stop. I shall leave Yalta not without pleasure: it is boring here, no spring, and besides I am not well. And I haven't yet had my teeth

fixed; yesterday I drove into town to see Ostrovsky,[1] but did not find him in, he had gone to Alushta. It is very tedious without a wife, but I haven't the courage to take a mistress. Yevtikhy Karpov, Suvorin's stage director, is here. Yesterday Ilyinskaya [2] visited me and said that he was planning to see me. It is raining. I had a letter from Lazarevsky, who is in Vladivostok. If, as you write, my letters reach you irregularly, yours play pranks like drunks. I receive two letters at once. Evidently your letters are detained somewhere and read. This is so necessary!

You ask: what is life? It is the same as asking what is a carrot. A carrot is a carrot, and that's all that's known.* * *

Keep well, don't be bored, don't be depressed, you will soon see your spouse. I embrace you and give your little leg a little tug.

Your A.

TO O. L. KNIPPER

Yalta, April 22, 1904

My darling, my wife, I am writing you my last letter,[1] and later, if need be, I shall wire you. Yesterday I was indisposed, today too, but still, I feel easier today; I eat nothing but eggs and soup. It is raining, the weather is nasty, cold. Nevertheless, in spite of my illness and the rain, I went to see the dentist.

The 22nd Siberian Infantry Regiment was on active duty the other day, and, as you know, that is Uncle Sasha's regiment! I can't get him out of my mind. It is reported that nine Company commanders were killed or wounded, and Uncle Sasha is just such a commander. Well, God is merciful, your dear uncle will come off unhurt. I can imagine how exhausted he is, how cross!

Yesterday I was visited by Yevtikhy Karpov, Suvorin's stage director, a playwright of no talent, but possessed of bottomlessly grandiose pretensions. These figures are superannuated, they bore me, they bore me to extinction by their insincere affability.

I shall reach Moscow in the morning. Express trains are already run-

[1] A dentist.
[2] Mariya Vasilyevna Ilyinskaya, an actress with the Aleksandrinsky Theater.
[1] A prophetic statement: it was his last letter to her.

ning. Oh, my blanket! Oh, the veal chop! Doggie, doggie, how I long for you!

I embrace and kiss you. Behave yourself. And if you have ceased to love me or have grown cold to me, say so, don't stand on ceremony.

I have written you about the dacha in Tsaritsyno. The letter from Sobolevsky on that subject I told you about.

Well, Christ be with you, my joy.

Your A.

TO L. I. LYUBIMOV[1]

Moscow, June 2, 1904

Much esteemed Leonid Ivanovich!

I am ill, since May 2 I have been confined to my bed, and tomorrow I am going abroad for treatment; nevertheless I shall still be able to do something for your son, Aleksandr Leonidovich.[2] Today I contacted a gentleman who will talk to the rector, and tomorrow I shall speak to another acquaintance.

I shall return at the end of July or early in August and then I will do all I can, so that your desire, with which I fully sympathize, should be realized.

Allow me to thank you for your kind, excellent letter and wish you and your family all the best.

Respectfully and devotedly,

A. Chekhov

TO M. P. CHEKHOVA

Berlin, June 6, 1904

Dear Masha,

I am writing you from Berlin, where I have been staying for the last twenty-four hours. In Moscow the weather turned very chilly after you left, it started snowing, and I probably caught cold. I felt rheumatic

[1] L. I. Lyubimov was a deacon who taught, presumably "God's law" (religion), in the Moscow city schools.

[2] The addressee had asked Chekhov to use his influence to enable the man's son to be transferred from the University of Yuriev (Dorpat, now Tartu) to that of Moscow. In another letter Chekhov set down his opinion that wire-pulling was unobjectionable if it were done to serve someone other than oneself.

pains in my arms and legs, couldn't sleep, got terribly thin, took morphine injections, swallowed thousands of various medicines, and I gratefully recall only heroin, which Altschuller had once prescribed for me. Nevertheless, by the time I was ready to leave I began to pick up strength, my appetite came back, I started taking injections of arsenic, etc., etc. On Thursday I finally went abroad, emaciated, with thin, scraggy legs, but I had a good, pleasant journey. Here in Berlin we have taken a cozy room in the best hotel and I greatly enjoy our stay here, and it has been a long time since I've eaten so well, with such appetite. The bread here is amazing, and I can't keep from eating too much of it, the coffee is excellent, the dinners are beyond words. If you've not been abroad, you don't know what good bread is. There isn't any decent tea here (we brought our own), no hors d'oeuvres, but then everything else is superb, and cheaper than at home. I have already put on weight, and today I even went on a long drive to the Tiergarten, although it was cool. And so you can tell Mama and everyone to whom this is of interest that I am convalescing and indeed, that I'm well, my legs no longer ache, I have no diarrhea, am beginning to grow stout, and am on my feet all day, don't lie down. Tomorrow I shall be examined by the local celebrity—Professor Ewald, a specialist in intestinal diseases. Dr. Taube wrote to him about me.

Yesterday I had some wonderful beer.

Is Vanya in Yalta? Two days before I left Moscow he came to see me and then vanished from sight. I confess that while I was traveling I was troubled by the thought of him; where is he and why did he suddenly disappear? Please write me what happened.

The day after tomorrow we leave for Badenweiler. I shall send you the address. Write to say if you have money. When shall I send a check? I like Berlin very much, though it is chilly here today. I read the German papers. The rumors that the local press is very hostile to Russians are exaggerated.

Keep well and be cheerful, may the angels of Heaven guard you. Greetings to Mamasha, tell her that everything is all right now. In August I'll come to Yalta. Greetings also to Grandmother, Arseny, and Nastya. To Varvara Konstantinovna as well. I kiss you.

Your A. Chekhov

We forgot to bring my dressing gown.

TO P. F. IORDANOV

Badenweiler, June 12, 1904

Much esteemed Pavel Fyodorovich!

Kindly let me know if you have received the package of books that I sent you from Moscow early in June. I left the books in Moscow with a request to mail them immediately, and then I departed. Early in May I fell ill, lost much weight, became weak, did not sleep nights, but now I am on a diet (I eat a great deal) and live abroad.* * *

I seem on the mend. It is emphysema that interferes with my walking properly. But, I thank the Germans, they have taught me how and what to eat. You know, ever since the age of twenty I have suffered from intestinal disorder. Oh, the Germans! How punctual they are (with very few exceptions)!

The Germans have forbidden me to drink coffee, which I love so much.

They insist that I drink wine, of which I have lost the habit.

Now, keep well, I wish you everything good. Is it true that in Taganrog it is cold? In Berlin it is very cold.

There is no such good bread anywhere as what the Germans have, and they feed you wonderfully well. In Moscow, I, an invalid, was given dry toast made of home-baked bread, for in *all Moscow* there is no decent wholesome bread.

However, forgive me, I have bored you with trifles.

I press your hand.

Your A. Chekhov

Badenweiler is a health resort in the Black Forest, southern Germany. In Moscow my arms and legs ached; I even thought that I was beginning to suffer from tabes. But it wasn't that, God was merciful, as soon as I left the Moscow apartment and got into the train the pains began to abate.

Dear Masha,

For the third day I am living in a place that has been chosen for me. Here, if you wish, is my exact address: Germany, Badenweiler, Herrn

Anton Tschechow, Villa Friederika.

Like all local houses and villas, this Villa Friederika stands apart in a luxuriant garden, facing the sun, which gives light and warmth until seven in the evening (later I retire to the rooms). We have room and board here. For 14 or 16 marks a day the two of us have a room flooded with sunlight, with washstands, beds, etc., etc., with a desk and, chiefly, with marvelous water which resembles seltzer. The impression made by the surroundings is of a large garden with wooded mountains behind it, few people, the street quiet, the garden and the flowers wonderfully tended, but today, unexpectedly, it rained and I keep indoors, and I begin to feel that in a day or two I shall start thinking about how to escape.

I continue eating tremendous quantities of butter and without any ill effects. Milk I can't stand. The local doctor, Schwöhrer (married to a Zhivago from Moscow), has turned out to be knowledgeable and decent.

From here we shall perhaps return to Yalta, taking the sea route, by way of Trieste or some other port. Health is pouring into me not by the teaspoonful but by the gallon. At least here I have learned how to feed myself. Coffee is forbidden altogether. They say it is laxative. I have already begun to eat eggs—some. Oh, how dreadfully German women dress!

I live on the ground floor. Oh, if you knew what the sunshine here is like! It doesn't burn, it caresses. I have a comfortable armchair in which I can sit or stretch out.

I shall certainly buy a watch, I haven't forgotten it. How is Mamasha's health? How does she feel otherwise? Write to me. Greet her for me. Olga is going to a dentist here, a very good one.

Keep well and cheerful. I'll write again shortly.

In Berlin I bought a lot of this paper and envelopes, too. I kiss you, press your hand.

Your A. Chekhov

Greetings to Arseny, Grandmother, and Nastya. Also, by the way, to Sinani.

Where is Vanya? Has he come to Yalta? If he is in Yalta, greet him too for me.

TO M. P. CHEKHOVA

Badenweiler, June 16, 1904

Dear Masha,

Today I received your first post card, thank you very much. I am living among Germans, am already used to my room and to the regimen, but I cannot get used to German tranquillity and calm. Not a sound either in or out of doors, only at 7 o'clock in the morning and at noon there is music in the garden, it is not cheap, but the performance is poor, not a trace of verve in anything, not a sign of taste but, to compensate, order and honesty to spare. Our Russian life is much more spirited and as for the Italians and the French, needless to say, they are far and away superior.

My health has improved and when I walk I no longer notice that I am ill, I walk and that's it, less marked shortness of breath, no pain, all that remains of the illness is extreme emaciation, my legs were never so thin before. The German doctors have turned my life topsy-turvy. At 7 o'clock in the morning I have tea in bed, for some reason unquestionably in bed, at half-past seven a German comes, a kind of masseur, and gives me a rubdown with water, and this, it appears, isn't bad, then I have to wait a while, and get up at 8 o'clock, drink acorn cocoa and swallow a huge amount of butter with it. At 10 o'clock thin oatmeal, extraordinarily delicious and aromatic, not at all like our own Russian oatmeal. Fresh air in the sun. Reading newspapers. At 1 o'clock dinner, not all the dishes of which I eat but only those prescribed by the German doctor and selected for me by Olga. At 4 o'clock cocoa again. At 7 o'clock supper. Before going to sleep a cup of strawberry tea as a sleeping potion. In all this, a lot of charlatanism, but much also that is really good, useful, for instance, the oatmeal. I shall take some of the local oatmeal home with me.

Olga has left for Switzerland, where she is having her teeth taken care of in Basel. She will be home at 5 o'clock in the evening.

I am longing furiously for Italy. I am very glad that Vanya is with the family. Greet him for me. Greet Mamasha too. What's going on in the girls' high school? * * *

I am glad that all is well with the family. I shall probably spend another three weeks here, then I shall go to Italy for a time, and then perhaps by sea to Yalta.

Write more often. Tell Vanya to write, too. Be well and prosper, I kiss you.

Your A.

* * * I don't need anything more.

TO K. P. PYATNITZKY[1]

Badenweiler, June 19, 1904

Much respected Konstantin Petrovich!

From May 2 on I was very ill, bedridden all the time, and, as I now realize, I did not think about what I, of all men, should have thought about, and therefore in this whole unpleasant incident [2] willy-nilly I must take a large share of the guilt. Your losses I perhaps can make up by returning the 4500 rubles that you paid me, which sum you can receive from me at the end of July when I return to Russia. Furthermore, I could assume a part of the losses your edition may suffer as a result of poor sales. Such is my decision and I earnestly beg you to abide by it.

Legally the case can be settled thus: you sue me (I give you my full consent in the belief that this will in no way alter our good relations); then I engage Grusenberg [3] as my lawyer, and he deals with Marx for me, seeking to recover the damages that you sustained and for which I am responsible.

[1] K. P. Pyatnitzky was one of the founders and managers of *Knowledge*, a publishing company in which Maxim Gorky figured largely. It issued, at irregular intervals, a literary miscellany under the same title.

[2] An oversight for which Chekhov, mortally ill, was partly responsible resulted in the simultaneous appearance, in the spring of 1904, of two editions of *The Cherry Orchard*. One, priced at 40 copecks, was brought out by A. F. Marx; the other, for which Chekhov received 4500 rubles from the *Knowledge* company, formed part of one of their miscellanies.

[3] Oskar Osipovich Grusenberg, an outstanding lawyer. His opinion, as reported by Pyatnitzky, was that Marx had no right whatsoever to publish the play.

And so: either I pay you 4500 and damages, out of court, or the case is settled in litigation. Of course, I favor the latter. Whatever I can write to Marx now is useless. I terminate all relations with him because I regard him as having cheated me in a paltry and foolish way. Furthermore, no matter what I would write him would have no meaning for him.

Forgive me for having disturbed the peace of your publishing activity in this way. Nothing to be done. Something adverse always happens with a play, and for some reason every one of my plays is born into the world marked by a scandal, and I never experience the usual feeling of an author, but something rather peculiar.

In any event, do not be upset, and do not be cross, I am in a worse condition than you.* * *

I am not well. I press your hand firmly and remain

With sincere respect,
A. Chekhov

TO M. P. CHEKHOVA[1]

Badenweiler, June 28, 1904

Dear Masha,

We are having a cruel spell of heat here and it has caught me unawares, since I have only my winter clothes with me. I am stifling and dream of leaving the place. But where could we go? I thought of Como in Italy, but the heat has chased everybody away from there. All southern Europe is hot. I would like to take a steamer from Trieste to Odessa, but I don't know if now, in June-July, it is possible. Would

[1] Chekhov's last letter. The same day, a Monday, he had written to Rossolimo to ask for details about going from Marseilles to Odessa by steamer, apologizing for putting his friend to trouble, and promising to reciprocate. He added, "These past days I had a high temperature but today all is well, I am in good health, especially when I don't move, i.e., am not short of breath." The following night and the night thereafter he had severe heart attacks. Thursday, July 1, passed without incident. In the course of it he composed a comic story which made Olga laugh. On Friday, July 2/15, he woke at 1 A.M. The doctor was called and ordered oxygen, which Chekhov refused, and then ordered champagne. According to Olga's account, Chekhov said to the doctor, "*Ich sterbe.*" Then he turned to Olga, smiled "his wonderful smile and said, 'I haven't had champagne in a long time.' He drank it off slowly, lay down on his left side and soon grew quiet forever."

Georgy find out what ships there are on that run? Are they comfortable? How long are the stops, is the food good, and so on? For me it would be an irreplaceable jaunt, if only the steamer were not bad, but a good one. Georgy would do me a great favor if he wired me *at my expense*. The wire should read as follows: "Badenweiler Tschechow. *Bien*. Sixteen. *Vendredi*." The meaning of the last three words is this: "bien"—the steamer is good. "Sixteen"—the number of days the journey takes. *"Vendredi"*—the day the ship sails from Trieste. Of course, if the steamer leaves on Thursday, the word *Vendredi* would be wrong.

It won't be a misfortune if the trip is somewhat hot. I shall have a flannel suit. I confess I am somewhat shy of railroad travel. In a coach you may suffocate, particularly with my shortness of breath, which the least trifle aggravates. Besides, there are no sleeping cars from Vienna to Odessa, so it would be a tiring trip. Then, too, a train takes one home faster than necessary, and I haven't had my fill of globe-trotting.

It is exceedingly hot, enough to make one strip. I just don't know what to do. Olga went to Freiburg to get me a flannel suit: here in Badenweiler there are neither tailors nor shoemakers. For a pattern, she took the suit Duchard made for me.

I eat delicious food, but very little of it, for my stomach is repeatedly upset. I may not eat the butter here. Obviously, my stomach is in a hopeless condition, and there is no help for it by any means short of fasting, that is, to stop eating entirely—and that's final. *Basta!* As for my shortness of breath, the only remedy is not to move.

Not a single decently dressed German woman, depressing bad taste.

Keep well and be happy. Greetings to Mamasha, Vanya, Georgy. Grandmother, and all the others. Write. I kiss you, press your hand.

Your A.

INDEX

Figures in *italics* indicate pages on which
letters addressed to the individual begin.

[*483*]

Red Sea, 170
Reinovo, 161
Religion, ix, 202, 411, 438, 453
Repin, Ilya Yefimovich, 131, 226, 366
"Requiem," 28
Resurrection (Tolstoy), 287, 369, 376
Revolutionary activity, viii. *See also* So-
   cialism; Student riots
Riviera. *See* Nice
Roche, Denis, 366
Rochefort, A., 299
Rome, 180–81, 182, 392
Roshchin-Insarov, Nikolay Petrovich, 329
Rossolimo, Grigory Ivanovich, *351*, 476n
Rozanov, Vasily Vasilyevich, 290, 411
Rozhansky, A. V. (Sekar), 312
Rudin (Turgenev), 100
Russian Bulletins, The, 198, 241, 242,
   291n
Russian Huntsman, 123
Russians and Russian culture, 97–99, 102–
   103, 145, 197, 245, 252, 297, 299, 300,
   308, 474
Russian Thought, 77, 134, 215, 224, 230,
   231n, 235, 241n, 252, 284, 309, 367n
Russian Veteran, The, 399
Russian Wealth, 43, 417
Russian Writers' Union of Mutual De-
   fense, 339n
Russo-Japanese War, 465–66, 469

Sablin, Mikhail Alekseyevich, 242
St. Petersburg, 6, 25, 36, 38–39, 43, 82,
   125–26, 229, 237, 262, 343, 391, 394–
   395, 445
Sakhalin: census, vii, 166, 169; Chekhov's
   impressions of visit, 165–68, 171–75;
   preparation and reasons for trip, 126–
   130; summary of visit, vi–viii; trip to
   and from, 136–64, 167–70; mentioned,
   196, 352. *See also Island of Sakhalin,
   The*
Saltykov, Mikhail Yevgrafovich (N.
   Schedrin; Saltykov-Shchedrin), 115,
   118, 289n
Salvini, 176
Sandher, 304
Sanin, 395
Sapieha, Count, 149
Savina, Mariya Gavrilovna, 96, 108, 440
Sazonova, Sofya Ivanovna, 227–28
Schechtel, Darya Karlovna, 45
Schechtel, Franz (Fyodor) Osipovich, *45*,
   47, 273
Scherer-Koestner, 305
Scholarships, 368
Scholz, August, 430
Schools, Chekhov's building of, vii, 261–
   262, 278–79, 289, 310–11, 342
Schwöhrer, 473
Science, ix, 91, 119, 226, 245–46, 336, 445.
   See also Medicine and literature

Sea Gull, The: articles on, 389, 437; censored, 267–68; Chekhov attempts to
   stop production, 437; Chekhov's reaction to, 269, 272, 275; inspiration for,
   187n; Knipper in, 342n, 404; recep-
   tion, 269–73, 322, 327, 353n; staging,
   271n, 327; writing, 261, 263–64; men-
   tioned, 325, 335n, 355n, 370, 444
Seifert, F. I., 402n
Sekar (A. V. Rozhansky), 312
Selected Letters, xii, 76n, 176n, 299n
Semashko, Marian Romualdovich, 137,
   159
Senger, Grigory Eduardovich, 426
Sergeyenko (writer), 259, 271, 311, 332
Sergeyevo, 395–96
Sergius, Bishop, 411
Serpukhov district, 200, 217, 219, 251,
   291, 337, 353, 363
Servants, 111
Sevastopol municipal theater company,
   467n
Sex, 240–41, 319
Shakespeare, William, 4, 40, 132
Shapovalov, Lev Nikolayevich, 441
Shavrova, Yelena Mikhailovna, *191*, 252,
   256, 275, 321
Shchedrin, N. *See* Saltykov, Mikhail Yev-
   grafovich
Shchepkina-Kupernik, Tatyana Lvovna,
   251
Shcherbak, Dr., 169
Shchurovsky, Dr., 404
Sheremetyev, Count A. D., 200
Shishkin, 226
Sholom Aleichem (Solomon Naumovich
   Rabinovich), *452*
Short-story writing, 5–6, 85, 86, 89–90,
   432, 444. *See also* Collected works, pub-
   lication of; Playwriting; specific short-
   story entries; Writing, Chekhov and
Siberia; Chekhov's trip to, vi, 141–69,
   171; railroad, 186
Sibiryakova, 118, 194
Sienkiewicz, Henry, 237n; *The Polaniet-
   ski Family*, 259–60
Simonov, A. M., 141
Sinani, Abram Isaakovich, *344*
Sinani, Isaak Abramovich, 313, 315,
   344n, 348, 403
Singapore, 169, 221
Skabichevsky, Aleksandr Mikhailovich,
   231, 233
Skin diseases, 390
Sklifasovsky, 261, 263
Slavyansk, 59–60
Sluchevsky (poet), 332
Smagin, Aleksandr Ivanovich, *198*, 205
Smagin family, 77
Smoke (Turgenev), 231
Smoking, 215, 235, 240, 245, 320
Snegirev, Vladimir Fyodorovich, 192
Snow Maiden, The (Ostrovsky), 382

Sobolevsky, Vasily Mikhailovich, 198, *291, 297–98*, 301, *366*, 470
Sochi, 288, 289
Socialism, 99
Society of Dramatic Writers and Operatic Composers, 91–92, 113, 114*n*
Society of Lovers of Russian Literature, 353*n*, 461
Socrates (Sergeyenko), 376
Soldatenkov, Kuzma Terentyevich, 261
Solovtzov, Nikolay Nikolayevich, 176, 398
Spectator, The, 6, 10, 36*n*
Speechmaking, Chekhov on, 341
Spiritualism, 249
Splinters, 5–7, 9, 12, 13–15, 20, 22, 27, 29, 30, 44, 255, 307, 309
Sredin, Aleksandr Valentinovich, 457
Sredin, Anatoly Leonidovich, 443
Sredin, Leonid Valentinovich, 348, *386*, 457*n*
Sredin family, 347*n*, 348
Sretensk, 153, 155, 157
Stackelberg, Baron, 214
Stakhovich, Aleksey Aleksandrovich, 425
Stanislavsky, Konstantin Sergeyevich (K. S. Alekseyev), 271*n*, 312, 315, 350–51, 356, 371, 379, 388, 409, 416, *420, 422, 434, 437, 441, 444*, 450, 451*n*, 454–55, *458, 460*
Staraya Ruza, 365, 368
Stasov, Vladimir Vasilyevich, 226, 231, 293
Steamer travel, 136–40, 158–69, 236, 379, 421–22
"Steppe, The," 66*n*
Stories, 120*n*
Stories from the Life of My Friends, 110–111
"Story of an Unknown Man, The," 222, 231
Stowe, Harriet Beecher, 4
Strauch, Dr., 419–20, 422, 427
"Strider, the Story of a Horse," (Tolstoy), 191
Stuart, Baron, 346*n*
Student riots, 129–30, 276, 336, 338
Students, Chekhov's advice to, 445; Chekhov's aid to, 250–51, 344–45, 367, 405, 425–27, 456*n*, 465–66, 470
Stulli, 30
Sudogda, 173*n*
Sulerzhitsky, Leopold Antonovich, 385
Sumbatov-Youzhin, Aleksandr Ivanovich (Youzhin), *446*
Sumy (Lintvarev estate), 70–71, 73*n*, 113
Surgery, 276, 294
Surgical Chronicle, 261–64
Suvorin, Aleksey Alekseyevich, 73*n*, 176*n*, 182
Suvorin, Aleksey Sergeyevich, 28, 70, 78, *85–91, 92–96, 107, 111–12, 113–14, 119, 124, 126, 128, 133,* 152, 163–65,

168, 171, 185–86, 188–90, 192–94, 201, 203, 207, 208, 211–14, 218–23, 225–228, 230, 233–36, 238, 240, *243–44, 248–49, 251, 252, 254, 255, 258–64, 266, 269, 272, 275–77, 278–79, 283, 285, 288–90, 291–93, 294, 299, 301, 303, 308, 311, 314, 317, 326, 332, 336, 339, 342, 345, 364, 375–76, 436*; controversy over Chekhov's collected works, 325, 332, 370–71; Chekhov's opinion of, 40, 73, 337, 393; relationship with Chekhov, viii, 25, 37, 79, 80, 82, 84, 196, 232, 370–71; visits and travel with Chekhov, 72–75, 176*n*; conflict over Dreyfus case, viii, 25*n*, 301, 303, 307, 362; family, 232, 270; interest in hospital for alcoholics, 292; letters, 118; politics, 276; contributes to school building, 289; stand on student riots, 276, 336–38; aids *Surgical Chronicle*, 261–64; *Tatyana Repina*, 94, 109; mentioned, 34, 42, 121*n*, 138, 173, 439, 469
Suvorina, Anna Ivanovna, 75, 244 275, 296, 370–71
Svobodin, Pavel Matveyevich, 121, 224
"Swan Song," 43
Syphilis, *175,* 256–57, 390
Syromyatnikov, Sergey Nikolayevich, 369
Sytin, Ivan Dmitriyevich, 264, 279, 309

Taganrog, 3*n*, 7, 11, 46–54, 61, 128*n*, 184*n*, 204, 248–50 *passim*, 280, 352, 359*n*, 366, 397*n*; Chekhov's bequest to, 405; Chekhov's civic activities, 47*n*, 308, 309*n*, 362–63
Talezh, 251
Tarakhovsky, Abram Borisovich, 359
Tarnovskaya, Praskovya Nikolayevna, 75
Tartars, 72–73, 93, 139, 145
Tartar Strait, 165, 166
Tatarinova, Mme., 439
Tatishchev, Sergey Spiridonovich, 184, 221
Tatyana, 203
Tatyana Repina (Suvorin), 94, 109
Taube, Dr., 420, 471
Tausch, Major, 304
Tchaikovsky, Modest Ilyich, 120, *130*
Tchaikovsky, Pyotr Ilyich, *120,* 130–31
Teleshev, Nikolay Dmitriyevich, 409
Tenants, The (Naidenov), 428
Theater, the, 91, 308, 320, 322, 327, 350, 359, 395; people's, 279–80, 287, 359–360, 458. *See also* Playwriting
Theater-Goer, The, 273
"Thief," 6
Thoreau, Henry David, 62
Three of Them (Gorky), 446
Three Sisters, 271*n*, 342*n*, 355*n*, 358, 378–381, 383–84, 388, 390–92, 398–99, 415*n*, 443
"Three Years," 229, 252